Get the eBooks FREE!

(PDF, ePub, Kindle, and liveBook all included)

We believe that once you buy a book from us, you should be able to read it in any format we have available. To get electronic versions of this book at no additional cost to you, purchase and then register this book at the Manning website.

Go to https://www.manning.com/freebook and follow the instructions to complete your pBook registration.

That's it!
Thanks from Manning!

C++ Concurrency in Action

C++ Concurrency in Action

PRACTICAL MULTITHREADING

ANTHONY WILLIAMS

MANNING
SHELTER ISLAND

For online information and ordering of this and other Manning books, please visit www.manning.com. The publisher offers discounts on this book when ordered in quantity. For more information, please contact

Special Sales Department
Manning Publications Co.
20 Baldwin Road
PO Box 261
Shelter Island, NY 11964
Email: orders@manning.com

♾ Recognizing the importance of preserving what has been written, it is Manning's policy to have the books we publish printed on acid-free paper, and we exert our best efforts to that end. Recognizing also our responsibility to conserve the resources of our planet, Manning books are printed on paper that is at least 15 percent recycled and processed without the use of elemental chlorine.

Manning Publications Co.
20 Baldwin Road
PO Box 261
Shelter Island, NY 11964

Development editor: Cynthia Kane
Technical proofreader: Jonathan Wakely
Copyeditor: Linda Recktenwald
Proofreader: Katie Tennant
Typesetter: Dennis Dalinnik
Cover designer: Marija Tudor

ISBN: 9781933988771
Printed in the United States of America
12 13 14 15 – EBM – 18 17

To Kim, Hugh, and Erin

contents

preface

I encountered the concept of multithreaded code while working at my first job after I left college. We were writing a data processing application that had to populate a database with incoming data records. There was a lot of data, but each record was independent and required a reasonable amount of processing before it could be inserted into the database. To take full advantage of the power of our 10-CPU UltraSPARC, we ran the code in multiple threads, each thread processing its own set of incoming records. We wrote the code in C++, using POSIX threads, and made a fair number of mistakes—multithreading was new to all of us—but we got there in the end. It was also while working on this project that I first became aware of the C++ Standards Committee and the freshly published C++ Standard.

I have had a keen interest in multithreading and concurrency ever since. Where others saw it as difficult, complex, and a source of problems, I saw it as a powerful tool that could enable your code to take advantage of the available hardware to run faster. Later on I would learn how it could be used to improve the responsiveness and performance of applications even on single-core hardware, by using multiple threads to hide the latency of time-consuming operations such as I/O. I also learned how it worked at the OS level and how Intel CPUs handled task switching.

Meanwhile, my interest in C++ brought me in contact with the ACCU and then the C++ Standards panel at BSI, as well as Boost. I followed the initial development of the Boost Thread Library with interest, and when it was abandoned by the original developer, I jumped at the chance to get involved. I have been the primary developer and maintainer of the Boost Thread Library ever since.

As the work of the C++ Standards Committee shifted from fixing defects in the existing standard to writing proposals for the next standard (named C++0x in the hope that it would be finished by 2009, and now officially C++11, because it was finally published in 2011), I got more involved with BSI and started drafting proposals of my own. Once it became clear that multithreading was on the agenda, I jumped in with both feet and authored or coauthored many of the multithreading and concurrency-related proposals that shaped this part of the new standard. I feel privileged to have had the opportunity to combine two of my major computer-related interests—C++ and multithreading—in this way.

This book draws on all my experience with both C++ and multithreading and aims to teach other C++ developers how to use the C++11 Thread Library safely and efficiently. I also hope to impart some of my enthusiasm for the subject along the way.

acknowledgments

I will start by saying a big "Thank you" to my wife, Kim, for all the love and support she has given me while writing this book. It has occupied a significant part of my spare time for the last four years, and without her patience, support, and understanding, I couldn't have managed it.

Second, I would like to thank the team at Manning who have made this book possible: Marjan Bace, publisher; Michael Stephens, associate publisher; Cynthia Kane, my development editor; Karen Tegtmeyer, review editor; Linda Recktenwald, my copyeditor; Katie Tennant, my proofreader; and Mary Piergies, the production manager. Without their efforts you would not be reading this book right now.

I would also like to thank the other members of the C++ Standards Committee who wrote committee papers on the multithreading facilities: Andrei Alexandrescu, Pete Becker, Bob Blainer, Hans Boehm, Beman Dawes, Lawrence Crowl, Peter Dimov, Jeff Garland, Kevlin Henney, Howard Hinnant, Ben Hutchings, Jan Kristofferson, Doug Lea, Paul McKenney, Nick McLaren, Clark Nelson, Bill Pugh, Raul Silvera, Herb Sutter, Detlef Vollmann, and Michael Wong, plus all those who commented on the papers, discussed them at the committee meetings, and otherwise helped shaped the multithreading and concurrency support in C++11.

Finally, I would like to thank the following people, whose suggestions have greatly improved this book: Dr. Jamie Allsop, Peter Dimov, Howard Hinnant, Rick Molloy, Jonathan Wakely, and Dr. Russel Winder, with special thanks to Russel for his detailed reviews and to Jonathan who, as technical proofreader, painstakingly checked all the content for outright errors in the final manuscript during production. (Any remaining mistakes are of course all mine.) In addition I'd like to thank my panel of reviewers: Ryan Stephens, Neil Horlock, John Taylor Jr., Ezra Jivan, Joshua Heyer, Keith S. Kim, Michele Galli, Mike Tian-Jian Jiang, David Strong, Roger Orr, Wagner Rick, Mike Buksas, and Bas Vodde. Also, thanks to the readers of the MEAP edition who took the time to point out errors or highlight areas that needed clarifying.

about this book

This book is an in-depth guide to the concurrency and multithreading facilities from the new C++ Standard, from the basic usage of `std::thread`, `std::mutex`, and `std::async`, to the complexities of atomic operations and the memory model.

Roadmap

The first four chapters introduce the various library facilities provided by the library and show how they can be used.

Chapter 5 covers the low-level nitty-gritty of the memory model and atomic operations, including how atomic operations can be used to impose ordering constraints on other code, and marks the end of the introductory chapters.

Chapters 6 and 7 start the coverage of higher-level topics, with some examples of how to use the basic facilities to build more complex data structures—lock-based data structures in chapter 6, and lock-free data structures in chapter 7.

Chapter 8 continues the higher-level topics, with guidelines for designing multithreaded code, coverage of the issues that affect performance, and example implementations of various parallel algorithms.

Chapter 9 covers thread management—thread pools, work queues, and interrupting operations.

Chapter 10 covers testing and debugging—types of bugs, techniques for locating them, how to test for them, and so forth.

The appendixes include a brief description of some of the new language facilities introduced with the new standard that are relevant to multithreading, the implementation details of the message-passing library mentioned in chapter 4, and a complete reference to the C++11 Thread Library.

Who should read this book

If you're writing multithreaded code in C++, you should read this book. If you're using the new multithreading facilities from the C++ Standard Library, this book is an essential guide. If you're using alternative thread libraries, the guidelines and techniques from the later chapters should still prove useful.

A good working knowledge of C++ is assumed, though familiarity with the new language features is not—these are covered in appendix A. Prior knowledge or experience of multithreaded programming is not assumed, though it may be useful.

How to use this book

If you've never written multithreaded code before, I suggest reading this book sequentially from beginning to end, though possibly skipping the more detailed parts of chapter 5. Chapter 7 relies heavily on the material in chapter 5, so if you skipped chapter 5, you should save chapter 7 until you've read it.

If you've not used the new C++11 language facilities before, it might be worth skimming appendix A before you start to ensure that you're up to speed with the examples in the book. The uses of the new language facilities are highlighted in the text, though, and you can always flip to the appendix if you encounter something you've not seen before.

If you have extensive experience with writing multithreaded code in other environments, the beginning chapters are probably still worth skimming so you can see how the facilities you know map onto the new standard C++ ones. If you're going to be doing any low-level work with atomic variables, chapter 5 is a must. Chapter 8 is worth reviewing to ensure that you're familiar with things like exception safety in multithreaded C++. If you have a particular task in mind, the index and table of contents should help you find a relevant section quickly.

Once you're up to speed on the use of the C++ Thread Library, appendix D should continue to be useful, such as for looking up the exact details of each class and function call. You may also like to dip back into the main chapters from time to time to refresh your use of a particular construct or look at the sample code.

Code conventions and downloads

All source code in listings or in text is in a `fixed-width font like this` to separate it from ordinary text. Code annotations accompany many of the listings, highlighting important concepts. In some cases, numbered bullets link to explanations that follow the listing.

Source code for all working examples in this book is available for download from the publisher's website at www.manning.com/CPlusPlusConcurrencyinAction.

Software requirements

To use the code from this book unchanged, you'll need a recent C++ compiler that supports the new C++11 language features used in the examples (see appendix A), and you'll need a copy of the C++ Standard Thread Library.

At the time of writing, g++ is the only compiler I'm aware of that ships with an implementation of the Standard Thread Library, although the Microsoft Visual Studio 2011 preview also includes an implementation. The g++ implementation of the Thread Library was first introduced in a basic form in g++ 4.3 and extended in subsequent releases. g++ 4.3 also introduced the first support for some of the new C++11 language features; more of the new language features are supported in each subsequent release. See the g++ C++11 status page for details.[1]

Microsoft Visual Studio 2010 provides some of the new C++11 language features, such as rvalue references and lambda functions, but doesn't ship with an implementation of the Thread Library.

My company, Just Software Solutions Ltd, sells a complete implementation of the C++11 Standard Thread Library for Microsoft Visual Studio 2005, Microsoft Visual Studio 2008, Microsoft Visual Studio 2010, and various versions of g++.[2] This implementation has been used for testing the examples in this book.

The Boost Thread Library[3] provides an API that's based on the C++11 Standard Thread Library proposals and is portable to many platforms. Most of the examples from the book can be modified to work with the Boost Thread Library by judicious replacement of `std::` with `boost::` and use of the appropriate `#include` directives. There are a few facilities that are either not supported (such as `std::async`) or have different names (such as `boost::unique_future`) in the Boost Thread Library.

Author Online

Purchase of *C++ Concurrency in Action* includes free access to a private web forum run by Manning Publications where you can make comments about the book, ask technical questions, and receive help from the author and from other users. To access the forum and subscribe to it, point your web browser to www.manning.com/CPlusPlusConcurrencyinAction. This page provides information on how to get on the forum once you're registered, what kind of help is available, and the rules of conduct on the forum.

Manning's commitment to our readers is to provide a venue where a meaningful dialogue between individual readers and between readers and the author can take place. It's not a commitment to any specific amount of participation on the part of the author, whose contribution to the book's forum remains voluntary (and unpaid). We suggest you try asking the author some challenging questions, lest his interest stray!

The Author Online forum and the archives of previous discussions will be accessible from the publisher's website as long as the book is in print.

---

1 GNU Compiler Collection C++0x/C++11 status page, http://gcc.gnu.org/projects/cxx0x.html.

2 The `just::thread` implementation of the C++ Standard Thread Library, http://www.stdthread.co.uk.

3 The Boost C++ library collection, http://www.boost.org.

about the cover illustration

The illustration on the cover of *C++ Concurrency in Action* is captioned "Habit of a Lady of Japan." The image is taken from the four-volume *Collection of the Dress of Different Nations* by Thomas Jefferys, published in London between 1757 and 1772. The collection includes beautiful hand-colored copperplate engravings of costumes from around the world and has influenced theatrical costume design since its publication. The diversity of the drawings in the compendium speaks vividly of the richness of the costumes presented on the London stage over 200 years ago. The costumes, both historical and contemporaneous, offered a glimpse into the dress customs of people living in different times and in different countries, making them come alive for London theater audiences.

Dress codes have changed in the last century and the diversity by region, so rich in the past, has faded away. It's now often hard to tell the inhabitant of one continent from another. Perhaps, trying to view it optimistically, we've traded a cultural and visual diversity for a more varied personal life—or a more varied and interesting intellectual and technical life.

We at Manning celebrate the inventiveness, the initiative, and the fun of the computer business with book covers based on the rich diversity of regional and theatrical life of two centuries ago, brought back to life by the pictures from this collection.

1 Hello, world of concurrency in C++!

This chapter covers

- What is meant by concurrency and multithreading
- Why you might want to use concurrency and multithreading in your applications
- Some of the history of the support for concurrency in C++
- What a simple multithreaded C++ program looks like

These are exciting times for C++ users. Thirteen years after the original C++ Standard was published in 1998, the C++ Standards Committee is giving the language and its supporting library a major overhaul. The new C++ Standard (referred to as C++11 or C++0x) was published in 2011 and brings with it a whole swathe of changes that will make working with C++ easier and more productive.

One of the most significant new features in the C++11 Standard is the support of multithreaded programs. For the first time, the C++ Standard will acknowledge the existence of multithreaded applications in the language and provide components in the library for writing multithreaded applications. This will make it possible to write multithreaded C++ programs without relying on platform-specific extensions and thus allow writing portable multithreaded code with guaranteed behavior. It also comes at a time when programmers are increasingly looking to concurrency in general, and multithreaded programming in particular, to improve application performance.

This book is about writing programs in C++ using multiple threads for concurrency and the C++ language features and library facilities that make that possible. I'll start by explaining what I mean by concurrency and multithreading and why you would want to use concurrency in your applications. After a quick detour into why you might *not* want to use it in your applications, I'll give an overview of the concurrency support in C++, and I'll round off this chapter with a simple example of C++ concurrency in action. Readers experienced with developing multithreaded applications may wish to skip the early sections. In subsequent chapters I'll cover more extensive examples and look at the library facilities in more depth. The book will finish with an in-depth reference to all the C++ Standard Library facilities for multithreading and concurrency.

So, what do I mean by *concurrency* and *multithreading*?

1.1 What is concurrency?

At the simplest and most basic level, concurrency is about two or more separate activities happening at the same time. We encounter concurrency as a natural part of life; we can walk and talk at the same time or perform different actions with each hand, and of course we each go about our lives independently of each other—you can watch football while I go swimming, and so on.

1.1.1 Concurrency in computer systems

When we talk about concurrency in terms of computers, we mean a single system performing multiple independent activities in parallel, rather than sequentially, or one after the other. It isn't a new phenomenon: multitasking operating systems that allow a single computer to run multiple applications at the same time through task switching have been commonplace for many years, and high-end server machines with multiple processors that enable genuine concurrency have been available for even longer. What *is* new is the increased prevalence of computers that can genuinely run multiple tasks in parallel rather than just giving the illusion of doing so.

Historically, most computers have had one processor, with a single processing unit or core, and this remains true for many desktop machines today. Such a machine can really only perform one task at a time, but it can switch between tasks many times per second. By doing a bit of one task and then a bit of another and so on, it appears that the tasks are happening concurrently. This is called *task switching*. We still talk about *concurrency* with such systems; because the task switches are so fast, you can't tell at which point a task may be suspended as the processor switches to another one. The task switching provides an illusion of concurrency to both the user and the applications themselves. Because there is only an *illusion* of concurrency, the behavior of applications may be subtly different when executing in a single-processor task-switching environment compared to when executing in an environment with true concurrency. In particular, incorrect assumptions about the memory model (covered in chapter 5) may not show up in such an environment. This is discussed in more depth in chapter 10.

Computers containing multiple processors have been used for servers and high-performance computing tasks for a number of years, and now computers based on processors with more than one core on a single chip (multicore processors) are becoming increasingly common as desktop machines too. Whether they have multiple processors or multiple cores within a processor (or both), these computers are capable of genuinely running more than one task in parallel. We call this *hardware concurrency*.

Figure 1.1 shows an idealized scenario of a computer with precisely two tasks to do, each divided into 10 equal-size chunks. On a dual-core machine (which has two processing cores), each task can execute on its own core. On a single-core machine doing task switching, the chunks from each task are interleaved. But they are also spaced out a bit (in the diagram this is shown by the gray bars separating the chunks being thicker than the separator bars shown for the dual-core machine); in order to do the interleaving, the system has to perform a *context switch* every time it changes from one task to another, and this takes time. In order to perform a context switch, the OS has to save the CPU state and instruction pointer for the currently running task, work out which task to switch to, and reload the CPU state for the task being switched to. The CPU will then potentially have to load the memory for the instructions and data for the new task into cache, which can prevent the CPU from executing any instructions, causing further delay.

Though the availability of concurrency in the hardware is most obvious with multiprocessor or multicore systems, some processors can execute multiple threads on a single core. The important factor to consider is really the number of *hardware threads*: the measure of how many independent tasks the hardware can genuinely run concurrently. Even with a system that has genuine hardware concurrency, it's easy to have more tasks than the hardware can run in parallel, so task switching is still used in these cases. For example, on a typical desktop computer there may be hundreds of tasks

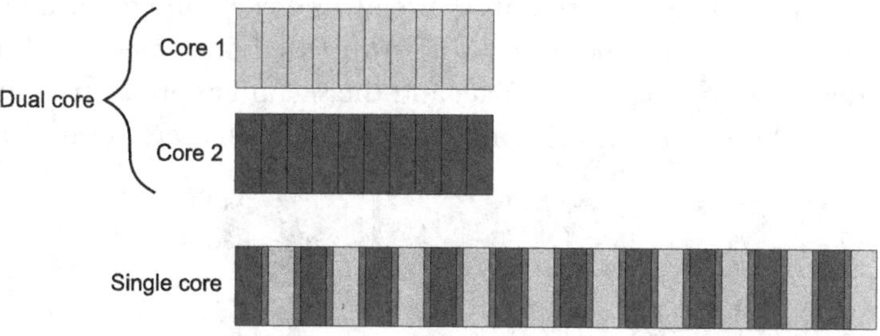

Figure 1.1 Two approaches to concurrency: parallel execution on a dual-core machine versus task switching on a single-core machine

running, performing background operations, even when the computer is nominally idle. It's the task switching that allows these background tasks to run and allows you to run your word processor, compiler, editor, and web browser (or any combination of applications) all at once. Figure 1.2 shows task switching among four tasks on a dual-core machine, again for an idealized scenario with the tasks divided neatly into equal-size chunks. In practice, many issues will make the divisions uneven and the scheduling irregular. Some of these issues are covered in chapter 8 when we look at factors affecting the performance of concurrent code.

All the techniques, functions, and classes covered in this book can be used whether your application is running on a machine with one single-core processor or on a machine with many multicore processors and are not affected by whether the concurrency is achieved through task switching or by genuine hardware concurrency. But as you may imagine, how you make use of concurrency in your application may well depend on the amount of hardware concurrency available. This is covered in chapter 8, where I cover the issues involved with designing concurrent code in C++.

1.1.2 Approaches to concurrency

Imagine for a moment a pair of programmers working together on a software project. If your developers are in separate offices, they can go about their work peacefully, without being disturbed by each other, and they each have their own set of reference manuals. However, communication is not straightforward; rather than just turning around and talking to each other, they have to use the phone or email or get up and walk to each other's office. Also, you have the overhead of two offices to manage and multiple copies of reference manuals to purchase.

Now imagine that you move your developers into the same office. They can now talk to each other freely to discuss the design of the application, and they can easily draw diagrams on paper or on a whiteboard to help with design ideas or explanations. You now have only one office to manage, and one set of resources will often suffice. On the negative side, they might find it harder to concentrate, and there may be issues with sharing resources ("Where's the reference manual gone now?").

These two ways of organizing your developers illustrate the two basic approaches to concurrency. Each developer represents a thread, and each office represents a process. The first approach is to have multiple single-threaded processes, which is similar to having each developer in their own office, and the second approach is to have multiple threads in a single process, which is like having two developers in the same office.

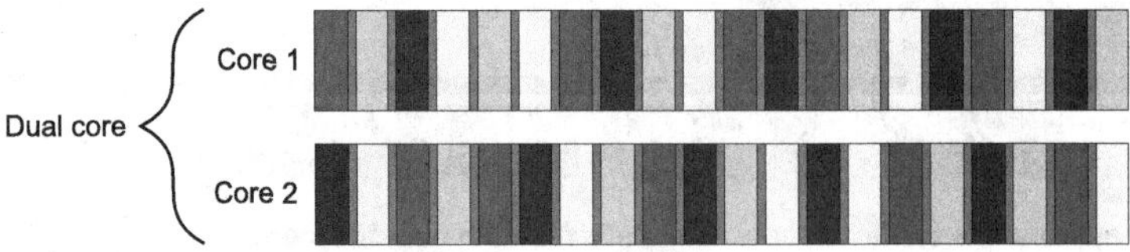

Figure 1.2 Task switching of four tasks on two cores

You can combine these in an arbitrary fashion and have multiple processes, some of which are multithreaded and some of which are single-threaded, but the principles are the same. Let's now have a brief look at these two approaches to concurrency in an application.

CONCURRENCY WITH MULTIPLE PROCESSES

The first way to make use of concurrency within an application is to divide the application into multiple, separate, single-threaded processes that are run at the same time, much as you can run your web browser and word processor at the same time. These separate processes can then pass messages to each other through all the normal interprocess communication channels (signals, sockets, files, pipes, and so on), as shown in figure 1.3. One downside is that such communication between processes is often either complicated to set up or slow or both, because operating systems typically provide a lot of protection between processes to avoid one process accidentally modifying data belonging to another process. Another downside is that there's an inherent overhead in running multiple processes: it takes time to start a process, the operating system must devote internal resources to managing the process, and so forth.

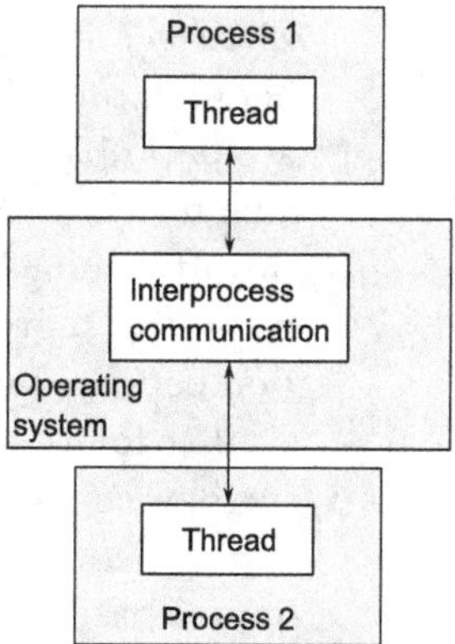

Figure 1.3 Communication between a pair of processes running concurrently

Of course, it's not all downside: the added protection operating systems typically provide between processes and the higher-level communication mechanisms mean that it can be easier to write *safe* concurrent code with processes rather than threads. Indeed, environments such as that provided for the Erlang programming language use processes as the fundamental building block of concurrency to great effect.

Using separate processes for concurrency also has an additional advantage—you can run the separate processes on distinct machines connected over a network. Though this increases the communication cost, on a carefully designed system it can be a cost-effective way of increasing the available parallelism and improving performance.

CONCURRENCY WITH MULTIPLE THREADS

The alternative approach to concurrency is to run multiple threads in a single process. Threads are much like lightweight processes: each thread runs independently of the others, and each thread may run a different sequence of instructions. But all threads in a process share the same address space, and most of the data can be accessed directly from all threads—global variables remain global, and pointers or references to objects or data can be passed around among threads. Although it's often possible to share memory among processes, this is complicated to set up and often hard to manage, because memory addresses of the same data aren't necessarily the same in different processes. Figure 1.4 shows two threads within a process communicating through shared memory.

The shared address space and lack of protection of data between threads makes the overhead associated with using multiple threads much smaller than that from using multiple processes, because the operating system has less bookkeeping to do. But the flexibility of shared memory also comes with a price: if data is accessed by multiple threads, the application programmer must ensure that the view of data seen by each thread is consistent whenever it is accessed. The issues surrounding sharing data between threads and the tools to use and guidelines to follow to avoid problems are covered throughout this book, notably in chapters 3, 4, 5, and 8. The problems are not insurmountable, provided suitable care is taken when writing the code, but they do mean that a great deal of thought must go into the communication between threads.

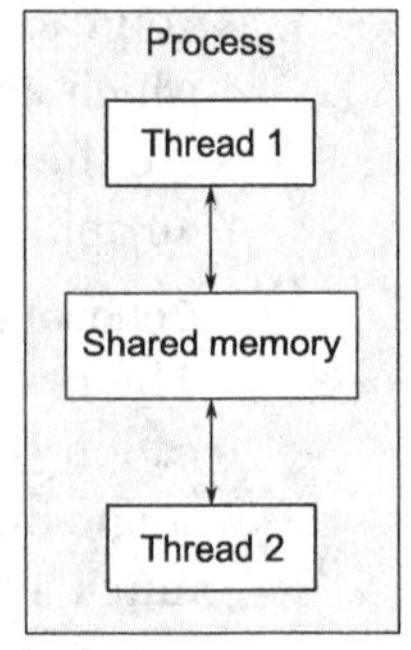

Figure 1.4 Communication between a pair of threads running concurrently in a single process

The low overhead associated with launching and communicating between multiple threads within a process compared to launching and communicating between multiple single-threaded processes means that this is the favored approach to concurrency in mainstream languages including C++, despite the potential problems arising from the shared memory. In addition, the C++ Standard doesn't provide any intrinsic support for communication between processes, so applications that use multiple processes will have to rely on platform-specific APIs to do so. This book therefore focuses exclusively on using multithreading for concurrency, and future references to concurrency assume that this is achieved by using multiple threads.

Having clarified what we mean by concurrency, let's now look at why you would use concurrency in your applications.

1.2 Why use concurrency?

There are two main reasons to use concurrency in an application: separation of concerns and performance. In fact, I'd go so far as to say that they're pretty much the *only* reasons to use concurrency; anything else boils down to one or the other (or maybe even both) when you look hard enough (well, except for reasons like "because I want to").

1.2.1 Using concurrency for separation of concerns

Separation of concerns is almost always a good idea when writing software; by grouping related bits of code together and keeping unrelated bits of code apart, you can make your programs easier to understand and test, and thus less likely to contain bugs. You can use concurrency to separate distinct areas of functionality, even when the operations in these distinct areas need to happen at the same time; without the explicit use of concurrency you either have to write a task-switching framework or actively make calls to unrelated areas of code during an operation.

Consider a processing-intensive application with a user interface, such as a DVD player application for a desktop computer. Such an application fundamentally has two sets of responsibilities: not only does it have to read the data from the disk, decode the images and sound, and send them to the graphics and sound hardware in a timely fashion so the DVD plays without glitches, but it must also take input from the user, such as when the user clicks Pause or Return To Menu, or even Quit. In a single thread, the application has to check for user input at regular intervals during the playback, thus conflating the DVD playback code with the user interface code. By using multithreading to separate these concerns, the user interface code and DVD playback code no longer have to be so closely intertwined; one thread can handle the user interface and another the DVD playback. There will have to be interaction between them, such as when the user clicks Pause, but now these interactions are directly related to the task at hand.

This gives the illusion of responsiveness, because the user interface thread can typically respond immediately to a user request, even if the response is simply to display a busy cursor or Please Wait message while the request is conveyed to the thread doing the work. Similarly, separate threads are often used to run tasks that must run continuously in the background, such as monitoring the filesystem for changes in a desktop search application. Using threads in this way generally makes the logic in each thread much simpler, because the interactions between them can be limited to clearly identifiable points, rather than having to intersperse the logic of the different tasks.

In this case, the number of threads is independent of the number of CPU cores available, because the division into threads is based on the conceptual design rather than an attempt to increase throughput.

1.2.2 Using concurrency for performance

Multiprocessor systems have existed for decades, but until recently they were mostly found only in supercomputers, mainframes, and large server systems. But chip manufacturers have increasingly been favoring multicore designs with 2, 4, 16, or more processors on a single chip over better performance with a single core. Consequently, multicore desktop computers, and even multicore embedded devices, are now increasingly prevalent. The increased computing power of these machines comes not from running a single task faster but from running multiple tasks in parallel. In the past, programmers have been able to sit back and watch their programs get faster with each new generation of processors, without any effort on their part. But now, as Herb Sutter put it, "The free lunch is over."[1] *If software is to take advantage of this increased computing power, it must be designed to run multiple tasks concurrently.* Programmers must therefore take heed, and those who have hitherto ignored concurrency must now look to add it to their toolbox.

There are two ways to use concurrency for performance. The first, and most obvious, is to divide a single task into parts and run each in parallel, thus reducing the total runtime. This is *task parallelism.* Although this sounds straightforward, it can be

---

1 "The Free Lunch Is Over: A Fundamental Turn Toward Concurrency in Software," Herb Sutter, *Dr. Dobb's Journal,* 30(3), March 2005. http://www.gotw.ca/publications/concurrency-ddj.htm.

quite a complex process, because there may be many dependencies between the various parts. The divisions may be either in terms of processing—one thread performs one part of the algorithm while another thread performs a different part—or in terms of data—each thread performs the same operation on different parts of the data. This latter approach is called *data parallelism*.

Algorithms that are readily susceptible to such parallelism are frequently called *embarrassingly parallel*. Despite the implications that you might be embarrassed to have code so easy to parallelize, this is a good thing: other terms I've encountered for such algorithms are *naturally parallel* and *conveniently concurrent*. Embarrassingly parallel algorithms have good scalability properties—as the number of available hardware threads goes up, the parallelism in the algorithm can be increased to match. Such an algorithm is the perfect embodiment of the adage, "Many hands make light work." For those parts of the algorithm that aren't embarrassingly parallel, you might be able to divide the algorithm into a fixed (and therefore not scalable) number of parallel tasks. Techniques for dividing tasks between threads are covered in chapter 8.

The second way to use concurrency for performance is to use the available parallelism to solve bigger problems; rather than processing one file at a time, process 2 or 10 or 20, as appropriate. Although this is really just an application of *data parallelism*, by performing the same operation on multiple sets of data concurrently, there's a different focus. It still takes the same amount of time to process one chunk of data, but now more data can be processed in the same amount of time. Obviously, there are limits to this approach too, and this won't be beneficial in all cases, but the increase in throughput that comes from such an approach can actually make new things possible—increased resolution in video processing, for example, if different areas of the picture can be processed in parallel.

1.2.3 When not to use concurrency

It's just as important to know *when not* to use concurrency as it is to know *when* to use it. Fundamentally, the only reason not to use concurrency is when the benefit is not worth the cost. Code using concurrency is harder to understand in many cases, so there's a direct intellectual cost to writing and maintaining multithreaded code, and the additional complexity can also lead to more bugs. Unless the potential performance gain is large enough or separation of concerns clear enough to justify the additional development time required to get it right and the additional costs associated with maintaining multithreaded code, don't use concurrency.

Also, the performance gain might not be as large as expected; there's an inherent overhead associated with launching a thread, because the OS has to allocate the associated kernel resources and stack space and then add the new thread to the scheduler, all of which takes time. If the task being run on the thread is completed quickly, the actual time taken by the task may be dwarfed by the overhead of launching the thread, possibly making the overall performance of the application worse than if the task had been executed directly by the spawning thread.

Furthermore, threads are a limited resource. If you have too many threads running at once, this consumes OS resources and may make the system as a whole run slower. Not only that, but using too many threads can exhaust the available memory or address space for a process, because each thread requires a separate stack space. This is particularly a problem for 32-bit processes with a flat architecture where there's a 4 GB limit in the available address space: if each thread has a 1 MB stack (as is typical on many systems), then the address space would be all used up with 4096 threads, without allowing for any space for code or static data or heap data. Although 64-bit (or larger) systems don't have this direct address-space limit, they still have finite resources: if you run too many threads, this will eventually cause problems. Though thread pools (see chapter 9) can be used to limit the number of threads, these are not a silver bullet, and they do have their own issues.

If the server side of a client/server application launches a separate thread for each connection, this works fine for a small number of connections, but can quickly exhaust system resources by launching too many threads if the same technique is used for a high-demand server that has to handle many connections. In this scenario, careful use of thread pools can provide optimal performance (see chapter 9).

Finally, the more threads you have running, the more context switching the operating system has to do. Each context switch takes time that could be spent doing useful work, so at some point adding an extra thread will actually *reduce* the overall application performance rather than increase it. For this reason, if you're trying to achieve the best possible performance of the system, it's necessary to adjust the number of threads running to take account of the available hardware concurrency (or lack of it).

Use of concurrency for performance is just like any other optimization strategy: it has potential to greatly improve the performance of your application, but it can also complicate the code, making it harder to understand and more prone to bugs. Therefore it's only worth doing for those performance-critical parts of the application where there's the potential for measurable gain. Of course, if the potential for performance gains is only secondary to clarity of design or separation of concerns, it may still be worth using a multithreaded design.

Assuming that you've decided you *do* want to use concurrency in your application, whether for performance, separation of concerns, or because it's "multithreading Monday," what does that mean for C++ programmers?

1.3 Concurrency and multithreading in C++

Standardized support for concurrency through multithreading is a new thing for C++. It's only with the upcoming C++11 Standard that you'll be able to write multithreaded code without resorting to platform-specific extensions. In order to understand the rationale behind lots of the decisions in the new Standard C++ Thread Library, it's important to understand the history.

1.3.1 History of multithreading in C++

The 1998 C++ Standard doesn't acknowledge the existence of threads, and the operational effects of the various language elements are written in terms of a sequential abstract machine. Not only that, but the memory model isn't formally defined, so you can't write multithreaded applications without compiler-specific extensions to the 1998 C++ Standard.

Of course, compiler vendors are free to add extensions to the language, and the prevalence of C APIs for multithreading—such as those in the POSIX C standard and the Microsoft Windows API—has led many C++ compiler vendors to support multithreading with various platform-specific extensions. This compiler support is generally limited to allowing the use of the corresponding C API for the platform and ensuring that the C++ Runtime Library (such as the code for the exception-handling mechanism) works in the presence of multiple threads. Although very few compiler vendors have provided a formal multithreading-aware memory model, the actual behavior of the compilers and processors has been sufficiently good that a large number of multithreaded C++ programs have been written.

Not content with using the platform-specific C APIs for handling multithreading, C++ programmers have looked to their class libraries to provide object-oriented multithreading facilities. Application frameworks such as MFC and general-purpose C++ libraries such as Boost and ACE have accumulated sets of C++ classes that wrap the underlying platform-specific APIs and provide higher-level facilities for multithreading that simplify tasks. Although the precise details of the class libraries have varied considerably, particularly in the area of launching new threads, the overall shape of the classes has had a lot in common. One particularly important design that's common to many C++ class libraries, and that provides considerable benefit to the programmer, has been the use of the *Resource Acquisition Is Initialization* (RAII) idiom with locks to ensure that mutexes are unlocked when the relevant scope is exited.

For many cases, the multithreading support of existing C++ compilers combined with the availability of platform-specific APIs and platform-independent class libraries such as Boost and ACE provide a solid foundation on which to write multithreaded C++ code, and as a result there are probably millions of lines of C++ code written as part of multithreaded applications. But the lack of standard support means that there are occasions where the lack of a thread-aware memory model causes problems, particularly for those who try to gain higher performance by using knowledge of the processor hardware or for those writing cross-platform code where the actual behavior of the compilers varies between platforms.

1.3.2 Concurrency support in the new standard

All this changes with the release of the new C++11 Standard. Not only is there a brand-new thread-aware memory model, but the C++ Standard Library has been extended to include classes for managing threads (see chapter 2), protecting shared data (see chapter 3), synchronizing operations between threads (see chapter 4), and low-level atomic operations (see chapter 5).

The new C++ Thread Library is heavily based on the prior experience accumulated through the use of the C++ class libraries mentioned previously. In particular, the Boost Thread Library has been used as the primary model on which the new library is based, with many of the classes sharing their names and structure with the corresponding ones from Boost. As the new standard has evolved, this has been a two-way flow, and the Boost Thread Library has itself changed to match the C++ Standard in many respects, so users transitioning from Boost should find themselves very much at home.

Concurrency support is just one of the changes with the new C++ Standard—as mentioned at the beginning of this chapter, there are many enhancements to the language itself to make programmers' lives easier. Although these are generally outside the scope of this book, some of those changes have had a direct impact on the Thread Library itself and the ways in which it can be used. Appendix A provides a brief introduction to these language features.

The support for atomic operations directly in C++ enables programmers to write efficient code with defined semantics without the need for platform-specific assembly language. This is a real boon for those trying to write efficient, portable code; not only does the compiler take care of the platform specifics, but the optimizer can be written to take into account the semantics of the operations, thus enabling better optimization of the program as a whole.

1.3.3 Efficiency in the C++ Thread Library

One of the concerns that developers involved in high-performance computing often raise regarding C++ in general, and C++ classes that wrap low-level facilities—such as those in the new Standard C++ Thread Library specifically is that of efficiency. If you're after the utmost in performance, then it's important to understand the implementation costs associated with using any high-level facilities, compared to using the underlying low-level facilities directly. This cost is the *abstraction penalty*.

The C++ Standards Committee has been very aware of this when designing the C++ Standard Library in general and the Standard C++ Thread Library in particular; one of the design goals has been that there should be little or no benefit to be gained from using the lower-level APIs directly, where the same facility is to be provided. The library has therefore been designed to allow for efficient implementation (with a very low abstraction penalty) on most major platforms.

Another goal of the C++ Standards Committee has been to ensure that C++ provides sufficient low-level facilities for those wishing to work close to the metal for the ultimate performance. To this end, along with the new memory model comes a comprehensive atomic operations library for direct control over individual bits and bytes and the inter-thread synchronization and visibility of any changes. These atomic types and the corresponding operations can now be used in many places where developers would previously have chosen to drop down to platform-specific assembly language. Code using the new standard types and operations is thus more portable and easier to maintain.

The C++ Standard Library also provides higher-level abstractions and facilities that make writing multithreaded code easier and less error prone. Sometimes the use of these facilities does come with a performance cost because of the additional code that must be executed. But this performance cost doesn't necessarily imply a higher abstraction penalty; in general the cost is no higher than would be incurred by writing equivalent functionality by hand, and the compiler may well inline much of the additional code anyway.

In some cases, the high-level facilities provide additional functionality beyond what may be required for a specific use. Most of the time this is not an issue: you don't pay for what you don't use. On rare occasions, this unused functionality will impact the performance of other code. If you're aiming for performance and the cost is too high, you may be better off handcrafting the desired functionality from lower-level facilities. In the vast majority of cases, the additional complexity and chance of errors far outweigh the potential benefits from a small performance gain. Even if profiling *does* demonstrate that the bottleneck is in the C++ Standard Library facilities, it may be due to poor application design rather than a poor library implementation. For example, if too many threads are competing for a mutex, it *will* impact the performance significantly. Rather than trying to shave a small fraction of time off the mutex operations, it would probably be more beneficial to restructure the application so that there's less contention on the mutex. Designing applications to reduce contention is covered in chapter 8.

In those very rare cases where the C++ Standard Library does not provide the performance or behavior required, it might be necessary to use platform-specific facilities.

1.3.4 Platform-specific facilities

Although the C++ Thread Library provides reasonably comprehensive facilities for multithreading and concurrency, on any given platform there will be platform-specific facilities that go beyond what's offered. In order to gain easy access to those facilities without giving up the benefits of using the Standard C++ Thread Library, the types in the C++ Thread Library may offer a `native_handle()` member function that allows the underlying implementation to be directly manipulated using a platform-specific API. By its very nature, any operations performed using the `native_handle()` are entirely platform dependent and out of the scope of this book (and the Standard C++ Library itself).

Of course, before even considering using platform-specific facilities, it's important to understand what the Standard Library provides, so let's get started with an example.

1.4 Getting started

OK, so you have a nice, shiny C++11-compatible compiler. What next? What does a multithreaded C++ program look like? It looks pretty much like any other C++ program, with the usual mix of variables, classes, and functions. The only real distinction is that some functions might be running concurrently, so you need to ensure that shared data is safe for concurrent access, as described in chapter 3. Of course, in order to run functions concurrently, specific functions and objects must be used to manage the different threads.

1.4.1 Hello, Concurrent World

Let's start with a classic example: a program to print "Hello World." A really simple Hello, World program that runs in a single thread is shown here, to serve as a baseline when we move to multiple threads:

```
#include <iostream>

int main()
{
    std::cout<<"Hello World\n";
}
```

All this program does is write "Hello World" to the standard output stream. Let's compare it to the simple Hello, Concurrent World program shown in the following listing, which starts a separate thread to display the message.

Listing 1.1 A simple Hello, Concurrent World program

```
#include <iostream>
#include <thread>                  <-1

void hello()                              <-2
{
    std::cout<<"Hello Concurrent World\n";
}

int main()
{
    std::thread t(hello);          <-3
    t.join();                             <-4
}
```

The first difference is the extra `#include <thread>` ❶. The declarations for the multithreading support in the Standard C++ Library are in new headers: the functions and classes for managing threads are declared in `<thread>`, whereas those for protecting shared data are declared in other headers.

Second, the code for writing the message has been moved to a separate function ❷. This is because every thread has to have an *initial function*, which is where the new thread of execution begins. For the initial thread in an application, this is `main()`, but for every other thread it's specified in the constructor of a `std::thread` object—in this case, the `std::thread` object named `t` ❸ has the new function `hello()` as its initial function.

This is the next difference: rather than just writing directly to standard output or calling `hello()` from `main()`, this program launches a whole new thread to do it, bringing the thread count to two—the initial thread that starts at `main()` and the new thread that starts at `hello()`.

After the new thread has been launched ❸, the initial thread continues execution. If it didn't wait for the new thread to finish, it would merrily continue to the end of `main()` and thus end the program—possibly before the new thread had had a chance to run. This is why the call to `join()` is there ❹—as described in chapter 2, this causes the calling thread (in `main()`) to wait for the thread associated with the `std::thread` object, in this case, `t`.

If this seems like a lot of work to go to just to write a message to standard output, it is—as described previously in section 1.2.3, it's generally not worth the effort to use multiple threads for such a simple task, especially if the initial thread has nothing to do in the meantime. Later in the book, we'll work through examples that show scenarios where there's a clear gain to using multiple threads.

1.5 Summary

In this chapter, I covered what is meant by concurrency and multithreading and why you'd choose to use it (or not) in your applications. I also covered the history of multithreading in C++ from the complete lack of support in the 1998 standard, through various platform-specific extensions, to proper multithreading support in the new C++ Standard, C++11. This support is coming just in time to allow programmers to take advantage of the greater hardware concurrency becoming available with newer CPUs, as chip manufacturers choose to add more processing power in the form of multiple cores that allow more tasks to be executed concurrently, rather than increasing the execution speed of a single core.

I also showed how simple using the classes and functions from the C++ Standard Library can be, in the examples in section 1.4. In C++, using multiple threads isn't complicated in and of itself; the complexity lies in designing the code so that it behaves as intended.

After the taster examples of section 1.4, it's time for something with a bit more substance. In chapter 2 we'll look at the classes and functions available for managing threads.

2 Managing threads

This chapter covers

- Starting threads, and various ways of specifying code to run on a new thread
- Waiting for a thread to finish versus leaving it to run
- Uniquely identifying threads

OK, so you've decided to use concurrency for your application. In particular, you've decided to use multiple threads. What now? How do you launch these threads, how do you check that they've finished, and how do you keep tabs on them? The C++ Standard Library makes most thread-management tasks relatively easy, with just about everything managed through the `std::thread` object associated with a given thread, as you'll see. For those tasks that aren't so straightforward, the library provides the flexibility to build what you need from the basic building blocks.

In this chapter, I'll start by covering the basics: launching a thread, waiting for it to finish, or running it in the background. We'll then proceed to look at passing additional parameters to the thread function when it's launched and how to transfer ownership of a thread from one `std::thread` object to another. Finally, we'll look at choosing the number of threads to use and identifying particular threads.

2.1 Basic thread management

Every C++ program has at least one thread, which is started by the C++ runtime: the thread running `main()`. Your program can then launch additional threads that have another function as the entry point. These threads then run concurrently with each other and with the initial thread. Just as the program exits when the program returns from `main()`, when the specified entry point function returns, the thread exits. As you'll see, if you have a `std::thread` object for a thread, you can wait for it to finish; but first you have to start it, so let's look at launching threads.

2.1.1 Launching a thread

As you saw in chapter 1, threads are started by constructing a `std::thread` object that specifies the task to run on that thread. In the simplest case, that task is just a plain, ordinary `void`-returning function that takes no parameters. This function runs on its own thread until it returns, and then the thread stops. At the other extreme, the task could be a function object that takes additional parameters and performs a series of independent operations that are specified through some kind of messaging system while it's running, and the thread stops only when it's signaled to do so, again via some kind of messaging system. It doesn't matter what the thread is going to do or where it's launched from, but starting a thread using the C++ Thread Library always boils down to constructing a `std::thread` object:

```
void do_some_work();
std::thread my_thread(do_some_work);
```

This is just about as simple as it gets. Of course, you have to make sure that the `<thread>` header is included so the compiler can see the definition of the `std::thread` class. As with much of the C++ Standard Library, `std::thread` works with any *callable* type, so you can pass an instance of a class with a function call operator to the `std::thread` constructor instead:

```
class background_task
{
public:
    void operator()() const
    {
        do_something();
        do_something_else();
    }
};
background_task f;
std::thread my_thread(f);
```

In this case, the supplied function object is *copied* into the storage belonging to the newly created thread of execution and invoked from there. It's therefore essential that the copy behave equivalently to the original, or the result may not be what's expected.

One thing to consider when passing a function object to the thread constructor is to avoid what is dubbed "C++'s most vexing parse." If you pass a temporary rather than a named variable, then the syntax can be the same as that of a function declaration, in which case the compiler interprets it as such, rather than an object definition. For example,

```
std::thread my_thread(background_task());
```

declares a function `my_thread` that takes a single parameter (of type pointer to a function taking no parameters and returning a `background_task` object) and returns a `std::thread` object, rather than launching a new thread. You can avoid this by naming your function object as shown previously, by using an extra set of parentheses, or by using the new uniform initialization syntax, for example:

```
std::thread my_thread((background_task()));        <-1
std::thread my_thread{background_task()};           <-2
```

In the first example ❶, the extra parentheses prevent interpretation as a function declaration, thus allowing `my_thread` to be declared as a variable of type `std::thread`. The second example ❷ uses the new uniform initialization syntax with braces rather than parentheses, and thus would also declare a variable.

One type of callable object that avoids this problem is a *lambda expression*. This is a new feature from C++11 which essentially allows you to write a local function, possibly capturing some local variables and avoiding the need of passing additional arguments (see section 2.2). For full details on lambda expressions, see appendix A, section A.5. The previous example can be written using a lambda expression as follows:

```
std::thread my_thread([](
    do_something();
    do_something_else();
});
```

Once you've started your thread, you need to explicitly decide whether to wait for it to finish (by joining with it—see section 2.1.2) or leave it to run on its own (by detaching it—see section 2.1.3). If you don't decide before the `std::thread` object is destroyed, then your program is terminated (the `std::thread` destructor calls `std::terminate()`). It's therefore imperative that you ensure that the thread is correctly joined or detached, even in the presence of exceptions. See section 2.1.3 for a technique to handle this scenario. Note that you only have to make this decision before the `std::thread` object is destroyed—the thread itself may well have finished long before you join with it or detach it, and if you detach it, then the thread may continue running long after the `std::thread` object is destroyed.

If you don't wait for your thread to finish, then you need to ensure that the data accessed by the thread is valid until the thread has finished with it. This isn't a new problem—even in single-threaded code it is undefined behavior to access an object after it's been destroyed—but the use of threads provides an additional opportunity to encounter such lifetime issues.

One situation in which you can encounter such problems is when the thread function holds pointers or references to local variables and the thread hasn't finished when the function exits. The following listing shows an example of just such a scenario.

Listing 2.1 A function that returns while a thread still has access to local variables

```
struct func
{
    int& i;

    func(int& i_):i(i_){}

    void operator()()
    {
        for(unsigned j=0;j<1000000;++j)
        {
            do_something(i);            // 1 Potential access to dangling reference
        }
    }
};

void oops()
{
    int some_local_state=0;
    func my_func(some_local_state);
    std::thread my_thread(my_func);
    my_thread.detach();                 // 2 Don't wait for thread to finish
}                                       // 3 New thread might still be running
```

In this case, the new thread associated with `my_thread` will probably still be running when `oops` exits ❸, because you've explicitly decided not to wait for it by calling `detach()` ❷. If the thread *is* still running, then the next call to `do_something(i)` ❶ will access an already destroyed variable. This is just like normal single-threaded code—allowing a pointer or reference to a local variable to persist beyond the function exit is never a good idea—but it's easier to make the mistake with multithreaded code, because it isn't necessarily immediately apparent that this has happened.

One common way to handle this scenario is to make the thread function self-contained and *copy* the data into the thread rather than sharing the data. If you use a callable object for your thread function, that object is itself copied into the thread, so the original object can be destroyed immediately. But you still need to be wary of objects containing pointers or references, such as that from listing 2.1. In particular, it's a bad idea to create a thread within a function that has access to the local variables in that function, unless the thread is guaranteed to finish before the function exits.

Alternatively, you can ensure that the thread has completed execution before the function exits by *joining* with the thread.

2.1.2 Waiting for a thread to complete

If you need to wait for a thread to complete, you can do this by calling `join()` on the associated `std::thread` instance. In the case of listing 2.1, replacing the call to `my_thread.detach()` before the closing brace of the function body with a call to `my_thread.join()`

would therefore be sufficient to ensure that the thread was finished before the function was exited and thus before the local variables were destroyed. In this case, it would mean there was little point running the function on a separate thread, because the first thread wouldn't be doing anything useful in the meantime, but in real code the original thread would either have work to do itself or it would have launched several threads to do useful work before waiting for all of them to complete.

`join()` is simple and brute force—either you wait for a thread to finish or you don't. If you need more fine-grained control over waiting for a thread, such as to check whether a thread is finished, or to wait only a certain period of time, then you have to use alternative mechanisms such as condition variables and futures, which we'll look at in chapter 4. The act of calling `join()` also cleans up any storage associated with the thread, so the `std::thread` object is no longer associated with the now-finished thread; it isn't associated with any thread. This means that you can call `join()` only once for a given thread; once you've called `join()`, the `std::thread` object is no longer joinable, and `joinable()` will return `false`.

2.1.3 *Waiting in exceptional circumstances*

As mentioned earlier, you need to ensure that you've called either `join()` or `detach()` before a `std::thread` object is destroyed. If you're detaching a thread, you can usually call `detach()` immediately after the thread has been started, so this isn't a problem. But if you're intending to wait for the thread, you need to pick carefully the place in the code where you call `join()`. This means that the call to `join()` is liable to be skipped if an exception is thrown after the thread has been started but before the call to `join()`.

To avoid your application being terminated when an exception is thrown, you therefore need to make a decision on what to do in this case. In general, if you were intending to call `join()` in the non-exceptional case, you also need to call `join()` in the presence of an exception to avoid accidental lifetime problems. The next listing shows some simple code that does just that.

Listing 2.2 Waiting for a thread to finish

```
struct func;                          <-- See definition
                                          in listing 2.1
void f()
{
    int some_local_state=0;
    func my_func(some_local_state);
    std::thread t(my_func);
    try
    {
        do_something_in_current_thread();
    }
    catch(...)
    {
        t.join();               <-- 1
```

```
        throw;
    }
    t.join();                  <-- 2
}
```

The code in listing 2.2 uses a `try/catch` block to ensure that a thread with access to local state is finished before the function exits, whether the function exits normally ❷ or by an exception ❶. The use of `try/catch` blocks is verbose, and it's easy to get the scope slightly wrong, so this isn't an ideal scenario. If it's important to ensure that the thread must complete before the function exits—whether because it has a reference to other local variables or for any other reason—then it's important to ensure this is the case for all possible exit paths, whether normal or exceptional, and it's desirable to provide a simple, concise mechanism for doing so.

One way of doing this is to use the standard Resource Acquisition Is Initialization (RAII) idiom and provide a class that does the `join()` in its destructor, as in the following listing. See how it simplifies the function `f()`.

Listing 2.3 Using RAII to wait for a thread to complete

```
class thread_guard
{
    std::thread& t;
public:
    explicit thread_guard(std::thread& t_):
        t(t_)
    {}
    ~thread_guard()
    {
        if(t.joinable())                    <-- 1
        {
            t.join();                       <-- 2
        }
    }
    thread_guard(thread_guard const&)=delete;                <-- 3
    thread_guard& operator=(thread_guard const&)=delete;
};

struct func;                                <-- See definition
                                                in listing 2.1
void f()
{
    int some_local_state=0;
    func my_func(some_local_state);
    std::thread t(my_func);
    thread_guard g(t);

    do_something_in_current_thread();
}                                           <-- 4
```

When the execution of the current thread reaches the end of `f` ❹, the local objects are destroyed in reverse order of construction. Consequently, the `thread_guard` object `g` is destroyed first, and the thread is joined with in the destructor ❷. This even happens if the function exits because `do_something_in_current_thread` throws an exception.

The destructor of `thread_guard` in listing 2.3 first tests to see if the `std::thread` object is `joinable()` ❶ before calling `join()` ❷. This is important, because `join()` can be called only once for a given thread of execution, so it would therefore be a mistake to do so if the thread had already been joined.

The copy constructor and copy-assignment operator are marked `=delete` ❸ to ensure that they're not automatically provided by the compiler. Copying or assigning such an object would be dangerous, because it might then outlive the scope of the thread it was joining. By declaring them as deleted, any attempt to copy a `thread_guard` object will generate a compilation error. See appendix A, section A.2, for more about deleted functions.

If you don't need to wait for a thread to finish, you can avoid this exception-safety issue by *detaching* it. This breaks the association of the thread with the `std::thread` object and ensures that `std::terminate()` won't be called when the `std::thread` object is destroyed, even though the thread is still running in the background.

2.1.4 Running threads in the background

Calling `detach()` on a `std::thread` object leaves the thread to run in the background, with no direct means of communicating with it. It's no longer possible to wait for that thread to complete; if a thread becomes detached, it isn't possible to obtain a `std::thread` object that references it, so it can no longer be joined. Detached threads truly run in the background; ownership and control are passed over to the C++ Runtime Library, which ensures that the resources associated with the thread are correctly reclaimed when the thread exits.

Detached threads are often called *daemon threads* after the UNIX concept of a *daemon process* that runs in the background without any explicit user interface. Such threads are typically long-running; they may well run for almost the entire lifetime of the application, performing a background task such as monitoring the filesystem, clearing unused entries out of object caches, or optimizing data structures. At the other extreme, it may make sense to use a detached thread where there's another mechanism for identifying when the thread has completed or where the thread is used for a "fire and forget" task.

As you've already seen in section 2.1.2, you detach a thread by calling the `detach()` member function of the `std::thread` object. After the call completes, the `std::thread` object is no longer associated with the actual thread of execution and is therefore no longer joinable:

```
std::thread t(do_background_work);
t.detach();
assert(!t.joinable());
```

In order to detach the thread from a `std::thread` object, there must be a thread to detach: you can't call `detach()` on a `std::thread` object with no associated thread of execution. This is exactly the same requirement as for `join()`, and you can check it in exactly the same way—you can only call `t.detach()` for a `std::thread` object `t` when `t.joinable()` returns `true`.

Consider an application such as a word processor that can edit multiple documents at once. There are many ways to handle this, both at the UI level and internally. One way that seems to be increasingly common at the moment is to have multiple independent top-level windows, one for each document being edited. Although these windows appear to be completely independent, each with its own menus and so forth, they're running within the same instance of the application. One way to handle this internally is to run each document-editing window in its own thread; each thread runs the same code but with different data relating to the document being edited and the corresponding window properties. Opening a new document therefore requires starting a new thread. The thread handling the request isn't going to care about waiting for that other thread to finish, because it's working on an unrelated document, so this makes it a prime candidate for running a detached thread.

The following listing shows a simple code outline for this approach.

Listing 2.4 Detaching a thread to handle other documents

```
void edit_document(std::string const& filename)
{
    open_document_and_display_gui(filename);
    while(!done_editing())
    {
        user_command cmd=get_user_input();
        if(cmd.type==open_new_document)
        {
            std::string const new_name=get_filename_from_user();
            std::thread t(edit_document,new_name);                    <-1
            t.detach();                                        <-2
        }
        else
        {
            process_user_input(cmd);
        }
    }
}
```

If the user chooses to open a new document, you prompt them for the document to open, start a new thread to open that document ❶, and then detach it ❷. Because the new thread is doing the same operation as the current thread but on a different file, you can reuse the same function (`edit_document`) with the newly chosen filename as the supplied argument.

This example also shows a case where it's helpful to pass arguments to the function used to start a thread: rather than just passing the name of the function to the `std::thread` constructor ❶, you also pass in the filename parameter. Although other mechanisms could be used to do this, such as using a function object with member data instead of an ordinary function with parameters, the Thread Library provides you with an easy way of doing it.

2.2 Passing arguments to a thread function

As shown in listing 2.4, passing arguments to the callable object or function is fundamentally as simple as passing additional arguments to the `std::thread` constructor. But it's important to bear in mind that by default the arguments are *copied* into internal storage, where they can be accessed by the newly created thread of execution, even if the corresponding parameter in the function is expecting a reference. Here's a simple example:

```
void f(int i,std::string const& s);
std::thread t(f,3,"hello");
```

This creates a new thread of execution associated with `t`, which calls `f(3,"hello")`. Note that even though `f` takes a `std::string` as the second parameter, the string literal is passed as a `char const*` and converted to a `std::string` only in the context of the new thread. This is particularly important when the argument supplied is a pointer to an automatic variable, as follows:

```
void f(int i,std::string const& s);

void oops(int some_param)
{
    char buffer[1024];                          <-❶
    sprintf(buffer, "%i",some_param);
    std::thread t(f,3,buffer);                  <-❷
    t.detach();
}
```

In this case, it's the pointer to the local variable `buffer` ❶ that's passed through to the new thread ❷, and there's a significant chance that the function oops will exit before the buffer has been converted to a `std::string` on the new thread, thus leading to undefined behavior. The solution is to cast to `std::string` *before* passing the buffer to the `std::thread` constructor:

```
void f(int i,std::string const& s);

void not_oops(int some_param)
{
    char buffer[1024];
    sprintf(buffer,"%i",some_param);
    std::thread t(f,3,std::string(buffer));     <-  Using std::string avoids
    t.detach();                                     dangling pointer
}
```

In this case, the problem is that you were relying on the implicit conversion of the pointer to the buffer into the `std::string` object expected as a function parameter, because the `std::thread` constructor copies the supplied values as is, without converting to the expected argument type.

It's also possible to get the reverse scenario: the object is copied, and what you wanted was a reference. This might happen if the thread is updating a data structure that's passed in by reference, for example:

```
void update_data_for_widget(widget_id w,widget_data& data);    <-1

void oops_again(widget_id w)
{
    widget_data data;
    std::thread t(update_data_for_widget,w,data);    <-2
    display_status();
    t.join();
    process_widget_data(data);    <-3
}
```

Although `update_data_for_widget` ❶ expects the second parameter to be passed by reference, the `std::thread` constructor ❷ doesn't know that; it's oblivious to the types of the arguments expected by the function and blindly copies the supplied values. When it calls `update_data_for_widget`, it will end up passing a reference to the internal copy of `data` and not a reference to `data` itself. Consequently, when the thread finishes, these updates will be discarded as the internal copies of the supplied arguments are destroyed, and `process_widget_data` will be passed an unchanged `data` ❸ rather than a correctly updated version. For those of you familiar with `std::bind`, the solution will be readily apparent: you need to wrap the arguments that really need to be references in `std::ref`. In this case, if you change the thread invocation to

```
std::thread t(update_data_for_widget,w,std::ref(data));
```

and then `update_data_for_widget` will be correctly passed a reference to `data` rather than a reference to a *copy* of `data`.

If you're familiar with `std::bind`, the parameter-passing semantics will be unsurprising, because both the operation of the `std::thread` constructor and the operation of `std::bind` are defined in terms of the same mechanism. This means that, for example, you can pass a member function pointer as the function, provided you supply a suitable object pointer as the first argument:

```
class X
{
public:
    void do_lengthy_work();
};

X my_x;
std::thread t(&X::do_lengthy_work,&my_x);    <-1
```

This code will invoke `my_x.do_lengthy_work()` on the new thread, because the address of `my_x` is supplied as the object pointer ❶. You can also supply arguments to such a member function call: the third argument to the `std::thread` constructor will be the first argument to the member function and so forth.

Another interesting scenario for supplying arguments is where the arguments can't be copied but can only be *moved*: the data held within one object is transferred over to another, leaving the original object "empty." An example of such a type is `std::unique_ptr`, which provides automatic memory management for dynamically allocated objects. Only one `std::unique_ptr` instance can point to a given object at a time, and when that instance is destroyed, the pointed-to object is deleted. The *move constructor* and *move assignment operator* allow the ownership of an object to be transferred around between `std::unique_ptr` instances (see appendix A, section A.1.1, for more on move semantics). Such a transfer leaves the source object with a `NULL` pointer. This moving of values allows objects of this type to be accepted as function parameters or returned from functions. Where the source object is a temporary, the move is automatic, but where the source is a named value, the transfer must be requested directly by invoking `std::move()`. The following example shows the use of `std::move` to transfer ownership of a dynamic object into a thread:

```
void process_big_object(std::unique_ptr<big_object>);

std::unique_ptr<big_object> p(new big_object);
p->prepare_data(42);
std::thread t(process_big_object,std::move(p));
```

By specifying `std::move(p)` in the `std::thread` constructor, the ownership of the `big_object` is transferred first into internal storage for the newly created thread and then into `process_big_object`.

Several of the classes in the Standard Thread Library exhibit the same ownership semantics as `std::unique_ptr`, and `std::thread` is one of them. Though `std::thread` instances don't own a dynamic object in the same way as `std::unique_ptr` does, they do own a resource: each instance is responsible for managing a thread of execution. This ownership can be transferred between instances, because instances of `std::thread` are *movable*, even though they aren't *copyable*. This ensures that only one object is associated with a particular thread of execution at any one time while allowing programmers the option of transferring that ownership between objects.

2.3 Transferring ownership of a thread

Suppose you want to write a function that creates a thread to run in the background but passes back ownership of the new thread to the calling function rather than waiting for it to complete, or maybe you want to do the reverse: create a thread and pass ownership in to some function that should wait for it to complete. In either case, you need to transfer ownership from one place to another.

This is where the move support of `std::thread` comes in. As described in the previous section, many resource-owning types in the C++ Standard Library such as `std::ifstream` and `std::unique_ptr` are *movable* but not *copyable*, and `std::thread` is one of them. This means that the ownership of a particular thread of execution can be moved between `std::thread` instances, as in the following example. The example shows the creation of two threads of execution and the transfer of ownership of those threads among three `std::thread` instances, `t1`, `t2`, and `t3`:

```
void some_function();
void some_other_function();
std::thread t1(some_function);            <-1
std::thread t2=std::move(t1);                  <-2
t1=std::thread(some_other_function);      <-3
std::thread t3;                                <-4
t3=std::move(t2);                         <-5
t1=std::move(t3);                              <-6
```

6 **This assignment will terminate program!**

First, a new thread is started ❶ and associated with `t1`. Ownership is then transferred over to `t2` when `t2` is constructed, by invoking `std::move()` to explicitly move ownership ❷. At this point, `t1` no longer has an associated thread of execution; the thread running `some_function` is now associated with `t2`.

Then, a new thread is started and associated with a temporary `std::thread` object ❸. The subsequent transfer of ownership into `t1` doesn't require a call to `std::move()` to explicitly move ownership, because the owner is a temporary object—moving from temporaries is automatic and implicit.

`t3` is default constructed ❹, which means that it's created without any associated thread of execution. Ownership of the thread currently associated with `t2` is transferred into `t3` ❺, again with an explicit call to `std::move()`, because `t2` is a named object. After all these moves, `t1` is associated with the thread running `some_other_function`, `t2` has no associated thread, and `t3` is associated with the thread running `some_function`.

The final move ❻ transfers ownership of the thread running `some_function` back to `t1` where it started. But in this case `t1` already had an associated thread (which was running `some_other_function`), so `std::terminate()` is called to terminate the program. This is done for consistency with the `std::thread` destructor. You saw in section 2.1.1 that you must explicitly wait for a thread to complete or detach it before destruction, and the same applies to assignment: you can't just "drop" a thread by assigning a new value to the `std::thread` object that manages it.

The move support in `std::thread` means that ownership can readily be transferred out of a function, as shown in the following listing.

Listing 2.5 Returning a `std::thread` from a function

```
std::thread f()
{
    void some_function();
    return std::thread(some_function);
}
std::thread g()
{
    void some_other_function(int);
    std::thread t(some_other_function,42);
    return t;
}
```

Likewise, if ownership should be transferred into a function, it can just accept an instance of `std::thread` by value as one of the parameters, as shown here:

```
void f(std::thread t);
void g()
{
    void some_function();
    f(std::thread(some_function));
    std::thread t(some_function);
    f(std::move(t));
}
```

One benefit of the move support of `std::thread` is that you can build on the `thread_guard` class from listing 2.3 and have it actually take ownership of the thread. This avoids any unpleasant consequences should the `thread_guard` object outlive the thread it was referencing, and it also means that no one else can join or detach the thread once ownership has been transferred into the object. Because this would primarily be aimed at ensuring threads are completed before a scope is exited, I named this class `scoped_thread`. The implementation is shown in the following listing, along with a simple example.

Listing 2.6 `scoped_thread` and example usage

```
class scoped_thread
{
    std::thread t;
public:
    explicit scoped_thread(std::thread t_):                ❶
        t(std::move(t_))
    {
        if(!t.joinable())                                  ❷
            throw std::logic_error("No thread");
    }
    ~scoped_thread()
    {
        t.join();          ❸
    }
    scoped_thread(scoped_thread const&)=delete;
    scoped_thread& operator=(scoped_thread const&)=delete;
};

struct func;                    See listing 2.1

void f()
{
    int some_local_state;
    scoped_thread t(std::thread(func(some_local_state)));     ❹

    do_something_in_current_thread();
}                                                ❺
```

The example is similar to that from listing 2.3, but the new thread is passed in directly to the `scoped_thread` ❹ rather than having to create a separate named variable for it.

When the initial thread reaches the end of `f` ❺, the `scoped_thread` object is destroyed and then joins with ❸ the thread supplied to the constructor ❶. Whereas with the `thread_guard` class from listing 2.3 the destructor had to check that the thread was still joinable, you can do that in the constructor ❷ and throw an exception if it's not.

The move support in `std::thread` also allows for containers of `std::thread` objects, if those containers are move aware (like the updated `std::vector<>`). This means that you can write code like that in the following listing, which spawns a number of threads and then waits for them to finish.

Listing 2.7 Spawn some threads and wait for them to finish

```
void do_work(unsigned id);

void f()
{
    std::vector<std::thread> threads;
    for(unsigned i=0;i<20;++i)
    {
        threads.push_back(std::thread(do_work,i));      // Spawn threads
    }
    std::for_each(threads.begin(),threads.end(),
                  std::mem_fn(&std::thread::join));     // Call join() on each thread in turn
}
```

If the threads are being used to subdivide the work of an algorithm, this is often just what's required; before returning to the caller, all threads must have finished. Of course, the simple structure of listing 2.7 implies that the work done by the threads is self-contained, and the result of their operations is purely the side effects on shared data. If `f()` were to return a value to the caller that depended on the results of the operations performed by these threads, then as written this return value would have to be determined by examining the shared data after the threads had terminated. Alternative schemes for transferring the results of operations between threads are discussed in chapter 4.

Putting `std::thread` objects in a `std::vector` is a step toward automating the management of those threads: rather than creating separate variables for those threads and joining with them directly, they can be treated as a group. You can take this a step further by creating a dynamic number of threads determined at runtime, rather than creating a fixed number as in listing 2.7.

2.4 Choosing the number of threads at runtime

One feature of the C++ Standard Library that helps here is `std::thread::hardware_concurrency()`. This function returns an indication of the number of threads that can truly run concurrently for a given execution of a program. On a multicore system it might be the number of CPU cores, for example. This is only a hint, and the function might return 0 if this information is not available, but it can be a useful guide for splitting a task among threads.

Listing 2.8 shows a simple implementation of a parallel version of `std::accumulate`. It divides the work among the threads, with a minimum number of elements per thread in order to avoid the overhead of too many threads. Note that this implementation assumes that none of the operations will throw an exception, even though exceptions are possible; the `std::thread` constructor will throw if it can't start a new thread of execution, for example. Handling exceptions in such an algorithm is beyond the scope of this simple example and will be covered in chapter 8.

Listing 2.8 A naïve parallel version of `std::accumulate`

```
template<typename Iterator,typename T>
struct accumulate_block
{
    void operator()(Iterator first,Iterator last,T& result)
    {
        result=std::accumulate(first,last,result);
    }
};

template<typename Iterator,typename T>
T parallel_accumulate(Iterator first,Iterator last,T init)
{
    unsigned long const length=std::distance(first,last);

    if(!length)                                              (1)
        return init;

    unsigned long const min_per_thread=25;
    unsigned long const max_threads=
        (length+min_per_thread-1)/min_per_thread;        (2)

    unsigned long const hardware_threads=
        std::thread::hardware_concurrency();
                                                      (3)
    unsigned long const num_threads=
        std::min(hardware_threads!=0?hardware_threads:2,max_threads);

    unsigned long const block_size=length/num_threads;       (4)

    std::vector<T> results(num_threads);
    std::vector<std::thread>  threads(num_threads-1);        (5)

    Iterator block_start=first;
    for(unsigned long i=0;i<(num_threads-1);++i)
    {
        Iterator block_end=block_start;
        std::advance(block_end,block_size);                  (6)
        threads[i]=std::thread(                     (7)
            accumulate_block<Iterator,T>(),
            block_start,block_end,std::ref(results[i]));
        block_start=block_end;                               (8)
    }
    accumulate_block<Iterator,T>()(
        block_start,last,results[num_threads-1]);        (9)
```

```
    std::for_each(threads.begin(),threads.end(),
        std::mem_fn(&std::thread::join));              <-10

    return std::accumulate(results.begin(),results.end(),init);    <-11
}
```

Although this is quite a long function, it's actually straightforward. If the input range is empty ❶, you just return the initial value `init`. Otherwise, there's at least one element in the range, so you can divide the number of elements to process by the minimum block size in order to give the maximum number of threads ❷. This is to avoid creating 32 threads on a 32-core machine when you have only five values in the range.

The number of threads to run is the minimum of your calculated maximum and the number of hardware threads ❸. You don't want to run more threads than the hardware can support (which is called *oversubscription*), because the context switching will mean that more threads will decrease the performance. If the call to `std::thread::hardware_concurrency()` returned 0, you'd simply substitute a number of your choice; in this case I've chosen 2. You don't want to run too many threads, because that would slow things down on a single-core machine, but likewise you don't want to run too few, because then you'd be passing up the available concurrency.

The number of entries for each thread to process is the length of the range divided by the number of threads ❹. If you're worrying about the case where the number doesn't divide evenly, don't—you'll handle that later.

Now that you know how many threads you have, you can create a `std::vector<T>` for the intermediate results and a `std::vector<std::thread>` for the threads ❺. Note that you need to launch one fewer thread than `num_threads`, because you already have one.

Launching the threads is just a simple loop: advance the `block_end` iterator to the end of the current block ❻ and launch a new thread to accumulate the results for this block ❼. The start of the next block is the end of this one ❽.

After you've launched all the threads, this thread can then process the final block ❾. This is where you take account of any uneven division: you know the end of the final block must be `last`, and it doesn't matter how many elements are in that block.

Once you've accumulated the results for the last block, you can wait for all the threads you spawned with `std::for_each` ❿, as in listing 2.7, and then add up the results with a final call to `std::accumulate` ⓫.

Before you leave this example, it's worth pointing out that where the addition operator for the type `T` is not associative (such as for `float` or `double`), the results of this `parallel_accumulate` may vary from those of `std::accumulate`, because of the grouping of the range into blocks. Also, the requirements on the iterators are slightly more stringent: they must be at least *forward iterators*, whereas `std::accumulate` can work with single-pass *input iterators*, and `T` must be *default constructible* so that you can create the `results` vector. These sorts of requirement changes are common with parallel algorithms; by their very nature they're different in some manner in order to make them parallel, and this has consequences on the results and requirements. Parallel algorithms are covered in more depth in chapter 8. It's also worth noting that because you can't return a value directly from a thread, you must pass in a reference to the relevant entry in the `results` vector. Alternative ways of returning results from threads are addressed through the use of *futures* in chapter 4.

In this case, all the information required by each thread was passed in when the thread was started, including the location in which to store the result of its calculation. This isn't always the case: sometimes it's necessary to be able to identify the threads in some way for part of the processing. You could pass in an identifying number, such as the value of `i` in listing 2.7, but if the function that needs the identifier is several levels deep in the call stack and could be called from any thread, it's inconvenient to have to do it that way. When we were designing the C++ Thread Library we foresaw this need, and so each thread has a unique identifier.

2.5 Identifying threads

Thread identifiers are of type `std::thread::id` and can be retrieved in two ways. First, the identifier for a thread can be obtained from its associated `std::thread` object by calling the `get_id()` member function. If the `std::thread` object doesn't have an associated thread of execution, the call to `get_id()` returns a default-constructed `std::thread::id` object, which indicates "not any thread." Alternatively, the identifier for the current thread can be obtained by calling `std::this_thread::get_id()`, which is also defined in the `<thread>` header.

Objects of type `std::thread::id` can be freely copied and compared; they wouldn't be of much use as identifiers otherwise. If two objects of type `std::thread::id` are equal, they represent the same thread, or both are holding the "not any thread" value. If two objects aren't equal, they represent different threads, or one represents a thread and the other is holding the "not any thread" value.

The Thread Library doesn't limit you to checking whether thread identifiers are the same or not; objects of type `std::thread::id` offer the complete set of comparison operators, which provide a total ordering for all distinct values. This allows them to be used as keys in associative containers, or sorted, or compared in any other way that you as a programmer may see fit. The comparison operators provide a total order for all non-equal values of `std::thread::id`, so they behave as you'd intuitively expect: if `a<b` and `b<c`, then `a<c`, and so forth. The Standard Library also provides `std::hash<std::thread::id>` so that values of type `std::thread::id` can be used as keys in the new unordered associative containers too.

Instances of `std::thread::id` are often used to check whether a thread needs to perform some operation. For example, if threads are used to divide work as in listing 2.8, the initial thread that launched the others might need to perform its work slightly differently in the middle of the algorithm. In this case it could store the result of `std::this_thread::get_id()` before launching the other threads, and then the core part of the algorithm (which is common to all threads) could check its own thread ID against the stored value:

```
std::thread::id master_thread;
void some_core_part_of_algorithm()
{
    if(std::this_thread::get_id()==master_thread)
    {
        do_master_thread_work();
    }
    do_common_work();
}
```

Alternatively, the `std::thread::id` of the current thread could be stored in a data structure as part of an operation. Later operations on that same data structure could then check the stored ID against the ID of the thread performing the operation to determine what operations are permitted/required.

Similarly, thread IDs could be used as keys into associative containers where specific data needs to be associated with a thread and alternative mechanisms such as thread-local storage aren't appropriate. Such a container could, for example, be used by a controlling thread to store information about each of the threads under its control or for passing information between threads.

The idea is that `std::thread::id` will suffice as a generic identifier for a thread in most circumstances; it's only if the identifier has semantic meaning associated with it (such as being an index into an array) that alternatives should be necessary. You can even write out an instance of `std::thread::id` to an output stream such as `std::cout`:

```
std::cout<<std::this_thread::get_id();
```

The exact output you get is strictly implementation dependent; the only guarantee given by the standard is that thread IDs that compare as equal should produce the same output, and those that are not equal should give different output. This is therefore primarily useful for debugging and logging, but the values have no semantic meaning, so there's not much more that could be said anyway.

2.6 Summary

In this chapter I covered the basics of thread management with the C++ Standard Library: starting threads, waiting for them to finish, and *not* waiting for them to finish because you want them to run in the background. You also saw how to pass arguments into the thread function when a thread is started, how to transfer the responsibility for managing a thread from one part of the code to another, and how groups of threads can be used to divide work. Finally, I discussed identifying threads in order to associate data or behavior with specific threads that's inconvenient to associate through alternative means. Although you can do quite a lot with purely independent threads that each operate on separate data, as in listing 2.8 for example, sometimes it's desirable to share data among threads while they're running. Chapter 3 discusses the issues surrounding sharing data directly among threads, while chapter 4 covers more general issues surrounding synchronizing operations with and without shared data.

Sharing data between threads

This chapter covers

- Problems with sharing data between threads
- Protecting data with mutexes
- Alternative facilities for protecting shared data

One of the key benefits of using threads for concurrency is the potential to easily and directly share data between them, so now that we've covered starting and managing threads, let's look at the issues surrounding shared data.

Imagine for a moment that you're sharing an apartment with a friend. There's only one kitchen and only one bathroom. Unless you're particularly friendly, you can't both use the bathroom at the same time, and if your roommate occupies the bathroom for a long time, it can be frustrating if you need to use it. Likewise, though it might be possible to both cook meals at the same time, if you have a combined oven and grill, it's just not going to end well if one of you tries to grill some sausages at the same time as the other is baking a cake. Furthermore, we all know the frustration of sharing a space and getting halfway through a task only to find that someone has borrowed something we need or changed something from the way we left it.

It's the same with threads. If you're sharing data between threads, you need to have rules for which thread can access which bit of data when, and how any updates are communicated to the other threads that care about that data. The ease with which data can be shared between multiple threads in a single process is not just a benefit—it can also be a big drawback. Incorrect use of shared data is one of the biggest causes of concurrency-related bugs, and the consequences can be far worse than sausage-flavored cakes.

This chapter is about sharing data safely between threads in C++, avoiding the potential problems that can arise, and maximizing the benefits.

3.1 Problems with sharing data between threads

When it comes down to it, the problems with sharing data between threads are all due to the consequences of modifying data. *If all shared data is read-only, there's no problem, because the data read by one thread is unaffected by whether or not another thread is reading the same data.* However, if data is shared between threads, and one or more threads start modifying the data, there's a lot of potential for trouble. In this case, you must take care to ensure that everything works out OK.

One concept that's widely used to help programmers reason about their code is that of *invariants*—statements that are always true about a particular data structure, such as "this variable contains the number of items in the list." These invariants are often broken during an update, especially if the data structure is of any complexity or the update requires modification of more than one value.

Consider a doubly linked list, where each node holds a pointer to both the next node in the list and the previous one. One of the invariants is that if you follow a "next" pointer from one node (A) to another (B), the "previous" pointer from that node (B) points back to the first node (A). In order to remove a node from the list, the nodes on either side have to be updated to point to each other. Once one has been updated, the invariant is broken until the node on the other side has been updated too; after the update has completed, the invariant holds again.

The steps in deleting an entry from such a list are shown in figure 3.1:

1. Identify the node to delete (N).
2. Update the link from the node prior to N to point to the node after N.
3. Update the link from the node after N to point to the node prior to N.
4. Delete node N.

As you can see, between steps b and c, the links going in one direction are inconsistent with the links going in the opposite direction, and the invariant is broken.

The simplest potential problem with modifying data that's shared between threads is that of broken invariants. If you don't do anything special to ensure otherwise, if one thread is reading the doubly linked list while another is removing a node, it's quite possible for the reading thread to see the list with a node only partially removed (because only one of the links has been changed, as in step b of figure 3.1), so the invariant is broken. The consequences of this broken invariant can vary; if the other thread is just reading the list items from left to right in the diagram, it will skip the node being

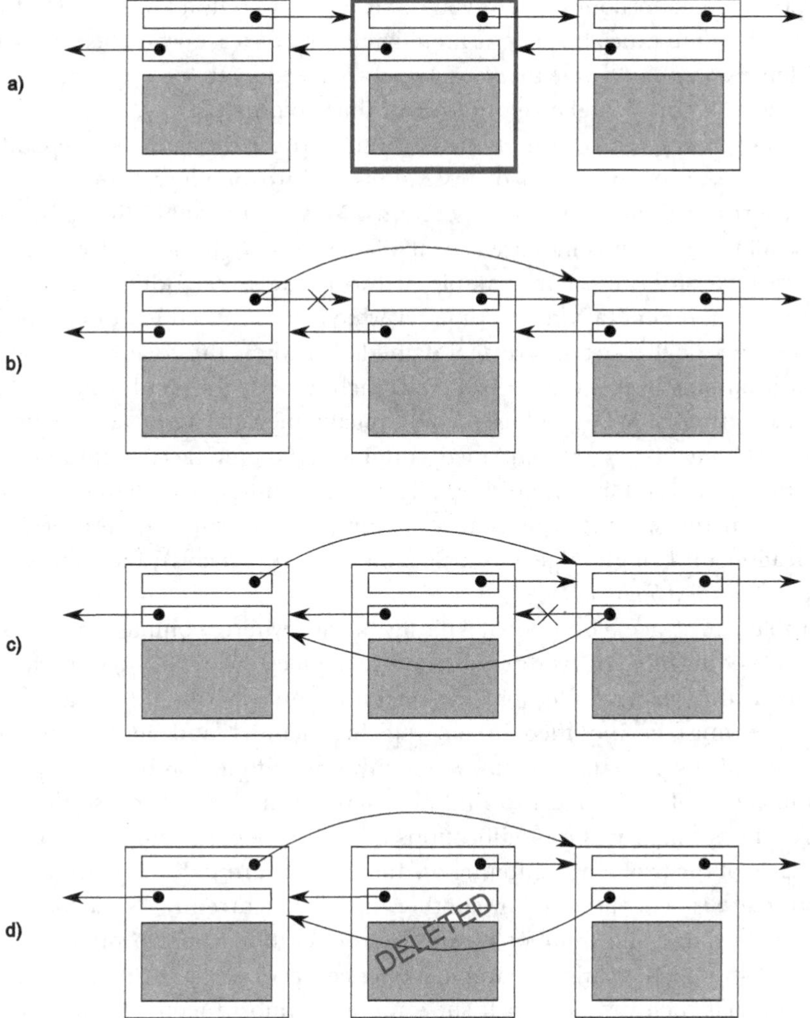

Figure 3.1 Deleting a node from a doubly linked list

deleted. On the other hand, if the second thread is trying to delete the rightmost node in the diagram, it might end up permanently corrupting the data structure and eventually crashing the program. Whatever the outcome, this is an example of one of the most common causes of bugs in concurrent code: a *race condition*.

3.1.1 Race conditions

Suppose you're buying tickets to see a movie at the cinema. If it's a big cinema, multiple cashiers will be taking money, so more than one person can buy tickets at the same time. If someone at another cashier's desk is also buying tickets for the same movie as you are, which seats are available for you to choose from depends on whether the other person actually books first or you do. If there are only a few seats left, this difference can be quite crucial: it might literally be a race to see who gets the last tickets. This is an example of a *race condition*: which seats you get (or even whether you get tickets) depends on the relative ordering of the two purchases.

In concurrency, a race condition is anything where the outcome depends on the relative ordering of execution of operations on two or more threads; the threads race to perform their respective operations. Most of the time, this is quite benign because all possible outcomes are acceptable, even though they may change with different relative orderings. For example, if two threads are adding items to a queue for processing, it generally doesn't matter which item gets added first, provided that the invariants of the system are maintained. It's when the race condition leads to broken invariants that there's a problem, such as with the doubly linked list example just mentioned. When talking about concurrency, the term *race condition* is usually used to mean a *problematic* race condition; benign race conditions aren't so interesting and aren't a cause of bugs. The C++ Standard also defines the term *data race* to mean the specific type of race condition that arises because of concurrent modification to a single object (see section 5.1.2 for details); data races cause the dreaded *undefined behavior*.

Problematic race conditions typically occur where completing an operation requires modification of two or more distinct pieces of data, such as the two link pointers in the example. Because the operation must access two separate pieces of data, these must be modified in separate instructions, and another thread could potentially access the data structure when only one of them has been completed. Race conditions can often be hard to find and hard to duplicate because the window of opportunity is small. If the modifications are done as consecutive CPU instructions, the chance of the problem exhibiting on any one run-through is very small, even if the data structure is being accessed by another thread concurrently. As the load on the system increases, and the number of times the operation is performed increases, the chance of the problematic execution sequence occurring also increases. It's almost inevitable that such problems will show up at the most inconvenient time. Because race conditions are generally timing sensitive, they can often disappear entirely when the application is run under the debugger, because the debugger affects the timing of the program, even if only slightly.

If you're writing multithreaded programs, race conditions can easily be the bane of your life; a great deal of the complexity in writing software that uses concurrency comes from avoiding problematic race conditions.

3.1.2 Avoiding problematic race conditions

There are several ways to deal with problematic race conditions. The simplest option is to wrap your data structure with a protection mechanism, to ensure that only the thread actually performing a modification can see the intermediate states where the invariants are broken. From the point of view of other threads accessing that data structure, such modifications either haven't started or have completed. The C++ Standard Library provides several such mechanisms, which are described in this chapter.

Another option is to modify the design of your data structure and its invariants so that modifications are done as a series of indivisible changes, each of which preserves the invariants. This is generally referred to as *lock-free programming* and is difficult to get right. If you're working at this level, the nuances of the memory model and identifying which threads can potentially see which set of values can get complicated. The memory model is covered in chapter 5, and lock-free programming is discussed in chapter 7.

Another way of dealing with race conditions is to handle the updates to the data structure as a *transaction*, just as updates to a database are done within a transaction. The required series of data modifications and reads is stored in a transaction log and then committed in a single step. If the commit can't proceed because the data structure has been modified by another thread, the transaction is restarted. This is termed *software transactional memory (STM)*, and it's an active research area at the time of writing. This won't be covered in this book, because there's no direct support for STM in C++. However, the basic idea of doing something privately and then committing in a single step is something that I'll come back to later.

The most basic mechanism for protecting shared data provided by the C++ Standard is the *mutex*, so we'll look at that first.

3.2 Protecting shared data with mutexes

So, you have a shared data structure such as the linked list from the previous section, and you want to protect it from race conditions and the potential broken invariants that can ensue. Wouldn't it be nice if you could mark all the pieces of code that access the data structure as *mutually exclusive*, so that if any thread was running one of them, any other thread that tried to access that data structure had to wait until the first thread was finished? That would make it impossible for a thread to see a broken invariant except when it was the thread doing the modification.

Well, this isn't a fairy tale wish—it's precisely what you get if you use a synchronization primitive called a *mutex* (*mut*ual *ex*clusion). Before accessing a shared data structure, you *lock* the mutex associated with that data, and when you've finished accessing the data structure, you *unlock* the mutex. The Thread Library then ensures that once one thread has locked a specific mutex, all other threads that try to lock the same mutex have to wait until the thread that successfully locked the mutex unlocks it. This ensures that all threads see a self-consistent view of the shared data, without any broken invariants.

Mutexes are the most general of the data-protection mechanisms available in C++, but they're not a silver bullet; it's important to structure your code to protect the right data (see section 3.2.2) and avoid race conditions inherent in your interfaces (see section 3.2.3). Mutexes also come with their own problems, in the form of a *deadlock* (see section 3.2.4) and protecting either too much or too little data (see section 3.2.8). Let's start with the basics.

3.2.1 Using mutexes in C++

In C++, you create a mutex by constructing an instance of `std::mutex`, lock it with a call to the member function `lock()`, and unlock it with a call to the member function `unlock()`. However, it isn't recommended practice to call the member functions directly, because this means that you have to remember to call `unlock()` on every code path out of a function, including those due to exceptions. Instead, the Standard C++ Library provides the `std::lock_guard` class template, which implements that RAII idiom for a mutex; it locks the supplied mutex on construction and unlocks it on destruction, thus ensuring a locked mutex is always correctly unlocked. The following listing shows how to protect a list that can be accessed by multiple threads using a `std::mutex`, along with `std::lock_guard`. Both of these are declared in the `<mutex>` header.

Listing 3.1 Protecting a list with a mutex

```
#include <list>
#include <mutex>
#include <algorithm>

std::list<int> some_list;                         <-1
std::mutex some_mutex;                     <-2

void add_to_list(int new_value)
{
    std::lock_guard<std::mutex> guard(some_mutex);    <-3
    some_list.push_back(new_value);
}
bool list_contains(int value_to_find)
{
    std::lock_guard<std::mutex> guard(some_mutex);       <-4
    return std::find(some_list.begin(),some_list.end(),value_to_find)
        != some_list.end();
}
```

In listing 3.1, there's a single global variable ❶, and it's protected with a corresponding global instance of `std::mutex` ❷. The use of `std::lock_guard<std::mutex>` in `add_to_list()` ❸ and again in `list_contains()` ❹ means that the accesses in these functions are mutually exclusive: `list_contains()` will never see the list partway through a modification by `add_to_list()`.

Although there are occasions where this use of global variables is appropriate, in the majority of cases it's common to group the mutex and the protected data together in a class rather than use global variables. This is a standard application of object-oriented design rules: by putting them in a class, you're clearly marking them as related, and you can encapsulate the functionality and enforce the protection. In this case, the functions `add_to_list` and `list_contains` would become member functions of the class, and the mutex and protected data would both become `private` members of the class, making it much easier to identify which code has access to the data and thus which code needs to lock the mutex. If all the member functions of the class lock the mutex before accessing any other data members and unlock it when done, the data is nicely protected from all comers.

Well, that's not *quite* true, as the astute among you will have noticed: if one of the member functions returns a pointer or reference to the protected data, then it doesn't matter that the member functions all lock the mutex in a nice orderly fashion, because you've just blown a big hole in the protection. *Any code that has access to that pointer or reference can now access (and potentially modify) the protected data without locking the mutex.* Protecting data with a mutex therefore requires careful interface design, to ensure that the mutex is locked before there's any access to the protected data and that there are no backdoors.

3.2.2 Structuring code for protecting shared data

As you've just seen, protecting data with a mutex is not quite as easy as just slapping a `std::lock_guard` object in every member function; one stray pointer or reference, and all that protection is for nothing. At one level, checking for stray pointers or references is easy; as long as none of the member functions return a pointer or reference to the protected data to their caller either via their return value or via an out parameter, the data is safe. If you dig a little deeper, it's not that straightforward—nothing ever is. As well as checking that the member functions don't pass out pointers or references to their callers, it's also important to check that they don't pass such pointers or references *in* to functions they call that aren't under your control. This is just as dangerous: those functions might store the pointer or reference in a place where it can later be used without the protection of the mutex. Particularly dangerous in this regard are functions that are supplied at runtime via a function argument or other means, as in the next listing.

Listing 3.2 Accidentally passing out a reference to protected data

```
class some_data
{
    int a;
    std::string b;
public:
    void do_something();
};

class data_wrapper
{
private:
    some_data data;
    std::mutex m;
public:
    template<typename Function>
    void process_data(Function func)
    {
        std::lock_guard<std::mutex> l(m);
        func(data);                          ❶ Pass "protected" data to
    }                                           user-supplied function
};
```

```
some_data* unprotected;

void malicious_function(some_data& protected_data)
{
    unprotected=&protected_data;
}

data_wrapper x;

void foo()
{
    x.process_data(malicious_function);      ❷ Pass in a malicious function
    unprotected->do_something();             ❸ Unprotected access to protected data
}
```

In this example, the code in `process_data` looks harmless enough, nicely protected with `std::lock_guard`, but the call to the user-supplied function `func` ❶ means that `foo` can pass in `malicious_function` to bypass the protection ❷ and then call `do_something()` without the mutex being locked ❸.

Fundamentally, the problem with this code is that it hasn't done what you set out to do: mark all the pieces of code that access the data structure as *mutually exclusive*. In this case, it missed the code in `foo()` that calls `unprotected->do_something()`. Unfortunately, this part of the problem isn't something the C++ Thread Library can help you with; it's up to you as programmers to lock the right mutex to protect your data. On the upside, you have a guideline to follow, which will help you in these cases: *Don't pass pointers and references to protected data outside the scope of the lock, whether by returning them from a function, storing them in externally visible memory, or passing them as arguments to user-supplied functions.*

Although this is a common mistake when trying to use mutexes to protect shared data, it's far from the only potential pitfall. As you'll see in the next section, it's still possible to have race conditions, even when data is protected with a mutex.

3.2.3 Spotting race conditions inherent in interfaces

Just because you're using a mutex or other mechanism to protect shared data, you're not necessarily protected from race conditions; you still have to ensure that the appropriate data is protected. Consider the doubly linked list example again. In order for a thread to safely delete a node, you need to ensure that you're preventing concurrent accesses to three nodes: the node being deleted and the nodes on either side. If you protected accesses to the pointers of each node individually, you'd be no better off than with code that used no mutexes, because the race condition could still happen—it's not the individual nodes that need protecting for the individual steps but the whole data structure, for the whole delete operation. The easiest solution in this case is to have a single mutex that protects the entire list, as in listing 3.1.

Just because individual operations on the list are safe, you're not out of the woods yet; you can still get race conditions, even with a really simple interface. Consider a stack data structure like the `std::stack` container adapter shown in listing 3.3. Aside from the constructors and `swap()`, there are only five things you can do to a `std::stack`:

you can push() a new element onto the stack, pop() an element off the stack, read the top() element, check whether it's empty(), and read the number of elements—the size() of the stack. If you change top() so that it returns a copy rather than a reference (so you're following the guideline from section 3.2.2) and protect the internal data with a mutex, this interface is still inherently subject to race conditions. This problem is not unique to a mutex-based implementation; it's an interface problem, so the race conditions would still occur with a lock-free implementation.

Listing 3.3 The interface to the std::stack container adapter

```
template<typename T,typename Container=std::deque<T> >
class stack
{
public:
    explicit stack(const Container&);
    explicit stack(Container&& = Container());
    template <class Alloc> explicit stack(const Alloc&);
    template <class Alloc> stack(const Container&, const Alloc&);
    template <class Alloc> stack(Container&&, const Alloc&);
    template <class Alloc> stack(stack&&, const Alloc&);

    bool empty() const;
    size_t size() const;
    T& top();
    T const& top() const;
    void push(T const&);
    void push(T&&);
    void pop();
    void swap(stack&&);
};
```

The problem here is that the results of empty() and size() can't be relied on. Although they might be correct at the time of the call, once they've returned, other threads are free to access the stack and might push() new elements onto or pop() the existing ones off of the stack before the thread that called empty() or size() could use that information.

In particular, if the stack instance is *not shared*, it's safe to check for empty() and then call top() to access the top element if the stack is not empty, as follows:

```
stack<int> s;
if(!s.empty())                   <-1
{
    int const value=s.top();           <-2
    s.pop();                      <-3
    do_something(value);
}
```

Not only is it safe in single-threaded code, it's expected: calling top() on an empty stack is undefined behavior. With a shared stack object, *this call sequence is no longer safe*, because there might be a call to pop() from another thread that removes the last element in between the call to empty() 1 and the call to top() 2. This is therefore a classic race condition, and the use of a mutex internally to protect the stack contents doesn't prevent it; it's a consequence of the interface.

What's the solution? Well, this problem happens as a consequence of the design of the interface, so the solution is to change the interface. However, that still begs the question: what changes need to be made? In the simplest case, you could just declare that `top()` will throw an exception if there aren't any elements in the stack when it's called. Though this directly addresses this issue, it makes for more cumbersome programming, because now you need to be able to catch an exception, even if the call to `empty()` returned `false`. This essentially makes the call to `empty()` completely redundant.

If you look closely at the previous snippet, there's also potential for another race condition but this time between the call to `top()` ❷ and the call to `pop()` ❸. Consider two threads running the previous snippet of code and both referencing the same `stack` object, `s`. This isn't an unusual situation; when using threads for performance, it's quite common to have several threads running the same code on different data, and a shared `stack` object is ideal for dividing work between them. Suppose that initially the stack has two elements, so you don't have to worry about the race between `empty()` and `top()` on either thread, and consider the potential execution patterns.

If the stack is protected by a mutex internally, only one thread can be running a stack member function at any one time, so the calls get nicely interleaved, while the calls to `do_something()` can run concurrently. One possible execution is then as shown in table 3.1.

Table 3.1 A possible ordering of operations on a stack from two threads

Thread A	Thread B
`if(!s.empty())`	
	`if(!s.empty())`
`    int const value=s.top();`	
	`    int const value=s.top();`
`    s.pop();`	
`    do_something(value);`	`    s.pop();`
	`    do_something(value);`

As you can see, if these are the only threads running, there's nothing in between the two calls to `top()` to modify the stack, so both threads will see the same value. Not only that, but *there are no calls to* `top()` *between the calls to* `pop()`. Consequently, one of the two values on the stack is discarded without ever having been read, whereas the other is processed twice. This is yet another race condition and far more insidious than the undefined behavior of the `empty()`/`top()` race; there's never anything obviously wrong going on, and the consequences of the bug are likely far removed from the cause, although they obviously depend on exactly what `do_something()` really does.

This calls for a more radical change to the interface, one that combines the calls to `top()` and `pop()` under the protection of the mutex. Tom Cargill[1] pointed out that a combined call can lead to issues if the copy constructor for the objects on the stack can throw an exception. This problem was dealt with fairly comprehensively from an exception-safety point of view by Herb Sutter,[2] but the potential for race conditions brings something new to the mix.

For those of you who aren't aware of the issue, consider a `stack<vector<int>>`. Now, a `vector` is a dynamically sized container, so when you copy a `vector` the library has to allocate some more memory from the heap in order to copy the contents. If the system is heavily loaded, or there are significant resource constraints, this memory allocation can fail, so the copy constructor for `vector` might throw a `std::bad_alloc` exception. This is especially likely if the `vector` contains a lot of elements. If the `pop()` function was defined to return the value popped, as well as remove it from the stack, you have a potential problem: the value being popped is returned to the caller only *after* the stack has been modified, but the process of copying the data to return to the caller might throw an exception. If this happens, the data just popped is lost; it has been removed from the stack, but the copy was unsuccessful! The designers of the `std::stack` interface helpfully split the operation in two: get the top element (`top()`) and then remove it from the stack (`pop()`), so that if you can't safely copy the data, it stays on the stack. If the problem was lack of heap memory, maybe the application can free some memory and try again.

Unfortunately, it's precisely this split that you're trying to avoid in eliminating the race condition! Thankfully, there are alternatives, but they aren't without cost.

OPTION 1: PASS IN A REFERENCE

The first option is to pass a reference to a variable in which you wish to receive the popped value as an argument in the call to `pop()`:

```
std::vector<int> result;
some_stack.pop(result);
```

This works well for many cases, but it has the distinct disadvantage that it requires the calling code to construct an instance of the stack's value type prior to the call, in order to pass this in as the target. For some types this is impractical, because constructing an instance is expensive in terms of time or resources. For other types this isn't always possible, because the constructors require parameters that aren't necessarily available at this point in the code. Finally, it requires that the stored type is assignable. This is an important restriction: many user-defined types do not support assignment, though

---

1 Tom Cargill, "Exception Handling: A False Sense of Security," in *C++ Report* 6, no. 9 (November–December 1994). Also available at http://www.informit.com/content/images/020163371x/supplements/Exception_Handling_Article.html.

2 Herb Sutter, *Exceptional C++: 47 Engineering Puzzles, Programming Problems, and Solutions* (Addison Wesley Professional, 1999).

they may support move construction or even copy construction (and thus allow return by value).

OPTION 2: REQUIRE A NO-THROW COPY CONSTRUCTOR OR MOVE CONSTRUCTOR

There's only an exception safety problem with a value-returning `pop()` if the return by value can throw an exception. Many types have copy constructors that don't throw exceptions, and with the new rvalue-reference support in the C++ Standard (see appendix A, section A.1), many more types will have a move constructor that doesn't throw exceptions, even if their copy constructor does. One valid option is to restrict the use of your thread-safe stack to those types that can safely be returned by value without throwing an exception.

Although this is safe, it's not ideal. Even though you can detect at compile time the existence of a copy or move constructor that doesn't throw an exception using the `std::is_nothrow_copy_constructible` and `std::is_nothrow_move_constructible` type traits, it's quite limiting. There are many more user-defined types with copy constructors that can throw and don't have move constructors than there are types with copy and/or move constructors that can't throw (although this might change as people get used to the rvalue-reference support in C++11). It would be unfortunate if such types couldn't be stored in your thread-safe stack.

OPTION 3: RETURN A POINTER TO THE POPPED ITEM

The third option is to return a pointer to the popped item rather than return the item by value. The advantage here is that pointers can be freely copied without throwing an exception, so you've avoided Cargill's exception problem. The disadvantage is that returning a pointer requires a means of managing the memory allocated to the object, and for simple types such as integers, the overhead of such memory management can exceed the cost of just returning the type by value. For any interface that uses this option, `std::shared_ptr` would be a good choice of pointer type; not only does it avoid memory leaks, because the object is destroyed once the last pointer is destroyed, but the library is in full control of the memory allocation scheme and doesn't have to use `new` and `delete`. This can be important for optimization purposes: requiring that each object in the stack be allocated separately with `new` would impose quite an overhead compared to the original non-thread-safe version.

OPTION 4: PROVIDE BOTH OPTION 1 AND EITHER OPTION 2 OR 3

Flexibility should never be ruled out, especially in generic code. If you've chosen option 2 or 3, it's relatively easy to provide option 1 as well, and this provides users of your code the ability to choose whichever option is most appropriate for them for very little additional cost.

EXAMPLE DEFINITION OF A THREAD-SAFE STACK

Listing 3.4 shows the class definition for a stack with no race conditions in the interface and that implements options 1 and 3: there are two overloads of `pop()`, one that takes a reference to a location in which to store the value and one that returns a `std::shared_ptr<>`. It has a simple interface, with only two functions: `push()` and `pop()`.

Listing 3.4 An outline class definition for a thread-safe stack

```
#include <exception>
#include <memory>                                    <-- For std::shared_ptr<>

struct empty_stack: std::exception
{
    const char* what() const throw();
};

template<typename T>
class threadsafe_stack
{
public:
    threadsafe_stack();
    threadsafe_stack(const threadsafe_stack&);
    threadsafe_stack& operator=(const threadsafe_stack&) = delete;   <-- 1 Assignment operator is deleted

    void push(T new_value);
    std::shared_ptr<T> pop();
    void pop(T& value);
    bool empty() const;
};
```

By paring down the interface you allow for maximum safety; even operations on the whole stack are restricted. The stack itself can't' be assigned, because the assignment operator is deleted ❶ (see appendix A, section A.2), and there's no `swap()` function. It can, however, be copied, assuming the stack elements can be copied. The `pop()` functions throw an `empty_stack` exception if the stack is empty, so everything still works even if the stack is modified after a call to `empty()`. As mentioned in the description of option 3, the use of `std::shared_ptr` allows the stack to take care of the memory-allocation issues and avoid excessive calls to `new` and `delete` if desired. Your five stack operations have now become three: `push()`, `pop()`, and `empty()`. Even `empty()` is superfluous. This simplification of the interface allows for better control over the data; you can ensure that the mutex is locked for the entirety of an operation. The following listing shows a simple implementation that's a wrapper around `std::stack<>`.

Listing 3.5 A fleshed-out class definition for a thread-safe stack

```
#include <exception>
#include <memory>
#include <mutex>
#include <stack>

struct empty_stack: std::exception
{
    const char* what() const throw();
};

template<typename T>
class threadsafe_stack
{
```

```
private:
    std::stack<T> data;
    mutable std::mutex m;
public:
    threadsafe_stack(){}
    threadsafe_stack(const threadsafe_stack& other)
    {
        std::lock_guard<std::mutex> lock(other.m);
        data=other.data;                                    ❶ Copy performed in constructor body
    }
    threadsafe_stack& operator=(const threadsafe_stack&) = delete;

    void push(T new_value)
    {
        std::lock_guard<std::mutex> lock(m);
        data.push(new_value);
    }
    std::shared_ptr<T> pop()
    {
        std::lock_guard<std::mutex> lock(m);
        if(data.empty()) throw empty_stack();              Check for empty before trying to pop value
        std::shared_ptr<T> const res(std::make_shared<T>(data.top()));    Allocate return value before modifying stack
        data.pop();
        return res;
    }
    void pop(T& value)
    {
        std::lock_guard<std::mutex> lock(m);
        if(data.empty()) throw empty_stack();
        value=data.top();
        data.pop();
    }
    bool empty() const
    {
        std::lock_guard<std::mutex> lock(m);
        return data.empty();
    }
};
```

This stack implementation is actually *copyable*—the copy constructor locks the mutex in the source object and then copies the internal stack. You do the copy in the constructor body ❶ rather than the member initializer list in order to ensure that the mutex is held across the copy.

As the discussion of `top()` and `pop()` shows, problematic race conditions in interfaces essentially arise because of locking at too small a granularity; the protection doesn't cover the entirety of the desired operation. Problems with mutexes can also arise from locking at too large a granularity; the extreme situation is a single global mutex that protects all shared data. In a system where there's a significant amount of shared data, this can eliminate any performance benefits of concurrency, because the threads are forced to run one at a time, even when they're accessing different bits of data. The first versions of the Linux kernel that were designed to handle multiprocessor systems used a single global kernel lock. Although this worked, it meant that a two-processor system typically had much worse performance than two single-processor systems, and performance on a four-processor system was nowhere near that of four single-processor systems. There was too much contention for the kernel, so the threads running on the additional processors were unable to perform useful work. Later revisions of the Linux kernel have moved to a more fine-grained locking scheme, so the performance of a four-processor system is much nearer the ideal of four times that of a single-processor system, because there's far less contention.

One issue with fine-grained locking schemes is that sometimes you need more than one mutex locked in order to protect all the data in an operation. As described previously, sometimes the right thing to do is increase the granularity of the data covered by the mutexes, so that only one mutex needs to be locked. However, sometimes that's undesirable, such as when the mutexes are protecting separate instances of a class. In this case, locking at the next level up would mean either leaving the locking to the user or having a single mutex that protected all instances of that class, neither of which is particularly desirable.

If you end up having to lock two or more mutexes for a given operation, there's another potential problem lurking in the wings: *deadlock*. This is almost the opposite of a race condition: rather than two threads racing to be first, each one is waiting for the other, so neither makes any progress.

3.2.4 Deadlock: the problem and a solution

Imagine that you have a toy that comes in two parts, and you need both parts to play with it—a toy drum and drumstick, for example. Now imagine that you have two small children, both of whom like playing with it. If one of them gets both the drum and the drumstick, that child can merrily play the drum until tiring of it. If the other child wants to play, they have to wait, however sad that makes them. Now imagine that the drum and the drumstick are buried (separately) in the toy box, and your children both decide to play with them at the same time, so they go rummaging in the toy box. One finds the drum and the other finds the drumstick. Now they're stuck; unless one decides to be nice and let the other play, each will hold onto whatever they have and demand that the other give them the other piece, so neither gets to play.

Now imagine that you have not children arguing over toys but threads arguing over locks on mutexes: each of a pair of threads needs to lock both of a pair of mutexes to perform some operation, and each thread has one mutex and is waiting for the other. Neither thread can proceed, because each is waiting for the other to release its mutex. This scenario is called *deadlock*, and it's the biggest problem with having to lock two or more mutexes in order to perform an operation.

The common advice for avoiding deadlock is to always lock the two mutexes in the same order: if you always lock mutex A before mutex B, then you'll never deadlock. Sometimes this is straightforward, because the mutexes are serving different purposes, but other times it's not so simple, such as when the mutexes are each protecting a separate instance of the same class. Consider, for example, an operation that exchanges data between two instances of the same class; in order to ensure that the data is exchanged correctly, without being affected by concurrent modifications, the mutexes on both instances must be locked. However, if a fixed order is chosen (for example, the mutex for the instance supplied as the first parameter, then the mutex for the instance supplied as the second parameter), this can backfire: all it takes is for two threads to try to exchange data between the same two instances with the parameters swapped, and you have deadlock!

Thankfully, the C++ Standard Library has a cure for this in the form of `std::lock`—a function that can lock two or more mutexes at once without risk of deadlock. The example in the next listing shows how to use this for a simple swap operation.

Listing 3.6 Using `std::lock()` and `std::lock_guard` in a swap operation

```
class some_big_object;
void swap(some_big_object& lhs,some_big_object& rhs);

class X
{
private:
    some_big_object some_detail;
    std::mutex m;
public:
    X(some_big_object const& sd):some_detail(sd){}

    friend void swap(X& lhs, X& rhs)
    {
        if(&lhs==&rhs)
            return;
        std::lock(lhs.m,rhs.m);                                      ❶
        std::lock_guard<std::mutex> lock_a(lhs.m,std::adopt_lock);   ❷
        std::lock_guard<std::mutex> lock_b(rhs.m,std::adopt_lock);   ❸
        swap(lhs.some_detail,rhs.some_detail);
    }
};
```

First, the arguments are checked to ensure they are different instances, because attempting to acquire a lock on a `std::mutex` when you already hold it is undefined behavior. (A mutex that does permit multiple locks by the same thread is provided in the form of `std::recursive_mutex`. See section 3.3.3 for details.) Then, the call to `std::lock()` ❶ locks the two mutexes, and two `std::lock_guard` instances are constructed ❷, ❸, one for each mutex. The `std::adopt_lock` parameter is supplied in addition to the mutex to indicate to the `std::lock_guard` objects that the mutexes are already locked, and they should just adopt the ownership of the existing lock on the mutex rather than attempt to lock the mutex in the constructor.

This ensures that the mutexes are correctly unlocked on function exit in the general case where the protected operation might throw an exception; it also allows for a simple return. Also, it's worth noting that locking either `lhs.m` or `rhs.m` inside the call to `std::lock` can throw an exception; in this case, the exception is propagated out of `std::lock`. If `std::lock` has successfully acquired a lock on one mutex and an exception is thrown when it tries to acquire a lock on the other mutex, this first lock is released automatically: `std::lock` provides all-or-nothing semantics with regard to locking the supplied mutexes.

Although `std::lock` can help you avoid deadlock in those cases where you need to acquire two or more locks together, it doesn't help if they're acquired separately. In that case you have to rely on your discipline as developers to ensure you don't get deadlock. This isn't easy: deadlocks are one of the nastiest problems to encounter in multithreaded code and are often unpredictable, with everything working fine the majority of the time. There are, however, some relatively simple rules that can help you to write deadlock-free code.

3.2.5 Further guidelines for avoiding deadlock

Deadlock doesn't just occur with locks, although that's the most frequent cause; you can create deadlock with two threads and no locks just by having each thread call `join()` on the `std::thread` object for the other. In this case, neither thread can make progress because it's waiting for the other to finish, just like the children fighting over their toys. This simple cycle can occur anywhere that a thread can wait for another thread to perform some action if the other thread can simultaneously be waiting for the first thread, and it isn't limited to two threads: a cycle of three or more threads will still cause deadlock. The guidelines for avoiding deadlock all boil down to one idea: don't wait for another thread if there's a chance it's waiting for you. The individual guidelines provide ways of identifying and eliminating the possibility that the other thread is waiting for you.

AVOID NESTED LOCKS

The first idea is the simplest: don't acquire a lock if you already hold one. If you stick to this guideline, it's impossible to get a deadlock from the lock usage alone because each thread only ever holds a single lock. You could still get deadlock from other things (like the threads waiting for each other), but mutex locks are probably the most common cause of deadlock. If you need to acquire multiple locks, do it as a single action with `std::lock` in order to acquire them without deadlock.

AVOID CALLING USER-SUPPLIED CODE WHILE HOLDING A LOCK

This is a simple follow-on from the previous guideline. Because the code is user supplied, you have no idea what it could do; it could do anything, including acquiring a lock. If you call user-supplied code while holding a lock, and that code acquires a lock, you've violated the guideline on avoiding nested locks and could get deadlock. Sometimes this is unavoidable; if you're writing generic code such as the stack in section 3.2.3, every operation on the parameter type or types is user-supplied code. In this case, you need a new guideline.

ACQUIRE LOCKS IN A FIXED ORDER

If you absolutely must acquire two or more locks, and you can't acquire them as a single operation with `std::lock`, the next-best thing is to acquire them in the same order in every thread. I touched on this in section 3.2.4 as one way of avoiding deadlock when acquiring two mutexes: the key is to define the order in a way that's consistent between threads. In some cases, this is relatively easy. For example, look at the stack from section 3.2.3—the mutex is internal to each stack instance, but the operations on the data items stored in a stack require calling user-supplied code. You can, however, add the constraint that none of the operations on the data items stored in the stack should perform any operation on the stack itself. This puts the burden on the user of the stack, but it's rather uncommon for the data stored in a container to access that container, and it's quite apparent when this is happening, so it's not a particularly difficult burden to carry.

In other cases, this isn't so straightforward, as you discovered with the swap operation in section 3.2.4. At least in that case you could lock the mutexes simultaneously, but that's not always possible. If you look back at the linked list example from section 3.1, you'll see that one possibility for protecting the list is to have a mutex per node. Then, in order to access the list, threads must acquire a lock on every node they're interested in. For a thread to delete an item, it must then acquire the lock on three nodes: the node being deleted and the nodes on either side, because they're all being modified in some way. Likewise, to traverse the list a thread must keep hold of the lock on the current node while it acquires the lock on the next one in the sequence, in order to ensure that the next pointer isn't modified in the meantime. Once the lock on the next node has been acquired, the lock on the first can be released because it's no longer necessary.

This hand-over-hand locking style allows multiple threads to access the list, provided each is accessing a different node. However, in order to prevent deadlock, the nodes must always be locked in the same order: if two threads tried to traverse the list in reverse order using hand-over-hand locking, they could deadlock with each other in the middle of the list. If nodes A and B are adjacent in the list, the thread going one way will try to hold the lock on node A and try to acquire the lock on node B. A thread going the other way would be holding the lock on node B and trying to acquire the lock on node A—a classic scenario for deadlock.

Likewise, when deleting node B that lies between nodes A and C, if that thread acquires the lock on B before the locks on A and C, it has the potential to deadlock with a thread traversing the list. Such a thread would try to lock either A or C first (depending on the direction of traversal) but would then find that it couldn't obtain a lock on B because the thread doing the deleting was holding the lock on B and trying to acquire the locks on A and C.

One way to prevent deadlock here is to define an order of traversal, so a thread must always lock A before B and B before C. This would eliminate the possibility of deadlock at the expense of disallowing reverse traversal. Similar conventions can often be established for other data structures.

USE A LOCK HIERARCHY

Although this is really a particular case of defining lock ordering, a lock hierarchy can provide a means of checking that the convention is adhered to at runtime. The idea is that you divide your application into layers and identify all the mutexes that may be locked in any given layer. When code tries to lock a mutex, it isn't permitted to lock that mutex if it already holds a lock from a lower layer. You can check this at runtime by assigning layer numbers to each mutex and keeping a record of which mutexes are locked by each thread. The following listing shows an example of two threads using a hierarchical mutex.

Listing 3.7 Using a lock hierarchy to prevent deadlock

```
hierarchical_mutex high_level_mutex(10000);          <-1
hierarchical_mutex low_level_mutex(5000);                  <-2

int do_low_level_stuff();

int low_level_func()
{
    std::lock_guard<hierarchical_mutex> lk(low_level_mutex);    <-3
    return do_low_level_stuff();
}

void high_level_stuff(int some_param);

void high_level_func()
{
    std::lock_guard<hierarchical_mutex> lk(high_level_mutex);    <-4
    high_level_stuff(low_level_func());        <-5
}

void thread_a()          <-6
{
    high_level_func();
}

hierarchical_mutex other_mutex(100);     <-7
void do_other_stuff();

void other_stuff()
{
    high_level_func();       <-8
    do_other_stuff();
}

void thread_b()          <-9
{
    std::lock_guard<hierarchical_mutex> lk(other_mutex);    <-10
    other_stuff();
}
```

thread_a() 6 abides by the rules, so it runs fine. On the other hand, thread_b() 9 disregards the rules and therefore will fail at runtime. thread_a() calls high_level_func(), which locks the high_level_mutex 4 (with a hierarchy value of 10000 1) and then calls low_level_func() 5 with this mutex locked in order to get the parameter for high_level_stuff().low_level_func() then locks the low_level_mutex ❸, but that's fine because this mutex has a lower hierarchy value of 5000 ❷.

thread_b() on the other hand is *not* fine. First off, it locks the other_mutex ❿, which has a hierarchy value of only 100 ❼. This means it should really be protecting ultra-low-level data. When other_stuff() calls high_level_func() ❽, it's thus violating the hierarchy: high_level_func() tries to acquire the high_level_mutex, which has a value of 10000, considerably more than the current hierarchy value of 100. The hierarchical_mutex will therefore report an error, possibly by throwing an exception or aborting the program. Deadlocks between hierarchical mutexes are thus impossible, because the mutexes themselves enforce the lock ordering. This does mean that you can't hold two locks at the same time if they're the same level in the hierarchy, so hand-over-hand locking schemes require that each mutex in the chain have a lower hierarchy value than the prior one, which may be impractical in some cases.

This example also demonstrates another point, the use of the std::lock_guard<> template with a user-defined mutex type. hierarchical_mutex is not part of the standard but is easy to write; a simple implementation is shown in listing 3.8. Even though it's a user-defined type, it can be used with std::lock_guard<> because it implements the three member functions required to satisfy the mutex concept: lock(), unlock(), and try_lock(). You haven't yet seen try_lock() used directly, but it's fairly simple: if the lock on the mutex is held by another thread, it returns false rather than waiting until the calling thread can acquire the lock on the mutex. It may also be used by std::lock() internally, as part of the deadlock-avoidance algorithm.

Listing 3.8 A simple hierarchical mutex

```
class hierarchical_mutex
{
    std::mutex internal_mutex;
    unsigned long const hierarchy_value;
    unsigned long previous_hierarchy_value;
    static thread_local unsigned long this_thread_hierarchy_value;     <-❶

    void check_for_hierarchy_violation()
    {
        if(this_thread_hierarchy_value <= hierarchy_value)     <-❷
        {
            throw std::logic_error("mutex hierarchy violated");
        }
    }
    void update_hierarchy_value()
    {
        previous_hierarchy_value=this_thread_hierarchy_value;     <-❸
        this_thread_hierarchy_value=hierarchy_value;
    }
public:
    explicit hierarchical_mutex(unsigned long value):
        hierarchy_value(value),
        previous_hierarchy_value(0)
    {}
```

```
    void lock()
    {
        check_for_hierarchy_violation();
        internal_mutex.lock();                          ◁—❹
        update_hierarchy_value();                            ◁—❺
    }
    void unlock()
    {
        this_thread_hierarchy_value=previous_hierarchy_value;    ◁—❻
        internal_mutex.unlock();
    }
    bool try_lock()
    {
        check_for_hierarchy_violation();
        if(!internal_mutex.try_lock())                       ◁—❼
            return false;
        update_hierarchy_value();
        return true;
    }
};
thread_local unsigned long                                       ❽
    hierarchical_mutex::this_thread_hierarchy_value(ULONG_MAX);  ◁┘
```

The key here is the use of the `thread_local` value representing the hierarchy value for the current thread: `this_thread_hierarchy_value` ❶. It's initialized to the maximum value ❽, so initially any mutex can be locked. Because it's declared `thread_local`, every thread has its own copy, so the state of the variable in one thread is entirely independent of the state of the variable when read from another thread. See appendix A, section A.8, for more information about `thread_local`.

So, the first time a thread locks an instance of `hierarchical_mutex` the value of `this_thread_hierarchy_value` is `ULONG_MAX`. By its very nature, this is greater than any other value, so the check in `check_for_hierarchy_violation()` ❷ passes. With that check out of the way, `lock()` delegates to the internal mutex for the actual locking ❹. Once this lock has succeeded, you can update the hierarchy value ❺.

If you now lock *another* `hierarchical_mutex` while holding the lock on this first one, the value of `this_thread_hierarchy_value` reflects the hierarchy value of the first mutex. The hierarchy value of this second mutex must now be less than that of the mutex already held in order for the check ❷ to pass.

Now, it's important to save the previous value of the hierarchy value for the current thread so you can restore it in `unlock()` ❻; otherwise you'd never be able to lock a mutex with a higher hierarchy value again, even if the thread didn't hold any locks. Because you store this previous hierarchy value only when you hold the `internal_mutex` ❸, and you restore it *before* you unlock the internal mutex ❻, you can safely store it in the `hierarchical_mutex` itself, because it's safely protected by the lock on the internal mutex.

`try_lock()` works the same as `lock()` except that if the call to `try_lock()` on the `internal_mutex` fails ❼, then you don't own the lock, so you don't update the hierarchy value and return `false` rather than `true`.

Although detection is a runtime check, it's at least not timing dependent—you don't have to wait around for the rare conditions that cause deadlock to show up. Also, the design process required to divide the application and mutexes in this way can help eliminate many possible causes of deadlock before they even get written. It might be worth performing the design exercise even if you then don't go as far as actually writing the runtime checks.

EXTENDING THESE GUIDELINES BEYOND LOCKS

As I mentioned back at the beginning of this section, deadlock doesn't just occur with locks; it can occur with any synchronization construct that can lead to a wait cycle. It's therefore worth extending these guidelines to cover those cases too. For example, just as you should avoid acquiring nested locks if possible, it's a bad idea to wait for a thread while holding a lock, because that thread might need to acquire the lock in order to proceed. Similarly, if you're going to wait for a thread to finish, it might be worth identifying a thread hierarchy, such that a thread waits only for threads lower down the hierarchy. One simple way to do this is to ensure that your threads are joined in the same function that started them, as described in sections 3.1.2 and 3.3.

Once you've designed your code to avoid deadlock, `std::lock()` and `std::lock_guard` cover most of the cases of simple locking, but sometimes more flexibility is required. For those cases, the Standard Library provides the `std::unique_lock` template. Like `std::lock_guard`, this is a class template parameterized on the mutex type, and it also provides the same RAII-style lock management as `std::lock_guard` but with a bit more flexibility.

3.2.6 *Flexible locking with std::unique_lock*

`std::unique_lock` provides a bit more flexibility than `std::lock_guard` by relaxing the invariants; a `std::unique_lock` instance doesn't always own the mutex that it's associated with. First off, just as you can pass `std::adopt_lock` as a second argument to the constructor to have the lock object manage the lock on a mutex, you can also pass `std::defer_lock` as the second argument to indicate that the mutex should remain unlocked on construction. The lock can then be acquired later by calling `lock()` on the `std::unique_lock` object (*not* the mutex) or by passing the `std::unique_lock` object itself to `std::lock()`. Listing 3.6 could just as easily have been written as shown in listing 3.9, using `std::unique_lock` and `std::defer_lock` ❶ rather than `std::lock_guard` and `std::adopt_lock`. The code has the same line count and is essentially equivalent, apart from one small thing: `std::unique_lock` takes more space and is a fraction slower to use than `std::lock_guard`. The flexibility of allowing a `std::unique_lock` instance *not* to own the mutex comes at a price: this information has to be stored, and it has to be updated.

Listing 3.9 Using `std::lock()` and `std::unique_lock` in a swap operation

```
class some_big_object;
void swap(some_big_object& lhs,some_big_object& rhs);
```

```
class X
{
private:
    some_big_object some_detail;
    std::mutex m;
public:
    X(some_big_object const& sd):some_detail(sd){}

    friend void swap(X& lhs, X& rhs)
    {
        if(&lhs==&rhs)
            return;
        std::unique_lock<std::mutex> lock_a(lhs.m,std::defer_lock);
        std::unique_lock<std::mutex> lock_b(rhs.m,std::defer_lock);
        std::lock(lock_a,lock_b);
        swap(lhs.some_detail,rhs.some_detail);
    }
};
```

std::defer_lock leaves mutexes unlocked ❶

❷ **Mutexes are locked here**

In listing 3.9, the `std::unique_lock` objects could be passed to `std::lock()` ❷ because `std::unique_lock` provides `lock()`, `try_lock()`, and `unlock()` member functions. These forward to the member functions of the same name on the underlying mutex to do the actual work and just update a flag inside the `std::unique_lock` instance to indicate whether the mutex is currently owned by that instance. This flag is necessary in order to ensure that `unlock()` is called correctly in the destructor. If the instance *does* own the mutex, the destructor *must* call `unlock()`, and if the instance *does not* own the mutex, it *must not* call `unlock()`. This flag can be queried by calling the `owns_lock()` member function.

As you might expect, this flag has to be stored somewhere. Therefore, the size of a `std::unique_lock` object is typically larger than that of a `std::lock_guard` object, and there's also a slight performance penalty when using `std::unique_lock` over `std::lock_guard` because the flag has to be updated or checked, as appropriate. If `std::lock_guard` is sufficient for your needs, I'd therefore recommend using it in preference. That said, there are cases where `std::unique_lock` is a better fit for the task at hand, because you need to make use of the additional flexibility. One example is deferred locking, as you've already seen; another case is where the ownership of the lock needs to be transferred from one scope to another.

3.2.7 Transferring mutex ownership between scopes

Because `std::unique_lock` instances don't have to own their associated mutexes, the ownership of a mutex can be transferred between instances by *moving* the instances around. In some cases such transfer is automatic, such as when returning an instance from a function, and in other cases you have to do it explicitly by calling `std::move()`. Fundamentally this depends on whether the source is an *lvalue*—a real variable or reference to one—or an *rvalue*—a temporary of some kind. Ownership transfer is automatic if the source is an rvalue and must be done explicitly for an lvalue in order to avoid accidentally transferring ownership away from a variable. `std::unique_lock` is an example of a type that's *movable* but not *copyable*. See appendix A, section A.1.1, for more about move semantics.

One possible use is to allow a function to lock a mutex and transfer ownership of that lock to the caller, so the caller can then perform additional actions under the protection of the same lock. The following code snippet shows an example of this: the function `get_lock()` locks the mutex and then prepares the data before returning the lock to the caller:

```
std::unique_lock<std::mutex> get_lock()
{
    extern std::mutex some_mutex;
    std::unique_lock<std::mutex> lk(some_mutex);
    prepare_data();
    return lk;                 <-1
}
void process_data()
{
    std::unique_lock<std::mutex> lk(get_lock());        <-2
    do_something();
}
```

Because `lk` is an automatic variable declared within the function, it can be returned directly ❶ without a call to `std:move()`; the compiler takes care of calling the move constructor. The `process_data()` function can then transfer ownership directly into its own `std::unique_lock` instance ❷, and the call to `do_something()` can rely on the data being correctly prepared without another thread altering the data in the meantime.

Typically this sort of pattern would be used where the mutex to be locked is dependent on the current state of the program or on an argument passed in to the function that returns the `std::unique_lock` object. One such usage is where the lock isn't returned directly but is a data member of a gateway class used to ensure correctly locked access to some protected data. In this case, all access to the data is through this gateway class: when you wish to access the data, you obtain an instance of the gateway class (by calling a function such as `get_lock()` in the preceding example), which acquires the lock. You can then access the data through member functions of the gateway object. When you're finished, you destroy the gateway object, which releases the lock and allows other threads to access the protected data. Such a gateway object may well be movable (so that it can be returned from a function), in which case the lock object data member also needs to be movable.

The flexibility of `std::unique_lock` also allows instances to relinquish their locks before they're destroyed. You can do this with the `unlock()` member function, just like for a mutex: `std::unique_lock` supports the same basic set of member functions for locking and unlocking as a mutex does, in order that it can be used with generic functions such as `std::lock`. The ability to release a lock before the `std::unique_lock` instance is destroyed means that you can optionally release it in a specific code branch if it's apparent that the lock is no longer required. This can be important for the performance of the application; holding a lock for longer than required can cause a drop in performance, because other threads waiting for the lock are prevented from proceeding for longer than necessary.

3.2.8 Locking at an appropriate granularity

The granularity of a lock is something I touched on earlier, in section 3.2.3: the lock granularity is a hand-waving term to describe the amount of data protected by a single lock. A fine-grained lock protects a small amount of data, and a coarse-grained lock protects a large amount of data. Not only is it important to choose a sufficiently coarse lock granularity to ensure the required data is protected, but it's also important to ensure that a lock is held only for the operations that actually require it. We all know the frustration of waiting in the checkout line in a supermarket with a cart full of groceries only for the person currently being served to suddenly realize that they forgot some cranberry sauce and then leave everybody waiting while they go and find some, or for the cashier to be ready for payment and the customer to only then start rummaging in their purse for their wallet. Everything proceeds much more easily if everybody gets to the checkout with everything they want and with an appropriate means of payment ready.

The same applies to threads: if multiple threads are waiting for the same resource (the cashier at the checkout), then if any thread holds the lock for longer than necessary, it will increase the total time spent waiting (don't wait until you've reached the checkout to start looking for the cranberry sauce). Where possible, lock a mutex only while actually accessing the shared data; try to do any processing of the data outside the lock. In particular, don't do any really time-consuming activities like file I/O while holding a lock. File I/O is typically hundreds (if not thousands) of times slower than reading or writing the same volume of data from memory. So unless the lock is really intended to protect access to the file, performing I/O while holding the lock will delay *other* threads unnecessarily (because they'll block while waiting to acquire the lock), potentially eliminating any performance gain from the use of multiple threads.

`std::unique_lock` works well in this situation, because you can call `unlock()` when the code no longer needs access to the shared data and then call `lock()` again if access is required later in the code:

```
void get_and_process_data()
{
    std::unique_lock<std::mutex> my_lock(the_mutex);
    some_class data_to_process=get_next_data_chunk();
    my_lock.unlock();                                    ❶
    result_type result=process(data_to_process);
    my_lock.lock();                                      ❷
    write_result(data_to_process,result);
}
```

❶ Don't need mutex locked across call to process()

❷ Relock mutex to write result

You don't need the mutex locked across the call to `process()`, so you manually unlock it before the call ❶ and then lock it again afterward ❷.

Hopefully it's obvious that if you have one mutex protecting an entire data structure, not only is there likely to be more contention for the lock, but also the potential for reducing the time that the lock is held is less. More of the operation steps will require a lock on the same mutex, so the lock must be held longer. This double whammy of a cost is thus also a double incentive to move toward finer-grained locking wherever possible.

As this example shows, locking at an appropriate granularity isn't only about the amount of data locked; it's also about how long the lock is held and what operations are performed while the lock is held. *In general, a lock should be held for only the minimum possible time needed to perform the required operations.* This also means that time-consuming operations such as acquiring another lock (even if you know it won't deadlock) or waiting for I/O to complete shouldn't be done while holding a lock unless absolutely necessary.

In listings 3.6 and 3.9, the operation that required locking the two mutexes was a swap operation, which obviously requires concurrent access to both objects. Suppose instead you were trying to compare a simple data member that was just a plain `int`. Would this make a difference? `int`s are cheap to copy, so you could easily copy the data for each object being compared while only holding the lock for that object and then compare the copied values. This would mean that you were holding the lock on each mutex for the minimum amount of time and also that you weren't holding one lock while locking another. The following listing shows a class `Y` for which this is the case and a sample implementation of the equality comparison operator.

Listing 3.10 Locking one mutex at a time in a comparison operator

```
class Y
{
private:
    int some_detail;
    mutable std::mutex m;

    int get_detail() const
    {
        std::lock_guard<std::mutex> lock_a(m);        <-1
        return some_detail;
    }
public:
    Y(int sd):some_detail(sd){}

    friend bool operator==(Y const& lhs, Y const& rhs)
    {
        if(&lhs==&rhs)
            return true;
        int const lhs_value=lhs.get_detail();              <-2
        int const rhs_value=rhs.get_detail();         <-3
        return lhs_value==rhs_value;              <-4
    }
};
```

In this case, the comparison operator first retrieves the values to be compared by calling the `get_detail()` member function ❷, ❸. This function retrieves the value while protecting it with a lock ❶. The comparison operator then compares the retrieved values ❹. Note, however, that as well as reducing the locking periods so that only one lock is held at a time (and thus eliminating the possibility of deadlock), *this has subtly changed the semantics of the operation* compared to holding both locks together. In listing 3.10, if the operator returns `true`, it means that the value of `lhs.some_detail` at one point in time is equal to the value of `rhs.some_detail` at another point in time. The two values could have been changed in any way in between the two reads; the values could have been swapped in between ❷ and ❸, for example, thus rendering the comparison meaningless. The equality comparison might thus return `true` to indicate that the values were equal, even though there was never an instant in time when the values were actually equal. It's therefore important to be careful when making such changes that the semantics of the operation are not changed in a problematic fashion: *if you don't hold the required locks for the entire duration of an operation, you're exposing yourself to race conditions.*

Sometimes, there just isn't an appropriate level of granularity because not all accesses to the data structure require the same level of protection. In this case, it might be appropriate to use an alternative mechanism, instead of a plain `std::mutex`.

3.3 Alternative facilities for protecting shared data

Although they're the most general mechanism, mutexes aren't the only game in town when it comes to protecting shared data; there are alternatives that provide more appropriate protection in specific scenarios.

One particularly extreme (but remarkably common) case is where the shared data needs protection only from concurrent access while it's being initialized, but after that no explicit synchronization is required. This might be because the data is read-only once created, and so there are no possible synchronization issues, or it might be because the necessary protection is performed implicitly as part of the operations on the data. In either case, locking a mutex after the data has been initialized, purely in order to protect the initialization, is unnecessary and a needless hit to performance. It's for this reason that the C++ Standard provides a mechanism purely for protecting shared data during initialization.

3.3.1 Protecting shared data during initialization

Suppose you have a shared resource that's so expensive to construct that you want to do so only if it's actually required; maybe it opens a database connection or allocates a lot of memory. *Lazy initialization* such as this is common in single-threaded code—each operation that requires the resource first checks to see if it has been initialized and then initializes it before use if not:

```
std::shared_ptr<some_resource> resource_ptr;
void foo()
{
    if(!resource_ptr)
    {
```

```
        resource_ptr.reset(new some_resource);      <-1
    }
    resource_ptr->do_something();
}
```

If the shared resource itself is safe for concurrent access, the only part that needs protecting when converting this to multithreaded code is the initialization ❶, but a naïve translation such as that in the following listing can cause unnecessary serialization of threads using the resource. This is because each thread must wait on the mutex in order to check whether the resource has already been initialized.

Listing 3.11 Thread-safe lazy initialization using a mutex

```
std::shared_ptr<some_resource> resource_ptr;
std::mutex resource_mutex;
void foo()
{                                                       All threads are
    std::unique_lock<std::mutex> lk(resource_mutex);   <- serialized here
    if(!resource_ptr)
    {
        resource_ptr.reset(new some_resource);     <- Only the initialization
    }                                                  needs protection
    lk.unlock();
    resource_ptr->do_something();
}
```

This code is common enough, and the unnecessary serialization problematic enough, that many people have tried to come up with a better way of doing this, including the infamous *Double-Checked Locking* pattern: the pointer is first read without acquiring the lock ❶ (in the code below), and the lock is acquired only if the pointer is NULL. The pointer is then checked *again* once the lock has been acquired ❷ (hence the *double-checked* part) in case another thread has done the initialization between the first check and this thread acquiring the lock:

```
void undefined_behaviour_with_double_checked_locking()
{
    if(!resource_ptr)                          <-1
    {
        std::lock_guard<std::mutex> lk(resource_mutex);
        if(!resource_ptr)                                 <-2
        {
            resource_ptr.reset(new some_resource);      <-3
        }
    }
    resource_ptr->do_something();    <-4
}
```

Unfortunately, this pattern is infamous for a reason: it has the potential for nasty race conditions, because the read outside the lock ❶ isn't synchronized with the write done by another thread inside the lock ❸. This therefore creates a race condition that covers not just the pointer itself but also the object pointed to; even if a thread sees the pointer written by another thread, it might not see the newly created instance of some_resource, resulting in the call to do_something() ❹ operating on incorrect values. This is an example of the type of race condition defined as a *data race* by the C++ Standard and thus specified as *undefined behavior.* It's is therefore quite definitely something to avoid. See chapter 5 for a detailed discussion of the memory model, including what constitutes a *data race.*

The C++ Standards Committee also saw that this was an important scenario, and so the C++ Standard Library provides std::once_flag and std::call_once to handle this situation. Rather than locking a mutex and explicitly checking the pointer, every thread can just use std::call_once, safe in the knowledge that the pointer will have been initialized by some thread (in a properly synchronized fashion) by the time std::call_once returns. Use of std::call_once will typically have a lower overhead than using a mutex explicitly, especially when the initialization has already been done, so should be used in preference where it matches the required functionality. The following example shows the same operation as listing 3.11, rewritten to use std::call_once. In this case, the initialization is done by calling a function, but it could just as easily have been done with an instance of a class with a function call operator. Like most of the functions in the standard library that take functions or predicates as arguments, std::call_once works with any function or callable object.

```
std::shared_ptr<some_resource> resource_ptr;
std::once_flag resource_flag;                          ❶

void init_resource()
{
    resource_ptr.reset(new some_resource);
}

void foo()
{
    std::call_once(resource_flag,init_resource);     Initialization is
    resource_ptr->do_something();                    called exactly once
}
```

In this example, both the std::once_flag ❶ and data being initialized are namespace-scope objects, but std::call_once() can just as easily be used for lazy initialization of class members, as in the following listing.

Listing 3.12 Thread-safe lazy initialization of a class member using std::call_once

```
class X
{
private:
    connection_info connection_details;
    connection_handle connection;
    std::once_flag connection_init_flag;

    void open_connection()
    {
        connection=connection_manager.open(connection_details);
    }
public:
```

```
    X(connection_info const& connection_details_):
        connection_details(connection_details_)
    {}
    void send_data(data_packet const& data)          <-❶
    {
        std::call_once(connection_init_flag,&X::open_connection,this);  <-┐
        connection.send_data(data);                                       │
    }                                                                     ❷
    data_packet receive_data()             <-❸                            │
    {                                                                     │
        std::call_once(connection_init_flag,&X::open_connection,this);  <-┘
        return connection.receive_data();
    }
};
```

In that example, the initialization is done either by the first call to `send_data()` ❶ or by the first call to `receive_data()` ❸. The use of the member function `open_connection()` to initialize the data also requires that the `this` pointer be passed in. Just as for other functions in the Standard Library that accept callable objects, such as the constructor for `std::thread` and `std::bind()`, this is done by passing an additional argument to `std::call_once()` ❷.

It's worth noting that, like `std::mutex`, `std::once_flag` instances can't be copied or moved, so if you use them as a class member like this, you'll have to explicitly define these special member functions should you require them.

One scenario where there's a potential race condition over initialization is that of a local variable declared with `static`. The initialization of such a variable is defined to occur the first time control passes through its declaration; for multiple threads calling the function, this means there's the potential for a race condition to define first. On many pre-C++11 compilers this race condition is problematic in practice, because multiple threads may believe they're first and try to initialize the variable, or threads may try to use it after initialization has started on another thread but before it's finished. In C++11 this problem is solved: the initialization is defined to happen on exactly one thread, and no other threads will proceed until that initialization is complete, so the race condition is just over which thread gets to do the initialization rather than anything more problematic. This can be used as an alternative to `std::call_once` for those cases where a single global instance is required:

```
class my_class;
my_class& get_my_class_instance()
{
    static my_class instance;          <-❶ Initialization guaranteed
    return instance;                       to be thread-safe
}
```

Multiple threads can then call `get_my_class_instance()` safely ❶, without having to worry about race conditions on the initialization.

Protecting data only for initialization is a special case of a more general scenario: that of a rarely updated data structure. For most of the time, such a data structure is read-only and can therefore be merrily read by multiple threads concurrently, but on occasion the data structure may need updating. What's needed here is a protection mechanism that acknowledges this fact.

3.3.2 Protecting rarely updated data structures

Consider a table used to store a cache of DNS entries for resolving domain names to their corresponding IP addresses. Typically, a given DNS entry will remain unchanged for a long period of time—in many cases DNS entries remain unchanged for years. Although new entries may be added to the table from time to time as users access different websites, this data will therefore remain largely unchanged throughout its life. It's important that the validity of the cached entries be checked periodically, but this still requires an update only if the details have actually changed.

Although updates are rare, they can still happen, and if this cache is to be accessed from multiple threads, it will need to be appropriately protected during updates to ensure that none of the threads reading the cache see a broken data structure.

In the absence of a special-purpose data structure that exactly fits the desired usage and that's specially designed for concurrent updates and reads (such as those in chapters 6 and 7), such an update requires that the thread doing the update have exclusive access to the data structure until it has completed the operation. Once the change is complete, the data structure is again safe for multiple threads to access concurrently. Using a `std::mutex` to protect the data structure is therefore overly pessimistic, because it will eliminate the possible concurrency in reading the data structure when it isn't undergoing modification; what's needed is a different kind of mutex. This new kind of mutex is typically called a *reader-writer* mutex, because it allows for two different kinds of usage: exclusive access by a single "writer" thread or shared, concurrent access by multiple "reader" threads.

The new C++ Standard Library doesn't provide such a mutex out of the box, although one was proposed to the Standards Committee.[3] Because the proposal wasn't accepted, the examples in this section use the implementation provided by the Boost library, which is based on the proposal. As you'll see in chapter 8, the use of such a mutex isn't a panacea, and the performance is dependent on the number of processors involved and the relative workloads of the reader and updater threads. It's therefore important to profile the performance of the code on the target system to ensure that there's actually a benefit to the additional complexity.

Rather than using an instance of `std::mutex` for the synchronization, you use an instance of `boost::shared_mutex`. For the update operations, `std::lock_guard<boost::shared_mutex>` and `std::unique_lock<boost::shared_mutex>` can be used for the locking, in place of the corresponding `std::mutex` specializations. These ensure exclusive access, just as with `std::mutex`. Those threads that don't need to update the data structure can instead use `boost::shared_lock<boost::shared_mutex>`

[3] Howard E. Hinnant, "Multithreading API for C++0X—A Layered Approach," C++ Standards Committee Paper N2094, http://www.open-std.org/jtc1/sc22/wg21/docs/papers/2006/n2094.html.

to obtain *shared* access. This is used just the same as std::unique_lock, except that multiple threads may have a shared lock on the same boost::shared_mutex at the same time. The only constraint is that if any thread has a shared lock, a thread that tries to acquire an exclusive lock will block until all other threads have relinquished their locks, and likewise if any thread has an exclusive lock, no other thread may acquire a shared or exclusive lock until the first thread has relinquished its lock.

The following listing shows a simple DNS cache like the one just described, using a std::map to hold the cached data, protected using a boost::shared_mutex.

Listing 3.13 Protecting a data structure with a boost::shared_mutex

```
#include <map>
#include <string>
#include <mutex>
#include <boost/thread/shared_mutex.hpp>

class dns_entry;

class dns_cache
{
    std::map<std::string,dns_entry> entries;
    mutable boost::shared_mutex entry_mutex;
public:
    dns_entry find_entry(std::string const& domain) const
    {
        boost::shared_lock<boost::shared_mutex> lk(entry_mutex);     ❶
        std::map<std::string,dns_entry>::const_iterator const it=
            entries.find(domain);
        return (it==entries.end())?dns_entry():it->second;
    }
    void update_or_add_entry(std::string const& domain,
                             dns_entry const& dns_details)
    {
        std::lock_guard<boost::shared_mutex> lk(entry_mutex);        ❷
        entries[domain]=dns_details;
    }
};
```

In listing 3.13, find_entry() uses an instance of boost::shared_lock<> to protect it for shared, read-only access ❶; multiple threads can therefore call find_entry() simultaneously without problems. On the other hand, update_or_add_entry() uses an instance of std::lock_guard<> to provide exclusive access while the table is updated ❷; not only are other threads prevented from doing updates in a call update_or_add_entry(), but threads that call find_entry() are blocked too.

3.3.3 Recursive locking

With std::mutex, it's an error for a thread to try to lock a mutex it already owns, and attempting to do so will result in *undefined behavior*. However, in some circumstances it would be desirable for a thread to reacquire the same mutex several times without having first released it. For this purpose, the C++ Standard Library provides std::recursive_mutex. It works just like std::mutex, except that you can acquire multiple locks on a single instance from the same thread. You must release all your locks before the mutex can be locked by another thread, so if you call lock() three times, you must also call unlock() three times. Correct use of std::lock_guard <std::recursive_mutex> and std::unique_lock<std::recursive_mutex> will handle this for you.

Most of the time, if you think you want a recursive mutex, you probably need to change your design instead. A common use of recursive mutexes is where a class is designed to be accessible from multiple threads concurrently, so it has a mutex protecting the member data. Each public member function locks the mutex, does the work, and then unlocks the mutex. However, sometimes it's desirable for one public member function to call another as part of its operation. In this case, the second member function will also try to lock the mutex, thus leading to undefined behavior. The quick-and-dirty solution is to change the mutex to a recursive mutex. This will allow the mutex lock in the second member function to succeed and the function to proceed.

However, such usage is *not recommended*, because it can lead to sloppy thinking and bad design. In particular, the class invariants are typically broken while the lock is held, which means that the second member function needs to work even when called with the invariants broken. It's usually better to extract a new private member function that's called from both member functions, which does not lock the mutex (it expects it to already be locked). You can then think carefully about the circumstances under which that new function can be called and the state of the data under those circumstances.

3.4 Summary

In this chapter I discussed how problematic race conditions can be disastrous when sharing data between threads and how to use std::mutex and careful interface design to avoid them. You saw that mutexes aren't a panacea and do have their own problems in the form of deadlock, though the C++ Standard Library provides a tool to help avoid that in the form of std::lock(). You then looked at some further techniques for avoiding deadlock, followed by a brief look at transferring lock ownership and issues surrounding choosing the appropriate granularity for locking. Finally, I covered the alternative data-protection facilities provided for specific scenarios, such as std::call_once(), and boost::shared_mutex.

One thing that I haven't covered yet, however, is waiting for input from other threads. Our thread-safe stack just throws an exception if the stack is empty, so if one thread wanted to wait for another thread to push a value on the stack (which is, after all, one of the primary uses for a thread-safe stack), it would have to repeatedly try to pop a value, retrying if an exception gets thrown. This consumes valuable processing time in performing the check, without actually making any progress; indeed, the constant checking might *hamper* progress by preventing the other threads in the system from running. What's needed is some way for a thread to wait for another thread to complete a task without consuming CPU time in the process. Chapter 4 builds on the facilities I've discussed for protecting shared data and introduces the various mechanisms for synchronizing operations between threads in C++; chapter 6 shows how these can be used to build larger reusable data structures.

4 Synchronizing concurrent operations

This chapter covers

- Waiting for an event
- Waiting for one-off events with futures
- Waiting with a time limit
- Using synchronization of operations to simplify code

In the last chapter, we looked at various ways of protecting data that's shared between threads. But sometimes you don't just need to protect the data but also to synchronize actions on separate threads. One thread might need to wait for another thread to complete a task before the first thread can complete its own, for example. In general, it's common to want a thread to wait for a specific event to happen or a condition to be `true`. Although it would be possible to do this by periodically checking a "task complete" flag or something similar stored in shared data, this is far from ideal. The need to synchronize operations between threads like this is such a common scenario that the C++ Standard Library provides facilities to handle it, in the form of *condition variables* and *futures*.

In this chapter I'll discuss how to wait for events with condition variables and futures and how to use them to simplify the synchronization of operations.

4.1 Waiting for an event or other condition

Suppose you're traveling on an overnight train. One way to ensure you get off at the right station would be to stay awake all night and pay attention to where the train stops. You wouldn't miss your station, but you'd be tired when you got there. Alternatively, you could look at the timetable to see when the train is supposed to arrive, set your alarm a bit before, and go to sleep. That would be OK; you wouldn't miss your stop, but if the train got delayed, you'd wake up too early. There's also the possibility that your alarm clock's batteries would die, and you'd sleep too long and miss your station. What would be ideal is if you could just go to sleep and have somebody or something wake you up when the train gets to your station, whenever that is.

How does that relate to threads? Well, if one thread is waiting for a second thread to complete a task, it has several options. First, it could just keep checking a flag in shared data (protected by a mutex) and have the second thread set the flag when it completes the task. This is wasteful on two counts: the thread consumes valuable processing time repeatedly checking the flag, and when the mutex is locked by the waiting thread, it can't be locked by any other thread. Both of these work against the thread doing the waiting, because they limit the resources available to the thread being waited for and even prevent it from setting the flag when it's done. This is akin to staying awake all night talking to the train driver: he has to drive the train more slowly because you keep distracting him, so it takes longer to get there. Similarly, the waiting thread is consuming resources that could be used by other threads in the system and may end up waiting longer than necessary.

A second option is to have the waiting thread sleep for small periods between the checks using the `std::this_thread::sleep_for()` function (see section 4.3):

```
bool flag;
std::mutex m;

void wait_for_flag()
{
    std::unique_lock<std::mutex> lk(m);
    while(!flag)
    {
        lk.unlock();                 // 1 Unlock the mutex
        std::this_thread::sleep_for(std::chrono::milliseconds(100));   // 2 Sleep for 100 ms
        lk.lock();                   // 3 Relock the mutex
    }
}
```

In the loop, the function unlocks the mutex ❶ before the sleep ❷ and locks it again afterward ❸, so another thread gets a chance to acquire it and set the flag.

This is an improvement, because the thread doesn't waste processing time while it's sleeping, but it's hard to get the sleep period right. Too short a sleep in between checks and the thread still wastes processing time checking; too long a sleep and the thread will keep on sleeping even when the task it's waiting for is complete, introducing a delay. It's rare that this oversleeping will have a direct impact on the operation of the program, but it could mean dropped frames in a fast-paced game or overrunning a time slice in a real-time application.

The third, and preferred, option is to use the facilities from the C++ Standard Library to wait for the event itself. The most basic mechanism for waiting for an event to be triggered by another thread (such as the presence of additional work in the pipeline mentioned previously) is the *condition variable*. Conceptually, a condition variable is associated with some event or other *condition*, and one or more threads can *wait* for that condition to be satisfied. When some thread has determined that the condition is satisfied, it can then *notify* one or more of the threads waiting on the condition variable, in order to wake them up and allow them to continue processing.

4.1.1 *Waiting for a condition with condition variables*

The Standard C++ Library provides not one but *two* implementations of a condition variable: `std::condition_variable` and `std::condition_variable_any`. Both of these are declared in the `<condition_variable>` library header. In both cases, they need to work with a mutex in order to provide appropriate synchronization; the former is limited to working with `std::mutex`, whereas the latter can work with anything that meets some minimal criteria for being mutex-like, hence the `_any` suffix. Because `std::condition_variable_any` is more general, there's the potential for additional costs in terms of size, performance, or operating system resources, so `std::condition_variable` should be preferred unless the additional flexibility is required.

So, how do you use a `std::condition_variable` to handle the example in the introduction—how do you let the thread that's waiting for work sleep until there's data to process? The following listing shows one way you could do this with a condition variable.

Listing 4.1 Waiting for data to process with a `std::condition_variable`

```
std::mutex mut;
std::queue<data_chunk> data_queue;      <-1
std::condition_variable data_cond;

void data_preparation_thread()
{
    while(more_data_to_prepare())
    {
        data_chunk const data=prepare_data();
        std::lock_guard<std::mutex> lk(mut);
        data_queue.push(data);              <-2
        data_cond.notify_one();     <-3
    }
}

void data_processing_thread()
{
    while(true)
    {
        std::unique_lock<std::mutex> lk(mut);     <-4
```

```
        data_cond.wait(
            lk,[]{return !data_queue.empty();});    <-5
        data_chunk data=data_queue.front();
        data_queue.pop();
        lk.unlock();          <-6
        process(data);
        if(is_last_chunk(data))
            break;
    }
}
```

First off, you have a queue ❶ that's used to pass the data between the two threads. When the data is ready, the thread preparing the data locks the mutex protecting the queue using a `std::lock_guard` and pushes the data onto the queue ❷. It then calls the `notify_one()` member function on the `std::condition_variable` instance to notify the waiting thread (if there is one) ❸.

On the other side of the fence, you have the processing thread. This thread first locks the mutex, but this time with a `std::unique_lock` rather than a `std::lock_guard` ❹—you'll see why in a minute. The thread then calls `wait()` on the `std::condition_variable`, passing in the lock object and a lambda function that expresses the condition being waited for ❺. Lambda functions are a new feature in C++11 that allows you to write an anonymous function as part of another expression, and they're ideally suited for specifying predicates for standard library functions such as `wait()`. In this case, the simple lambda function `[]{return !data_queue.empty();}` checks to see if the `data_queue` is not `empty()`—that is, there's some data in the queue ready for processing. Lambda functions are described in more detail in appendix A, section A.5.

The implementation of `wait()` then checks the condition (by calling the supplied lambda function) and returns if it's satisfied (the lambda function returned `true`). If the condition isn't satisfied (the lambda function returned `false`), `wait()` unlocks the mutex and puts the thread in a blocked or waiting state. When the condition variable is notified by a call to `notify_one()` from the data-preparation thread, the thread wakes from its slumber (unblocks it), reacquires the lock on the mutex, and checks the condition again, returning from `wait()` with the mutex still locked if the condition has been satisfied. If the condition hasn't been satisfied, the thread unlocks the mutex and resumes waiting. This is why you need the `std::unique_lock` rather than the `std::lock_guard`—the waiting thread must unlock the mutex while it's waiting and lock it again afterward, and `std::lock_guard` doesn't provide that flexibility. If the mutex remained locked while the thread was sleeping, the data-preparation thread wouldn't be able to lock the mutex to add an item to the queue, and the waiting thread would never be able to see its condition satisfied.

Listing 4.1 uses a simple lambda function for the wait ❺, which checks to see if the queue is not empty, but any function or callable object could be passed. If you already have a function to check the condition (perhaps because it's more complicated than a simple test like this), then this function can be passed in directly; there's no need to wrap it in a lambda. During a call to `wait()`, a condition variable may check the supplied condition any number of times; however, it always does so with the mutex locked and will return immediately if (and only if) the function provided to test the condition returns `true`. When the waiting thread reacquires the mutex and checks the condition, if it isn't in direct response to a notification from another thread, it's called a *spurious wake*. Because the number and frequency of any such spurious wakes are by definition indeterminate, it isn't advisable to use a function with side effects for the condition check. If you do so, you must be prepared for the side effects to occur multiple times.

The flexibility to unlock a `std::unique_lock` isn't just used for the call to `wait()`; it's also used once you have the data to process but before processing it ❻. Processing data can potentially be a time-consuming operation, and as you saw in chapter 3, it's a bad idea to hold a lock on a mutex for longer than necessary.

Using a queue to transfer data between threads as in listing 4.1 is a common scenario. Done well, the synchronization can be limited to the queue itself, which greatly reduces the possible number of synchronization problems and race conditions. In view of this, let's now work on extracting a generic thread-safe queue from listing 4.1.

4.1.2 Building a thread-safe queue with condition variables

If you're going to be designing a generic queue, it's worth spending a few minutes thinking about the operations that are likely to be required, as you did with the thread-safe stack back in section 3.2.3. Let's look at the C++ Standard Library for inspiration, in the form of the `std::queue<>` container adaptor shown in the following listing.

Listing 4.2 `std::queue` interface

```
template <class T, class Container = std::deque<T> >
class queue {
public:
    explicit queue(const Container&);
    explicit queue(Container&& = Container());

    template <class Alloc> explicit queue(const Alloc&);
    template <class Alloc> queue(const Container&, const Alloc&);
    template <class Alloc> queue(Container&&, const Alloc&);
    template <class Alloc> queue(queue&&, const Alloc&);

    void swap(queue& q);

    bool empty() const;
    size_type size() const;

    T& front();
    const T& front() const;
    T& back();
    const T& back() const;

    void push(const T& x);
    void push(T&& x);
```

```
    void pop();
    template <class... Args> void emplace(Args&&... args);
};
```

If you ignore the construction, assignment and swap operations, you're left with three groups of operations: those that query the state of the whole queue (`empty()` and `size()`), those that query the elements of the queue (`front()` and `back()`), and those that modify the queue (`push()`, `pop()` and `emplace()`). This is the same as you had back in section 3.2.3 for the stack, and therefore you have the same issues regarding race conditions inherent in the interface. Consequently, you need to combine `front()` and `pop()` into a single function call, much as you combined `top()` and `pop()` for the stack. The code from listing 4.1 adds a new nuance, though: when using a queue to pass data between threads, the receiving thread often needs to wait for the data. Let's provide two variants on `pop()`: `try_pop()`, which tries to pop the value from the queue but always returns immediately (with an indication of failure) even if there wasn't a value to retrieve, and `wait_and_pop()`, which will wait until there's a value to retrieve. If you take your lead for the signatures from the stack example, your interface looks like the following.

Listing 4.3 The interface of your `threadsafe_queue`

```
#include <memory>                        <-- For std::shared_ptr

template<typename T>
class threadsafe_queue
{
public:
    threadsafe_queue();
    threadsafe_queue(const threadsafe_queue&);
    threadsafe_queue& operator=(
        const threadsafe_queue&) = delete;        <-- Disallow assignment
                                                      for simplicity
    void push(T new_value);

    bool try_pop(T& value);           <-- 1
    std::shared_ptr<T> try_pop();         <-- 2

    void wait_and_pop(T& value);
    std::shared_ptr<T> wait_and_pop();

    bool empty() const;
};
```

As you did for the stack, you've cut down on the constructors and eliminated assignment in order to simplify the code. You've also provided two versions of both `try_pop()` and `wait_for_pop()`, as before. The first overload of `try_pop()` ❶ stores the retrieved value in the referenced variable, so it can use the return value for status; it returns `true` if it retrieved a value and `false` otherwise (see section A.2). The second overload ❷ can't do this, because it returns the retrieved value directly. But the returned pointer can be set to `NULL` if there's no value to retrieve.

So, how does all this relate to listing 4.1? Well, you can extract the code for `push()` and `wait_and_pop()` from there, as shown in the next listing.

Listing 4.4 Extracting `push()` and `wait_and_pop()` from listing 4.1

```
#include <queue>
#include <mutex>
#include <condition_variable>

template<typename T>
class threadsafe_queue
{
private:
    std::mutex mut;
    std::queue<T> data_queue;
    std::condition_variable data_cond;
public:
    void push(T new_value)
    {
        std::lock_guard<std::mutex> lk(mut);
        data_queue.push(new_value);
        data_cond.notify_one();
    }

    void wait_and_pop(T& value)
    {
        std::unique_lock<std::mutex> lk(mut);
        data_cond.wait(lk,[this]{return !data_queue.empty();});
        value=data_queue.front();
        data_queue.pop();
    }
};

threadsafe_queue<data_chunk> data_queue;      ❶

void data_preparation_thread()
{
    while(more_data_to_prepare())
    {
        data_chunk const data=prepare_data();
        data_queue.push(data);                 ❷
    }
}

void data_processing_thread()
{
    while(true)
    {
        data_chunk data;
        data_queue.wait_and_pop(data);      ❸
        process(data);
        if(is_last_chunk(data))
            break;
    }
}
```

The mutex and condition variable are now contained within the `threadsafe_queue` instance, so separate variables are no longer required ❶, and no external synchronization is required for the call to `push()` ❷. Also, `wait_and_pop()` takes care of the condition variable wait ❸.

The other overload of `wait_and_pop()` is now trivial to write, and the remaining functions can be copied almost verbatim from the stack example in listing 3.5. The final queue implementation is shown here.

Listing 4.5 Full class definition for a thread-safe queue using condition variables

```
#include <queue>
#include <memory>
#include <mutex>
#include <condition_variable>

template<typename T>
class threadsafe_queue
{
private:
    mutable std::mutex mut;                  ❶ The mutex must be mutable
    std::queue<T> data_queue;
    std::condition_variable data_cond;
public:
    threadsafe_queue()
    {}
    threadsafe_queue(threadsafe_queue const& other)
    {
        std::lock_guard<std::mutex> lk(other.mut);
        data_queue=other.data_queue;
    }

    void push(T new_value)
    {
        std::lock_guard<std::mutex> lk(mut);
        data_queue.push(new_value);
        data_cond.notify_one();
    }

    void wait_and_pop(T& value)
    {
        std::unique_lock<std::mutex> lk(mut);
        data_cond.wait(lk,[this]{return !data_queue.empty();});
        value=data_queue.front();
        data_queue.pop();
    }

    std::shared_ptr<T> wait_and_pop()
    {
        std::unique_lock<std::mutex> lk(mut);
        data_cond.wait(lk,[this]{return !data_queue.empty();});
        std::shared_ptr<T> res(std::make_shared<T>(data_queue.front()));
        data_queue.pop();
        return res;
    }
```

```
    bool try_pop(T& value)
    {
        std::lock_guard<std::mutex> lk(mut);
        if(data_queue.empty())
            return false;
        value=data_queue.front();
        data_queue.pop();
        return true;
    }

    std::shared_ptr<T> try_pop()
    {
        std::lock_guard<std::mutex> lk(mut);
        if(data_queue.empty())
            return std::shared_ptr<T>();
        std::shared_ptr<T> res(std::make_shared<T>(data_queue.front()));
        data_queue.pop();
        return res;
    }

    bool empty() const
    {
        std::lock_guard<std::mutex> lk(mut);
        return data_queue.empty();
    }
};
```

Even though `empty()` is a `const` member function, and the `other` parameter to the copy constructor is a `const` reference, other threads may have non-`const` references to the object, and be calling mutating member functions, so we still need to lock the mutex. Since locking a mutex is a mutating operation, the mutex object must be marked `mutable` ❶ so it can be locked in `empty()` and in the copy constructor.

Condition variables are also useful where there's more than one thread waiting for the same event. If the threads are being used to divide the workload, and thus only one thread should respond to a notification, exactly the same structure as shown in listing 4.1 can be used; just run multiple instances of the data—processing thread. When new data is ready, the call to `notify_one()` will trigger one of the threads currently executing `wait()` to check its condition and thus return from `wait()` (because you've just added an item to the `data_queue`). There's no guarantee which thread will be notified or even if there's a thread waiting to be notified; all the processing threads might be still processing data.

Another possibility is that several threads are waiting for the same event, and all of them need to respond. This can happen where shared data is being initialized, and the processing threads can all use the same data but need to wait for it to be initialized (although there are better mechanisms for this; see section 3.3.1 in chapter 3), or where the threads need to wait for an update to shared data, such as a periodic reinitialization. In these cases, the thread preparing the data can call the `notify_all()` member function on the condition variable rather than `notify_one()`. As the name suggests, this causes *all* the threads currently executing `wait()` to check the condition they're waiting for.

If the waiting thread is going to wait only once, so when the condition is `true` it will never wait on this condition variable again, a condition variable might not be the best choice of synchronization mechanisms. This is especially true if the condition being waited for is the availability of a particular piece of data. In this scenario, a *future* might be more appropriate.

4.2 Waiting for one-off events with futures

Suppose you?re going on vacation abroad by plane. Once you get to the airport and clear the various check-in procedures, you still have to wait for notification that your flight is ready for boarding, possibly for several hours. Yes, you might be able to find some means of passing the time, such as reading a book, surfing the internet, or eating in an overpriced airport café, but fundamentally you?re just waiting for one thing: the signal that it?s time to get on the plane. Not only that, but a given flight goes only once; the next time you?re going on vacation, you?ll be waiting for a different flight.

The C++ Standard Library models this sort of one-off event with something called a *future*. If a thread needs to wait for a specific one-off event, it somehow obtains a future representing this event. The thread can then periodically wait on the future for short periods of time to see if the event has occurred (check the departures board) while performing some other task (eating in the overpriced café) in between checks. Alternatively, it can do another task until it needs the event to have happened before it can proceed and then just wait for the future to become *ready*. A future may have data associated with it (such as which gate your flight is boarding at), or it may not. Once an event has happened (and the future has become *ready*), the future can't be reset.

There are two sorts of futures in the C++ Standard Library, implemented as two class templates declared in the `<future>` library header: *unique futures* (`std::future<>`) and *shared futures* (`std::shared_future<>`). These are modeled after `std::unique_ptr` and `std::shared_ptr`. An instance of `std::future` is the one and only instance that refers to its associated event, whereas multiple instances of `std::shared_future` may refer to the same event. In the latter case, all the instances will become *ready* at the same time, and they may all access any data associated with the event. This associated data is the reason these are templates; just like `std::unique_ptr` and `std::shared_ptr`, the template parameter is the type of the associated data. The `std:future<void>`, `std::shared_future<void>` template specializations should be used where there's no associated data. Although futures are used to communicate between threads, the future objects themselves don't provide synchronized accesses. If multiple threads need to access a single future object, they must protect access via a mutex or other synchronization mechanism, as described in chapter 3. However, as you'll see in section 4.2.5, multiple threads may each access their own copy of a `std::shared_future<>` without further synchronization, even if they all refer to the same asynchronous result.

The most basic of one-off events is the result of a calculation that has been run in the background. Back in chapter 2 you saw that `std::thread` doesn't provide an easy means of returning a value from such a task, and I promised that this would be addressed in chapter 4 with futures—now it's time to see how.

4.2.1 Returning values from background tasks

Suppose you have a long-running calculation that you expect will eventually yield a useful result but for which you don't currently need the value. Maybe you've found a way to determine the answer to Life, the Universe, and Everything, to pinch an example from Douglas Adams.[1] You could start a new thread to perform the calculation, but that means you have to take care of transferring the result back, because `std::thread` doesn't provide a direct mechanism for doing so. This is where the `std::async` function template (also declared in the `<future>` header) comes in.

You use `std::async` to start an *asynchronous task* for which you don't need the result right away. Rather than giving you back a `std::thread` object to wait on, `std::async` returns a `std::future` object, which will eventually hold the return value of the function. When you need the value, you just call `get()` on the future, and the thread blocks until the future is *ready* and then returns the value. The following listing shows a simple example.

Listing 4.6 Using `std::future` to get the return value of an asynchronous task

```
#include <future>
#include <iostream>

int find_the_answer_to_ltuae();
void do_other_stuff();
int main()
{
    std::future<int> the_answer=std::async(find_the_answer_to_ltuae);
    do_other_stuff();
    std::cout<<"The answer is "<<the_answer.get()<<std::endl;
}
```

`std::async` allows you to pass additional arguments to the function by adding extra arguments to the call, in the same way that `std::thread` does. If the first argument is a pointer to a member function, the second argument provides the object on which to apply the member function (either directly, or via a pointer, or wrapped in `std::ref`), and the remaining arguments are passed as arguments to the member function. Otherwise, the second and subsequent arguments are passed as arguments to the function or callable object specified as the first argument. Just as with `std::thread`, if the arguments are rvalues, the copies are created by *moving* the originals. This allows the use of move-only types as both the function object and the arguments. See the following listing.

Listing 4.7 Passing arguments to a function with `std::async`

```
#include <string>
#include <future>
```

---

[1] In *The Hitchhiker's Guide to the Galaxy*, the computer Deep Thought is built to determine "the answer to Life, the Universe and Everything." The answer is 42.

```
struct X
{
    void foo(int,std::string const&);
    std::string bar(std::string const&);
};
X x;
auto f1=std::async(&X::foo,&x,42,"hello");      <-- Calls p->foo(42,"hello") where p is &x
auto f2=std::async(&X::bar,x,"goodbye");        <-- Calls tmpx.bar("goodbye") where tmpx is a copy of x
struct Y
{
    double operator()(double);
};
Y y;
auto f3=std::async(Y(),3.141);                  <-- Calls tmpy(3.141) where tmpy is move-constructed from Y()
auto f4=std::async(std::ref(y),2.718);          <-- Calls y(2.718)
X baz(X&);
std::async(baz,std::ref(x));                    <-- Calls baz(x)
class move_only
{
public:
    move_only();
    move_only(move_only&&)
    move_only(move_only const&) = delete;
    move_only& operator=(move_only&&);
    move_only& operator=(move_only const&) = delete;

    void operator()();
};
auto f5=std::async(move_only());                <-- Calls tmp() where tmp is constructed from std::move(move_only())
```

By default, it's up to the implementation whether `std::async` starts a new thread, or whether the task runs synchronously when the future is waited for. In most cases this is what you want, but you can specify which to use with an additional parameter to `std::async` before the function to call. This parameter is of the type `std::launch`, and can either be `std::launch::deferred` to indicate that the function call is to be deferred until either `wait()` or `get()` is called on the future, `std::launch::async` to indicate that the function must be run on its own thread, or `std::launch::deferred | std::launch::async` to indicate that the implementation may choose. This last option is the default. If the function call is deferred, it may never actually run. For example:

```
auto f6=std::async(std::launch::async,Y(),1.2);              <-- Run in new thread
auto f7=std::async(std::launch::deferred,baz,std::ref(x));   <-- Run in wait() or get()
auto f8=std::async(                                          <-- Implementation chooses
   std::launch::deferred | std::launch::async,
   baz,std::ref(x));
auto f9=std::async(baz,std::ref(x));                         <-- Implementation chooses
f7.wait();                                                   <-- Invoke deferred function
```

As you'll see later in this chapter and again in chapter 8, the use of `std::async` makes it easy to divide algorithms into tasks that can be run concurrently. However, it's not the only way to associate a `std::future` with a task; you can also do it by wrapping the task in an instance of the `std::packaged_task<>` class template or by writing code to explicitly set the values using the `std::promise<>` class template. `std::packaged_task` is a higher-level abstraction than `std::promise`, so I'll start with that.

4.2.2 Associating a task with a future

`std::packaged_task<>` ties a future to a function or callable object. When the `std::packaged_task<>` object is invoked, it calls the associated function or callable object and makes the future *ready*, with the return value stored as the associated data. This can be used as a building block for thread pools (see chapter 9) or other task management schemes, such as running each task on its own thread, or running them all sequentially on a particular background thread. If a large operation can be divided into self-contained sub-tasks, each of these can be wrapped in a `std::packaged_task<>` instance, and then that instance passed to the task scheduler or thread pool. This abstracts out the details of the tasks; the scheduler just deals with `std::packaged_task<>` instances rather than individual functions.

The template parameter for the `std::packaged_task<>` class template is a function signature, like `void()` for a function taking no parameters with no return value, or `int(std::string&,double*)` for a function that takes a non-`const` reference to a `std::string` and a pointer to a `double` and returns an `int`. When you construct an instance of `std::packaged_task`, you must pass in a function or callable object that can accept the specified parameters and that returns a type convertible to the specified return type. The types don't have to match exactly; you can construct a `std::packaged_task<double(double)>` from a function that takes an `int` and returns a `float` because the types are implicitly convertible.

The return type of the specified function signature identifies the type of the `std::future<>` returned from the `get_future()` member function, whereas the argument list of the function signature is used to specify the signature of the packaged task's function call operator. For example, a partial class definition for `std::packaged_task<std::string(std::vector<char>*,int)>` would be as shown in the following listing.

Listing 4.8 Partial class definition for a specialization of `std::packaged_task< >`

```
template<>
class packaged_task<std::string(std::vector<char>*,int)>
{
public:
    template<typename Callable>
    explicit packaged_task(Callable&& f);
    std::future<std::string> get_future();
    void operator()(std::vector<char>*,int);
};
```

The `std::packaged_task` object is thus a callable object, and it can be wrapped in a `std::function` object, passed to a `std::thread` as the thread function, passed to another function that requires a callable object, or even invoked directly. When the `std::packaged_task` is invoked as a function object, the arguments supplied to the function call operator are passed on to the contained function, and the return value is stored as the asynchronous result in the `std::future` obtained from `get_future()`. You can thus wrap a task in a `std::packaged_task` and retrieve the future before passing the `std::packaged_task` object elsewhere to be invoked in due course. When you need the result, you can wait for the future to become ready. The following example shows this in action.

PASSING TASKS BETWEEN THREADS

Many GUI frameworks require that updates to the GUI be done from specific threads, so if another thread needs to update the GUI, it must send a message to the right thread in order to do so. `std:packaged_task` provides one way of doing this without requiring a custom message for each and every GUI-related activity, as shown here.

Listing 4.9 Running code on a GUI thread using `std::packaged_task`

```
#include <deque>
#include <mutex>
#include <future>
#include <thread>
#include <utility>

std::mutex m;
std::deque<std::packaged_task<void()> > tasks;

bool gui_shutdown_message_received();
void get_and_process_gui_message();

void gui_thread()                                    ❶
{
    while(!gui_shutdown_message_received())          ❷
    {
        get_and_process_gui_message();               ❸
        std::packaged_task<void()> task;
        {
            std::lock_guard<std::mutex> lk(m);
            if(tasks.empty())                        ❹
                continue;
            task=std::move(tasks.front());           ❺
            tasks.pop_front();
        }
        task();     ❻
    }
}

std::thread gui_bg_thread(gui_thread);

template<typename Func>
std::future<void> post_task_for_gui_thread(Func f)
{
    std::packaged_task<void()> task(f);              ❼
    std::future<void> res=task.get_future();              ❽
    std::lock_guard<std::mutex> lk(m);
    tasks.push_back(std::move(task));                ❾
    return res;                                  ❿
}
```

This code is very simple: the GUI thread ❶ loops until a message has been received telling the GUI to shut down ❷, repeatedly polling for GUI messages to handle ❸, such as user clicks, and for tasks on the task queue. If there are no tasks on the queue ❹, it loops again; otherwise, it extracts the task from the queue ❺, releases the lock on the queue, and then runs the task ❻. The future associated with the task will then be made ready when the task completes.

Posting a task on the queue is equally simple: a new packaged task is created from the supplied function ❼, the future is obtained from that task ❽ by calling the `get_future()` member function, and the task is put on the list ❾ before the future is returned to the caller ❿. The code that posted the message to the GUI thread can then wait for the future if it needs to know that the task has been completed, or it can discard the future if it doesn't need to know.

This example uses `std::packaged_task<void()>` for the tasks, which wraps a function or other callable object that takes no parameters and returns `void` (if it returns anything else, the return value is discarded). This is the simplest possible task, but as you saw earlier, `std::packaged_task` can also be used in more complex situations—by specifying a different function signature as the template parameter, you can change the return type (and thus the type of data stored in the future's associated state) and also the argument types of the function call operator. This example could easily be extended to allow for tasks that are to be run on the GUI thread to accept arguments and return a value in the `std::future` rather than just a completion indicator.

What about those tasks that can't be expressed as a simple function call or those tasks where the result may come from more than one place? These cases are dealt with by the third way of creating a future: using a `std::promise` to set the value explicitly.

4.2.3 Making (std::)promises

When you have an application that needs to handle a lot of network connections, it's often tempting to handle each connection on a separate thread, because this can make the network communication easier to think about and easier to program. This works well for low numbers of connections (and thus low numbers of threads). Unfortunately, as the number of connections rises, this becomes less suitable; the large numbers of threads consequently consume large numbers of operating system resources and potentially cause a lot of context switching (when the number of threads exceeds the available hardware concurrency), impacting performance. In the extreme case, the operating system may run out of resources for running new threads before its capacity for network connections is exhausted. In applications with very large numbers of network connections, it's therefore common to have a small number of threads (possibly only one) handling the connections, each thread dealing with multiple connections at once.

Consider one of these threads handling the connections. Data packets will come in from the various connections being handled in essentially random order, and likewise data packets will be queued to be sent in random order. In many cases, other parts of the application will be waiting either for data to be successfully sent or for a new batch of data to be successfully received via a specific network connection.

std::promise<T> provides a means of setting a value (of type T), which can later be read through an associated std::future<T> object. A std::promise/std::future pair would provide one possible mechanism for this facility; the waiting thread could block on the future, while the thread providing the data could use the promise half of the pairing to set the associated value and make the future *ready*.

You can obtain the std::future object associated with a given std::promise by calling the get_future() member function, just like with std::packaged_task. When the value of the promise is set (using the set_value() member function), the future becomes *ready* and can be used to retrieve the stored value. If you destroy the std::promise without setting a value, an exception is stored instead. Section 4.2.4 describes how exceptions are transferred across threads.

Listing 4.10 shows some example code for a thread processing connections as just described. In this example, you use a std::promise<bool>/std::future<bool> pair to identify the successful transmission of a block of outgoing data; the value associated with the future is a simple success/failure flag. For incoming packets, the data associated with the future is the payload of the data packet.

Listing 4.10 Handling multiple connections from a single thread using promises

```
#include <future>

void process_connections(connection_set& connections)
{
    while(!done(connections))                              <-1
    {
        for(connection_iterator                            <-2
                connection=connections.begin(),end=connections.end();
            connection!=end;
            ++connection)
        {
            if(connection->has_incoming_data())            <-3
            {
                data_packet data=connection->incoming();
                std::promise<payload_type>& p=
                    connection->get_promise(data.id);      <-4
                p.set_value(data.payload);
            }
            if(connection->has_outgoing_data())            <-5
            {
                outgoing_packet data=
                    connection->top_of_outgoing_queue();
                connection->send(data.payload);
                data.promise.set_value(true);              <-6
            }
        }
    }
}
```

The function process_connections() loops until done() returns true ❶. Every time through the loop, it checks each connection in turn ❷, retrieving incoming data if there is any ❸ or sending any queued outgoing data ❺. This assumes that an incoming packet has some ID and a payload with the actual data in it. The ID is mapped to a `std::promise` (perhaps by a lookup in an associative container) ❹, and the value is set to the packet's payload. For outgoing packets, the packet is retrieved from the outgoing queue and actually sent through the connection. Once the send has completed, the promise associated with the outgoing data is set to `true` to indicate successful transmission ❻. Whether this maps nicely to the actual network protocol depends on the protocol; this promise/future style structure may not work for a particular scenario, although it does have a similar structure to the asynchronous I/O support of some operating systems.

All the code up to now has completely disregarded exceptions. Although it might be nice to imagine a world in which everything worked all the time, this isn't actually the case. Sometimes disks fill up, sometimes what you're looking for just isn't there, sometimes the network fails, and sometimes the database goes down. If you were performing the operation in the thread that needed the result, the code could just report an error with an exception, so it would be unnecessarily restrictive to require that everything go well just because you wanted to use a `std::packaged_task` or a `std::promise`. The C++ Standard Library therefore provides a clean way to deal with exceptions in such a scenario and allows them to be saved as part of the associated result.

4.2.4 Saving an exception for the future

Consider the following short snippet of code. If you pass in `-1` to the `square_root()` function, it throws an exception, and this gets seen by the caller:

```
double square_root(double x)
{
    if(x<0)
    {
        throw std::out_of_range("x<0");
    }
    return sqrt(x);
}
```

Now suppose that instead of just invoking `square_root()` from the current thread,

```
double y=square_root(-1);
```

you run the call as an asynchronous call:

```
std::future<double> f=std::async(square_root,-1);
double y=f.get();
```

It would be ideal if the behavior was exactly the same; just as `y` gets the result of the function call in either case, it would be great if the thread that called `f.get()` could see the exception too, just as it would in the single-threaded case.

Well, that's exactly what happens: if the function call invoked as part of `std::async` throws an exception, that exception is stored in the future in place of a stored value, the future becomes *ready*, and a call to `get()` rethrows that stored exception.

(Note: the standard leaves it unspecified whether it is the original exception object that's rethrown or a copy; different compilers and libraries make different choices on this matter.) The same happens if you wrap the function in a `std::packaged_task`—when the task is invoked, if the wrapped function throws an exception, that exception is stored in the future in place of the result, ready to be thrown on a call to `get()`.

Naturally, `std::promise` provides the same facility, with an explicit function call. If you wish to store an exception rather than a value, you call the `set_exception()` member function rather than `set_value()`. This would typically be used in a `catch` block for an exception thrown as part of the algorithm, to populate the promise with that exception:

```
extern std::promise<double> some_promise;

try
{
    some_promise.set_value(calculate_value());
}
catch(...)
{
    some_promise.set_exception(std::current_exception());
}
```

This uses `std::current_exception()` to retrieve the thrown exception; the alternative here would be to use `std::copy_exception()` to store a new exception directly without throwing:

```
some_promise.set_exception(std::copy_exception(std::logic_error("foo ")));
```

This is much cleaner than using a `try/catch` block if the type of the exception is known, and it should be used in preference; not only does it simplify the code, but it also provides the compiler with greater opportunity to optimize the code.

Another way to store an exception in a future is to destroy the `std::promise` or `std::packaged_task` associated with the future without calling either of the set functions on the promise or invoking the packaged task. In either case, the destructor of the `std::promise` or `std::packaged_task` will store a `std::future_error` exception with an error code of `std::future_errc::broken_promise` in the associated state if the future isn't already *ready*; by creating a future you make a promise to provide a value or exception, and by destroying the source of that value or exception without providing one, you break that promise. If the compiler didn't store anything in the future in this case, waiting threads could potentially wait forever.

Up until now all the examples have used `std::future`. However, `std::future` has its limitations, not the least of which being that only one thread can wait for the result. If you need to wait for the same event from more than one thread, you need to use `std::shared_future` instead.

4.2.5 Waiting from multiple threads

Although `std::future` handles all the synchronization necessary to transfer data from one thread to another, calls to the member functions of a particular `std::future` instance are not synchronized with each other. If you access a single `std::future` object from multiple threads without additional synchronization, you have a *data race* and undefined behavior. This is by design: `std::future` models unique ownership of the asynchronous result, and the one-shot nature of `get()` makes such concurrent access pointless anyway—only one thread can retrieve the value, because after the first call to `get()` there's no value left to retrieve.

If your fabulous design for your concurrent code requires that multiple threads can wait for the same event, don't despair just yet; `std::shared_future` allows exactly that. Whereas `std::future` is only *moveable*, so ownership can be transferred between instances, but only one instance refers to a particular asynchronous result at a time, `std::shared_future` instances are *copyable*, so you can have multiple objects referring to the same associated state.

Now, with `std::shared_future`, member functions on an individual object are still unsynchronized, so to avoid data races when accessing a single object from multiple threads, you must protect accesses with a lock. The preferred way to use it would be to take a copy of the object instead and have each thread access its own copy. Accesses to the shared asynchronous state from multiple threads are safe if each thread accesses that state through its own `std::shared_future` object. See figure 4.1.

One potential use of `std::shared_future` is for implementing parallel execution of something akin to a complex spreadsheet; each cell has a single final value, which may be used by the formulas in multiple other cells. The formulas for calculating the results of the dependent cells can then use a `std::shared_future` to reference the first cell. If all the formulas for the individual cells are then executed in parallel, those tasks that can proceed to completion will do so, whereas those that depend on others will block until their dependencies are ready. This will thus allow the system to make maximum use of the available hardware concurrency.

Instances of `std::shared_future` that reference some asynchronous state are constructed from instances of `std::future` that reference that state. Since `std::future` objects don't share ownership of the asynchronous state with any other object, the ownership must be transferred into the `std::shared_future` using `std::move`, leaving the `std::future` in an empty state, as if it was default constructed:

```
std::promise<int> p;
std::future<int> f(p.get_future());
assert(f.valid());                               ❶ The future f is valid
std::shared_future<int> sf(std::move(f));
assert(!f.valid());                              ❷ f is no longer valid
assert(sf.valid());          ❸ sf is now valid
```

Here, the future `f` is initially valid ❶ because it refers to the asynchronous state of the promise `p`, but after transferring the state to `sf`, `f` is no longer valid ❷, whereas `sf` is ❸.

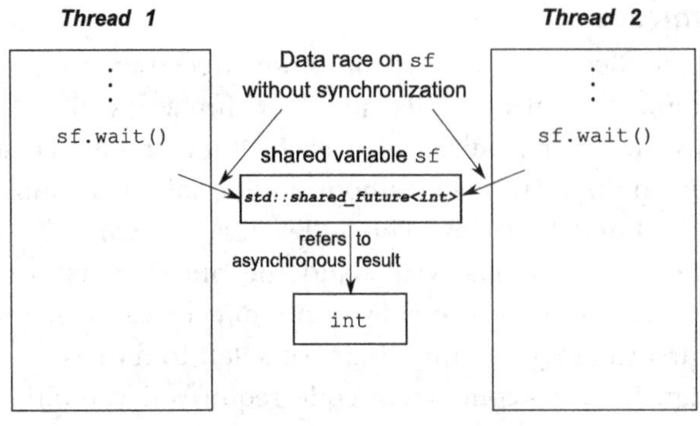

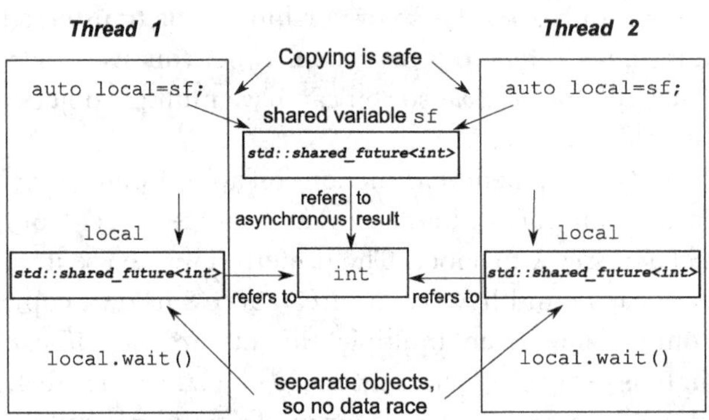

Figure 4.1 Using multiple `std::shared_future` objects to avoid data races

Just as with other movable objects, the transfer of ownership is implicit for rvalues, so you can construct a `std::shared_future` directly from the return value of the `get_future()` member function of a `std::promise` object, for example:

```
std::promise<std::string> p;
std::shared_future<std::string> sf(p.get_future());    // ❶ Implicit transfer of ownership
```

Here, the transfer of ownership is implicit; the `std::shared_future<>` is constructed from an rvalue of type `std::future<std::string>` ❶.

`std::future` also has an additional feature to facilitate the use of `std::shared_future` with the new facility for automatically deducing the type of a variable from its initializer (see appendix A, section A.6). `std::future` has a `share()` member function that creates a new `std::shared_future` and transfers ownership to it directly. This can save a lot of typing and makes code easier to change:

```
std::promise< std::map< SomeIndexType, SomeDataType, SomeComparator,
    SomeAllocator>::iterator> p;
auto sf=p.get_future().share();
```

In this case, the type of `sf` is deduced to be `std::shared_future< std::map< SomeIndexType, SomeDataType, SomeComparator, SomeAllocator>::iterator>`, which is rather a mouthful. If the comparator or allocator is changed, you only need to change the type of the promise; the type of the future is automatically updated to match.

Sometimes you want to limit the amount of time you're waiting for an event, either because you have a hard time limit on how long a particular section of code may take, or because there's other useful work that the thread can be doing if the event isn't going to happen soon. To handle this facility, many of the waiting functions have variants that allow a timeout to be specified.

4.3 Waiting with a time limit

All the blocking calls introduced previously will block for an indefinite period of time, suspending the thread until the event being waited for occurs. In many cases this is fine, but in some cases you want to put a limit on how long you wait. This might be to allow you to send some form of "I'm still alive" message either to an interactive user or another process or indeed to allow you to abort the wait if the user has given up waiting and pressed Cancel.

There are two sorts of timeouts you may wish to specify: a *duration-based* timeout, where you wait for a specific amount of time (for example, 30 milliseconds), or an *absolute* timeout, where you wait until a specific point in time (for example, 17:30:15.045987023 UTC on November 30, 2011). Most of the waiting functions provide variants that handle both forms of timeouts. The variants that handle the duration-based timeouts have a `_for` suffix, and those that handle the absolute timeouts have a `_until` suffix.

So, for example, `std::condition_variable` has two overloads of the `wait_for()` member function and two overloads of the `wait_until()` member function that correspond to the two overloads of `wait()`—one overload that just waits until signaled, or the timeout expires, or a spurious wakeup occurs, and another that will check the supplied predicate when woken and will return only when the supplied predicate is `true` (and the condition variable has been signaled) or the timeout expires.

Before we look at the details of the functions that use the timeouts, let's examine the way that times are specified in C++, starting with clocks.

4.3.1 Clocks

As far as the C++ Standard Library is concerned, a clock is a source of time information. In particular, a clock is a class that provides four distinct pieces of information:

- The time *now*
- The type of the value used to represent the times obtained from the clock
- The tick period of the clock
- Whether or not the clock ticks at a uniform rate and is thus considered to be a *steady* clock

The current time of a clock can be obtained by calling the static member function `now()` for that clock class; for example, `std::chrono::system_clock::now()` will return the current time of the system clock. The type of the time points for a particular clock is specified by the `time_point` member `typedef`, so the return type of `some_clock::now()` is `some_clock::time_point`.

The tick period of the clock is specified as a fractional number of seconds, which is given by the `period` member `typedef` of the clock—a clock that ticks 25 times per second thus has a `period` of `std::ratio<1,25>`, whereas a clock that ticks every 2.5 seconds has a `period` of `std::ratio<5,2>`. If the tick period of a clock can't be known until runtime, or it may vary during a given run of the application, the `period` may be specified as the average tick period, smallest possible tick period, or some other value that the library writer deems appropriate. There's no guarantee that the observed tick period in a given run of the program matches the specified `period` for that clock.

If a clock *ticks at a uniform rate* (whether or not that rate matches the `period`) and *can't be adjusted*, the clock is said to be a *steady* clock. The `is_steady` static data member of the clock class is `true` if the clock is steady and `false` otherwise. Typically, `std::chrono::system_clock` will *not* be steady, because the clock can be adjusted, even if such adjustment is done automatically to take account of local clock drift. Such an adjustment may cause a call to `now()` to return a value earlier than that returned by a prior call to `now()`, which is in violation of the requirement for a uniform tick rate. Steady clocks are important for timeout calculations, as you'll see shortly, so the C++ Standard Library provides one in the form of `std::chrono::steady_clock`. The other clocks provided by the C++ Standard Library are `std::chrono::system_clock` (mentioned above), which represents the "real time" clock of the system and which provides functions for converting its time points to and from `time_t` values, and `std::chrono::high_resolution_clock`, which provides the smallest possible tick period (and thus the highest possible resolution) of all the library-supplied clocks. It may actually be a `typedef` to one of the other clocks. These clocks are defined in the `<chrono>` library header, along with the other time facilities.

We'll look at the representation of time points shortly, but first let's look at how durations are represented.

4.3.2 Durations

Durations are the simplest part of the time support; they're handled by the `std::chrono::duration<>` class template (all the C++ time-handling facilities used by the Thread Library are in the `std::chrono` namespace). The first template parameter is the type of the representation (such as `int`, `long`, or `double`), and the second is a fraction specifying how many seconds each unit of the duration represents. For example, a number of minutes stored in a `short` is `std::chrono::duration<short,std::ratio<60,1>>`, because there are 60 seconds in a minute. On the other hand, a count of milliseconds stored in a `double` is `std::chrono::duration<double,std::ratio<1,1000>>`, because each millisecond is 1/1000 of a second.

The Standard Library provides a set of predefined `typedef`s in the `std::chrono` namespace for various durations: `nanoseconds`, `microseconds`, `milliseconds`, `seconds`, `minutes`, and `hours`. They all use a sufficiently large integral type for the representation chosen such that you can represent a duration of over 500 *years* in the appropriate units if you so desire. There are also `typedef`s for all the SI ratios from `std::atto`

(10^{-18}) to `std::exa` (10^{18}) (and beyond, if your platform has 128-bit integer types) for use when specifying custom durations such as `std::duration<double,std::centi>` for a count of 1/100 of a second represented in a `double`.

Conversion between durations is implicit where it does not require truncation of the value (so converting hours to seconds is OK, but converting seconds to hours is not). Explicit conversions can be done with `std::chrono::duration_cast<>`:

```
std::chrono::milliseconds ms(54802);
std::chrono::seconds s=
    std::chrono::duration_cast<std::chrono::seconds>(ms);
```

The result is truncated rather than rounded, so `s` will have a value of 54 in this example.

Durations support arithmetic, so you can add and subtract durations to get new durations or multiply or divide by a constant of the underlying representation type (the first template parameter). Thus `5*seconds(1)` is the same as `seconds(5)` or `minutes(1) - seconds(55)`. The count of the number of units in the duration can be obtained with the `count()` member function. Thus `std::chrono::milliseconds(1234).count()` is 1234.

Duration-based waits are done with instances of `std::chrono::duration<>`. For example, you can wait for up to 35 milliseconds for a future to be ready:

```
std::future<int> f=std::async(some_task);
if(f.wait_for(std::chrono::milliseconds(35))==std::future_status::ready)
    do_something_with(f.get());
```

The wait functions all return a status to indicate whether the wait timed out or the waited-for event occurred. In this case, you're waiting for a future, so the function returns `std::future_status::timeout` if the wait times out, `std::future_status::ready` if the future is ready, or `std::future_status::deferred` if the future's task is deferred. The time for a duration-based wait is measured using a steady clock internal to the library, so 35 milliseconds means 35 milliseconds of elapsed time, even if the system clock was adjusted (forward or back) during the wait. Of course, the vagaries of system scheduling and the varying precisions of OS clocks means that the actual time between the thread issuing the call and returning from it may be much longer than 35 ms.

With durations under our belt, we can now move on to time points.

4.3.3 Time points

The time point for a clock is represented by an instance of the `std::chrono::time_point<>` class template, which specifies which clock it refers to as the first template parameter and the units of measurement (a specialization of `std::chrono::duration<>`) as the second template parameter. The value of a time point is the length of time (in multiples of the specified duration) since a specific point in time called the *epoch* of the clock. The epoch of a clock is a basic property but not something that's directly available to query or specified by the C++ Standard. Typical epochs include 00:00 on January 1, 1970 and the instant when the computer running the application booted up. Clocks may share an epoch or have independent epochs. If two clocks share an epoch, the `time_point typedef` in one class may specify the other as the clock type associated with the time_point. Although you can't find out when the epoch is, you *can* get the time_since_epoch() for a given time_point. This member function returns a duration value specifying the length of time since the clock epoch to that particular time point.

For example, you might specify a time point as std::chrono::time_point<std::chrono::system_clock, std::chrono::minutes>. This would hold the time relative to the system clock but measured in minutes as opposed to the native precision of the system clock (which is typically seconds or less).

You can add durations and subtract durations from instances of std::chrono::time_point<> to produce new time points, so std::chrono::high_resolution_clock::now() + std::chrono::nanoseconds(500) will give you a time 500 nanoseconds in the future. This is good for calculating an absolute timeout when you know the maximum duration of a block of code, but there are multiple calls to waiting functions within it or nonwaiting functions that precede a waiting function but take up some of the time budget.

You can also subtract one time point from another that shares the same clock. The result is a duration specifying the length of time between the two time points. This is useful for timing blocks of code, for example:

```
auto start=std::chrono::high_resolution_clock::now();
do_something();
auto stop=std::chrono::high_resolution_clock::now();
std::cout<<"do_something() took "
  <<std::chrono::duration<double,std::chrono::seconds>(stop-start).count()
  <<" seconds"<<std::endl;
```

The clock parameter of a std::chrono::time_point<> instance does more than just specify the epoch, though. When you pass the time point to a wait function that takes an absolute timeout, the clock parameter of the time point is used to measure the time. This has important consequences when the clock is changed, because the wait tracks the clock change and won't return until the clock's now() function returns a value later than the specified timeout. If the clock is adjusted forward, this may reduce the total length of the wait (as measured by a steady clock), and if it's adjusted backward, this may increase the total length of the wait.

As you may expect, time points are used with the _until variants of the wait functions. The typical use case is as an offset from *some-clock*::now() at a fixed point in the program, although time points associated with the system clock can be obtained by converting from a time_t using the std::chrono::system_clock::to_time_point() static member function for scheduling operations at a user-visible time. For example, if you have a maximum of 500 milliseconds to wait for an event associated with a condition variable, you might do something like in the following listing.

Listing 4.11 Waiting for a condition variable with a timeout

```
#include <condition_variable>
#include <mutex>
#include <chrono>
```

```
std::condition_variable cv;
bool done;
std::mutex m;

bool wait_loop()
{
    auto const timeout= std::chrono::steady_clock::now()+
        std::chrono::milliseconds(500);
    std::unique_lock<std::mutex> lk(m);
    while(!done)
    {
        if(cv.wait_until(lk,timeout)==std::cv_status::timeout)
            break;
    }
    return done;
}
```

This is the recommended way to wait for condition variables with a time limit, if you're not passing a predicate to the wait. This way, the overall length of the loop is bounded. As you saw in section 4.1.1, you need to loop when using condition variables if you don't pass in the predicate, in order to handle spurious wakeups. If you use `wait_for()` in a loop, you might end up waiting almost the full length of time before a spurious wake, and the next time through the wait time starts again. This may repeat any number of times, making the total wait time unbounded.

With the basics of specifying timeouts under your belt, let's look at the functions that you can use the timeout with.

4.3.4 Functions that accept timeouts

The simplest use for a timeout is to add a delay to the processing of a particular thread, so that it doesn't take processing time away from other threads when it has nothing to do. You saw an example of this in section 4.1, where you polled a "done" flag in a loop. The two functions that handle this are `std::this_thread::sleep_for()` and `std::this_thread::sleep_until()`. They work like a basic alarm clock: the thread goes to sleep either for the specified duration (with `sleep_for()`) or until the specified point in time (with `sleep_until()`). `sleep_for()` makes sense for examples like that from section 4.1, where something must be done periodically, and the elapsed time is what matters. On the other hand, `sleep_until()` allows you to schedule the thread to wake at a particular point in time. This could be used to trigger the backups at midnight, or the payroll print run at 6:00 a.m., or to suspend the thread until the next frame refresh when doing a video playback.

Of course, sleeping isn't the only facility that takes a timeout; you already saw that you can use timeouts with condition variables and futures. You can even use timeouts when trying to acquire a lock on a mutex if the mutex supports it. Plain `std::mutex` and `std::recursive_mutex` don't support timeouts on locking, but `std::timed_mutex` does, as does `std::recursive_timed_mutex`. Both these types support `try_lock_for()` and `try_lock_until()` member functions that try to obtain the lock within a specified time period or before a specified time point. Table 4.1 shows the functions from the C++ Standard Library that can accept timeouts, their parameters, and their return values. Parameters listed as *duration* must be an instance of `std::duration<>`, and those listed as *time_point* must be an instance of `std::time_point<>`.

Table 4.1 Functions that accept timeouts

Class/Namespace	Functions	Return values
`std::this_thread` namespace	`sleep_for(`*duration*`)` `sleep_until(`*time_point*`)`	N/A
`std::condition_variable` or `std::condition_variable_any`	`wait_for(`*lock*`, `*duration*`)` `wait_until(`*lock*`, `*time_point*`)`	`std::cv_status::timeout` or `std::cv_status::no_timeout`
	`wait_for(`*lock*`, `*duration*`, `*predicate*`)` `wait_until(`*lock*`, `*time_point*`, `*predicate*`)`	`bool`—the return value of the *predicate* when awakened
`std::timed_mutex` or `std::recursive_timed_mutex`	`try_lock_for(`*duration*`)` `try_lock_until(`*time_point*`)`	`bool`—`true` if the lock was acquired, `false` otherwise
`std::unique_lock<`*TimedLockable*`>`	`unique_lock(`*lockable*`, `*duration*`)` `unique_lock(`*lockable*`, `*time_point*`)`	N/A—`owns_lock()` on the newly constructed object; returns `true` if the lock was acquired, `false` otherwise
	`try_lock_for(`*duration*`)` `try_lock_until(time_point)`	`bool`—`true` if the lock was acquired, `false` otherwise
`std::future<`*ValueType*`>` or `std::shared_future<`*ValueType*`>`	`wait_for(`*duration*`)` `wait_until(`*time_point*`)`	`std::future_status::timeout` if the wait timed out, `std::future_status::ready` if the future is ready, or `std::future_status::deferred` if the future holds a deferred function that hasn't yet started

Now that I've covered the mechanics of condition variables, futures, promises, and packaged tasks, it's time to look at the wider picture and how they can be used to simplify the synchronization of operations between threads.

4.4 Using synchronization of operations to simplify code

Using the synchronization facilities described so far in this chapter as building blocks allows you to focus on the operations that need synchronizing rather than the mechanics. One way this can help simplify your code is that it accommodates a much more *functional* (in the sense of *functional programming*) approach to programming concurrency. Rather than sharing data directly between threads, each task can be provided with the data it needs, and the result can be disseminated to any other threads that need it through the use of futures.

4.4.1 Functional programming with futures

The term *functional programming* (FP) refers to a style of programming where the result of a function call depends solely on the parameters to that function and doesn't depend on any external state. This is related to the mathematical concept of a function, and it means that if you invoke a function twice with the same parameters, the result is exactly the same. This is a property of many of the mathematical functions in the C++ Standard Library, such as `sin`, `cos`, and `sqrt`, and simple operations on basic types, such as `3+3`, `6*9`, or `1.3/4.7`. A *pure* function doesn't *modify* any external state either; the effects of the function are entirely limited to the return value.

This makes things easy to think about, especially when concurrency is involved, because many of the problems associated with shared memory discussed in chapter 3 disappear. If there are no modifications to shared data, there can be no race conditions and thus no need to protect shared data with mutexes either. This is such a powerful simplification that programming languages such as Haskell,[2] where all functions are pure *by default*, are becoming increasingly popular for programming concurrent systems. Because most things are pure, the *impure* functions that actually *do* modify the shared state stand out all the more, and it's therefore easier to reason about how they fit into the overall structure of the application.

The benefits of functional programming aren't limited to those languages where it's the default paradigm, however. C++ is a multiparadigm language, and it's entirely possible to write programs in the FP style. This is even easier in C++11 than it was in C++98, with the advent of lambda functions (see appendix A, section A.6), the incorporation of `std::bind` from Boost and TR1, and the introduction of automatic type deduction for variables (see appendix A, section A.7). Futures are the final piece of the puzzle that makes FP-style concurrency viable in C++; a future can be passed around between threads to allow the result of one computation to depend on the result of another, *without any explicit access to shared data.*

FP-STYLE QUICKSORT

To illustrate the use of futures for FP-style concurrency, let's look at a simple implementation of the Quicksort algorithm. The basic idea of the algorithm is simple: given a list of values, take an element to be the pivot element, and then partition the

---

[2] See http://www.haskell.org/.

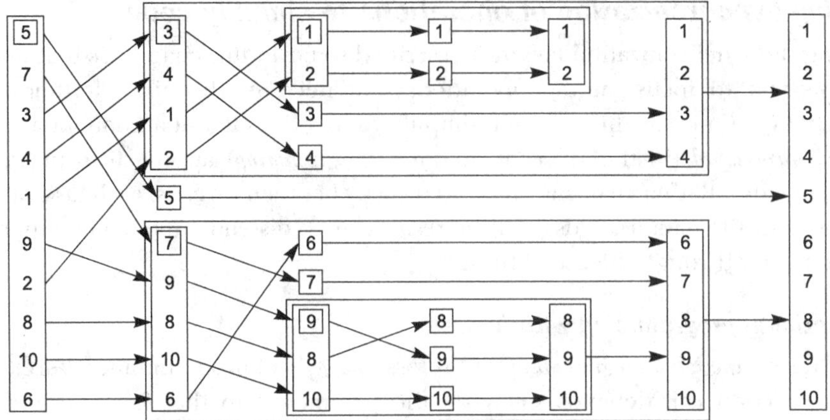

Figure 4.2 FP-style recursive sorting

list into two sets—those less than the pivot and those greater than or equal to the pivot. A sorted copy of the list is obtained by sorting the two sets and returning the sorted list of values less than the pivot, followed by the pivot, followed by the sorted list of values greater than or equal to the pivot. Figure 4.2 shows how a list of 10 integers is sorted under this scheme. An FP-style sequential implementation is shown in the following listing; it takes and returns a list by value rather than sorting in place like `std::sort()` does.

Listing 4.12 A sequential implementation of Quicksort

```
template<typename T>
std::list<T> sequential_quick_sort(std::list<T> input)
{
    if(input.empty())
    {
        return input;
    }
    std::list<T> result;
    result.splice(result.begin(),input,input.begin());      ❶
    T const& pivot=*result.begin();                          ❷

    auto divide_point=std::partition(input.begin(),input.end(),
            [&](T const& t){return t<pivot;});               ❸

    std::list<T> lower_part;
    lower_part.splice(lower_part.end(),input,input.begin(),
        divide_point);                                       ❹

    auto new_lower(
        sequential_quick_sort(std::move(lower_part)));       ❺
    auto new_higher(
        sequential_quick_sort(std::move(input)));            ❻

    result.splice(result.end(),new_higher);                  ❼
```

```
    result.splice(result.begin(),new_lower);        <-8
    return result;
}
```

Although the interface is FP-style, if you used FP-style throughout you'd do a lot of copying, so you use "normal" imperative style for the internals. You take the first element as the pivot by slicing it off the front of the list using `splice()` ❶. Although this can potentially result in a suboptimal sort (in terms of numbers of comparisons and exchanges), doing anything else with a `std::list` can add quite a bit of time because of the list traversal. You know you're going to want it in the result, so you can splice it directly into the list you'll be using for that. Now, you're also going to want to use it for comparisons, so let's take a reference to it to avoid copying ❷. You can then use `std::partition` to divide the sequence into those values *less than* the pivot and those *not* less than the pivot ❸. The easiest way to specify the partition criteria is to use a lambda function; you use a reference capture to avoid copying the `pivot` value (see appendix A, section A.5 for more on lambda functions).

`std::partition()` rearranges the list in place and returns an iterator marking the first element that's *not* less than the pivot value. The full type for an iterator can be quite long-winded, so you just use the `auto` type specifier to force the compiler to work it out for you (see appendix A, section A.7).

Now, you've opted for an FP-style interface, so if you're going to use recursion to sort the two "halves," you'll need to create two lists. You can do this by using `splice()` again to move the values from `input` up to the `divide_point` into a new list: `lower_part` ❹. This leaves the remaining values alone in `input`. You can then sort the two lists with recursive calls ❺, ❻. By using `std::move()` to pass the lists in, you can avoid copying here too—the result is implicitly moved out anyway. Finally, you can use `splice()` yet again to piece the `result` together in the right order. The `new_higher` values go on the end ❼, after the pivot, and the `new_lower` values go at the beginning, before the pivot ❽.

FP-STYLE PARALLEL QUICKSORT

Because this uses a functional style already, it's now easy to convert this to a parallel version using futures, as shown in the next listing. The set of operations is the same as before, except that some of them now run in parallel. This version uses an implementation of the Quicksort algorithm using futures and a functional style.

Listing 4.13 Parallel Quicksort using futures

```
template<typename T>
std::list<T> parallel_quick_sort(std::list<T> input)
{
    if(input.empty())
    {
        return input;
    }
    std::list<T> result;
    result.splice(result.begin(),input,input.begin());
    T const& pivot=*result.begin();
```

```
    auto divide_point=std::partition(input.begin(),input.end(),
            [&](T const& t){return t<pivot;});

    std::list<T> lower_part;
    lower_part.splice(lower_part.end(),input,input.begin(),
        divide_point);
                                                                   ❶
    std::future<std::list<T> > new_lower(                        <-
        std::async(&parallel_quick_sort<T>,std::move(lower_part)));

    auto new_higher(
        parallel_quick_sort(std::move(input)));          <- ❷

    result.splice(result.end(),new_higher);              <- ❸
    result.splice(result.begin(),new_lower.get());             <- ❹
    return result;
}
```

The big change here is that rather than sorting the lower portion on the current thread, you sort it on another thread using `std::async()` ❶. The upper portion of the list is sorted with direct recursion as before ❷. By recursively calling `parallel_quick_sort()`, you can take advantage of the available hardware concurrency. If `std::async()` starts a new thread every time, then if you recurse down three times, you'll have eight threads running; if you recurse down 10 times (for ~1000 elements), you'll have 1024 threads running if the hardware can handle it. If the library decides there are too many spawned tasks (perhaps because the number of tasks has exceeded the available hardware concurrency), it may switch to spawning the new tasks synchronously. They will run in the thread that calls `get()` rather than on a new thread, thus avoiding the overhead of passing the task to another thread when this won't help the performance. It's worth noting that it's perfectly conforming for an implementation of `std::async` to start a new thread for each task (even in the face of massive oversubscription) unless `std::launch::deferred` is explicitly specified or to run all tasks synchronously unless `std::launch::async` is explicitly specified. If you're relying on the library for automatic scaling, you're advised to check the documentation for your implementation to see what behavior it exhibits.

Rather than using `std::async()`, you could write your own `spawn_task()` function as a simple wrapper around `std::packaged_task` and `std::thread`, as shown in listing 4.14; you'd create a `std::packaged_task` for the result of the function call, get the future from it, run it on a thread, and return the future. This wouldn't itself offer much advantage (and indeed would likely lead to massive oversubcription), but it would pave the way to migrate to a more sophisticated implementation that adds the task to a queue to be run by a pool of worker threads. We'll look at thread pools in chapter 9. It's probably worth going this way in preference to using `std::async` only if you really know what you're doing and want complete control over the way the thread pool is built and executes tasks.

Anyway, back to `parallel_quick_sort`. Because you just used direct recursion to get `new_higher`, you can just splice it into place as before ❸. But `new_lower` is now a `std::future<std::list<T>>` rather than just a list, so you need to call `get()` to retrieve the value before you can call `splice()` ❹. This then waits for the background task to complete and *moves* the result into the `splice()` call; `get()` returns an rvalue reference to the contained result, so it can be moved out (see appendix A, section A.1.1 for more on rvalue references and move semantics).

Even assuming that `std::async()` makes optimal use of the available hardware concurrency, this still isn't an ideal parallel implementation of Quicksort. For one thing, `std::partition` does a lot of the work, and that's still a sequential call, but it's good enough for now. If you're interested in the fastest possible parallel implementation, check the academic literature.

Listing 4.14 A sample implementation of `spawn_task`

```
template<typename F,typename A>
std::future<std::result_of<F(A&&)>::type>
    spawn_task(F&& f,A&& a)
{
    typedef std::result_of<F(A&&)>::type result_type;
    std::packaged_task<result_type(A&&)>
        task(std::move(f)));
    std::future<result_type> res(task.get_future());
    std::thread t(std::move(task),std::move(a));
    t.detach();
    return res;
}
```

Functional programming isn't the only concurrent programming paradigm that eschews shared mutable data; another paradigm is CSP (Communicating Sequential Processes),[3] where threads are conceptually entirely separate, with no shared data but with communication channels that allow messages to be passed between them. This is the paradigm adopted by the programming language Erlang (http://www.erlang.org/) and by the MPI (Message Passing Interface) (http://www.mpi-forum.org/) environment commonly used for high-performance computing in C and C++. I'm sure that by now you'll be unsurprised to learn that this can also be supported in C++ with a bit of discipline; the following section discusses one way to achieve this.

4.4.2 Synchronizing operations with message passing

The idea of CSP is simple: if there's no shared data, each thread can be reasoned about entirely independently, purely on the basis of how it behaves in response to the messages that it received. Each thread is therefore effectively a state machine: when it receives a message, it updates its state in some manner and maybe sends one or more messages to other threads, with the processing performed depending on the initial state. One way to write such threads would be to formalize this and implement a Finite State Machine model, but this isn't the only way; the state machine can be implicit in the structure of the application. Which method works better in any given scenario

[3] *Communicating Sequential Processes*, C.A.R. Hoare, Prentice Hall, 1985. Available free online at http://www.usingcsp.com/cspbook.pdf.

depends on the exact behavioral requirements of the situation and the expertise of the programming team. However you choose to implement each thread, the separation into independent processes has the potential to remove much of the complication from shared-data concurrency and therefore make programming easier, lowering the bug rate.

True communicating sequential processes have no shared data, with all communication passed through the message queues, but because C++ threads share an address space, it's not possible to enforce this requirement. This is where the discipline comes in: as application or library authors, it's our responsibility to ensure that we don't share data between the threads. Of course, the message queues must be shared in order for the threads to communicate, but the details can be wrapped in the library.

Imagine for a moment that you're implementing the code for an ATM. This code needs to handle interaction with the person trying to withdraw money and interaction with the relevant bank, as well as control the physical machinery to accept the person's card, display appropriate messages, handle key presses, issue money, and return their card.

One way to handle everything would be to split the code into three independent threads: one to handle the physical machinery, one to handle the ATM logic, and one to communicate with the bank. These threads could communicate purely by passing messages rather than sharing any data. For example, the thread handling the machinery would send a message to the logic thread when the person at the machine entered their card or pressed a button, and the logic thread would send a message to the machinery thread indicating how much money to dispense, and so forth.

One way to model the ATM logic would be as a state machine. In each state the thread waits for an acceptable message, which it then processes. This may result in transitioning to a new state, and the cycle continues. The states involved in a simple implementation are shown in figure 4.3. In this simplified implementation, the system waits for a card to be inserted. Once the card is inserted, it then waits for the user to enter their PIN, one digit at a time. They can delete the last digit entered. Once enough digits have been entered, the PIN is verified. If the PIN is not OK, you're finished, so you return the card to the customer and resume waiting for someone to enter their card. If the PIN is OK, you wait for them to either cancel the transaction or select an amount to withdraw. If they cancel, you're finished, and you return their card. If they select an amount, you wait for confirmation from the bank before issuing the cash and returning the card or displaying an "insufficient funds" message and returning their card. Obviously, a real ATM is considerably more complex, but this is enough to illustrate the idea.

Having designed a state machine for your ATM logic, you can implement it with a class that has a member function to represent each state. Each member function can then wait for specific sets of incoming messages and handle them when they arrive, possibly triggering a switch to another state. Each distinct message type is represented by a separate `struct`. Listing 4.15 shows part of a simple implementation of the ATM logic in such a system, with the main loop and the implementation of the first state, waiting for the card to be inserted.

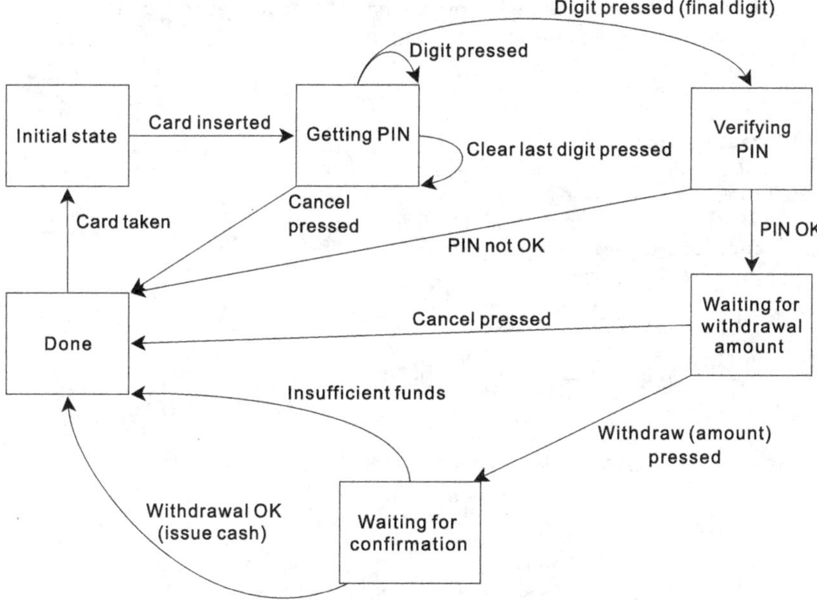

Figure 4.3 A simple state machine model for an ATM

As you can see, all the necessary synchronization for the message passing is entirely hidden inside the message-passing library (a basic implementation of which is given in appendix C, along with the full code for this example).

Listing 4.15 A simple implementation of an ATM logic class

```
struct card_inserted
{
    std::string account;
};
class atm
{
    messaging::receiver incoming;
    messaging::sender bank;
    messaging::sender interface_hardware;
    void (atm::*state)();

    std::string account;
    std::string pin;

    void waiting_for_card()                  ❶
    {
        interface_hardware.send(display_enter_card());      ❷
        incoming.wait()                             ❸
            .handle<card_inserted>(
                [&](card_inserted const& msg)          ❹
                {
                    account=msg.account;
                    pin="";
```

```
                    interface_hardware.send(display_enter_pin());
                    state=&atm::getting_pin;
                }
                );
    }
    void getting_pin();
public:
    void run()                   ❺
    {
        state=&atm::waiting_for_card;      ❻
        try
        {
            for(;;)
            {
                (this->*state)();      ❼
            }
        }
        catch(messaging::close_queue const&)
        {
        }
    }
};
```

As already mentioned, the implementation described here is grossly simplified from the real logic that would be required in an ATM, but it does give you a feel for the message-passing style of programming. There's no need to think about synchronization and concurrency issues, just which messages may be received at any given point and which messages to send. The state machine for this ATM logic runs on a single thread, with other parts of the system such as the interface to the bank and the terminal interface running on separate threads. This style of program design is called the *Actor model*—there are several discrete *actors* in the system (each running on a separate thread), which send messages to each other to perform the task at hand, and there's no shared state except that directly passed via messages.

Execution starts with the `run()` member function ❺, which sets the initial state to `waiting_for_card` ❻ and then repeatedly executes the member function representing the current state (whatever it is) ❼. The state functions are simple member functions of the `atm` class. The `waiting_for_card` state function ❶ is also simple: it sends a message to the interface to display a "waiting for card" message ❷ and then waits for a message to handle ❸. The only type of message that can be handled here is a `card_inserted` message, which you handle with a lambda function ❹. You could pass any function or function object to the `handle` function, but for a simple case like this, it's easiest to use a lambda. Note that the `handle()` function call is chained onto the `wait()` function; if a message is received that doesn't match the specified type, it's discarded, and the thread continues to wait until a matching message is received.

The lambda function itself just caches the account number from the card in a member variable, clears the current PIN, sends a message to the interface hardware to display something asking the user to enter their PIN, and changes to the "getting PIN" state. Once the message handler has completed, the state function returns, and the main loop then calls the new state function ❼.

The `getting_pin` state function is a bit more complex in that it can handle three distinct types of message, as in figure 4.3. This is shown in the following listing.

Listing 4.16 The `getting_pin` state function for the simple ATM implementation

```
void atm::getting_pin()
{
    incoming.wait()
        .handle<digit_pressed>(                          ❶
            [&](digit_pressed const& msg)
            {
                unsigned const pin_length=4;
                pin+=msg.digit;
                if(pin.length()==pin_length)
                {
                    bank.send(verify_pin(account,pin,incoming));
                    state=&atm::verifying_pin;
                }
            }
            )
        .handle<clear_last_pressed>(                     ❷
            [&](clear_last_pressed const& msg)
            {
                if(!pin.empty())
                {
                    pin.resize(pin.length()-1);
                }
            }
            )
        .handle<cancel_pressed>(                         ❸
            [&](cancel_pressed const& msg)
            {
                state=&atm::done_processing;
            }
            );
}
```

This time, there are three message types you can process, so the `wait()` function has three `handle()` calls chained on the end ❶, ❷, ❸. Each call to `handle()` specifies the message type as the template parameter and then passes in a lambda function that takes that particular message type as a parameter. Because the calls are chained together in this way, the `wait()` implementation knows that it's waiting for a `digit_pressed` message, a `clear_last_pressed` message, or a `cancel_pressed` message. Messages of any other type are again discarded.

This time, you don't necessarily change state when you get a message. For example, if you get a `digit_pressed` message, you just add it to the `pin` unless it's the final digit. The main loop ❼ in listing 4.15) will then call `getting_pin()` again to wait for the next digit (or clear or cancel).

This corresponds to the behavior shown in figure 4.3. Each state box is implemented by a distinct member function, which waits for the relevant messages and updates the state as appropriate.

As you can see, this style of programming can greatly simplify the task of designing a concurrent system, because each thread can be treated entirely independently. It is thus an example of using multiple threads to separate concerns and as such requires you to explicitly decide how to divide the tasks between threads.

4.5 Summary

Synchronizing operations between threads is an important part of writing an application that uses concurrency: if there's no synchronization, the threads are essentially independent and might as well be written as separate applications that are run as a group because of their related activities. In this chapter, I've covered various ways of synchronizing operations from the basic condition variables, through futures, promises, and packaged tasks. I've also discussed ways of approaching the synchronization issues: functional-style programming where each task produces a result entirely dependent on its input rather than on the external environment, and message passing where communication between threads is via asynchronous messages sent through a messaging subsystem that acts as an intermediary.

Having discussed many of the high-level facilities available in C++, it's now time to look at the low-level facilities that make it all work: the C++ memory model and atomic operations.

5 The C++ memory model and operations on atomic types

This chapter covers

- The details of the C++11 memory model
- The atomic types provided by the C++ Standard Library
- The operations that are available on those types
- How those operations can be used to provide synchronization between threads

One of the most important features of the C++11 Standard is something most programmers won't even notice. It's not the new syntax features, nor is it the new library facilities, but the new multithreading-aware memory model. Without the memory model to define exactly how the fundamental building blocks work, none of the facilities I've covered could be relied on to work. Of course, there's a reason that most programmers won't notice: if you use mutexes to protect your data and condition variables or futures to signal events, the details of *why* they work aren't important. It's only when you start trying to get "close to the machine" that the precise details of the memory model matter.

Whatever else it is, C++ is a systems programming language. One of the goals of the Standards Committee is that there shall be no need for a lower-level language than C++. Programmers should be provided with enough flexibility within C++ to do whatever they need without the language getting in the way, allowing them to get "close to the machine" when the need arises. The atomic types and operations allow just that, providing facilities for low-level synchronization operations that will commonly reduce to one or two CPU instructions.

In this chapter, I'll start by covering the basics of the memory model, then move on to the atomic types and operations, and finally cover the various types of synchronization available with the operations on atomic types. This is quite complex: unless you're planning on writing code that uses the atomic operations for synchronization (such as the lock-free data structures in chapter 7), you won't need to know these details.

Let's ease into things with a look at the basics of the memory model.

5.1 Memory model basics

There are two aspects to the memory model: the basic *structural* aspects, which relate to how things are laid out in memory, and then the *concurrency* aspects. The structural aspects are important for concurrency, especially when you're looking at low-level atomic operations, so I'll start with those. In C++, it's all about objects and memory locations.

5.1.1 Objects and memory locations

All data in a C++ program is made up of *objects*. This is not to say that you can create a new class derived from `int`, or that the fundamental types have member functions, or any of the other consequences often implied when people say "everything is an object" when discussing a language like Smalltalk or Ruby. It's just a statement about the building blocks of data in C++. The C++ Standard defines an object as "a region of storage," although it goes on to assign properties to these objects, such as their type and lifetime.

Some of these objects are simple values of a fundamental type such as `int` or `float`, whereas others are instances of user-defined classes. Some objects (such as arrays, instances of derived classes, and instances of classes with non-`static` data members) have subobjects, but others don't.

Whatever its type, an object is stored in one or more *memory locations*. Each such memory location is either an object (or subobject) of a scalar type such as `unsigned short` or `my_class*` or a sequence of adjacent bit fields. If you use bit fields, this is an important point to note: though adjacent bit fields are distinct objects, they're still counted as the same memory location. Figure 5.1 shows how a `struct` divides into objects and memory locations.

First, the entire `struct` is one object, which consists of several subobjects, one for each data member. The bit fields `bf1` and `bf2` share a memory location, and the `std::string` object `s` consists of several memory locations internally, but otherwise each member has its own memory location. Note how the zero-length bit field `bf3` separates `bf4` into its own memory location.

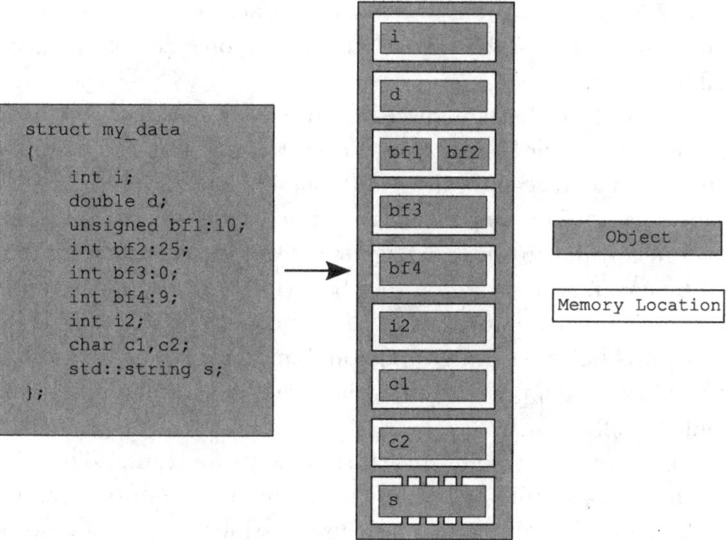
struct my_data
{
int i;
double d;
unsigned bf1:10;
int bf2:25;
int bf3:0;
int bf4:9;
int i2;
char c1,c2;
std::string s;
};
i
d
bf1
bf2
bf3
bf4
i2
c1
c2
s
Object
Memory Location

Figure 5.1 The division of a `struct` into objects and memory locations

There are four important things to take away from this:

- Every variable is an object, including those that are members of other objects.
- Every object occupies *at least one* memory location.
- Variables of fundamental type such as `int` or `char` are *exactly one* memory location, whatever their size, even if they're adjacent or part of an array.
- Adjacent bit fields are part of the same memory location.

I'm sure you're wondering what this has to do with concurrency, so let's take a look.

5.1.2 Objects, memory locations, and concurrency

Now, here's the part that's crucial for multithreaded applications in C++: everything hinges on those memory locations. If two threads access *separate* memory locations, there's no problem: everything works fine. On the other hand, if two threads access the *same* memory location, then you have to be careful. If neither thread is updating the memory location, you're fine; read-only data doesn't need protection or synchronization. If either thread is modifying the data, there's a potential for a race condition, as described in chapter 3.

In order to avoid the race condition, there has to be an enforced ordering between the accesses in the two threads. One way to ensure there's a defined ordering is to use mutexes as described in chapter 3; if the same mutex is locked prior to both accesses, only one thread can access the memory location at a time, so one must happen before the other. The other way is to use the synchronization properties of *atomic* operations (see section 5.2 for the definition of atomic operations) either on the same or other memory locations to enforce an ordering between the accesses in the two threads. The use of atomic operations to enforce an ordering is described in section 5.3. If more than two threads access the same memory location, each pair of accesses must have a defined ordering.

If there's no enforced ordering between two accesses to a single memory location from separate threads, one or both of those accesses is not atomic, and one or both is a write, then this is a data race and causes undefined behavior.

This statement is crucially important: undefined behavior is one of the nastiest corners of C++. According to the language standard, once an application contains any undefined behavior, all bets are off; the behavior of the complete application is now undefined, and it may do anything at all. I know of one case where a particular instance of undefined behavior caused someone's monitor to catch on fire. Although this is rather unlikely to happen to you, a data race is definitely a serious bug and should be avoided at all costs.

There's another important point in that statement: you can also avoid the undefined behavior by using atomic operations to access the memory location involved in the race. This doesn't prevent the race itself—which of the atomic operations touches the memory location first is still not specified—but it does bring the program back into the realm of defined behavior.

Before we look at atomic operations, there's one more concept that's important to understand about objects and memory locations: modification orders.

5.1.3 Modification orders

Every object in a C++ program has a defined *modification order* composed of all the writes to that object from all threads in the program, starting with the object's initialization. In most cases this order will vary between runs, but in any given execution of the program all threads in the system must agree on the order. If the object in question isn't one of the atomic types described in section 5.2, you're responsible for making certain that there's sufficient synchronization to ensure that threads agree on the modification order of each variable. If different threads see distinct sequences of values for a single variable, you have a data race and undefined behavior (see section 5.1.2). If you do use atomic operations, the compiler is responsible for ensuring that the necessary synchronization is in place.

This requirement means that certain kinds of speculative execution aren't permitted, because once a thread has seen a particular entry in the modification order, subsequent reads from that thread must return later values, and subsequent writes from that thread to that object must occur later in the modification order. Also, a read of an object that follows a write to that object in the same thread must either return the value written or another value that occurs later in the modification order of that object. Although all threads must agree on the modification orders of each individual object in a program, they don't necessarily have to agree on the relative order of operations on separate objects. See section 5.3.3 for more on the ordering of operations between threads.

So, what constitutes an atomic operation, and how can these be used to enforce ordering?

5.2 Atomic operations and types in C++

An *atomic operation* is an indivisible operation. You can't observe such an operation half-done from any thread in the system; it's either done or not done. If the load operation that reads the value of an object is *atomic*, and all modifications to that object are also *atomic*, that load will retrieve either the initial value of the object or the value stored by one of the modifications.

The flip side of this is that a nonatomic operation might be seen as half-done by another thread. If that operation is a store, the value observed by another thread might be neither the value before the store nor the value stored but something else. If the nonatomic operation is a load, it might retrieve part of the object, have another thread modify the value, and then retrieve the remainder of the object, thus retrieving neither the first value nor the second but some combination of the two. This is a simple problematic race condition, as described in chapter 3, but at this level it may constitute a *data race* (see section 5.1) and thus cause undefined behavior.

In C++, you need to use an atomic type to get an atomic operation in most cases, so let's look at those.

5.2.1 The standard atomic types

The standard *atomic types* can be found in the `<atomic>` header. All operations on such types are atomic, and only operations on these types are atomic in the sense of the language definition, although you can use mutexes to make other operations *appear* atomic. In actual fact, the standard atomic types themselves might use such emulation: they (almost) all have an `is_lock_free()` member function, which allows the user to determine whether operations on a given type are done directly with atomic instructions (`x.is_lock_free()` returns `true`) or done by using a lock internal to the compiler and library (`x.is_lock_free()` returns `false`).

The only type that doesn't provide an `is_lock_free()` member function is `std::atomic_flag`. This type is a really simple Boolean flag, and operations on this type are *required* to be lock-free; once you have a simple lock-free Boolean flag, you can use that to implement a simple lock and thus implement all the other atomic types using that as a basis. When I said *really simple*, I meant it: objects of type `std::atomic_flag` are initialized to clear, and they can then either be queried and set (with the `test_and_set()` member function) or cleared (with the `clear()` member function). That's it: no assignment, no copy construction, no test and clear, no other operations at all.

The remaining atomic types are all accessed through specializations of the `std::atomic<>` class template and are a bit more full-featured but may not be lock-free (as explained previously). On most popular platforms it's expected that the atomic variants of all the built-in types (such as `std::atomic<int>` and `std::atomic<void*>`) are indeed lock-free, but it isn't required. As you'll see shortly, the interface of each specialization reflects the properties of the type; bitwise operations such as `&=` aren't defined for plain pointers, so they aren't defined for atomic pointers either, for example.

In addition to using the `std::atomic<>` class template directly, you can use the set of names shown in table 5.1 to refer to the implementation-supplied atomic types. Because of the history of how atomic types were added to the C++ Standard, these alternative type names may refer either to the corresponding `std::atomic<>` specialization or to a base class of that specialization. Mixing these alternative names with direct naming of `std::atomic<>` specializations in the same program can therefore lead to nonportable code.

Table 5.1 The alternative names for the standard atomic types and their corresponding `std::atomic<>` specializations

Atomic type	Corresponding specialization
atomic_bool	std::atomic<bool>
atomic_char	std::atomic<char>
atomic_schar	std::atomic<signed char>
atomic_uchar	std::atomic<unsigned char>
atomic_int	std::atomic<int>
atomic_uint	std::atomic<unsigned>
atomic_short	std::atomic<short>
atomic_ushort	std::atomic<unsigned short>
atomic_long	std::atomic<long>
atomic_ulong	std::atomic<unsigned long>
atomic_llong	std::atomic<long long>
atomic_ullong	std::atomic<unsigned long long>
atomic_char16_t	std::atomic<char16_t>
atomic_char32_t	std::atomic<char32_t>
atomic_wchar_t	std::atomic<wchar_t>

As well as the basic atomic types, the C++ Standard Library also provides a set of `typedef`s for the atomic types corresponding to the various nonatomic Standard Library `typedef`s such as `std::size_t`. These are shown in table 5.2.

That's a lot of types! There's a rather simple pattern to it; for a standard `typedef T`, the corresponding atomic type is the same name with an `atomic_` prefix: `atomic_T`. The same applies to the built-in types, except that `signed` is abbreviated as just `s`, `unsigned` as

Table 5.2 The standard atomic `typedef`s and their corresponding built-in `typedef`s

Atomic `typedef`	Corresponding Standard Library `typedef`
`atomic_int_least8_t`	`int_least8_t`
`atomic_uint_least8_t`	`uint_least8_t`
`atomic_int_least16_t`	`int_least16_t`
`atomic_uint_least16_t`	`uint_least16_t`
`atomic_int_least32_t`	`int_least32_t`
`atomic_uint_least32_t`	`uint_least32_t`
`atomic_int_least64_t`	`int_least64_t`
`atomic_uint_least64_t`	`uint_least64_t`
`atomic_int_fast8_t`	`int_fast8_t`
`atomic_uint_fast8_t`	`uint_fast8_t`
`atomic_int_fast16_t`	`int_fast16_t`
`atomic_uint_fast16_t`	`uint_fast16_t`
`atomic_int_fast32_t`	`int_fast32_t`
`atomic_uint_fast32_t`	`uint_fast32_t`
`atomic_int_fast64_t`	`int_fast64_t`
`atomic_uint_fast64_t`	`uint_fast64_t`
`atomic_intptr_t`	`intptr_t`
`atomic_uintptr_t`	`uintptr_t`
`atomic_size_t`	`size_t`
`atomic_ptrdiff_t`	`ptrdiff_t`
`atomic_intmax_t`	`intmax_t`
`atomic_uintmax_t`	`uintmax_t`

just `u`, and `long long` as `llong`. It's generally just simpler to say `std::atomic<T>` for whichever `T` you wish to work with, rather than use the alternative names.

The standard atomic types are not copyable or assignable in the conventional sense, in that they have no copy constructors or copy assignment operators. They *do*, however, support assignment from and implicit conversion to the corresponding built-in types as well as direct `load()` and `store()` member functions, `exchange()`, `compare_exchange_weak()`, and `compare_exchange_strong()`. They also support the compound assignment operators where appropriate: `+=`, `-=`, `*=`, `|=`, and so on, and the integral types and `std::atomic<>` specializations for pointers support `++` and `--`.

These operators also have corresponding named member functions with the same functionality: `fetch_add()`, `fetch_or()`, and so on. The return value from the assignment operators and member functions is either the value stored (in the case of the assignment operators) or the value prior to the operation (in the case of the named functions). This avoids the potential problems that could stem from the usual habit of such assignment operators returning a reference to the object being assigned to. In order to get the stored value from such a reference, the code would have to perform a separate read, thus allowing another thread to modify the value between the assignment and the read and opening the door for a race condition.

The `std::atomic<>` class template isn't just a set of specializations, though. It does have a primary template that can be used to create an atomic variant of a user-defined type. Because it's a generic class template, the operations are limited to `load()`, `store()` (and assignment from and conversion to the user-defined type), `exchange()`, `compare_exchange_weak()`, and `compare_exchange_strong()`.

Each of the operations on the atomic types has an optional memory-ordering argument that can be used to specify the required memory-ordering semantics. The precise semantics of the memory-ordering options are covered in section 5.3. For now, it suffices to know that the operations are divided into three categories:

- *Store* operations, which can have `memory_order_relaxed`, `memory_order_release`, or `memory_order_seq_cst` ordering
- *Load* operations, which can have `memory_order_relaxed`, `memory_order_consume`, `memory_order_acquire`, or `memory_order_seq_cst` ordering
- *Read-modify-write* operations, which can have `memory_order_relaxed`, `memory_order_consume`, `memory_order_acquire`, `memory_order_release`, `memory_order_acq_rel`, or `memory_order_seq_cst` ordering

The default ordering for all operations is `memory_order_seq_cst`.

Let's now look at the operations you can actually do on each of the standard atomic types, starting with `std::atomic_flag`.

5.2.2 Operations on std::atomic_flag

`std::atomic_flag` is the simplest standard atomic type, which represents a Boolean flag. Objects of this type can be in one of two states: set or clear. It's deliberately basic and is intended as a building block only. As such, I'd never expect to see it in use, except under very special circumstances. Even so, it will serve as a starting point for discussing the other atomic types, because it shows some of the general policies that apply to the atomic types.

Objects of type `std::atomic_flag` *must* be initialized with `ATOMIC_FLAG_INIT`. This initializes the flag to a *clear* state. There's no choice in the matter; the flag always starts clear:

```
std::atomic_flag f=ATOMIC_FLAG_INIT;
```

This applies wherever the object is declared and whatever scope it has. It's the only atomic type to require such special treatment for initialization, but it's also the only type guaranteed to be lock-free. If the `std::atomic_flag` object has static storage duration, it's guaranteed to be statically initialized, which means that there are no initialization-order issues; it will always be initialized by the time of the first operation on the flag.

Once you have your flag object initialized, there are only three things you can do with it: destroy it, clear it, or set it and query the previous value. These correspond to the destructor, the `clear()` member function, and the `test_and_set()` member function, respectively. Both the `clear()` and `test_and_set()` member functions can have a memory order specified. `clear()` is a *store* operation and so can't have `memory_order_acquire` or `memory_order_acq_rel` semantics, but `test_and_set()` is a read-modify-write operation and so can have any of the memory-ordering tags applied. As with every atomic operation, the default for both is `memory_order_seq_cst`. For example:

```
f.clear(std::memory_order_release);        <-1
bool x=f.test_and_set();                <-2
```

Here, the call to `clear()` ❶ explicitly requests that the flag is cleared with release semantics, while the call to `test_and_set()` ❷ uses the default memory ordering for setting the flag and retrieving the old value.

You can't copy-construct another `std::atomic_flag` object from the first, and you can't assign one `std::atomic_flag` to another. This isn't something peculiar to `std::atomic_flag` but something common with all the atomic types. All operations on an atomic type are defined as atomic, and assignment and copy-construction involve two objects. A single operation on two distinct objects can't be atomic. In the case of copy-construction or copy-assignment, the value must first be read from one object and then written to the other. These are two separate operations on two separate objects, and the combination can't be atomic. Therefore, these operations aren't permitted.

The limited feature set makes `std::atomic_flag` ideally suited to use as a spin-lock mutex. Initially the flag is clear and the mutex is unlocked. To lock the mutex, loop on `test_and_set()` until the old value is `false`, indicating that *this* thread set the value to `true`. Unlocking the mutex is simply a matter of clearing the flag. Such an implementation is shown in the following listing.

Listing 5.1 Implementation of a spinlock mutex using `std::atomic_flag`

```
class spinlock_mutex
{
    std::atomic_flag flag;
public:
    spinlock_mutex():
        flag(ATOMIC_FLAG_INIT)
    {}
    void lock()
    {
        while(flag.test_and_set(std::memory_order_acquire));
    }
```

```
    void unlock()
    {
        flag.clear(std::memory_order_release);
    }
};
```

Such a mutex is very basic, but it's enough to use with `std::lock_guard<>` (see chapter 3). By its very nature it does a busy-wait in `lock()`, so it's a poor choice if you expect there to be any degree of contention, but it's enough to ensure mutual exclusion. When we look at the memory-ordering semantics, you'll see how this guarantees the necessary enforced ordering that goes with a mutex lock. This example is covered in section 5.3.6.

`std::atomic_flag` is so limited that it can't even be used as a general Boolean flag, because it doesn't have a simple nonmodifying query operation. For that you're better off using `std::atomic<bool>`, so I'll cover that next.

5.2.3 Operations on std::atomic<bool>

The most basic of the atomic integral types is `std::atomic<bool>`. This is a more full-featured Boolean flag than `std::atomic_flag`, as you might expect. Although it's still not copy-constructible or copy-assignable, you can construct it from a nonatomic `bool`, so it can be initially `true` or `false`, and you can also assign to instances of `std::atomic<bool>` from a nonatomic `bool`:

```
std::atomic<bool> b(true);
b=false;
```

One other thing to note about the assignment operator from a nonatomic `bool` is that it differs from the general convention of returning a reference to the object it's assigned to: it returns a `bool` with the value assigned instead. This is another common pattern with the atomic types: the assignment operators they support return values (of the corresponding nonatomic type) rather than references. If a reference to the atomic variable was returned, any code that depended on the result of the assignment would then have to explicitly load the value, potentially getting the result of a modification by another thread. By returning the result of the assignment as a nonatomic value, you can avoid this additional load, and you know that the value obtained is the actual value stored.

Rather than using the restrictive `clear()` function of `std::atomic_flag`, writes (of either `true` or `false`) are done by calling `store()`, although the memory-order semantics can still be specified. Similarly, `test_and_set()` has been replaced with the more general `exchange()` member function that allows you to replace the stored value with a new one of your choosing and atomically retrieve the original value. `std::atomic<bool>` also supports a plain nonmodifying query of the value with an implicit conversion to plain `bool` or with an explicit call to `load()`. As you might expect, `store()` is a store operation, whereas `load()` is a load operation. `exchange()` is a read-modify-write operation:

```
std::atomic<bool> b;
bool x=b.load(std::memory_order_acquire);
b.store(true);
x=b.exchange(false,std::memory_order_acq_rel);
```

`exchange()` isn't the only read-modify-write operation supported by `std::atomic<bool>`; it also introduces an operation to store a new value if the current value is equal to an expected value.

STORING A NEW VALUE (OR NOT) DEPENDING ON THE CURRENT VALUE

This new operation is called compare/exchange, and it comes in the form of the `compare_exchange_weak()` and `compare_exchange_strong()` member functions. The compare/exchange operation is the cornerstone of programming with atomic types; it compares the value of the atomic variable with a supplied expected value and stores the supplied desired value if they're equal. If the values aren't equal, the expected value is updated with the actual value of the atomic variable. The return type of the compare/exchange functions is a `bool`, which is `true` if the store was performed and `false` otherwise.

For `compare_exchange_weak()`, the store might not be successful even if the original value was equal to the expected value, in which case the value of the variable is unchanged and the return value of `compare_exchange_weak()` is `false`. This is most likely to happen on machines that lack a single compare-and-exchange instruction, if the processor can't guarantee that the operation has been done atomically—possibly because the thread performing the operation was switched out in the middle of the necessary sequence of instructions and another thread scheduled in its place by the operating system where there are more threads than processors. This is called a *spurious failure*, because the reason for the failure is a function of timing rather than the values of the variables.

Because `compare_exchange_weak()` can fail spuriously, it must typically be used in a loop:

```
bool expected=false;
extern atomic<bool> b; // set somewhere else
while(!b.compare_exchange_weak(expected,true) && !expected);
```

In this case, you keep looping as long as `expected` is still `false`, indicating that the `compare_exchange_weak()` call failed spuriously.

On the other hand, `compare_exchange_strong()` is guaranteed to return `false` only if the actual value wasn't equal to the `expected` value. This can eliminate the need for loops like the one shown where you just want to know whether you successfully changed a variable or whether another thread got there first.

If you want to change the variable whatever the initial value is (perhaps with an updated value that depends on the current value), the update of `expected` becomes useful; each time through the loop, `expected` is reloaded, so if no other thread modifies the value in the meantime, the `compare_exchange_weak()` or `compare_exchange_strong()` call should be successful the next time around the loop. If the calculation of the value to be stored is simple, it may be beneficial to use compare_exchange_weak() in order to avoid a double loop on platforms where compare_exchange_weak() *can* fail spuriously (and so compare_exchange_strong() contains a loop). On the other hand, if the calculation of the value to be stored is itself time consuming, it may make sense to use compare_exchange_strong() to avoid having to recalculate the value to store when the expected value hasn't changed. For std::atomic<bool> this isn't so important—there are only two possible values after all—but for the larger atomic types this can make a difference.

The compare/exchange functions are also unusual in that they can take *two* memory-ordering parameters. This allows for the memory-ordering semantics to differ in the case of success and failure; it might be desirable for a successful call to have memory_order_acq_rel semantics whereas a failed call has memory_order_relaxed semantics. A failed compare/exchange doesn't do a store, so it can't have memory_order_release or memory_order_acq_rel semantics. It's therefore not permitted to supply these values as the ordering for failure. You also can't supply stricter memory ordering for failure than for success; if you want memory_order_acquire or memory_order_seq_cst semantics for failure, you must specify those for success as well.

If you don't specify an ordering for failure, it's assumed to be the same as that for success, except that the release part of the ordering is stripped: memory_order_release becomes memory_order_relaxed, and memory_order_acq_rel becomes memory_order_acquire. If you specify neither, they default to memory_order_seq_cst as usual, which provides the full sequential ordering for both success and failure. The following two calls to compare_exchange_weak() are equivalent:

```
std::atomic<bool> b;
bool expected;
b.compare_exchange_weak(expected,true,
    memory_order_acq_rel,memory_order_acquire);
b.compare_exchange_weak(expected,true,memory_order_acq_rel);
```

I'll leave the consequences of the choice of memory ordering to section 5.3.

One further difference between std::atomic<bool> and std::atomic_flag is that std::atomic<bool> may not be lock-free; the implementation may have to acquire a mutex internally in order to ensure the atomicity of the operations. For the rare case when this matters, you can use the is_lock_free() member function to check whether operations on std::atomic<bool> are lock-free. This is another feature common to all atomic types other than std::atomic_flag.

The next-simplest of the atomic types are the atomic pointer specializations std::atomic<T*>, so we'll look at those next.

5.2.4 Operations on std::atomic<T*>: pointer arithmetic

The atomic form of a pointer to some type T is std::atomic<T*>, just as the atomic form of bool is std::atomic<bool>. The interface is essentially the same, although it operates on values of the corresponding pointer type rather than bool values. Just like std::atomic<bool>, it's neither copy-constructible nor copy-assignable, although it can be both constructed and assigned from the suitable pointer values. As well as the obligatory is_lock_free() member function, std::atomic<T*> also has load(), store(), exchange(), compare_exchange_weak(), and compare_exchange_strong() member functions, with similar semantics to those of std::atomic<bool>, again taking and returning T* rather than bool.

The new operations provided by std::atomic<T*> are the pointer arithmetic operations. The basic operations are provided by the fetch_add() and fetch_sub() member functions, which do atomic addition and subtraction on the stored address, and the operators += and -=, and both pre- and post-increment and decrement with ++ and --, which provide convenient wrappers. The operators work just as you'd expect from the built-in types: if x is std::atomic<Foo*> to the first entry of an array of Foo objects, then x+=3 changes it to point to the fourth entry and returns a plain Foo* that also points to that fourth entry. fetch_add() and fetch_sub() are slightly different in that they return the original value (so x.fetch_add(3) will update x to point to the fourth value but return a pointer to the first value in the array). This operation is also known as *exchange-and-add*, and it's an atomic read-modify-write operation, like exchange() and compare_exchange_weak()/compare_exchange_strong(). Just as with the other operations, the return value is a plain T* value rather than a reference to the std::atomic<T*> object, so that the calling code can perform actions based on what the previous value was:

```
class Foo{};
Foo some_array[5];
std::atomic<Foo*> p(some_array);
Foo* x=p.fetch_add(2);                      // Add 2 to p and return old value
assert(x==some_array);
assert(p.load()==&some_array[2]);
x=(p-=1);                                   // Subtract 1 from p and return new value
assert(x==&some_array[1]);
assert(p.load()==&some_array[1]);
```

The function forms also allow the memory-ordering semantics to be specified as an additional function call argument:

```
p.fetch_add(3,std::memory_order_release);
```

Because both fetch_add() and fetch_sub() are read-modify-write operations, they can have any of the memory-ordering tags and can participate in a *release sequence*. Specifying the ordering semantics isn't possible for the operator forms, because there's no way of providing the information: these forms therefore always have memory_order_seq_cst semantics.

The remaining basic atomic types are essentially all the same: they're all atomic integral types and have the same interface as each other, except that the associated built-in type is different. We'll look at them as a group.

5.2.5 Operations on standard atomic integral types

As well as the usual set of operations (load(), store(), exchange(), compare_exchange_weak(), and compare_exchange_strong()), the atomic integral types such as std::atomic<int> or std::atomic<unsigned long long> have quite a comprehensive set of operations available: fetch_add(), fetch_sub(), fetch_and(), fetch_or(), fetch_xor(), compound-assignment forms of these operations (+=, -=, &=, |=, and ^=), and pre- and post-increment and decrement (++x, x++, –x, and x--). It's not quite the full set of compound-assignment operations you could do on a normal integral type, but it's close enough: only division, multiplication, and shift operators are missing. Because atomic integral values are typically used either as counters or as bitmasks, this isn't a particularly noticeable loss; additional operations can easily be done using compare_exchange_weak() in a loop, if required.

The semantics match closely to those of fetch_add() and fetch_sub() for std::atomic<T*>; the named functions atomically perform their operation and return the *old* value, whereas the compound-assignment operators return the *new* value. Pre- and post- increment and decrement work as usual: ++x increments the variable and returns the new value, whereas x++ increments the variable and returns the old value. As you'll be expecting by now, the result is a value of the associated integral type in both cases.

We've now looked at all the basic atomic types; all that remains is the generic std::atomic<> primary class template rather than the specializations, so let's look at that next.

5.2.6 The std::atomic<> primary class template

The presence of the primary template allows a user to create an atomic variant of a user-defined type, in addition to the standard atomic types. You can't use just any user-defined type with std::atomic<>, though; the type has to fulfill certain criteria. In order to use std::atomic<UDT> for some user-defined type UDT, this type must have a *trivial* copy-assignment operator. This means that the type must not have any virtual functions or virtual base classes and must use the compiler-generated copy-assignment operator. Not only that, but every base class and non-static data member of a user-defined type must also have a trivial copy-assignment operator. This essentially permits the compiler to use memcpy() or an equivalent operation for assignment operations, because there's no user-written code to run.

Finally, the type must be *bitwise equality comparable*. This goes alongside the assignment requirements; not only must you be able to copy an object of type UDT using memcpy(), but you must be able to compare instances for equality using memcmp(). This guarantee is required in order for compare/exchange operations to work.

The reasoning behind these restrictions goes back to one of the guidelines from chapter 3: don't pass pointers and references to protected data outside the scope of the lock by passing them as arguments to user-supplied functions. In general, the compiler isn't going to be able to generate lock-free code for std::atomic<UDT>, so it will have to use an internal lock for all the operations. If user-supplied copy-assignment or comparison operators were permitted, this would require passing a reference to the protected data as an argument to a user-supplied function, thus violating the guideline. Also, the library is entirely at liberty to use a single lock for all atomic operations that need it, and allowing user-supplied functions to be called while holding that lock might cause deadlock or cause other threads to block because a comparison operation took a long time. Finally, these restrictions increase the chance that the compiler will be able to make use of atomic instructions directly for `std::atomic<UDT>` (and thus make a particular instantiation lock-free), because it can just treat the user-defined type as a set of raw bytes.

Note that although you can use `std::atomic<float>` or `std::atomic<double>`, because the built-in floating point types do satisfy the criteria for use with `memcpy` and `memcmp`, the behavior may be surprising in the case of `compare_exchange_strong`. The operation may fail even though the old stored value was equal in value to the comparand, if the stored value had a different representation. Note that there are no atomic arithmetic operations on floating-point values. You'll get similar behavior with `compare_exchange_strong` if you use `std::atomic<>` with a user-defined type that has an equality-comparison operator defined, and that operator differs from the comparison using `memcmp`—the operation may fail because the otherwise-equal values have a different representation.

If your `UDT` is the same size as (or smaller than) an `int` or a `void*`, most common platforms will be able to use atomic instructions for `std::atomic<UDT>`. Some platforms will also be able to use atomic instructions for user-defined types that are twice the size of an `int` or `void*`. These platforms are typically those that support a so-called *double-word-compare-and-swap (DWCAS)* instruction corresponding to the `compare_exchange_xxx` functions. As you'll see in chapter 7, such support can be helpful when writing lock-free code.

These restrictions mean that you can't, for example, create a `std::atomic<std::vector<int>>`, but you can use it with classes containing counters or flags or pointers or even just arrays of simple data elements. This isn't particularly a problem; the more complex the data structure, the more likely you'll want to do operations on it other than simple assignment and comparison. If that's the case, you're better off using a `std::mutex` to ensure that the data is appropriately protected for the desired operations, as described in chapter 3.

When instantiated with a user-defined type `T`, the interface of `std::atomic<T>` is limited to the set of operations available for `std::atomic<bool>`: `load()`, `store()`, `exchange()`, `compare_exchange_weak()`, `compare_exchange_strong()`, and assignment from and conversion to an instance of type `T`.

Table 5.3 shows the operations available on each atomic type.

5.2.7 Free functions for atomic operations

Up until now I've limited myself to describing the member function forms of the operations on the atomic types. However, there are also equivalent nonmember functions for all the operations on the various atomic types. For the most part the nonmember functions are named after the corresponding member functions but with an

Table 5.3 The operations available on atomic types

Operation	atomic_flag	atomic<bool>	atomic<T*>	atomic<integral-type>	atomic<other-type>
test_and_set	✓				
clear	✓				
is_lock_free		✓	✓	✓	✓
load		✓	✓	✓	✓
store		✓	✓	✓	✓
exchange		✓	✓	✓	✓
compare_exchange_weak, compare_exchange_strong		✓	✓	✓	✓
fetch_add, +=			✓	✓	
fetch_sub, -=			✓	✓	
fetch_or, |=				✓	
fetch_and, &=				✓	
fetch_xor, ^=				✓	
++, --			✓	✓	

`atomic_` prefix (for example, `std::atomic_load()`). These functions are then overloaded for each of the atomic types. Where there's opportunity for specifying a memory-ordering tag, they come in two varieties: one without the tag and one with an `_explicit` suffix and an additional parameter or parameters for the memory-ordering tag or tags (for example, `std::atomic_store(&atomic_var,new_value)` versus `std::atomic_store_explicit(&atomic_var,new_value,std::memory_order_release)`. Whereas the atomic object being referenced by the member functions is implicit, all the free functions take a pointer to the atomic object as the first parameter.

For example, `std::atomic_is_lock_free()` comes in just one variety (though overloaded for each type), and `std::atomic_is_lock_free(&a)` returns the same value as `a.is_lock_free()` for an object of atomic type `a`. Likewise, `std::atomic_load(&a)` is the same as `a.load()`, but the equivalent of `a.load(std::memory_order_acquire)` is `std::atomic_load_explicit(&a, std::memory_order_acquire)`.

The free functions are designed to be C-compatible, so they use pointers rather than references in all cases. For example, the first parameter of the `compare_exchange_weak()` and `compare_exchange_strong()` member functions (the expected value) is a reference, whereas the second parameter of `std::atomic_compare_exchange_weak()` (the first is the object pointer) is a pointer. `std::atomic_compare_exchange_weak_explicit()` also requires both the success and failure memory orders to be specified, whereas the compare/exchange member functions have both a single memory order form (with a default of `std::memory_order_seq_cst`) and an overload that takes the success and failure memory orders separately.

The operations on `std::atomic_flag` buck the trend, in that they spell out the "flag" part in the names: `std::atomic_flag_test_and_set()`, `std::atomic_flag_clear()`, although the additional variants that specify the memory ordering again have the `_explicit` suffix: `std::atomic_flag_test_and_set_explicit()` and `std::atomic_flag_clear_explicit()`.

The C++ Standard Library also provides free functions for accessing instances of `std::shared_ptr<>` in an atomic fashion. This is a break from the principle that only the atomic types support atomic operations, because `std::shared_ptr<>` is quite definitely *not* an atomic type. However, the C++ Standards Committee felt it was sufficiently important to provide these extra functions. The atomic operations available are *load*, *store*, *exchange*, and *compare/exchange*, which are provided as overloads of the same operations on the standard atomic types, taking a `std::shared_ptr<>*` as the first argument:

```
std::shared_ptr<my_data> p;
void process_global_data()
{
    std::shared_ptr<my_data> local=std::atomic_load(&p);
    process_data(local);
}
void update_global_data()
{
    std::shared_ptr<my_data> local(new my_data);
    std::atomic_store(&p,local);
}
```

As with the atomic operations on other types, the `_explicit` variants are also provided to allow you to specify the desired memory ordering, and the `std::atomic_is_lock_free()` function can be used to check whether the implementation uses locks to ensure the atomicity.

As described in the introduction, the standard atomic types do more than just avoid the undefined behavior associated with a data race; they allow the user to enforce an ordering of operations between threads. This enforced ordering is the basis of the facilities for protecting data and synchronizing operations such as `std::mutex` and `std::future<>`. With that in mind, let's move on to the real meat of this chapter: the details of the concurrency aspects of the memory model and how atomic operations can be used to synchronize data and enforce ordering.

5.3 Synchronizing operations and enforcing ordering

Suppose you have two threads, one of which is populating a data structure to be read by the second. In order to avoid a problematic race condition, the first thread sets a flag to indicate that the data is ready, and the second thread doesn't read the data until the flag is set. The following listing shows such a scenario.

Listing 5.2 Reading and writing variables from different threads

```
#include <vector>
#include <atomic>
#include <iostream>

std::vector<int> data;
std::atomic<bool> data_ready(false);

void reader_thread()
{
    while(!data_ready.load())      <-❶
    {
        std::this_thread::sleep(std::milliseconds(1));
    }
    std::cout<<"The answer="<<data[0]<<"\n";      <-❷
}
void writer_thread()
{
    data.push_back(42);      <-❸
    data_ready=true;      <-❹
}
```

Leaving aside the inefficiency of the loop waiting for the data to be ready ❶, you really need this to work, because otherwise sharing data between threads becomes impractical: every item of data is forced to be atomic. You've already learned that it's undefined behavior to have nonatomic reads ❷ and writes ❸ accessing the same data without an enforced ordering, so for this to work there must be an enforced ordering somewhere.

The required enforced ordering comes from the operations on the `std::atomic<bool>` variable `data_ready`; they provide the necessary ordering by virtue of the memory model relations *happens-before* and *synchronizes-with*. The write of the data ❸ happens-before the write to the `data_ready` flag ❹, and the read of the flag ❶ happens-before the read of the data ❷. When the value read from `data_ready` ❶ is `true`, the write synchronizes-with that read, creating a happens-before relationship. Because happens-before is transitive, the write to the data ❸ happens-before the write to the flag ❹, which happens-before the read of the `true` value from the flag ❶, which happens-before the read of the data ❷, and you have an enforced ordering: the write of the data happens-before the read of the data and everything is OK. Figure 5.2 shows the important happens-before relationships in the two threads. I've added a couple of iterations of the `while` loop from the reader thread.

All this might seem fairly intuitive: of course the operation that writes a value happens before an operation that reads that value! With the default atomic operations, that's indeed true (which is why this is the default), but it does need spelling out: the atomic operations also have other options for the ordering requirements, which I'll come to shortly.

Now that you've seen happens-before and synchronizes-with in action, it's time to look at what they really mean. I'll start with synchronizes-with.

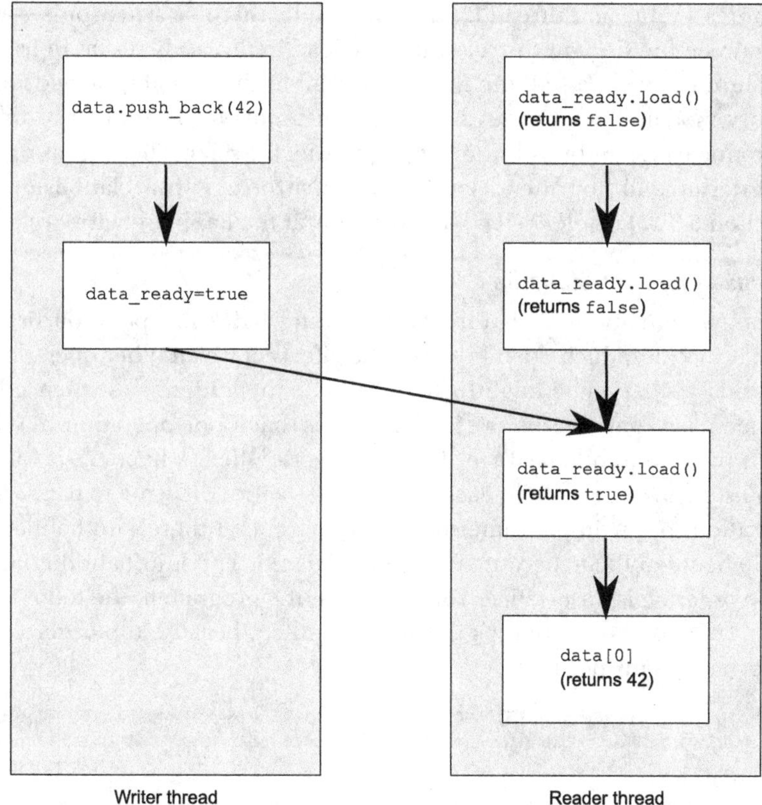

Figure 5.2 Enforcing an ordering between nonatomic operations using atomic operations

5.3.1 *The synchronizes-with relationship*

The synchronizes-with relationship is something that you can get only between operations on atomic types. Operations on a data structure (such as locking a mutex) might provide this relationship if the data structure contains atomic types and the operations on that data structure perform the appropriate atomic operations internally, but fundamentally it comes only from operations on atomic types.

The basic idea is this: a suitably tagged atomic write operation `W` on a variable `x` synchronizes-with a suitably tagged atomic read operation on `x` that reads the value stored by either that write (`W`), or a subsequent atomic write operation on `x` by the same thread that performed the initial write `W`, or a sequence of atomic read-modify-write operations on `x` (such as `fetch_add()` or `compare_exchange_weak()`) by any thread, where the value read by the first thread in the sequence is the value written by `W` (see section 5.3.4).

Leave the "suitably tagged" part aside for now, because all operations on atomic types are suitably tagged by default. This essentially means what you might expect: if thread A stores a value and thread B reads that value, there's a synchronizes-with relationship between the store in thread A and the load in thread B, just as in listing 5.2.

As I'm sure you've guessed, the nuances are all in the "suitably tagged" part. The C++ memory model allows various ordering constraints to be applied to the operations on atomic types, and this is the tagging to which I refer. The various options for memory ordering and how they relate to the synchronizes-with relationship are covered in section 5.3.3. First, let's step back and look at the happens-before relationship.

5.3.2 The happens-before relationship

The *happens-before* relationship is the basic building block of operation ordering in a program; it specifies which operations see the effects of which other operations. For a single thread, it's largely straightforward: if one operation is sequenced before another, then it also happens-before it. This means that if one operation (A) occurs in a statement prior to another (B) in the source code, then A happens-before B. You saw that in listing 5.2: the write to `data` ❸ happens-before the write to `data_ready` ❹. If the operations occur in the same statement, in general there's no happens-before relationship between them, because they're unordered. This is just another way of saying that the ordering is unspecified. You know that the program in the following listing will output `"1,2"` or `"2,1"`, but it's unspecified which, because the order of the two calls to `get_num()` is unspecified.

Listing 5.3 Order of evaluation of arguments to a function call is unspecified

```
#include <iostream>

void foo(int a,int b)
{
    std::cout<<a<<","<<b<<std::endl;
}

int get_num()
{
    static int i=0;
    return ++i;
}

int main()
{
    foo(get_num(),get_num());     <-- Calls to get_num() are unordered
}
```

There are circumstances where operations within a single statement are sequenced such as where the built-in comma operator is used or where the result of one expression is used as an argument to another expression. But in general, operations within a single statement are nonsequenced, and there's no sequenced-before (and thus no happens-before) relationship between them. Of course, all operations in a statement happen before all of the operations in the next statement.

This is really just a restatement of the single-threaded sequencing rules you're used to, so what's new? The new part is the interaction between threads: if operation A on one thread inter-thread happens-before operation B on another thread, then A happens-before B. This doesn't really help much: you've just added a new relationship (inter-thread happens-before), but this is an important relationship when you're writing multithreaded code.

At the basic level, inter-thread happens-before is relatively simple and relies on the synchronizes-with relationship introduced in section 5.3.1: if operation A in one thread synchronizes-with operation B in another thread, then A inter-thread happens-before B. It's also a transitive relation: if A inter-thread happens-before B and B inter-thread happens-before C, then A inter-thread happens-before C. You saw this in listing 5.2 as well.

Inter-thread happens-before also combines with the sequenced-before relation: if operation A is sequenced before operation B, and operation B inter-thread happens-before operation C, then A inter-thread happens-before C. Similarly, if A synchronizes-with B and B is sequenced before C, then A inter-thread happens-before C. These two together mean that if you make a series of changes to data in a single thread, you need only one synchronizes-with relationship for the data to be visible to subsequent operations on the thread that executed C.

These are the crucial rules that enforce ordering of operations between threads and make everything in listing 5.2 work. There are some additional nuances with data dependency, as you'll see shortly. In order for you to understand this, I need to cover the memory-ordering tags used for atomic operations and how they relate to the synchronizes-with relation.

5.3.3 Memory ordering for atomic operations

There are six memory ordering options that can be applied to operations on atomic types: `memory_order_relaxed`, `memory_order_consume`, `memory_order_acquire`, `memory_order_release`, `memory_order_acq_rel`, and `memory_order_seq_cst`. Unless you specify otherwise for a particular operation, the memory-ordering option for all operations on atomic types is `memory_order_seq_cst`, which is the most stringent of the available options. Although there are six ordering options, they represent three models: *sequentially consistent* ordering (`memory_order_seq_cst`), *acquire-release* ordering (`memory_order_consume`, `memory_order_acquire`, `memory_order_release`, and `memory_order_acq_rel`), and *relaxed* ordering (`memory_order_relaxed`).

These distinct memory-ordering models can have varying costs on different CPU architectures. For example, on systems based on architectures with fine control over the visibility of operations by processors other than the one that made the change, additional synchronization instructions can be required for sequentially consistent ordering over acquire-release ordering or relaxed ordering and for acquire-release ordering over relaxed ordering. If these systems have many processors, these additional synchronization instructions may take a significant amount of time, thus reducing the overall performance of the system. On the other hand, CPUs that use the x86 or x86-64 architectures (such as the Intel and AMD processors common in desktop PCs) don't require any additional instructions for acquire-release ordering beyond those necessary for ensuring atomicity, and even sequentially-consistent ordering doesn't require any special treatment for load operations, although there's a small additional cost on stores.

The availability of the distinct memory-ordering models allows experts to take advantage of the increased performance of the more fine-grained ordering relationships where they're advantageous while allowing the use of the default sequentially-consistent ordering (which is considerably easier to reason about than the others) for those cases that are less critical.

In order to choose which ordering model to use, or to understand the ordering relationships in code that uses the different models, it's important to know how the choices affect the program behavior. Let's therefore look at the consequences of each choice for operation ordering and synchronizes-with.

SEQUENTIALLY CONSISTENT ORDERING

The default ordering is named *sequentially consistent* because it implies that the behavior of the program is consistent with a simple sequential view of the world. If all operations on instances of atomic types are sequentially consistent, the behavior of a multithreaded program is as if all these operations were performed in some particular sequence by a single thread. This is by far the easiest memory ordering to understand, which is why it's the default: all threads must see the same order of operations. This makes it easy to reason about the behavior of code written with atomic variables. You can write down all the possible sequences of operations by different threads, eliminate those that are inconsistent, and verify that your code behaves as expected in the others. It also means that operations can't be reordered; if your code has one operation before another in one thread, that ordering must be seen by all other threads.

From the point of view of synchronization, a sequentially consistent store synchronizes-with a sequentially consistent load of the same variable that reads the value stored. This provides one ordering constraint on the operation of two (or more) threads, but sequential consistency is more powerful than that. Any sequentially consistent atomic operations done after that load must also appear after the store to other threads in the system using sequentially consistent atomic operations. The example in listing 5.4 demonstrates this ordering constraint in action. This constraint doesn't carry forward to threads that use atomic operations with relaxed memory orderings; they can still see the operations in a different order, so you must use sequentially consistent operations on all your threads in order to get the benefit.

This ease of understanding can come at a price, though. On a weakly ordered machine with many processors, it can impose a noticeable performance penalty, because the overall sequence of operations must be kept consistent between the processors, possibly requiring extensive (and expensive!) synchronization operations between the processors. That said, some processor architectures (such as the common x86 and x86-64 architectures) offer sequential consistency relatively cheaply, so if you're concerned about the performance implications of using sequentially consistent ordering, check the documentation for your target processor architectures.

The following listing shows sequential consistency in action. The loads and stores to x and y are explicitly tagged with memory_order_seq_cst, although this tag could be omitted in this case because it's the default.

Listing 5.4 Sequential consistency implies a total ordering

```
#include <atomic>
#include <thread>
#include <assert.h>

std::atomic<bool> x,y;
std::atomic<int> z;

void write_x()
{
    x.store(true,std::memory_order_seq_cst);          ❶
}

void write_y()
{
    y.store(true,std::memory_order_seq_cst);          ❷
}

void read_x_then_y()
{
    while(!x.load(std::memory_order_seq_cst));
    if(y.load(std::memory_order_seq_cst))             ❸
        ++z;
}

void read_y_then_x()
{
    while(!y.load(std::memory_order_seq_cst));
    if(x.load(std::memory_order_seq_cst))             ❹
        ++z;
}

int main()
{
    x=false;
    y=false;
    z=0;
    std::thread a(write_x);
    std::thread b(write_y);
    std::thread c(read_x_then_y);
    std::thread d(read_y_then_x);
    a.join();
    b.join();
    c.join();
    d.join();
    assert(z.load()!=0);          ❺
}
```

The assert ❺ can never fire, because either the store to x ❶ or the store to y ❷ must happen first, even though it's not specified which. If the load of y in read_x_then_y ❸ returns false, the store to x must occur before the store to y, in which case the load of x in read_y_then_x ❹ must return true, because the while loop ensures that the y is true at this point. Because the semantics of memory_order_seq_cst require a single total ordering over all operations tagged memory_order_seq_cst, there's an implied ordering relationship between a load of y that returns false ❸ and the store to y ❶. For there to be a single total order, if one thread sees x==true and then subsequently sees y==false, this implies that the store to x occurs before the store to y in this total order.

Of course, because everything is symmetrical, it could also happen the other way around, with the load of x ❹ returning false, forcing the load of y ❸ to return true. In both cases, z is equal to 1. Both loads can return true, leading to z being 2, but under no circumstances can z be zero.

The operations and happens-before relationships for the case that read_x_then_y sees x as true and y as false are shown in figure 5.3. The dashed line from the load of y in read_x_then_y to the store to y in write_y shows the implied ordering relationship required in order to maintain sequential consistency: the load must occur before the store in the global order of memory_order_seq_cst operations in order to achieve the outcomes given here.

Sequential consistency is the most straightforward and intuitive ordering, but it's also the most expensive memory ordering because it requires global synchronization between all threads. On a multiprocessor system this may require quite extensive and time-consuming communication between processors.

In order to avoid this synchronization cost, you need to step outside the world of sequential consistency and consider using other memory orderings.

NON-SEQUENTIALLY CONSISTENT MEMORY ORDERINGS

Once you step outside the nice sequentially consistent world, things start to get complicated. Probably the single biggest issue to come to grips with is the fact that *there's no longer*

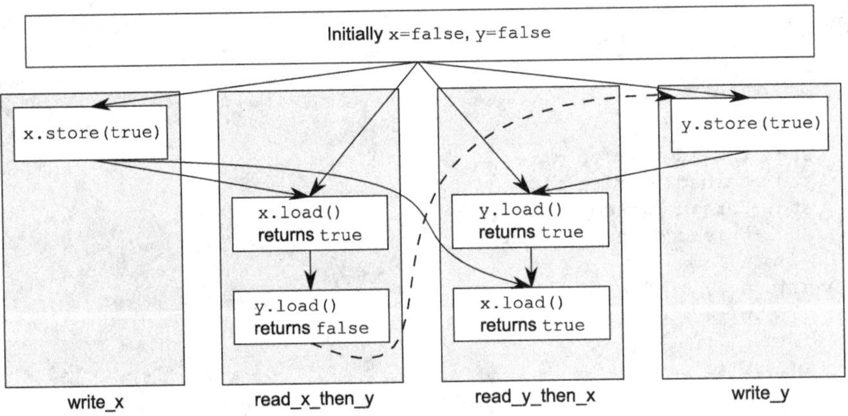

Figure 5.3 Sequential consistency and happens-before

a single global order of events. This means that different threads can see different views of the same operations, and any mental model you have of operations from different threads neatly interleaved one after the other must be thrown away. Not only do you have to account for things happening truly concurrently, but *threads don't have to agree on the order of events*. In order to write (or even just to understand) any code that uses a memory ordering other than the default `memory_order_seq_cst`, it's absolutely vital to get your head around this. It's not just that the compiler can reorder the instructions. Even if the threads are running the same bit of code, they can disagree on the order of events because of operations in other threads in the absence of explicit ordering constraints, because the different CPU caches and internal buffers can hold different values for the same memory. It's so important I'll say it again: *threads don't have to agree on the order of events*.

Not only do you have to throw out mental models based on interleaving operations, you also have to throw out mental models based on the idea of the compiler or processor reordering the instructions. *In the absence of other ordering constraints, the only requirement is that all threads agree on the modification order of each individual variable*. Operations on distinct variables can appear in different orders on different threads, provided the values seen are consistent with any additional ordering constraints imposed.

This is best demonstrated by stepping completely outside the sequentially consistent world and using `memory_order_relaxed` for all operations. Once you've come to grips with that, you can move back to acquire-release ordering, which allows you to selectively introduce ordering relationships between operations and claw back some of your sanity.

RELAXED ORDERING

Operations on atomic types performed with relaxed ordering don't participate in synchronizes-with relationships. Operations on the same variable within a single thread still obey happens-before relationships, but there's almost no requirement on ordering relative to other threads. The only requirement is that accesses to a single atomic variable from the same thread can't be reordered; once a given thread has seen a particular value of an atomic variable, a subsequent read by that thread can't retrieve an earlier value of the variable. Without any additional synchronization, the modification order of each variable is the only thing shared between threads that are using `memory_order_relaxed`.

To demonstrate just how relaxed your relaxed operations can be, you need only two threads, as shown in the following listing.

Listing 5.5 Relaxed operations have very few ordering requirements

```
#include <atomic>
#include <thread>
#include <assert.h>

std::atomic<bool> x,y;
std::atomic<int> z;

void write_x_then_y()
{
    x.store(true,std::memory_order_relaxed);    <-❶
```

```
    y.store(true,std::memory_order_relaxed);      ❷
}
void read_y_then_x()
{
    while(!y.load(std::memory_order_relaxed));    ❸
    if(x.load(std::memory_order_relaxed))       ❹
        ++z;
}
int main()
{
    x=false;
    y=false;
    z=0;
    std::thread a(write_x_then_y);
    std::thread b(read_y_then_x);
    a.join();
    b.join();
    assert(z.load()!=0);    ❺
}
```

This time the assert ❺ *can* fire, because the load of x ❹ can read `false`, even though the load of y ❸ reads `true` and the store of x ❶ happens-before the store of y ❷. x and y are different variables, so there are no ordering guarantees relating to the visibility of values arising from operations on each.

Relaxed operations on different variables can be freely reordered provided they obey any happens-before relationships they're bound by (for example, within the same thread). They don't introduce synchronizes-with relationships. The happens-before relationships from listing 5.5 are shown in figure 5.4, along with a possible outcome. Even though there's a happens-before relationship between the stores and between the loads, there isn't one between either store and either load, and so the loads can see the stores out of order.

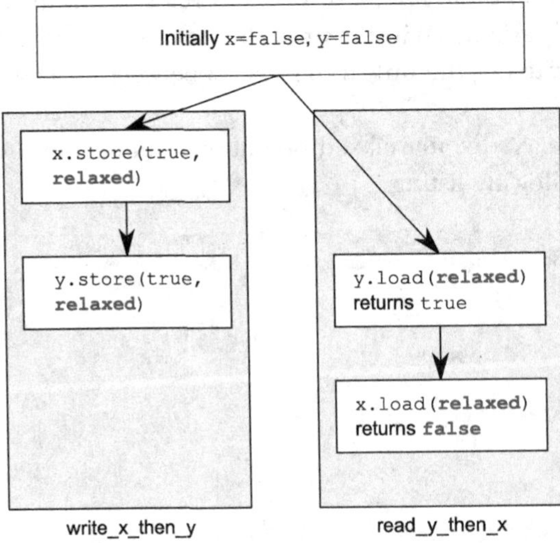

Figure 5.4 Relaxed atomics and happens-before

Let's look at the slightly more complex example with three variables and five threads in the next listing.

Listing 5.6 Relaxed operations on multiple threads

```
#include <thread>
#include <atomic>
#include <iostream>

std::atomic<int> x(0),y(0),z(0);                    ❶
std::atomic<bool> go(false);                        ❷

unsigned const loop_count=10;

struct read_values
{
    int x,y,z;
};

read_values values1[loop_count];
read_values values2[loop_count];
read_values values3[loop_count];
read_values values4[loop_count];
read_values values5[loop_count];

void increment(std::atomic<int>* var_to_inc,read_values* values)
{
    while(!go)                                      ❸ Spin, waiting
        std::this_thread::yield();                    for the signal
    for(unsigned i=0;i<loop_count;++i)
    {
        values[i].x=x.load(std::memory_order_relaxed);
        values[i].y=y.load(std::memory_order_relaxed);
        values[i].z=z.load(std::memory_order_relaxed);
        var_to_inc->store(i+1,std::memory_order_relaxed);      ❹
        std::this_thread::yield();
    }
}

void read_vals(read_values* values)
{
    while(!go)                                      ❺ Spin, waiting
        std::this_thread::yield();                    for the signal
    for(unsigned i=0;i<loop_count;++i)
    {
        values[i].x=x.load(std::memory_order_relaxed);
        values[i].y=y.load(std::memory_order_relaxed);
        values[i].z=z.load(std::memory_order_relaxed);
        std::this_thread::yield();
    }
}

void print(read_values* v)
{
    for(unsigned i=0;i<loop_count;++i)
    {
        if(i)
```

```
            std::cout<<",";
        std::cout<<"("<<v[i].x<<","<<v[i].y<<","<<v[i].z<<")";
    }
    std::cout<<std::endl;
}

int main()
{
    std::thread t1(increment,&x,values1);
    std::thread t2(increment,&y,values2);
    std::thread t3(increment,&z,values3);
    std::thread t4(read_vals,values4);
    std::thread t5(read_vals,values5);

    go=true;                  <-- 6 Signal to start execution of main loop

    t5.join();
    t4.join();
    t3.join();
    t2.join();
    t1.join();
                              7 Print the final values
    print(values1);        <--
    print(values2);
    print(values3);
    print(values4);
    print(values5);
}
```

This is a really simple program in essence. You have three shared global atomic variables ❶ and five threads. Each thread loops 10 times, reading the values of the three atomic variables using `memory_order_relaxed` and storing them in an array. Three of the threads each update one of the atomic variables each time through the loop ❹, while the other two threads just read. Once all the threads have been joined, you print the values from the arrays stored by each thread ❼.

The atomic variable `go` ❷ is used to ensure that the threads all start the loop as near to the same time as possible. Launching a thread is an expensive operation, and without the explicit delay, the first thread may be finished before the last one has started. Each thread waits for `go` to become `true` before entering the main loop ❸, ❺, and `go` is set to `true` only once all the threads have started ❻.

One possible output from this program is as follows:

```
(0,0,0),(1,0,0),(2,0,0),(3,0,0),(4,0,0),(5,7,0),(6,7,8),(7,9,8),(8,9,8),
    (9,9,10)
(0,0,0),(0,1,0),(0,2,0),(1,3,5),(8,4,5),(8,5,5),(8,6,6),(8,7,9),(10,8,9),
    (10,9,10)
(0,0,0),(0,0,1),(0,0,2),(0,0,3),(0,0,4),(0,0,5),(0,0,6),(0,0,7),(0,0,8),
    (0,0,9)
(1,3,0),(2,3,0),(2,4,1),(3,6,4),(3,9,5),(5,10,6),(5,10,8),(5,10,10),
    (9,10,10),(10,10,10)
(0,0,0),(0,0,0),(0,0,0),(6,3,7),(6,5,7),(7,7,7),(7,8,7),(8,8,7),(8,8,9),
    (8,8,9)
```

The first three lines are the threads doing the updating, and the last two are the threads doing just reading. Each triplet is a set of the variables x, y and z in that order from one pass through the loop. There are a few things to notice from this output:

- The first set of values shows x increasing by one with each triplet, the second set has y increasing by one, and the third has z increasing by one.
- The x elements of each triplet only increase within a given set, as do the y and z elements, but the increments are uneven, and the relative orderings vary between all threads.
- Thread 3 doesn't see any of the updates to x or y; it sees only the updates it makes to z. This doesn't stop the other threads from seeing the updates to z mixed in with the updates to x and y though.

This is a valid outcome for relaxed operations, but it's not the only valid outcome. Any set of values that's consistent with the three variables each holding the values 0 to 10 in turn and that has the thread incrementing a given variable printing the values 0 to 9 for that variable is valid.

UNDERSTANDING RELAXED ORDERING

To understand how this works, imagine that each variable is a man in a cubicle with a notepad. On his notepad is a list of values. You can phone him and ask him to give you a value, or you can tell him to write down a new value. If you tell him to write down a new value, he writes it at the bottom of the list. If you ask him for a value, he reads you a number from the list.

The first time you talk to this man, if you ask him for a value, he may give you *any* value from the list he has on his pad at the time. If you then ask him for another value, he may give you the same one again or a value from farther down the list. He'll never give you a value from farther up the list. If you tell him to write down a number and then subsequently ask him for a value, he'll give you either the number you told him to write down or a number below that on the list.

Imagine for a moment that his list starts with the values 5, 10, 23, 3, 1, 2. If you ask for a value, you could get any of those. If he gives you 10, then the next time you ask he could give you 10 again, or any of the later ones, but not 5. If you call him five times, he could say "10, 10, 1, 2, 2," for example. If you tell him to write down 42, he'll add it to the end of the list. If you ask him for a number again, he'll keep telling you "42" until he has another number on his list and he feels like telling it to you.

Now, imagine your friend Carl also has this man's number. Carl can also phone him and either ask him to write down a number or ask for one, and he applies the same rules to Carl as he does to you. He has only one phone, so he can only deal with one of you at a time, so the list on his pad is a nice straightforward list. However, just because you got him to write down a new number doesn't mean he has to tell it to Carl, and vice versa. If Carl asked him for a number and was told "23," then just because you asked the man to write down 42 doesn't mean he'll tell that to Carl next time. He may tell Carl any of the numbers 23, 3, 1, 2, 42, or even the 67 that Fred told him to write down after you called. He could very well tell Carl "23, 3, 3, 1, 67" without being inconsistent with what he told you. It's like he keeps track of which number he told to whom with a little movable sticky note for each person, like in figure 5.5.

Now imagine that there's not just one man in a cubicle but a whole cubicle farm, with loads of men with phones and notepads. These are all our atomic variables. Each variable has its own modification order (the list of values on the pad), but there's no relationship between them at all. If each caller (you, Carl, Anne, Dave, and Fred) is a thread, then this is what you get when every operation uses `memory_order_relaxed`. There are a few additional things you can tell the man in the cubicle, such as "write down this number, and tell me what was at the bottom of the list" (`exchange`) and "write down *this* number if the number on the bottom of the list is *that*; otherwise tell me what I should have guessed" (`compare_exchange_strong`), but that doesn't affect the general principle.

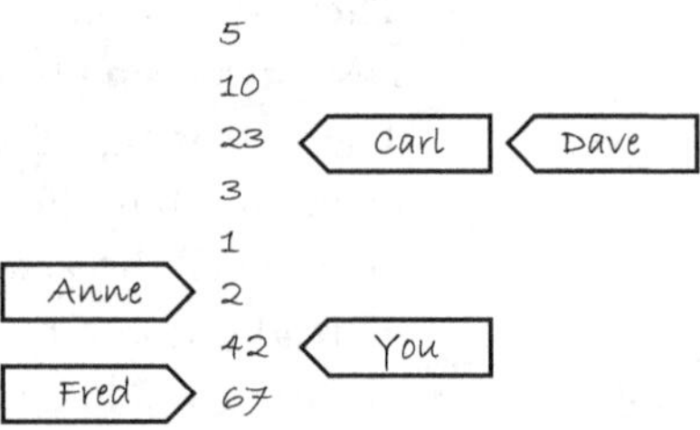

Figure 5.5 The notebook for the man in the cubicle

If you think about the program logic from listing 5.5, then `write_x_then_y` is like some guy calling up the man in cubicle `x` and telling him to write `true` and then calling up the man in cubicle `y` and telling *him* to write `true`. The thread running `read_y_then_x` repeatedly calls up the man in cubicle `y` asking for a value until he says `true` and then calls the man in cubicle `x` to ask for a value. The man in cubicle `x` is under no obligation to tell you any specific value off his list and is quite within his rights to say `false`.

This makes relaxed atomic operations difficult to deal with. They must be used in combination with atomic operations that feature stronger ordering semantics in order to be useful for inter-thread synchronization. I strongly recommend avoiding relaxed atomic operations unless they're absolutely necessary and even then using them only with extreme caution. Given the unintuitive results that can be achieved with just two threads and two variables in listing 5.5, it's not hard to imagine the possible complexity when more threads and more variables are involved.

One way to achieve additional synchronization without the overhead of full-blown sequential consistency is to use *acquire-release ordering.*

ACQUIRE-RELEASE ORDERING

Acquire-release ordering is a step up from relaxed ordering; there's still no total order of operations, but it does introduce some synchronization. Under this ordering model, atomic loads are *acquire* operations (`memory_order_acquire`), atomic stores are *release* operations (`memory_order_release`), and atomic read-modify-write operations (such as `fetch_add()` or `exchange()`) are either *acquire, release,* or both (`memory_order_acq_rel`). Synchronization is pairwise, between the thread that does the release and the thread that does the acquire. *A release operation synchronizes-with an acquire operation that reads the value written*. This means that different threads can *still* see different orderings, but these orderings are restricted. The following listing is a rework of listing 5.4 using acquire-release semantics rather than sequentially consistent ones.

Listing 5.7 Acquire-release doesn't imply a total ordering

```
#include <atomic>
#include <thread>
#include <assert.h>

std::atomic<bool> x,y;
std::atomic<int> z;

void write_x()
{
    x.store(true,std::memory_order_release);
}

void write_y()
{
    y.store(true,std::memory_order_release);
}

void read_x_then_y()
{
    while(!x.load(std::memory_order_acquire));
    if(y.load(std::memory_order_acquire))          <-❶
        ++z;
}

void read_y_then_x()
{
    while(!y.load(std::memory_order_acquire));
    if(x.load(std::memory_order_acquire))          <-❷
        ++z;
}

int main()
{
    x=false;
    y=false;
    z=0;
    std::thread a(write_x);
    std::thread b(write_y);
    std::thread c(read_x_then_y);
    std::thread d(read_y_then_x);
    a.join();
    b.join();
    c.join();
    d.join();
    assert(z.load()!=0);    <-❸
}
```

In this case the assert ❸ *can* fire (just like in the relaxed-ordering case), because it's possible for both the load of `x` ❷ and the load of `y` ❶ to read `false`. `x` and `y` are written

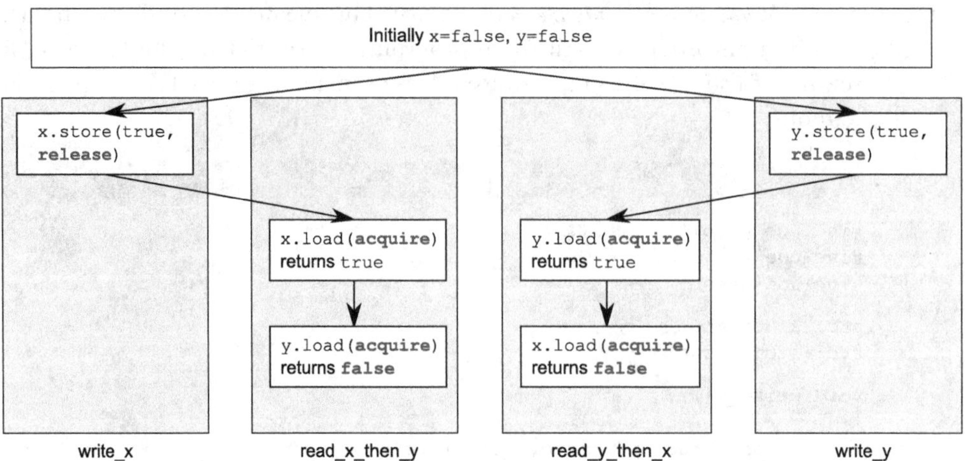

Figure 5.6 Acquire-release and happens-before

by different threads, so the ordering from the release to the acquire in each case has no effect on the operations in the other threads.

Figure 5.6 shows the happens-before relationships from listing 5.7, along with a possible outcome where the two reading threads each have a different view of the world. This is possible because there's no happens-before relationship to force an ordering, as described previously.

In order to see the benefit of acquire-release ordering, you need to consider two stores from the same thread, like in listing 5.5. If you change the store to y to use memory_order_release and the load from y to use memory_order_acquire like in the following listing, then you actually impose an ordering on the operations on x.

Listing 5.8 Acquire-release operations can impose ordering on relaxed operations

```
#include <atomic>
#include <thread>
#include <assert.h>

std::atomic<bool> x,y;
std::atomic<int> z;

void write_x_then_y()
{
    x.store(true,std::memory_order_relaxed);      ❶
    y.store(true,std::memory_order_release);      ❷
}

void read_y_then_x()
{
    while(!y.load(std::memory_order_acquire));    ❸
    if(x.load(std::memory_order_relaxed))         ❹
        ++z;
}
```

❶ Spin, waiting for y to be set to true

```
int main()
{
    x=false;
    y=false;
    z=0;
    std::thread a(write_x_then_y);
    std::thread b(read_y_then_x);
    a.join();
    b.join();
    assert(z.load()!=0);       <-5
}
```

Eventually, the load from `y` ❸ will see `true` as written by the store ❷. Because the store uses `memory_order_release` and the load uses `memory_order_acquire`, the store synchronizes-with the load. The store to `x` ❶ happens-before the store to `y` ❷, because they're in the same thread. Because the store to `y` synchronizes-with the load from `y`, the store to `x` also happens-before the load from `y` and by extension happens-before the load from `x` ❹. Thus the load from `x` *must* read `true`, and the assert ❺ *can't* fire. If the load from `y` wasn't in a `while` loop, this wouldn't necessarily be the case; the load from `y` might read `false`, in which case there'd be no requirement on the value read from `x`. In order to provide any synchronization, acquire and release operations must be paired up. The value stored by a release operation must be seen by an acquire operation for either to have any effect. If either the store at ❷ or the load at ❸ was a relaxed operation, there'd be no ordering on the accesses to `x`, so there'd be no guarantee that the load at ❹ would read `true`, and the `assert` could fire.

You can still think about acquire-release ordering in terms of our men with notepads in their cubicles, but you have to add more to the model. First, imagine that every store that's done is part of some batch of updates, so when you call a man to tell him to write down a number, you also tell him which batch this update is part of: "Please write down 99, as part of batch 423." For the last store in a batch, you tell this to the man too: "Please write down 147, which is the last store in batch 423." The man in the cubicle will then duly write down this information, along with who gave him the value. This models a store-release operation. The next time you tell someone to write down a value, you increase the batch number: "Please write down 41, as part of batch 424."

When you ask for a value, you now have a choice: you can either just ask for a value (which is a relaxed load), in which case the man just gives you the number, or you can ask for a value and information about whether it's the last in a batch (which models a load-acquire). If you ask for the batch information, and the value wasn't the last in a batch, the man will tell you something like, "The number is 987, which is just a 'normal' value," whereas if it *was* the last in a batch, he'll tell you something like "The number is 987, which is the last number in batch 956 from Anne." Now, here's where the acquire-release semantics kick in: if you tell the man all the batches you know about when you ask for a value, he'll look down his list for the last value from any of the batches you know about and either give you that number or one further down the list.

How does this model acquire-release semantics? Let's look at our example and see. First off, thread a is running write_x_then_y and says to the man in cubicle x, "Please write true as part of batch 1 from thread a," which he duly writes down. Thread a then says to the man in cubicle y, "Please write true as the last write of batch 1 from thread a," which he duly writes down. In the meantime, thread b is running read_y_then_x. Thread b keeps asking the man in box y for a value with batch information until he says "true." He may have to ask many times, but eventually the man will say "true." The man in box y doesn't *just* say "true" though; he also says, "This is the last write in batch 1 from thread a."

Now, thread b goes on to ask the man in box x for a value, but this time he says, "Please can I have a value, and by the way I know about batch 1 from thread a." So now, the man from cubicle x has to look down his list for the last mention of batch 1 from thread a. The only mention he has is the value true, which is also the last value on his list, so he *must* read out that value; otherwise, he's breaking the rules of the game.

If you look at the definition of *inter-thread happens-before* back in section 5.3.2, one of the important properties is that it's transitive: *if A inter-thread happens-before B and B inter-thread happens-before C, then A inter-thread happens-before C.* This means that acquire-release ordering can be used to synchronize data across several threads, even when the "intermediate" threads haven't actually touched the data.

TRANSITIVE SYNCHRONIZATION WITH ACQUIRE-RELEASE ORDERING

In order to think about transitive ordering, you need at least three threads. The first thread modifies some shared variables and does a store-release to one of them. A second thread then reads the variable subject to the store-release with a load-acquire and performs a store-release on a second shared variable. Finally, a third thread does a load-acquire on that second shared variable. Provided that the load-acquire operations see the values written by the store-release operations to ensure the synchronizes-with relationships, this third thread can read the values of the other variables stored by the first thread, even if the intermediate thread didn't touch any of them. This scenario is shown in the next listing.

Listing 5.9 Transitive synchronization using acquire and release ordering

```
std::atomic<int> data[5];
std::atomic<bool> sync1(false),sync2(false);

void thread_1()
{
    data[0].store(42,std::memory_order_relaxed);
    data[1].store(97,std::memory_order_relaxed);
    data[2].store(17,std::memory_order_relaxed);
    data[3].store(-141,std::memory_order_relaxed);
    data[4].store(2003,std::memory_order_relaxed);
    sync1.store(true,std::memory_order_release);      <-- 1 Set sync1
}

void thread_2()
{
```

```
    while(!sync1.load(std::memory_order_acquire));     <-2 Loop until sync1 is set
    sync2.store(true,std::memory_order_release);       <-3 Set sync2
}
void thread_3()
{
    while(!sync2.load(std::memory_order_acquire));     <-4 Loop until sync2 is set
    assert(data[0].load(std::memory_order_relaxed)==42);
    assert(data[1].load(std::memory_order_relaxed)==97);
    assert(data[2].load(std::memory_order_relaxed)==17);
    assert(data[3].load(std::memory_order_relaxed)==-141);
    assert(data[4].load(std::memory_order_relaxed)==2003);
}
```

Even though thread_2 only touches the variables sync1 ❷ and sync2 ❸, this is enough for synchronization between thread_1 and thread_3 to ensure that the asserts don't fire. First off, the stores to data from thread_1 happens-before the store to sync1 ❶, because they're sequenced-before it in the same thread. Because the load from sync1 ❶ is in a while loop, it will eventually see the value stored from thread_1 and thus form the second half of the release-acquire pair. Therefore, the store to sync1 happens-before the final load from sync1 in the while loop. This load is sequenced-before (and thus happens-before) the store to sync2 ❸, which forms a release-acquire pair with the final load from the while loop in thread_3 ❹. The store to sync2 ❸ thus happens-before the load ❹, which happens-before the loads from data. Because of the transitive nature of happens-before, you can chain it all together: the stores to data happen-before the store to sync1 ❶, which happens-before the load from sync1 ❷, which happens-before the store to sync2 ❸, which happens-before the load from sync2 ❹, which happens-before the loads from data. Thus the stores to data in thread_1 happen-before the loads from data in thread_3, and the asserts can't fire.

In this case, you could combine sync1 and sync2 into a single variable by using a read-modify-write operation with memory_order_acq_rel in thread_2. One option would be to use compare_exchange_strong() to ensure that the value is updated only once the store from thread_1 has been seen:

```
std::atomic<int> sync(0);
void thread_1()
{
    // ...
    sync.store(1,std::memory_order_release);
}
void thread_2()
{
    int expected=1;
    while(!sync.compare_exchange_strong(expected,2,
                                        std::memory_order_acq_rel))
        expected=1;
}
void thread_3()
{
```

```
    while(sync.load(std::memory_order_acquire)<2);
    // ...
}
```

If you use read-modify-write operations, it's important to pick which semantics you desire. In this case, you want both acquire and release semantics, so `memory_order_acq_rel` is appropriate, but you can use other orderings too. A `fetch_sub` operation with `memory_order_acquire` semantics doesn't synchronize-with anything, even though it stores a value, because it isn't a release operation. Likewise, a store can't synchronize-with a `fetch_or` with `memory_order_release` semantics, because the read part of the `fetch_or` isn't an acquire operation. Read-modify-write operations with `memory_order_acq_rel` semantics behave as both an acquire and a release, so a prior store can synchronize-with such an operation, and it can synchronize-with a subsequent load, as is the case in this example.

If you mix acquire-release operations with sequentially consistent operations, the sequentially consistent loads behave like loads with acquire semantics, and sequentially consistent stores behave like stores with release semantics. Sequentially consistent read-modify-write operations behave as both acquire and release operations. Relaxed operations are still relaxed but are bound by the additional synchronizes-with and consequent happens-before relationships introduced through the use of acquire-release semantics.

Despite the potentially non-intuitive outcomes, anyone who's used locks has had to deal with the same ordering issues: locking a mutex is an acquire operation, and unlocking the mutex is a release operation. With mutexes, you learn that you must ensure that the same mutex is locked when you read a value as was locked when you wrote it, and the same applies here; your acquire and release operations have to be on the same variable to ensure an ordering. If data is protected with a mutex, the exclusive nature of the lock means that the result is indistinguishable from what it would have been had the lock and unlock been sequentially consistent operations. Similarly, if you use acquire and release orderings on atomic variables to build a simple lock, then from the point of view of code that *uses* the lock, the behavior will appear sequentially consistent, even though the internal operations are not.

If you don't need the stringency of sequentially consistent ordering for your atomic operations, the pair-wise synchronization of acquire-release ordering has the potential for a much lower synchronization cost than the global ordering required for sequentially consistent operations. The trade-off here is the mental cost required to ensure that the ordering works correctly and that the non-intuitive behavior across threads isn't problematic.

DATA DEPENDENCY WITH ACQUIRE-RELEASE ORDERING AND MEMORY_ORDER_CONSUME

In the introduction to this section I said that `memory_order_consume` was part of the acquire-release ordering model, but it was conspicuously absent from the preceding description. This is because `memory_order_consume` is special: it's all about data dependencies, and it introduces the data-dependency nuances to the inter-thread happens-before relationship mentioned in section 5.3.2.

There are two new relations that deal with data dependencies: *dependency-ordered-before* and *carries-a-dependency-to*. Just like sequenced-before, carries-a-dependency-to applies strictly within a single thread and essentially models the data dependency between operations; if the result of an operation A is used as an operand for an operation B, then A carries-a-dependency-to B. If the result of operation A is a value of a scalar type such as an `int`, then the relationship still applies if the result of A is stored in a variable, and that variable is then used as an operand for operation B. This operation is also transitive, so if A carries-a-dependency-to B, and B carries-a-dependency-to C, then A carries-a-dependency-to C.

On the other hand, the dependency-ordered-before relationship can apply between threads. It's introduced by using atomic load operations tagged with `memory_order_consume`. This is a special case of `memory_order_acquire` that limits the synchronized data to direct dependencies; a store operation A tagged with `memory_order_release`, `memory_order_acq_rel`, or `memory_order_seq_cst` is dependency-ordered-before a load operation B tagged with `memory_order_consume` if the consume reads the value stored. This is as opposed to the synchronizes-with relationship you get if the load uses `memory_order_acquire`. If this operation B then carries-a-dependency-to some operation C, then A is also dependency-ordered-before C.

This wouldn't actually do you any good for synchronization purposes if it didn't affect the inter-thread happens-before relation, but it does: if A is dependency-ordered-before B, then A also inter-thread happens-before B.

One important use for this kind of memory ordering is where the atomic operation loads a pointer to some data. By using `memory_order_consume` on the load and `memory_order_release` on the prior store, you ensure that the pointed-to data is correctly synchronized, without imposing any synchronization requirements on any other nondependent data. The following listing shows an example of this scenario.

Listing 5.10 Using `std::memory_order_consume` to synchronize data

```
struct X
{
    int i;
    std::string s;
};

std::atomic<X*> p;
std::atomic<int> a;

void create_x()
{
    X* x=new X;
    x->i=42;
    x->s="hello";
    a.store(99,std::memory_order_relaxed);        ❶
    p.store(x,std::memory_order_release);      ❷
}

void use_x()
{
```

```
    X* x;
    while(!(x=p.load(std::memory_order_consume)))       ❸
        std::this_thread::sleep(std::chrono::microseconds(1));
    assert(x->i==42);                                    ❹
    assert(x->s=="hello");                  ❺
    assert(a.load(std::memory_order_relaxed)==99);    ❻
}

int main()
{
    std::thread t1(create_x);
    std::thread t2(use_x);
    t1.join();
    t2.join();
}
```

Even though the store to a ❶ is sequenced before the store to p ❷, and the store to p is tagged `memory_order_release`, the load of p ❸ is tagged `memory_order_consume`. This means that the store to p only happens-before those expressions that are dependent on the value loaded from p. This means that the asserts on the data members of the X structure ❹, ❺ are guaranteed not to fire, because the load of p carries a dependency to those expressions through the variable x. On the other hand, the assert on the value of a ❻ may or may not fire; this operation isn't dependent on the value loaded from p, and so there's no guarantee on the value that's read. This is particularly apparent because it's tagged with `memory_order_relaxed`, as you'll see.

Sometimes, you don't want the overhead of carrying the dependency around. You want the compiler to be able to cache values in registers and reorder operations to optimize the code rather than fussing about the dependencies. In these scenarios, you can use `std::kill_dependency()` to explicitly break the dependency chain. `std::kill_dependency()` is a simple function template that copies the supplied argument to the return value but breaks the dependency chain in doing so. For example, if you have a global read-only array, and you use `std::memory_order_consume` when retrieving an index into that array from another thread, you can use `std::kill_dependency()` to let the compiler know that it doesn't need to reread the contents of the array entry, as in the following example:

```
int global_data[]={ … };
std::atomic<int> index;
void f()
{
    int i=index.load(std::memory_order_consume);
    do_something_with(global_data[std::kill_dependency(i)]);
}
```

Of course, you wouldn't normally use `std::memory_order_consume` at all in such a simple scenario, but you might call on `std::kill_dependency()` in a similar situation with more complex code. You must remember that this is an optimization, so it should only be used with care and where profiling has demonstrated the need.

Now that I've covered the basics of the memory orderings, it's time to look at the more complex parts of the synchronizes-with relation, which manifest in the form of *release sequences*.

5.3.4 Release sequences and synchronizes-with

Back in section 5.3.1, I mentioned that you could get a synchronizes-with relationship between a store to an atomic variable and a load of that atomic variable from another thread, even when there's a sequence of read-modify-write operations between the store and the load, provided all the operations are suitably tagged. Now that I've covered the possible memory-ordering "tags," I can elaborate on this. If the store is tagged with `memory_order_release`, `memory_order_acq_rel`, or `memory_order_seq_cst`, and the load is tagged with `memory_order_consume`, `memory_order_acquire`, or `memory_order_seq_cst`, and each operation in the chain loads the value written by the previous operation, then the chain of operations constitutes a *release sequence* and the initial store synchronizes-with (for `memory_order_acquire` or `memory_order_seq_cst`) or is dependency-ordered-before (for `memory_order_consume`) the final load. Any atomic read-modify-write operations in the chain can have *any* memory ordering (even `memory_order_relaxed`).

To see what this means and why it's important, consider an `atomic<int>` being used as a count of the number of items in a shared queue, as in the following listing.

Listing 5.11 Reading values from a queue with atomic operations

```
#include <atomic>
#include <thread>

std::vector<int> queue_data;
std::atomic<int> count;

void populate_queue()
{
    unsigned const number_of_items=20;
    queue_data.clear();
    for(unsigned i=0;i<number_of_items;++i)
    {
        queue_data.push_back(i);
    }

    count.store(number_of_items,std::memory_order_release);    ❶ The initial store
}

void consume_queue_items()
{
    while(true)
    {
        int item_index;
        if((item_index=count.fetch_sub(1,std::memory_order_acquire))<=0)    ❷ An RMW operation
        {
            wait_for_more_items();    ❸ Wait for more items
            continue;
```

```
        }
        process(queue_data[item_index-1]);     ④ Reading queue_data is safe
    }
}

int main()
{
    std::thread a(populate_queue);
    std::thread b(consume_queue_items);
    std::thread c(consume_queue_items);
    a.join();
    b.join();
    c.join();
}
```

One way to handle things would be to have the thread that's producing the data store the items in a shared buffer and then do `count.store(number_of_items, memory_order_release)` ❶ to let the other threads know that data is available. The threads consuming the queue items might then do `count.fetch_sub(1,memory_order_acquire)` ❷ to claim an item from the queue, prior to actually reading the shared buffer ❹. Once the `count` becomes zero, there are no more items, and the thread must wait ❸.

If there's one consumer thread, this is fine; the `fetch_sub()` is a read, with `memory_order_acquire` semantics, and the store had `memory_order_release` semantics, so the store synchronizes-with the load and the thread can read the item from the buffer. If there are two threads reading, the second `fetch_sub()` will see the value written by the first and not the value written by the `store`. Without the rule about the release sequence, this second thread wouldn't have a happens-before relationship with the first thread, and it wouldn't be safe to read the shared buffer unless the first `fetch_sub()` also had `memory_order_release` semantics, which would introduce unnecessary synchronization between the two consumer threads. Without the release sequence rule or `memory_order_release` on the `fetch_sub` operations, there would be nothing to require that the stores to the `queue_data` were visible to the second consumer, and you would have a data race. Thankfully, the first `fetch_sub()` *does* participate in the release sequence, and so the `store()` synchronizes-with the second `fetch_sub()`. There's still no synchronizes-with relationship between the two consumer threads. This is shown in figure 5.7. The dotted lines in figure 5.7 show the release sequence, and the solid lines show the happens-before relationships.

There can be any number of links in the chain, but provided they're all read-modify-write operations such as `fetch_sub()`, the `store()` will still synchronize-with each one that's tagged `memory_order_acquire`. In this example, all the links are the same, and all are acquire operations, but they could be a mix of different operations with different memory-ordering semantics.

Although most of the synchronization relationships come from the memory-ordering semantics applied to operations on atomic variables, it's also possible to introduce additional ordering constraints by using *fences*.

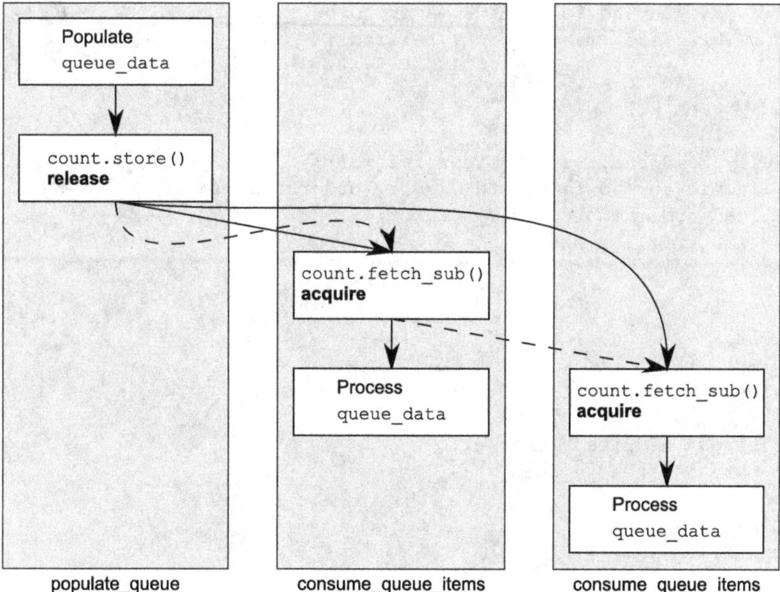

Figure 5.7 The release sequence for the queue operations from listing 5.11

5.3.5 Fences

An atomic operations library wouldn't be complete without a set of fences. These are operations that enforce memory-ordering constraints without modifying any data and are typically combined with atomic operations that use the memory_order_relaxed ordering constraints. Fences are global operations and affect the ordering of other atomic operations in the thread that executed the fence. Fences are also commonly called *memory barriers*, and they get their name because they put a line in the code that certain operations can't cross. As you may recall from section 5.3.3, relaxed operations on separate variables can usually be freely reordered by the compiler or the hardware. Fences restrict this freedom and introduce happens-before and synchronizes-with relationships that weren't present before.

Let's start by adding a fence between the two atomic operations on each thread in listing 5.5, as shown in the following listing.

Listing 5.12 Relaxed operations can be ordered with fences

```
#include <atomic>
#include <thread>
#include <assert.h>

std::atomic<bool> x,y;
std::atomic<int> z;

void write_x_then_y()
{
    x.store(true,std::memory_order_relaxed);    <-1
```

```
    std::atomic_thread_fence(std::memory_order_release);      <-2
    y.store(true,std::memory_order_relaxed);                  <-3
}

void read_y_then_x()
{
    while(!y.load(std::memory_order_relaxed));                <-4
    std::atomic_thread_fence(std::memory_order_acquire);      <-5
    if(x.load(std::memory_order_relaxed))                     <-6
        ++z;
}

int main()
{
    x=false;
    y=false;
    z=0;
    std::thread a(write_x_then_y);
    std::thread b(read_y_then_x);
    a.join();
    b.join();
    assert(z.load()!=0);    <-7
}
```

The release fence ❷ synchronizes-with the acquire fence ❺, because the load from y at ❹ reads the value stored at ❸. This means that the store to x at ❶ happens-before the load from x at ❻, so the value read must be true and the assert at ❼ won't fire. This is in contrast to the original case without the fences where the store to and load from x weren't ordered, and so the assert could fire. Note that both fences are necessary: you need a release in one thread and an acquire in another to get a synchronizes-with relationship.

In this case, the release fence ❷ has the same effect as if the store to y ❸ was tagged with memory_order_release rather than memory_order_relaxed. Likewise, the acquire fence ❺ makes it as if the load from y ❹ was tagged with memory_order_acquire. This is the general idea with fences: if an acquire operation sees the result of a store that takes place after a release fence, the fence synchronizes-with that acquire operation; and if a load that takes place before an acquire fence sees the result of a release operation, the release operation synchronizes-with the acquire fence. Of course, you can have fences on both sides, as in the example here, in which case if a load that takes place before the acquire fence sees a value written by a store that takes place after the release fence, the release fence synchronizes-with the acquire fence.

Although the fence synchronization depends on the values read or written by operations before or after the fence, it's important to note that the synchronization point is the fence itself. If you take write_x_then_y from listing 5.12 and move the write to x after the fence as follows, the condition in the assert is no longer guaranteed to be true, even though the write to x comes before the write to y:

```
void write_x_then_y()
{
    std::atomic_thread_fence(std::memory_order_release);
```

```
    x.store(true,std::memory_order_relaxed);
    y.store(true,std::memory_order_relaxed);
}
```

These two operations are no longer separated by the fence and so are no longer ordered. It's only when the fence comes *between* the store to x and the store to y that it imposes an ordering. Of course, the presence or absence of a fence doesn't affect any enforced orderings on happens-before relations that exist because of other atomic operations.

This example, and almost every other example so far in this chapter, is built entirely from variables with an atomic type. However, the real benefit to using atomic operations to enforce an ordering is that they can enforce an ordering on nonatomic operations and thus avoid the undefined behavior of a data race, as you saw back in listing 5.2.

5.3.6 Ordering nonatomic operations with atomics

If you replace x from listing 5.12 with an ordinary nonatomic `bool` (as in the following listing), the behavior is guaranteed to be the same.

Listing 5.13 Enforcing ordering on nonatomic operations

```
#include <atomic>
#include <thread>
#include <assert.h>

bool x=false;                          <-- x is now a plain nonatomic variable
std::atomic<bool> y;
std::atomic<int> z;

void write_x_then_y()
{
    x=true;                            <-- 1 Store to x before the fence
    std::atomic_thread_fence(std::memory_order_release);
    y.store(true,std::memory_order_relaxed);     <-- 2 Store to y after the fence
}

void read_y_then_x()
{
    while(!y.load(std::memory_order_relaxed));   <-- 3 Wait until you see the write from #2
    std::atomic_thread_fence(std::memory_order_acquire);
    if(x)                              <-- 4 This will read the value written by #1
        ++z;
}

int main()
{
    x=false;
    y=false;
    z=0;
    std::thread a(write_x_then_y);
    std::thread b(read_y_then_x);
    a.join();
    b.join();
    assert(z.load()!=0);               <-- 5 This assert won't fire
}
```

The fences still provide an enforced ordering of the store to `x` ❶ and the store to `y` ❷ and the load from `y` ❸ and the load from `x` ❹, and there's still a happens-before relationship between the store to `x` and the load from `x`, so the assert ❺ still won't fire. The store to ❷ and load from ❸ `y` still have to be atomic; otherwise, there would be a data race on `y`, but the fences enforce an ordering on the operations on `x`, once the reading thread has seen the stored value of `y`. This enforced ordering means that there's no data race on `x`, even though it's modified by one thread and read by another.

It's not just fences that can order nonatomic operations. You saw the ordering effects back in listing 5.10 with a `memory_order_release`/`memory_order_consume` pair ordering nonatomic accesses to a dynamically allocated object, and many of the examples in this chapter could be rewritten with some of the `memory_order_relaxed` operations replaced with plain nonatomic operations instead.

Ordering of nonatomic operations through the use of atomic operations is where the sequenced-before part of happens-before becomes so important. If a nonatomic operation is sequenced-before an atomic operation, and that atomic operation happens-before an operation in another thread, the nonatomic operation also happens-before that operation in the other thread. This is where the ordering on the operations on `x` in listing 5.13 comes from and why the example in listing 5.2 works. This is also the basis for the higher-level synchronization facilities in the C++ Standard Library, such as mutexes and condition variables. To see how this works, consider the simple spin-lock mutex from listing 5.1.

The `lock()` operation is a loop on `flag.test_and_set()` using `std::memory_order_acquire` ordering, and the `unlock()` is a call to `flag.clear()` with `std::memory_order_release` ordering. When the first thread calls `lock()`, the flag is initially clear, so the first call to `test_and_set()` will set the flag and return `false`, indicating that this thread now has the lock, and terminating the loop. The thread is then free to modify any data protected by the mutex. Any other thread that calls `lock()` at this time will find the flag already set and will be blocked in the `test_and_set()` loop.

When the thread with the lock has finished modifying the protected data, it calls `unlock()`, which calls `flag.clear()` with `std::memory_order_release` semantics. This then synchronizes-with (see section 5.3.1) a subsequent call to `flag.test_and_set()` from an invocation of `lock()` on another thread, because this call has `std::memory_order_acquire` semantics. Because the modification of the protected data is necessarily sequenced before the `unlock()` call, this modification happens-before the `unlock()` and thus happens-before the subsequent `lock()` call from the second thread (because of the synchronizes-with relationship between the `unlock()` and the `lock()`) and happens-before any accesses to that data from this second thread once it has acquired the lock.

Although other mutex implementations will have different internal operations, the basic principle is the same: `lock()` is an acquire operation on an internal memory location, and `unlock()` is a release operation on that same memory location.

5.4 Summary

In this chapter I've covered the low-level details of the C++11 memory model and the atomic operations that provide the basis for synchronization between threads. This includes the basic atomic types provided by specializations of the `std::atomic<>` class template as well as the generic atomic interface provided by the primary `std::atomic<>` template, the operations on these types, and the complex details of the various memory-ordering options.

We've also looked at fences and how they can be paired with operations on atomic types to enforce an ordering. Finally, we've come back to the beginning with a look at how the atomic operations can be used to enforce an ordering between nonatomic operations on separate threads.

In the next chapter we'll look at using the high-level synchronization facilities alongside atomic operations to design efficient containers for concurrent access, and we'll write algorithms that process data in parallel.

6 Designing lock-based concurrent data structures

This chapter covers

- What it means to design data structures for concurrency
- Guidelines for doing so
- Example implementations of data structures designed for concurrency

In the last chapter we looked at the low-level details of atomic operations and the memory model. In this chapter we'll take a break from the low-level details (although we'll need them for chapter 7) and think about data structures.

The choice of data structure to use for a programming problem can be a key part of the overall solution, and parallel programming problems are no exception. If a data structure is to be accessed from multiple threads, either it must be completely immutable so the data never changes and no synchronization is necessary, or the program must be designed to ensure that changes are correctly synchronized between threads. One option is to use a separate mutex and external locking to protect the data, using the techniques we looked at in chapters 3 and 4, and another is to design the data structure itself for concurrent access.

When designing a data structure for concurrency, you can use the basic building blocks of multithreaded applications from earlier chapters, such as mutexes and condition variables. Indeed, you've already seen a couple of examples showing how to combine these building blocks to write data structures that are safe for concurrent access from multiple threads.

In this chapter we'll start by looking at some general guidelines for designing data structures for concurrency. We'll then take the basic building blocks of locks and condition variables and revisit the design of those basic data structures before moving on to more complex data structures. In chapter 7 we'll look at how to go right back to basics and use the atomic operations described in chapter 5 to build data structures without locks.

So, without further ado, let's look at what's involved in designing a data structure for concurrency.

6.1 What does it mean to design for concurrency?

At the basic level, designing a data structure for concurrency means that multiple threads can access the data structure concurrently, either performing the same or distinct operations, and each thread will see a self-consistent view of the data structure. No data will be lost or corrupted, all invariants will be upheld, and there'll be no problematic race conditions. Such a data structure is said to be *thread-safe*. In general, a data structure will be safe only for particular types of concurrent access. It may be possible to have multiple threads performing one type of operation on the data structure concurrently, whereas another operation requires exclusive access by a single thread. Alternatively, it may be safe for multiple threads to access a data structure concurrently if they're performing *different* actions, whereas multiple threads performing the *same* action would be problematic.

Truly designing for concurrency means more than that, though: it means providing the *opportunity for concurrency* to threads accessing the data structure. By its very nature, a mutex provides *mutual exclusion*: only one thread can acquire a lock on the mutex at a time. A mutex protects a data structure by explicitly *preventing* true concurrent access to the data it protects.

This is called *serialization*: threads take turns accessing the data protected by the mutex; they must access it serially rather than concurrently. Consequently, you must put careful thought into the design of the data structure to enable true concurrent access. Some data structures have more scope for true concurrency than others, but in all cases the idea is the same: the smaller the protected region, the fewer operations are serialized, and the greater the potential for concurrency.

Before we look at some data structure designs, let's have a quick look at some simple guidelines for what to consider when designing for concurrency.

6.1.1 Guidelines for designing data structures for concurrency

As I just mentioned, you have two aspects to consider when designing data structures for concurrent access: ensuring that the accesses are *safe* and *enabling* genuine concurrent access. I covered the basics of how to make the data structure thread-safe back in chapter 3:

- Ensure that no thread can see a state where the invariants of the data structure have been broken by the actions of another thread.
- Take care to avoid race conditions inherent in the interface to the data structure by providing functions for complete operations rather than for operation steps.
- Pay attention to how the data structure behaves in the presence of exceptions to ensure that the invariants are not broken.
- Minimize the opportunities for deadlock when using the data structure by restricting the scope of locks and avoiding nested locks where possible.

Before you think about any of these details, it's also important to think about what constraints you wish to put on the users of the data structure; if one thread is accessing the data structure through a particular function, which functions are safe to call from other threads?

This is actually quite a crucial question to consider. Generally constructors and destructors require exclusive access to the data structure, but it's up to the user to ensure that they're not accessed before construction is complete or after destruction has started. If the data structure supports assignment, `swap()`, or copy construction, then as the designer of the data structure, you need to decide whether these operations are safe to call concurrently with other operations or whether they require the user to ensure exclusive access even though the majority of functions for manipulating the data structure may be called from multiple threads concurrently without problem.

The second aspect to consider is that of enabling genuine concurrent access. I can't offer much in the way of guidelines here; instead, here's a list of questions to ask yourself as the data structure designer:

- Can the scope of locks be restricted to allow some parts of an operation to be performed outside the lock?
- Can different parts of the data structure be protected with different mutexes?
- Do all operations require the same level of protection?
- Can a simple change to the data structure improve the opportunities for concurrency without affecting the operational semantics?

All these questions are guided by a single idea: how can you minimize the amount of serialization that must occur and enable the greatest amount of true concurrency? It's not uncommon for data structures to allow concurrent access from multiple threads that merely read the data structure, whereas a thread that can modify the data structure must have exclusive access. This is supported by using constructs like `boost::shared_mutex`. Likewise, as you'll see shortly, it's quite common for a data structure to support concurrent access from threads performing different operations while serializing threads that try to perform the same operation.

The simplest thread-safe data structures typically use mutexes and locks to protect the data. Although there are issues with this, as you saw in chapter 3, it's relatively easy to ensure that only one thread is accessing the data structure at a time. To ease you into the design of thread-safe data structures, we'll stick to looking at such lock-based data structures in this chapter and leave the design of concurrent data structures without locks for chapter 7.

6.2 Lock-based concurrent data structures

The design of lock-based concurrent data structures is all about ensuring that the right mutex is locked when accessing the data and ensuring that the lock is held for a minimum amount of time. This is hard enough when there's just one mutex protecting a data structure. You need to ensure that data can't be accessed outside the protection of the mutex lock and that there are no race conditions inherent in the interface, as you saw in chapter 3. If you use separate mutexes to protect separate parts of the data structure, these issues are compounded, and there's now also the possibility of deadlock if the operations on the data structure require more than one mutex to be locked. You therefore need to consider the design of a data structure with multiple mutexes even more carefully than the design of a data structure with a single mutex.

In this section you'll apply the guidelines from section 6.1.1 to the design of several simple data structures, using mutexes and locks to protect the data. In each case you'll seek out the opportunities for enabling greater concurrency while ensuring that the data structure remains thread-safe.

Let's start by looking at the stack implementation from chapter 3; it's one of the simplest data structures around, and it uses only a single mutex. Is it really thread-safe? How does it fare from the point of view of achieving true concurrency?

6.2.1 A thread-safe stack using locks

The thread-safe stack from chapter 3 is reproduced in the following listing. The intent is to write a thread-safe data structure akin to `std::stack<>`, which supports pushing data items onto the stack and popping them off again.

Listing 6.1 A class definition for a thread-safe stack

```
#include <exception>

struct empty_stack: std::exception
{
    const char* what() const throw();
};

template<typename T>
class threadsafe_stack
{
private:
    std::stack<T> data;
    mutable std::mutex m;
public:
    threadsafe_stack(){}
    threadsafe_stack(const threadsafe_stack& other)
    {
        std::lock_guard<std::mutex> lock(other.m);
        data=other.data;
```

```
    }
    threadsafe_stack& operator=(const threadsafe_stack&) = delete;

    void push(T new_value)
    {
        std::lock_guard<std::mutex> lock(m);
        data.push(std::move(new_value));         ⊲—❶
    }
    std::shared_ptr<T> pop()
    {
        std::lock_guard<std::mutex> lock(m);
        if(data.empty()) throw empty_stack();      ⊲—❷
        std::shared_ptr<T> const res(
           std::make_shared<T>(std::move(data.top())));     ⊲—❸
        data.pop();                        ⊲—❹
        return res;
    }
    void pop(T& value)
    {
        std::lock_guard<std::mutex> lock(m);
        if(data.empty()) throw empty_stack();
        value=std::move(data.top());             ⊲—❺
        data.pop();                        ⊲—❻
    }
    bool empty() const
    {
        std::lock_guard<std::mutex> lock(m);
        return data.empty();
    }
};
```

Let's look at each of the guidelines in turn, and see how they apply here.

First, as you can see, the basic thread safety is provided by protecting each member function with a lock on the mutex, `m`. This ensures that only one thread is actually accessing the data at any one time, so provided each member function maintains the invariants, no thread can see a broken invariant.

Second, there's a potential for a race condition between `empty()` and either of the `pop()` functions, but because the code explicitly checks for the contained stack being empty while holding the lock in `pop()`, this race condition isn't problematic. By returning the popped data item directly as part of the call to `pop()`, you avoid a potential race condition that would be present with separate `top()` and `pop()` member functions such as those in `std::stack<>`.

Next, there are a few potential sources of exceptions. Locking a mutex may throw an exception, but not only is this likely to be exceedingly rare (because it indicates a problem with the mutex or a lack of system resources), it's also the first operation in each member function. Because no data has been modified, this is safe. Unlocking a mutex can't fail, so that's always safe, and the use of `std::lock_guard<>` ensures that the mutex is never left locked.

The call to `data.push()` ❶ may throw an exception if either copying/moving the data value throws an exception or not enough memory can be allocated to extend the underlying data structure. Either way, `std::stack<>` guarantees it will be safe, so that's not a problem either.

In the first overload of `pop()`, the code itself might throw an `empty_stack` exception ❷, but nothing has been modified, so that's safe. The creation of `res` ❸ might throw an exception though for a couple of reasons: the call to `std::make_shared` might throw because it can't allocate memory for the new object and the internal data required for reference counting, or the copy constructor or move constructor of the data item to be returned might throw when copying/moving into the freshly allocated memory. In both cases, the C++ runtime and Standard Library ensure that there are no memory leaks and the new object (if any) is correctly destroyed. Because you *still* haven't modified the underlying stack, you're still OK. The call to `data.pop()` ❹ is guaranteed not to throw, as is the return of the result, so this overload of `pop()` is exception-safe.

The second overload of `pop()` is similar, except this time it's the copy assignment or move assignment operator that can throw ❺ rather than the construction of a new object and a `std::shared_ptr` instance. Again, you don't actually modify the data structure until the call to `data.pop()` ❻, which is still guaranteed not to throw, so this overload is exception-safe too.

Finally, `empty()` doesn't modify any data, so that's exception-safe.

There are a couple of opportunities for deadlock here, because you call user code while holding a lock: the copy constructor or move constructor ❶, ❸ and copy assignment or move assignment operator ❺ on the contained data items, as well as potentially a user-defined `operator new`. If these functions either call member functions on the stack that the item is being inserted into or removed from or require a lock of any kind and another lock was held when the stack member function was invoked, there's the possibility of deadlock. However, it's sensible to require that users of the stack be responsible for ensuring this; you can't reasonably expect to add an item onto a stack or remove it from a stack without copying it or allocating memory for it.

Because all the member functions use a `std::lock_guard<>` to protect the data, it's safe for any number of threads to call the `stack` member functions. The only member functions that aren't safe are the constructors and destructors, but this isn't a particular problem; the object can be constructed only once and destroyed only once. Calling member functions on an incompletely constructed object or a partially destructed object is never a good idea whether done concurrently or not. As a consequence, the user must ensure that other threads aren't able to access the stack until it's fully constructed and must ensure that all threads have ceased accessing the stack before it's destroyed.

Although it's safe for multiple threads to call the member functions concurrently, because of the use of locks, only one thread is ever actually doing any work in the stack data structure at a time. This *serialization* of threads can potentially limit the performance of an application where there's significant contention on the `stack`: while a thread is waiting for the lock, it isn't doing any useful work. Also, the stack doesn't provide any means for waiting for an item to be added, so if a thread needs to wait, it must periodically call `empty()` or just call `pop()` and catch the `empty_stack` exceptions. This makes this stack implementation a poor choice if such a scenario is required, because a waiting thread must either consume precious resources checking for data or the user must write external wait and notification code (for example, using condition variables), which might render the internal locking unnecessary and therefore wasteful. The queue from chapter 4 shows a way of incorporating such waiting into the data structure itself using a condition variable inside the data structure, so let's look at that next.

6.2.2 A thread-safe queue using locks and condition variables

The thread-safe queue from chapter 4 is reproduced in listing 6.2. Much like the stack was modeled after `std::stack<>`, this queue is modeled after `std::queue<>`. Again, the interface differs from that of the standard container adaptor because of the constraints of writing a data structure that's safe for concurrent access from multiple threads.

Listing 6.2 The full class definition for a thread-safe queue using condition variables

```
template<typename T>
class threadsafe_queue
{
private:
    mutable std::mutex mut;
    std::queue<T> data_queue;
    std::condition_variable data_cond;
public:
    threadsafe_queue()
    {}

    void push(T new_value)
    {
        std::lock_guard<std::mutex> lk(mut);
        data_queue.push(std::move(data));
        data_cond.notify_one();              ❶
    }

    void wait_and_pop(T& value)    ❷
    {
        std::unique_lock<std::mutex> lk(mut);
        data_cond.wait(lk,[this]{return !data_queue.empty();});
        value=std::move(data_queue.front());
        data_queue.pop();
    }

    std::shared_ptr<T> wait_and_pop()    ❸
    {
        std::unique_lock<std::mutex> lk(mut);
        data_cond.wait(lk,[this]{return !data_queue.empty();});    ❹
        std::shared_ptr<T> res(
            std::make_shared<T>(std::move(data_queue.front())));
```

```
        data_queue.pop();
        return res;
    }

    bool try_pop(T& value)
    {
        std::lock_guard<std::mutex> lk(mut);
        if(data_queue.empty())
            return false;
        value=std::move(data_queue.front());
        data_queue.pop();
        return true;
    }

    std::shared_ptr<T> try_pop()
    {
        std::lock_guard<std::mutex> lk(mut);
        if(data_queue.empty())
            return std::shared_ptr<T>();       <-5
        std::shared_ptr<T> res(
            std::make_shared<T>(std::move(data_queue.front())));
        data_queue.pop();
        return res;
    }

    bool empty() const
    {
        std::lock_guard<std::mutex> lk(mut);
        return data_queue.empty();
    }
};
```

The structure of the queue implementation shown in listing 6.2 is similar to the stack from listing 6.1, except for the call to `data_cond.notify_one()` in `push()` ❶ and the `wait_and_pop()` functions ❷, ❸. The two overloads of `try_pop()` are almost identical to the `pop()` functions from listing 6.1, except that they don't throw an exception if the queue is empty. Instead, they return either a `bool` value indicating whether a value was retrieved or a `NULL` pointer if no value could be retrieved by the pointer-returning overload ❺. This would also have been a valid way of implementing the stack. So, if you exclude the `wait_and_pop()` functions, the analysis you did for the stack applies just as well here.

The new `wait_and_pop()` functions are a solution to the problem of waiting for a queue entry that you saw with the stack; rather than continuously calling `empty()`, the waiting thread can just call `wait_and_pop()` and the data structure will handle the waiting with a condition variable. The call to `data_cond.wait()` won't return until the underlying queue has at least one element, so you don't have to worry about the possibility of an empty queue at this point in the code, and the data is still protected with the lock on the mutex. These functions don't therefore add any new race conditions or possibilities for deadlock, and the invariants will be upheld.

There's a slight twist with regard to exception safety in that if more than one thread is waiting when an entry is pushed onto the queue, only one thread will be woken by the call to `data_cond.notify_one()`. However, if that thread then throws an exception in `wait_and_pop()`, such as when the new `std::shared_ptr<>` is constructed ❹, none of the other threads will be woken. If this isn't acceptable, the call is readily replaced with `data_cond.notify_all()`, which will wake all the threads but at the cost of most of them then going back to sleep when they find that the queue is empty after all. A second alternative is to have `wait_and_pop()` call `notify_one()` if an exception is thrown, so that another thread can attempt to retrieve the stored value. A third alternative is to move the `std::shared_ptr<>` initialization to the `push()` call and store `std::shared_ptr<>` instances rather than direct data values. Copying the `std::shared_ptr<>` out of the internal `std::queue<>` then can't throw an exception, so `wait_and_pop()` is safe again. The following listing shows the queue implementation revised with this in mind.

Listing 6.3 A thread-safe queue holding `std::shared_ptr<>` instances

```
template<typename T>
class threadsafe_queue
{
private:
    mutable std::mutex mut;
    std::queue<std::shared_ptr<T> > data_queue;
    std::condition_variable data_cond;
public:
    threadsafe_queue()
    {}

    void wait_and_pop(T& value)
    {
        std::unique_lock<std::mutex> lk(mut);
        data_cond.wait(lk,[this]{return !data_queue.empty();});
        value=std::move(*data_queue.front());           ❶
        data_queue.pop();
    }

    bool try_pop(T& value)
    {
        std::lock_guard<std::mutex> lk(mut);
        if(data_queue.empty())
            return false;
        value=std::move(*data_queue.front());           ❷
        data_queue.pop();
        return true;
    }

    std::shared_ptr<T> wait_and_pop()
    {
        std::unique_lock<std::mutex> lk(mut);
        data_cond.wait(lk,[this]{return !data_queue.empty();});
        std::shared_ptr<T> res=data_queue.front();       ❸
        data_queue.pop();
        return res;
    }
```

```
    std::shared_ptr<T> try_pop()
    {
        std::lock_guard<std::mutex> lk(mut);
        if(data_queue.empty())
            return std::shared_ptr<T>();
        std::shared_ptr<T> res=data_queue.front();      <-4
        data_queue.pop();
        return res;
    }

    void push(T new_value)
    {
        std::shared_ptr<T> data(
            std::make_shared<T>(std::move(new_value)));      <-5
        std::lock_guard<std::mutex> lk(mut);
        data_queue.push(data);
        data_cond.notify_one();
    }

    bool empty() const
    {
        std::lock_guard<std::mutex> lk(mut);
        return data_queue.empty();
    }
};
```

The basic consequences of holding the data by `std::shared_ptr<>` are straightforward: the pop functions that take a reference to a variable to receive the new value now have to dereference the stored pointer ❶, ❷, and the pop functions that return a `std::shared_ptr<>` instance can just retrieve it from the queue ❸, ❹ before returning it to the caller.

If the data is held by `std::shared_ptr<>`, there's an additional benefit: the allocation of the new instance can now be done outside the lock in `push()` ❺, whereas in listing 6.2 it had to be done while holding the lock in `pop()`. Because memory allocation is typically quite an expensive operation, this can be very beneficial for the performance of the queue, because it reduces the time the mutex is held, allowing other threads to perform operations on the queue in the meantime.

Just like in the stack example, the use of a mutex to protect the entire data structure limits the concurrency supported by this queue; although multiple threads might be blocked on the queue in various member functions, only one thread can be doing any work at a time. However, part of this restriction comes from the use of `std::queue<>` in the implementation; by using the standard container you now have essentially one data item that's either protected or not. By taking control of the detailed implementation of the data structure, you can provide more fine-grained locking and thus allow a higher level of concurrency.

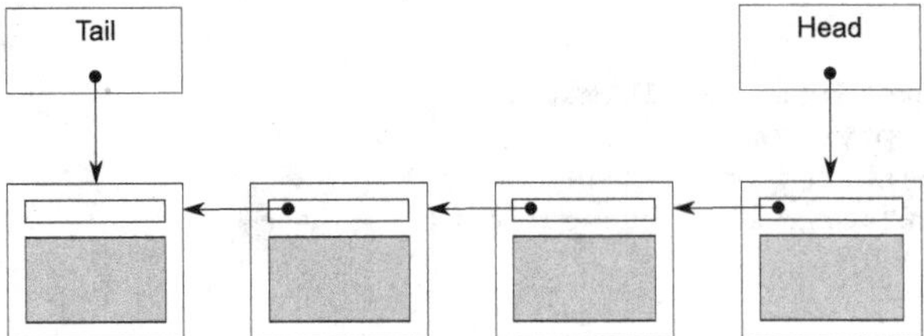

Figure 6.1 A queue represented using a single-linked list

6.2.3 A thread-safe queue using fine-grained locks and condition variables

In listings 6.2 and 6.3 you have one protected data item (`data_queue`) and thus one mutex. In order to use finer-grained locking, you need to look inside the queue at its constituent parts and associate one mutex with each distinct data item.

The simplest data structure for a queue is a singly linked list, as shown in figure 6.1. The queue contains a *head* pointer, which points to the first item in the list, and each item then points to the next item. Data items are removed from the queue by replacing the head pointer with the pointer to the next item and then returning the data from the old head.

Items are added to the queue at the other end. In order to do this, the queue also contains a *tail* pointer, which refers to the last item in the list. New nodes are added by changing the *next* pointer of the last item to point to the new node and then updating the tail pointer to refer to the new item. When the list is empty, both the head and tail pointers are `NULL`.

The following listing shows a simple implementation of such a queue based on a cut-down version of the interface to the queue in listing 6.2; you have only one `try_pop()` function and no `wait_and_pop()` because this queue supports only single-threaded use.

Listing 6.4 A simple single-threaded queue implementation

```
template<typename T>
class queue
{
private:
    struct node
    {
        T data;
        std::unique_ptr<node> next;

        node(T data_):
            data(std::move(data_))
        {}
    };

    std::unique_ptr<node> head;     ❶
    node* tail;     ❷

public:
    queue()
    {}
```

```
    queue(const queue& other)=delete;
    queue& operator=(const queue& other)=delete;

    std::shared_ptr<T> try_pop()
    {
        if(!head)
        {
            return std::shared_ptr<T>();
        }
        std::shared_ptr<T> const res(
            std::make_shared<T>(std::move(head->data)));
        std::unique_ptr<node> const old_head=std::move(head);
        head=std::move(old_head->next);          ❸
        return res;
    }

    void push(T new_value)
    {
        std::unique_ptr<node> p(new node(std::move(new_value)));
        node* const new_tail=p.get();
        if(tail)
        {
            tail->next=std::move(p);          ❹
        }
        else
        {
            head=std::move(p);          ❺
        }
        tail=new_tail;          ❻
    }
};
```

First off, note that listing 6.4 uses `std::unique_ptr<node>` to manage the nodes, because this ensures that they (and the data they refer to) get deleted when they're no longer needed, without having to write an explicit `delete`. This ownership chain is managed from `head`, with `tail` being a raw pointer to the last node.

Although this implementation works fine in a single-threaded context, a couple of things will cause you problems if you try to use fine-grained locking in a multi-threaded context. Given that you have two data items (`head` ❶ and `tail` ❷), you could in principle use two mutexes, one to protect `head` and one to protect `tail`, but there are a couple of problems with that.

The most obvious problem is that `push()` can modify both `head` ❺ and `tail` ❻, so it would have to lock both mutexes. This isn't too much of a problem, although it's unfortunate, because locking both mutexes would be possible. The critical problem is that both `push()` and `pop()` access the `next` pointer of a node: `push()` updates `tail->next` ❹, and `try_pop()` reads `head->next` ❸. If there's a single item in the queue, then `head==tail`, so both `head->next` and `tail->next` are the same object, which therefore requires protection. Because you can't tell if it's the same object without reading both `head` and `tail`, you now have to lock the same mutex in both `push()` and `try_pop()`, so you're no better off than before. Is there a way out of this dilemma?

ENABLING CONCURRENCY BY SEPARATING DATA

You can solve this problem by preallocating a dummy node with no data to ensure that there's always at least one node in the queue to separate the node being accessed at the head from that being accessed at the tail. For an empty queue, `head` and `tail` now both point to the dummy node rather than being `NULL`. This is fine, because `try_pop()` doesn't access `head->next` if the queue is empty. If you add a node to the queue (so there's one real node), then `head` and `tail` now point to separate nodes, so there's no race on `head->next` and `tail->next`. The downside is that you have to add an extra level of indirection to store the data by pointer in order to allow the dummy nodes. The following listing shows how the implementation looks now.

Listing 6.5 A simple queue with a dummy node

```
template<typename T>
class queue
{
private:
    struct node
    {
        std::shared_ptr<T> data;          <-1
        std::unique_ptr<node> next;
    };

    std::unique_ptr<node> head;
    node* tail;

public:
    queue():
        head(new node),tail(head.get())        <-2
    {}

    queue(const queue& other)=delete;
    queue& operator=(const queue& other)=delete;

    std::shared_ptr<T> try_pop()
    {
        if(head.get()==tail)          <-3
        {
            return std::shared_ptr<T>();
        }
        std::shared_ptr<T> const res(head->data);              <-4
        std::unique_ptr<node> old_head=std::move(head);
        head=std::move(old_head->next);                        <-5
        return res;                  <-6
    }

    void push(T new_value)
    {
        std::shared_ptr<T> new_data(
            std::make_shared<T>(std::move(new_value)));          <-7
        std::unique_ptr<node> p(new node);                       <-8
        tail->data=new_data;                   <-9
        node* const new_tail=p.get();
        tail->next=std::move(p);
```

```
        tail=new_tail;
    }
};
```

The changes to `try_pop()` are fairly minimal. First, you're comparing `head` against `tail` ❸ rather than checking for `NULL`, because the dummy node means that `head` is never `NULL`. Because `head` is a `std::unique_ptr<node>`, you need to call `head.get()` to do the comparison. Second, because the `node` now stores the data by pointer ❶, you can retrieve the pointer directly ❹ rather than having to construct a new instance of `T`. The big changes are in `push()`: you must first create a new instance of `T` on the heap and take ownership of it in a `std::shared_ptr<>` ❼ (note the use of `std::make_shared` to avoid the overhead of a second memory allocation for the reference count). The new node you create is going to be the new dummy node, so you don't need to supply the `new_value` to the constructor ❽. Instead, you set the data on the old dummy node to your newly allocated copy of the `new_value` ❾. Finally, in order to have a dummy node, you have to create it in the constructor ❷.

By now, I'm sure you're wondering what these changes buy you and how they help with making the queue thread-safe. Well, `push()` now accesses only `tail`, not `head`, which is an improvement. `try_pop()` accesses both `head` and `tail`, but `tail` is needed only for the initial comparison, so the lock is short-lived. The big gain is that the dummy node means `try_pop()` and `push()` are never operating on the same node, so you no longer need an overarching mutex. So, you can have one mutex for `head` and one for `tail`. Where do you put the locks?

You're aiming for the maximum opportunities for concurrency, so you want to hold the locks for the smallest possible length of time. `push()` is easy: the mutex needs to be locked across all accesses to `tail`, which means you lock the mutex after the new node is allocated ❽ and before you assign the data to the current tail node ❾. The lock then needs to be held until the end of the function.

`try_pop()` isn't so easy. First off, you need to lock the mutex on `head` and hold it until you're finished with `head`. In essence, this is the mutex to determine which thread does the popping, so you want to do that first. Once `head` is changed ❺, you can unlock the mutex; it doesn't need to be locked when you return the result ❻. That leaves the access to `tail` needing a lock on the tail mutex. Because you need to access `tail` only once, you can just acquire the mutex for the time it takes to do the read. This is best done by wrapping it in a function. In fact, because the code that needs the `head` mutex locked is only a subset of the member, it's clearer to wrap that in a function too. The final code is shown here.

Listing 6.6 A thread-safe queue with fine-grained locking

```
template<typename T>
class threadsafe_queue
{
private:
    struct node
```

```
    {
        std::shared_ptr<T> data;
        std::unique_ptr<node> next;
    };

    std::mutex head_mutex;
    std::unique_ptr<node> head;
    std::mutex tail_mutex;
    node* tail;

    node* get_tail()
    {
        std::lock_guard<std::mutex> tail_lock(tail_mutex);
        return tail;
    }

    std::unique_ptr<node> pop_head()
    {
        std::lock_guard<std::mutex> head_lock(head_mutex);

        if(head.get()==get_tail())
        {
            return nullptr;
        }
        std::unique_ptr<node> old_head=std::move(head);
        head=std::move(old_head->next);
        return old_head;
    }
public:
    threadsafe_queue():
        head(new node),tail(head.get())
    {}

    threadsafe_queue(const threadsafe_queue& other)=delete;
    threadsafe_queue& operator=(const threadsafe_queue& other)=delete;

    std::shared_ptr<T> try_pop()
    {
        std::unique_ptr<node> old_head=pop_head();
        return old_head?old_head->data:std::shared_ptr<T>();
    }

    void push(T new_value)
    {
        std::shared_ptr<T> new_data(
            std::make_shared<T>(std::move(new_value)));
        std::unique_ptr<node> p(new node);
        node* const new_tail=p.get();
        std::lock_guard<std::mutex> tail_lock(tail_mutex);
        tail->data=new_data;
        tail->next=std::move(p);
        tail=new_tail;
    }
};
```

Let's look at this code with a critical eye, thinking about the guidelines listed in section 6.1.1. Before you look for broken invariants, you should be sure what they are:

- tail->next==nullptr.
- tail->data==nullptr.
- head==tail implies an empty list.
- A single element list has head->next==tail.
- For each node x in the list, where x!=tail, x->data points to an instance of T and x->next points to the next node in the list. x->next==tail implies x is the last node in the list.
- Following the next nodes from head will eventually yield tail.

On its own, push() is straightforward: the only modifications to the data structure are protected by tail_mutex, and they uphold the invariant because the new tail node is an empty node and data and next are correctly set for the old tail node, which is now the last real node in the list.

The interesting part is try_pop(). It turns out that not only is the lock on tail_mutex necessary to protect the read of tail itself, but it's also necessary to ensure that you don't get a data race reading the data from the head. If you didn't have that mutex, it would be quite possible for a thread to call try_pop() and a thread to call push() concurrently, and there'd be no defined ordering on their operations. Even though each member function holds a lock on a mutex, they hold locks on *different* mutexes, and they potentially access the same data; all data in the queue originates from a call to push(), after all. Because the threads would be potentially accessing the same data without a defined ordering, this would be a data race, as you saw in chapter 5, and undefined behavior. Thankfully the lock on the tail_mutex in get_tail() solves everything. Because the call to get_tail() locks the same mutex as the call to push(), there's a defined order between the two calls. Either the call to get_tail() occurs before the call to push(), in which case it sees the old value of tail, or it occurs after the call to push(), in which case it sees the new value of tail *and the new data attached to the previous value of* tail.

It's also important that the call to get_tail() occurs inside the lock on head_mutex. If it didn't, the call to pop_head() could be stuck in between the call to get_tail() and the lock on the head_mutex, because other threads called try_pop() (and thus pop_head()) and acquired the lock first, thus preventing your initial thread from making progress:

```
std::unique_ptr<node> pop_head()        <-- This is a broken implementation
{
    node* const old_tail=get_tail();                    <-- (1) Get old tail value outside lock on head_mutex
    std::lock_guard<std::mutex> head_lock(head_mutex);

    if(head.get()==old_tail)    <-- (2)
    {
        return nullptr;
    }
    std::unique_ptr<node> old_head=std::move(head);
    head=std::move(old_head->next);        <-- (3)
    return old_head;
}
```

In this *broken* scenario, where the call to `get_tail()` ❶ is made outside the scope of the lock, you might find that both `head` and `tail` have changed by the time your initial thread can acquire the lock on `head_mutex`, and not only is the returned tail node no longer the tail, but it's no longer even part of the list. This could then mean that the comparison of `head` to `old_tail` ❷ fails, even if `head` really is the last node. Consequently, when you update `head` ❸ you may end up moving `head` beyond `tail` and off the end of the list, destroying the data structure. In the `correct` implementation from listing 6.6, you keep the call to `get_tail()` inside the lock on `head_mutex`. This ensures that no other threads can change `head`, and `tail` only ever moves further away (as new nodes are added in calls to `push()`), which is perfectly safe. `head` can never pass the value returned from `get_tail()`, so the invariants are upheld.

Once `pop_head()` has removed the node from the queue by updating `head`, the mutex is unlocked, and `try_pop()` can extract the data and delete the node if there was one (and return a `NULL` instance of `std::shared_ptr<>` if not), safe in the knowledge that it's the only thread that can access this node.

Next up, the external interface is a subset of that from listing 6.2, so the same analysis applies: there are no race conditions inherent in the interface.

Exceptions are more interesting. Because you've changed the data allocation patterns, the exceptions can now come from different places. The only operations in `try_pop()` that can throw exceptions are the mutex locks, and the data isn't modified until the locks are acquired. Therefore `try_pop()` is exception-safe. On the other hand, `push()` allocates a new instance of `T` on the heap and a new instance of `node`, either of which might throw an exception. However, both of the newly allocated objects are assigned to smart pointers, so they'll be freed if an exception is thrown. Once the lock is acquired, none of the remaining operations in `push()` can throw an exception, so again you're home and dry and `push()` is exception-safe too.

Because you haven't changed the interface, there are no new external opportunities for deadlock. There are no internal opportunities either; the only place that two locks are acquired is in `pop_head()`, which always acquires the `head_mutex` and then the `tail_mutex`, so this will never deadlock.

The remaining question concerns the actual possibilities for concurrency. This data structure actually has considerably more scope for concurrency than that from listing 6.2, because the locks are more fine-grained and *more is done outside the locks*. For example, in `push()`, the new node and new data item are allocated with no locks held. This means that multiple threads can be allocating new nodes and data items concurrently without a problem. Only one thread can add its new node to the list at a time, but the code to do so is only a few simple pointer assignments, so the lock isn't held for much time at all compared to the `std::queue<>`-based implementation where the lock is held around all the memory allocation operations internal to the `std::queue<>`.

Also, `try_pop()` holds the `tail_mutex` for only a short time, to protect a read from `tail`. Consequently, almost the entirety of a call to `try_pop()` can occur concurrently with a call to `push()`. Also, the operations performed while holding the `head_mutex` are also quite minimal; the expensive `delete` (in the destructor of the node pointer) is outside the lock. This will increase the number of calls to `try_pop()` that can happen concurrently; only one thread can call `pop_head()` at a time, but multiple threads can then delete their old nodes and return the data safely.

WAITING FOR AN ITEM TO POP

OK, so listing 6.6 provides a thread-safe queue with fine-grained locking, but it supports only `try_pop()` (and only one overload at that). What about the handy `wait_and_pop()` functions back in listing 6.2? Can you implement an identical interface with your fine-grained locking?

Of course, the answer is, yes, but the real question is, how? Modifying `push()` is easy: just add the `data_cond.notify_one()` call at the end of the function, just like in listing 6.2. Actually, it's not quite that simple; you're using fine-grained locking because you want the maximum possible amount of concurrency. If you leave the mutex locked across the call to `notify_one()` (as in listing 6.2), then if the notified thread wakes up before the mutex has been unlocked, it will have to wait for the mutex. On the other hand, if you unlock the mutex *before* you call `notify_one()`, then the mutex is available for the waiting thread to acquire when it wakes up (assuming no other thread locks it first). This is a minor improvement, but it might be important in some cases.

`wait_and_pop()` is more complicated, because you have to decide where to wait, what the predicate is, and which mutex needs to be locked. The condition you're waiting for is "queue not empty," which is represented by `head!=tail`. Written like that, it would require both `head_mutex` and `tail_mutex` to be locked, but you've already decided in listing 6.6 that you only need to lock `tail_mutex` for the read of `tail` and not for the comparison itself, so you can apply the same logic here. If you make the predicate `head!=get_tail()`,you only need to hold the `head_mutex`, so you can use your lock on that for the call to `data_cond.wait()`. Once you've added the wait logic, the implementation is the same as `try_pop()`.

The second overload of `try_pop()` and the corresponding `wait_and_pop()` overload require careful thought. If you just replace the return of the `std::shared_ptr<>` retrieved from `old_head` with a copy assignment to the `value` parameter, there's a potential exception-safety issue. At this point, the data item has been removed from the queue and the mutex unlocked; all that remains is to return the data to the caller. However, if the copy assignment throws an exception (as it very well might), the data item is lost because it can't be returned to the queue in the same place.

If the actual type `T` used for the template argument has a no-throw move-assignment operator or a no-throw swap operation, you could use that, but you'd really like a general solution that could be used for any type `T`. In this case, you have to move the potential throwing inside the locked region, before the node is removed from the list. This means you need an extra overload of `pop_head()` that retrieves the stored value prior to modifying the list.

In comparison, `empty()` is trivial: just lock `head_mutex` and check for `head== get_tail()` (see listing 6.10). The final code for the queue is shown in listings 6.7, 6.8, 6.9, and 6.10.

Listing 6.7 A thread-safe queue with locking and waiting: internals and interface

```
template<typename T>
class threadsafe_queue
{
private:
    struct node
    {
        std::shared_ptr<T> data;
        std::unique_ptr<node> next;
    };

    std::mutex head_mutex;
    std::unique_ptr<node> head;
    std::mutex tail_mutex;
    node* tail;
    std::condition_variable data_cond;
public:
    threadsafe_queue():
        head(new node),tail(head.get())
    {}
    threadsafe_queue(const threadsafe_queue& other)=delete;
    threadsafe_queue& operator=(const threadsafe_queue& other)=delete;

    std::shared_ptr<T> try_pop();
    bool try_pop(T& value);
    std::shared_ptr<T> wait_and_pop();
    void wait_and_pop(T& value);
    void push(T new_value);
    void empty();
};
```

Pushing new nodes onto the queue is fairly straightforward—the implementation (shown in the following listing) is close to that shown previously.

Listing 6.8 A thread-safe queue with locking and waiting: pushing new values

```
template<typename T>
void threadsafe_queue<T>::push(T new_value)
{
    std::shared_ptr<T> new_data(
        std::make_shared<T>(std::move(new_value)));
    std::unique_ptr<node> p(new node);
    {
        std::lock_guard<std::mutex> tail_lock(tail_mutex);
        tail->data=new_data;
        node* const new_tail=p.get();
        tail->next=std::move(p);
        tail=new_tail;
    }
    data_cond.notify_one();
}
```

As already mentioned, the complexity is all in the *pop* side, which makes use of a series of helper functions to simplify matters. The next listing shows the implementation of `wait_and_pop()` and the associated helper functions.

Listing 6.9 A thread-safe queue with locking and waiting: `wait_and_pop()`

```
template<typename T>
class threadsafe_queue
{
private:
    node* get_tail()
    {
        std::lock_guard<std::mutex> tail_lock(tail_mutex);
        return tail;
    }

    std::unique_ptr<node> pop_head()        <-1
    {
        std::unique_ptr<node> old_head=std::move(head);
        head=std::move(old_head->next);
        return old_head;
    }

    std::unique_ptr<node> wait_for_data()        <-2
    {
        std::unique_lock<std::mutex> head_lock(head_mutex);
        data_cond.wait(head_lock,[&]{return head.get()!=get_tail();});
        return std::move(head_lock);        <-3
    }

    std::unique_ptr<node> wait_pop_head()
    {
        std::unique_lock<std::mutex> head_lock(wait_for_data());        <-4
        return pop_head();
    }

    std::unique_ptr<node> wait_pop_head(T& value)
    {
        std::unique_lock<std::mutex> head_lock(wait_for_data());        <-5
        value=std::move(*head->data);
        return pop_head();
    }
public:
    std::shared_ptr<T> wait_and_pop()
    {
        std::unique_ptr<node> const old_head=wait_pop_head();
        return old_head->data;
    }

    void wait_and_pop(T& value)
    {
        std::unique_ptr<node> const old_head=wait_pop_head(value);
    }
};
```

The implementation of the pop side shown in listing 6.9 has several little helper functions to simplify the code and reduce duplication, such as `pop_head()` ❶ and `wait_for_data()` ❷, which modify the list to remove the head item and wait for the queue to have some data to pop, respectively. `wait_for_data()` is particularly noteworthy, because not only does it wait on the condition variable using a lambda function for the predicate, but it also returns the lock instance to the caller ❸. This is to ensure that the same lock is held while the data is modified by the relevant `wait_pop_head()` overload ❹, ❺. `pop_head()` is also reused by the `try_pop()` code shown in the next listing.

Listing 6.10 A thread-safe queue with locking and waiting: `try_pop()` and `empty()`

```
template<typename T>
class threadsafe_queue
{
private:
    std::unique_ptr<node> try_pop_head()
    {
        std::lock_guard<std::mutex> head_lock(head_mutex);
        if(head.get()==get_tail())
        {
            return std::unique_ptr<node>();
        }
        return pop_head();
    }

    std::unique_ptr<node> try_pop_head(T& value)
    {
        std::lock_guard<std::mutex> head_lock(head_mutex);
        if(head.get()==get_tail())
        {
            return std::unique_ptr<node>();
        }
        value=std::move(*head->data);
        return pop_head();
    }

public:
    std::shared_ptr<T> try_pop()
    {
        std::unique_ptr<node> old_head=try_pop_head();
        return old_head?old_head->data:std::shared_ptr<T>();
    }

    bool try_pop(T& value)
    {
        std::unique_ptr<node> const old_head=try_pop_head(value);
        return old_head;
    }

    void empty()
    {
        std::lock_guard<std::mutex> head_lock(head_mutex);
```

```
        return (head.get()==get_tail());
    }
};
```

This queue implementation will serve as the basis for the lock-free queue covered in chapter 7. It's an *unbounded* queue; threads can continue to push new values onto the queue as long as there's available memory, even if no values are removed. The alternative to an unbounded queue is a *bounded* queue, in which the maximum length of the queue is fixed when the queue is created. Once a bounded queue is full, attempts to push further elements onto the queue will either fail or block, until an element has been popped from the queue to make room. Bounded queues can be useful for ensuring an even spread of work when dividing work between threads based on tasks to be performed (see chapter 8). This prevents the thread(s) populating the queue from running too far ahead of the thread(s) reading items from the queue.

The unbounded queue implementation shown here can easily be extended to limit the length of the queue by waiting on the condition variable in `push()`. Rather than waiting for the queue to have items (as is done in `pop()`), you need to wait for the queue to have fewer than the maximum number of items. Further discussion of bounded queues is outside the scope of this book; for now let's move beyond queues and on to more complex data structures.

6.3 Designing more complex lock-based data structures

Stacks and queues are simple: the interface is exceedingly limited, and they're very tightly focused on a specific purpose. Not all data structures are that simple; most data structures support a variety of operations. In principle, this can then lead to greater opportunities for concurrency, but it also makes the task of protecting the data that much harder because the multiple access patterns need to be taken into account. The precise nature of the various operations that can be performed is important when designing such data structures for concurrent access.

To see some of the issues involved, let's look at the design of a lookup table.

6.3.1 Writing a thread-safe lookup table using locks

A lookup table or dictionary associates values of one type (the key type) with values of either the same or a different type (the mapped type). In general, the intention behind such a structure is to allow code to query the data associated with a given key. In the C++ Standard Library, this facility is provided by the associative containers: `std::map<>`, `std::multimap<>`, `std::unordered_map<>`, and `std::unordered_multimap<>`.

A lookup table has a different usage pattern than a stack or a queue. Whereas almost every operation on a stack or a queue modifies it in some way, either to add an element or remove one, a lookup table might be modified rarely. The simple DNS cache in listing 3.13 is one example of such a scenario, which features a greatly reduced interface compared to `std::map<>`. As you saw with the stack and queue, the interfaces of the standard containers aren't suitable when the data structure is to be accessed from multiple threads concurrently, because there are inherent race conditions in the interface design, so they need to be cut down and revised.

The biggest problem with the `std::map<>` interface from a concurrency perspective is the iterators. Although it's possible to have an iterator that provides safe access into a container even when other threads can access (and modify) the container, this is a tricky proposition. Correctly handling iterators requires you to deal with issues such as another thread deleting the element that the iterator is referring to, which can get rather involved. For the first cut at a thread-safe lookup table interface, you'll skip the iterators. Given that the interface to `std::map<>` (and the other associative containers in the standard library) is so heavily iterator-based, it's probably worth setting them aside and designing the interface from the ground up.

There are only a few basic operations on a lookup table:

- Add a new key/value pair.
- Change the value associated with a given key.
- Remove a key and its associated value.
- Obtain the value associated with a given key if any.

There are also a few container-wide operations that might be useful, such as a check on whether the container is empty, a snapshot of the complete list of keys, or a snapshot of the complete set of key/value pairs.

If you stick to the simple thread-safety guidelines such as not returning references and put a simple mutex lock around the entirety of each member function, all of these are safe; they either come before some modification from another thread or come after it. The biggest potential for a race condition is when a new key/value pair is being added; if two threads add a new value, only one will be first, and the second will therefore fail. One possibility is to combine add and change into a single member function, as you did for the DNS cache in listing 3.13.

The only other interesting point from an interface perspective is the *if any* part of obtaining an associated value. One option is to allow the user to provide a "default" result that's returned in the case when the key isn't present:

```
mapped_type get_value(key_type const& key, mapped_type default_value);
```

In this case, a default-constructed instance of `mapped_type` could be used if the `default_value` wasn't explicitly provided. This could also be extended to return a `std::pair<mapped_type,bool>` instead of just an instance of `mapped_type`, where the `bool` indicates whether the value was present. Another option is to return a smart pointer referring to the value; if the pointer value is `NULL`, there was no value to return.

As already mentioned, once the interface has been decided, then (assuming no interface race conditions) the thread safety could be guaranteed by using a single mutex and a simple lock around every member function to protect the underlying data structure. However, this would squander the possibilities for concurrency provided by the separate functions for reading the data structure and modifying it. One option is to use a mutex that supports multiple reader threads or a single writer thread, such as the `boost::shared_mutex` used in listing 3.13. Although this would indeed improve the possibilities for concurrent access, only one thread could modify the data structure at a time. Ideally, you'd like to do better than that.

DESIGNING A MAP DATA STRUCTURE FOR FINE-GRAINED LOCKING

As with the queue discussed in section 6.2.3, in order to permit fine-grained locking you need to look carefully at the details of the data structure rather than just wrapping a preexisting container such as `std::map<>`. There are three common ways of implementing an associative container like your lookup table:

- A binary tree, such as a red-black tree
- A sorted array
- A hash table

A binary tree doesn't provide much scope for extending the opportunities for concurrency; every lookup or modification has to start by accessing the root node, which therefore has to be locked. Although this lock can be released as the accessing thread moves down the tree, this isn't much better than a single lock across the whole data structure.

A sorted array is even worse, because you can't tell in advance where in the array a given data value is going to be, so you need a single lock for the whole array.

That leaves the hash table. Assuming a fixed number of buckets, which bucket a key belongs to is purely a property of the key and its hash function. This means you can safely have a separate lock per bucket. If you again use a mutex that supports multiple readers or a single writer, you increase the opportunities for concurrency *N*-fold, where *N* is the number of buckets. The downside is that you need a good hash function for the key. The C++ Standard Library provides the `std::hash<>` template, which you can use for this purpose. It's already specialized for the fundamental types such as `int` and common library types such as `std::string`, and the user can easily specialize it for other key types. If you follow the lead of the standard unordered containers and take the type of the function object to use for doing the hashing as a template parameter, the user can choose whether to specialize `std::hash<>` for their key type or provide a separate hash function.

So, let's look at some code. What might the implementation of a thread-safe lookup table look like? One possibility is shown here.

Listing 6.11 A thread-safe lookup table

```
template<typename Key,typename Value,typename Hash=std::hash<Key> >
class threadsafe_lookup_table
{
private:
    class bucket_type
    {
    private:
        typedef std::pair<Key,Value> bucket_value;
```

```
        typedef std::list<bucket_value> bucket_data;
        typedef typename bucket_data::iterator bucket_iterator;

        bucket_data data;
        mutable boost::shared_mutex mutex;                    ❶

        bucket_iterator find_entry_for(Key const& key) const      ❷
        {
            return std::find_if(data.begin(),data.end(),
                                [&](bucket_value const& item)
                                {return item.first==key;});
        }
    public:
        Value value_for(Key const& key,Value const& default_value) const
        {
            boost::shared_lock<boost::shared_mutex> lock(mutex);      ❸
            bucket_iterator const found_entry=find_entry_for(key);
            return (found_entry==data.end())?
                default_value:found_entry->second;
        }

        void add_or_update_mapping(Key const& key,Value const& value)
        {
            std::unique_lock<boost::shared_mutex> lock(mutex);        ❹
            bucket_iterator const found_entry=find_entry_for(key);
            if(found_entry==data.end())
            {
                data.push_back(bucket_value(key,value));
            }
            else
            {
                found_entry->second=value;
            }
        }

        void remove_mapping(Key const& key)
        {
            std::unique_lock<boost::shared_mutex> lock(mutex);        ❺
            bucket_iterator const found_entry=find_entry_for(key);
            if(found_entry!=data.end())
            {
                data.erase(found_entry);
            }
        }
    };

    std::vector<std::unique_ptr<bucket_type> > buckets;          ❻
    Hash hasher;

    bucket_type& get_bucket(Key const& key) const           ❼
    {
        std::size_t const bucket_index=hasher(key)%buckets.size();
        return *buckets[bucket_index];
    }

public:
    typedef Key key_type;
```

```
    typedef Value mapped_type;
    typedef Hash hash_type;

    threadsafe_lookup_table(
        unsigned num_buckets=19,Hash const& hasher_=Hash()):
        buckets(num_buckets),hasher(hasher_)
    {
        for(unsigned i=0;i<num_buckets;++i)
        {
            buckets[i].reset(new bucket_type);
        }
    }

    threadsafe_lookup_table(threadsafe_lookup_table const& other)=delete;
    threadsafe_lookup_table& operator=(
        threadsafe_lookup_table const& other)=delete;

    Value value_for(Key const& key,
                    Value const& default_value=Value()) const
    {
        return get_bucket(key).value_for(key,default_value);       <-- 8
    }

    void add_or_update_mapping(Key const& key,Value const& value)
    {
        get_bucket(key).add_or_update_mapping(key,value);       <-- 9
    }

    void remove_mapping(Key const& key)
    {
        get_bucket(key).remove_mapping(key);       <-- 10
    }
};
```

This implementation uses a `std::vector<std::unique_ptr<bucket_type>>` ❻ to hold the buckets, which allows the number of buckets to be specified in the constructor. The default is 19, which is an arbitrary prime number; hash tables work best with a prime number of buckets. Each bucket is protected with an instance of `boost::shared_mutex` ❶ to allow many concurrent reads or a single call to either of the modification functions *per bucket*.

Because the number of buckets is fixed, the `get_bucket()` function ❼ can be called without any locking ❽, ❾, ❿, and then the bucket mutex can be locked either for shared (read-only) ownership ❸ or unique (read/write) ownership ❹, ❺ as appropriate for each function.

All three functions make use of the `find_entry_for()` member function ❷ on the bucket to determine whether the entry is in the bucket. Each bucket contains just a `std::list<>` of key/value pairs, so adding and removing entries is easy.

I've already covered the concurrency angle, and everything is suitably protected with mutex locks, so what about exception safety? `value_for` doesn't modify anything, so that's fine; if it throws an exception, it won't affect the data structure. `remove_mapping` modifies the list with the call to `erase`, but this is guaranteed not to throw, so that's safe. This leaves `add_or_update_mapping`, which might throw in either of the two branches of the if. push_back is exception-safe and will leave the list in the original state if it throws, so that branch is fine. The only problem is with the assignment in the case where you're replacing an existing value; if the assignment throws, you're relying on it leaving the original unchanged. However, this doesn't affect the data structure as a whole and is entirely a property of the user-supplied type, so you can safely leave it up to the user to handle this.

At the beginning of this section, I mentioned that one nice-to-have feature of such a lookup table would be the option of retrieving a snapshot of the current state into, for example, a std::map<>. This would require locking the entire container in order to ensure that a consistent copy of the state is retrieved, which requires locking all the buckets. Because the "normal" operations on the lookup table require a lock on only one bucket at a time, this would be the only operation that requires a lock on all the buckets. Therefore, provided you lock them in the same order every time (for example, increasing bucket index), there'll be no opportunity for deadlock. Such an implementation is shown in the following listing.

Listing 6.12 Obtaining contents of a threadsafe_lookup_table as a std::map<>

```
std::map<Key,Value> threadsafe_lookup_table::get_map() const
{
    std::vector<std::unique_lock<boost::shared_mutex> > locks;
    for(unsigned i=0;i<buckets.size();++i)
    {
        locks.push_back(
            std::unique_lock<boost::shared_mutex>(buckets[i].mutex));
    }
    std::map<Key,Value> res;
    for(unsigned i=0;i<buckets.size();++i)
    {
        for(bucket_iterator it=buckets[i].data.begin();
            it!=buckets[i].data.end();
            ++it)
        {
            res.insert(*it);
        }
    }
    return res;
}
```

The lookup table implementation from listing 6.11 increases the opportunity for concurrency of the lookup table as a whole by locking each bucket separately and by using a boost::shared_mutex to allow reader concurrency on each bucket. But what if you could increase the potential for concurrency on a bucket by even finer-grained locking? In the next section, you'll do just that by using a thread-safe list container with iterator support.

6.3.2 *Writing a thread-safe list using locks*

A list is one of the most basic data structures, so it should be straightforward to write a thread-safe one, shouldn't it? Well, that depends on what facilities you're after, and you need one that offers iterator support, something I shied away from adding to your map on the basis that it was too complicated. The basic issue with STL-style iterator support is that the iterator must hold some kind of reference into the internal data structure of the container. If the container can be modified from another thread, this reference must somehow remain valid, which essentially requires that the iterator hold a lock on some part of the structure. Given that the lifetime of an STL-style iterator is completely outside the control of the container, this is a bad idea.

The alternative is to provide iteration functions such as `for_each` as part of the container itself. This puts the container squarely in charge of the iteration and locking, but it does fall foul of the deadlock avoidance guidelines from chapter 3. In order for `for_each` to do anything useful, it must call user-supplied code while holding the internal lock. Not only that, but it must also pass a reference to each item to this user-supplied code in order for the user-supplied code to work on this item. You could avoid this by passing a copy of each item to the user-supplied code, but that would be expensive if the data items were large.

So, for now you'll leave it up to the user to ensure that they don't cause deadlock by acquiring locks in the user-supplied operations and don't cause data races by storing the references for access outside the locks. In the case of the list being used by the lookup table, this is perfectly safe, because you know you're not going to do anything naughty.

That leaves you with the question of which operations to supply for your list. If you cast your eyes back on listings 6.11 and 6.12, you can see the sorts of operations you require:

- Add an item to the list.
- Remove an item from the list if it meets a certain condition.
- Find an item in the list that meets a certain condition.
- Update an item that meets a certain condition.
- Copy each item in the list to another container.

For this to be a good general-purpose list container, it would be helpful to add further operations such as a positional insert, but this is unnecessary for your lookup table, so I'll leave it as an exercise for the reader.

The basic idea with fine-grained locking for a linked list is to have one mutex per node. If the list gets big, that's a lot of mutexes! The benefit here is that operations on separate parts of the list are truly concurrent: each operation holds only the locks on the nodes it's actually interested in and unlocks each node as it moves on to the next. The next listing shows an implementation of just such a list.

Listing 6.13 A thread-safe list with iteration support

```
template<typename T>
class threadsafe_list
{
    struct node                                    // 1
    {
        std::mutex m;
        std::shared_ptr<T> data;
        std::unique_ptr<node> next;

        node():                                    // 2
            next()
        {}

        node(T const& value):                      // 3
            data(std::make_shared<T>(value))
        {}
    };

    node head;

public:
    threadsafe_list()
    {}

    ~threadsafe_list()
    {
        remove_if([](node const&){return true;});
    }

    threadsafe_list(threadsafe_list const& other)=delete;
    threadsafe_list& operator=(threadsafe_list const& other)=delete;

    void push_front(T const& value)
    {
        std::unique_ptr<node> new_node(new node(value));      // 4
        std::lock_guard<std::mutex> lk(head.m);
        new_node->next=std::move(head.next);                  // 5
        head.next=std::move(new_node);                        // 6
    }

    template<typename Function>
    void for_each(Function f)                                 // 7
    {
        node* current=&head;
        std::unique_lock<std::mutex> lk(head.m);              // 8
        while(node* const next=current->next.get())           // 9
        {
            std::unique_lock<std::mutex> next_lk(next->m);    // 10
            lk.unlock();                                      // 11
            f(*next->data);                                   // 12
            current=next;
            lk=std::move(next_lk);                            // 13
        }
    }

    template<typename Predicate>
    std::shared_ptr<T> find_first_if(Predicate p)             // 14
```

```
    {
        node* current=&head;
        std::unique_lock<std::mutex> lk(head.m);
        while(node* const next=current->next.get())
        {
            std::unique_lock<std::mutex> next_lk(next->m);
            lk.unlock();
            if(p(*next->data))         <-⓯
            {
                return next->data;        <-⓰
            }
            current=next;
            lk=std::move(next_lk);
        }
        return std::shared_ptr<T>();
    }

    template<typename Predicate>
    void remove_if(Predicate p)         <-⓱
    {
        node* current=&head;
        std::unique_lock<std::mutex> lk(head.m);
        while(node* const next=current->next.get())
        {
            std::unique_lock<std::mutex> next_lk(next->m);
            if(p(*next->data))                             <-⓲
            {
                std::unique_ptr<node> old_next=std::move(current->next);
                current->next=std::move(next->next);                <-⓳
                next_lk.unlock();
            }                          <-⓴
            else
            {
                lk.unlock();         <-㉑
                current=next;
                lk=std::move(next_lk);
            }
        }
    }
};
```

The `threadsafe_list<>` from listing 6.13 is a singly linked list, where each entry is a `node` structure ❶. A default-constructed `node` is used for the `head` of the list, which starts with a `NULL next` pointer ❷. New nodes are added with the `push_front()` function; first a new node is constructed ❹, which allocates the stored data on the heap ❸, while leaving the `next` pointer as `NULL`. You then need to acquire the lock on the mutex for the `head` node in order to get the appropriate `next` value ❺ and insert the node at the front of the list by setting `head.next` to point to your new node ❻. So far, so good: you only need to lock one mutex in order to add a new item to the list, so there's no risk of deadlock. Also, the slow memory allocation happens outside the lock, so the lock is only protecting the update of a couple of pointer values that can't fail. On to the iterative functions.

First up, let's look at `for_each()` ❼. This operation takes a `Function` of some type to apply to each element in the list; in common with most standard library algorithms, it takes this function by value and will work with either a genuine function or an object of a type with a function call operator. In this case, the function must accept a value of type `T` as the sole parameter. Here's where you do the hand-over-hand locking. To start with, you lock the mutex on the `head` node ❽. It's then safe to obtain the pointer to the `next` node (using `get()` because you're not taking ownership of the pointer). If that pointer isn't `NULL` ❾, you lock the mutex on that node ❿ in order to process the data. Once you have the lock on that node, you can release the lock on the previous node ⓫ and call the specified function ⓬. Once the function completes, you can update the `current` pointer to the node you just processed and `move` the ownership of the lock from `next_lk` out to `lk` ⓭. Because `for_each` passes each data item directly to the supplied `Function`, you can use this to update the items if necessary or copy them into another container, or whatever. This is entirely safe if the function is well behaved, because the mutex for the node holding the data item is held across the call.

`find_first_if()` ⓮ is similar to `for_each()`; the crucial difference is that the supplied `Predicate` must return `true` to indicate a match or `false` to indicate no match ⓯. Once you have a match, you just return the found data ⓰ rather than continuing to search. You could do this with `for_each()`, but it would needlessly continue processing the rest of the list even once a match had been found.

`remove_if()` ⓱ is slightly different, because this function has to actually update the list; you can't use `for_each()` for this. If the `Predicate` returns `true` ⓲, you remove the node from the list by updating `current->next` ⓳. Once you've done that, you can release the lock held on the mutex for the `next` node. The node is deleted when the `std::unique_ptr<node>` you moved it into goes out of scope ⓴. In this case, you don't update `current` because you need to check the new `next` node. If the `Predicate` returns `false`, you just want to move on as before ㉑.

So, are there any deadlocks or race conditions with all these mutexes? The answer here is quite definitely *no*, provided that the supplied predicates and functions are well behaved. The iteration is always one way, always starting from the `head` node, and always locking the next mutex before releasing the current one, so there's no possibility of different lock orders in different threads. The only potential candidate for a race condition is the deletion of the removed node in `remove_if()` ⓴ because you do this after you've unlocked the mutex (it's undefined behavior to destroy a locked mutex). However, a few moments' thought reveals that this is indeed safe, because you still hold the mutex on the previous node (`current`), so no new thread can try to acquire the lock on the node you're deleting.

What about opportunities for concurrency? The whole point of such fine-grained locking was to improve the possibilities for concurrency over a single mutex, so have you achieved that? Yes, you have: different threads can be working on different nodes in the list at the same time, whether they're just processing each item with `for_each()`, searching with `find_first_if()`, or removing items with `remove_if()`. But because the mutex for each node must be locked in turn, the threads can't pass each other. If one thread is spending a long time processing a particular node, other threads will have to wait when they reach that particular node.

6.4 Summary

This chapter started by looking at what it means to design a data structure for concurrency and providing some guidelines for doing so. We then worked through several common data structures (stack, queue, hash map, and linked list), looking at how to apply those guidelines to implement them in a way designed for concurrent access, using locks to protect the data and prevent data races. You should now be able to look at the design of your own data structures to see where the opportunities for concurrency lie and where there's potential for race conditions.

In chapter 7 we'll look at ways of avoiding locks entirely, using the low-level atomic operations to provide the necessary ordering constraints, while sticking to the same set of guidelines.

7 Designing lock-free concurrent data structures

This chapter covers

- Implementations of data structures designed for concurrency without using locks
- Techniques for managing memory in lock-free data structures
- Simple guidelines to aid in the writing of lock-free data structures

In the last chapter we looked at general aspects of designing data structures for concurrency, with guidelines for thinking about the design to ensure they're safe. We then examined several common data structures and looked at example implementations that used mutexes and locks to protect the shared data. The first couple of examples used one mutex to protect the entire data structure, but later ones used more than one to protect various smaller parts of the data structure and allow greater levels of concurrency in accesses to the data structure.

Mutexes are powerful mechanisms for ensuring that multiple threads can safely access a data structure without encountering race conditions or broken invariants. It's also relatively straightforward to reason about the behavior of code that uses them: either the code has the lock on the mutex protecting the data or it doesn't. However, it's not all a bed of roses; you saw in chapter 3 how the incorrect use of locks can lead to deadlock, and you've just seen with the lock-based queue and lookup table examples how the granularity of locking can affect the potential for true concurrency. If you can write data structures that are safe for concurrent access without locks, there's the potential to avoid these problems. Such a data structure is called a *lock-free* data structure.

In this chapter we'll look at how the memory-ordering properties of the atomic operations introduced in chapter 5 can be used to build lock-free data structures. You need to take extreme care when designing such data structures, because they're hard to get right, and the conditions that cause the design to fail may occur very rarely. We'll start by looking at what it means for data structures to be lock-free; then we'll move on to the reasons for using them before working through some examples and drawing out some general guidelines.

7.1 Definitions and consequences

Algorithms and data structures that use mutexes, condition variables, and futures to synchronize the data are called *blocking* data structures and algorithms. The application calls library functions that will suspend the execution of a thread until another thread performs an action. Such library calls are termed *blocking* calls because the thread can't progress past this point until the block is removed. Typically, the OS will suspend a blocked thread completely (and allocate its time slices to another thread) until it's *unblocked* by the appropriate action of another thread, whether that's unlocking a mutex, notifying a condition variable, or making a future *ready*.

Data structures and algorithms that don't use blocking library functions are said to be *nonblocking*. Not all such data structures are *lock-free,* though, so let's look at the various types of nonblocking data structures.

7.1.1 Types of nonblocking data structures

Back in chapter 5, we implemented a basic mutex using `std::atomic_flag` as a spin lock. The code is reproduced in the following listing.

Listing 7.1 Implementation of a spin-lock mutex using `std::atomic_flag`

```
class spinlock_mutex
{
    std::atomic_flag flag;
public:
    spinlock_mutex():
        flag(ATOMIC_FLAG_INIT)
    {}
    void lock()
    {
        while(flag.test_and_set(std::memory_order_acquire));
    }
    void unlock()
    {
        flag.clear(std::memory_order_release);
    }
};
```

This code doesn't call any blocking functions; `lock()` just keeps looping until the call to `test_and_set()` returns `false`. This is why it gets the name *spin lock*—the code "spins" around the loop. Anyway, there are no blocking calls, so any code that uses this mutex to protect shared data is consequently *nonblocking*. It's not *lock-free*, though. It's still a mutex and can still be locked by only one thread at a time. Let's look at the definition of *lock-free* so you can see what kinds of data structures *are* covered.

7.1.2 Lock-free data structures

For a data structure to qualify as lock-free, more than one thread must be able to access the data structure concurrently. They don't have to be able to do the same operations; a lock-free queue might allow one thread to push and one to pop but break if two threads try to push new items at the same time. Not only that, but if one of the threads accessing the data structure is suspended by the scheduler midway through its operation, the other threads must still be able to complete their operations without waiting for the suspended thread.

Algorithms that use compare/exchange operations on the data structure often have loops in them. The reason for using a compare/exchange operation is that another thread might have modified the data in the meantime, in which case the code will need to redo part of its operation before trying the compare/exchange again. Such code can still be lock-free if the compare/exchange would eventually succeed if the other threads were suspended. If it wouldn't, you'd essentially have a spin lock, which is nonblocking but not lock-free.

Lock-free algorithms with such loops can result in one thread being subject to *starvation*. If another thread performs operations with the "wrong" timing, the other thread might make progress while the first thread continually has to retry its operation. Data structures that avoid this problem are wait-free as well as lock-free.

7.1.3 Wait-free data structures

A wait-free data structure is a lock-free data structure with the additional property that every thread accessing the data structure can complete its operation within a bounded number of steps, regardless of the behavior of other threads. Algorithms that can involve an unbounded number of retries because of clashes with other threads are thus not wait-free.

Writing wait-free data structures correctly is extremely hard. In order to ensure that every thread can complete its operations within a bounded number of steps, you have to ensure that each operation can be performed in a single pass and that the steps performed by one thread don't cause an operation on another thread to fail. This can make the overall algorithms for the various operations considerably more complex.

Given how hard it is to get a lock-free or wait-free data structure right, you need some pretty good reasons to write one; you need to be sure that the benefit outweighs the cost. Let's therefore examine the points that affect the balance.

7.1.4 The pros and cons of lock-free data structures

When it comes down to it, the primary reason for using lock-free data structures is to enable maximum concurrency. With lock-based containers, there's always the potential for one thread to have to block and wait for another to complete its operation before the first thread can proceed; preventing concurrency through mutual exclusion is the entire purpose of a mutex lock. With a lock-free data structure, *some* thread makes progress with every step. With a wait-free data structure, every thread can make forward progress, regardless of what the other threads are doing; there's no need for waiting. This is a desirable property to have but hard to achieve. It's all too easy to end up writing what's essentially a spin lock.

A second reason to use lock-free data structures is robustness. If a thread dies while holding a lock, that data structure is broken forever. But if a thread dies partway through an operation on a lock-free data structure, nothing is lost except that thread's data; other threads can proceed normally.

The flip side here is that if you can't exclude threads from accessing the data structure, then you must be careful to ensure that the invariants are upheld or choose alternative invariants that can be upheld. Also, you must pay attention to the ordering constraints you impose on the operations. To avoid the undefined behavior associated with a data race, you must use atomic operations for the modifications. But that alone isn't enough; you must ensure that changes become visible to other threads in the correct order. All this means that writing thread-safe data structures without using locks is considerably harder than writing them with locks.

Because there aren't any locks, deadlocks are impossible with lock-free data structures, although there is the possibility of live locks instead. A *live lock* occurs when two threads each try to change the data structure, but for each thread the changes made by the other require the operation to be restarted, so both threads loop and try again. Imagine two people trying to go through a narrow gap. If they both go at once, they get stuck, so they have to come out and try again. Unless someone gets there first (either by agreement, by being quicker, or by sheer luck), the cycle will repeat. As in this simple example, live locks are typically short lived because they depend on the exact scheduling of threads. They therefore sap performance rather than cause long-term problems, but they're still something to watch out for. By definition, wait-free code can't suffer from live lock because there's always an upper limit on the number of steps needed to perform an operation. The flip side here is that the algorithm is likely more complex than the alternative and may require more steps even when no other thread is accessing the data structure.

This brings us to another downside of lock-free and wait-free code: although it can increase the potential for concurrency of operations on a data structure and reduce the time an individual thread spends waiting, it may well *decrease* overall performance. First, the atomic operations used for lock-free code can be much slower than nonatomic operations, and there'll likely be more of them in a lock-free data structure than in the mutex locking code for a lock-based data structure. Not only that, but the hardware must synchronize data between threads that access the same atomic variables. As you'll see in chapter 8, the cache ping-pong associated with multiple threads accessing the same atomic variables can be a significant performance drain. As with everything, it's important to check the relevant performance aspects (whether that's worst-case wait time, average wait time, overall execution time, or something else) both with a lock-based data structure and a lock-free one before committing either way.

Now let's look at some examples.

7.2 Examples of lock-free data structures

In order to demonstrate some of the techniques used in designing lock-free data structures, we'll look at the lock-free implementation of a series of simple data structures. Not only will each example describe the implementation of a useful data structure, but I'll use the examples to highlight particular aspects of lock-free data structure design.

As already mentioned, lock-free data structures rely on the use of atomic operations and the associated memory-ordering guarantees in order to ensure that data becomes visible to other threads in the correct order. Initially, we'll use the default `memory_order_seq_cst` memory ordering for all atomic operations, because that's the easiest to reason about (remember that all `memory_order_seq_cst` operations form a total order). But for later examples we'll look at reducing some of the ordering constraints to `memory_order_acquire`, `memory_order_release`, or even `memory_order_relaxed`. Although none of these examples use mutex locks directly, it's worth bearing in mind that only `std::atomic_flag` is guaranteed not to use locks in the implementation. On some platforms what appears to be lock-free code might actually be using locks internal to the C++ Standard Library implementation (see chapter 5 for more details). On these platforms, a simple lock-based data structure might actually be more appropriate, but there's more to it than that; before choosing an implementation, you must identify your requirements and profile the various options that meet those requirements.

So, back to the beginning with the simplest of data structures: a stack.

7.2.1 Writing a thread-safe stack without locks

The basic premise of a stack is relatively simple: nodes are retrieved in the reverse order to which they were added—last in, first out (LIFO). It's therefore important to ensure that once a value is added to the stack, it can safely be retrieved immediately by another thread, and it's also important to ensure that only one thread returns a given value. The simplest stack is just a linked list; the `head` pointer identifies the first node (which will be the next to retrieve), and each node then points to the next node in turn.

Under such a scheme, adding a node is relatively simple:

1. Create a new node.
2. Set its `next` pointer to the current `head` node.
3. Set the `head` node to point to it.

This works fine in a single-threaded context, but if other threads are also modifying the stack, it's not enough. Crucially, if two threads are adding nodes, there's a race condition between steps 2 and 3: a second thread could modify the value of head between when your thread reads it in step 2 and you update it in step 3. This would then result in the changes made by that other thread being discarded or even worse consequences. Before we look at addressing this race condition, it's also important to note that once head has been updated to point to your new node, another thread could read that node. It's therefore vital that your new node is thoroughly prepared *before* head is set to point to it; you can't modify the node afterward.

OK, so what can you do about this nasty race condition? The answer is to use an atomic compare/exchange operation at step 3 to ensure that head hasn't been modified since you read it in step 2. If it has, you can loop and try again. The following listing shows how you can implement a thread-safe push() without locks.

Listing 7.2 Implementing push() without locks

```
template<typename T>
class lock_free_stack
{
private:
    struct node
    {
        T data;
        node* next;

        node(T const& data_):          <-1
            data(data_)
        {}
    };

    std::atomic<node*> head;
public:
    void push(T const& data)
    {
        node* const new_node=new node(data);     <-2        3
        new_node->next=head.load();                      <-
        while(!head.compare_exchange_weak(new_node->next,new_node));      <-4
    }
};
```

This code neatly matches the three-point plan from above: create a new node ❷, set the node's next pointer to the current head ❸, and set the head pointer to the new node ❹. By populating the data in the node structure itself from the node constructor ❶, you've ensured that the node is ready to roll as soon as it's constructed, so that's the easy problem down. Then you use compare_exchange_weak() to ensure that the head pointer still has the same value as you stored in new_node->next ❸, and you set it to new_node if so. This bit of code also uses a nifty part of the compare/exchange functionality: if it returns false to indicate that the comparison failed (for example, because head was modified by another thread), the value supplied as the first parameter (new_node->next) is updated to the current value of head. You therefore don't have to reload head each time through the loop, because the compiler does that for you. Also, because you're just looping directly on failure, you can use compare_exchange_weak, which can result in more optimal code than compare_exchange_strong on some architectures (see chapter 5).

So, you might not have a pop() operation yet, but you can quickly check push() against the guidelines. The only place that can throw an exception is the construction of the new node ❶, but this will clean up after itself, and the list hasn't been modified yet, so that's perfectly safe. Because you build the data to be stored as part of the node, and you use compare_exchange_weak() to update the head pointer, there are no problematic race conditions here. Once the compare/exchange succeeds, the node is on the list and ready for the taking. There are no locks, so there's no possibility of deadlock, and your push() function passes with flying colors.

Of course, now that you have a means of adding data to the stack, you need a way of getting it off again. On the face of it, this is quite simple:

1. Read the current value of head.
2. Read head->next.
3. Set head to head->next.
4. Return the data from the retrieved node.
5. Delete the retrieved node.

However, in the presence of multiple threads, this isn't so simple. If there are two threads removing items from the stack, they both might read the same value of head at step 1. If one thread then proceeds all the way through to step 5 before the other gets to step 2, the second thread will be dereferencing a dangling pointer. This is one of the biggest issues in writing lock-free code, so for now you'll just leave out step 5 and leak the nodes.

This doesn't resolve all the problems, though. There's another problem: if two threads read the same value of head, they'll return the same node. This violates the intent of the stack data structure, so you need to avoid this. You can resolve this the same way you resolved the race in push(): use compare/exchange to update head. If the compare/exchange fails, either a new node has been pushed on or another thread just popped the node you were trying to pop. Either way, you need to return to step 1 (although the compare/exchange call rereads head for you).

Once the compare/exchange call succeeds, you know you're the only thread that's popping the given node off the stack, so you can safely execute step 4. Here's a first cut at pop():

```
template<typename T>
class lock_free_stack
{
public:
    void pop(T& result)
    {
```

```
        node* old_head=head.load();
        while(!head.compare_exchange_weak(old_head,old_head->next));
        result=old_head->data;
    }
};
```

Although this is nice and succinct, there are still a couple of problems aside from the leaking node. First, it doesn't work on an empty list: if `head` is a null pointer, it will cause undefined behavior as it tries to read the `next` pointer. This is easily fixed by checking for `nullptr` in the `while` loop and either throwing an exception on an empty stack or returning a `bool` to indicate success or failure.

The second problem is an exception-safety issue. When we first introduced the thread-safe stack back in chapter 3, you saw how just returning the object by value left you with an exception safety issue: if an exception is thrown when copying the return value, the value is lost. In that case, passing in a reference to the result was an acceptable solution because you could ensure that the stack was left unchanged if an exception was thrown. Unfortunately, here you don't have that luxury; you can only safely copy the data once you know you're the only thread returning the node, *which means the node has already been removed from the queue.* Consequently, passing in the target for the return value by reference is no longer an advantage: you might as well just return by value. If you want to return the value safely, you have to use the other option from chapter 3: return a (smart) pointer to the data value.

If you return a smart pointer, you can just return `nullptr` to indicate that there's no value to return, but this requires that the data be allocated on the heap. If you do the heap allocation as part of the `pop()`,you're *still* no better off, because the heap allocation might throw an exception. Instead, you can allocate the memory when you `push()` the data onto the stack—you have to allocate memory for the `node` anyway. Returning a `std::shared_ptr<>` won't throw an exception, so `pop()` is now safe. Putting all this together gives the following listing.

Listing 7.3 A lock-free stack that leaks nodes

```
template<typename T>
class lock_free_stack
{
private:
    struct node
    {
        std::shared_ptr<T> data;          <-- 1 Data is now held by pointer
        node* next;

        node(T const& data_):
            data(std::make_shared<T>(data_))      <-- 2 Create std::shared_ptr for newly allocated T
        {}
    };

    std::atomic<node*> head;
public:
    void push(T const& data)
```

```
    {
        node* const new_node=new node(data);
        new_node->next=head.load();
        while(!head.compare_exchange_weak(new_node->next,new_node));
    }
    std::shared_ptr<T> pop()
    {                                                  ❸ Check old_head is not a null
        node* old_head=head.load();                      pointer before you dereference it
        while(old_head &&
            !head.compare_exchange_weak(old_head,old_head->next));
        return old_head ? old_head->data : std::shared_ptr<T>();     ❹
    }
};
```

The data is held by the pointer now ❶, so you have to allocate the data on the heap in the node constructor ❷. You also have to check for a null pointer before you dereference `old_head` in the `compare_exchange_weak()` loop ❸. Finally, you either return the data associated with your node, if there is one, or a null pointer if not ❹. Note that although this is *lock-free*, it's not *wait-free*, because the `while` loops in both `push()` and `pop()` could in theory loop forever if the `compare_exchange_weak()` keeps failing.

If you have a garbage collector picking up after you (like in managed languages such as C# or Java), you're finished; the old node will be collected and recycled once it's no longer being accessed by any threads. However, not many C++ compilers ship with a garbage collector, so you generally have to tidy up after yourself.

7.2.2 Stopping those pesky leaks: managing memory in lock-free data structures

When we first looked at `pop()`, we opted to leak nodes in order to avoid the race condition where one thread deletes a node while another thread still holds a pointer to it that it's just about to dereference. However, leaking memory isn't acceptable in any sensible C++ program, so we have to do something about that. Now it's time to look at the problem and work out a solution.

The basic problem is that you want to free a node, but you can't do so until you're sure there are no other threads that still hold pointers to it. If only one thread ever calls `pop()` on a particular stack instance, you're home free. `push()` doesn't touch the node once it's been added to the stack, so the thread that called `pop()` must be the only thread that can touch the node, and it can safely delete it.

On the other hand, if you need to handle multiple threads calling `pop()` on the same stack instance, you need some way to track when it's safe to delete a node. This essentially means you need to write a special-purpose garbage collector just for `node`s. Now, this might sound scary, but although it's certainly tricky, it's not *that* bad: you're only checking for `node`s, and you're only checking for `node`s accessed from `pop()`. You're not worried about nodes in `push()`, because they're only accessible from one thread until they're on the stack, whereas multiple threads might be accessing the same node in `pop()`.

If there are no threads calling `pop()`,it's perfectly safe to delete all the nodes currently awaiting deletion. Therefore, if you add the nodes to a "to be deleted" list when you've extracted the data, then you can delete them all when there are no threads calling pop(). How do you know there aren't any threads calling pop()? Simple—count them. If you increment a counter on entry and decrement that counter on exit, it's safe to delete the nodes from the "to be deleted" list when the counter is zero. Of course, it will have to be an atomic counter so it can safely be accessed from multiple threads. The following listing shows the amended pop() function, and listing 7.5 shows the supporting functions for such an implementation.

Listing 7.4 Reclaiming nodes when no threads are in pop()

```
template<typename T>
class lock_free_stack
{
private:
    std::atomic<unsigned> threads_in_pop;          // 1 Atomic variable
    void try_reclaim(node* old_head);
public:
    std::shared_ptr<T> pop()
    {
        ++threads_in_pop;                          // 2 Increase counter before doing anything else
        node* old_head=head.load();
        while(old_head &&
              !head.compare_exchange_weak(old_head,old_head->next));
        std::shared_ptr<T> res;
        if(old_head)
        {
            res.swap(old_head->data);              // 3 Reclaim deleted nodes if you can
        }
        try_reclaim(old_head);                     // 4 Extract data from node rather than copying pointer
        return res;
    }
};
```

The atomic variable threads_in_pop ❶ is used to count the threads currently trying to pop an item off the stack. It's incremented at the start of pop() ❷ and decremented inside try_reclaim(), which is called once the node has been removed ❹. Because you're going to potentially delay the deletion of the node itself, you can use swap() to remove the data from the node ❸ rather than just copying the pointer, so that the data will be deleted automatically when you no longer need it rather than it being kept alive because there's still a reference in a not-yet-deleted node. The next listing shows what goes into try_reclaim().

Listing 7.5 The reference-counted reclamation machinery

```
template<typename T>
class lock_free_stack
{
private:
    std::atomic<node*> to_be_deleted;

    static void delete_nodes(node* nodes)
    {
```

```
        while(nodes)
        {
            node* next=nodes->next;
            delete nodes;
            nodes=next;
        }
    }
    void try_reclaim(node* old_head)
    {
        if(threads_in_pop==1)                                        ❶
        {
            node* nodes_to_delete=to_be_deleted.exchange(nullptr);   ❷ Claim list of to-be-deleted nodes
            if(!--threads_in_pop)                                    ❸ Are you the only thread in pop()?
            {
                delete_nodes(nodes_to_delete);                       ❹
            }
            else if(nodes_to_delete)                                 ❺
            {
                chain_pending_nodes(nodes_to_delete);                ❻
            }
            delete old_head;                                         ❼
        }
        else
        {
            chain_pending_node(old_head);                            ❽
            --threads_in_pop;
        }
    }
    void chain_pending_nodes(node* nodes)
    {
        node* last=nodes;
        while(node* const next=last->next)                           ❾ Follow the next pointer chain to the end
        {
            last=next;
        }
        chain_pending_nodes(nodes,last);
    }
    void chain_pending_nodes(node* first,node* last)
    {
        last->next=to_be_deleted;                                    ❿
        while(!to_be_deleted.compare_exchange_weak(                  ⓫ Loop to guarantee that last->next is correct
                  last->next,first));
    }
    void chain_pending_node(node* n)
    {
        chain_pending_nodes(n,n);                                    ⓬
    }
};
```

If the count of threads_in_pop is 1 when you're trying to reclaim the node ❶, you're the only thread currently in pop(), which means it's safe to delete the node you just removed ❼, and it *may* also be safe to delete the pending nodes. If the count is *not* 1, it's not safe to delete any nodes, so you have to add the node to the pending list ❽.

Assume for a moment that `threads_in_pop` is 1. You now need to try to reclaim the pending nodes; if you don't, they'll stay pending until you destroy the stack. To do this, you first claim the list for yourself with an atomic `exchange` operation ❷ and then decrement the count of `threads_in_pop` ❸. If the count is zero after the decrement, you know that no other thread can be accessing this list of pending nodes. There may be new pending nodes, but you're not bothered about them for now, as long as it's safe to reclaim your list. You can then just call `delete_nodes` to iterate down the list and delete them ❹.

If the count is *not* zero after the decrement, it's not safe to reclaim the nodes, so if there are any ❺, you must chain them back onto the list of nodes pending deletion ❻. This can happen if there are multiple threads accessing the data structure concurrently. Other threads might have called `pop()` in between the first test of `threads_in_pop` ❶ and the "claiming" of the list ❷, potentially adding new nodes to the list that are still being accessed by one or more of those other threads. In figure 7.1, thread C adds node Y to the `to_be_deleted` list, even though thread B is still referencing it as `old_head`, and will thus try and read its `next` pointer. Thread A can't therefore delete the nodes without potentially causing undefined behavior for thread B.

To chain the nodes that are pending deletion onto the pending list, you reuse the `next` pointer from the nodes to link them together. In the case of relinking an existing chain back onto the list, you traverse the chain to find the end ❾, replace the `next` pointer from the last node with the current `to_be_deleted` pointer ❿, and store the first node in the chain as the new `to_be_deleted` pointer ⓫. You have to use `compare_exchange_weak` in a loop here in order to ensure that you don't leak any nodes that have been added by another thread. This has the benefit of updating the `next` pointer from the end of the chain if it has been changed. Adding a single node onto the list is a special case where the first node in the chain to be added is the same as the last one ⓬.

This works reasonably well in low-load situations, where there are suitable *quiescent* points at which no threads are in `pop()`. However, this is potentially a transient situation, which is why you need to test that the `threads_in_pop` count decrements to zero ❸ before doing the reclaim and why this test occurs *before* you delete the just-removed node ❼. Deleting a node is potentially a time-consuming operation, and you want the window in which other threads can modify the list to be as small as possible. The longer the time between when the thread first finds `threads_in_pop` to be equal to 1 and the attempt to delete the nodes, the more chance there is that another thread has called `pop()`, and that `threads_in_pop` is no longer equal to 1, thus preventing the nodes from actually being deleted.

In high-load situations, there may *never* be such a quiescent state, because other threads have entered `pop()` before all the threads initially in `pop()` have left. Under such a scenario, the `to_be_deleted` list would grow without bounds, and you'd be essentially leaking memory again. If there aren't going to be any quiescent periods, you need to find an alternative mechanism for reclaiming the nodes. The key is to identify when no more threads are accessing a particular node so that it can be reclaimed. By far the easiest such mechanism to reason about is the use of *hazard pointers.*

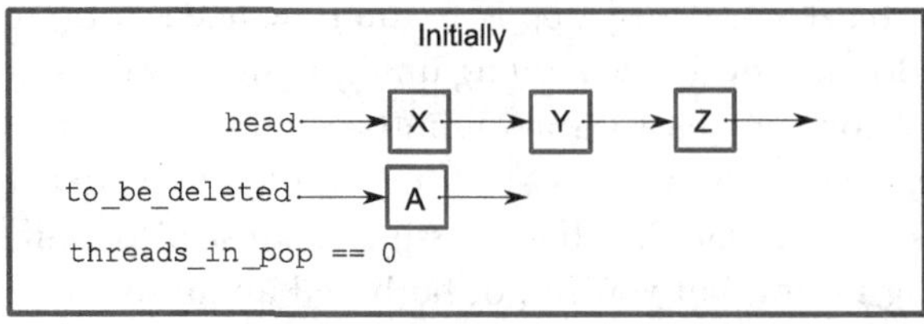

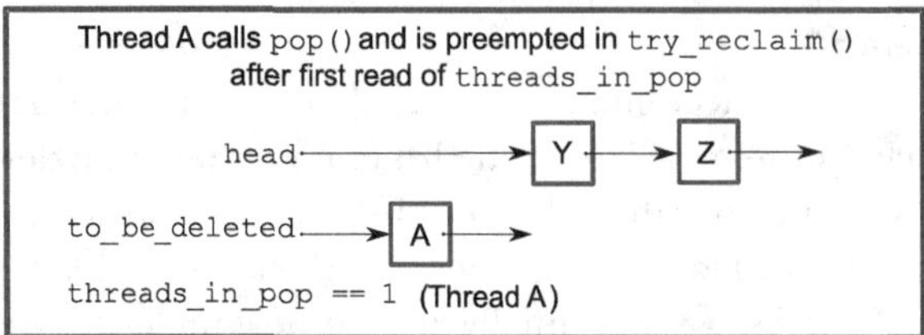

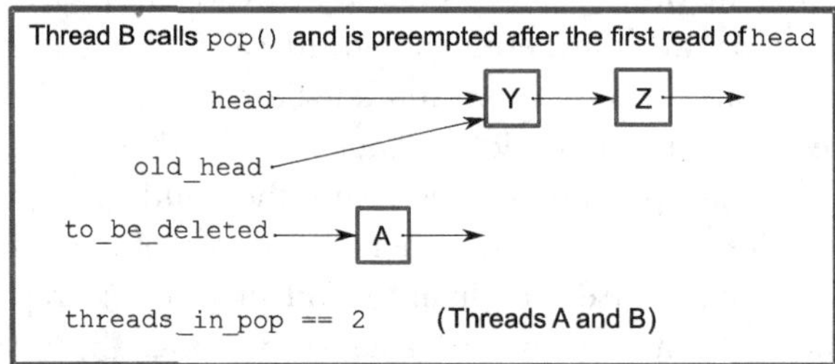

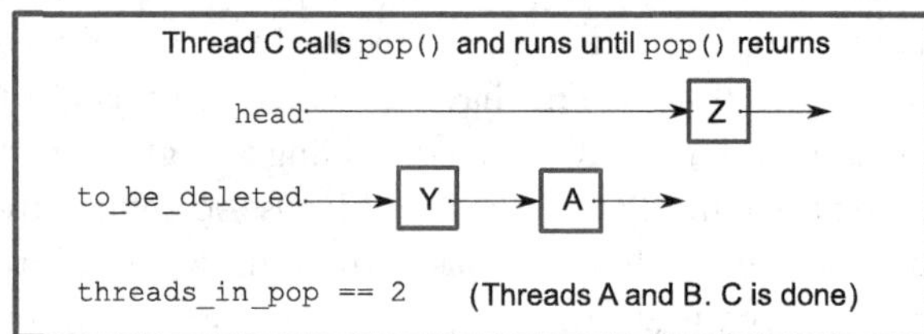

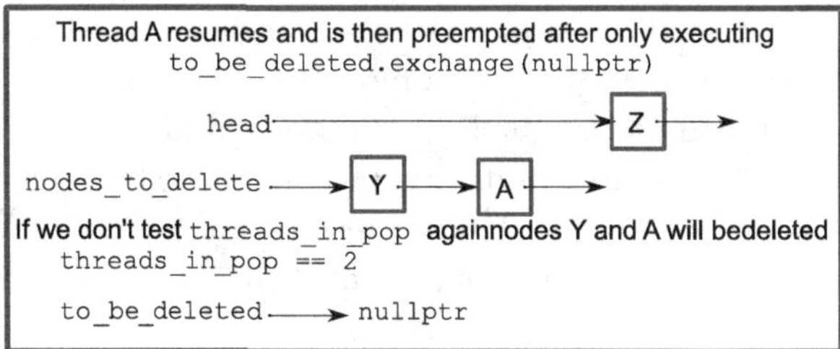

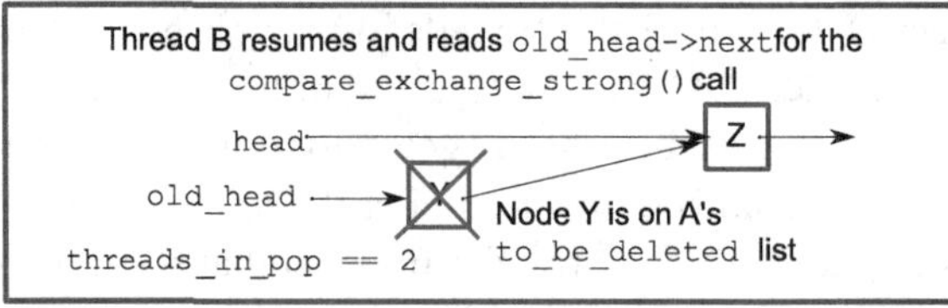

Figure 7.1 Three threads call `pop()` concurrently, showing why you must check `threads_in_pop` after claiming the nodes to be deleted in `try_reclaim()`.

7.2.3 Detecting nodes that can't be reclaimed using hazard pointers

The term *hazard pointers* is a reference to a technique discovered by Maged Michael.[1] They are so called because deleting a node that might still be referenced by other threads is hazardous. If other threads do indeed hold references to that node and proceed to access the node through that reference, you have undefined behavior. The basic idea is that if a thread is going to access an object that another thread might want to delete, it first sets a hazard pointer to reference the object, thus informing the other thread that deleting the object would indeed be hazardous. Once the object is no longer needed, the hazard pointer is cleared. If you've ever watched the Oxford/Cambridge boat race, you've seen a similar mechanism used when starting the race: the cox of either boat can raise their hand to indicate that they aren't ready. While either cox has their hand raised, the umpire may not start the race. If both coxes have their hands down, the race may start, but a cox may raise their hand again if the race hasn't started and they feel the situation has changed.

When a thread wishes to delete an object, it must first check the hazard pointers belonging to the other threads in the system. If none of the hazard pointers reference the object, it can safely be deleted. Otherwise, it must be left until later. Periodically, the list of objects that have been left until later is checked to see if any of them can now be deleted.

Described at such a high level, it sounds relatively straightforward, so how do you do this in C++?

Well, first off you need a location in which to store the pointer to the object you're accessing, the *hazard pointer* itself. This location must be visible to all threads, and you need one of these for each thread that might access the data structure. Allocating them correctly and efficiently can be a challenge, so you'll leave that for later and assume you have a function `get_hazard_pointer_for_current_thread()` that returns a reference to your hazard pointer. You then need to set it when you read a pointer that you intend to dereference—in this case the `head` value from the list:

```
std::shared_ptr<T> pop()
{
    std::atomic<void*>& hp=get_hazard_pointer_for_current_thread();
    node* old_head=head.load();        ❶
    node* temp;
    do
    {
        temp=old_head;
        hp.store(old_head);            ❷
        old_head=head.load();
    } while(old_head!=temp);           ❸
    // ...
}
```

[1] "Safe Memory Reclamation for Dynamic Lock-Free Objects Using Atomic Reads and Writes," Maged M. Michael, in *PODC '02: Proceedings of the Twenty-first Annual Symposium on Principles of Distributed Computing* (2002), ISBN 1-58113-485-1.

You have to do this in a while loop to ensure that the node hasn't been deleted between the reading of the old head pointer ❶ and the setting of the hazard pointer ❷. During this window no other thread knows you're accessing this particular node. Fortunately, if the old head node is going to be deleted, head itself must have changed, so you can check this and keep looping until you know that the head pointer still has the same value you set your hazard pointer to ❸. Using hazard pointers like this relies on the fact that it's safe to use the value of a pointer after the object it references has been deleted. This is technically undefined behavior if you are using the default implementation of new and delete, so either you need to ensure that your implementation permits it, or you need to use a custom allocator that permits such usage.

Now that you've set your hazard pointer, you can proceed with the rest of pop(), safe in the knowledge that no other thread will delete the nodes from under you. Well, almost: every time you reload old_head, you need to update the hazard pointer before you dereference the freshly read pointer value. Once you've extracted a node from the list, you can clear your hazard pointer. If there are no other hazard pointers referencing your node, you can safely delete it; otherwise, you have to add it to a list of nodes to be deleted later. The following listing shows a full implementation of pop() using such a scheme.

Listing 7.6 An implementation of pop() using hazard pointers

```
std::shared_ptr<T> pop()
{
    std::atomic<void*>& hp=get_hazard_pointer_for_current_thread();
    node* old_head=head.load();
    do
    {
        node* temp;
        do                                        ❶ Loop until you've set the
        {                                            hazard pointer to head
            temp=old_head;
            hp.store(old_head);
            old_head=head.load();
        } while(old_head!=temp);
    }
    while(old_head &&
          !head.compare_exchange_strong(old_head,old_head->next));
    hp.store(nullptr);                        ❷ Clear hazard pointer
    std::shared_ptr<T> res;                      once you're finished
    if(old_head)
    {                                                     ❸ Check for hazard
        res.swap(old_head->data);                            pointers referencing
        if(outstanding_hazard_pointers_for(old_head))        a node before you
        {                                                    delete it
            reclaim_later(old_head);          ❹
        }
        else
        {
            delete old_head;          ❺
        }
        delete_nodes_with_no_hazards();       ❻
```

```
    }
    return res;
}
```

First off, you've moved the loop that sets the hazard pointer *inside* the outer loop for reloading `old_head` if the compare/exchange fails ❶. You're using `compare_exchange_strong()` here because you're actually doing work inside the `while` loop: a spurious failure on `compare_exchange_weak()` would result in resetting the hazard pointer unnecessarily. This ensures that the hazard pointer is correctly set before you dereference `old_head`. Once you've claimed the node as yours, you can clear your hazard pointer ❷. If you did get a node, you need to check the hazard pointers belonging to other threads to see if they reference it ❸. If so, you can't delete it just yet, so you must put it on a list to be reclaimed later ❹; otherwise, you can delete it right away ❺. Finally, you put in a call to check for any nodes for which you had to call `reclaim_later()`. If there are no longer any hazard pointers referencing those nodes, you can safely delete them ❻. Any nodes for which there are still outstanding hazard pointers will be left for the next thread that calls `pop()`.

Of course, there's still a lot of detail hidden in these new functions—`get_hazard_pointer_for_current_thread()`, `reclaim_later()`, `outstanding_hazard_pointers_for()`, and `delete_nodes_with_no_hazards()`—so let's draw back the curtain and look at how they work.

The exact scheme for allocating hazard pointer instances to threads used by `get_hazard_pointer_for_current_thread()` doesn't really matter for the program logic (although it can affect the efficiency, as you'll see later). So for now you'll go with a simple structure: a fixed-size array of pairs of thread IDs and pointers. `get_hazard_pointer_for_current_thread()` then searches through the array to find the first free slot and sets the ID entry of that slot to the ID of the current thread. When the thread exits, the slot is freed by resetting the ID entry to a default-constructed `std::thread::id()`. This is shown in the following listing.

Listing 7.7 A simple implementation of `get_hazard_pointer_for_current_thread()`

```
unsigned const max_hazard_pointers=100;
struct hazard_pointer
{
    std::atomic<std::thread::id> id;
    std::atomic<void*> pointer;
};
hazard_pointer hazard_pointers[max_hazard_pointers];

class hp_owner
{
    hazard_pointer* hp;

public:
    hp_owner(hp_owner const&)=delete;
    hp_owner operator=(hp_owner const&)=delete;
```

```
    hp_owner():
        hp(nullptr)
    {
        for(unsigned i=0;i<max_hazard_pointers;++i)
        {
            std::thread::id old_id;
            if(hazard_pointers[i].id.compare_exchange_strong(     <-
                old_id,std::this_thread::get_id()))
            {
                hp=&hazard_pointers[i];            Try to claim ownership
                break;                               of a hazard pointer
            }
        }
        if(!hp)      <-1
        {
            throw std::runtime_error("No hazard pointers available");
        }
    }

    std::atomic<void*>& get_pointer()
    {
        return hp->pointer;
    }

    ~hp_owner()      <-2
    {
        hp->pointer.store(nullptr);
        hp->id.store(std::thread::id());
    }
};

std::atomic<void*>& get_hazard_pointer_for_current_thread()      <-3
{
    thread_local static hp_owner hazard;          <-  Each thread has its
    return hazard.get_pointer();         <-5      4   own hazard pointer
}
```

The actual implementation of `get_hazard_pointer_for_current_thread()` itself is deceptively simple ❸: it has a `thread_local` variable of type `hp_owner` ❹ that stores the hazard pointer for the current thread. It then just returns the pointer from that object ❺. This works as follows: The first time *each thread* calls this function, a new instance of `hp_owner` is created. The constructor for this new instance ❶ then searches through the table of owner/pointer pairs looking for an entry without an owner. It uses `compare_exchange_strong()` to check for an entry without an owner and claim it in one go ❷. If the `compare_exchange_strong()` fails, another thread owns that entry, so you move on to the next. If the exchange succeeds, you've successfully claimed the entry for the current thread, so you store it and stop the search ❸. If you get to the end of the list without finding a free entry ❹, there are too many threads using hazard pointers, so you throw an exception.

Once the `hp_owner` instance has been created for a given thread, further accesses are much faster because the pointer is cached, so the table doesn't have to be scanned again.

When each thread exits, if an instance of `hp_owner` was created for that thread, then it's destroyed. The destructor then resets the actual pointer to `nullptr` before setting the owner ID to `std::thread::id()`, allowing another thread to reuse the entry later ❺.

With this implementation of `get_hazard_pointer_for_current_thread()`, the implementation of `outstanding_hazard_pointers_for()` is really simple: just scan through the hazard pointer table looking for entries:

```
bool outstanding_hazard_pointers_for(void* p)
{
    for(unsigned i=0;i<max_hazard_pointers;++i)
    {
        if(hazard_pointers[i].pointer.load()==p)
        {
            return true;
        }
    }
    return false;
}
```

It's not even worth checking whether each entry has an owner: unowned entries will have a null pointer, so the comparison will return `false` anyway, and it simplifies the code.

`reclaim_later()` and `delete_nodes_with_no_hazards()` can then work on a simple linked list; `reclaim_later()` just adds nodes to the list, and `delete_nodes_with_no_hazards()` scans through the list, deleting entries with no outstanding hazards. The next listing shows just such an implementation.

Listing 7.8 A simple implementation of the reclaim functions

```
template<typename T>
void do_delete(void* p)
{
    delete static_cast<T*>(p);
}

struct data_to_reclaim
{
    void* data;
    std::function<void(void*)> deleter;
    data_to_reclaim* next;

    template<typename T>
    data_to_reclaim(T* p):          <-- 1
        data(p),
        deleter(&do_delete<T>),
        next(0)
    {}

    ~data_to_reclaim()
    {
        deleter(data);          <-- 2
    }
};

std::atomic<data_to_reclaim*> nodes_to_reclaim;
```

```
void add_to_reclaim_list(data_to_reclaim* node)        ❸
{
    node->next=nodes_to_reclaim.load();
    while(!nodes_to_reclaim.compare_exchange_weak(node->next,node));
}
template<typename T>
void reclaim_later(T* data)        ❹
{
    add_to_reclaim_list(new data_to_reclaim(data));        ❺
}
void delete_nodes_with_no_hazards()
{
    data_to_reclaim* current=nodes_to_reclaim.exchange(nullptr);        ❻
    while(current)
    {
        data_to_reclaim* const next=current->next;
        if(!outstanding_hazard_pointers_for(current->data))        ❼
        {
            delete current;        ❽
        }
        else
        {
            add_to_reclaim_list(current);        ❾
        }
        current=next;
    }
}
```

First off, I expect you've spotted that `reclaim_later()` is a function template rather than a plain function ❹. This is because hazard pointers are a general-purpose utility, so you don't want to tie yourselves to stack nodes. You've been using `std::atomic<void*>` for storing the pointers already. You therefore need to handle any pointer type, but you can't use `void*` because you want to delete the data items when you can, and `delete` requires the real type of the pointer. The constructor of `data_to_reclaim` handles that nicely, as you'll see in a minute: `reclaim_later()` just creates a new instance of `data_to_reclaim` for your pointer and adds it to the reclaim list ❺. `add_to_reclaim_list()` itself ❸ is just a simple `compare_exchange_weak()` loop on the list head like you've seen before.

So, back to the constructor of `data_to_reclaim` ❶: the constructor is also a template. It stores the data to be deleted as a `void*` in the `data` member and then stores a pointer to the appropriate instantiation of `do_delete()`—a simple function that casts the supplied `void*` to the chosen pointer type and then deletes the pointed-to object. `std::function<>` wraps this function pointer safely, so that the destructor of `data_to_reclaim` can then delete the data just by invoking the stored function ❷.

The destructor of `data_to_reclaim` isn't called when you're adding nodes to the list; it's called when there are no more hazard pointers to that node. This is the responsibility of `delete_nodes_with_no_hazards()`.

`delete_nodes_with_no_hazards()` first claims the entire list of nodes to be reclaimed for itself with a simple `exchange()` ❻. This simple but crucial step ensures that this is the only thread trying to reclaim this particular set of nodes. Other threads are now free to add further nodes to the list or even try to reclaim them without impacting the operation of this thread.

Then, as long as there are still nodes left in the list, you check each node in turn to see if there are any outstanding hazard pointers ❼. If there aren't, you can safely delete the entry (and thus clean up the stored data) ❽. Otherwise, you just add the item back on the list for reclaiming later ❾.

Although this simple implementation does indeed safely reclaim the deleted nodes, it adds quite a bit of overhead to the process. Scanning the hazard pointer array requires checking `max_hazard_pointers` atomic variables, and this is done for every `pop()` call. Atomic operations are inherently slow—often 100 times slower than an equivalent non-atomic operation on desktop CPUs—so this makes `pop()` an expensive operation. Not only do you scan the hazard pointer list for the node you're about to remove, but you also scan it for each node in the waiting list. Clearly this is a bad idea. There may well be `max_hazard_pointers` nodes in the list, and you're checking all of them against `max_hazard_pointers` stored hazard pointers. Ouch! There has to be a better way.

BETTER RECLAMATION STRATEGIES USING HAZARD POINTERS

Of course, there *is* a better way. What I've shown here is a simple and naïve implementation of hazard pointers to help explain the technique. The first thing you can do is trade memory for performance. Rather than checking every node on the reclamation list every time you call `pop()`, you don't try to reclaim any nodes at all unless there are more than `max_hazard_pointers` nodes on the list. That way you're guaranteed to be able to reclaim at least one node. If you just wait until there are `max_hazard_pointers+1` nodes on the list, you're not much better off. Once you get to `max_hazard_pointers` nodes, you'll be trying to reclaim nodes for most calls to `pop()`, so you're not doing much better. But if you wait until there are `2*max_hazard_pointers` nodes on the list, you're guaranteed to be able to reclaim at least `max_hazard_pointers` nodes, and it will then be at least `max_hazard_pointers` calls to `pop()` before you try to reclaim any nodes again. This is much better. Rather than checking around `max_hazard_pointers` nodes every call to `push()` (and not necessarily reclaiming any), you're checking `2*max_hazard_pointers` nodes every `max_hazard_pointers` calls to `pop()` and reclaiming at least `max_hazard_pointers` nodes. That's effectively two nodes checked for every `pop()`, one of which is reclaimed.

Even this has a downside (beyond the increased memory usage): you now have to count the nodes on the reclamation list, which means using an atomic count, and you still have multiple threads competing to access the reclamation list itself. If you have memory to spare, you can trade increased memory usage for an even better reclamation scheme: each thread keeps its own reclamation list in a thread-local variable. There's thus no need for atomic variables for the count or the list access. Instead, you have `max_hazard_pointers*max_hazard_pointers` nodes allocated. If a thread exits before all its nodes have been reclaimed, they can be stored in the global list as before and added to the local list of the next thread doing a reclamation process.

Another downside of hazard pointers is that they're covered by a patent application submitted by IBM.[2] If you write software for use in a country where the patents are valid, you need to make sure you have a suitable licensing arrangement in place. This is something common to many of the lock-free memory reclamation techniques; this is an active research area, so large companies are taking out patents where they can. You may well be asking why I've devoted so many pages to a technique that many people will be unable to use, and that's a fair question. First, it may be possible to use the technique without paying for a license. For example, if you're developing free software licensed under the GPL,[3] your software may be covered by IBM's statement of non-assertion.[4] Second, and most important, the explanation of the techniques shows some of the things that are important to think about when writing lock-free code, such as the costs of atomic operations.

So, are there any unpatented memory reclamation techniques that can be used with lock-free code? Luckily, there are. One such mechanism is reference counting.

7.2.4 Detecting nodes in use with reference counting

Back in section 7.2.2, you saw that the problem with deleting nodes is detecting which nodes are still being accessed by reader threads. If you could safely identify precisely which nodes were being referenced and when no threads were accessing these nodes, you could delete them. Hazard pointers tackle the problem by storing a list of the nodes in use. Reference counting tackles the problem by storing a count of the number of threads accessing each node.

This may seem nice and straightforward, but it's quite hard to manage in practice. At first, you might think that something like `std::shared_ptr<>` would be up to the task; after all, it's a reference-counted pointer. Unfortunately, although some operations on `std::shared_ptr<>` are atomic, they aren't guaranteed to be lock-free. Although by itself this is no different than any of the operations on the atomic types, `std::shared_ptr<>` is intended for use in many contexts, and making the atomic operations lock-free would likely impose an overhead on all uses of the class. If your platform supplies an implementation for which `std::atomic_is_lock_free(&some_shared_ptr)` returns `true`, the whole memory reclamation issue goes away. Just use `std::shared_ptr<node>` for the list, as in the following listing.

Listing 7.9 A lock-free stack using a lock-free `std::shared_ptr<>` implementation

```
template<typename T>
class lock_free_stack
{
private:
```

---

[2] Maged M. Michael, U.S. Patent and Trademark Office application number 20040107227, "Method for efficient implementation of dynamic lock-free data structures with safe memory reclamation."

[3] GNU General Public License http://www.gnu.org/licenses/gpl.html.

[4] IBM Statement of Non-Assertion of Named Patents Against OSS, http://www.ibm.com/ibm/licensing/patents/pledgedpatents.pdf.

```
    struct node
    {
        std::shared_ptr<T> data;
        std::shared_ptr<node> next;

        node(T const& data_):
            data(std::make_shared<T>(data_))
        {}
    };

    std::shared_ptr<node> head;
public:
    void push(T const& data)
    {
        std::shared_ptr<node> const new_node=std::make_shared<node>(data);
        new_node->next=head.load();
        while(!std::atomic_compare_exchange_weak(&head,
                  &new_node->next,new_node));
    }
    std::shared_ptr<T> pop()
    {
        std::shared_ptr<node> old_head=std::atomic_load(&head);
        while(old_head && !std::atomic_compare_exchange_weak(&head,
                  &old_head,old_head->next));
        return old_head ? old_head->data : std::shared_ptr<T>();
    }
};
```

In the probable case that your `std::shared_ptr<>` implementation isn't lock-free, you need to manage the reference counting manually.

One possible technique involves the use of not one but two reference counts for each node: an internal count and an external count. The sum of these values is the total number of references to the node. The external count is kept alongside the pointer to the node and is increased every time the pointer is read. When the reader is finished with the node, it decreases the *internal* count. A simple operation that reads the pointer will thus leave the external count increased by one and the internal count decreased by one when it's finished.

When the external count/pointer pairing is no longer required (that is, the node is no longer accessible from a location accessible to multiple threads), the internal count is increased by the value of the external count minus one and the external counter is discarded. Once the internal count is equal to zero, there are no outstanding references to the node and it can be safely deleted. It's still important to use atomic operations for updates of shared data. Let's now look at an implementation of a lock-free stack that uses this technique to ensure that the nodes are reclaimed only when it's safe to do so.

The following listing shows the internal data structure and the implementation of `push()`, which is nice and straightforward.

Listing 7.10 Pushing a node on a lock-free stack using split reference counts

```
template<typename T>
class lock_free_stack
```

```
{
private:
    struct node;

    struct counted_node_ptr        <-1
    {
        int external_count;
        node* ptr;
    };

    struct node
    {
        std::shared_ptr<T> data;                    2
        std::atomic<int> internal_count;         <--
        counted_node_ptr next;              <-3

        node(T const& data_):
            data(std::make_shared<T>(data_)),
            internal_count(0)
        {}
    };

    std::atomic<counted_node_ptr> head;      <-4

public:
    ~lock_free_stack()
    {
        while(pop());
    }

    void push(T const& data)        <-5
    {
        counted_node_ptr new_node;
        new_node.ptr=new node(data);
        new_node.external_count=1;
        new_node.ptr->next=head.load();
        while(!head.compare_exchange_weak(new_node.ptr->next,new_node));
    }
};
```

First, the external count is wrapped together with the node pointer in the `counted_node_ptr` structure ❶. This can then be used for the `next` pointer in the `node` structure ❸ alongside the internal count ❷. Because `counted_node_ptr` is just a simple `struct`, you can use it with the `std::atomic<>` template for the `head` of the list ❹.

On those platforms that support a double-word-compare-and-swap operation, this structure will be small enough for `std::atomic<counted_node_ptr>` to be lock-free. If it isn't on your platform, you might be better off using the `std::shared_ptr<>` version from listing 7.9, because `std::atomic<>` will use a mutex to guarantee atomicity when the type is too large for the platform's atomic instructions (thus rendering your "lock-free" algorithm lock-based after all). Alternatively, if you're willing to limit the size of the counter, and you know that your platform has spare bits in a pointer (for example, because the address space is only 48 bits but a pointer is 64 bits), you can store the count inside the spare bits of the pointer to fit it all back in a single machine word. Such tricks require platform-specific knowledge and are thus outside the scope of this book.

push() is relatively simple ❺. You construct a counted_node_ptr that refers to a freshly allocated node with associated data and set the next value of the node to the current value of head. You can then use compare_exchange_weak() to set the value of head, just as in the previous listings. The counts are set up so the internal_count is zero, and the external_count is one. Because this is a new node, there's currently only one external reference to the node (the head pointer itself).

As usual, the complexities come to light in the implementation of pop(), which is shown in the following listing.

Listing 7.11 Popping a node from a lock-free stack using split reference counts

```
template<typename T>
class lock_free_stack
{
private:
    void increase_head_count(counted_node_ptr& old_counter)
    {
        counted_node_ptr new_counter;

        do
        {
            new_counter=old_counter;
            ++new_counter.external_count;
        }
        while(!head.compare_exchange_strong(old_counter,new_counter));   ❶

        old_counter.external_count=new_counter.external_count;
    }

public:
    std::shared_ptr<T> pop()#
    {
        counted_node_ptr old_head=head.load();
        for(;;)
        {
            increase_head_count(old_head);
            node* const ptr=old_head.ptr;     ❷
            if(!ptr)
            {
                return std::shared_ptr<T>();
            }
            if(head.compare_exchange_strong(old_head,ptr->next))     ❸
            {
                std::shared_ptr<T> res;
                res.swap(ptr->data);     ❹

                int const count_increase=old_head.external_count-2;     ❺

                if(ptr->internal_count.fetch_add(count_increase)==     ❻
                   -count_increase)
                {
                    delete ptr;
                }

                return res;     ❼
```

```
            }
            else if(ptr->internal_count.fetch_sub(1)==1)
            {
                delete ptr;          <-8
            }
        }
    }
};
```

This time, once you've loaded the value of head, you must first increase the count of external references to the head node to indicate that you're referencing it and to ensure that it's safe to dereference it. If you dereference the pointer *before* increasing the reference count, another thread could free the node before you access it, thus leaving you with a dangling pointer. *This is the primary reason for using the split reference count:* by incrementing the external reference count, you ensure that the pointer remains valid for the duration of your access. The increment is done with a compare_exchange_strong() loop ❶ that compares and sets the whole structure to ensure that the pointer hasn't been changed by another thread in the meantime.

Once the count has been increased, you can safely dereference the ptr field of the value loaded from head in order to access the pointed-to node ❷. If the pointer is a null pointer, you're at the end of the list: no more entries. If the pointer isn't a null pointer, you can try to remove the node by a compare_exchange_strong() call on head ❸.

If the compare_exchange_strong() succeeds, you've taken ownership of the node and can swap out the data in preparation for returning it ❹. This ensures that the data isn't kept alive just because other threads accessing the stack happen to still have pointers to its node. Then you can add the external count to the internal count on the node with an atomic fetch_add ❻. If the reference count is now zero, the *previous* value (which is what fetch_add returns) was the negative of what you just added, in which case you can delete the node. It's important to note that the value you add is actually *two less* than the external count ❺; you've removed the node from the list, so you drop one off the count for that, and you're no longer accessing the node from this thread, so you drop another off the count for that. Whether or not you deleted the node, you've finished, so you can return the data ❼.

If the compare/exchange ❸ *fails*, another thread removed your node before you did, or another thread added a new node to the stack. Either way, you need to start again with the fresh value of head returned by the compare/exchange call. But first you must decrease the reference count on the node you were trying to remove. This thread won't access it anymore. If you're the last thread to hold a reference (because another thread removed it from the stack), the internal reference count will be 1, so subtracting 1 will set the count to zero. In this case, you can delete the node here before you loop ❽.

So far, you've been using the default std::memory_order_seq_cst memory ordering for all your atomic operations. On most systems these are more expensive in terms of execution time and synchronization overhead than the other memory orderings, and on some systems considerably so. Now that you have the logic of your data structure right, you can think about relaxing some of these memory-ordering requirements; you don't want to impose any unnecessary overhead on the users of the stack. So, before leaving your stack behind and moving on to the design of a lock-free queue, let's examine the stack operations and ask ourselves, can we use more relaxed memory orderings for some operations and still get the same level of safety?

7.2.5 Applying the memory model to the lock-free stack

Before you go about changing the memory orderings, you need to examine the operations and identify the required relationships between them. You can then go back and find the minimum memory orderings that provide these required relationships. In order to do this, you'll have to look at the situation from the point of view of threads in several different scenarios. The simplest possible scenario has to be where one thread pushes a data item onto the stack and another thread then pops that data item off the stack some time later, so we'll start from there.

In this simple case, three important pieces of data are involved. First is the `counted_node_ptr` used for transferring the data: `head`. Second is the `node` structure that `head` refers to, and third is the data item pointed to by that node.

The thread doing the `push()` first constructs the data item and the `node` and then sets `head`. The thread doing the `pop()` first loads the value of `head`, then does a compare/exchange loop on `head` to increase the reference count, and then reads the `node` structure to obtain the `next` value. Right here you can see a required relationship; the `next` value is a plain nonatomic object, so in order to read this safely, there must be a happens-before relationship between the store (by the pushing thread) and the load (by the popping thread). Because the only atomic operation in the `push()` is the `compare_exchange_weak()`, and you need a *release* operation to get a happens-before relationship between threads, the `compare_exchange_weak()` must be `std::memory_order_release` or stronger. If the `compare_exchange_weak()` call fails, nothing has changed and you keep looping, so you need only `std::memory_order_relaxed` in that case:

```
void push(T const& data)
{
    counted_node_ptr new_node;
    new_node.ptr=new node(data);
    new_node.external_count=1;
    new_node.ptr->next=head.load(std::memory_order_relaxed)
    while(!head.compare_exchange_weak(new_node.ptr->next,new_node,
        std::memory_order_release,std::memory_order_relaxed));
}
```

What about the `pop()` code? In order to get the happens-before relationship you need, you must have an operation that's `std::memory_order_acquire` or stronger before the access to `next`. The pointer you dereference to access the `next` field is the old value read by the `compare_exchange_strong()` in `increase_head_count()`, so you need the ordering on that if it succeeds. As with the call in `push()`, if the exchange fails, you just loop again, so you can use relaxed ordering on failure:

```
void increase_head_count(counted_node_ptr& old_counter)
{
    counted_node_ptr new_counter;

    do
    {
        new_counter=old_counter;
        ++new_counter.external_count;
    }
    while(!head.compare_exchange_strong(old_counter,new_counter,
        std::memory_order_acquire,std::memory_order_relaxed));

    old_counter.external_count=new_counter.external_count;
}
```

If the `compare_exchange_strong()` call succeeds, you know that the value read had the `ptr` field set to what's now stored in `old_counter`. Because the store in `push()` was a release operation, and this `compare_exchange_strong()` is an acquire operation, the store synchronizes with the load and you have a happens-before relationship. Consequently, the store to the `ptr` field in the `push()` happens before the `ptr->next` access in `pop()`, and you're safe.

Note that the memory ordering on the initial `head.load()` didn't matter to this analysis, so you can safely use `std::memory_order_relaxed` for that.

Next up, the `compare_exchange_strong()` to set `head` to `old_head.ptr->next`. Do you need anything from this operation to guarantee the data integrity of this thread? If the exchange succeeds, you access `ptr->data`, so you need to ensure that the store to `ptr->data` in the `push()` thread happens before the load. However, you already have that guarantee: the acquire operation in `increase_head_count()` ensures that there's a synchronizes-with relationship between the store in the `push()` thread and that compare/exchange. Because the store to `data` in the `push()` thread is sequenced before the store to `head` and the call to `increase_head_count()` is sequenced before the load of `ptr->data`, there's a happens-before relationship, and all is well even if this compare/exchange in `pop()` uses `std::memory_order_relaxed`. The only other place where `ptr->data` is changed is the very call to `swap()` that you're looking at, and no other thread can be operating on the same node; that's the whole point of the compare/exchange.

If the `compare_exchange_strong()` fails, the new value of `old_head` isn't touched until next time around the loop, and you already decided that the `std::memory_order_acquire` in `increase_head_count()` was enough, so `std::memory_order_relaxed` is enough there also.

What about other threads? Do you need anything stronger here to ensure other threads are still safe? The answer is, no, because `head` is only ever modified by compare/exchange operations. Because these are read-modify-write operations, they form part of the release sequence headed by the compare/exchange in `push()`. Therefore, the `compare_exchange_weak()` in `push()` synchronizes with a call to `compare_exchange_strong()` in `increase_head_count()`, which reads the value stored, even if many other threads modify `head` in the meantime.

So you've nearly finished: the only remaining operations to deal with are the fetch_add() operations for modifying the reference count. The thread that got to return the data from this node can proceed, safe in the knowledge that no other thread can have modified the node data. However, any thread that did *not* successfully retrieve the data knows that another thread *did* modify the node data; it used swap() to extract the referenced data item. Therefore you need to ensure that the swap() happens-before the delete in order to avoid a data race. The easy way to do this is to make the fetch_add() in the successful-return branch use std::memory_order_release and the fetch_add() in the loop-again branch use std::memory_order_acquire. However, this is still overkill: only one thread does the delete (the one that sets the count to zero), so only that thread needs to do an acquire operation. Thankfully, because fetch_add() is a read-modify-write operation, it forms part of the release sequence, so you can do that with an additional load(). If the loop-again branch decreases the reference count to zero, it can reload the reference count with std::memory_order_acquire in order to ensure the required synchronizes-with relationship, and the fetch_add() itself can use std::memory_order_relaxed. The final stack implementation with the new version of pop() is shown here.

Listing 7.12 A lock-free stack with reference counting and relaxed atomic operations

```
template<typename T>
class lock_free_stack
{
private:
    struct node;

    struct counted_node_ptr
    {
        int external_count;
        node* ptr;
    };

    struct node
    {
        std::shared_ptr<T> data;
        std::atomic<int> internal_count;
        counted_node_ptr next;

        node(T const& data_):
            data(std::make_shared<T>(data_)),
            internal_count(0)
        {}
    };

    std::atomic<counted_node_ptr> head;

    void increase_head_count(counted_node_ptr& old_counter)
    {
        counted_node_ptr new_counter;

        do
        {
```

```
            new_counter=old_counter;
            ++new_counter.external_count;
        }
        while(!head.compare_exchange_strong(old_counter,new_counter,
                                            std::memory_order_acquire,
                                            std::memory_order_relaxed));

        old_counter.external_count=new_counter.external_count;
    }

public:
    ~lock_free_stack()
    {
        while(pop());
    }

    void push(T const& data)
    {
        counted_node_ptr new_node;
        new_node.ptr=new node(data);
        new_node.external_count=1;
        new_node.ptr->next=head.load(std::memory_order_relaxed)
        while(!head.compare_exchange_weak(new_node.ptr->next,new_node,
                                          std::memory_order_release,
                                          std::memory_order_relaxed));
    }
    std::shared_ptr<T> pop()
    {
        counted_node_ptr old_head=
            head.load(std::memory_order_relaxed);
        for(;;)
        {
            increase_head_count(old_head);
            node* const ptr=old_head.ptr;
            if(!ptr)
            {
                return std::shared_ptr<T>();
            }
            if(head.compare_exchange_strong(old_head,ptr->next,
                                            std::memory_order_relaxed))
            {
                std::shared_ptr<T> res;
                res.swap(ptr->data);

                int const count_increase=old_head.external_count-2;

                if(ptr->internal_count.fetch_add(count_increase,
                       std::memory_order_release)==-count_increase)
                {
                    delete ptr;
                }

                return res;
            }
            else if(ptr->internal_count.fetch_add(-1,
                        std::memory_order_relaxed)==1)
            {
```

```
                    ptr->internal_count.load(std::memory_order_acquire);
                    delete ptr;
                }
            }
        }
};
```

That was quite a workout, but you got there in the end, and the stack is better for it. By using more relaxed operations in a carefully thought-through manner, the performance is improved without impacting the correctness. As you can see, the implementation of `pop()` is now 37 lines rather than the 8 lines of the equivalent `pop()` in the lock-based stack of listing 6.1 and the 7 lines of the basic lock-free stack without memory management in listing 7.2. As we move on to look at writing a lock-free queue, you'll see a similar pattern: lots of the complexity in lock-free code comes from managing memory.

7.2.6 Writing a thread-safe queue without locks

A queue offers a slightly different challenge to a stack, because the `push()` and `pop()` operations access different parts of the data structure in a queue, whereas they both access the same head node for a stack. Consequently, the synchronization needs are different. You need to ensure that changes made to one end are correctly visible to accesses at the other. However, the structure of `try_pop()` for the queue in listing 6.6 isn't actually that far off that of `pop()` for the simple lock-free stack in listing 7.2, so you can reasonably assume that the lock-free code won't be that dissimilar. Let's see how.

If you take listing 6.6 as a basis, you need two `node` pointers: one for the `head` of the list and one for the `tail`. You're going to be accessing these from multiple threads, so they'd better be atomic in order to allow you to do away with the corresponding mutexes. Let's start by making that small change and see where it gets you. The following listing shows the result.

Listing 7.13 A single-producer, single-consumer lock-free queue

```
template<typename T>
class lock_free_queue
{
private:
    struct node
    {
        std::shared_ptr<T> data;
        node* next;

        node():
            next(nullptr)
        {}
    };

    std::atomic<node*> head;
    std::atomic<node*> tail;
```

```
    node* pop_head()
    {
        node* const old_head=head.load();
        if(old_head==tail.load())                  <-1
        {
            return nullptr;
        }
        head.store(old_head->next);
        return old_head;
    }
public:
    lock_free_queue():
        head(new node),tail(head.load())
    {}

    lock_free_queue(const lock_free_queue& other)=delete;
    lock_free_queue& operator=(const lock_free_queue& other)=delete;

    ~lock_free_queue()
    {
        while(node* const old_head=head.load())
        {
            head.store(old_head->next);
            delete old_head;
        }
    }
    std::shared_ptr<T> pop()
    {
        node* old_head=pop_head();
        if(!old_head)
        {
            return std::shared_ptr<T>();
        }

        std::shared_ptr<T> const res(old_head->data);          <-2
        delete old_head;
        return res;
    }

    void push(T new_value)
    {
        std::shared_ptr<T> new_data(std::make_shared<T>(new_value));
        node* p=new node;                                      <-3
        node* const old_tail=tail.load();        <-4
        old_tail->data.swap(new_data);                 <-5
        old_tail->next=p;                    <-6
        tail.store(p);            <-7
    }
};
```

At first glance, this doesn't seem too bad, and if there's only one thread calling `push()` at a time, and only one thread calling `pop()`, then this is actually perfectly fine. The important thing in that case is the happens-before relationship between the `push()` and the `pop()` to ensure that it's safe to retrieve the `data`. The store to `tail` ❼ synchronizes with the load from `tail` ❶; the store to the preceding node's `data` pointer ❺ is sequenced before the store to `tail`; and the load from `tail` is sequenced before the load from the `data` pointer ❷, so the store to `data` happens before the load, and everything is OK. This is therefore a perfectly serviceable *single-producer, single-consumer (SPSC)* queue.

The problems come when multiple threads call `push()` concurrently or multiple threads call `pop()` concurrently. Let's look at `push()` first. If you have two threads calling `push()` concurrently, they both allocate new nodes to be the new dummy node ❸, both read the *same* value for `tail` ❹, and consequently both update the data members of the same node when setting the `data` and `next` pointers ❺, ❻. This is a data race!

There are similar problems in `pop_head()`. If two threads call concurrently, they will both read the same value of `head`, and both then overwrite the old value with the same `next` pointer. Both threads will now think they've retrieved the same node—a recipe for disaster. Not only do you have to ensure that only one thread `pop()`s a given item, but you also need to ensure that other threads can safely access the `next` member of the node they read from `head`. This is exactly the problem you saw with `pop()` for your lock-free stack, so any of the solutions for that could be used here.

So if `pop()` is a "solved problem," what about `push()`? The problem here is that in order to get the required happens-before relationship between `push()` and `pop()`, you need to set the data items on the dummy node before you update `tail`. But this then means that concurrent calls to `push()` are racing over those very same data items, because they've read the same `tail` pointer.

HANDLING MULTIPLE THREADS IN PUSH()

One option is to add a dummy node between the real nodes. This way, the only part of the current `tail` node that needs updating is the `next` pointer, which could therefore be made atomic. If a thread manages to successfully change the `next` pointer from `nullptr` to its new node, then it has successfully added the pointer; otherwise, it would have to start again and reread the `tail`. This would then require a minor change to `pop()` in order to discard nodes with a null data pointer and loop again. The downside here is that every `pop()` call will typically have to remove two nodes, and there are twice as many memory allocations.

A second option is to make the `data` pointer atomic and set that with a call to compare/exchange. If the call succeeds, this is your tail node, and you can safely set the `next` pointer to your new node and then update `tail`. If the compare/exchange fails because another thread has stored the data, you loop around, reread `tail`, and start again. If the atomic operations on `std::shared_ptr<>` are lock-free, you're home free. If not, you need an alternative. One possibility is to have `pop()` return a `std::unique_ptr<>` (after all, it's the only reference to the object) and store the data as a plain pointer in the queue. This would allow you to store it as a `std::atomic<T*>`, which would then support the necessary `compare_exchange_strong()` call. If you're using the reference-counting scheme from listing 7.11 to handle multiple threads in `pop()`,`push()` now looks like this.

Listing 7.14 A (broken) first attempt at revising push()

```
void push(T new_value)
{
    std::unique_ptr<T> new_data(new T(new_value));
    counted_node_ptr new_next;
    new_next.ptr=new node;
    new_next.external_count=1;
    for(;;)
    {
        node* const old_tail=tail.load();              ❶
        T* old_data=nullptr;
        if(old_tail->data.compare_exchange_strong(
            old_data,new_data.get()))                       ❷
        {
            old_tail->next=new_next;
            tail.store(new_next.ptr);              ❸
            new_data.release();
            break;
        }
    }
}
```

Using the reference-counting scheme avoids this particular race, but it's not the only race in push(). If you look at the revised version of push() in listing 7.14, you'll see a pattern you saw in the stack: load an atomic pointer ❶ and dereference that pointer ❷. In the meantime, another thread could update the pointer ❸, eventually leading to the node being deallocated (in pop()). If the node is deallocated before you dereference the pointer, you have undefined behavior. Ouch! It's tempting to add an external count in tail the same as you did for head, but each node already has an external count in the next pointer of the previous node in the queue. Having two external counts for the same node requires a modification to the reference-counting scheme to avoid deleting the node too early. You can address this by also counting the number of external counters inside the node structure and decreasing this number when each external counter is destroyed (as well as adding the corresponding external count to the internal count). If the internal count is zero and there are no external counters, you know the node can safely be deleted. This is a technique I first encountered through Joe Seigh's Atomic Ptr Plus Project.[5] The following listing shows how push() looks under this scheme.

Listing 7.15 Implementing push() for a lock-free queue with a reference-counted tail

```
template<typename T>
class lock_free_queue
{
private:
    struct node;

    struct counted_node_ptr
    {
```

[5] Atomic Ptr Plus Project, http://atomic-ptr-plus.sourceforge.net/.

```
        int external_count;
        node* ptr;
    };

    std::atomic<counted_node_ptr> head;
    std::atomic<counted_node_ptr> tail;          <-1

    struct node_counter
    {
        unsigned internal_count:30;
        unsigned external_counters:2;            <-2
    };

    struct node
    {
        std::atomic<T*> data;
        std::atomic<node_counter> count;         <-3
        counted_node_ptr next;

        node()
        {
            node_counter new_count;
            new_count.internal_count=0;
            new_count.external_counters=2;       <-4
            count.store(new_count);

            next.ptr=nullptr;
            next.external_count=0;
        }
    };
public:
    void push(T new_value)
    {
        std::unique_ptr<T> new_data(new T(new_value));
        counted_node_ptr new_next;
        new_next.ptr=new node;
        new_next.external_count=1;
        counted_node_ptr old_tail=tail.load();

        for(;;)
        {
            increase_external_count(tail,old_tail);        <-5

            T* old_data=nullptr;
            if(old_tail.ptr->data.compare_exchange_strong(    <-6
               old_data,new_data.get()))
            {
                old_tail.ptr->next=new_next;
                old_tail=tail.exchange(new_next);
                free_external_counter(old_tail);       <-7
                new_data.release();
                break;
            }
            old_tail.ptr->release_ref();
        }
    }
};
```

In listing 7.15, tail is now an atomic<counted_node_ptr> the same as head ❶, and the node structure has a count member to replace the internal_count from before ❸. This count is a structure containing the internal_count and an additional external_counters member ❷. Note that you need only 2 bits for the external_counters because there are at most two such counters. By using a bit field for this and specifying internal_count as a 30-bit value, you keep the total counter size to 32 bits. This gives you plenty of scope for large internal count values while ensuring that the whole structure fits inside a machine word on 32-bit and 64-bit machines. It's important to update these counts together as a single entity in order to avoid race conditions, as you'll see shortly. Keeping the structure within a machine word makes it more likely that the atomic operations can be lock-free on many platforms.

The node is initialized with the internal_count set to zero and the external_counters set to 2 ❹ because every new node starts out referenced from tail and from the next pointer of the previous node once you've actually added it to the queue. push() itself is similar to listing 7.14, except that before you dereference the value loaded from tail in order to call to compare_exchange_strong() on the data member of the node ❻, you call a new function increase_external_count() to increase the count ❺, and then afterward you call free_external_counter() on the old tail value ❼.

With the push() side dealt with, let's take a look at pop(). This is shown in the following listing and blends the reference-counting logic from the pop() implementation in listing 7.11 with the queue-pop logic from listing 7.13.

Listing 7.16 Popping a node from a lock-free queue with a reference-counted tail

```
template<typename T>
class lock_free_queue
{
private:
    struct node
    {
        void release_ref();
    };
public:
    std::unique_ptr<T> pop()
    {
        counted_node_ptr old_head=head.load(std::memory_order_relaxed);   ❶
        for(;;)
        {
            increase_external_count(head,old_head);   ❷
            node* const ptr=old_head.ptr;
            if(ptr==tail.load().ptr)
            {
                ptr->release_ref();   ❸
                return std::unique_ptr<T>();
            }
            if(head.compare_exchange_strong(old_head,ptr->next))   ❹
            {
```

```
                T* const res=ptr->data.exchange(nullptr);
                free_external_counter(old_head);            <-5
                return std::unique_ptr<T>(res);
            }
            ptr->release_ref();         <-6
        }
    }
};
```

You prime the pump by loading the old_head value before you enter the loop ❶ and before you increase the external count on the loaded value ❷. If the head node is the same as the tail node, you can release the reference ❸ and return a null pointer because there's no data in the queue. If there is data, you want to try to claim it for yourself, and you do this with the call to compare_exchange_strong() ❹. As with the stack in listing 7.11, this compares the external count and pointer as a single entity; if either changes, you need to loop again, after releasing the reference ❻. If the exchange succeeded, you've claimed the data in the node as yours, so you can return that to the caller after you've released the external counter to the popped node ❺. Once both the external reference counts have been freed and the internal count has dropped to zero, the node itself can be deleted. The reference-counting functions that take care of all this are shown in listings 7.17, 7.18, and 7.19.

Listing 7.17 Releasing a node reference in a lock-free queue

```
template<typename T>
class lock_free_queue
{
private:
    struct node
    {
        void release_ref()
        {
            node_counter old_counter=
                count.load(std::memory_order_relaxed);
            node_counter new_counter;
            do
            {
                new_counter=old_counter;
                --new_counter.internal_count;       <-1
            }
            while(!count.compare_exchange_strong(       <-2
                   old_counter,new_counter,
                   std::memory_order_acquire,std::memory_order_relaxed));

            if(!new_counter.internal_count &&
               !new_counter.external_counters)
            {
                delete this;      <-3
            }
        }
    };
};
```

The implementation of `node::release_ref()` is only slightly changed from the equivalent code in the implementation of `lock_free_stack::pop()` from listing 7.11. Whereas the code in listing 7.11 only has to handle a single external count, so you could just use a simple `fetch_sub`, the whole `count` structure now has to be updated atomically, even though you only want to modify the `internal_count` field ❶. This therefore requires a compare/exchange loop ❷. Once you've decremented the `internal_count`, if both the internal and external counts are now zero, this is the last reference, so you can delete the node ❸.

Listing 7.18 Obtaining a new reference to a node in a lock-free queue

```
template<typename T>
class lock_free_queue
{
private:
    static void increase_external_count(
        std::atomic<counted_node_ptr>& counter,
        counted_node_ptr& old_counter)
    {
        counted_node_ptr new_counter;

        do
        {
            new_counter=old_counter;
            ++new_counter.external_count;
        }
        while(!counter.compare_exchange_strong(
              old_counter,new_counter,
              std::memory_order_acquire,std::memory_order_relaxed));

        old_counter.external_count=new_counter.external_count;
    }
};
```

Listing 7.18 is the other side. This time, rather than releasing a reference, you're obtaining a fresh one and increasing the external count. `increase_external_count()` is similar to the `increase_head_count()` function from listing 7.12, except that it has been made into a `static` member function that takes the external counter to update as the first parameter rather than operating on a fixed counter.

Listing 7.19 Freeing an external counter to a node in a lock-free queue

```
template<typename T>
class lock_free_queue
{
private:
    static void free_external_counter(counted_node_ptr &old_node_ptr)
    {
        node* const ptr=old_node_ptr.ptr;
        int const count_increase=old_node_ptr.external_count-2;

        node_counter old_counter=
            ptr->count.load(std::memory_order_relaxed);
```

```
        node_counter new_counter;
        do
        {
            new_counter=old_counter;                    ❶
            --new_counter.external_counters;         <─┘
            new_counter.internal_count+=count_increase;     <─❷
        }
        while(!ptr->count.compare_exchange_strong(     <─❸
              old_counter,new_counter,
              std::memory_order_acquire,std::memory_order_relaxed));

        if(!new_counter.internal_count &&
           !new_counter.external_counters)
        {
            delete ptr;     <─❹
        }
    }
};
```

The counterpart to `increase_external_count()` is `free_external_counter()`. This is similar to the equivalent code from `lock_free_stack::pop()` in listing 7.11 but modified to handle the `external_counters` count. It updates the two counts using a single `compare_exchange_strong()` on the whole count structure ❸, just as you did when decreasing the `internal_count` in `release_ref()`. The `internal_count` value is updated as in listing 7.11 ❷, and the `external_counters` value is decreased by one ❶. If *both* the values are now zero, there are no more references to the node, so it can be safely deleted ❹. This has to be done as a single action (which therefore requires the compare/exchange loop) to avoid a race condition. If they're updated separately, two threads may both think they are the last one and thus both delete the node, resulting in undefined behavior.

Although this now works and is race-free, there's still a performance issue. Once one thread has started a `push()` operation by successfully completing the `compare_exchange_strong()` on `old_tail.ptr->data` (❺ from listing 7.15), no other thread can perform a `push()` operation. Any thread that tries will see the new value rather than `nullptr`, which will cause the `compare_exchange_strong()` call to fail and make that thread loop again. This is a busy wait, which consumes CPU cycles without achieving anything. Consequently, this is effectively a lock. The first `push()` call blocks other threads until it has completed, so *this code is no longer lock-free.* Not only that, but whereas the operating system can give priority to the thread that holds the lock on a mutex if there are blocked threads, it can't do so in this case, so the blocked threads will waste CPU cycles until the first thread is done. This calls for the next trick from the lock-free bag of tricks: the waiting thread can help the thread that's doing the `push()`.

MAKING THE QUEUE LOCK-FREE BY HELPING OUT ANOTHER THREAD

In order to restore the lock-free property of the code, you need to find a way for a waiting thread to make progress even if the thread doing the `push()` is stalled. One way to do this is to help the stalled thread by doing its work for it.

In this case, you know exactly what needs to be done: the next pointer on the tail node needs to be set to a new dummy node, and then the tail pointer itself must be updated. The thing about dummy nodes is that they're all equivalent, so it doesn't matter if you use the dummy node created by the thread that successfully pushed the data or the dummy node from one of the threads that's waiting to push. If you make the next pointer in a node atomic, you can then use compare_exchange_strong() to set the pointer. Once the next pointer is set, you can then use a compare_exchange_weak() loop to set the tail while ensuring that it's still referencing the same original node. If it isn't, someone else has updated it, and you can stop trying and loop again. This requires a minor change to pop() as well in order to load the next pointer; this is shown in the following listing.

Listing 7.20 pop() modified to allow helping on the push() side

```
template<typename T>
class lock_free_queue
{
private:
    struct node
    {
        std::atomic<T*> data;
        std::atomic<node_counter> count;
        std::atomic<counted_node_ptr> next;          ❶
    };
public:
    std::unique_ptr<T> pop()
    {
        counted_node_ptr old_head=head.load(std::memory_order_relaxed);
        for(;;)
        {
            increase_external_count(head,old_head);
            node* const ptr=old_head.ptr;
            if(ptr==tail.load().ptr)
            {
                return std::unique_ptr<T>();
            }
            counted_node_ptr next=ptr->next.load();          ❷
            if(head.compare_exchange_strong(old_head,next))
            {
                T* const res=ptr->data.exchange(nullptr);
                free_external_counter(old_head);
                return std::unique_ptr<T>(res);
            }
            ptr->release_ref();
        }
    }
};
```

As I mentioned, the changes here are simple: the next pointer is now atomic ❶, so the load at ❷ is atomic. In this example, you're using the default memory_order_seq_cst ordering, so you could omit the explicit call to load() and rely on the load in the implicit conversion to counted_node_ptr, but putting in the explicit call reminds you where to add the explicit memory ordering later.

The code for push() is more involved and is shown here.

Listing 7.21 A sample push() with helping for a lock-free queue

```
template<typename T>
class lock_free_queue
{
private:
    void set_new_tail(counted_node_ptr &old_tail,              <-1
                      counted_node_ptr const &new_tail)
    {
        node* const current_tail_ptr=old_tail.ptr;
        while(!tail.compare_exchange_weak(old_tail,new_tail) &&       <-2
              old_tail.ptr==current_tail_ptr);
        if(old_tail.ptr==current_tail_ptr)          <-3
            free_external_counter(old_tail);            <-4
        else
            current_tail_ptr->release_ref();        <-5
    }
public:
    void push(T new_value)
    {
        std::unique_ptr<T> new_data(new T(new_value));
        counted_node_ptr new_next;
        new_next.ptr=new node;
        new_next.external_count=1;
        counted_node_ptr old_tail=tail.load();

        for(;;)
        {
            increase_external_count(tail,old_tail);

            T* old_data=nullptr;
            if(old_tail.ptr->data.compare_exchange_strong(        <-6
                   old_data,new_data.get()))
            {
                counted_node_ptr old_next={0};
                if(!old_tail.ptr->next.compare_exchange_strong(        <-7
                       old_next,new_next))
                {
                    delete new_next.ptr;          <-8
                    new_next=old_next;      <-9
                }
                set_new_tail(old_tail, new_next);
                new_data.release();
                break;
            }
            else        <-10
            {
                counted_node_ptr old_next={0};
                if(old_tail.ptr->next.compare_exchange_strong(        <-11
                       old_next,new_next))
```

```
            {
                old_next=new_next;        <-12
                new_next.ptr=new node;          <-13
            }
            set_new_tail(old_tail, old_next);     <-14
        }
    }
}
};
```

This is similar to the original push() from listing 7.15, but there are a few crucial differences. If you *do* set the data pointer ❻, you need to handle the case where another thread has helped you, and there's now an else clause to do the helping ❿.

Having set the data pointer in the node ❻, this new version of push() updates the next pointer using compare_exchange_strong() ❼. You use compare_exchange_strong() to avoid looping. If the exchange fails, you know that another thread has already set the next pointer, so you don't need the new node you allocated at the beginning, and you can delete it ❽. You also want to use the next value that the other thread set for updating tail ❾.

The actual update of the tail pointer has been extracted into set_new_tail() ❶. This uses a compare_exchange_weak() loop ❷ to update the tail, because if other threads are trying to push() a new node, the external_count part may have changed, and you don't want to lose it. However, you also need to take care that you don't replace the value if another thread has successfully changed it already; otherwise, you may end up with loops in the queue, which would be a rather bad idea. Consequently, you need to ensure that the ptr part of the loaded value is the same if the compare/exchange fails. If the ptr is the same once the loop has exited ❸, then you must have successfully set the tail, so you need to free the old external counter ❹. If the ptr value is different, then another thread will have freed the counter, so you just need to release the single reference held by this thread ❺.

If the thread calling push() failed to set the data pointer this time through the loop, it can help the successful thread to complete the update. First off, you try to update the next pointer to the new node allocated on this thread ⓫. If this succeeds, you want to use the node you allocated as the new tail node ⓬, and you need to allocate another new node in anticipation of actually managing to push an item on the queue ⓭. You can then try to set the tail node by calling set_new_tail before looping around again ⓮.

You may have noticed that there are rather a lot of new and delete calls for such a small piece of code, because new nodes are allocated on push() and destroyed in pop(). The efficiency of the memory allocator therefore has a considerable impact on the performance of this code; a poor allocator can completely destroy the scalability properties of a lock-free container such as this. The selection and implementation of such allocators is beyond the scope of this book, but it's important to bear in mind that the only way to know that an allocator is better is to try it and measure the performance of the code before and after. Common techniques for optimizing memory allocation include having a separate memory allocator on each thread and using free lists to recycle nodes rather than returning them to the allocator.

That's enough examples for now; instead, let's look at extracting some guidelines for writing lock-free data structures from the examples.

7.3 Guidelines for writing lock-free data structures

If you've followed through all the examples in this chapter, you'll appreciate the complexities involved in getting lock-free code right. If you're going to design your own data structures, it helps to have some guidelines to focus on. The general guidelines regarding concurrent data structures from the beginning of chapter 6 still apply, but you need more than that. I've pulled a few useful guidelines out from the examples, which you can then refer to when designing your own lock-free data structures.

7.3.1 Guideline: use std::memory_order_seq_cst for prototyping

`std::memory_order_seq_cst` is much easier to reason about than any other memory ordering because all such operations form a total order. In all the examples in this chapter, you've started with `std::memory_order_seq_cst` and only relaxed the memory-ordering constraints once the basic operations were working. In this sense, using other memory orderings is an *optimization*, and as such you need to avoid doing it prematurely. In general, you can only determine which operations can be relaxed when you can see the full set of code that can operate on the guts of the data structure. Attempting to do otherwise just makes your life harder. This is complicated by the fact that the code may work when tested but isn't guaranteed. Unless you have an algorithm checker that can systematically test all possible combinations of thread visibilities that are consistent with the specified ordering guarantees (and such things do exist), just running the code isn't enough.

7.3.2 Guideline: use a lock-free memory reclamation scheme

One of the biggest difficulties with lock-free code is managing memory. It's essential to avoid deleting objects when other threads might still have references to them, but you still want to delete the object as soon as possible in order to avoid excessive memory consumption. In this chapter you've seen three techniques for ensuring that memory can safely be reclaimed:

- Waiting until no threads are accessing the data structure and deleting all objects that are pending deletion
- Using hazard pointers to identify that a thread is accessing a particular object
- Reference counting the objects so that they aren't deleted until there are no outstanding references

In all cases the key idea is to use some method to keep track of how many threads are accessing a particular object and only delete each object when it's no longer referenced from anywhere. There are many other ways of reclaiming memory in lock-free data structures. For example, this is the ideal scenario for using a garbage collector. It's much easier to write the algorithms if you know that the garbage collector will free the nodes when they're no longer used, but not before.

Another alternative is to recycle nodes and only free them completely when the data structure is destroyed. Because the nodes are reused, the memory never becomes invalid, so some of the difficulties in avoiding undefined behavior go away. The downside here is that another problem becomes more prevalent. This is the so-called *ABA problem*.

7.3.3 Guideline: watch out for the ABA problem

The ABA problem is something to be wary of in any compare/exchange–based algorithm. It goes like this:

1. Thread 1 reads an atomic variable `x` and finds it has value `A`.
2. Thread 1 performs some operation based on this value, such as dereferencing it (if it's a pointer) or doing a lookup or something.
3. Thread 1 is stalled by the operating system.
4. Another thread performs some operations on `x` that changes its value to `B`.
5. A thread then changes the data associated with the value `A` such that the value held by thread 1 is no longer valid. This may be as drastic as freeing the pointed-to memory or just changing an associated value.
6. A thread then changes `x` back to `A` based on this new data. If this is a pointer, it may be a new object that just happens to share the same address as the old one.
7. Thread 1 resumes and performs a compare/exchange on `x`, comparing against `A`. The compare/exchange succeeds (because the value is indeed `A`), but this is *the wrong* `A` *value*. The data originally read at step 2 is no longer valid, but thread 1 has no way of telling and will thus corrupt the data structure.

None of the algorithms presented here suffer from this problem, but it's easy to write lock-free algorithms that do. The most common way to avoid the problem is to include an ABA counter alongside the variable `x`. The compare/exchange operation is then done on the combined structure of `x` plus the counter as a single unit. Every time the value is replaced, the counter is incremented, so even if `x` has the same value, the compare/exchange will fail if another thread has modified `x`.

The ABA problem is particularly prevalent in algorithms that use free lists or otherwise recycle nodes rather than returning them to the allocator.

7.3.4 Guideline: identify busy-wait loops and help the other thread

In the final queue example you saw how a thread performing a push operation had to wait for another thread also performing a push to complete its operation before it could proceed. Left alone, this would have been a busy-wait loop, with the waiting thread wasting CPU time while failing to proceed. If you end up with a busy-wait loop, you effectively have a blocking operation and might as well use mutexes and locks. By modifying the algorithm so that the waiting thread performs the incomplete steps if it's scheduled to run before the original thread completes the operation, you can remove the busy-wait and the operation is no longer blocking. In the queue example this required changing a data member to be an atomic variable rather than a nonatomic variable and using compare/exchange operations to set it, but in more complex data structures it might require more extensive changes.

7.4 Summary

Following from the lock-based data structures of chapter 6, this chapter has described simple implementations of various lock-free data structures, starting with a stack and a queue, as before. You saw how you must take care with the memory ordering on your atomic operations to ensure that there are no data races and that each thread sees a coherent view of the data structure. You also saw how memory management becomes much harder for lock-free data structures than lock-based ones and examined a couple of mechanisms for handling it. You also saw how to avoid creating wait loops by helping the thread you're waiting for to complete its operation.

Designing lock-free data structures is a difficult task, and it's easy to make mistakes, but such data structures have scalability properties that are important in some situations. Hopefully, by following through the examples in this chapter and reading the guidelines, you'll be better equipped to design your own lock-free data structure, implement one from a research paper, or find the bug in the one your former colleague wrote just before he left the company.

Wherever data is shared between threads, you need to think about the data structures used and how the data is synchronized between threads. By designing data structures for concurrency, you can encapsulate that responsibility in the data structure itself, so the rest of the code can focus on the task it's trying to perform *with* the data rather than the data synchronization. You'll see this in action in chapter 8 as we move on from concurrent data structures to concurrent code in general. Parallel algorithms use multiple threads to improve their performance, and the choice of concurrent data structure is crucial where the algorithms need their worker threads to share data.

8 Designing concurrent code

This chapter covers

- Techniques for dividing data between threads
- Factors that affect the performance of concurrent code
- How performance factors affect the design of data structures
- Exception safety in multithreaded code
- Scalability
- Example implementations of several parallel algorithms

Most of the preceding chapters have focused on the tools you have in your new C++11 toolbox for writing concurrent code. In chapters 6 and 7 we looked at how to use those tools to design basic data structures that are safe for concurrent access by multiple threads. Much as a carpenter needs to know more than just how to build a hinge or a joint in order to make a cupboard or a table, there's more to designing concurrent code than the design and use of basic data structures. You now need to look at the wider context so you can build bigger structures that perform useful work. I'll be using multithreaded implementations of some of the C++

Standard Library algorithms as examples, but the same principles apply at all scales of an application.

Just as with any programming project, it's vital to think carefully about the design of concurrent code. However, with multithreaded code, there are even more factors to consider than with sequential code. Not only must you think about the usual factors such as encapsulation, coupling, and cohesion (which are amply described in the many books on software design), but you also need to consider which data to share, how to synchronize accesses to that data, which threads need to wait for which other threads to complete certain operations, and so forth.

In this chapter we'll be focusing on these issues, from the high-level (but fundamental) considerations of how many threads to use, which code to execute on which thread, and how this can affect the clarity of the code, to the low-level details of how to structure the shared data for optimal performance.

Let's start by looking at techniques for dividing work between threads.

8.1 Techniques for dividing work between threads

Imagine for a moment that you've been tasked with building a house. In order to complete the job, you'll need to dig the foundation, build walls, put in plumbing, add the wiring, and so forth. Theoretically, you could do it all yourself with sufficient training, but it would probably take a long time, and you'd be continually switching tasks as necessary. Alternatively, you could hire a few other people to help out. You now have to choose how many people to hire and decide what skills they need. You could, for example, hire a couple of people with general skills and have everybody chip in with everything. You'd still all switch tasks as necessary, but now things can be done more quickly because there are more of you.

Alternatively, you could hire a team of specialists: a bricklayer, a carpenter, an electrician, and a plumber, for example. Your specialists just do whatever their specialty is, so if there's no plumbing needed, your plumber sits around drinking tea or coffee. Things still get done quicker than before, because there are more of you, and the plumber can put the toilet in while the electrician wires up the kitchen, but there's more waiting around when there's no work for a particular specialist. Even with the idle time, you might find that the work is done faster with specialists than with a team of general handymen. Your specialists don't need to keep changing tools, and they can probably each do their tasks quicker than the generalists can. Whether or not this is the case depends on the particular circumstances—you'd have to try it and see.

Even if you hire specialists, you can still choose to hire different numbers of each. It might make sense to have more bricklayers than electricians, for example. Also, the makeup of your team and the overall efficiency might change if you had to build more than one house. Even though your plumber might not have lots of work to do on any given house, you might have enough work to keep him busy all the time if you're building many houses at once. Also, if you don't have to pay your specialists when there's no work for them to do, you might be able to afford a larger team overall even if you have only the same number of people working at any one time.

OK, enough about building; what does all this have to do with threads? Well, with threads the same issues apply. You need to decide how many threads to use and what tasks they should be doing. You need to decide whether to have "generalist" threads that do whatever work is necessary at any point in time or "specialist" threads that do one thing well, or some combination. You need to make these choices whatever the driving reason for using concurrency, and quite how you do this will have a crucial effect on the performance and clarity of the code. It's therefore vital to understand the options so you can make an appropriately informed decision when designing the structure of your application. In this section, we'll look at several techniques for dividing the tasks, starting with dividing data between threads before we do any other work.

8.1.1 Dividing data between threads before processing begins

The easiest algorithms to parallelize are simple algorithms such as `std::for_each` that perform an operation on each element in a data set. In order to parallelize such an algorithm, you can assign each element to one of the processing threads. How the elements are best divided for optimal performance depends very much on the details of the data structure, as you'll see later in this chapter when we look at performance issues.

The simplest means of dividing the data is to allocate the first *N* elements to one thread, the next *N* elements to another thread, and so on, as shown in figure 8.1, but other patterns could be used too. No matter how the data is divided, each thread then processes just the elements it has been assigned without any communication with the other threads until it has completed its processing.

This structure will be familiar to anyone who has programmed using the Message Passing Interface (MPI)[1] or OpenMP[2] frameworks: a task is split into a set of parallel tasks, the worker threads run these tasks independently, and the results are combined in a final *reduction* step. It's the approach used by the `accumulate` example from section 2.4; in this

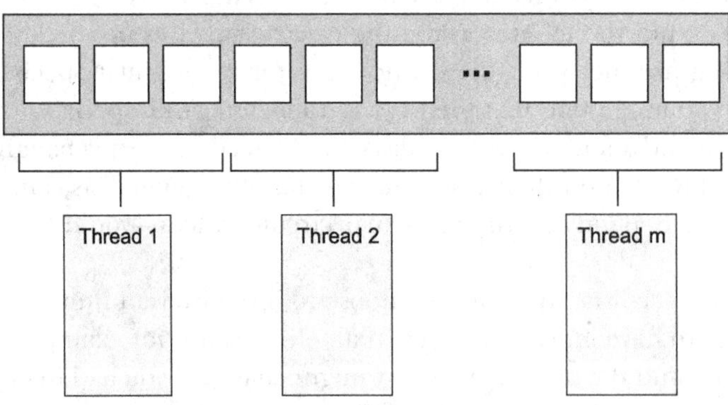

Figure 8.1 Distributing consecutive chunks of data between threads

---

1 http://www.mpi-forum.org/
2 http://www.openmp.org/

case, both the parallel tasks and the final reduction step are accumulations. For a simple `for_each`, the final step is a no-op because there are no results to reduce.

Identifying this final step as a reduction is important; a naïve implementation such as listing 2.8 will perform this reduction as a final serial step. However, this step can often be parallelized as well; `accumulate` actually *is* a reduction operation itself, so listing 2.8 could be modified to call itself recursively where the number of threads is larger than the minimum number of items to process on a thread, for example. Alternatively, the worker threads could be made to perform some of the reduction steps as each one completes its task, rather than spawning new threads each time.

Although this technique is powerful, it can't be applied to everything. Sometimes the data can't be divided neatly up front because the necessary divisions become apparent only as the data is processed. This is particularly apparent with recursive algorithms such as Quicksort; they therefore need a different approach.

8.1.2 Dividing data recursively

The Quicksort algorithm has two basic steps: partition the data into items that come before or after one of the elements (the pivot) in the final sort order and recursively sort those two "halves." You can't parallelize this by simply dividing the data up front, because it's only by processing the items that you know which "half" they go in. If you're going to parallelize such an algorithm, you need to make use of the recursive nature. With each level of recursion there are *more* calls to the `quick_sort` function, because you have to sort both the elements that belong before the pivot *and* those that belong after it. These recursive calls are entirely independent, because they access separate sets of elements, and so are prime candidates for concurrent execution. Figure 8.2 shows such recursive division.

In chapter 4, you saw such an implementation. Rather than just performing two recursive calls for the higher and lower chunks, you used `std::async()` to spawn asynchronous tasks for the lower chunk at each stage. By using `std::async()`, you ask the C++ Thread Library to decide when to actually run the task on a new thread and when to run it synchronously.

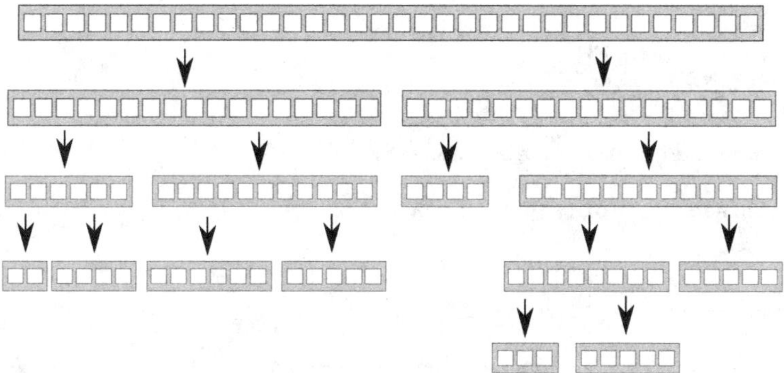

Figure 8.2 Recursively dividing data

This is important: if you're sorting a large set of data, spawning a new thread for each recursion would quickly result in a lot of threads. As you'll see when we look at performance, if you have too many threads, you might actually *slow down* the application. There's also a possibility of running out of threads if the data set is very large. The idea of dividing the overall task in a recursive fashion like this is a good one; you just need to keep a tighter rein on the number of threads. `std::async()` can handle this in simple cases, but it's not the only choice.

One alternative is to use the `std::thread::hardware_concurrency()` function to choose the number of threads, as you did with the parallel version of `accumulate()` from listing 2.8. Then, rather than starting a new thread for the recursive calls, you can just push the chunk to be sorted onto a thread-safe stack such as one of those described in chapters 6 and 7. If a thread has nothing else to do, either because it has finished processing all its chunks or because it's waiting for a chunk to be sorted, it can take a chunk from the stack and sort that.

The following listing shows a sample implementation that uses this technique.

Listing 8.1 Parallel Quicksort using a stack of pending chunks to sort

```
template<typename T>
struct sorter                    <-1
{
    struct chunk_to_sort
    {
        std::list<T> data;
        std::promise<std::list<T> > promise;
    };

    thread_safe_stack<chunk_to_sort> chunks;           <-2
    std::vector<std::thread> threads;              <-3
    unsigned const max_thread_count;
    std::atomic<bool> end_of_data;

    sorter():
        max_thread_count(std::thread::hardware_concurrency()-1),
        end_of_data(false)
    {}

    ~sorter()            <-4
    {
        end_of_data=true;        <-5

        for(unsigned i=0;i<threads.size();++i)
        {
            threads[i].join();       <-6
        }
    }

    void try_sort_chunk()
    {
        boost::shared_ptr<chunk_to_sort > chunk=chunks.pop();      <-7
        if(chunk)
        {
```

```
            sort_chunk(chunk);          ⑧
        }
    }

    std::list<T> do_sort(std::list<T>& chunk_data)      ⑨
    {
        if(chunk_data.empty())
        {
            return chunk_data;
        }

        std::list<T> result;
        result.splice(result.begin(),chunk_data,chunk_data.begin());
        T const& partition_val=*result.begin();

        typename std::list<T>::iterator divide_point=          ⑩
            std::partition(chunk_data.begin(),chunk_data.end(),
                           [&](T const& val){return val<partition_val;});

        chunk_to_sort new_lower_chunk;
        new_lower_chunk.data.splice(new_lower_chunk.data.end(),
                                    chunk_data,chunk_data.begin(),
                                    divide_point);

        std::future<std::list<T> > new_lower=
            new_lower_chunk.promise.get_future();
        chunks.push(std::move(new_lower_chunk));          ⑪
        if(threads.size()<max_thread_count)        ⑫
        {
            threads.push_back(std::thread(&sorter<T>::sort_thread,this));
        }

        std::list<T> new_higher(do_sort(chunk_data));

        result.splice(result.end(),new_higher);
        while(new_lower.wait_for(std::chrono::seconds(0)) !=
              std::future_status::ready)          ⑬
        {
            try_sort_chunk();          ⑭
        }

        result.splice(result.begin(),new_lower.get());
        return result;
    }

    void sort_chunk(boost::shared_ptr<chunk_to_sort > const& chunk)
    {
        chunk->promise.set_value(do_sort(chunk->data));          ⑮
    }

    void sort_thread()
    {
        while(!end_of_data)          ⑯
        {
            try_sort_chunk();          ⑰
            std::this_thread::yield();          ⑱
        }
    }
};
```

```
template<typename T>
std::list<T> parallel_quick_sort(std::list<T> input)     <-19
{
    if(input.empty())
    {
        return input;
    }
    sorter<T> s;

    return s.do_sort(input);     <-20
}
```

Here, the parallel_quick_sort function ⓳ delegates most of the functionality to the sorter class ❶, which provides an easy way of grouping the stack of unsorted chunks ❷ and the set of threads ❸. The main work is done in the do_sort member function ❾, which does the usual partitioning of the data ❿. This time, rather than spawning a new thread for one chunk, it pushes it onto the stack ⓫ and spawns a new thread while you still have processors to spare ⓬. Because the lower chunk might be handled by another thread, you then have to wait for it to be ready ⓭. In order to help things along (in case you're the only thread or all the others are already busy), you try to process chunks from the stack on this thread while you're waiting ⓮. try_sort_chunk just pops a chunk off the stack ❼ and sorts it ❽, storing the result in the promise, ready to be picked up by the thread that posted the chunk on the stack ⓯.

Your freshly spawned threads sit in a loop trying to sort chunks off the stack ⓱ while the end_of_data flag isn't set ⓰. In between checking, they yield to other threads ⓲ to give them a chance to put some more work on the stack. This code relies on the destructor of your sorter class ❹ to tidy up these threads. When all the data has been sorted, do_sort will return (even though the worker threads are still running), so your main thread will return from parallel_quick_sort ⓴ and thus destroy your sorter object. This sets the end_of_data flag ❺ and waits for the threads to finish ❻. Setting the flag terminates the loop in the thread function ⓰.

With this approach you no longer have the problem of unbounded threads that you have with a spawn_task that launches a new thread, and you're no longer relying on the C++ Thread Library to choose the number of threads for you, as it does with std::async(). Instead, you limit the number of threads to the value of std::thread::hardware_concurrency() in order to avoid excessive task switching. You do, however, have another potential problem: the management of these threads and the communication between them add quite a lot of complexity to the code. Also, although the threads are processing separate data elements, they all access the stack to add new chunks and to remove chunks for processing. This heavy contention can reduce performance, even if you use a lock-free (and hence nonblocking) stack, for reasons that you'll see shortly.

This approach is a specialized version of a *thread pool*—there's a set of threads that each take work to do from a list of pending work, do the work, and then go back to the list for more. Some of the potential problems with thread pools (including the contention on the work list) and ways of addressing them are covered in chapter 9.

The problems of scaling your application to multiple processors are discussed in more detail later in this chapter (see section 8.2.1).

Both dividing the data before processing begins and dividing it recursively presume that the data itself is fixed beforehand, and you're just looking at ways of dividing it. This isn't always the case; if the data is dynamically generated or is coming from external input, this approach doesn't work. In this case, it might make more sense to divide the work by task type rather than dividing based on the data.

8.1.3 Dividing work by task type

Dividing work between threads by allocating different chunks of data to each thread (whether up front or recursively during processing) still rests on the assumption that the threads are going to be doing essentially the same work on each chunk of data. An alternative to dividing the work is to make the threads specialists, where each performs a distinct task, just as plumbers and electricians perform distinct tasks when building a house. Threads may or may not work on the same data, but if they do, it's for different purposes.

This is the sort of division of work that results from separating concerns with concurrency; each thread has a different task, which it carries out independently of other threads. Occasionally other threads may give it data or trigger events that it needs to handle, but in general each thread focuses on doing one thing well. In itself, this is basic good design; each piece of code should have a single responsibility.

DIVIDING WORK BY TASK TYPE TO SEPARATE CONCERNS

A single-threaded application has to handle conflicts with the single responsibility principle where there are multiple tasks that need to be run continuously over a period of time, or where the application needs to be able to handle incoming events (such as user key presses or incoming network data) in a timely fashion, even while other tasks are ongoing. In the single-threaded world you end up manually writing code that performs a bit of task A, performs a bit of task B, checks for key presses, checks for incoming network packets, and then loops back to perform another bit of task A. This means that the code for task A ends up being complicated by the need to save its state and return control to the main loop periodically. If you add too many tasks to the loop, things might slow down too far, and the user may find it takes too long to respond to the key press. I'm sure you've all seen the extreme form of this in action with some application or other: you set it doing some task, and the interface freezes until it has completed the task.

This is where threads come in. If you run each of the tasks in a separate thread, the operating system handles this for you. In the code for task A, you can focus on performing the task and not worry about saving state and returning to the main loop or how long you spend before doing so. The operating system will automatically save the state and switch to task B or C when appropriate, and if the target system has multiple cores or processors, tasks A and B may well be able to run truly concurrently. The code for handling the key press or network packet will now be run in a timely fashion, and everybody wins: the user gets timely responses, and you as developer have simpler code because each thread can focus on doing operations related directly to its responsibilities, rather than getting mixed up with control flow and user interaction.

That sounds like a nice, rosy vision. Can it really be like that? As with everything, it depends on the details. If everything really is independent, and the threads have no need to communicate with each other, then it really is this easy. Unfortunately, the world is rarely like that. These nice background tasks are often doing something that the user requested, and they need to let the user know when they're done by updating the user interface in some manner. Alternatively, the user might want to cancel the task, which therefore requires the user interface to somehow send a message to the background task telling it to stop. Both these cases require careful thought and design and suitable synchronization, but the concerns are still separate. The user interface thread still just handles the user interface, but it might have to update it when asked to do so by other threads. Likewise, the thread running the background task still just focuses on the operations required for that task; it just happens that one of them is "allow task to be stopped by another thread." In neither case do the threads care where the request came from, only that it was intended for them and relates directly to their responsibilities.

There are two big dangers with separating concerns with multiple threads. The first is that you'll end up separating the *wrong* concerns. The symptoms to check for are that there is a lot of data shared between the threads or the different threads end up waiting for each other; both cases boil down to too much communication between threads. If this happens, it's worth looking at the reasons for the communication. If all the communication relates to the same issue, maybe that should be the key responsibility of a single thread and extracted from all the threads that refer to it. Alternatively, if two threads are communicating a lot with each other but much less with other threads, maybe they should be combined into a single thread.

When dividing work across threads by task type, you don't have to limit yourself to completely isolated cases. If multiple sets of input data require the same *sequence* of operations to be applied, you can divide the work so each thread performs one stage from the overall sequence.

DIVIDING A SEQUENCE OF TASKS BETWEEN THREADS

If your task consists of applying the same sequence of operations to many independent data items, you can use a *pipeline* to exploit the available concurrency of your system. This is by analogy to a physical pipeline: data flows in at one end through a series of operations (pipes) and out at the other end.

To divide the work this way, you create a separate thread for each stage in the pipeline—one thread for each of the operations in the sequence. When the operation is completed, the data element is put on a queue to be picked up by the next thread. This allows the thread performing the first operation in the sequence to start on the next data element while the second thread in the pipeline is working on the first element.

This is an alternative to just dividing the data between threads, as described in section 8.1.1, and is appropriate in circumstances where the input data itself isn't all known when the operation is started. For example, the data might be coming in over a network, or the first operation in the sequence might be to scan a filesystem in order to identify files to process.

Pipelines are also good where each operation in the sequence is time consuming; by dividing the tasks between threads rather than the data, you change the performance profile. Suppose you have 20 data items to process, on four cores, and each data item requires four steps, which take 3 seconds each. If you divide the data between four threads, then each thread has 5 items to process. Assuming there's no other processing that might affect the timings, after 12 seconds you'll have 4 items processed, after 24 seconds 8 items processed, and so forth. All 20 items will be done after 1 minute. With a pipeline, things work differently. Your four steps can be assigned one to each processing core. Now the first item has to be processed by each core, so it still takes the full 12 seconds. Indeed, after 12 seconds you only have one item processed, which isn't as good as with the division by data. However, once the pipeline is *primed*, things proceed a bit differently; after the first core has processed the first item, it moves on to the second, so once the final core has processed the first item, it can perform its step on the second. You now get one item processed every 3 seconds rather than having the items processed in batches of four every 12 seconds.

The overall time to process the entire batch takes longer because you have to wait 9 seconds before the final core starts processing the first item. But smoother, more regular processing can be beneficial in some circumstances. Consider, for example, a system for watching high-definition digital videos. In order for the video to be watchable, you typically need at least 25 frames per second and ideally more. Also, the viewer needs these to be evenly spaced to give the impression of continuous movement; an application that can decode 100 frames per second is still no use if it pauses for a second, then displays 100 frames, then pauses for another second, and displays another 100 frames. On the other hand, viewers are probably happy to accept a delay of a couple of seconds when they *start* watching a video. In this case, parallelizing using a pipeline that outputs frames at a nice steady rate is probably preferable.

Having looked at various techniques for dividing the work between threads, let's take a look at the factors affecting the performance of a multithreaded system and how that can impact your choice of techniques.

8.2 Factors affecting the performance of concurrent code

If you're using concurrency in order to improve the performance of your code on systems with multiple processors, you need to know what factors are going to affect the performance. Even if you're just using multiple threads to separate concerns, you need to ensure that this doesn't adversely affect the performance. Customers won't thank you if your application runs *more slowly* on their shiny new 16-core machine than it did on their old single-core one.

As you'll see shortly, many factors affect the performance of multithreaded code—even something as simple as changing *which* data elements are processed by each thread (while keeping everything else identical) can have a dramatic effect on performance. So, without further ado, let's look at some of these factors, starting with the obvious one: how many processors does your target system have?

8.2.1 How many processors?

The number (and structure) of processors is the first big factor that affects the performance of a multithreaded application, and it's quite a crucial one. In some cases you do know exactly what the target hardware is and can thus design with this in mind, taking real measurements on the target system or an exact duplicate. If so, you're one of the lucky ones; in general you don't have that luxury. You might be developing on a *similar* system, but the differences can be crucial. For example, you might be developing on a dual- or quad-core system, but your customers' systems may have one multicore processor (with any number of cores), or multiple single-core processors, or even multiple multicore processors. The behavior and performance characteristics of a concurrent program can vary considerably under such different circumstances, so you need to think carefully about what the impact may be and test things where possible.

To a first approximation, a single 16-core processor is the same as 4 quad-core processors or 16 single-core processors: in each case the system can run 16 threads concurrently. If you want to take advantage of this, your application must have at least 16 threads. If it has fewer than 16, you're leaving processor power on the table (unless the system is running other applications too, but we'll ignore that possibility for now). On the other hand, if you have more than 16 threads actually ready to run (and not blocked, waiting for something), your application will waste processor time switching between the threads, as discussed in chapter 1. When this happens, the situation is called *oversubscription*.

To allow applications to scale the number of threads in line with the number of threads the hardware can run concurrently, the C++11 Standard Thread Library provides `std::thread::hardware_concurrency()`. You've already seen how that can be used to scale the number of threads to the hardware.

Using `std::thread::hardware_concurrency()` directly requires care; your code doesn't take into account any of the other threads that are running on the system unless you explicitly share that information. In the worst case, if multiple threads call a function that uses `std::thread::hardware_concurrency()` for scaling at the same time, there will be huge oversubscription. `std::async()` avoids this problem because the library is aware of all calls and can schedule appropriately. Careful use of thread pools can also avoid this problem.

However, even if you take into account all threads running in your application, you're still subject to the impact of other applications running at the same time. Although the use of multiple CPU-intensive applications simultaneously is rare on single-user systems, there are some domains where it's more common. Systems designed to handle this scenario typically offer mechanisms to allow each application to choose an appropriate number of threads, although these mechanisms are outside the scope of the C++ Standard. One option is for a `std::async()`-like facility to take into account the total number of asynchronous tasks run by all applications when choosing the number of threads. Another is to limit the number of processing cores that can be used by a given application. I'd expect such a limit to be reflected in the value returned by `std::thread::hardware_concurrency()` on such platforms, although this isn't guaranteed. If you need to handle this scenario, consult your system documentation to see what options are available to you.

One additional twist to this situation is that the ideal algorithm for a problem can depend on the size of the problem compared to the number of processing units. If you have a *massively parallel* system with many processing units, an algorithm that performs more operations overall may finish more quickly than one that performs fewer operations, because each processor performs only a few operations.

As the number of processors increases, so does the likelihood and performance impact of another problem: that of multiple processors trying to access the same data.

8.2.2 Data contention and cache ping-pong

If two threads are executing concurrently on different processors and they're both *reading* the same data, this usually won't cause a problem; the data will be copied into their respective caches, and both processors can proceed. However, if one of the threads *modifies* the data, this change then has to propagate to the cache on the other core, which takes time. Depending on the nature of the operations on the two threads, and the memory orderings used for the operations, such a modification may cause the second processor to stop in its tracks and wait for the change to propagate through the memory hardware. In terms of CPU instructions, this can be a *phenomenally* slow operation, equivalent to many hundreds of individual instructions, although the exact timing depends primarily on the physical structure of the hardware.

Consider the following simple piece of code:

```
std::atomic<unsigned long> counter(0);
void processing_loop()
{
    while(counter.fetch_add(1,std::memory_order_relaxed)<100000000)
    {
        do_something();
    }
}
```

The `counter` is global, so any threads that call `processing_loop()` are modifying the same variable. Therefore, for each increment the processor must ensure it has an up-to-date copy of `counter` in its cache, modify the value, and publish it to other processors. Even though you're using `std::memory_order_relaxed`, so the compiler doesn't have to synchronize any other data, `fetch_add` is a read-modify-write operation and therefore needs to retrieve the most recent value of the variable. If another thread on another processor is running the same code, the data for `counter` must therefore be passed back and forth between the two processors and their corresponding caches so that each processor has the latest value for `counter` when it does the increment. If `do_something()` is short enough, or if there are too many processors running this code, the processors might actually find themselves *waiting* for each other; one processor is ready to update the value, but another processor is currently doing that, so it has to wait until the second processor has completed its update and the change has propagated. This situation is called *high contention*. If the processors rarely have to wait for each other, you have *low contention*.

In a loop like this one, the data for `counter` will be passed back and forth between the caches many times. This is called *cache ping-pong*, and it can seriously impact the performance of the application. If a processor stalls because it has to wait for a cache transfer, it can't do *any* work in the meantime, even if there are other threads waiting that could do useful work, so this is bad news for the whole application.

You might think that this won't happen to you; after all, you don't have any loops like that. Are you sure? What about mutex locks? If you acquire a mutex in a loop, your code is similar to the previous code from the point of view of data accesses. In order to lock the mutex, another thread must transfer the data that makes up the mutex to its processor and modify it. When it's done, it modifies the mutex again to unlock it, and the mutex data has to be transferred to the next thread to acquire the mutex. This transfer time is *in addition to* any time that the second thread has to wait for the first to release the mutex:

```
std::mutex m;
my_data data;
void processing_loop_with_mutex()
{
    while(true)
    {
        std::lock_guard<std::mutex> lk(m);
        if(done_processing(data)) break;
    }
}
```

Now, here's the worst part: if the data and mutex really are accessed by more than one thread, then as you add more cores and processors to the system, it becomes *more likely* that you will get high contention and one processor having to wait for another. If you're using multiple threads to process the same data more quickly, the threads are competing for the data and thus competing for the same mutex. The more of them there are, the more likely they'll try to acquire the mutex at the same time, or access the atomic variable at the same time, and so forth.

The effects of contention with mutexes are usually different from the effects of contention with atomic operations for the simple reason that the use of a mutex naturally serializes threads at the operating system level rather than at the processor level. If you have enough threads ready to run, the operating system can schedule another thread to run while one thread is waiting for the mutex, whereas a processor stall prevents any threads from running on that processor. However, it will still impact the performance of those threads that *are* competing for the mutex; they can only run one at a time, after all.

Back in chapter 3, you saw how a rarely updated data structure can be protected with a single-writer, multiple-reader mutex (see section 3.3.2). Cache ping-pong effects can nullify the benefits of such a mutex if the workload is unfavorable, because all threads accessing the data (even reader threads) still have to modify the mutex itself. As the number of processors accessing the data goes up, the contention on the mutex itself increases, and the cache line holding the mutex must be transferred between cores, thus potentially increasing the time taken to acquire and release locks to undesirable levels. There are techniques to ameliorate this problem, essentially by spreading out the mutex across multiple cache lines, but unless you implement your own such mutex, you are subject to whatever your system provides.

If this cache ping-pong is bad, how can you avoid it? As you'll see later in the chapter, the answer ties in nicely with general guidelines for improving the potential for concurrency: do what you can to reduce the potential for two threads competing for the same memory location.

It's not quite that simple, though; things never are. Even if a particular memory location is only ever accessed by one thread, you can *still* get cache ping-pong due to an effect known as *false sharing*.

8.2.3 False sharing

Processor caches don't generally deal in individual memory locations; instead, they deal in blocks of memory called *cache lines*. These blocks of memory are typically 32 or 64 bytes in size, but the exact details depend on the particular processor model being used. Because the cache hardware only deals in cache-line-sized blocks of memory, small data items in adjacent memory locations will be in the same cache line. Sometimes this is good: if a set of data accessed by a thread is in the same cache line, this is better for the performance of the application than if the same set of data was spread over multiple cache lines. However, if the data items in a cache line are unrelated and need to be accessed by different threads, this can be a major cause of performance problems.

Suppose you have an array of `int` values and a set of threads that each access their own entry in the array but do so repeatedly, including updates. Since an `int` is typically much smaller than a cache line, quite a few of those array entries will be in the same cache line. Consequently, even though each thread only accesses its own array entry, the cache hardware *still* has to play cache ping-pong. Every time the thread accessing entry 0 needs to update the value, ownership of the cache line needs to be transferred to the processor running that thread, only to be transferred to the cache for the processor running the thread for entry 1 when that thread needs to update its data item. The cache line is shared, even though none of the data is, hence the term *false sharing*. The solution here is to structure the data so that data items to be accessed by the same thread are close together in memory (and thus more likely to be in the same cache line), whereas those that are to be accessed by separate threads are far apart in memory and thus more likely to be in separate cache lines. You'll see how this affects the design of the code and data later in this chapter.

If having multiple threads access data from the same cache line is bad, how does the memory layout of data accessed by a single thread affect things?

8.2.4 How close is your data?

Whereas false sharing is caused by having data accessed by one thread too close to data accessed by another thread, another pitfall associated with data layout directly impacts the performance of a single thread on its own. The issue is data proximity: if the data accessed by a single thread is spread out in memory, it's likely that it lies on separate cache lines. On the flip side, if the data accessed by a single thread is close together in memory, it's more likely to lie on the same cache line. Consequently, if data is spread out, more cache lines must be loaded from memory onto the processor cache, which can increase memory access latency and reduce performance compared to data that's located close together.

Also, if the data is spread out, there's an increased chance that a given cache line containing data for the current thread also contains data that's *not* for the current thread. At the extreme there'll be more data in the cache that you don't care about than data that you do. This wastes precious cache space and thus increases the chance that the processor will experience a cache miss and have to fetch a data item from main memory even if it once held it in the cache, because it had to remove the item from the cache to make room for another.

Now, this is important with single-threaded code, so why am I bringing it up here? The reason is *task switching*. If there are more threads than cores in the system, each core is going to be running multiple threads. This increases the pressure on the cache, as you try to ensure that different threads are accessing different cache lines in order to avoid false sharing. Consequently, when the processor switches threads, it's more likely to have to reload the cache lines if each thread uses data spread across multiple cache lines than if each thread's data is close together in the same cache line.

If there are more threads than cores or processors, the operating system might also choose to schedule a thread on one core for one time slice and then on another core for the next time slice. This will therefore require transferring the cache lines for that thread's data from the cache for the first core to the cache for the second; the more cache lines that need transferring, the more time consuming this will be. Although operating systems typically avoid this when they can, it does happen and does impact performance when it happens.

Task-switching problems are particularly prevalent when lots of threads are *ready to run* as opposed to *waiting*. This is an issue we've already touched on: oversubscription.

8.2.5 Oversubscription and excessive task switching

In multithreaded systems, it's typical to have more threads than processors, unless you're running on *massively parallel* hardware. However, threads often spend time waiting for external I/O to complete or blocked on mutexes or waiting for condition variables and so forth, so this isn't a problem. Having the extra threads enables the application to perform useful work rather than having processors sitting idle while the threads wait.

This isn't always a good thing. If you have *too many* additional threads, there will be more threads *ready to run* than there are available processors, and the operating system will have to start task switching quite heavily in order to ensure they all get a fair time slice. As you saw in chapter 1, this can increase the overhead of the task switching as well as compound any cache problems resulting from lack of proximity. Oversubscription can arise when you have a task that repeatedly spawns new threads without limits, as the recursive quick sort from chapter 4 did, or where the natural number of threads when you separate by task type is more than the number of processors and the work is naturally CPU bound rather than I/O bound.

If you're simply spawning too many threads because of data division, you can limit the number of worker threads, as you saw in section 8.1.2. If the oversubscription is due to the natural division of work, there's not a lot you can do to ameliorate the problem save for choosing a different division. In that case, choosing the appropriate division may require more knowledge of the target platform than you have available and is only worth doing if performance is unacceptable and it can be demonstrated that changing the division of work does improve performance.

Other factors can affect the performance of multithreaded code. The cost of cache ping-pong can vary quite considerably between two single-core processors and a single dual-core processor, even if they're the same CPU type and clock speed, for example, but these are the major ones that will have a very visible impact. Let's now look at how that affects the design of the code and data structures.

8.3 Designing data structures for multithreaded performance

In section 8.1 we looked at various ways of dividing work between threads, and in section 8.2 we looked at various factors that can affect the performance of your code. How can you use this information when designing data structures for multithreaded performance? This is a different question than that addressed in chapters 6 and 7, which were about designing data structures that are safe for concurrent access. As you've just seen in section 8.2, the layout of the data used by a single thread can have an impact, even if that data isn't shared with any other threads.

The key things to bear in mind when designing your data structures for multithreaded performance are *contention*, *false sharing*, and *data proximity*. All three of these can have a big impact on performance, and you can often improve things just by altering the data layout or changing which data elements are assigned to which thread. First off, let's look at an easy win: dividing array elements between threads.

8.3.1 Dividing array elements for complex operations

Suppose you're doing some heavy-duty math, and you need to multiply two large square matrices together. To multiply matrices, you multiply each element in the first *row* of the first matrix with the corresponding element of the first *column* of the second matrix and add up the products to give the top-left element of the result. You then repeat this with the second row and the first column to give the second element in the first column of the result, and with the first row and second column to give the first element in the second column of the result, and so forth. This is shown in figure 8.3; the highlighting shows that the second row of the first matrix is paired with the third column of the second matrix to give the entry in the second row of the third column of the result.

Now let's assume that these are *large* matrices with several thousand rows and columns, in order to make it worthwhile using multiple threads to optimize the multiplication. Typically, a non-sparse matrix is represented by a big array in memory, with all the elements of the first row followed by all the elements of the second row, and so forth. To multiply your matrices you thus have three of these huge arrays. In order to get optimal performance, you need to pay careful attention to the data access patterns, particularly the writes to the third array.

There are many ways you can divide the work between threads. Assuming you have more rows/columns than available processors, you could have each thread calculate the values for a number of columns in the result matrix, or have each thread calculate the results for a number of rows, or even have each thread calculate the results for a rectangular subset of the matrix.

Back in sections 8.2.3 and 8.2.4, you saw that it's better to access contiguous elements from an array rather than values all over the place, because this reduces cache usage and the chance of false sharing. If you have each thread handle a set of columns, it needs to read every value from the first matrix and the values from the corresponding columns in the second matrix, but you only have to write the column values. Given that the matrices are stored with the rows contiguous, this means that you're accessing N elements from the first row, N elements from the second, and so forth (where N is the number of columns you're processing). Since other threads will be accessing the other elements of each row, it's clear that you ought to be accessing adjacent columns, so the N

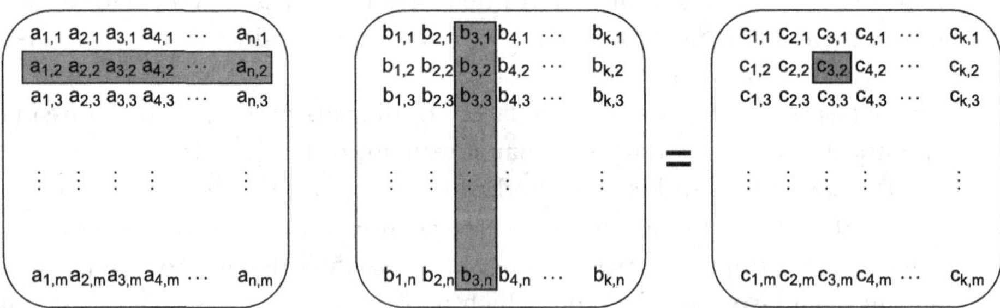

Figure 8.3 Matrix multiplication

elements from each row are adjacent, and you minimize false sharing. Of course, if the space occupied by your *N* elements is an exact number of cache lines, there'll be no false sharing because threads will be working on separate cache lines.

On the other hand, if you have each thread handle a set of *rows*, then it needs to read every value from the *second* matrix and the values from the corresponding *rows* of the *first* matrix, but it only has to write the row values. Because the matrices are stored with the rows contiguous, you're now accessing *all* elements from *N* rows. If you again choose adjacent rows, this means that the thread is now the *only* thread writing to those *N* rows; it has a contiguous block of memory that's not touched by any other thread. This is likely an improvement over having each thread handle a set of columns, because the only possibility of false sharing is for the last few elements of one block with the first few of the next, but it's worth timing it on the target architecture to confirm.

What about your third option—dividing into rectangular blocks? This can be viewed as dividing into columns and then dividing into rows. As such, it has the same false-sharing potential as division by columns. If you can choose the number of columns in the block to avoid this possibility, there's an advantage to rectangular division from the *read* side: you don't need to read the entirety of either source matrix. You only need to read the values corresponding to the rows and columns of the target rectangle. To look at this in concrete terms, consider multiplying two matrices that have 1,000 rows and 1,000 columns. That's 1 million elements. If you have 100 processors, they can handle 10 rows each for a nice round 10,000 elements. However, to calculate the results of those 10,000 elements, they need to access the entirety of the second matrix (1 million elements) plus the 10,000 elements from the corresponding rows in the first matrix, for a grand total of 1,010,000 elements. On the other hand, if they each handle a block of 100 elements by 100 elements (which is still 10,000 elements total), they need to access the values from 100 rows of the first matrix (100 x 1,000 = 100,000 elements) and 100 columns of the second matrix (another 100,000). This is only 200,000 elements, which is a five-fold reduction in the number of elements read. If you're reading fewer elements, there's less chance of a cache miss and the potential for greater performance.

It may therefore be better to divide the result matrix into small square or almost-square blocks rather than have each thread handle the entirety of a small number of rows. Of course, you can adjust the size of each block at runtime, depending on the size of the matrices and the available number of processors. As ever, if performance is important, it's vital to profile various options on the target architecture.

Chances are you're not doing matrix multiplication, so how does this apply to you? The same principles apply to any situation where you have large blocks of data to divide between threads; look at all the aspects of the data access patterns carefully, and identify the potential causes of performance hits. There may be similar circumstances in your problem domain where changing the division of work can improve performance without requiring any change to the basic algorithm.

OK, so we've looked at how access patterns in arrays can affect performance. What about other types of data structures?

8.3.2 Data access patterns in other data structures

Fundamentally, the same considerations apply when trying to optimize the data access patterns of other data structures as when optimizing access to arrays:

- Try to adjust the data distribution between threads so that data that's close together is worked on by the same thread.
- Try to minimize the data required by any given thread.
- Try to ensure that data accessed by separate threads is sufficiently far apart to avoid false sharing.

Of course, that's not easy to apply to other data structures. For example, binary trees are inherently difficult to subdivide in any unit other than a subtree, which may or may not be useful, depending on how balanced the tree is and how many sections you need to divide it into. Also, the nature of the trees means that the nodes are likely dynamically allocated and thus end up in different places on the heap.

Now, having data end up in different places on the heap isn't a particular problem in itself, but it does mean that the processor has to keep more things in cache. This can actually be beneficial. If multiple threads need to traverse the tree, then they all need to access the tree nodes, but if the tree nodes only contain *pointers* to the real data held at the node, then the processor only has to load the data from memory if it's actually needed. If the data is being modified by the threads that need it, this can avoid the performance hit of false sharing between the node data itself and the data that provides the tree structure.

There's a similar issue with data protected by a mutex. Suppose you have a simple class that contains a few data items and a mutex used to protect accesses from multiple threads. If the mutex and the data items are close together in memory, this is ideal for a thread that acquires the mutex; the data it needs may well already be in the processor cache, because it was just loaded in order to modify the mutex. But there's also a downside: if other threads try to lock the mutex while it's held by the first thread, they'll need access to that memory. Mutex locks are typically implemented as a read-modify-write atomic operation on a memory location within the mutex to try to acquire the mutex, followed by a call to the operating system kernel if the mutex is already locked. This read-modify-write operation may well cause the data held in the cache by the thread that owns the mutex to be invalidated. As far as the mutex goes, this isn't a problem; that thread isn't going to touch the mutex until it unlocks it. However, if the mutex shares a cache line with the data being used by the thread, the thread that owns the mutex can take a performance hit *because another thread tried to lock the mutex*!

One way to test whether this kind of false sharing is a problem is to add huge blocks of padding between the data elements that can be concurrently accessed by different threads. For example, you can use

```
struct protected_data
{
    std::mutex m;
    char padding[65536];
    my_data data_to_protect;
};
```

65536 bytes is orders of magnitude larger than a cache line

to test the mutex contention issue or

```
struct my_data
{
    data_item1 d1;
    data_item2 d2;
    char padding[65536];
};
my_data some_array[256];
```

to test for false sharing of array data. If this improves the performance, you know that false sharing was a problem, and you can either leave the padding in or work to eliminate the false sharing in another way by rearranging the data accesses.

Of course, there's more than just the data access patterns to consider when designing for concurrency, so let's look at some of these additional considerations.

8.4 Additional considerations when designing for concurrency

So far in this chapter we've looked at ways of dividing work between threads, factors affecting performance, and how these factors affect your choice of data access patterns and data structures. There's more to designing code for concurrency than just that, though. You also need to consider things such as exception safety and scalability. Code is said to be *scalable* if the performance (whether in terms of reduced speed of execution or increased throughput) increases as more processing cores are added to the system. Ideally, the performance increase is linear, so a system with 100 processors performs 100 times better than a system with one processor.

Although code can work even if it isn't scalable—a single-threaded application is certainly not scalable, for example—exception safety is a matter of correctness. If your code isn't exception safe, you can end up with broken invariants or race conditions, or your application might terminate unexpectedly because an operation threw an exception. With this in mind, we'll look at exception safety first.

8.4.1 Exception safety in parallel algorithms

Exception safety is an essential aspect of good C++ code, and code that uses concurrency is no exception. In fact, parallel algorithms often require that you take more care with regard to exceptions than normal sequential algorithms. If an operation in a sequential algorithm throws an exception, the algorithm only has to worry about ensuring that it tidies up after itself to avoid resource leaks and broken invariants; it can merrily allow the exception to propagate to the caller for them to handle. By contrast, in a parallel algorithm many of the operations will be running on separate threads. In this case, the exception can't be allowed to propagate because it's on the wrong call stack. If a function spawned on a new thread exits with an exception, the application is terminated.

As a concrete example, let's revisit the `parallel_accumulate` function from listing 2.8, which is reproduced here.

Listing 8.2 A naïve parallel version of `std::accumulate` (from listing 2.8)

```
template<typename Iterator,typename T>
struct accumulate_block
{
    void operator()(Iterator first,Iterator last,T& result)
    {
        result=std::accumulate(first,last,result);           ❶
    }
};

template<typename Iterator,typename T>
T parallel_accumulate(Iterator first,Iterator last,T init)
{
    unsigned long const length=std::distance(first,last);      ❷

    if(!length)
        return init;

    unsigned long const min_per_thread=25;
    unsigned long const max_threads=
        (length+min_per_thread-1)/min_per_thread;

    unsigned long const hardware_threads=
        std::thread::hardware_concurrency();

    unsigned long const num_threads=
        std::min(hardware_threads!=0?hardware_threads:2,max_threads);

    unsigned long const block_size=length/num_threads;

    std::vector<T> results(num_threads);                  ❸
    std::vector<std::thread>  threads(num_threads-1);         ❹

    Iterator block_start=first;                           ❺
    for(unsigned long i=0;i<(num_threads-1);++i)
    {
        Iterator block_end=block_start;              ❻
        std::advance(block_end,block_size);
        threads[i]=std::thread(                      ❼
            accumulate_block<Iterator,T>(),
            block_start,block_end,std::ref(results[i]));
        block_start=block_end;                             ❽
    }
    accumulate_block()(block_start,last,results[num_threads-1]);     ❾

    std::for_each(threads.begin(),threads.end(),
        std::mem_fn(&std::thread::join));

    return std::accumulate(results.begin(),results.end(),init);     ❿
}
```

Now let's go through and identify the places where an exception can be thrown: basically anywhere where you call a function you know can throw or you perform an operation on a user-defined type that may throw.

First up, you have the call to `distance` ❷, which performs operations on the user-supplied iterator type. Because you haven't yet done any work, and this is on the calling thread, it's fine. Next up, you have the allocation of the `results` vector ❸ and the `threads` vector ❹. Again, these are on the calling thread, and you haven't done any work or spawned any threads, so this is fine. Of course, if the construction of `threads` throws, the memory allocated for `results` will have to be cleaned up, but the destructor will take care of that for you.

Skipping over the initialization of `block_start` ❺ because that's similarly safe, you come to the operations in the thread-spawning loop ❻, ❼, ❽. Once you've been through the creation of the first thread at ❼, you're in trouble if you throw any exceptions; the destructors of your new `std::thread` objects will call `std::terminate` and abort your program. This isn't a good place to be.

The call to `accumulate_block` ❾ can potentially throw, with similar consequences; your thread objects will be destroyed and call `std::terminate`. On the other hand, the final call to `std::accumulate` ❿ can throw without causing any hardship, because all the threads have been joined by this point.

That's it for the main thread, but there's more: the calls to `accumulate_block` on the new threads might throw at ❶. There aren't any `catch` blocks, so this exception will be left unhandled and cause the library to call `std::terminate()` to abort the application.

In case it's not glaringly obvious, *this code isn't exception-safe.*

ADDING EXCEPTION SAFETY

OK, so we've identified all the possible `throw` points and the nasty consequences of exceptions. What can you do about it? Let's start by addressing the issue of the exceptions thrown on your new threads.

You encountered the tool for this job in chapter 4. If you look carefully at what you're trying to achieve with new threads, it's apparent that you're trying to calculate a result to return while allowing for the possibility that the code might throw an exception. This is *precisely* what the combination of `std::packaged_task` and `std::future` is designed for. If you rearrange your code to use `std::packaged_task`, you end up the following code.

Listing 8.3 A parallel version of `std::accumulate` using `std::packaged_task`

```
template<typename Iterator,typename T>
struct accumulate_block
{
    T operator()(Iterator first,Iterator last)          ❶
    {
        return std::accumulate(first,last,T());          ❷
    }
};
```

```
template<typename Iterator,typename T>
T parallel_accumulate(Iterator first,Iterator last,T init)
{
    unsigned long const length=std::distance(first,last);

    if(!length)
        return init;

    unsigned long const min_per_thread=25;
    unsigned long const max_threads=
        (length+min_per_thread-1)/min_per_thread;

    unsigned long const hardware_threads=
        std::thread::hardware_concurrency();

    unsigned long const num_threads=
        std::min(hardware_threads!=0?hardware_threads:2,max_threads);

    unsigned long const block_size=length/num_threads;

    std::vector<std::future<T> > futures(num_threads-1);        ❸
    std::vector<std::thread> threads(num_threads-1);

    Iterator block_start=first;
    for(unsigned long i=0;i<(num_threads-1);++i)
    {
        Iterator block_end=block_start;
        std::advance(block_end,block_size);
        std::packaged_task<T(Iterator,Iterator)> task(        ❹
            accumulate_block<Iterator,T>());
        futures[i]=task.get_future();                          ❺
        threads[i]=std::thread(std::move(task),block_start,block_end);   ❻
        block_start=block_end;
    }
    T last_result=accumulate_block()(block_start,last);       ❼

    std::for_each(threads.begin(),threads.end(),
        std::mem_fn(&std::thread::join));

    T result=init;                                          ❽
    for(unsigned long i=0;i<(num_threads-1);++i)
    {
        result+=futures[i].get();      ❾
    }
    result += last_result;      ❿
    return result;
}
```

The first change is that the function call operator of accumulate_block now returns the result directly, rather than taking a reference to somewhere to store it ❶. You're using std::packaged_task and std::future for the exception safety, so you can use it to transfer the result too. This does require that you explicitly pass in a default-constructed T in the call to std::accumulate ❷ rather than reusing the supplied result value, but that's a minor change.

The next change is that rather than having a vector of results, you have a vector of futures ❸ to store a std::future<T> for each spawned thread. In the thread-spawning loop, you first create a task for `accumulate_block` ❹. `std::packaged_task<T(Iterator, Iterator)>` declares a task that takes two `Iterator`s and returns a `T`, which is what your function does. You then get the future for that task ❺ and run that task on a new thread, passing in the start and end of the block to process ❻. When the task runs, the result will be captured in the future, as will any exception thrown.

Since you've been using futures, you don't have a result array, so you must store the result from the final block in a variable ❼ rather than in a slot in the array. Also, because you have to get the values out of the futures, it's now simpler to use a basic `for` loop rather than `std::accumulate`, starting with the supplied initial value ❽ and adding in the result from each future ❾. If the corresponding task threw an exception, this will have been captured in the future and will now be thrown again by the call to `get()`. Finally, you add the result from the last block ❿ before returning the overall result to the caller.

So, that's removed one of the potential problems: exceptions thrown in the worker threads are rethrown in the main thread. If more than one of the worker threads throws an exception, only one will be propagated, but that's not too big a deal. If it really matters, you can use something like `std::nested_exception` to capture all the exceptions and throw that instead.

The remaining problem is the leaking threads if an exception is thrown between when you spawn the first thread and when you've joined with them all. The simplest solution is just to catch any exceptions, join with the threads that are still `joinable()`, and rethrow the exception:

```
try
{
    for(unsigned long i=0;i<(num_threads-1);++i)
    {
        // ... as before
    }
    T last_result=accumulate_block()(block_start,last);

    std::for_each(threads.begin(),threads.end(),
        std::mem_fn(&std::thread::join));
}
catch(...)
{
    for(unsigned long i=0;i<(num_thread-1);++i)
    {
        if(threads[i].joinable())
            thread[i].join();
    }
    throw;
}
```

Now this works. All the threads will be joined, no matter how the code leaves the block. However, `try-catch` blocks are ugly, and you have duplicate code. You're joining the threads both in the "normal" control flow *and* in the `catch` block. Duplicate code is rarely a good thing, because it means more places to change. Instead, let's extract this out into the destructor of an object; it is, after all, the idiomatic way of cleaning up resources in C++. Here's your class:

```
class join_threads
{
    std::vector<std::thread>& threads;
public:
    explicit join_threads(std::vector<std::thread>& threads_):
        threads(threads_)
    {}
    ~join_threads()
    {
        for(unsigned long i=0;i<threads.size();++i)
        {
            if(threads[i].joinable())
                threads[i].join();
        }
    }
};
```

This is similar to your thread_guard class from listing 2.3, except it's extended for the whole vector of threads. You can then simplify your code as follows.

Listing 8.4 An exception-safe parallel version of `std::accumulate`

```
template<typename Iterator,typename T>
T parallel_accumulate(Iterator first,Iterator last,T init)
{
    unsigned long const length=std::distance(first,last);

    if(!length)
        return init;

    unsigned long const min_per_thread=25;
    unsigned long const max_threads=
        (length+min_per_thread-1)/min_per_thread;

    unsigned long const hardware_threads=
        std::thread::hardware_concurrency();

    unsigned long const num_threads=
        std::min(hardware_threads!=0?hardware_threads:2,max_threads);

    unsigned long const block_size=length/num_threads;

    std::vector<std::future<T> > futures(num_threads-1);
    std::vector<std::thread> threads(num_threads-1);
    join_threads joiner(threads);                          ❶

    Iterator block_start=first;
    for(unsigned long i=0;i<(num_threads-1);++i)
    {
        Iterator block_end=block_start;
        std::advance(block_end,block_size);
        std::packaged_task<T(Iterator,Iterator)> task(
            accumulate_block<Iterator,T>());
        futures[i]=task.get_future();
```

```
        threads[i]=std::thread(std::move(task),block_start,block_end);
        block_start=block_end;
    }
    T last_result=accumulate_block()(block_start,last);
    T result=init;
    for(unsigned long i=0;i<(num_threads-1);++i)
    {
        result+=futures[i].get();      <-2
    }
    result += last_result;
    return result;
}
```

Once you've created your container of threads, you create an instance of your new class ❶ to join with all the threads on exit. You can then remove your explicit join loop, safe in the knowledge that the threads will be joined however the function exits. Note that the calls to `futures[i].get()` ❷ will block until the results are ready, so you don't need to have explicitly joined with the threads at this point. This is unlike the original from listing 8.2, where you needed to have joined with the threads to ensure that the `results` vector was correctly populated. Not only do you get exception-safe code, but your function is actually shorter because you've extracted the join code into your new (reusable) class.

EXCEPTION SAFETY WITH STD::ASYNC()

Now that you've seen what's required for exception safety when explicitly managing the threads, let's take a look at the same thing done with `std::async()`. As you've already seen, in this case the library takes care of managing the threads for you, and any threads spawned are completed when the future is *ready*. The key thing to note for exception safety is that if you destroy the future without waiting for it, the destructor will wait for the thread to complete. This neatly avoids the problem of leaked threads that are still executing and holding references to the data. The next listing shows an exception-safe implementation using `std::async()`.

Listing 8.5 An exception-safe parallel version of `std::accumulate` using `std::async`

```
template<typename Iterator,typename T>
T parallel_accumulate(Iterator first,Iterator last,T init)
{
    unsigned long const length=std::distance(first,last);      <-1
    unsigned long const max_chunk_size=25;
    if(length<=max_chunk_size)
    {
        return std::accumulate(first,last,init);      <-2
    }
    else
    {
    Iterator mid_point=first;
        std::advance(mid_point,length/2);      <-3
        std::future<T> first_half_result=
            std::async(parallel_accumulate<Iterator,T>,      <-4
                       first,mid_point,init);
```

```
        T second_half_result=parallel_accumulate(mid_point,last,T());   ⑤
        return first_half_result.get()+second_half_result;              ⑥
    }
}
```

This version uses recursive division of the data rather than pre-calculating the division of the data into chunks, but it's a whole lot simpler than the previous version, and it's *still exception safe*. As before, you start by finding the length of the sequence ❶, and if it's smaller than the maximum chunk size, you resort to calling `std::accumulate` directly ❷. If there are more elements than your chunk size, you find the midpoint ❸ and then spawn an asynchronous task to handle that half ❹. The second half of the range is handled with a direct recursive call ❺, and then the results from the two chunks are added together ❻. The library ensures that the `std::async` calls make use of the hardware threads that are available without creating an overwhelming number of threads. Some of the "asynchronous" calls will actually be executed synchronously in the call to `get()` ❻.

The beauty of this is that not only can it take advantage of the hardware concurrency, but it's also trivially exception safe. If an exception is thrown by the recursive call ❺, the future created from the call to `std::async` ❹ will be destroyed as the exception propagates. This will in turn wait for the asynchronous task to finish, thus avoiding a dangling thread. On the other hand, if the asynchronous call throws, this is captured by the future, and the call to `get()` ❻ will rethrow the exception.

What other considerations do you need to take into account when designing concurrent code? Let's look at *scalability*. How much does the performance improve if you move your code to a system with more processors?

8.4.2 Scalability and Amdahl's law

Scalability is all about ensuring that your application can take advantage of additional processors in the system it's running on. At one extreme you have a single-threaded application that's completely unscalable; even if you add 100 processors to your system, the performance will remain unchanged. At the other extreme you have something like the SETI@Home[3] project, which is designed to take advantage of thousands of additional processors (in the form of individual computers added to the network by users) as they become available.

For any given multithreaded program, the number of threads that are performing useful work will vary as the program runs. Even if every thread is doing useful work for the entirety of its existence, the application may initially have only one thread, which will then have the task of spawning all the others. But even that's a highly unlikely scenario. Threads often spend time waiting for each other or waiting for I/O operations to complete.

[3] http://setiathome.ssl.berkeley.edu/

Every time one thread has to wait for something (whatever that something is), unless there's another thread ready to take its place on the processor, you have a processor sitting idle that could be doing useful work.

A simplified way of looking at this is to divide the program into "serial" sections where only one thread is doing any useful work and "parallel" sections where all the available processors are doing useful work. If you run your application on a system with more processors, the "parallel" sections will theoretically be able to complete more quickly, because the work can be divided between more processors, whereas the "serial" sections will remain serial. Under such a simplified set of assumptions, you can therefore estimate the potential performance gain to be achieved by increasing the number of processors: if the "serial" sections constitute a fraction f_s of the program, then the performance gain P from using N processors can be estimated as

$$P = \frac{1}{f_S + \frac{1 - f_S}{N}}$$

This is *Amdahl's law*, which is often cited when talking about the performance of concurrent code. If everything can be parallelized, so the serial fraction is 0, the speedup is simply N. Alternatively, if the serial fraction is one third, even with an infinite number of processors you're not going to get a speedup of more than 3.

However, this paints a naïve picture, because tasks are rarely infinitely divisible in the way that would be required for the equation to hold, and it's also rare for everything to be CPU bound in the way that's assumed. As you've just seen, threads may wait for many things while executing.

One thing that's clear from Amdahl's law is that when you're using concurrency for performance, it's worth looking at the overall design of the application to maximize the potential for concurrency and ensure that there's always useful work for the processors to be doing. If you can reduce the size of the "serial" sections or reduce the potential for threads to wait, you can improve the potential for performance gains on systems with more processors. Alternatively, if you can provide more data for the system to process, and thus keep the parallel sections primed with work, you can reduce the serial fraction and increase the performance gain P.

Essentially, scalability is about *reducing the time it takes to perform an action or increasing the amount of data that can be processed in a given time* as more processors are added. Sometimes these are equivalent (you can process more data if each element is processed faster) but not always. Before choosing the techniques to use for dividing work between threads, it's important to identify which of these aspects of scalability are important to you.

I mentioned at the beginning of this section that threads don't always have useful work to do. Sometimes they have to wait for other threads, or for I/O to complete, or for something else. If you give the system something useful to do during this wait, you can effectively "hide" the waiting.

8.4.3 Hiding latency with multiple threads

For lots of the discussions of the performance of multithreaded code, we've been assuming that the threads are running "flat out" and always have useful work to do when they're actually running on a processor. This is of course not true; in application code threads frequently block while waiting for something. For example, they may be waiting for some I/O to complete, waiting to acquire a mutex, waiting for another thread to complete some operation and notify a condition variable or populate a future, or even just sleeping for a period of time.

Whatever the reason for the waits, if you have only as many threads as there are physical processing units in the system, having blocked threads means you're wasting CPU time. The processor that would otherwise be running a blocked thread is instead doing nothing. Consequently, if you know that one of your threads is likely to spend a considerable portion of its time waiting around, you can make use of that spare CPU time by running one or more additional threads.

Consider a virus scanner application, which divides the work across threads using a pipeline. The first thread searches the filesystem for files to check and puts them on a queue. Meanwhile, another thread takes filenames from the queue, loads the files, and scans them for viruses. You know that the thread searching the filesystem for files to scan is definitely going to be I/O bound, so you make use of the "spare" CPU time by running an additional scanning thread. You'd then have one file-searching thread and as many scanning threads as there are physical cores or processors in the system. Since the scanning thread may also have to read significant portions of the files off the disk in order to scan them, it might make sense to have even more scanning threads. But at some point there'll be too many threads, and the system will slow down again as it spends more and more time task switching, as described in section 8.2.5.

As ever, this is an optimization, so it's important to measure performance before and after any change in the number of threads; the optimal number of threads will be highly dependent on the nature of the work being done and the percentage of time the thread spends waiting.

Depending on the application, it might be possible to use up this spare CPU time without running additional threads. For example, if a thread is blocked because it's waiting for an I/O operation to complete, it might make sense to use asynchronous I/O if that's available, and then the thread can perform other useful work while the I/O is performed in the background. In other cases, if a thread is waiting for another thread to perform an operation, then rather than blocking, the waiting thread might be able to perform that operation itself, as you saw with the lock-free queue in chapter 7. In an extreme case, if a thread is waiting for a task to be completed and that task hasn't yet been started by any thread, the waiting thread might perform the task in entirety itself or another task that's incomplete. You saw an example of this in listing 8.1, where the sort function repeatedly tries to sort outstanding chunks as long as the chunks it needs are not yet sorted.

Rather than adding threads to ensure that all available processors are being used, sometimes it pays to add threads to ensure that external events are handled in a timely manner, to increase the *responsiveness* of the system.

8.4.4 Improving responsiveness with concurrency

Most modern graphical user interface frameworks are *event driven*; the user performs actions on the user interface by pressing keys or moving the mouse, which generate a series of events or messages that the application then handles. The system may also generate messages or events on its own. In order to ensure that all events and messages are correctly handled, the application typically has an event loop that looks like this:

```
while(true)
{
    event_data event=get_event();
    if(event.type==quit)
        break;
    process(event);
}
```

Obviously, the details of the API will vary, but the structure is generally the same: wait for an event, do whatever processing is necessary to handle it, and then wait for the next one. If you have a single-threaded application, this can make long-running tasks hard to write, as described in section 8.1.3. In order to ensure that user input is handled in a timely manner, `get_event()` and `process()` must be called with reasonable frequency, whatever the application is doing. This means that either the task must periodically suspend itself and return control to the event loop, or the `get_event()`/`process()` code must be called from within the code at convenient points. Either option complicates the implementation of the task.

By separating the concerns with concurrency, you can put the lengthy task on a whole new thread and leave a dedicated GUI thread to process the events. The threads can then communicate through simple mechanisms rather than having to somehow mix the event-handling code in with the task code. The following listing shows a simple outline for such a separation.

Listing 8.6 Separating GUI thread from task thread

```
std::thread task_thread;
std::atomic<bool> task_cancelled(false);

void gui_thread()
{
    while(true)
    {
        event_data event=get_event();
        if(event.type==quit)
            break;
        process(event);
    }
}
```

```
void task()
{
    while(!task_complete() && !task_cancelled)
    {
        do_next_operation();
    }
    if(task_cancelled)
    {
        perform_cleanup();
    }
    else
    {
        post_gui_event(task_complete);
    }
}

void process(event_data const& event)
{
    switch(event.type)
    {
    case start_task:
        task_cancelled=false;
        task_thread=std::thread(task);
        break;
    case stop_task:
        task_cancelled=true;
        task_thread.join();
        break;
    case task_complete:
        task_thread.join();
        display_results();
        break;
    default:
        //...
    }
}
```

By separating the concerns in this way, the user thread is always able to respond to the events in a timely fashion, even if the task takes a long time. This *responsiveness* is often key to the user experience when using an application; applications that completely lock up whenever a particular operation is being performed (whatever that may be) are inconvenient to use. By providing a dedicated event-handling thread, the GUI can handle GUI-specific messages (such as resizing or repainting the window) without interrupting the execution of the time-consuming processing, while still passing on the relevant messages where they *do* affect the long-running task.

So far in this chapter you've had a thorough look at the issues that need to be considered when designing concurrent code. Taken as a whole, these can be quite overwhelming, but as you get used to working with your "multithreaded programming hat" on, most of them will become second nature. If these considerations are new to you, hopefully they'll become clearer as you look at how they impact some concrete examples of multithreaded code.

8.5 Designing concurrent code in practice

When designing concurrent code for a particular task, the extent to which you'll need to consider each of the issues described previously will depend on the task. To demonstrate how they apply, we'll look at the implementation of parallel versions of three functions from the C++ Standard Library. This will give you a familiar basis on which to build, while providing a platform for looking at the issues. As a bonus, we'll also have usable implementations of the functions, which could be used to help with parallelizing a larger task.

I've primarily selected these implementations to demonstrate particular techniques rather than to be state-of-the-art implementations; more advanced implementations that make better use of the available hardware concurrency may be found in the academic literature on parallel algorithms or in specialist multithreading libraries such as Intel's Threading Building Blocks.[4]

The simplest parallel algorithm conceptually is a parallel version of `std::for_each`, so we'll start with that.

8.5.1 A parallel implementation of std::for_each

`std::for_each` is simple in concept; it calls a user-supplied function on every element in a range in turn. The big difference between a parallel implementation and the sequential `std::for_each` is the order of the function calls. `std::for_each` calls the function with the first element in the range, then the second, and so on, whereas with a parallel implementation there's no guarantee as to the order in which the elements will be processed, and they may (indeed we hope they *will*) be processed concurrently.

To implement a parallel version of this, you just need to divide the range into sets of elements to process on each thread. You know the number of elements in advance, so you can divide the data before processing begins (section 8.1.1). We'll assume that this is the only parallel task running, so you can use `std::thread::hardware_concurrency()` to determine the number of threads. You also know that the elements can be processed entirely independently, so you can use contiguous blocks to avoid false sharing (section 8.2.3).

This algorithm is similar in concept to the parallel version of `std::accumulate` described in section 8.4.1, but rather than computing the sum of each element, you merely have to apply the specified function. Although you might imagine this would greatly simplify the code, because there's no result to return, if you wish to pass on exceptions to the caller, you still need to use the `std::packaged_task` and `std::future` mechanisms to transfer the exception between threads. A sample implementation is shown here.

Listing 8.7 A parallel version of `std::for_each`

```
template<typename Iterator,typename Func>
void parallel_for_each(Iterator first,Iterator last,Func f)
```

[4] http://threadingbuildingblocks.org/

```
{
    unsigned long const length=std::distance(first,last);

    if(!length)
        return;

    unsigned long const min_per_thread=25;
    unsigned long const max_threads=
        (length+min_per_thread-1)/min_per_thread;

    unsigned long const hardware_threads=
        std::thread::hardware_concurrency();

    unsigned long const num_threads=
        std::min(hardware_threads!=0?hardware_threads:2,max_threads);

    unsigned long const block_size=length/num_threads;

    std::vector<std::future<void> > futures(num_threads-1);     ❶
    std::vector<std::thread> threads(num_threads-1);
    join_threads joiner(threads);

    Iterator block_start=first;
    for(unsigned long i=0;i<(num_threads-1);++i)
    {
        Iterator block_end=block_start;
        std::advance(block_end,block_size);
        std::packaged_task<void(void)> task(     ❷
            [=]()
            {
                std::for_each(block_start,block_end,f);
            });
        futures[i]=task.get_future();
        threads[i]=std::thread(std::move(task));     ❸
        block_start=block_end;
    }
    std::for_each(block_start,last,f);
    for(unsigned long i=0;i<(num_threads-1);++i)
    {
        futures[i].get();     ❹
    }
}
```

The basic structure of the code is identical to that of listing 8.4, which is unsurprising. The key difference is that the futures vector stores `std::future<void>` ❶ because the worker threads don't return a value, and a simple lambda function that invokes the function `f` on the range from `block_start` to `block_end` is used for the task ❷. This avoids having to pass the range into the thread constructor ❸. Since the worker threads don't return a value, the calls to `futures[i].get()` ❹ just provide a means of retrieving any exceptions thrown on the worker threads; if you don't wish to pass on the exceptions, you could omit this.

Just as your parallel implementation of `std::accumulate` could be simplified using `std::async`, so can your `parallel_for_each`. Such an implementation follows.

Listing 8.8 A parallel version of `std::for_each` using `std::async`

```
template<typename Iterator,typename Func>
void parallel_for_each(Iterator first,Iterator last,Func f)
{
    unsigned long const length=std::distance(first,last);

    if(!length)
        return;

    unsigned long const min_per_thread=25;

    if(length<(2*min_per_thread))
    {
        std::for_each(first,last,f);                  <-1
    }
    else
    {
        Iterator const mid_point=first+length/2;
        std::future<void> first_half=                              <-2
            std::async(&parallel_for_each<Iterator,Func>,
                       first,mid_point,f);
        parallel_for_each(mid_point,last,f);          <-3
        first_half.get();                        <-4
    }
}
```

As with your `std::async`-based `parallel_accumulate` from listing 8.5, you split the data recursively rather than before execution, because you don't know how many threads the library will use. As before, you divide the data in half at each stage, running one half asynchronously ❷ and the other directly ❸ until the remaining data is too small to be worth dividing, in which case you defer to `std::for_each` ❶. Again, the use of `std::async` and the `get()` member function of `std::future` ❹ provides the exception propagation semantics.

Let's move on from algorithms that must perform the same operation on each element (of which there are several; `std::count` and `std::replace` spring to mind for starters) to a slightly more complicated example in the shape of `std::find`.

8.5.2 A parallel implementation of std::find

`std::find` is a useful algorithm to consider next, because it's one of several algorithms that can complete without every element having been processed. For example, if the first element in the range matches the search criterion, there's no need to examine any other elements. As you'll see shortly, this is an important property for performance, and it has direct consequences for the design of the parallel implementation. It's a particular example of how data access patterns can affect the design of your code (section 8.3.2). Other algorithms in this category include `std::equal` and `std::any_of`.

If you were searching for an old photograph through the boxes of keepsakes in your attic with your wife or partner, you wouldn't let them continue searching if you found the photograph. Instead, you'd let them know you'd found the photograph (perhaps by shouting, "Found it!"), so that they could stop searching and move on to something else. The nature of many algorithms requires that they process every element, so they have no equivalent to shouting, "Found it!" For algorithms such as std::find the ability to complete "early" is an important property and not something to squander. You therefore need to design your code to make use of it—to interrupt the other tasks in some way when the answer is known, so that the code doesn't have to wait for the other worker threads to process the remaining elements.

If you don't interrupt the other threads, the serial version may well outperform your parallel implementation, because the serial algorithm can just stop searching and return once a match is found. If, for example, the system can support four concurrent threads, each thread will have to examine one quarter of the elements in the range, and our naïve parallel implementation would thus take approximately one quarter of the time a single thread would take to check every element. If the matching element lies in the first quarter of the range, the sequential algorithm will return first, because it doesn't need to check the remainder of the elements.

One way in which you can interrupt the other threads is by making use of an atomic variable as a flag and checking the flag after processing every element. If the flag is set, one of the other threads has found a match, so you can cease processing and return. By interrupting the threads in this way, you preserve the property that you don't have to process every value and thus improve the performance compared to the serial version in more circumstances. The downside to this is that atomic loads can be slow operations, so this can impede the progress of each thread.

Now you have two choices as to how to return the values and how to propagate any exceptions. You can use an array of futures, use std::packaged_task for transferring the values and exceptions, and then process the results back in the main thread; or you can use std::promise to set the final result directly from the worker threads. It all depends on how you wish to handle exceptions from the worker threads. If you want to stop on the first exception (even if you haven't processed all elements), you can use std::promise to set both the value and the exception. On the other hand, if you want to allow the other workers to keep searching, you can use std::packaged_task, store all the exceptions, and then rethrow one of them if a match isn't found.

In this case I've opted to use std::promise because the behavior matches that of std::find more closely. One thing to watch out for here is the case where the element being searched for isn't in the supplied range. You therefore need to wait for all the threads to finish *before* getting the result from the future. If you just block on the future, you'll be waiting forever if the value isn't there. The result is shown here.

Listing 8.9 An implementation of a parallel find algorithm

```
template<typename Iterator,typename MatchType>
Iterator parallel_find(Iterator first,Iterator last,MatchType match)
{
    struct find_element      ❶
    {
```

```
    void operator()(Iterator begin,Iterator end,
                    MatchType match,
                    std::promise<Iterator>* result,
                    std::atomic<bool>* done_flag)
    {
        try
        {
            for(;(begin!=end) && !done_flag->load();++begin)      ❷
            {
                if(*begin==match)
                {
                    result->set_value(begin);      ❸
                    done_flag->store(true);      ❹
                    return;
                }
            }
        }
        catch(...)      ❺
        {
            try
            {
                result->set_exception(std::current_exception());      ❻
                done_flag->store(true);
            }
            catch(...)      ❼
            {}
        }
    }
};

unsigned long const length=std::distance(first,last);

if(!length)
    return last;

unsigned long const min_per_thread=25;
unsigned long const max_threads=
    (length+min_per_thread-1)/min_per_thread;

unsigned long const hardware_threads=
    std::thread::hardware_concurrency();

unsigned long const num_threads=
    std::min(hardware_threads!=0?hardware_threads:2,max_threads);

unsigned long const block_size=length/num_threads;

std::promise<Iterator> result;      ❽
std::atomic<bool> done_flag(false);      ❾
std::vector<std::thread> threads(num_threads-1);
{      ❿
    join_threads joiner(threads);

    Iterator block_start=first;
    for(unsigned long i=0;i<(num_threads-1);++i)
    {
        Iterator block_end=block_start;
        std::advance(block_end,block_size);
```

```
            threads[i]=std::thread(find_element(),                    ⑪
                                   block_start,block_end,match,
                                   &result,&done_flag);
            block_start=block_end;
        }
        find_element()(block_start,last,match,&result,&done_flag);     ⑫
    }
    if(!done_flag.load())         ⑬
    {
        return last;
    }
    return result.get_future().get();        ⑭
}
```

The main body of listing 8.9 is similar to the previous examples. This time, the work is done in the function call operator of the local `find_element` class ❶. This loops through the elements in the block it's been given, checking the flag at each step ❷. If a match is found, it sets the final result value in the promise ❸ and then sets the `done_flag` ❹ before returning.

If an exception is thrown, this is caught by the catchall handler ❺, and you try to store the exception in the promise ❻ before setting the `done_flag`. Setting the value on the promise might throw an exception if the promise is already set, so you catch and discard any exceptions that happen here ❼.

This means that if a thread calling `find_element` either finds a match or throws an exception, all other threads will see `done_flag` set and will stop. If multiple threads find a match or throw at the same time, they'll race to set the result in the promise. But this is a benign race condition; whichever succeeds is therefore nominally "first" and is therefore an acceptable result.

Back in the main `parallel_find` function itself, you have the promise ❽ and flag ❾ used to stop the search, both of which are passed in to the new threads along with the range to search ⓫. The main thread also uses `find_element` to search the remaining elements ⓬. As already mentioned, you need to wait for all threads to finish before you check the result, because there might not be *any* matching elements. You do this by enclosing the thread launching-and-joining code in a block ❿, so all threads are joined when you check the flag to see whether a match was found ⓭. If a match was found, you can get the result or throw the stored exception by calling `get()` on the `std::future<Iterator>` you can get from the promise ⓮.

Again, this implementation assumes that you're going to be using all available hardware threads or that you have some other mechanism to determine the number of threads to use for the up-front division of work between threads. Just as before, you can use `std::async` and recursive data division to simplify your implementation, while using the automatic scaling facility of the C++ Standard Library. An implementation of `parallel_find` using `std::async` is shown in the following listing.

Listing 8.10 An implementation of a parallel find algorithm using `std::async`

```
template<typename Iterator,typename MatchType>                          ❶
Iterator parallel_find_impl(Iterator first,Iterator last,MatchType match,
                            std::atomic<bool>& done)
{
    try
    {
        unsigned long const length=std::distance(first,last);
        unsigned long const min_per_thread=25;                      ❷
        if(length<(2*min_per_thread))                  ❸
        {
            for(;(first!=last) && !done.load();++first)        ❹
            {
                if(*first==match)
                {
                    done=true;      ❺
                    return first;
                }
            }
            return last;     ❻
        }
        else
        {
            Iterator const mid_point=first+(length/2);        ❼
            std::future<Iterator> async_result=
                std::async(&parallel_find_impl<Iterator,MatchType>,     ❽
                           mid_point,last,match,std::ref(done));
            Iterator const direct_result=
                    parallel_find_impl(first,mid_point,match,done);     ❾
            return (direct_result==mid_point)?
                async_result.get():direct_result;       ❿
        }
    }
    catch(...)
    {
        done=true;      ⓫
        throw;
    }
}

template<typename Iterator,typename MatchType>
Iterator parallel_find(Iterator first,Iterator last,MatchType match)
{
    std::atomic<bool> done(false);
    return parallel_find_impl(first,last,match,done);      ⓬
}
```

The desire to finish early if you find a match means that you need to introduce a flag that is shared between all threads to indicate that a match has been found. This therefore needs to be passed in to all recursive calls. The simplest way to achieve this is by delegating to an implementation function ❶ that takes an additional parameter—a reference to the done flag, which is passed in from the main entry point ⓬.

The core implementation then proceeds along familiar lines. In common with many of the implementations here, you set a minimum number of items to process on a single thread ❷; if you can't cleanly divide into two halves of at least that size, you run everything on the current thread ❸. The actual algorithm is a simple loop through the specified range, looping until you reach the end of the range or the done flag is set ❹. If you do find a match, the done flag is set before returning ❺. If you stop searching either because you got to the end of the list or because another thread set the done flag, you return `last` to indicate that no match was found here ❻.

If the range can be divided, you first find the midpoint ❼ before using `std::async` to run the search in the second half of the range ❽, being careful to use `std::ref` to pass a reference to the done flag. In the meantime, you can search in the first half of the range by doing a direct recursive call ❾. Both the asynchronous call and the direct recursion may result in further subdivisions if the original range is big enough.

If the direct search returned `mid_point`, then it failed to find a match, so you need to get the result of the asynchronous search. If no result was found in that half, the result will be `last`, which is the correct return value to indicate that the value was not found ❿. If the "asynchronous" call was deferred rather than truly asynchronous, it will actually run here in the call to `get()`; in such circumstances the search of the top half of the range is skipped if the search in the bottom half was successful. If the asynchronous search is really running on another thread, the destructor of the `async_result` variable will wait for the thread to complete, so you don't have any leaking threads.

As before, the use of `std::async` provides you with exception-safety and exception-propagation features. If the direct recursion throws an exception, the future's destructor will ensure that the thread running the asynchronous call has terminated before the function returns, and if the asynchronous call throws, the exception is propagated through the `get()` call ❿. The use of a `try/catch` block around the whole thing is only there to set the done flag on an exception and ensure that all threads terminate quickly if an exception is thrown ⓫. The implementation would still be correct without it but would keep checking elements until every thread was finished.

A key feature that both implementations of this algorithm share with the other parallel algorithms you've seen is that there's no longer the guarantee that items are processed in the sequence that you get from `std::find`. This is essential if you're going to parallelize the algorithm. You can't process elements concurrently if the order matters. If the elements are independent, it doesn't matter for things like `parallel_for_each`, but it means that your `parallel_find` might return an element toward the end of the range even when there's a match toward the beginning, which might be surprising if you're not expecting it.

OK, so you've managed to parallelize `std::find`. As I stated at the beginning of this section, there are other similar algorithms that can complete without processing every data element, and the same techniques can be used for those. We'll also look further at the issue of interrupting threads in chapter 9.

To complete our trio of examples, we'll go in a different direction and look at `std::partial_sum`. This algorithm doesn't get a lot of press, but it's an interesting algorithm to parallelize and highlights some additional design choices.

8.5.3 A parallel implementation of std::partial_sum

`std::partial_sum` calculates the running totals in a range, so each element is replaced by the sum of that element and all the elements prior to it in the original sequence. Thus the sequence 1, 2, 3, 4, 5 becomes 1, (1+2)=3, (1+2+3)=6, (1+2+3+4)=10, (1+2+3+4+5)=15. This is interesting to parallelize because you can't just divide the range into chunks and calculate each chunk independently. For example, the initial value of the first element needs to be added to every other element.

One approach to determining the partial sum of a range is to calculate the partial sum of individual chunks and then add the resulting value of the last element in the first chunk onto the elements in the next chunk, and so forth. If you have the elements 1, 2, 3, 4, 5, 6, 7, 8, 9 and you're splitting into three chunks, you get {1, 3, 6}, {4, 9, 15}, {7, 15, 24} in the first instance. If you then add 6 (the sum for the last element in the first chunk) onto the elements in the second chunk, you get {1, 3, 6}, {10, 15, 21}, {7, 15, 24}. Then you add the last element of the second chunk (21) onto the elements in the third and final chunk to get the final result: {1, 3, 6}, {10, 15, 21}, {28, 36, 55}.

As well as the original division into chunks, the addition of the partial sum from the previous block can also be parallelized. If the last element of each block is updated first, the remaining elements in a block can be updated by one thread while a second thread updates the next block, and so forth. This works well when there are many more elements in the list than processing cores, because each core has a reasonable number of elements to process at each stage.

If you have a lot of processing cores (as many or more than the number of elements), this doesn't work so well. If you divide the work among the processors, you end up working in pairs of elements at the first step. Under these conditions, this forward propagation of results means that many processors are left waiting, so you need to find some work for them to do. You can then take a different approach to the problem. Rather than doing the full forward propagation of the sums from one chunk to the next, you do a partial propagation: first sum adjacent elements as before, but then add those sums to those two elements away, then add the next set of results to the results from four elements away, and so forth. If you start with the same initial nine elements, you get 1, 3, 5, 7, 9, 11, 13, 15, 17 after the first round, which gives you the final results for the first two elements. After the second you then have 1, 3, 6, 10, 14, 18, 22, 26, 30, which is correct for the first four elements. After round three you have 1, 3, 6, 10, 15, 21, 28, 36, 44, which is correct for the first eight elements, and finally after round four you have 1, 3, 6, 10, 15, 21, 28, 36, 45, which is the final answer. Although there are more total steps than in the first approach, there's greater scope for parallelism if you have many processors; each processor can update one entry with each step.

Overall, the second approach takes $\log_2(N)$ steps of around N operations (one per processor), where N is the number of elements in the list. This compares to the first algorithm where each thread has to perform N/k operations for the initial partial sum of the chunk allocated to it and then further N/k operations to do the forward propagation, where k is the number of threads. Thus the first approach is $O(N)$, whereas the second is $O(N\log(N))$ in terms of total number of operations. However, if you have as many processors as list elements, the second approach requires only $\log(N)$ operations *per processor*, whereas the first essentially serializes the operations when k gets large, because of the forward propagation. For small numbers of processing units, the first approach will therefore finish faster, whereas for massively parallel systems, the second will finish faster. This is an extreme example of the issues discussed in section 8.2.1.

Anyway, efficiency issues aside, let's look at some code. The following listing shows the first approach.

Listing 8.11 Calculating partial sums in parallel by dividing the problem

```
template<typename Iterator>
void parallel_partial_sum(Iterator first,Iterator last)
{
    typedef typename Iterator::value_type value_type;

    struct process_chunk                                          <-1
    {
        void operator()(Iterator begin,Iterator last,
                        std::future<value_type>* previous_end_value,
                        std::promise<value_type>* end_value)
        {
            try
            {
                Iterator end=last;
                ++end;
                std::partial_sum(begin,end,begin);                <-2
                if(previous_end_value)                            <-3
                {
                    value_type& addend=previous_end_value->get();      <-4
                    *last+=addend;                                <-5
                    if(end_value)
                    {
                        end_value->set_value(*last);              <-6
                    }
                    std::for_each(begin,last,[addend](value_type& item)  <-7
                                  {
                                      item+=addend;
                                  });
                }
                else if(end_value)
                {
                    end_value->set_value(*last);                  <-8
                }
            }
            catch(...)                                            <-9
```

```
            {
                if(end_value)
                {
                    end_value->set_exception(std::current_exception()); ◁— 10
                }
                else
                {
                    throw;     ◁— 11
                }
            }
        }
    };

    unsigned long const length=std::distance(first,last);

    if(!length)
        return last;

    unsigned long const min_per_thread=25;     ◁— 12
    unsigned long const max_threads=
        (length+min_per_thread-1)/min_per_thread;

    unsigned long const hardware_threads=
        std::thread::hardware_concurrency();

    unsigned long const num_threads=
        std::min(hardware_threads!=0?hardware_threads:2,max_threads);

    unsigned long const block_size=length/num_threads;

    typedef typename Iterator::value_type value_type;

    std::vector<std::thread> threads(num_threads-1);      ◁— 13
    std::vector<std::promise<value_type> >
         end_values(num_threads-1);     ◁— 14
    std::vector<std::future<value_type> >
         previous_end_values;     ◁— 15
    previous_end_values.reserve(num_threads-1);     ◁— 16
    join_threads joiner(threads);

    Iterator block_start=first;
    for(unsigned long i=0;i<(num_threads-1);++i)
    {
        Iterator block_last=block_start;
        std::advance(block_last,block_size-1);     ◁— 17
        threads[i]=std::thread(process_chunk(),     ◁— 18
                               block_start,block_last,
                               (i!=0)?&previous_end_values[i-1]:0,
                               &end_values[i]);
        block_start=block_last;               19
        ++block_start;                     ◁—┘
        previous_end_values.push_back(end_values[i].get_future());     ◁— 20
    }
    Iterator final_element=block_start;
    std::advance(final_element,std::distance(block_start,last)-1);     ◁— 21
    process_chunk()(block_start,final_element,     ◁— 22
                    (num_threads>1)?&previous_end_values.back():0,
                    0);
}
```

In this instance, the general structure is the same as with the previous algorithms, dividing the problem into chunks, with a minimum chunk size per thread ⓬. In this case, as well as the vector of threads ⓭, you have a vector of promises ⓮, which is used to store the value of the last element in the chunk, and a vector of futures ⓯, which is used to retrieve the last value from the previous chunk. You can reserve the space for the futures ⓰ to avoid a reallocation while spawning threads, because you know how many you're going to have.

The main loop is the same as before, except this time you actually want the iterator that *points to* the last element in each block, rather than being the usual one past the end ⓱, so that you can do the forward propagation of the last element in each range. The actual processing is done in the `process_chunk` function object, which we'll look at shortly; the start and end iterators for this chunk are passed in as arguments alongside the future for the end value of the previous range (if any) and the promise to hold the end value of this range ⓲.

After you've spawned the thread, you can update the block start, remembering to advance it past that last element ⓳, and store the future for the last value in the current chunk into the vector of futures so it will be picked up next time around the loop ⓴.

Before you process the final chunk, you need to get an iterator for the last element ㉑, which you can pass in to `process_chunk` ㉒. `std::partial_sum` doesn't return a value, so you don't need to do anything once the final chunk has been processed. The operation is complete once all the threads have finished.

OK, now it's time to look at the `process_chunk` function object that actually does all the work ❶. You start by calling `std::partial_sum` for the entire chunk, including the final element ❷, but then you need to know if you're the first chunk or not ❸. If you are *not* the first chunk, then there was a `previous_end_value` from the previous chunk, so you need to wait for that ❹. In order to maximize the parallelism of the algorithm, you then update the last element first ❺, so you can pass the value on to the next chunk (if there is one) ❻. Once you've done that, you can just use `std::for_each` and a simple lambda function ❼ to update all the remaining elements in the range.

If there was *not* a `previous_end_value`, you're the first chunk, so you can just update the `end_value` for the next chunk (again, if there is one—you might be the only chunk) ❽.

Finally, if any of the operations threw an exception, you catch it ❾ and store it in the promise ❿ so it will propagate to the next chunk when it tries to get the previous end value ❹. This will propagate all exceptions into the final chunk, which then just rethrows ⓫, because you know you're running on the main thread.

Because of the synchronization between the threads, this code isn't readily amenable to rewriting with `std::async`. The tasks wait on results made available partway through the execution of other tasks, so all tasks must be running concurrently.

With the block-based, forward-propagation approach out of the way, let's look at the second approach to computing the partial sums of a range.

IMPLEMENTING THE INCREMENTAL PAIRWISE ALGORITHM FOR PARTIAL SUMS

This second approach to calculating the partial sums by adding elements increasingly further away works best where your processors can execute the additions in lockstep. In this case, no further synchronization is necessary because all the intermediate results can be propagated directly to the next processor that needs them. But in practice you rarely have such systems to work with except for those cases where a single processor can execute the same instruction across a small number of data elements simultaneously with so-called Single-Instruction/Multiple-Data (SIMD) instructions. Therefore, you must design your code for the general case and explicitly synchronize the threads at each step.

One way to do this is to use a *barrier*—a synchronization mechanism that causes threads to wait until the required number of threads has reached the barrier. Once all the threads have reached the barrier, they're all unblocked and may proceed. The C++11 Thread Library doesn't offer such a facility directly, so you have to design one yourself.

Imagine a roller coaster at the fairground. If there's a reasonable number of people waiting, the fairground staff will ensure that every seat is filled before the roller coaster leaves the platform. A barrier works the same way: you specify up front the number of "seats," and threads have to wait until all the "seats" are filled. Once there are enough waiting threads, they can all proceed; the barrier is reset and starts waiting for the next batch of threads. Often, such a construct is used in a loop, where the same threads come around and wait next time. The idea is to keep the threads in lockstep, so one thread doesn't run away in front of the others and get out of step. For an algorithm such as this one, that would be disastrous, because the runaway thread would potentially modify data that was still being used by other threads or use data that hadn't been correctly updated yet.

Anyway, the following listing shows a simple implementation of a barrier.

Listing 8.12 A simple barrier class

```
class barrier
{
    unsigned const count;
    std::atomic<unsigned> spaces;
    std::atomic<unsigned> generation;
public:
    explicit barrier(unsigned count_):            // 1
        count(count_),spaces(count),generation(0)
    {}
    void wait()
    {
        unsigned const my_generation=generation;      // 2
        if(!--spaces)                                 // 3
        {
            spaces=count;       // 4
            ++generation;       // 5
        }
        else
```

```
        {
            while(generation==my_generation)        ⑥
                std::this_thread::yield();       ⑦
        }
    }
};
```

With this implementation, you construct a `barrier` with the number of "seats" ❶, which is stored in the `count` variable. Initially, the number of `spaces` at the barrier is equal to this count. As each thread waits, the number of `spaces` is decremented ❸. When it reaches zero, the number of spaces is reset back to `count` ❹, and the `generation` is increased to signal to the other threads that they can continue ❺. If the number of free `spaces` does not reach zero, you have to wait. This implementation uses a simple spin lock ❻, checking the `generation` against the value you retrieved at the beginning of `wait()` ❷. Because the `generation` is only updated when all the threads have reached the barrier ❺, you `yield()` while waiting ❼ so the waiting thread doesn't hog the CPU in a busy wait.

When I said this implementation was simple, I meant it: it uses a spin wait, so it's not ideal for cases where threads are likely to be waiting a long time, and it doesn't work if there's more than `count` threads that can potentially call `wait()` at any one time. If you need to handle either of those scenarios, you must use a more robust (but more complex) implementation instead. I've also stuck to sequentially consistent operations on the atomic variables, because that makes everything easier to reason about, but you could potentially relax some of the ordering constraints. Such global synchronization is expensive on massively parallel architectures, because the cache line holding the barrier state must be shuttled between all the processors involved (see the discussion of cache ping-pong in section 8.2.2), so you must take great care to ensure that this really is the best choice here.

Anyway, this is just what you need here; you have a fixed number of threads that need to run in a lockstep loop. Well, it's *almost* a fixed number of threads. As you may remember, the items at the beginning of the list acquire their final values after a couple of steps. This means that either you have to keep those threads looping until the entire range has been processed, or you need to allow your barrier to handle threads dropping out, and thus decreasing `count`. I opted for the latter option, because it avoids having threads doing unnecessary work just looping until the final step is done.

This means you have to change `count` to be an atomic variable, so you can update it from multiple threads without external synchronization:

```
std::atomic<unsigned> count;
```

The initialization remains the same, but now you have to explicitly `load()` from `count` when you reset the number of `spaces`:

```
spaces=count.load();
```

These are all the changes that you need on the `wait()` front; now you need a new member function to decrement `count`. Let's call it `done_waiting()`, because a thread is declaring that it is done with waiting:

```
void done_waiting()
{
    --count;                  ❶
    if(!--spaces)             ❷
    {
        spaces=count.load();  ❸
        ++generation;
    }
}
```

The first thing you do is decrement the `count` ❶ so that the next time `spaces` is reset it reflects the new lower number of waiting threads. Then you need to decrease the number of free `spaces` ❷. If you don't do this, the other threads will be waiting forever, because `spaces` was initialized to the old, larger value. If you're the last thread through on this batch, you need to reset the counter and increase the `generation` ❸, just as you do in `wait()`. The key difference here is that if you're the last thread in the batch, you don't have to wait. You're finished with waiting after all!

You're now ready to write your second implementation of partial sum. At each step, every thread calls `wait()` on the barrier to ensure the threads step through together, and once each thread is done, it calls `done_waiting()` on the barrier to decrement the count. If you use a second buffer alongside the original range, the barrier provides all the synchronization you need. At each step the threads read from either the original range or the buffer and write the new value to the corresponding element of the other. If the threads read from the original range on one step, they read from the buffer on the next, and vice versa. This ensures there are no race conditions between the reads and writes by separate threads. Once a thread has finished looping, it must ensure that the correct final value has been written to the original range. The following listing pulls this all together.

Listing 8.13 A parallel implementation of `partial_sum` by pairwise updates

```
struct barrier
{
    std::atomic<unsigned> count;
    std::atomic<unsigned> spaces;
    std::atomic<unsigned> generation;

    barrier(unsigned count_):
        count(count_),spaces(count_),generation(0)
    {}

    void wait()
    {
        unsigned const gen=generation.load();
        if(!--spaces)
        {
```

```
                spaces=count.load();
                ++generation;
            }
            else
            {
                while(generation.load()==gen)
                {
                    std::this_thread::yield();
                }
            }
        }

        void done_waiting()
        {
            --count;
            if(!--spaces)
            {
                spaces=count.load();
                ++generation;
            }
        }
    };

    template<typename Iterator>
    void parallel_partial_sum(Iterator first,Iterator last)
    {
        typedef typename Iterator::value_type value_type;

        struct process_element                    <-1
        {
            void operator()(Iterator first,Iterator last,
                            std::vector<value_type>& buffer,
                            unsigned i,barrier& b)
            {
                value_type& ith_element=*(first+i);
                bool update_source=false;

                for(unsigned step=0,stride=1;stride<=i;++step,stride*=2)
                {
                    value_type const& source=(step%2)?       <-2
                        buffer[i]:ith_element;
                    value_type& dest=(step%2)?
                        ith_element:buffer[i];
                    value_type const& addend=(step%2)?       <-3
                        buffer[i-stride]:*(first+i-stride);

                    dest=source+addend;              <-4
                    update_source=!(step%2);
                    b.wait();                        <-5
                }
                if(update_source)               <-6
                {
                    ith_element=buffer[i];
                }
                b.done_waiting();               <-7
            }
        };
```

```
    unsigned long const length=std::distance(first,last);

    if(length<=1)
        return;

    std::vector<value_type> buffer(length);
    barrier b(length);

    std::vector<std::thread> threads(length-1);         ⑧
    join_threads joiner(threads);

    Iterator block_start=first;
    for(unsigned long i=0;i<(length-1);++i)
    {
        threads[i]=std::thread(process_element(),first,last,     ⑨
                               std::ref(buffer),i,std::ref(b));
    }
    process_element()(first,last,buffer,length-1,b);        ⑩
}
```

The overall structure of this code is probably becoming familiar by now. You have a class with a function call operator (`process_element`) for doing the work ❶, which you run on a bunch of threads ❾ stored in a vector ❽ and which you also call from the main thread ❿. The key difference this time is that the number of threads is dependent on the number of items in the list rather than on `std::thread::hardware_concurrency`. As I said already, unless you're on a massively parallel machine where threads are cheap, this is probably a bad idea, but it shows the overall structure. It would be possible to have fewer threads, with each thread handling several values from the source range, but there will come a point where there are sufficiently few threads that this is less efficient than the forward-propagation algorithm.

Anyway, the key work is done in the function call operator of `process_element`. At each step you either take the *i*th element from the original range or the *i*th element from the buffer ❷ and add it to the value `stride` elements prior ❸, storing it in the buffer if you started in the original range or back in the original range if you started in the buffer ❹. You then wait on the barrier ❺ before starting the next step. You've finished when the `stride` takes you off the start of the range, in which case you need to update the element in the original range if your final result was stored in the buffer ❻. Finally, you tell the barrier that you're `done_waiting()` ❼.

Note that this solution isn't exception safe. If an exception is thrown in `process_element` on one of the worker threads, it will terminate the application. You could deal with this by using a `std::promise` to store the exception, as you did for the `parallel_find` implementation from listing 8.9, or even just using a `std::exception_ptr` protected by a mutex.

That concludes our three examples. Hopefully, they've helped to crystallize some of the design considerations highlighted in sections 8.1, 8.2, 8.3, and 8.4 and have demonstrated how these techniques can be brought to bear in real code.

8.6 Summary

We've covered quite a lot of ground in this chapter. We started with various techniques for dividing work between threads, such as dividing the data beforehand or using a number of threads to form a pipeline. We then looked at the issues surrounding the performance of multithreaded code from a low-level perspective, with a look at false sharing and data contention before moving on to how the patterns of data access can affect the performance of a bit of code. We then looked at additional considerations in the design of concurrent code, such as exception safety and scalability. Finally, we ended with a number of examples of parallel algorithm implementations, each of which highlighted particular issues that can occur when designing multithreaded code.

One item that has cropped up a couple of times in this chapter is the idea of a thread pool—a preconfigured group of threads that run tasks assigned to the pool. Quite a lot of thought goes into the design of a good thread pool, so we'll look at some of the issues in the next chapter, along with other aspects of advanced thread management.

9 Advanced thread management

This chapter covers

- Thread pools
- Handling dependencies between pool tasks
- Work stealing for pool threads
- Interrupting threads

In earlier chapters, we've been explicitly managing threads by creating `std::thread` objects for every thread. In a couple of places you've seen how this can be undesirable, because you then have to manage the lifetime of the thread objects, determine the number of threads appropriate to the problem and to the current hardware, and so forth. The ideal scenario would be that you could just divide the code into the smallest pieces that can be executed concurrently, pass them over to the compiler and library, and say, "Parallelize this for optimal performance."

Another recurring theme in several of the examples is that you might use several threads to solve a problem but require that they finish early if some condition is met. This might be because the result has already been determined, or because an error has occurred, or even because the user has explicitly requested that the operation be aborted. Whatever the reason, the threads need to be sent a "Please stop" request so that they can give up on the task they were given, tidy up, and finish as soon as possible.

In this chapter, we'll look at mechanisms for managing threads and tasks, starting with the automatic management of the number of threads and the division of tasks between them.

9.1 Thread pools

In many companies, employees who would normally spend their time in the office are occasionally required to visit clients or suppliers or attend a trade show or conference. Although these trips might be necessary, and on any given day there might be several people making such a trip, it may well be months or even years between such trips for any particular employee. Since it would therefore be rather expensive and impractical for each employee to have a company car, companies often offer a *car pool* instead; they have a limited number of cars that are available to all employees. When an employee needs to make an off-site trip, they book one of the pool cars for the appropriate time and return it for others to use when they return to the office. If there are no pool cars free on a given day, the employee will have to reschedule their trip for a subsequent date.

A *thread pool* is a similar idea, except that *threads* are being shared rather than cars. On most systems, it's impractical to have a separate thread for every task that can potentially be done in parallel with other tasks, but you'd still like to take advantage of the available concurrency where possible. A thread pool allows you to accomplish this; tasks that can be executed concurrently are submitted to the pool, which puts them on a queue of pending work. Each task is then taken from the queue by one of the *worker threads*, which executes the task before looping back to take another from the queue.

There are several key design issues when building a thread pool, such as how many threads to use, the most efficient way to allocate tasks to threads, and whether or not you can wait for a task to complete. In this section we'll look at some thread pool implementations that address these design issues, starting with the simplest possible thread pool.

9.1.1 The simplest possible thread pool

At its simplest, a thread pool is a fixed number of *worker threads* (typically the same number as the value returned by `std::thread::hardware_concurrency()`) that process work. When you have work to do, you call a function to put it on the queue of pending work. Each worker thread takes work off the queue, runs the specified task, and then goes back to the queue for more work. In the simplest case there's no way to wait for the task to complete. If you need to do this, you have to manage the synchronization yourself.

The following listing shows a sample implementation of such a thread pool.

Listing 9.1 Simple thread pool

```
class thread_pool
{
    std::atomic_bool done;
    thread_safe_queue<std::function<void()> > work_queue;     ❶
    std::vector<std::thread> threads;                        ❷
    join_threads joiner;                ❸

    void worker_thread()
    {
        while(!done)          ❹
        {
            std::function<void()> task;
            if(work_queue.try_pop(task))        ❺
            {
                task();        ❻
            }
            else
            {
                std::this_thread::yield();       ❼
            }
        }
    }
public:
    thread_pool():
        done(false),joiner(threads)
    {
        unsigned const thread_count=std::thread::hardware_concurrency();    ❽

        try
        {
            for(unsigned i=0;i<thread_count;++i)
            {
                threads.push_back(
                    std::thread(&thread_pool::worker_thread,this));    ❾
            }
        }
        catch(...)
        {
            done=true;        ❿
            throw;
        }
    }

    ~thread_pool()
    {
        done=true;        ⓫
    }

    template<typename FunctionType>
    void submit(FunctionType f)
    {
        work_queue.push(std::function<void()>(f));      ⓬
    }
};
```

This implementation has a vector of worker threads ❷ and uses one of the thread-safe queues from chapter 6 ❶ to manage the queue of work. In this case, users can't wait for the tasks, and they can't return any values, so you can use `std::function<void()>` to encapsulate your tasks. The `submit()` function then wraps whatever function or callable object is supplied inside a `std::function<void()>` instance and pushes it on the queue ⓬.

The threads are started in the constructor: you use `std::thread::hardware_concurrency()` to tell you how many concurrent threads the hardware can support ❽, and you create that many threads running your `worker_thread()` member function ❾.

Starting a thread can fail by throwing an exception, so you need to ensure that any threads you've already started are stopped and cleaned up nicely in this case. This is achieved with a `try-catch` block that sets the `done` flag when an exception is thrown ❿, alongside an instance of the `join_threads` class from chapter 8 ❸ to join all the threads. This also works with the destructor: you can just set the `done` flag ⓫, and the `join_threads` instance will ensure that all the threads have completed before the pool is destroyed. Note that the order of declaration of the members is important: both the `done` flag and the `worker_queue` must be declared before the `threads` vector, which must in turn be declared before the `joiner`. This ensures that the members are destroyed in the right order; you can't destroy the queue safely until all the threads have stopped, for example.

The `worker_thread` function itself is quite simple: it sits in a loop waiting until the `done` flag is set ❹, pulling tasks off the queue ❺ and executing them ❻ in the meantime. If there are no tasks on the queue, the function calls `std::this_thread::yield()` to take a small break ❼ and give another thread a chance to put some work on the queue before it tries to take some off again the next time around.

For many purposes such a simple thread pool will suffice, especially if the tasks are entirely independent and don't return any values or perform any blocking operations. But there are also many circumstances where such a simple thread pool may not adequately address your needs and yet others where it can cause problems such as deadlock. Also, in the simple cases you may well be better served using `std::async` as in many of the examples in chapter 8. Throughout this chapter, we'll look at more complex thread pool implementations that have additional features either to address user needs or reduce the potential for problems. First up: waiting for the tasks we've submitted.

9.1.2 *Waiting for tasks submitted to a thread pool*

In the examples in chapter 8 that explicitly spawned threads, after dividing the work between threads, the master thread always waited for the newly spawned threads to finish, to ensure that the overall task was complete before returning to the caller. With thread pools, you'd need to wait for the *tasks* submitted to the thread pool to complete, rather than the worker threads themselves. This is similar to the way that the `std::async`-based examples in chapter 8 waited for the futures. With the simple thread pool from listing 9.1, you'd have to do this manually using the techniques from chapter 4: condition variables and futures. This adds complexity to the code; it would be better if you could wait for the tasks directly.

By moving that complexity into the thread pool itself, you *can* wait for the tasks directly. You can have the `submit()` function return a task handle of some description that you can then use to wait for the task to complete. This task handle would wrap the use of condition variables or futures, thus simplifying the code that uses the thread pool.

A special case of having to wait for the spawned task to finish occurs when the main thread needs a result computed by the task. You've seen this in examples throughout the book, such as the `parallel_accumulate()` function from chapter 2. In this case, you can combine the waiting with the result transfer through the use of futures. Listing 9.2 shows the changes required to the simple thread pool that allows you to wait for tasks to complete and then pass return values from the task to the waiting thread. Since `std::packaged_task<>` instances are not *copyable*, just *movable*, you can no longer use `std::function<>` for the queue entries, because `std::function<>` requires that the stored function objects are copy-constructible. Instead, you must use a custom function wrapper that can handle move-only types. This is a simple type-erasure class with a function call operator. You only need to handle functions that take no parameters and return `void`, so this is a straightforward virtual call in the implementation.

Listing 9.2 A thread pool with waitable tasks

```
class function_wrapper
{
    struct impl_base {
        virtual void call()=0;
        virtual ~impl_base() {}
    };
    std::unique_ptr<impl_base> impl;
    template<typename F>
    struct impl_type: impl_base
    {
        F f;
        impl_type(F&& f_): f(std::move(f_)) {}
        void call() { f(); }
    };
public:
    template<typename F>
    function_wrapper(F&& f):
        impl(new impl_type<F>(std::move(f)))
    {}

    void operator()() { impl->call(); }

    function_wrapper() = default;

    function_wrapper(function_wrapper&& other):
        impl(std::move(other.impl))
    {}
```

```
    function_wrapper& operator=(function_wrapper&& other)
    {
        impl=std::move(other.impl);
        return *this;
    }

    function_wrapper(const function_wrapper&)=delete;
    function_wrapper(function_wrapper&)=delete;
    function_wrapper& operator=(const function_wrapper&)=delete;
};

class thread_pool
{
    thread_safe_queue<function_wrapper> work_queue;      <-- Use function_
                                                             wrapper rather
    void worker_thread()                                     than std::function
    {
        while(!done)
        {
            function_wrapper task;                       <--
            if(work_queue.try_pop(task))
            {
                task();
            }
            else
            {
                std::this_thread::yield();
            }
        }
    }
public:
    template<typename FunctionType>
    std::future<typename std::result_of<FunctionType()>::type>     <-- 1
        submit(FunctionType f)
    {
        typedef typename std::result_of<FunctionType()>::type
            result_type;                                            <-- 2

        std::packaged_task<result_type()> task(std::move(f));       <-- 3
        std::future<result_type> res(task.get_future());            <-- 4
        work_queue.push(std::move(task));                <-- 5
        return res;                  <-- 6
    }
    // rest as before
};
```

First, the modified submit() function ❶ returns a std::future<> to hold the return value of the task and allow the caller to wait for the task to complete. This requires that you know the return type of the supplied function f, which is where std::result_of<> comes in: std::result_of<FunctionType()>::type is the type of the result of invoking an instance of type FunctionType (such as f) with no arguments. You use the same std::result_of<> expression for the result_type typedef ❷ inside the function.

You then wrap the function f in a std::packaged_task<result_type()> ❸, because f is a function or callable object that takes no parameters and returns an instance of type `result_type`, as we just deduced. You can now get your future from the `std::packaged_task<>` ❹, before pushing the task onto the queue ❺ and returning the future ❻. Note that you have to use `std::move()` when pushing the task onto the queue, because `std::packaged_task<>` isn't copyable. The queue now stores `function_wrapper` objects rather than `std::function<void()>` objects in order to handle this.

This pool thus allows you to wait for your tasks and have them return results. The next listing shows what the `parallel_accumulate` function looks like with such a thread pool.

Listing 9.3 `parallel_accumulate` using a thread pool with waitable tasks

```
template<typename Iterator,typename T>
T parallel_accumulate(Iterator first,Iterator last,T init)
{
    unsigned long const length=std::distance(first,last);

    if(!length)
        return init;

    unsigned long const block_size=25;
    unsigned long const num_blocks=(length+block_size-1)/block_size;    ❶

    std::vector<std::future<T> > futures(num_blocks-1);
    thread_pool pool;

    Iterator block_start=first;
    for(unsigned long i=0;i<(num_blocks-1);++i)
    {
        Iterator block_end=block_start;
        std::advance(block_end,block_size);
        futures[i]=pool.submit(accumulate_block<Iterator,T>());    ❷
        block_start=block_end;
    }
    T last_result=accumulate_block<Iterator,T>()(block_start,last);
    T result=init;
    for(unsigned long i=0;i<(num_blocks-1);++i)
    {
        result+=futures[i].get();
    }
    result += last_result;
    return result;
}
```

When you compare this against listing 8.4, there are a couple of things to notice. First, you're working in terms of the number of blocks to use (`num_blocks` ❶) rather than the number of threads. In order to make the most use of the scalability of your thread pool, you need to divide the work into the smallest blocks that it's worth working with concurrently. When there are only a few threads in the pool, each thread will process many blocks, but as the number of threads grows with the hardware, the number of blocks processed in parallel will also grow.

You need to be careful when choosing the "smallest blocks that it's worth working with concurrently." There's an inherent overhead to submitting a task to a thread pool, having the worker thread run it, and passing the return value through a `std::future<>`, and for small tasks it's not worth the payoff. *If you choose too small a task size, the code may run more slowly with a thread pool than with one thread.*

Assuming the block size is sensible, you don't have to worry about packaging the tasks, obtaining the futures, or storing the `std::thread` objects so you can join with the threads later; the thread pool takes care of that. All you need to do is call `submit()` with your task ❷.

The thread pool takes care of the exception safety too. Any exception thrown by the task gets propagated through the future returned from `submit()`, and if the function exits with an exception, the thread pool destructor abandons any not-yet-completed tasks and waits for the pool threads to finish.

This works well for simple cases like this, where the tasks are independent. But it's not so good for situations where the tasks depend on other tasks also submitted to the thread pool.

9.1.3 Tasks that wait for other tasks

The Quicksort algorithm is an example that I've used throughout this book. It's simple in concept: the data to be sorted is partitioned into those items that go before a pivot item and those that go after it in the sorted sequence. These two sets of items are recursively sorted and then stitched back together to form a fully sorted set. When parallelizing this algorithm, you need to ensure that these recursive calls make use of the available concurrency.

Back in chapter 4, when I first introduced this example, we used `std::async` to run one of the recursive calls at each stage, letting the library choose between running it on a new thread and running it synchronously when the relevant `get()` was called. This works well, because each task is either running on its own thread or will be invoked when required.

When we revisited the implementation in chapter 8, you saw an alternative structure that used a fixed number of threads related to the available hardware concurrency. In this case, you used a stack of pending chunks that needed sorting. As each thread partitioned the data it was sorting, it added a new chunk to the stack for one of the sets of data and then sorted the other one directly. At this point, a straightforward wait for the sorting of the other chunk to complete would potentially deadlock, because you'd be consuming one of your limited number of threads waiting. It would be very easy to end up in a situation where all of the threads were waiting for chunks to be sorted and no threads were actually doing any sorting. We addressed this issue by having the threads pull chunks off the stack and sort them while the particular chunk they were waiting for was unsorted.

You'd get the same problem if you substituted a simple thread pool like the ones you've seen so far in this chapter instead of `std::async` in the example from chapter 4. There are now only a limited number of threads, and they might end up all waiting for tasks that haven't been scheduled because there are no free threads. You therefore need to use a solution similar to the one you used in chapter 8: process outstanding chunks while you're waiting for your chunk to complete. If you're using the thread pool to manage the list of tasks and their association with threads—which is, after all, the whole point of using a thread pool—you don't have access to the task list to do this. What you need to do is modify the thread pool to do this automatically.

The simplest way to do this is to add a new function on `thread_pool` to run a task from the queue and manage the loop yourself, so we'll go with that. Advanced thread pool implementations might add logic into the wait function or additional wait functions to handle this case, possibly prioritizing the task being waited for. The following listing shows the new `run_pending_task()` function, and a modified Quicksort to make use of it is shown in listing 9.5.

Listing 9.4 An implementation of `run_pending_task()`

```
void thread_pool::run_pending_task()
{
    function_wrapper task;
    if(work_queue.try_pop(task))
    {
        task();
    }
    else
    {
        std::this_thread::yield();
    }
}
```

This implementation of `run_pending_task()` is lifted straight out of the main loop of the `worker_thread()` function, which can now be modified to call the extracted `run_pending_task()`. This tries to take a task of the queue and run it if there is one; otherwise, it yields to allow the OS to reschedule the thread. The Quicksort implementation next is a lot simpler than the corresponding version from listing 8.1, because all the thread-management logic has been moved to the thread pool.

Listing 9.5 A thread pool–based implementation of Quicksort

```
template<typename T>
struct sorter                    <-1
{
    thread_pool pool;            <-2

    std::list<T> do_sort(std::list<T>& chunk_data)
    {
        if(chunk_data.empty())
        {
            return chunk_data;
        }

        std::list<T> result;
        result.splice(result.begin(),chunk_data,chunk_data.begin());
        T const& partition_val=*result.begin();
```

```
        typename std::list<T>::iterator divide_point=
            std::partition(chunk_data.begin(),chunk_data.end(),
                           [&](T const& val){return val<partition_val;});

        std::list<T> new_lower_chunk;
        new_lower_chunk.splice(new_lower_chunk.end(),
                               chunk_data,chunk_data.begin(),
                               divide_point);

        std::future<std::list<T> > new_lower=                  <-3
            pool.submit(std::bind(&sorter::do_sort,this,
                                  std::move(new_lower_chunk)));

        std::list<T> new_higher(do_sort(chunk_data));

        result.splice(result.end(),new_higher);
        while(!new_lower.wait_for(std::chrono::seconds(0)) ==
            std::future_status::timeout)
        {
            pool.run_pending_task();      <-4
        }

        result.splice(result.begin(),new_lower.get());
        return result;
    }
};

template<typename T>
std::list<T> parallel_quick_sort(std::list<T> input)
{
    if(input.empty())
    {
        return input;
    }
    sorter<T> s;

    return s.do_sort(input);
}
```

Just as in listing 8.1, you've delegated the real work to the `do_sort()` member function of the `sorter` class template ❶, although in this case the class is only there to wrap the `thread_pool` instance ❷.

Your thread and task management is now reduced to submitting a task to the pool ❸ and running pending tasks while waiting ❹. This is much simpler than in listing 8.1, where you had to explicitly manage the threads and the stack of chunks to sort. When submitting the task to the pool, you use `std::bind()` to bind the `this` pointer to `do_sort()` and to supply the chunk to sort. In this case, you call `std::move()` on the `new_lower_chunk` as you pass it in, to ensure that the data is moved rather than copied.

Although this has now addressed the crucial deadlock-causing problem with tasks that wait for other tasks, this thread pool is still far from ideal. For starters, every call to `submit()` and every call to `run_pending_task()` accesses the same queue. You saw in chapter 8 how having a single set of data modified by multiple threads can have a detrimental effect on performance, so you need to somehow address this problem.

9.1.4 Avoiding contention on the work queue

Every time a thread calls `submit()` on a particular instance of the thread pool, it has to push a new item onto the single shared work queue. Likewise, the worker threads are continually popping items off the queue in order to run the tasks. This means that as the number of processors increases, there's increasing contention on the queue. This can be a real performance drain; even if you use a lock-free queue so there's no explicit waiting, cache ping-pong can be a substantial time sink.

One way to avoid cache ping-pong is to use a separate work queue per thread. Each thread then posts new items to its own queue and takes work from the global work queue only if there's no work on its own individual queue. The following listing shows an implementation that makes use of a `thread_local` variable to ensure that each thread has its own work queue, as well as the global one.

Listing 9.6 A thread pool with thread-local work queues

```
class thread_pool
{
    thread_safe_queue<function_wrapper> pool_work_queue;

    typedef std::queue<function_wrapper> local_queue_type;        ❶
    static thread_local std::unique_ptr<local_queue_type>
        local_work_queue;                                        ❷

    void worker_thread()
    {
        local_work_queue.reset(new local_queue_type);           ❸

        while(!done)
        {
            run_pending_task();
        }
    }

public:
    template<typename FunctionType>
    std::future<typename std::result_of<FunctionType()>::type>
        submit(FunctionType f)
    {
        typedef typename std::result_of<FunctionType()>::type result_type;

        std::packaged_task<result_type()> task(f);
        std::future<result_type> res(task.get_future());
        if(local_work_queue)                                    ❹
        {
            local_work_queue->push(std::move(task));
        }
        else
        {
            pool_work_queue.push(std::move(task));             ❺
        }
        return res;
    }
```

```
    void run_pending_task()
    {
        function_wrapper task;
        if(local_work_queue && !local_work_queue->empty())      ⑥
        {
            task=std::move(local_work_queue->front());
            local_work_queue->pop();
            task();
        }
        else if(pool_work_queue.try_pop(task))      ⑦
        {
            task();
        }
        else
        {
            std::this_thread::yield();
        }
    }
    // rest as before
};
```

We've used a `std::unique_ptr<>` to hold the thread-local work queue ❷ because we don't want non-pool threads to have one; this is initialized in the `worker_thread()` function before the processing loop ❸. The destructor of `std::unique_ptr<>` will ensure that the work queue is destroyed when the thread exits.

`submit()` then checks to see if the current thread has a work queue ❹. If it does, it's a pool thread, and you can put the task on the local queue; otherwise, you need to put the task on the pool queue as before ❺.

There's a similar check in `run_pending_task()` ❻, except this time you also need to check to see if there are any items on the local queue. If there are, you can take the front one and process it; notice that the local queue can be a plain `std::queue<>` ❶ because it's only ever accessed by the one thread. If there are no tasks on the local queue, you try the pool queue as before ❼.

This works fine for reducing contention, but when the distribution of work is uneven, it can easily result in one thread having a lot of work on its queue while the others have no work do to. For example, with the Quicksort example, only the topmost chunk would make it to the pool queue, because the remaining chunks would end up on the local queue of the worker thread that processed that one. This defeats the purpose of using a thread pool.

Thankfully, there is a solution to this: allow the threads to *steal* work from each other's queues if there's no work in their queue and no work in the global queue.

9.1.5 Work stealing

In order to allow a thread with no work to do to take work from another thread with a full queue, the queue must be accessible to the thread doing the stealing from `run_pending_tasks()`. This requires that each thread register its queue with the thread pool or be given one by the thread pool. Also, you must ensure that the data in the work queue is suitably synchronized and protected, so that your invariants are protected.

It's possible to write a lock-free queue that allows the owner thread to push and pop at one end while other threads can steal entries from the other, but the implementation of such a queue is beyond the scope of this book. In order to demonstrate the idea, we'll stick to using a mutex to protect the queue's data. We hope work stealing is a rare event, so there should be little contention on the mutex, and such a simple queue should therefore have minimal overhead. A simple lock-based implementation is shown here.

Listing 9.7 Lock-based queue for work stealing

```
class work_stealing_queue
{
private:
    typedef function_wrapper data_type;
    std::deque<data_type> the_queue;            <-1
    mutable std::mutex the_mutex;

public:
    work_stealing_queue()
    {}

    work_stealing_queue(const work_stealing_queue& other)=delete;
    work_stealing_queue& operator=(
        const work_stealing_queue& other)=delete;

    void push(data_type data)           <-2
    {
        std::lock_guard<std::mutex> lock(the_mutex);
        the_queue.push_front(std::move(data));
    }

    bool empty() const
    {
        std::lock_guard<std::mutex> lock(the_mutex);
        return the_queue.empty();
    }

    bool try_pop(data_type& res)          <-3
    {
        std::lock_guard<std::mutex> lock(the_mutex);
        if(the_queue.empty())
        {
            return false;
        }

        res=std::move(the_queue.front());
        the_queue.pop_front();
        return true;
    }

    bool try_steal(data_type& res)          <-4
    {
        std::lock_guard<std::mutex> lock(the_mutex);
        if(the_queue.empty())
```

```
        {
            return false;
        }
        res=std::move(the_queue.back());
        the_queue.pop_back();
        return true;
    }
};
```

This queue is a simple wrapper around a `std::deque<function_wrapper>` ❶ that protects all accesses with a mutex lock. Both `push()` ❷ and `try_pop()` ❸ work on the front of the queue, while `try_steal()` ❹ works on the back.

This actually means that this "queue" is a last-in-first-out stack for its own thread; the task most recently pushed on is the first one off again. This can help improve performance from a cache perspective, because the data related to that task is more likely to still be in the cache than the data related to a task pushed on the queue previously. Also, it maps nicely to algorithms such as Quicksort. In the previous implementation, each call to `do_sort()` pushes one item on the stack and then waits for it. By processing the most recent item first, you ensure that the chunk needed for the current call to complete is processed before the chunks needed for the other branches, thus reducing the number of active tasks and the total stack usage. `try_steal()` takes items from the opposite end of the queue to `try_pop()` in order to minimize contention; you could potentially use the techniques discussed in chapters 6 and 7 to enable concurrent calls to `try_pop()` and `try_steal()`.

OK, so you have your nice sparkly work queue that permits stealing; how do you use it in your thread pool? Here's one potential implementation.

Listing 9.8 A thread pool that uses work stealing

```
class thread_pool
{
    typedef function_wrapper task_type;

    std::atomic_bool done;
    thread_safe_queue<task_type> pool_work_queue;
    std::vector<std::unique_ptr<work_stealing_queue> > queues;      ❶

    std::vector<std::thread> threads;
    join_threads joiner;

    static thread_local work_stealing_queue* local_work_queue;      ❷
    static thread_local unsigned my_index;

    void worker_thread(unsigned my_index_)
    {
        my_index=my_index_;
        local_work_queue=queues[my_index].get();      ❸
        while(!done)
        {
            run_pending_task();
        }
    }
```

```
    bool pop_task_from_local_queue(task_type& task)
    {
        return local_work_queue && local_work_queue->try_pop(task);
    }

    bool pop_task_from_pool_queue(task_type& task)
    {
        return pool_work_queue.try_pop(task);
    }

    bool pop_task_from_other_thread_queue(task_type& task)        <-4
    {
        for(unsigned i=0;i<queues.size();++i)
        {
            unsigned const index=(my_index+i+1)%queues.size();     <-5
            if(queues[index]->try_steal(task))
            {
                return true;
            }
        }

        return false;
    }

public:
    thread_pool():
        done(false),joiner(threads)
    {
        unsigned const thread_count=std::thread::hardware_concurrency();

        try
        {
            for(unsigned i=0;i<thread_count;++i)
            {
                queues.push_back(std::unique_ptr<work_stealing_queue>(   <-6
                                     new work_stealing_queue));
                threads.push_back(
                    std::thread(&thread_pool::worker_thread,this,i));
            }
        }
        catch(...)
        {
            done=true;
            throw;
        }
    }

    ~thread_pool()
    {
        done=true;
    }

    template<typename FunctionType>
    std::future<typename std::result_of<FunctionType()>::type> submit(
        FunctionType f)
    {
        typedef typename std::result_of<FunctionType()>::type result_type;
```

```
        std::packaged_task<result_type()> task(f);
        std::future<result_type> res(task.get_future());
        if(local_work_queue)
        {
            local_work_queue->push(std::move(task));
        }
        else
        {
            pool_work_queue.push(std::move(task));
        }
        return res;
    }

    void run_pending_task()
    {
        task_type task;
        if(pop_task_from_local_queue(task) ||               ❼
           pop_task_from_pool_queue(task) ||                ❽
           pop_task_from_other_thread_queue(task))          ❾
        {
            task();
        }
        else
        {
            std::this_thread::yield();
        }
    }
};
```

This code is very similar to listing 9.6. The first difference is that each thread has a `work_stealing_queue` rather than a plain `std::queue<>` ❷. When each thread is created, rather than allocating its own work queue, the pool constructor allocates one ❻, which is then stored in the list of work queues for this pool ❶. The index of the queue in the list is then passed in to the thread function and used to retrieve the pointer to the queue ❸. This means that the thread pool can access the queue when trying to steal a task for a thread that has no work to do. `run_pending_task()` will now try to take a task from its thread's own queue ❼, take a task from the pool queue ❽, or take a task from the queue of another thread ❾.

`pop_task_from_other_thread_queue()` ❹ iterates through the queues belonging to all the threads in the pool, trying to steal a task from each in turn. In order to avoid every thread trying to steal from the first thread in the list, each thread starts at the next thread in the list, by offsetting the index of the queue to check by its own index ❺.

Now you have a working thread pool that's good for many potential uses. Of course, there are still a myriad of ways to improve it for any particular usage, but that's left as an exercise for the reader. One aspect in particular that hasn't been explored is the idea of dynamically resizing the thread pool to ensure that there's optimal CPU usage even when threads are blocked waiting for something such as I/O or a mutex lock.

Next on the list of "advanced" thread-management techniques is interrupting threads.

9.2 Interrupting threads

In many situations it's desirable to signal to a long-running thread that it's time to stop. This might be because it's a worker thread for a thread pool and the pool is now being destroyed, or it might be because the work being done by the thread has been explicitly canceled by the user, or a myriad of other reasons. Whatever the reason, the idea is the same: you need to signal from one thread that another should stop before it reaches the natural end of its processing, and you need to do this in a way that allows that thread to terminate nicely rather than abruptly pulling the rug from under it.

You could potentially design a separate mechanism for every case where you need to do this, but that would be overkill. Not only does a common mechanism make it easier to write the code on subsequent occasions, but it can allow you to write code that can be interrupted, without having to worry about where that code is being used. The C++11 Standard doesn't provide such a mechanism, but it's relatively straightforward to build one. Let's look at how you can do that, starting from the point of view of the interface for launching and interrupting a thread rather than that of the thread being interrupted.

9.2.1 Launching and interrupting another thread

To start with, let's look at the external interface. What do you need from an interruptible thread? At the basic level, all you need is the same interface as you have for `std::thread`, with an additional `interrupt()` function:

```
class interruptible_thread
{
public:
    template<typename FunctionType>
    interruptible_thread(FunctionType f);
    void join();
    void detach();
    bool joinable() const;
    void interrupt();
};
```

Internally, you can use `std::thread` to manage the thread itself and use some custom data structure to handle the interruption. Now, what about from the point of view of the thread itself? At the most basic level you want to be able to say, "I can be interrupted here"—you want an *interruption point*. For this to be usable without having to pass down additional data, it needs to be a simple function that can be called without any parameters: `interruption_point()`. This implies that the interruption-specific data structure needs to be accessible through a `thread_local` variable that's set when the thread is started, so that when a thread calls your `interruption_point()` function, it checks the data structure for the currently executing thread. We'll look at the implementation of `interruption_point()` later.

This `thread_local` flag is the primary reason you can't just use plain `std::thread` to manage the thread; it needs to be allocated in a way that the `interruptible_thread` instance can access, as well as the newly started thread. You can do this by wrapping the supplied function before you pass it to std::thread to actually launch the thread in the constructor, as shown in the next listing.

Listing 9.9 Basic implementation of interruptible_thread

```
class interrupt_flag
{
public:
    void set();
    bool is_set() const;
};
thread_local interrupt_flag this_thread_interrupt_flag;          ❶

class interruptible_thread
{
    std::thread internal_thread;
    interrupt_flag* flag;
public:
    template<typename FunctionType>
    interruptible_thread(FunctionType f)
    {
        std::promise<interrupt_flag*> p;        ❷
        internal_thread=std::thread([f,&p]{            ❸
                p.set_value(&this_thread_interrupt_flag);
                f();                                   ❹
            });
        flag=p.get_future().get();     ❺
    }
    void interrupt()
    {
        if(flag)
        {
            flag->set();      ❻
        }
    }
};
```

The supplied function f is wrapped in a lambda function ❸ that holds a copy of f and a reference to the local promise p ❷. The lambda sets the value of the promise to the address of the this_thread_interrupt_flag (which is declared thread_local ❶) for the new thread before invoking the copy of the supplied function ❹. The calling thread then waits for the future associated with the promise to become ready and stores the result in the flag member variable ❺. Note that even though the lambda is running on the new thread and has a dangling reference to the local variable p, this is OK because the interruptible_thread constructor waits until p is no longer referenced by the new thread before returning. Note that this implementation doesn't take account of handling joining with the thread, or detaching it. You need to ensure that the flag variable is cleared when the thread exits, or is detached, to avoid a dangling pointer.

The interrupt() function is then relatively straightforward: if you have a valid pointer to an interrupt flag, you have a thread to interrupt, so you can just set the flag ❻. It's then up to the interrupted thread what it does with the interruption. Let's explore that next.

9.2.2 *Detecting that a thread has been interrupted*

You can now set the interruption flag, but that doesn't do you any good if the thread doesn't actually check whether it's being interrupted. In the simplest case you can do this with an `interruption_point()` function; you can call this function at a point where it's safe to be interrupted, and it throws a `thread_interrupted` exception if the flag is set:

```
void interruption_point()
{
    if(this_thread_interrupt_flag.is_set())
    {
        throw thread_interrupted();
    }
}
```

You can use such a function by calling it at convenient points within your code:

```
void foo()
{
    while(!done)
    {
        interruption_point();
        process_next_item();
    }
}
```

Although this works, it's not ideal. Some of the best places for interrupting a thread are where it's blocked waiting for something, which means that the thread isn't running in order to call `interruption_point()`! What you need here is a means for waiting for something in an interruptible fashion.

9.2.3 *Interrupting a condition variable wait*

OK, so you can detect interruptions at carefully chosen places in your code, with explicit calls to `interruption_point()`, but that doesn't help when you want to do a blocking wait, such as waiting for a condition variable to be notified. You need a new function—`interruptible_wait()`—which you can then overload for the various things you might want to wait for, and you can work out how to interrupt the waiting. I've already mentioned that one thing you might be waiting for is a condition variable, so let's start there: what do you need to do in order to be able to interrupt a wait on a condition variable? The simplest thing that would work is to notify the condition variable once you've set the interrupt flag, and put an interruption point immediately after the wait. But for this to work, you'd have to notify all threads waiting on the condition variable in order to ensure that your thread of interest wakes up. Waiters have to handle spurious wake-ups anyway, so other threads would handle this the same as a spurious wake-up—they wouldn't be able to tell the difference. The `interrupt_flag` structure would need to be able to store a pointer to a condition variable so that it can be notified in a call to `set()`. One possible implementation of `interruptible_wait()` for condition variables might look like the following listing.

Listing 9.10 A broken version of `interruptible_wait` for `std::condition_variable`

```
void interruptible_wait(std::condition_variable& cv,
                        std::unique_lock<std::mutex>& lk)
{
    interruption_point();
    this_thread_interrupt_flag.set_condition_variable(cv);        <-1
    cv.wait(lk);                                                 <-2
    this_thread_interrupt_flag.clear_condition_variable();        <-3
    interruption_point();
}
```

Assuming the presence of some functions for setting and clearing an association of a condition variable with an interrupt flag, this code is nice and simple. It checks for interruption, associates the condition variable with the `interrupt_flag` for the current thread ❶, waits on the condition variable ❷, clears the association with the condition variable ❸, and checks for interruption again. If the thread is interrupted during the wait on the condition variable, the interrupting thread will broadcast the condition variable and wake you from the wait, so you can check for interruption. Unfortunately, this code is *broken*: there are two problems with it. The first problem is relatively obvious if you have your exception safety hat on: `std::condition_variable::wait()` can throw an exception, so you might exit the function without removing the association of the interrupt flag with the condition variable. This is easily fixed with a structure that removes the association in its destructor.

The second, less-obvious problem is that there's a race condition. If the thread is interrupted after the initial call to `interruption_point()`, but before the call to `wait()`, then it doesn't matter whether the condition variable has been associated with the interrupt flag, because *the thread isn't waiting and so can't be woken by a notify on the condition variable.* You need to ensure that the thread can't be notified between the last check for interruption and the call to `wait()`. Without delving into the internals of `std::condition_variable`, you have only one way of doing that: use the mutex held by `lk` to protect this too, which requires passing it in on the call to `set_condition_variable()`. Unfortunately, this creates its own problems: you'd be passing a reference to a mutex whose lifetime you don't know to another thread (the thread doing the interrupting) for that thread to lock (in the call to `interrupt()`), without knowing whether that thread has locked the mutex already when it makes the call. This has the potential for deadlock *and* the potential to access a mutex after it has already been destroyed, so it's a nonstarter. It would be rather too restrictive if you couldn't *reliably* interrupt a condition variable wait—you can do almost as well without a special `interruptible_wait()`—so what other options do you have? One option is to put a timeout on the wait; use `wait_for()` rather than `wait()` with a small timeout value (such as 1 ms). This puts an upper limit on how long the thread will have to wait before it sees the interruption (subject to the tick granularity of the clock). If you do this, the waiting thread will see rather more "spurious" wakes resulting from the timeout, but it can't easily be helped. Such an implementation is shown in the next listing, along with the corresponding implementation of `interrupt_flag`.

Listing 9.11 Using a timeout in `interruptible_wait` for `std::condition_variable`

```
class interrupt_flag
{
    std::atomic<bool> flag;
    std::condition_variable* thread_cond;
    std::mutex set_clear_mutex;

public:
    interrupt_flag():
        thread_cond(0)
    {}

    void set()
    {
        flag.store(true,std::memory_order_relaxed);
        std::lock_guard<std::mutex> lk(set_clear_mutex);
        if(thread_cond)
        {
            thread_cond->notify_all();
        }
    }

    bool is_set() const
    {
        return flag.load(std::memory_order_relaxed);
    }

    void set_condition_variable(std::condition_variable& cv)
    {
        std::lock_guard<std::mutex> lk(set_clear_mutex);
        thread_cond=&cv;
    }

    void clear_condition_variable()
    {
        std::lock_guard<std::mutex> lk(set_clear_mutex);
        thread_cond=0;
    }

    struct clear_cv_on_destruct
    {
        ~clear_cv_on_destruct()
        {
            this_thread_interrupt_flag.clear_condition_variable();
        }
    };
};

void interruptible_wait(std::condition_variable& cv,
                        std::unique_lock<std::mutex>& lk)
{
```

```
    interruption_point();
    this_thread_interrupt_flag.set_condition_variable(cv);
    interrupt_flag::clear_cv_on_destruct guard;
    interruption_point();
    cv.wait_for(lk,std::chrono::milliseconds(1));
    interruption_point();
}
```

If you have the predicate that's being waited for, then the 1 ms timeout can be completely hidden inside the predicate loop:

```
template<typename Predicate>
void interruptible_wait(std::condition_variable& cv,
                        std::unique_lock<std::mutex>& lk,
                        Predicate pred)
{
    interruption_point();
    this_thread_interrupt_flag.set_condition_variable(cv);
    interrupt_flag::clear_cv_on_destruct guard;
    while(!this_thread_interrupt_flag.is_set() && !pred())
    {
        cv.wait_for(lk,std::chrono::milliseconds(1));
    }
    interruption_point();
}
```

This will result in the predicate being checked more often than it might otherwise be, but it's easily used in place of a plain call to `wait()`. The variants with timeouts are easily implemented: wait either for the time specified, or 1 ms, whichever is shortest. OK, so `std::condition_variable` waits are now taken care of; what about `std::condition_variable_any`? Is this the same, or can you do better?

9.2.4 Interrupting a wait on std::condition_variable_any

`std::condition_variable_any` differs from `std::condition_variable` in that it works with *any* lock type rather than just `std::unique_lock<std::mutex>`. It turns out that this makes things much easier, and you *can* do better with `std::condition_variable_any` than you could with `std::condition_variable`. Because it works with *any* lock type, you can build your own lock type that locks/unlocks both the internal `set_clear_mutex` in your `interrupt_flag` *and* the lock supplied to the wait call, as shown here.

Listing 9.12 `interruptible_wait` for `std::condition_variable_any`

```
class interrupt_flag
{
    std::atomic<bool> flag;
    std::condition_variable* thread_cond;
    std::condition_variable_any* thread_cond_any;
    std::mutex set_clear_mutex;

public:
    interrupt_flag():
```

```
        thread_cond(0),thread_cond_any(0)
    {}

    void set()
    {
        flag.store(true,std::memory_order_relaxed);
        std::lock_guard<std::mutex> lk(set_clear_mutex);
        if(thread_cond)
        {
            thread_cond->notify_all();
        }
        else if(thread_cond_any)
        {
            thread_cond_any->notify_all();
        }
    }

    template<typename Lockable>
    void wait(std::condition_variable_any& cv,Lockable& lk)
    {
        struct custom_lock
        {
            interrupt_flag* self;
            Lockable& lk;

            custom_lock(interrupt_flag* self_,
                        std::condition_variable_any& cond,
                        Lockable& lk_):
                self(self_),lk(lk_)
            {
                self->set_clear_mutex.lock();        ❶
                self->thread_cond_any=&cond;         ❷
            }

            void unlock()          ❸
            {
                lk.unlock();
                self->set_clear_mutex.unlock();
            }

            void lock()
            {
                std::lock(self->set_clear_mutex,lk);      ❹
            }

            ~custom_lock()
            {
                self->thread_cond_any=0;          ❺
                self->set_clear_mutex.unlock();
            }
        };
        custom_lock cl(this,cv,lk);
        interruption_point();
        cv.wait(cl);
        interruption_point();
    }
```

```
    // rest as before
};

template<typename Lockable>
void interruptible_wait(std::condition_variable_any& cv,
                        Lockable& lk)
{
    this_thread_interrupt_flag.wait(cv,lk);
}
```

Your custom lock type acquires the lock on the internal `set_clear_mutex` when it's constructed ❶ and then sets the `thread_cond_any` pointer to refer to the `std::condition_variable_any` passed in to the constructor ❷. The `Lockable` reference is stored for later; this must already be locked. You can now check for an interruption without worrying about races. If the interrupt flag is set at this point, it was set before you acquired the lock on `set_clear_mutex`. When the condition variable calls your `unlock()` function inside `wait()`,you unlock the `Lockable` object *and the internal* `set_clear_mutex` ❸. This allows threads that are trying to interrupt you to acquire the lock on `set_clear_mutex` and check the `thread_cond_any` pointer *once you're inside the* `wait()` *call* but not before. This is exactly what you were after (but couldn't manage) with `std::condition_variable`. Once `wait()` has finished waiting (either because it was notified or because of a spurious wake), it will call your `lock()` function, which again acquires the lock on the internal `set_clear_mutex` and the lock on the `Lockable` object ❹. You can now check again for interruptions that happened during the `wait()` call before clearing the `thread_cond_any` pointer in your `custom_lock` destructor ❺, where you also unlock the `set_clear_mutex`.

9.2.5 *Interrupting other blocking calls*

That rounds up interrupting condition variable waits, but what about other blocking waits: mutex locks, waiting for futures, and the like? In general you have to go for the timeout option you used for `std::condition_variable` because there's no way to interrupt the wait short of actually fulfilling the condition being waited for, without access to the internals of the mutex or future. But with those other things you do know what you're waiting for, so you can loop within the `interruptible_wait()` function. As an example, here's an overload of `interruptible_wait()` for a `std::future<>`:

```
template<typename T>
void interruptible_wait(std::future<T>& uf)
{
    while(!this_thread_interrupt_flag.is_set())
    {
        if(uf.wait_for(lk,std::chrono::milliseconds(1)==
            std::future_status::ready)
            break;
    }
    interruption_point();
}
```

This waits until either the interrupt flag is set or the future is ready but does a blocking wait on the future for 1 ms at a time. This means that on average it will be around

0.5 ms before an interrupt request is acknowledged, assuming a high-resolution clock. The `wait_for` will typically wait at least a whole clock tick, so if your clock ticks every 15 ms, you'll end up waiting around 15 ms rather than 1 ms. This may or may not be acceptable, depending on the circumstances. You can always reduce the timeout if necessary (and the clock supports it). The downside of reducing the timeout is that the thread will wake more often to check the flag, and this will increase the task-switching overhead.

OK, so we've looked at how you might detect interruption, with the `interruption_point()` and `interruptible_wait()` functions, but how do you handle that?

9.2.6 *Handling interruptions*

From the point of view of the thread being interrupted, an interruption is just a `thread_interrupted` exception, which can therefore be handled just like any other exception. In particular, you can catch it in a standard `catch` block:

```
try
{
    do_something();
}
catch(thread_interrupted&)
{
    handle_interruption();
}
```

This means that you could catch the interruption, handle it in some way, and then carry on regardless. If you do this, and another thread calls `interrupt()` again, your thread will be interrupted again the next time it calls an interruption point. You might want to do this if your thread is performing a series of independent tasks; interrupting one task will cause that task to be abandoned, and the thread can then move on to performing the next task in the list.

Because `thread_interrupted` is an exception, all the usual exception-safety precautions must also be taken when calling code that can be interrupted, in order to ensure that resources aren't leaked, and your data structures are left in a coherent state. Often, it will be desirable to let the interruption terminate the thread, so you can just let the exception propagate up. But if you let exceptions propagate out of the thread function passed to the `std::thread` constructor, `std::terminate()` will be called, and the whole program will be terminated. In order to avoid having to remember to put a `catch (thread_interrupted)` handler in every function you pass to `interruptible_thread`, you can instead put that `catch` block inside the wrapper you use for initializing the `interrupt_flag`. This makes it safe to allow the interruption exception to propagate unhandled, because it will then terminate just that individual thread. The initialization of the thread in the `interruptible_thread` constructor now looks like this:

```
internal_thread=std::thread([f,&p]{
        p.set_value(&this_thread_interrupt_flag);
```

```
        try
        {
            f();
        }
        catch(thread_interrupted const&)
        {}
    });
```

Let's now look at a concrete example where interruption is useful.

9.2.7 Interrupting background tasks on application exit

Consider for a moment a desktop search application. As well as interacting with the user, the application needs to monitor the state of the filesystem, identifying any changes and updating its index. Such processing is typically left to a background thread, in order to avoid affecting the responsiveness of the GUI. This background thread needs to run for the entire lifetime of the application; it will be started as part of the application initialization and left to run until the application is shut down. For such an application this is typically only when the machine itself is being shut down, because the application needs to run the whole time in order to maintain an up-to-date index. In any case, when the application is being shut down, you need to close down the background threads in an orderly manner; one way to do this is by interrupting them.

The following listing shows a sample implementation of the thread-management parts of such a system.

Listing 9.13 Monitoring the filesystem in the background

```
std::mutex config_mutex;
std::vector<interruptible_thread> background_threads;

void background_thread(int disk_id)
{
    while(true)
    {
        interruption_point();                    <-- 1
        fs_change fsc=get_fs_changes(disk_id);       <-- 2
        if(fsc.has_changes())
        {
            update_index(fsc);        <-- 3
        }
    }
}

void start_background_processing()
{
    background_threads.push_back(
        interruptible_thread(background_thread,disk_1));
    background_threads.push_back(
        interruptible_thread(background_thread,disk_2));
}

int main()
{
```

```
        start_background_processing();           ❹
        process_gui_until_exit();                    ❺
        std::unique_lock<std::mutex> lk(config_mutex);
        for(unsigned i=0;i<background_threads.size();++i)
        {
            background_threads[i].interrupt();       ❻
        }
        for(unsigned i=0;i<background_threads.size();++i)
        {
            background_threads[i].join();        ❼
        }
}
```

At startup, the background threads are launched ❹. The main thread then proceeds with handling the GUI ❺. When the user has requested that the application exit, the background threads are interrupted ❻, and then the main thread waits for each background thread to complete before exiting ❼. The background threads sit in a loop, checking for disk changes ❷ and updating the index ❸. Every time around the loop they check for interruption by calling `interruption_point()` ❶.

Why do you interrupt all the threads before waiting for any? Why not interrupt each and then wait for it before moving on to the next? The answer is *concurrency*. Threads will likely not finish immediately when they're interrupted, because they have to proceed to the next interruption point and then run any destructor calls and exception-handling code necessary before they exit. By joining with each thread immediately, you therefore cause the interrupting thread to wait, *even though it still has useful work it could do*—interrupt the other threads. Only when you have no more work to do (all the threads have been interrupted) do you wait. This also allows all the threads being interrupted to process their interruptions in parallel and potentially finish sooner.

This interruption mechanism could easily be extended to add further interruptible calls or to disable interruptions across a specific block of code, but this is left as an exercise for the reader.

9.3 Summary

In this chapter, we've looked at various "advanced" thread-management techniques: thread pools and interrupting threads. You've seen how the use of local work queues and work stealing can reduce the synchronization overhead and potentially improve the throughput of the thread pool and how running other tasks from the queue while waiting for a subtask to complete can eliminate the potential for deadlock.

We've also looked at various ways of allowing one thread to interrupt the processing of another, such as the use of specific interruption points and functions that perform what would otherwise be a blocking wait in a way that can be interrupted.

10 Testing and debugging multithreaded applications

This chapter covers

- Concurrency-related bugs
- Locating bugs through testing and code review
- Designing multithreaded tests
- Testing the performance of multithreaded code

Up to now, I've focused on what's involved in writing concurrent code—the tools that are available, how to use them, and the overall design and structure of the code. But there's a crucial part of software development that I haven't addressed yet: testing and debugging. If you're reading this chapter hoping for an easy way to test concurrent code, you're going to be sorely disappointed. Testing and debugging concurrent code is *hard*. What I *am* going to give you are some techniques that will make things easier, alongside issues that are important to think about.

Testing and debugging are like two sides of a coin—you subject your code to tests in order to find any bugs that might be there, and you debug it to remove those bugs. With luck, you only have to remove the bugs found by your own tests rather than bugs found by the end users of your application. Before we look at either testing or debugging, it's important to understand the problems that might arise, so let's look at those.

10.1 Types of concurrency-related bugs

You can get just about any sort of bug in concurrent code; it's not special in that regard. But some types of bugs are directly related to the use of concurrency and therefore of particular relevance to this book. Typically, these concurrency-related bugs fall into two primary categories:

- Unwanted blocking
- Race conditions

These are huge categories, so let's divide them up a bit. First, let's look at unwanted blocking.

10.1.1 Unwanted blocking

What do I mean by unwanted blocking? First, a thread is *blocked* when it's unable to proceed because it's waiting for something. This is typically something like a mutex, a condition variable, or a future, but it could be waiting for I/O. This is a natural part of multithreaded code, but it's not always desirable—hence the problem of unwanted blocking. This leads us to the next question: why is this blocking unwanted? Typically, this is because some other thread is also waiting for the blocked thread to perform some action, and so that thread in turn is blocked. There are several variations on this theme:

- *Deadlock*—As you saw in chapter 3, in the case of deadlock one thread is waiting for another, which is in turn waiting for the first. If your threads deadlock, the tasks they're supposed to be doing won't get done. In the most visible cases, one of the threads involved is the thread responsible for the user interface, in which case the interface will cease to respond. In other cases, the interface will remain responsive, but some required task won't complete, such as a search not returning or a document not printing.
- *Livelock*—Livelock is similar to deadlock in that one thread is waiting for another, which is in turn waiting for the first. The key difference here is that the wait is not a blocking wait but an active checking loop, such as a spin lock. In serious cases, the symptoms are the same as deadlock (the app doesn't make any progress), except that the CPU usage is high because threads are still running but blocking each other. In not-so-serious cases, the livelock will eventually resolve because of the random scheduling, but there will be a long delay in the task that got livelocked, with a high CPU usage during that delay.
- *Blocking on I/O or other external input*—If your thread is blocked waiting for external input, it can't proceed, even if the waited-for input is never going to come. It's therefore undesirable to block on external input from a thread that also performs tasks that other threads may be waiting for.

That briefly covers unwanted blocking. What about race conditions?

10.1.2 Race conditions

Race conditions are the most common cause of problems in multithreaded code—many deadlocks and livelocks only actually manifest because of a race condition. Not all race conditions are problematic—a race condition occurs anytime the behavior depends on the relative scheduling of operations in separate threads. A large number of race conditions are entirely benign; for example, which worker thread processes the next task in the task queue is largely irrelevant. However, many concurrency bugs are due to race conditions. In particular, race conditions often cause the following types of problems:

- *Data races*—A data race is the specific type of race condition that results in undefined behavior because of unsynchronized concurrent access to a shared memory location. I introduced data races in chapter 5 when we looked at the C++ memory model. Data races usually occur through incorrect usage of atomic operations to synchronize threads or through access to shared data without locking the appropriate mutex.
- *Broken invariants*—These can manifest as dangling pointers (because another thread deleted the data being accessed), random memory corruption (due to a thread reading inconsistent values resulting from partial updates), and double-free (such as when two threads pop the same value from a queue, and so both delete some associated data), among others. The invariants being broken can be temporal- as well as value-based. If operations on separate threads are required to execute in a particular order, incorrect synchronization can lead to a race condition in which the required order is sometimes violated.
- *Lifetime issues*—Although you could bundle these problems in with broken invariants, this really is a separate category. The basic problem with bugs in this category is that the thread outlives the data that it accesses, so it is accessing data that has been deleted or otherwise destroyed, and potentially the storage is even reused for another object. You typically get lifetime issues where a thread references local variables that go out of scope before the thread function has completed, but they aren't limited to that scenario. Whenever the lifetime of the thread and the data it operates on aren't tied together in some way, there's the potential for the data to be destroyed before the thread has finished and for the thread function to have the rug pulled out from under its feet. If you manually call `join()` in order to wait for the thread to complete, you need to ensure that the call to `join()` can't be skipped if an exception is thrown. This is basic exception safety applied to threads.

It's the problematic race conditions that are the killers. With deadlock and livelock, the application appears to hang and become completely unresponsive or takes too long to complete a task. Often, you can attach a debugger to the running process to identify which threads are involved in the deadlock or livelock and which synchronization objects they're fighting over. With data races, broken invariants, and lifetime issues, the visible symptoms of the problem (such as random crashes or incorrect output) can manifest anywhere in the code—the code may overwrite memory used by another part of the system that isn't touched until much later. The fault will then manifest in code completely unrelated to the location of the buggy code, possibly much later in the execution of the program. This is the true curse of shared memory systems—however much you try to limit which data is accessible by which thread and try to ensure that correct synchronization is used, any thread can overwrite the data being used by any other thread in the application.

Now that we've briefly identified the sorts of problems we're looking for, let's look at what you can do to locate any instances in your code so you can fix them.

10.2 Techniques for locating concurrency-related bugs

In the previous section we looked at the types of concurrency-related bugs you might see and how they might manifest in your code. With that information in mind, you can then look at your code to see where bugs might lie and how you can attempt to determine whether there are any bugs in a particular section.

Perhaps the most obvious and straightforward thing to do is *look at the code*. Although this might seem obvious, it's actually difficult to do in a thorough way. When you read code you've just written, it's all too easy to read what you intended to write rather than what's actually there. Likewise, when reviewing code that others have written, it's tempting to just give it a quick read-through, check it off against your local coding standards, and highlight any glaringly obvious problems. What's needed is to spend the time really going through the code with a fine-tooth comb, thinking about the concurrency issues—and the non-concurrency issues as well. (You might as well, while you're doing it. After all, a bug is a bug.) We'll cover specific things to think about when reviewing code shortly.

Even after thoroughly reviewing your code, you still might have missed some bugs, and in any case you need to confirm that it does indeed work, for peace of mind if nothing else. Consequently, we'll continue on from reviewing the code to a few techniques to employ when testing multithreaded code.

10.2.1 Reviewing code to locate potential bugs

As I've already mentioned, when reviewing multithreaded code to check for concurrency-related bugs, it's important to review it thoroughly, with a fine-tooth comb. If possible, get someone else to review it. Because they haven't written the code, they'll have to think through how it works, and this will help uncover any bugs that may be there. It's important that the reviewer have the time to do the review properly—not a casual two-minute quick glance, but a proper, considered review. Most concurrency bugs require more than a quick glance to spot—they usually rely on subtle timing issues to actually manifest.

If you get one of your colleagues to review the code, they'll be coming at it fresh. They'll therefore see things from a different point of view and may well spot things that you don't. If you don't have colleagues you can ask, ask a friend, or even post the code on the internet (taking care not to upset your company lawyers). If you can't get anybody to review your code for you, or they don't find anything, don't worry—there's still more you can do. For starters, it might be worth leaving the code alone for a while—work on another part of the application, read a book, or go for a walk. If you take a break, your subconscious can work on the problem in the background while you're consciously focused on something else. Also, the code will be less familiar when you come back to it—you might manage to look at it from a different perspective yourself.

An alternative to getting someone else to review your code is to do it yourself. One useful technique is to try to explain how it works *in detail* to someone else. They don't even have to be physically there—many teams have a bear or rubber chicken for this purpose, and I personally find that writing detailed notes can be hugely beneficial. As you explain, think about each line, what could happen, which data it accesses, and so forth. Ask yourself questions about the code, and explain the answers. I find this to be an incredibly powerful technique—by asking myself these questions and thinking carefully about the answers, the problem often reveals itself. These questions can be helpful for *any* code review, not just when reviewing your own code.

QUESTIONS TO THINK ABOUT WHEN REVIEWING MULTITHREADED CODE

As I've already mentioned, it can be useful for a reviewer (whether the code's author or someone else) to think about specific questions relating to the code being reviewed. These questions can focus the reviewer's mind on the relevant details of the code and can help identify potential problems. The questions I like to ask include the following, though this is most definitely not a comprehensive list. You might find other questions that help you to focus better. Anyway, here are the questions:

- Which data needs to be protected from concurrent access?
- How do you ensure that the data is protected?
- Where in the code could other threads be at this time?
- Which mutexes does this thread hold?
- Which mutexes might other threads hold?
- Are there any ordering requirements between the operations done in this thread and those done in another? How are those requirements enforced?
- Is the data loaded by this thread still valid? Could it have been modified by other threads?
- If you assume that another thread could be modifying the data, what would that mean and how could you ensure that this never happens?

This last question is my favorite, because it really makes me think about the relationships between the threads. By assuming the existence of a bug related to a particular line of code, you can then act as a detective and track down the cause. In order to convince yourself that there's no bug, you have to consider every corner case and possible ordering. This is particularly useful where the data is protected by more than one mutex over its lifetime, such as with the thread-safe queue from chapter 6 where we had separate mutexes for the head and tail of the queue: in order to be sure that an access is safe while holding one mutex, you have to be certain that a thread holding the *other* mutex can't also access the same element. It also makes it obvious that public data, or data for which other code can readily obtain a pointer or reference, has to come under particular scrutiny.

The penultimate question in the list is also important, because it addresses what's an easy mistake to make: if you release and then reacquire a mutex, you must assume that other threads may have modified the shared data. Although this is obvious, if the mutex locks aren't immediately visible—perhaps because they're internal to an object—you may unwittingly be doing exactly that. In chapter 6 you saw how this can lead to race conditions and bugs where the functions provided on a thread-safe data structure are too fine-grained. Whereas for a non-thread-safe stack it makes sense to have separate `top()` and `pop()` operations, for a stack that may be accessed by multiple threads concurrently, this is no longer the case because the lock on the internal mutex is released between the two calls, and so another thread can modify the stack. As you saw in chapter 6, the solution is to combine the two operations so they are both performed under the protection of the same mutex lock, thus eliminating the potential race condition.

OK, so you've reviewed your code (or got someone else to review it). You're sure there are no bugs. The proof of the pudding is, as they say, in the eating—how can you test your code to confirm or deny your belief in its lack of bugs?

10.2.2 Locating concurrency-related bugs by testing

When developing single-threaded applications, testing your applications is relatively straightforward, if time consuming. You could, in principle, identify all the possible sets of input data (or at least all the interesting cases) and run them through the application. If the application produced the correct behavior and output, you'd know it works for that given set of input. Testing for error states such as the handling of disk-full errors is more complicated than that, but the idea is the same—set up the initial conditions and allow the application to run.

Testing multithreaded code is an order of magnitude harder, because the precise scheduling of the threads is indeterminate and may vary from run to run. Consequently, even if you run the application with the same input data, it might work correctly some times and fail at other times if there's a race condition lurking in the code. Just because there's a potential race condition doesn't mean the code will fail *always*, just that it *might* fail *sometimes*.

Given the inherent difficulty of reproducing concurrency-related bugs, it pays to design your tests carefully. You want each test to run the smallest amount of code that could potentially demonstrate a problem, so that you can best isolate the code that's faulty if the test fails—it's better to test a concurrent queue directly to verify that concurrent pushes and pops work rather than testing it through a whole chunk of code that uses the queue. It can help if you think about how code should be tested when designing it—see the section on designing for testability later in this chapter.

It's also worth eliminating the concurrency from the test in order to verify that the problem is concurrency-related. If you have a problem when everything is running in a single thread, it's just a plain common or garden-variety bug rather than a concurrency-related bug. This is particularly important when trying to track down a bug that occurs "in the wild" as opposed to being detected in your test harness. Just because a bug occurs in the multithreaded portion of your application doesn't mean it's automatically concurrency-related. If you're using thread pools to manage the level of concurrency, there's usually a configuration parameter you can set to specify the number of worker threads. If you're managing threads manually, you'll have to modify the code to use a single thread for the test. Either way, if you can reduce your application to a single thread, you can eliminate concurrency as a cause. On the flip side, if the problem goes away on a *single-core* system (even with multiple threads running) but is present on *multicore* systems or *multiprocessor* systems, you have a race condition and possibly a synchronization or memory-ordering issue.

There's more to testing concurrent code than the structure of the code being tested; the structure of the test is just as important, as is the test environment. If you continue on with the example of testing a concurrent queue, you have to think about various scenarios:

- One thread calling `push()` or `pop()` on its own to verify that the queue does work at a basic level
- One thread calling `push()` on an empty queue while another thread calls `pop()`
- Multiple threads calling `push()` on an empty queue
- Multiple threads calling `push()` on a full queue
- Multiple threads calling `pop()` on an empty queue
- Multiple threads calling `pop()` on a full queue
- Multiple threads calling `pop()` on a partially full queue with insufficient items for all threads
- Multiple threads calling `push()` while one thread calls `pop()` on an empty queue
- Multiple threads calling `push()` while one thread calls `pop()` on a full queue
- Multiple threads calling `push()` while multiple threads call `pop()` on an empty queue
- Multiple threads calling `push()` while multiple threads call `pop()` on a full queue

Having thought about all these scenarios and more, you then need to consider additional factors about the test environment:

- What you mean by "multiple threads" in each case (3, 4, 1024?)
- Whether there are enough processing cores in the system for each thread to run on its own core
- Which processor architectures the tests should be run on
- How you ensure suitable scheduling for the "while" parts of your tests

There are additional factors to think about specific to your particular situation. Of these four environmental considerations, the first and last affect the structure of the test itself (and are covered in section 10.2.5), whereas the other two are related to the physical test system being used. The number of threads to use relates to the particular code being tested, but there are various ways of structuring tests to obtain suitable scheduling. Before we look at these techniques, let's look at how you can design your application code to be easier to test.

10.2.3 Designing for testability

Testing multithreaded code is difficult, so you want to do what you can to make it easier. One of the most important things you can do is *design* the code for testability. A lot has been written about designing single-threaded code for testability, and much of the advice still applies. In general, code is easier to test if the following factors apply:

- The responsibilities of each function and class are clear.
- The functions are short and to the point.
- Your tests can take complete control of the environment surrounding the code being tested.
- The code that performs the particular operation being tested is close together rather than spread throughout the system.
- You thought about how to test the code before you wrote it.

All of these are still true for multithreaded code. In fact, I'd argue that it's even more important to pay attention to the testability of multithreaded code than for single-threaded code, because it's inherently that much harder to test. That last point is important: even if you don't go as far as writing your tests before the code, it's well worth thinking about how you can test the code before you write it—what inputs to use, which conditions are likely to be problematic, how to stimulate the code in potentially problematic ways, and so on.

One of the best ways to design concurrent code for testing is to eliminate the concurrency. If you can break down the code into those parts that are responsible for the communication paths between threads and those parts that operate on the communicated data within a single thread, then you've greatly reduced the problem. Those parts of the application that operate on data that's being accessed by only that one thread can then be tested using the normal single-threaded techniques. The hard-to-test concurrent code that deals with communicating between threads and ensuring that only one thread at a time *is* accessing a particular block of data is now much smaller and the testing more tractable.

For example, if your application is designed as a multithreaded state machine, you could split it into several parts. The state logic for each thread, which ensures that the transitions and operations are correct for each possible set of input events, can be tested independently with single-threaded techniques, with the test harness providing the input events that would be coming from other threads. Then, the core state machine and message routing code that ensures that events are correctly delivered to the right thread in the right order can be tested independently, but with multiple concurrent threads and simple state logic designed specifically for the tests.

Alternatively, if you can divide your code into multiple blocks of *read shared data/transform data/update shared data*, you can test the *transform data* portions using all the usual single-threaded techniques, because this is now just single-threaded code. The hard problem of testing a multithreaded transformation will be reduced to testing the reading and updating of the shared data, which is much simpler.

One thing to watch out for is that library calls can use internal variables to store state, which then becomes shared if multiple threads use the same set of library calls. This can be a problem because it's not immediately apparent that the code accesses shared data. However, with time you learn which library calls these are, and they stick out like sore thumbs. You can then either add appropriate protection and synchronization or use an alternate function that's safe for concurrent access from multiple threads.

There's more to designing multithreaded code for testability than structuring your code to minimize the amount of code that needs to deal with concurrency-related issues and paying attention to the use of non-thread-safe library calls. It's also helpful to bear in mind the same set of questions you ask yourself when reviewing the code, from section 10.2.1. Although these questions aren't directly about testing and testability, if you think about the issues with your "testing hat" on and consider how to test the code, it will affect which design choices you make and will make testing easier.

Now that we've looked at designing code to make testing easier, and potentially modified the code to separate the "concurrent" parts (such as the thread-safe containers or state machine event logic) from the "single-threaded" parts (which may still interact with other threads through the concurrent chunks), let's look at the techniques for testing concurrency-aware code.

10.2.4 Multithreaded testing techniques

So, you've thought through the scenario you wish to test and written a small amount of code that exercises the functions being tested. How do you ensure that any potentially problematic scheduling sequences are exercised in order to flush out the bugs?

Well, there are a few ways of approaching this, starting with brute-force testing, or stress testing.

BRUTE-FORCE TESTING

The idea behind brute-force testing is to stress the code to see if it breaks. This typically means running the code many times, possibly with many threads running at once. If there's a bug that manifests only when the threads are scheduled in a particular fashion, then the more times the code is run, the more likely the bug is to appear. If you run the test once and it passes, you might feel a bit of confidence that the code works. If you run it ten times in a row and it passes every time, you'll likely feel more confident. If you run the test a billion times and it passes every time, you'll feel more confident still.

The confidence you have in the results does depend on the amount of code being tested by each test. If your tests are quite fine-grained, like the tests outlined previously for a thread-safe queue, such brute-force testing can give you a high degree of confidence in your code. On the other hand, if the code being tested is considerably larger, the number of possible scheduling permutations is so vast that even a billion test runs might yield a low level of confidence.

The downside to brute-force testing is that it might give you false confidence. If the way you've written the test means that the problematic circumstances can't occur, you can run the test as many times as you like and it won't fail, even if it would fail *every* time in slightly different circumstances. The worst example is where the problematic circumstances can't occur on your test system because of the way the particular system you're testing on happens to run. Unless your code is to run only on systems identical to the one being tested, the particular hardware and operating system combination may not allow the circumstances that would cause a problem to arise.

The classic example here is testing a multithreaded application on a single-processor system. Because every thread has to run on the same processor, everything is automatically serialized, and many race conditions and cache ping-pong problems that you may get with a true multiprocessor system evaporate. This isn't the only variable though; different processor architectures provide different synchronization and ordering facilities. For example, on x86 and x86-64 architectures, atomic load operations are always the same, whether tagged `memory_order_relaxed` or `memory_order_seq_cst` (see section 5.3.3). This means that code written using relaxed memory ordering may work on systems with an x86 architecture, where it would fail on a system with a finer-grained set of memory-ordering instructions such as SPARC.

If you need your application to be portable across a range of target systems, it's important to test it on representative instances of those systems. This is why I listed the processor architectures being used for testing as a consideration in section 10.2.2.

Avoiding the potential for false confidence is crucial to successful brute-force testing. This requires careful thought over test design, not just with respect to the choice of unit for the code being tested but also with respect to the design of the test harness and the choice of testing environment. You need to ensure that as many of the code paths as possible are tested and as many of the possible thread interactions as feasible. Not only that, but you need to know *which* options are covered and *which are left untested.*

Although brute-force testing does give you some degree of confidence in your code, it's not guaranteed to find all the problems. There's one technique that *is* guaranteed to find the problems, if you have the time to apply it to your code and the appropriate software. I call it *combination simulation testing.*

COMBINATION SIMULATION TESTING

That's a bit of a mouthful, so I'd best explain what I mean. The idea is that you run your code with a special piece of software that *simulates* the real runtime environment of the code. You may be aware of software that allows you to run multiple virtual machines on a single physical computer, where the characteristics of the virtual machine and its hardware are emulated by the supervisor software. The idea here is similar, except rather than just emulating the system, the simulation software records the sequences of data accesses, locks, and atomic operations from each thread. It then uses the rules of the C++ memory model to repeat the run with every permitted *combination* of operations and thus identify race conditions and deadlocks.

Although such exhaustive combination testing is guaranteed to find all the problems the system is designed to detect, for anything but the most trivial of programs it will take a huge amount of time, because the number of combinations increases exponentially with the number of threads and the number of operations performed by each thread. This technique is thus best reserved for fine-grained tests of individual pieces of code rather than an entire application. The other obvious downside is that it relies on the availability of simulation software that can handle the operations used in your code.

So, you have a technique that involves running your test many times under normal conditions but that might miss problems, and you have a technique that involves running your test many times under special conditions but that's more likely to find any problems that exist. Are there any other options?

A third option is to use a library that detects problems as they occur in the running of the tests.

DETECTING PROBLEMS EXPOSED BY TESTS WITH A SPECIAL LIBRARY

Although this option doesn't provide the exhaustive checking of a combination simulation test, you can identify many problems by using a special implementation of the library synchronization primitives such as mutexes, locks, and condition variables. For example, it's common to require that all accesses to a piece of shared data be done with a particular mutex locked. If you could check which mutexes were locked when the data was accessed, you could verify that the appropriate mutex was indeed locked by the calling thread when the data was accessed and report a failure if this was not the case. By marking your shared data in some way, you can allow the library to check this for you.

Such a library implementation can also record the sequence of locks if more than one mutex is held by a particular thread at once. If another thread locks the same mutexes in a different order, this could be recorded as a *potential* deadlock even if the test didn't actually deadlock while running.

Another type of special library that could be used when testing multithreaded code is one where the implementations of the threading primitives such as mutexes and condition variables give the test writer control over which thread gets the lock when multiple threads are waiting or which thread is notified by a `notify_one()` call on a condition variable. This would allow you to set up particular scenarios and verify that your code works as expected in those scenarios.

Some of these testing facilities would have to be supplied as part of the C++ Standard Library implementation, whereas others can be built on top of the Standard Library as part of your test harness.

Having looked at various ways of executing test code, let's now look at ways of structuring the code to achieve the scheduling you want.

10.2.5 Structuring multithreaded test code

Back in section 10.2.2 I said that you need to find ways of providing suitable scheduling for the "while" part of your tests. Now it's time to look at the issues involved in that.

The basic issue is that you need to arrange for a set of threads to each be executing a chosen piece of code at a time that you specify. In the most basic case you have two threads, but this could easily be extended to more. In the first step, you need to identify the distinct parts of each test:

- The general setup code that must be executed before anything else
- The thread-specific setup code that must run on each thread
- The actual code for each thread that you desire to run concurrently
- The code to be run after the concurrent execution has finished, possibly including assertions on the state of the code

To explain further, let's consider a specific example from the test list in section 10.2.2: one thread calling `push()` on an empty queue while another thread calls `pop()`.

The *general* setup code is simple: you must create the queue. The thread executing `pop()` has no *thread-specific* setup code. The thread-specific setup code for the thread executing `push()` depends on the interface to the queue and the type of object being stored. If the object being stored is expensive to construct or must be heap allocated, you want to do this as part of the thread-specific setup, so that it doesn't affect the test. On the other hand, if the queue is just storing plain `int`s, there's nothing to be gained by constructing an `int` in the setup code. The actual code being tested is relatively straightforward—a call to `push()` from one thread and a call to `pop()` from another—but what about the "after completion" code?

In this case, it depends on what you want `pop()` to do. If it's supposed to block until there is data, then clearly you want to see that the returned data is what was supplied to the `push()` call and that the queue is empty afterward. If `pop()` is *not* blocking and may complete even when the queue is empty, you need to test for two possibilities: either the `pop()` returned the data item supplied to the `push()` and the queue is empty or the `pop()` signaled that there was no data and the queue has one element. One or the other must be true; what you want to avoid is the scenario that `pop()` signaled "no data" but the queue is empty, or that `pop()` returned the value and the queue is *still* not empty. In order to simplify the test, assume you have a blocking `pop()`. The final code is therefore an assertion that the popped value is the pushed value and that the queue is empty.

Now, having identified the various chunks of code, you need to do the best you can to ensure that everything runs as planned. One way to do this is to use a set of `std::promises` to indicate when everything is ready. Each thread sets a promise to indicate that it's ready and then waits on a (copy of a) `std::shared_future` obtained from a third std::promise; the main thread waits for all the promises from all the threads to be set and then triggers the threads to go. This ensures that each thread has started and is just before the chunk of code that should be run concurrently; any thread-specific setup should be done before setting that thread's promise. Finally, the main thread waits for the threads to complete and checks the final state. You also need to be aware of exceptions and make sure you don't have any threads left waiting for the go signal when that's not going to happen. The following listing shows one way of structuring this test.

Listing 10.1 An example test for concurrent push() and pop() calls on a queue

```
void test_concurrent_push_and_pop_on_empty_queue()
{
    threadsafe_queue<int> q;                                  ❶

    std::promise<void> go,push_ready,pop_ready;               ❷
    std::shared_future<void> ready(go.get_future());          ❸

    std::future<void> push_done;                              ❹
    std::future<int> pop_done;

    try
    {
        push_done=std::async(std::launch::async,              ❺
                             [&q,ready,&push_ready]()
                             {
                                 push_ready.set_value();
                                 ready.wait();
                                 q.push(42);
                             }
            );
        pop_done=std::async(std::launch::async,               ❻
                            [&q,ready,&pop_ready]()
                            {
                                pop_ready.set_value();
                                ready.wait();
                                return q.pop();               ❼
                            }
            );
        push_ready.get_future().wait();                       ❽
        pop_ready.get_future().wait();
        go.set_value();                                       ❾

        push_done.get();                                      ❿
        assert(pop_done.get()==42);                           ⓫
        assert(q.empty());
    }
    catch(...)
    {
        go.set_value();                                       ⓬
        throw;
    }
}
```

The structure is pretty much as described previously. First, you create your empty queue as part of the general setup ❶. Then, you create all your promises for the "ready" signals ❷ and get a `std::shared_future` for the go signal ❸. Then, you create the futures you'll use to indicate that the threads have finished ❹. These have to go outside the `try` block so that you can set the go signal on an exception without waiting for the test threads to complete (which would deadlock—a deadlock in the test code would be rather less than ideal).

Inside the `try` block you can then start the threads ❺, ❻—you use `std::launch::async` to guarantee that the tasks are each running on their own thread. Note that the use of `std::async` makes your exception-safety task easier than it would be with plain `std::thread` because the destructor for the future will join with the thread. The lambda captures specify that each task will reference the queue and the relevant promise for signaling readiness, while taking a copy of the `ready` future you got from the go promise.

As described previously, each task sets its own `ready` signal and then waits for the general `ready` signal before running the actual test code. The main thread does the reverse—waiting for the signals from both threads ❽ before signaling them to start the real test ❾.

Finally, the main thread calls `get()` on the futures from the async calls to wait for the tasks to finish ❿, ⓫ and checks the results. Note that the *pop* task returns the retrieved value through the future ❼, so you can use that to get the result for the assert ⓫.

If an exception is thrown, you set the go signal to avoid any chance of a dangling thread and rethrow the exception ⓬. The futures corresponding to the tasks ❹ were declared last, so they'll be destroyed first, and their destructors will wait for the tasks to complete if they haven't already.

Although this seems like quite a lot of boilerplate just to test two simple calls, it's necessary to use something similar in order to have the best chance of testing what you actually want to test. For example, actually starting a thread can be quite a time-consuming process, so if you didn't have the threads wait for the go signal, then the push thread may have completed before the pop thread even started, which would completely defeat the point of the test. Using the futures in this way ensures that both threads are running and blocked on the same future. Unblocking the future then allows both threads to run. Once you're familiar with the structure, it should be relatively straightforward to create new tests in the same pattern. For tests that require more than two threads, this pattern is readily extended to additional threads.

So far, we've just been looking at the *correctness* of multithreaded code. Although this is the most important issue, it's not the only reason you test: it's also important to test the *performance* of multithreaded code, so let's look at that next.

10.2.6 Testing the performance of multithreaded code

One of the main reasons you might choose to use concurrency in an application is to make use of the increasing prevalence of multicore processors to improve the performance of your applications. It's therefore important to actually test your code to confirm that the performance does indeed improve, just as you'd do with any other attempt at optimization.

The particular issue with using concurrency for performance is the *scalability*—you want code that runs approximately 24 times faster or processes 24 times as much data on a 24-core machine than on a single-core machine, all else being equal. You don't want code that runs twice as fast on a dual-core machine but is actually slower on a 24-core machine. As you saw in section 8.4.2, if a significant section of your code runs on only one thread, this can limit the potential performance gain. It's therefore worth looking at the overall design of the code before you start testing, so you know whether you're hoping for a factor-of-24 improvement, or whether the serial portion of your code means you're limited to a maximum of a factor of 3.

As you've already seen in previous chapters, contention between processors for access to a data structure can have a big performance impact. Something that scales nicely with the number of processors when that number is small may actually perform badly when the number of processors is much larger because of the huge increase in contention.

Consequently, when testing for the performance of multithreaded code, it's best to check the performance on systems with as many different configurations as possible, so you get a picture of the scalability graph. At the very least, you ought to test on a single-processor system *and* a system with as many processing cores as are available to you.

10.3 Summary

In this chapter we looked at various types of concurrency-related bugs that you might encounter, from deadlocks and livelocks to data races and other problematic race conditions. We followed that with techniques for locating bugs. These included issues to think about during code reviews, guidelines for writing testable code, and how to structure tests for concurrent code. Finally, we looked at some utility components that can help with testing.

appendix A
Brief reference for some C++11 language features

The new C++ Standard brings more than just concurrency support; there are a whole host of other language features and new libraries as well. In this appendix I give a brief overview of the new language features that are used in the Thread Library and the rest of the book. Aside from `thread_local` (which is covered in section A.8), none of them are directly related to concurrency, though they are important and/or useful for multithreaded code. I've limited this list to those that are either necessary (such as rvalue references) or serve to make the code simpler or easier to understand. Code that uses these features may be difficult to understand at first because of lack of familiarity, but as you become familiar with them, they should generally make code easier to understand rather than harder. As the use of C++11 becomes more widespread, code making use of these features will become more common.

Without further ado, let's start by looking at *rvalue references*, which are used extensively by the Thread Library to facilitate transfer of ownership (of threads, locks, or whatever) between objects.

A.1 Rvalue references

If you've been doing C++ programming for any time, you'll be familiar with references; C++ references allow you to create a new name for an existing object. All accesses and modifications done through the new reference affect the original, for example:

```
int var=42;
int& ref=var;        <-- Create a reference to var
ref=99;
assert(var==99);     <-- Original updated because of assignment to reference
```

The references that we've all been using up to now are *lvalue references*—references to lvalues. The term *lvalue* comes from C and refers to things that can be on the left side of an assignment expression—named objects, objects allocated on the stack or heap, or members of other objects—things with a defined storage location. The term *rvalue* also comes from C and refers to things that can occur only on the right side of an assignment expression—literals and temporaries, for example. Lvalue references can only be bound to lvalues, not rvalues. You can't write

```
int& i=42;          // Won't compile
```

for example, because 42 is an rvalue. OK, that's not quite true; you've always been able to bind an rvalue to a const lvalue reference:

```
int const& i=42;
```

But this is a deliberate exception on the part of the standard, introduced before we had rvalue references in order to allow you to pass temporaries to functions taking references. This allows implicit conversions, so you can write things like this:

```
void print(std::string const& s);
print("hello");                    // Create temporary std::string object
```

Anyway, the C++11 Standard introduces *rvalue references*, which bind *only* to rvalues, not to lvalues, and are declared with two ampersands rather than one:

```
int&& i=42;
int j=42;
int&& k=j;          // Won't compile
```

You can thus use function overloading to determine whether function parameters are lvalues or rvalues by having one overload take an lvalue reference and another take an rvalue reference. This is the cornerstone of *move semantics*.

A.1.1 Move semantics

Rvalues are typically temporary and so can be freely modified; if you know that your function parameter is an rvalue, you can use it as temporary storage, or "steal" its contents without affecting program correctness. This means that rather than *copying* the contents of an rvalue parameter, you can just *move* the contents. For large dynamic structures, this saves a lot of memory allocation and provides a lot of scope for optimization. Consider a function that takes a std::vector<int> as a parameter and needs to have an internal copy for modification, without touching the original. The old way of doing this would be to take the parameter as a const lvalue reference and make the copy internally:

```
void process_copy(std::vector<int> const& vec_)
{
    std::vector<int> vec(vec_);
    vec.push_back(42);
}
```

This allows the function to take both lvalues and rvalues but forces the copy in every case. If you overload the function with a version that takes an rvalue reference, you can avoid the copy in the rvalue case, because you know you can freely modify the original:

```
void process_copy(std::vector<int> && vec)
{
    vec.push_back(42);
}
```

Now, if the function in question is the constructor of your class, you can pilfer the innards of the rvalue and use them for your new instance. Consider the class in the following listing. In the default constructor it allocates a large chunk of memory, which is freed in the destructor.

Listing A.1 A class with a move constructor

```
class X
{
private:
    int* data;
public:
    X():
        data(new int[1000000])
    {}
    ~X()
    {
        delete [] data;
    }
    X(const X& other):                  <-- 1
        data(new int[1000000])
    {
        std::copy(other.data,other.data+1000000,data);
    }
    X(X&& other):                    <-- 2
        data(other.data)
    {
        other.data=nullptr;
    }
};
```

The *copy constructor* ❶ is defined just as you might expect: allocate a new block of memory and copy the data across. However, you also have a new constructor that takes the old value by rvalue reference ❷. This is the *move constructor*. In this case you just copy the *pointer to* the data and leave the `other` instance with a null pointer, saving yourself a huge chunk of memory and time when creating variables from rvalues.

For class `X` the move constructor is just an optimization, but in some cases it makes sense to provide a move constructor even when it doesn't make sense to provide a copy constructor. For example, the whole point of `std::unique_ptr<>` is that each non-null instance is the one and only pointer to its object, so a copy constructor makes no sense. However, a move constructor allows ownership of the pointer to be transferred between instances and permits `std::unique_ptr<>` to be used as a function return value—the pointer is *moved* rather than *copied*.

If you wish to explicitly move from a named object that you know you'll no longer use, you can cast it to an rvalue either by using `static_cast<X&&>` or by calling `std::move()`:

```
X x1;
X x2=std::move(x1);
X x3=static_cast<X&&>(x2);
```

This can be beneficial when you wish to move the parameter value into a local or member variable without copying, because although an rvalue reference parameter can bind to rvalues, within the function itself it is treated as an lvalue:

```
void do_stuff(X&& x_)
{
    X a(x_);                    <-- Copies
    X b(std::move(x_));             <-- Moves
}
do_stuff(X());                  <-- OK, rvalue binds to rvalue reference
X x;
do_stuff(x);        <-- Error, lvalue can't bind to rvalue reference
```

Move semantics are used extensively in the Thread Library, both where copies make no semantic sense but resources can be transferred, and as an optimization to avoid expensive copies where the source is going to be destroyed anyway. You saw an example of this in section 2.2 where we used `std::move()` to transfer a `std::unique_ptr<>` instance into a newly constructed thread, and then again in section 2.3 where we looked at transferring ownership of threads between `std::thread` instances.

None of `std::thread`, `std::unique_lock<>`, `std::future<>`, `std::promise<>`, or `std::packaged_task<>` can be copied, but they all have move constructors to allow the associated resource to be transferred between instances and support their use as function return values. `std::string` and `std::vector<>` both can be copied as always, but they also have move constructors and move-assignment operators to avoid copying large quantities of data from an rvalue.

The C++ Standard Library never does anything with an object that has been explicitly moved into another object, except destroy it or assign *to* it (either with a copy or, more likely, a move). However, it's good practice to ensure that the invariant of the class encompasses the moved-from state. A `std::thread` instance that has been used as the source of a move is equivalent to a default-constructed `std::thread` instance, for example, and an instance of `std::string` that has been used as the source of a move will still have a valid state, although no guarantees are made as to what that state is (in terms of how long the string is or what characters it contains).

A.1.2 Rvalue references and function templates

There's a final nuance when you use rvalue references for parameters to a function template: if the function parameter is an rvalue reference to a template parameter, automatic template argument type deduction deduces the type to be an lvalue reference if an lvalue is supplied or a plain unadorned type if an rvalue is supplied. That's a bit of a mouthful, so let's look at an example. Consider the following function:

```
template<typename T>
void foo(T&& t)
{}
```

If you call it with an rvalue as follows, then `T` is deduced to be the type of the value:

```
foo(42);                    Calls foo<int>(42)
foo(3.14159);               Calls foo<double>(3.14159)
foo(std::string());         Calls foo<std::string>(std::string())
```

However, if you call `foo` with an *lvalue*, `T` is deduced to be an lvalue reference:

```
int i=42;
foo(i);                     Calls foo<int&>(i)
```

Because the function parameter is declared `T&&`, this is therefore a reference to a reference, which is treated as just the original reference type. The signature of `foo<int&>()` is thus

```
void foo<int&>(int& t);
```

This allows a single function template to accept both lvalue and rvalue parameters and is used by the `std::thread` constructor (sections 2.1 and 2.2) so that the supplied callable object can be moved into internal storage rather than copied if the parameter is an rvalue.

A.2 Deleted functions

Sometimes it doesn't make sense to allow a class to be copied. `std::mutex` is a prime example of this—what would it mean if you did copy a mutex? `std::unique_lock<>` is another—an instance is the one and only owner of the lock it holds. To truly copy it would mean that the copy also held the lock, which doesn't make sense. Moving ownership between instances, as described in section A.1.2, makes sense, but that's not copying. I'm sure you've met other examples.

The standard idiom for preventing copies of a class used to be to declare the copy constructor and copy assignment operator private and then not provide an implementation. This would cause a compile error if any code outside the class in question tried to copy an instance and a link-time error (due to lack of an implementation) if any of the class's member functions or friends tried to copy an instance:

```
class no_copies
{
public:
    no_copies(){}
private:
    no_copies(no_copies const&);
    no_copies& operator=(no_copies const&);      ❶ No implementation
};
```

```
no_copies a;
no_copies b(a);
```

2 Won't compile

With C++11, the committee realized that this was a common idiom but also realized that it's a bit of a hack. The committee therefore provided a more general mechanism that can be applied in other cases too: you can declare a function as *deleted* by adding `= delete` to the function declaration. `no_copies` can thus be written as

```
class no_copies
{
public:
    no_copies(){}
    no_copies(no_copies const&) = delete;
    no_copies& operator=(no_copies const&) = delete;
};
```

This is much more descriptive than the original code and clearly expresses the intent. It also allows the compiler to give more descriptive error messages and moves the error from link time to compile time if you try to perform the copy within a member function of your class.

If, as well as deleting the copy constructor and copy-assignment operator, you also explicitly write a move constructor and move-assignment operator, your class becomes move-only, the same as `std::thread` and `std::unique_lock<>`. The following listing shows an example of such a move-only type.

Listing A.2 A simple move-only type

```
class move_only
{
    std::unique_ptr<my_class> data;
public:
    move_only(const move_only&) = delete;
    move_only(move_only&& other):
        data(std::move(other.data))
    {}
    move_only& operator=(const move_only&) = delete;
    move_only& operator=(move_only&& other)
    {
        data=std::move(other.data);
        return *this;
    }
};
move_only m1;
move_only m2(m1);
move_only m3(std::move(m1));
```

Error, copy constructor is declared deleted

OK, move constructor found

Move-only objects can be passed as function parameters and returned from functions, but if you wish to move from an lvalue, you always have to be explicit and use `std::move()` or a `static_cast<T&&>`.

You can apply the `= delete` specifier to any function, not just copy constructors and assignment operators. This makes it clear that the function isn't available. It does a bit more than that too, though; a deleted function participates in overload resolution in the normal way and only causes a compilation error if it's selected. This can be used to remove specific overloads. For example, if your function takes a short parameter, you can prevent narrowing of int values by writing an overload that takes an int and declaring it deleted:

```
void foo(short);
void foo(int) = delete;
```

Any attempts to call foo with an int will now be met with a compilation error, and the caller will have to explicitly cast supplied values to short:

```
foo(42);                    <-- Error, int overload declared deleted
foo((short)42);             <-- OK
```

A.3 Defaulted functions

Whereas deleted functions allow you to explicitly declare that a function isn't implemented, *defaulted* functions are the opposite extreme: they allow you to specify that the compiler should write the function for you, with its "default" implementation. Of course, you can only do this for functions that the compiler can autogenerate anyway: default constructors, destructors, copy constructors, move constructors, copy-assignment operators, and move-assignment operators.

Why would you want to do that? There are several reasons why you might:

- *In order to change the accessibility of the function*—By default, the compiler-generated functions are public. If you wish to make them protected or even private, you must write them yourself. By declaring them as defaulted, you can get the compiler to write the function *and* change the access level.
- *As documentation*—If the compiler-generated version is sufficient, it might be worth explicitly declaring it as such so that when you or someone else looks at the code later, it's clear that this was intended.
- *In order to force the compiler to generate the function when it would not otherwise have done so*—This is typically done with default constructors, which are only normally compiler generated if there are no user-defined constructors. If you need to define a custom copy constructor (for example), you can still get a compiler-generated default constructor by declaring it as defaulted.
- *In order to make a destructor virtual while leaving it as compiler generated.*
- *To force a particular declaration of the copy constructor, such as having it take the source parameter by a non-*const *reference rather than by a* const *reference.*
- *To take advantage of the special properties of the compiler-generated function, which are lost if you provide an implementation*—More on this in a moment.

Just as deleted functions are declared by following the declaration with = delete, defaulted functions are declared by following the declaration by = default, for example:

```
class Y
{
```

```
private:
    Y() = default;          <-- Change access
public:
    Y(Y&) = default;        <-- Take a non-const reference
    T& operator=(const Y&) = default;   <-- Declare as defaulted for documentation
protected:
    virtual ~Y() = default; <-- Change access and add virtual
};
```

I mentioned previously that compiler-generated functions can have special properties that you can't get from a user-defined version. The biggest difference is that a compiler-generated function can be *trivial*. This has a few consequences, including the following:

- Objects with trivial copy constructors, trivial copy assignment operators, and trivial destructors can be copied with `memcpy` or `memmove`.
- Literal types used for `constexpr` functions (see section A.4) must have a trivial constructor, copy constructor, and destructor.
- Classes with a trivial default constructor, copy constructor, copy assignment operator, and destructor can be used in a union with a user-defined constructor and destructor.
- Classes with trivial copy assignment operators can be used with the `std::atomic<>` class template (see section 5.2.6) in order to provide a value of that type with atomic operations.

Just declaring the function as `= default` doesn't make it trivial—it will only be trivial if the class also supports all the other criteria for the corresponding function to be trivial—but explicitly writing the function in user code does *prevent* it from being trivial.

The second difference between classes with compiler-generated functions and user-supplied equivalents is that a class with no user-supplied constructors can be an *aggregate* and thus can be initialized with an aggregate initializer:

```
struct aggregate
{
    aggregate() = default;
    aggregate(aggregate const&) = default;

    int a;
    double b;
};
aggregate x={42,3.141};
```

In this case, `x.a` is initialized to `42` and `x.b` is initialized to `3.141`.

The third difference between a compiler-generated function and a user-supplied equivalent is quite esoteric and applies only to the default constructor and only to the default constructor of classes that meet certain criteria. Consider the following class:

```
struct X
{
    int a;
};
```

If you create an instance of class `X` without an initializer, the contained `int` (`a`) is *default initialized*. If the object has static storage duration, it's initialized to zero; otherwise, it has an indeterminate value that can potentially cause undefined behavior if it's accessed before being assigned a new value:

```
X x1;                                   x1.a has an indeterminate value
```

If, on the other hand, you initialize your instance of `X` by explicitly invoking the default constructor, then `a` is initialized to zero:

```
X x2=X();                               x2.a==0
```

This bizarre property also extends to base classes and members. If your class has a compiler-generated default constructor and any of your data members and base classes also have a compiler-generated default constructor, data members of those bases and members that are built-in types are also either left with an indeterminate value or initialized to zero, depending on whether or not the outer class has its default constructor explicitly invoked.

Although this rule is confusing and potentially error prone, it does have its uses, and if you write the default constructor yourself, you lose this property; either data members like `a` are always initialized (because you specify a value or explicitly default construct) or always uninitialized (because you don't):

```
X::X():a(){}          a==0 always
X::X():a(42){}                          a==42 always
X::X(){}              1
```

If you omit the initialization of `a` from the constructor of `X` as in the third example ❶, then `a` is left uninitialized for nonstatic instances of `X` and initialized to zero for instances of `X` with static storage duration.

Under normal circumstances, if you write any other constructor manually, the compiler will no longer generate the default constructor for you, so if you want one you have to write it, which means you lose this bizarre initialization property. However, by explicitly declaring the constructor as defaulted, you can force the compiler to generate the default constructor for you, and this property is retained:

```
X::X() = default;              Default initialization rules for a apply
```

This property is used for the atomic types (see section 5.2), which have their default constructor explicitly defaulted. Their initial value is always undefined unless either (a) they have static storage duration (and thus are statically initialized to zero), or (b) you explicitly invoke the default constructor to request zero initialization, or (c) you explicitly specify a value. Note that in the case of the atomic types, the constructor for initialization with a value is declared `constexpr` (see section A.4) in order to allow static initialization.

A.4 constexpr functions

Integer literals such as `42` are *constant expressions*. So are simple arithmetic expressions such as `23*2-4`. You can even use `const` variables of integral type that are themselves initialized with constant expressions as part of a new constant expression:

```
const int i=23;
const int two_i=i*2;
const int four=4;
const int forty_two=two_i-four;
```

Aside from using constant expressions to create variables that can be used in other constant expressions, there are a few things you can *only* do with constant expressions:

- Specify the bounds of an array:

  ```
  int bounds=99;
  int array[bounds];          // Error bounds is not a constant expression
  const int bounds2=99;
  int array2[bounds2];        // OK, bounds2 is a constant expression
  ```

- Specify the value of a nontype template parameter:

  ```
  template<unsigned size>
  struct test
  {};
  test<bounds> ia;            // Error bounds is not a constant expression
  test<bounds2> ia2;          // OK, bounds2 is a constant expression
  ```

- Provide an initializer for a `static const` class data member of integral type in the class definition:

  ```
  class X
  {
      static const int the_answer=forty_two;
  };
  ```

- Provide an initializer for a built-in type or aggregate that can be used for static initialization:

  ```
  struct my_aggregate
  {
      int a;
      int b;
  };
  static my_aggregate ma1={forty_two,123};    // Static initialization
  int dummy=257;
  static my_aggregate ma2={dummy,dummy};      // Dynamic initialization
  ```

- Static initialization like this can be used to avoid order-of-initialization problems and race conditions.

None of this is new—you could do all that with the 1998 edition of the C++ Standard. However, with the new Standard what constitutes a *constant expression* has been extended with the introduction of the `constexpr` keyword.

The `constexpr` keyword is primarily a function modifier. If the parameter and return type of a function meet certain requirements and the body is sufficiently simple, a function can be declared `constexpr`, in which case it can be used in constant expressions, for example:

```
constexpr int square(int x)
{
    return x*x;
}
int array[square(5)];
```

In this case, `array` will have 25 entries, because `square` is declared `constexpr`. Of course, just because the function *can* be used in a constant expression doesn't mean that all uses are automatically constant expressions:

```
int dummy=4;
int array[square(dummy)];
```

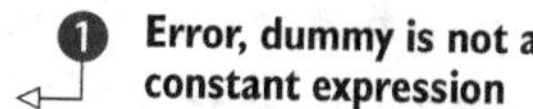
1 Error, dummy is not a constant expression

In this example, `dummy` is not a constant expression ❶, so `square(dummy)` isn't either—it's just a normal function call—and thus can't be used to specify the bounds of `array`.

A.4.1 constexpr and user-defined types

Up to now, all the examples have been with built-in types such as `int`. However, the new C++ Standard allows constant expressions to be of any type that satisfies the requirements for a *literal type*. For a class type to be classified as a literal type, the following must all be true:

- It must have a trivial copy constructor.
- It must have a trivial destructor.
- All non-`static` data members and base classes must be trivial types.
- It must have either a trivial default constructor or a `constexpr` constructor other than the copy constructor.

We'll look at `constexpr` constructors shortly. For now we'll focus on classes with a trivial default constructor, such as class `CX` in the following listing.

Listing A.3 A class with a trivial default constructor

```
class CX
{
private:
    int a;
    int b;
public:
    CX() = default;                ❶
    CX(int a_, int b_):                ❷
        a(a_),b(b_)
    {}
    int get_a() const
    {
        return a;
    }
    int get_b() const
```

```
    {
        return b;
    }
    int foo() const
    {
        return a+b;
    }
};
```

Note that we've explicitly declared the default constructor ❶ as *defaulted* (see section A.3) in order to preserve it as trivial in the face of the user-defined constructor ❷. This type therefore fits all the qualifications for being a literal type, and you can use it in constant expressions. You can, for example, provide a constexpr function that creates new instances:

```
constexpr CX create_cx()
{
    return CX();
}
```

You can also create a simple constexpr function that copies its parameter:

```
constexpr CX clone(CX val)
{
    return val;
}
```

But that's about all you can do—a constexpr function can only call other constexpr functions. What you *can* do, though, is apply constexpr to the member functions and constructor of CX:

```
class CX
{
private:
    int a;
    int b;
public:
    CX() = default;
    constexpr CX(int a_, int b_):
        a(a_),b(b_)
    {}
    constexpr int get_a() const          <-❶
    {
        return a;
    }
    constexpr int get_b()                <-❷
    {
        return b;
    }
    constexpr int foo()
    {
        return a+b;
    }
};
```

Note that the const qualification on get_a() ❶ is now superfluous, because it's implied by the use of constexpr. get_b() is thus const even though the const qualification is omitted ❷. This now allows more complex constexpr functions such as the following:

```
constexpr CX make_cx(int a)
{
    return CX(a,1);
}
constexpr CX half_double(CX old)
{
    return CX(old.get_a()/2,old.get_b()*2);
}
constexpr int foo_squared(CX val)
{
    return square(val.foo());
}
int array[foo_squared(half_double(make_cx(10)))];     <-- 49 elements
```

Interesting though this is, it's a lot of effort to go to if all you get is a fancy way of computing some array bounds or an integral constant. The key benefit of constant expressions and constexpr functions involving user-defined types is that objects of a literal type initialized with a constant expression are statically initialized, and so their initialization is free from race conditions and initialization order issues:

```
CX si=half_double(CX(42,19));            <-- Statically initialized
```

This covers constructors too. If the constructor is declared constexpr and the constructor parameters are constant expressions, the initialization is *constant initialization* and happens as part of the static initialization phase. *This is one of the most important changes in C++11 as far as concurrency goes:* by allowing user-defined constructors that can still undergo static initialization, you can avoid any race conditions over their initialization, because they're guaranteed to be initialized before any code is run.

This is particularly relevant for things like std::mutex (see section 3.2.1) or std::atomic<> (see section 5.2.6) where you might want to use a global instance to synchronize access to other variables and avoid race conditions in *that* access. This wouldn't be possible if the constructor of the mutex was subject to race conditions, so the default constructor of std::mutex is declared constexpr to ensure that mutex initialization is always done as part of the static initialization phase.

A.4.2 constexpr objects

So far we've looked at constexpr as applied to functions. constexpr can also be applied to objects. This is primarily for diagnostic purposes; it verifies that the object is initialized with a constant expression, constexpr constructor, or aggregate initializer made of constant expressions. It also declares the object as const:

```
constexpr int i=45;                       <-- OK
constexpr std::string s("hello");         <-- Error, std::string isn't a literal type
```

```
int foo();
constexpr int j=foo();
```

Error, foo() isn't declared constexpr

A.4.3 constexpr function requirements

In order to declare a function as `constexpr` it must meet a few requirements; if it doesn't meet these requirements, declaring it `constexpr` is a compilation error. The requirements for a `constexpr` function are as follows:

- All parameters must be of a literal type.
- The return type must be a literal type.
- The function body must consist of a single `return` statement.
- The expression in the `return` statement must qualify as a constant expression.
- Any constructor or conversion operator used to construct the return value from the expression must be `constexpr`.

This is straightforward; you must be able to inline the function into a constant expression and it will still be a constant expression, and you must not modify anything. `constexpr` functions are *pure functions* with no side effects.

For `constexpr` class member functions there are additional requirements:

- `constexpr` member functions can't be virtual.
- The class for which the function is a member must be a literal type.

The rules are different for `constexpr` constructors:

- The constructor body must be empty.
- Every base class must be initialized.
- Every non-`static` data member must be initialized.
- Any expressions used in the member initialization list must qualify as constant expressions.
- The constructors chosen for the initialization of the data members and base classes must be `constexpr` constructors.
- Any constructor or conversion operator used to construct the data members and base classes from their corresponding initialization expression must be `constexpr`.

This is the same set of rules as for functions, except that there's no return value, so no `return` statement. Instead, the constructor initializes all the bases and data members in the member initialization list. Trivial copy constructors are implicitly `constexpr`.

A.4.4 constexpr and templates

When `constexpr` is applied to a function template, or to a member function of a class template, it's ignored if the parameters and return types of a particular instantiation of the template aren't literal types. This allows you to write function templates that are `constexpr` if the type of the template parameters is appropriate and just plain `inline` functions otherwise, for example:

```
template<typename T>
constexpr T sum(T a,T b)
```

```
{
    return a+b;
}
constexpr int i=sum(3,42);          // OK, sum<int> is constexpr
std::string s=
    sum(std::string("hello"),
        std::string(" world"));     // OK, but sum<std::string> isn't constexpr
```

The function must satisfy all the other requirements for a `constexpr` function. You can't declare a function with multiple statements `constexpr` just because it's a function template; that's still a compilation error.

A.5 Lambda functions

Lambda functions are one of the most exciting features of the C++11 Standard, because they have the potential to greatly simplify code and eliminate much of the boilerplate associated with writing callable objects. The C++11 lambda function syntax allows a function to be defined at the point where it's needed in another expression. This works well for things like predicates provided to the wait functions of `std::condition_variable` (as in the example in section 4.1.1), because it allows the semantics to be quickly expressed in terms of the accessible variables rather than capturing the necessary state in the member variables of a class with a function call operator.

At its simplest, a *lambda expression* defines a self-contained function that takes no parameters and relies only on global variables and functions. It doesn't even have to return a value. Such a lambda expression is a series of statements enclosed in braces, prefixed with square brackets (the *lambda introducer*):

```
[]{                      // Start the lambda expression with []
    do_stuff();
    do_more_stuff();
}();                     // Finish the lambda, and call it
```

In this example, the lambda expression is called by following it with parentheses, but this is unusual. For one thing, if you're going to call it directly, you could usually do away with the lambda and write the statements directly in the source. It's more common to pass it as a parameter to a function template that takes a callable object as one of its parameters, in which case it likely needs to take parameters or return a value or both. If you need to take parameters, you can do this by following the lambda introducer with a parameter list just like for a normal function. For example, the following code writes all the elements of the vector to `std::cout` separated by newlines:

```
std::vector<int> data=make_data();
std::for_each(data.begin(),data.end(),[](int i){std::cout<<i<<"\n";});
```

Return values are almost as easy. If your lambda function body consists of a single `return` statement, the return type of the lambda is the type of the expression being returned. For example, you might use a simple lambda like this to wait for a flag to be set with a `std::condition_variable` (see section 4.1.1) as in the following listing.

Listing A.4 A simple lambda with a deduced return type

```
std::condition_variable cond;
bool data_ready;
std::mutex m;

void wait_for_data()
{
    std::unique_lock<std::mutex> lk(m);
    cond.wait(lk,[]{return data_ready;});      <-1
}
```

The return type of the lambda passed to `cond.wait()` ❶ is deduced from the type of `data_ready` and is thus `bool`. Whenever the condition variable wakes from waiting, it then calls the lambda with the mutex locked and only returns from the call to `wait()` once `data_ready` is `true`.

What if you can't write your lambda body as a single `return` statement? In that case you have to specify the return type explicitly. You can do this even if your body is a single `return` statement, but you *have* to do it if your lambda body is more complex. The return type is specified by following the lambda parameter list with an arrow (`->`) and the return type. If your lambda doesn't take any parameters, you must still include the (empty) parameter list in order to specify the return value explicitly. Your condition variable predicate can thus be written

```
cond.wait(lk,[]()->bool{return data_ready;});
```

By specifying the return type, you can expand the lambda to log messages or do some more complex processing:

```
cond.wait(lk,[]()->bool{
    if(data_ready)
    {
        std::cout<<"Data ready"<<std::endl;
        return true;
    }
    else
    {
        std::cout<<"Data not ready, resuming wait"<<std::endl;
        return false;
    }
});
```

Although simple lambdas like this are powerful and can simplify code quite a lot, the real power of lambdas comes when they capture local variables.

A.5.1 Lambda functions that reference local variables

Lambda functions with a *lambda introducer* of `[]` can't reference any local variables from the containing scope; they can only use global variables and anything passed in as a parameter. If you wish to access a local variable, you need to *capture* it. The simplest way to do this is to capture the entire set of variables within the local scope by using a lambda introducer of [=]. That's all there is to it—your lambda can now access *copies* of the local variables at the time the lambda was created.

To see this in action, consider the following simple function:

```
std::function<int(int)> make_offseter(int offset)
{
    return [=](int j){return offset+j;};
}
```

Every call to make_offseter returns a new lambda function object through the std::function<> function wrapper. This returned function adds the supplied offset to any parameter supplied. For example,

```
int main()
{
    std::function<int(int)> offset_42=make_offseter(42);
    std::function<int(int)> offset_123=make_offseter(123);
    std::cout<<offset_42(12)<<","<<offset_123(12)<<std::endl;
    std::cout<<offset_42(12)<<","<<offset_123(12)<<std::endl;
}
```

will write out 54,135 twice because the function returned from the first call to make_offseter always adds 42 to the supplied argument, whereas the function returned from the second call to make_offseter always adds 123 to the supplied argument.

This is the safest form of local variable capture; everything is copied, so you can return the lambda and call it outside the scope of the original function. It's not the only choice though; you can choose to capture everything by reference instead. In this case it's undefined behavior to call the lambda once the variables it references have been destroyed by exiting the function or block scope to which they belong, just as it's undefined behavior to reference a variable that has already been destroyed in any other circumstance.

A lambda function that captures all the local variables by reference is introduced using [&], as in the following example:

```
int main()
{
    int offset=42;                                                  ❶
    std::function<int(int)> offset_a=[&](int j){return offset+j;};    ❷
    offset=123;                                                     ❸
    std::function<int(int)> offset_b=[&](int j){return offset+j;};    ❹
    std::cout<<offset_a(12)<<","<<offset_b(12)<<std::endl;          ❺
    offset=99;                                                 ❻
    std::cout<<offset_a(12)<<","<<offset_b(12)<<std::endl;          ❼
}
```

Whereas in the make_offseter function from the previous example we used the [=] lambda introducer to capture a copy of the offset, the offset_a function in this example uses the [&] lambda introducer to capture offset by reference ❷. It doesn't matter that the initial value of offset is 42 ❶; the result of calling offset_a(12) will always depend on the current value of offset. Even though the value of offset is then changed to 123 ❸ before we produce the second (identical) lambda function `offset_b` ❹, this second lambda again captures by reference, so the result depends on the current value of `offset`.

Now, when we print the first line of output ❺, `offset` is still 123, so the output is `135,135`. However, at the second line of output ❼, `offset` has been changed to 99 ❻, so this time the output is `111,111`. Both `offset_a` and `offset_b` add the current value of `offset` (99) to the supplied argument (12).

Now, C++ being C++, you're not stuck with these all-or-nothing options; you can choose to capture some variables by copy and some by reference, and you can choose to capture only those variables you have explicitly chosen just by tweaking the lambda introducer. If you wish to *copy* all the used variables except for one or two, you can use the `[=]` form of the lambda introducer but follow the equals sign with a list of variables to capture by reference preceded with ampersands. The following example will thus print `1239`, because `i` is copied into the lambda, but `j` and `k` are captured by reference:

```
int main()
{
    int i=1234,j=5678,k=9;
    std::function<int()> f=[=,&j,&k]{return i+j+k;};
    i=1;
    j=2;
    k=3;
    std::cout<<f()<<std::endl;
}
```

Alternatively, you can capture by reference by default but capture a specific subset of variables by copying. In this case you use the `[&]` form of the lambda introducer but follow the ampersand with a list of variables to capture by copy. The following example thus prints `5688` because `i` is captured by reference, but `j` and `k` are copied:

```
int main()
{
    int i=1234,j=5678,k=9;
    std::function<int()> f=[&,j,k]{return i+j+k;};
    i=1;
    j=2;
    k=3;
    std::cout<<f()<<std::endl;
}
```

If you only want to capture the named variables, then you can omit the leading `=` or `&` and just list the variables to be captured, prefixing them with an ampersand to capture by reference rather than copy. The following code will thus print `5682` because `i` and `k` are captured by reference, but `j` is copied:

```
int main()
{
    int i=1234,j=5678,k=9;
    std::function<int()> f=[&i,j,&k]{return i+j+k;};
```

```
    i=1;
    j=2;
    k=3;
    std::cout<<f()<<std::endl;
}
```

This final variant allows you to ensure that only the intended variables are being captured, because any reference to a local variable not in the capture list will cause a compilation error. If you choose this option, you have to be careful when accessing class members if the function containing the lambda is a member function. Class members can't be captured directly; if you wish to access class members from your lambda, you have to capture the this pointer by adding it to the capture list. In the following example, the lambda captures `this` to allow access to the `some_data` class member:

```
struct X
{
    int some_data;
    void foo(std::vector<int>& vec)
    {
        std::for_each(vec.begin(),vec.end(),
            [this](int& i){i+=some_data;});
    }
};
```

In the context of concurrency, lambdas are most useful as predicates for `std::condition_variable::wait()` (section 4.1.1) and with `std::packaged_task<>` (section 4.2.1) or thread pools for packaging small tasks. They can also be passed to the `std::thread` constructor as a thread function (section 2.1.1) and as the function when using parallel algorithms such as `parallel_for_each()` (from section 8.5.1).

A.6 Variadic templates

Variadic templates are templates with a variable number of parameters. Just as you've always been able to have variadic functions such as `printf` that take a variable number of parameters, you can now have variadic templates that have a variable number of *template* parameters. Variadic templates are used throughout the C++ Thread Library. For example, the `std::thread` constructor for starting a thread (section 2.1.1) is a variadic function template, and `std::packaged_task<>` (section 4.2.2) is a variadic class template. From a user's point of view, it's enough to know that the template takes an unbounded number of parameters, but if you want to write such a template, or if you're just interested in how it all works, you need to know the details.

Just as variadic functions are declared with an ellipsis (`...`) in the function parameter list, variadic templates are declared with an ellipsis in the template parameter list:

```
template<typename ... ParameterPack>
class my_template
{};
```

You can use variadic templates for a partial specialization of a template too, even if the primary template isn't variadic. For example, the primary template for `std::packaged_task<>` (section 4.2.1) is just a simple template with a single template parameter:

```
template<typename FunctionType>
class packaged_task;
```

However, this primary template is never defined anywhere; it's just a placeholder for the partial specialization:

```
template<typename ReturnType,typename ... Args>
class packaged_task<ReturnType(Args...)>;
```

It's this partial specialization that contains the real definition of the class; you saw in chapter 4 that you can write `std::packaged_task<int(std::string,double)>` to declare a task that takes a `std::string` and a `double` as parameters when you call it and that provides the result through a `std::future<int>`.

This declaration shows two additional features of variadic templates. The first feature is relatively simple: you can have normal template parameters (such as `ReturnType`) as well as variadic ones (`Args`) in the same declaration. The second feature demonstrated is the use of `Args...` in the template argument list of the specialization to show that the types that make up `Args` when the template is instantiated are to be listed here. Actually, because this is a partial specialization, it works as a pattern match; the types that occur in this context in the actual instantiation are captured as `Args`. The variadic parameter `Args` is called a *parameter pack*, and the use of `Args...` is called a *pack expansion*.

Just like with variadic functions, the variadic part may be an empty list or may have many entries. For example, with `std::packaged_task<my_class()>` the `ReturnType` parameter is `my_class`, and the `Args` parameter pack is empty, whereas with `std::packaged_task<void(int,double,my_class&,std::string*)>` the `ReturnType` is `void`, and `Args` is the list `int`, `double`, `my_class&`, `std::string*`.

A.6.1 Expanding the parameter pack

The power of variadic templates comes from what you can do with that pack expansion: you aren't limited to just expanding the list of types as is. First off, you can use a pack expansion directly anywhere a list of types is required, such as in the argument list for another template:

```
template<typename ... Params>
struct dummy
{
    std::tuple<Params...> data;
};
```

In this case the single member variable `data` is an instantiation of `std::tuple<>` containing all the types specified, so `dummy<int,double,char>` has a member of type `std::tuple<int,double,char>`. You can combine pack expansions with normal types:

```
template<typename ... Params>
struct dummy2
{
    std::tuple<std::string,Params...> data;
};
```

This time, the tuple has an additional (first) member of type `std::string`. The nifty part is that you can create a pattern with the pack expansion, which is then copied for each element in the expansion. You do this by putting the `...` that marks the pack expansion at the end of the pattern. For example, rather than just creating a tuple of the elements supplied in your parameter pack, you can create a tuple of pointers to the elements or even a tuple of `std::unique_ptr<>`s to your elements:

```
template<typename ... Params>
struct dummy3
{
    std::tuple<Params* ...> pointers;
    std::tuple<std::unique_ptr<Params> ...> unique_pointers;
};
```

The type expression can be as complex as you like, provided the parameter pack occurs in the type expression, and provided the expression is followed by the `...` that marks the expansion. When the parameter pack is expanded, for each entry in the pack that type is substituted into the type expression to generate the corresponding entry in the resulting list. Thus, if your parameter pack `Params` contains the types `int,int,char`, then the expansion of `std::tuple<std::pair<std::unique_ptr<Params>,double> ... >` is `std::tuple<std::pair<std::unique_ptr<int>,double>, std::pair<std::unique_ptr<int>,double>, std::pair<std::unique_ptr<char>, double> >`. If the pack expansion is used as a template argument list, that template doesn't have to have variadic parameters, but if it doesn't, the size of the pack must exactly match the number of template parameters required:

```
template<typename ... Types>
struct dummy4
{
    std::pair<Types...> data;
};
dummy4<int,char> a;        ❶ OK, data is std::pair<int,char>
dummy4<int> b;             ❷ Error, no second type
dummy4<int,int,int> c;     ❸ Error, too many types
```

The second thing you can do with a pack expansion is use it to declare a list of function parameters:

```
template<typename ... Args>
void foo(Args ... args);
```

This creates a new parameter pack `args`, which is a list of the function parameters rather than a list of types, which you can expand with `...` as before. Now, you can use a pattern with the pack expansion for declaring the function parameters, just as you can use a pattern when you expand the pack elsewhere. For example, this is used by the `std::thread` constructor to take all the function arguments by rvalue reference (see section A.1):

```
template<typename CallableType,typename ... Args>
thread::thread(CallableType&& func,Args&& ... args);
```

The function parameter pack can then be used to call another function, by specifying the pack expansion in the argument list of the called function. Just as with the type expansions, you can use a pattern for each expression in the resulting argument list. For example, one common idiom with rvalue references is to use `std::forward<>` to preserve the rvalue-ness of the supplied function arguments:

```
template<typename ... ArgTypes>
void bar(ArgTypes&& ... args)
{
    foo(std::forward<ArgTypes>(args)...);
}
```

Note that in this case, the pack expansion contains both the type pack `ArgTypes` and the function parameter pack `args`, and the ellipsis follows the whole expression. If you call `bar` like this,

```
int i;
bar(i,3.141,std::string("hello "));
```

then the expansion becomes

```
template<>
void bar<int&,double,std::string>(
    int& args_1,
    double&& args_2,
    std::string&& args_3)
{
    foo(std::forward<int&>(args_1),
        std::forward<double>(args_2),
        std::forward<std::string>(args_3));
}
```

which correctly passes the first argument on to `foo` as an lvalue reference, while passing the others as rvalue references.

The final thing you can do with a parameter pack is find its size with the `sizeof...` operator. This is quite simple: `sizeof...(p)` is the number of elements in the parameter pack `p`. It doesn't matter whether this is a type parameter pack or a function argument parameter pack; the result is the same. This is probably the only case where you can use a parameter pack and not follow it with an ellipsis; the ellipsis is already part of the `sizeof...` operator. The following function returns the number of arguments supplied to it:

```
template<typename ... Args>
unsigned count_args(Args ... args)
{
    return sizeof... (Args);
}
```

Just as with the normal `sizeof` operator, the result of `sizeof...` is a constant expression, so it can be used for specifying array bounds and so forth.

A.7 Automatically deducing the type of a variable

C++ is a statically typed language: the type of every variable is known at compile time. Not only that, but as a programmer you have to actually specify the type of each variable. In some cases this can lead to quite unwieldy names, for example:

```
std::map<std::string,std::unique_ptr<some_data>> m;
std::map<std::string,std::unique_ptr<some_data>>::iterator
    iter=m.find("my key");
```

Traditionally, the solution has been to use `typedef`s to reduce the length of a type identifier and potentially eliminate problems due to inconsistent types. This still works in C++11, but there's now a new way: if a variable is initialized in its declaration from a value of the same type, then you can specify the type as `auto`. In this case, the compiler will automatically deduce the type of the variable to be the same as the initializer. Thus, the iterator example can be written as

```
auto iter=m.find("my key");
```

Now, you're not restricted to just plain `auto`; you can embellish it to declare `const` variables or pointer or reference variables too. Here are a few variable declarations using `auto` and the corresponding type of the variable:

```
auto i=42;         // int
auto& j=i;         // int&
auto const k=i;    // int const
auto* const p=&i;  // int * const
```

The rules for deducing the type of the variable are based on the rules for the only other place in the language where types are deduced: parameters of function templates. In a declaration of the form

```
some-type-expression-involving-auto var=some-expression;
```

the type of `var` is the same as the type deduced for the parameter of a function template declared with the same type expression, except replacing `auto` with the name of a template type parameter:

```
template<typename T>
void f(type-expression var);
f(some-expression);
```

This means that array types decay to pointers, and references are dropped unless the type expression explicitly declares the variable as a reference, for example:

```
int some_array[45];
auto p=some_array;    // int*
int& r=*p;
auto x=r;             // int
auto& y=r;            // int&
```

This can greatly simplify the declaration of variables, particularly where the full type identifier is long or possibly not even known (for example, the type of the result of a function call in a template).

A.8 Thread-local variables

Thread-local variables allow you to have a separate instance of a variable for each thread in your program. You mark a variable as being thread-local by declaring it with the `thread_local` keyword. Variables at namespace scope, static data members of classes, and local variables can be declared thread-local, and are said to have *thread storage duration*:

```
thread_local int x;                              <-- A thread-local variable at namespace scope

class X
{
    static thread_local std::string s;           <-- A thread-local static class data member
};
static thread_local std::string X::s;            <-- The definition of X::s is required

void foo()
{
    thread_local std::vector<int> v;             <-- A thread-local local variable
}
```

Thread-local variables at namespace scope and thread-local static class data members are constructed before the first use of a thread-local variable from the same translation unit, but it isn't specified *how much* before. Some implementations may construct thread-local variables when the thread is started; others may construct them immediately before their first use on each thread, and others may construct them at other times, or in some combination depending on their usage context. Indeed, if none of the thread-local variables from a given translation unit is used, there's no guarantee that they will be constructed at all. This allows for the dynamic loading of modules containing thread-local variables—these variables can be constructed on a given thread the first time that thread references a thread-local variable from the dynamically-loaded module.

Thread-local variables declared inside a function are initialized the first time the flow of control passes through their declaration on a given thread. If the function is not called by a given thread, any thread-local variables declared in that function are not constructed. This is just the same as the behaviour for local static variables, except it applies separately to each thread.

Thread-local variables share other properties with static variables—they're zero-initialized prior to any further initialization (such as dynamic initialization), and if the construction of a thread-local variable throws an exception, `std::terminate()` is called to abort the application.

The destructors for all thread-local variables that have been constructed on a given thread are run when the thread function returns, in the reverse order of construction. Since the order of initialization is unspecified, it's important to ensure that there are no interdependencies between the destructors of such variables. If the destructor of a thread-local variable exits with an exception, `std::terminate()` is called, just as for construction.

Thread-local variables are also destroyed for a thread if *that thread* calls `std::exit()` or returns from main() (which is equivalent to calling `std::exit()` with the return value of `main()`). If any other threads are still running when the application exits, the destructors of thread-local variables on those threads are *not* called.

Though thread-local variables have a different address on each thread, you can still obtain a normal pointer to such a variable. The pointer then references the object in the thread that took the address, and can be used to allow other threads to access that object. It's undefined behaviour to access an object after it's been destroyed (as always), so if you pass a pointer to a thread-local variable to another thread, you need to ensure it's not dereferenced once the owning thread has finished.

A.9 Summary

This appendix has only scratched the surface of the new language features introduced with the C++11 Standard, because we've only looked at those features that actively affect the usage of the Thread Library. Other new language features include static assertions, strongly typed enumerations, delegating constructors, Unicode support, template aliases, and a new uniform initialization sequence, along with a host of smaller changes. Describing all the new features in detail is outside the scope of this book; it would probably require a book in itself. The best overview of the entire set of changes to the standard at the time of writing is probably Bjarne Stroustrup's C++11 FAQ,[1] though popular C++ reference books will be revised to cover it in due course.

Hopefully the brief introduction to the new features covered in this appendix has provided enough depth to show how they relate to the Thread Library and to enable you to write and understand multithreaded code that uses these new features. Although this appendix should provide enough depth for simple uses of the features covered, this is still only a brief introduction and not a complete reference or tutorial for the use of these features. If you intend to make extensive use of them, I recommend acquiring such a reference or tutorial in order to gain the most benefit from them.

---

1 http://www.research.att.com/~bs/C++0xFAQ.html

appendix B
Brief comparison of concurrency libraries

Concurrency and multithreading support in programming languages and libraries aren't something new, even though standardized support in C++ is new. For example, Java has had multithreading support since it was first released, platforms that conform to the POSIX standard provide a C interface for multithreading, and Erlang provides support for message-passing concurrency. There are even C++ class libraries such as Boost that wrap the underlying programming interface for multithreading used on any given platform (whether it's the POSIX C interface or something else) to provide a portable interface across the supported platforms.

For those who are already experienced in writing multithreaded applications and would like to use that experience to write code using the new C++ multithreading facilities, this appendix provides a comparison between the facilities available in Java, POSIX C, C++ with the Boost Thread Library, and C++11, along with cross-references to the relevant chapters of this book.

Feature	Java	POSIX C	Boost threads	C++11	Chapter reference
Starting threads	java.lang.thread class	pthread_t type and associated API functions: pthread_create(), pthread_detach(), and pthread_join()	boost::thread class and member functions	std::thread class and member functions	Chapter 2
Mutual exclusion	synchronized blocks	pthread_mutex_t type and associated API functions: pthread_mutex_lock(), pthread_mutex_unlock(), etc.	boost::mutex class and member functions, boost::lock_guard<> and boost::unique_lock<> templates	std::mutex class and member functions, std::lock_guard<> and std::unique_lock<> templates	Chapter 3
Monitors/ waits for a predicate	wait() and notify() methods of the java.lang.Object class, used inside synchronized blocks	pthread_cond_t type and associated API functions: pthread_cond_wait(), pthread_cond_timed_wait(), etc.	boost::condition_variable and boost::condition_variable_any classes and member functions	std::condition_variable and std::condition_variable_any classes and member functions	Chapter 4
Atomic operations and concurrency-aware memory model	volatile variables, the types in the java.util.concurrent .atomic package	N/A	N/A	std::atomic_*xxx* types, std::atomic<> class template, std::atomic_thread_fence() function	Chapter 5
Thread-safe containers	The containers in the java.util.concurrent package	N/A	N/A	N/A	Chapters 6 and 7
Futures	java.util.concurrent .future interface and associated classes	N/A	boost::unique_future<> and boost::shared_future<> class templates	std::future<>, std::shared_future<> and std::atomic_future<> class templates	Chapter 4
Thread pools	java.util.concurrent .ThreadPoolExecutor class	N/A	N/A	N/A	Chapter 9
Thread interruption	interrupt() method of java.lang.Thread	pthread_cancel()	interrupt() member function of boost::thread class	N/A	Chapter 9

appendix C
A message-passing framework and complete ATM example

Back in chapter 4, I presented an example of sending messages between threads using a message-passing framework, using a simple implementation of the code in an ATM as an example. What follows is the complete code for this example, including the message-passing framework.

Listing C.1 shows the message queue. It stores a list of messages as pointers to a base class; the specific message type is handled with a template class derived from that base class. Pushing an entry constructs an appropriate instance of the wrapper class and stores a pointer to it; popping an entry returns that pointer. Because the `message_base` class doesn't have any member functions, the popping thread will need to cast the pointer to a suitable `wrapped_message<T>` pointer before it can access the stored message.

Listing C.1 A simple message queue

```
#include <mutex>
#include <condition_variable>
#include <queue>
#include <memory>

namespace messaging
{
    struct message_base
    {
        virtual ~message_base()
        {}
    };
```

Base class of our queue entries

```
    template<typename Msg>
    struct wrapped_message:                    <-- Each message type
        message_base                               has a specialization
    {
        Msg contents;

        explicit wrapped_message(Msg const& contents_):
            contents(contents_)
        {}
    };
                                   Our message
    class queue                <-- queue
    {
        std::mutex m;                                     Actual queue
        std::condition_variable c;                        stores pointers to
        std::queue<std::shared_ptr<message_base> > q;  <-- message_base
    public:
        template<typename T>                                        Wrap
        void push(T const& msg)                                     posted
        {                                                           message
            std::lock_guard<std::mutex> lk(m);                      and store
            q.push(std::make_shared<wrapped_message<T> >(msg));  <-- pointer
            c.notify_all();
        }

        std::shared_ptr<message_base> wait_and_pop()
        {
            std::unique_lock<std::mutex> lk(m);         Block until queue
            c.wait(lk,[&]{return !q.empty();});     <-- isn't empty
            auto res=q.front();
            q.pop();
            return res;
        }
    };
}
```

Sending messages is handled through an instance of the sender class shown in listing C.2. This is just a thin wrapper around a message queue that only allows messages to be pushed. Copying instances of sender just copies the pointer to the queue rather than the queue itself.

Listing C.2 The sender class

```
namespace messaging
{
    class sender
    {                       sender is wrapper
        queue*q;        <-- around queue pointer
    public:                                       Default-constructed
        sender():                             <-- sender has no queue
            q(nullptr)
        {}                                     Allow construction
        explicit sender(queue*q_):         <-- from pointer to queue
            q(q_)
        {}
```

```
        template<typename Message>
        void send(Message const& msg)
        {
            if(q)
            {                                   Sending pushes
                q->push(msg);              <--  message on the queue
            }
        }
    };
}
```

Receiving messages is a bit more complicated. Not only do you have to wait for a message from the queue, but you also have to check to see if the type matches any of the message types being waited on and call the appropriate handler function. This all starts with the `receiver` class shown in the following listing.

Listing C.3 The `receiver` class

```
namespace messaging
{
    class receiver
    {                      A receiver owns
        queue q;      <--  the queue
    public:                                  Allow implicit conversion
        operator sender()                    to a sender that
        {                                <-- references the queue
            return sender(&q);
        }
                                             Waiting for a queue
        dispatcher wait()                <-- creates a dispatcher
        {
            return dispatcher(&q);
        }
    };
}
```

Whereas a `sender` just references a message queue, a `receiver` owns it. You can obtain a `sender` that references the queue by using the implicit conversion. The complexity of doing the message dispatch starts with a call to `wait()`. This creates a `dispatcher` object that references the queue from the `receiver`. The `dispatcher` class is shown in the next listing; as you can see, the work is done in the *destructor*. In this case, that work consists of waiting for a message and dispatching it.

Listing C.4 The `dispatcher` class

```
namespace messaging
{                                  The message for
    class close_queue         <--  closing the queue
    {};

    class dispatcher
    {
```

```
    queue* q;
    bool chained;

    dispatcher(dispatcher const&)=delete;              <-- dispatcher instances
    dispatcher& operator=(dispatcher const&)=delete;       cannot be copied

    template<
        typename Dispatcher,
        typename Msg,                   Allow TemplateDispatcher
        typename Func>              <-- instances to access the internals
    friend class TemplateDispatcher;

    void wait_and_dispatch()
    {                                (1) Loop, waiting for and
        for(;;)                  <--     dispatching messages
        {
            auto msg=q->wait_and_pop();
            dispatch(msg);
        }                                   (2) dispatch() checks for a
    }                                           close_queue message,
                                                and throws
    bool dispatch(                      <--
        std::shared_ptr<message_base> const& msg)
    {
        if(dynamic_cast<wrapped_message<close_queue>*>(msg.get()))
        {
            throw close_queue();
        }
        return false;
    }
public:                                        dispatcher instances
    dispatcher(dispatcher&& other):        <-- can be moved
        q(other.q),chained(other.chained)
    {
        other.chained=true;            <-- The source mustn't
    }                                      wait for messages

    explicit dispatcher(queue* q_):
        q(q_),chained(false)
    {}

    template<typename Message,typename Func>         (3) Handle a specific type
    TemplateDispatcher<dispatcher,Message,Func>          of message with a
    handle(Func&& f)                             <--     TemplateDispatcher
    {
        return TemplateDispatcher<dispatcher,Message,Func>(
            q,this,std::forward<Func>(f));
    }

    ~dispatcher() noexcept(false)       <-- The destructor might
    {                                   (4) throw exceptions
        if(!chained)
        {
            wait_and_dispatch();
        }
    }
};
}
```

The dispatcher instance that's returned from wait() will be destroyed immediately, because it's a temporary, and as mentioned, the destructor does the work. The destructor calls wait_and_dispatch(), which is a loop ❶ that waits for a message and passes it to dispatch(). dispatch() itself ❷ is rather simple; it checks whether the message is a close_queue message and throws an exception if it is; otherwise, it returns false to indicate that the message was unhandled. This close_queue exception is why the destructor is marked noexcept(false); without this annotation the default exception specification for the destructor would be noexcept(true) ❹, indicating that no exceptions can be thrown, and the close_queue exception would thus terminate the program.

It's not often that you're going to call wait() on its own, though; most of the time you'll be wanting to handle a message. This is where the handle() member function ❸ comes in. It's a template, and the message type isn't deducible, so you must specify which message type to handle and pass in a function (or callable object) to handle it. handle() itself passes the queue, the current dispatcher object, and the handler function to a new instance of the TemplateDispatcher class template, to handle messages of the specified type. This is shown in listing C.5. This is why you test the chained value in the destructor before waiting for messages; not only does it prevent moved-from objects waiting for messages, but it also allows you to transfer the responsibility of waiting to your new TemplateDispatcher instance.

Listing C.5 The TemplateDispatcher class template

```
namespace messaging
{
    template<typename PreviousDispatcher,typename Msg,typename Func>
    class TemplateDispatcher
    {
        queue* q;
        PreviousDispatcher* prev;
        Func f;
        bool chained;

        TemplateDispatcher(TemplateDispatcher const&)=delete;
        TemplateDispatcher& operator=(TemplateDispatcher const&)=delete;

        template<typename Dispatcher,typename OtherMsg,typename OtherFunc>
        friend class TemplateDispatcher;            <-- TemplateDispatcher instantiations
                                                        are friends of each other
        void wait_and_dispatch()
        {
            for(;;)
            {
                auto msg=q->wait_and_pop();          ❶ If we handle the message,
                if(dispatch(msg))                   <-- break out of the loop
                    break;
            }
        }

        bool dispatch(std::shared_ptr<message_base> const& msg)
        {
```

```
            if(wrapped_message<Msg>* wrapper=
                dynamic_cast<wrapped_message<Msg>*>(msg.get()))
            {
                f(wrapper->contents);                   Check the message type,
                return true;                              and call the function 2
            }
            else
            {                                          3 Chain to the
                return prev->dispatch(msg);               previous dispatcher
            }
        }
    public:
        TemplateDispatcher(TemplateDispatcher&& other):
            q(other.q),prev(other.prev),f(std::move(other.f)),
            chained(other.chained)
        {
            other.chained=true;
        }
        TemplateDispatcher(queue* q_,PreviousDispatcher* prev_,Func&& f_):
            q(q_),prev(prev_),f(std::forward<Func>(f_)),chained(false)
        {
            prev_->chained=true;
        }

        template<typename OtherMsg,typename OtherFunc>
        TemplateDispatcher<TemplateDispatcher,OtherMsg,OtherFunc>
        handle(OtherFunc&& of)
        {                                                       Additional
            return TemplateDispatcher<                          handlers can
                TemplateDispatcher,OtherMsg,OtherFunc>(       4 be chained
                    q,this,std::forward<OtherFunc>(of));
        }

        ~TemplateDispatcher() noexcept(false)
        {                                              The destructor is
            if(!chained)                               noexcept(false)
            {                                        5 again
                wait_and_dispatch();
            }
        }
    };
}
```

The `TemplateDispatcher<>` class template is modeled on the `dispatcher` class and is almost identical. In particular, the destructor still calls `wait_and_dispatch()` to wait for a message.

Since you don't throw exceptions if you handle the message, you now need to check whether you did handle the message in your message loop ❶. Your message processing stops when you've successfully handled a message, so that you can wait for a different set of messages next time. If you do get a match for the specified message type, the supplied function is called ❷ rather than throwing an exception (although the handler function may throw an exception itself). If you don't get a match, you chain to the previous dispatcher ❸. In the first instance, this will be a `dispatcher`, but if you chain calls to handle() ❹ to allow multiple types of messages to be handled, this may be a prior instantiation of TemplateDispatcher<>, which will in turn chain to the previous handler if the message doesn't match. Because any of the handlers might throw an exception (including the dispatcher's default handler for close_queue messages), the destructor must once again be declared noexcept(false) ❺.

This simple framework allows you to push any type of message on the queue and then selectively match against messages you can handle on the receiving end. It also allows you to pass around a reference to the queue for pushing messages on, while keeping the receiving end private.

To complete the example from chapter 4, the messages are given in listing C.6, the various state machines in listings C.7, C.8, and C.9, and the driving code in listing C.10.

Listing C.6 ATM messages

```
struct withdraw
{
    std::string account;
    unsigned amount;
    mutable messaging::sender atm_queue;

    withdraw(std::string const& account_,
             unsigned amount_,
             messaging::sender atm_queue_):
        account(account_),amount(amount_),
        atm_queue(atm_queue_)
    {}
};

struct withdraw_ok
{};

struct withdraw_denied
{};

struct cancel_withdrawal
{
    std::string account;
    unsigned amount;

    cancel_withdrawal(std::string const& account_,
                      unsigned amount_):
        account(account_),amount(amount_)
    {}
};

struct withdrawal_processed
{
    std::string account;
    unsigned amount;

    withdrawal_processed(std::string const& account_,
                         unsigned amount_):
        account(account_),amount(amount_)
    {}
};
```

```
struct card_inserted
{
    std::string account;

    explicit card_inserted(std::string const& account_):
        account(account_)
    {}

};

struct digit_pressed
{
    char digit;

    explicit digit_pressed(char digit_):
        digit(digit_)
    {}

};

struct clear_last_pressed
{};

struct eject_card
{};

struct withdraw_pressed
{
    unsigned amount;

    explicit withdraw_pressed(unsigned amount_):
        amount(amount_)
    {}

};

struct cancel_pressed
{};

struct issue_money
{
    unsigned amount;
    issue_money(unsigned amount_):
        amount(amount_)
    {}
};

struct verify_pin
{
    std::string account;
    std::string pin;
    mutable messaging::sender atm_queue;

    verify_pin(std::string const& account_,std::string const& pin_,
               messaging::sender atm_queue_):
        account(account_),pin(pin_),atm_queue(atm_queue_)
    {}
};

struct pin_verified
{};
```

```
struct pin_incorrect
{};

struct display_enter_pin
{};

struct display_enter_card
{};

struct display_insufficient_funds
{};

struct display_withdrawal_cancelled
{};

struct display_pin_incorrect_message
{};

struct display_withdrawal_options
{};

struct get_balance
{
    std::string account;
    mutable messaging::sender atm_queue;

    get_balance(std::string const& account_,messaging::sender atm_queue_):
        account(account_),atm_queue(atm_queue_)
    {}
};

struct balance
{
    unsigned amount;

    explicit balance(unsigned amount_):
        amount(amount_)
    {}
};

struct display_balance
{
    unsigned amount;

    explicit display_balance(unsigned amount_):
        amount(amount_)
    {}
};

struct balance_pressed
{};
```

Listing C.7 The ATM state machine

```
class atm
{
    messaging::receiver incoming;
    messaging::sender bank;
    messaging::sender interface_hardware;
    void (atm::*state)();
```

```
    std::string account;
    unsigned withdrawal_amount;
    std::string pin;

    void process_withdrawal()
    {
        incoming.wait()
            .handle<withdraw_ok>(
                [&](withdraw_ok const& msg)
                {
                    interface_hardware.send(
                        issue_money(withdrawal_amount));
                    bank.send(
                        withdrawal_processed(account,withdrawal_amount));
                    state=&atm::done_processing;
                }
                )
            .handle<withdraw_denied>(
                [&](withdraw_denied const& msg)
                {
                    interface_hardware.send(display_insufficient_funds());
                    state=&atm::done_processing;
                }
                )
            .handle<cancel_pressed>(
                [&](cancel_pressed const& msg)
                {
                    bank.send(
                        cancel_withdrawal(account,withdrawal_amount));
                    interface_hardware.send(
                        display_withdrawal_cancelled());
                    state=&atm::done_processing;
                }
                );
    }

    void process_balance()
    {
        incoming.wait()
            .handle<balance>(
                [&](balance const& msg)
                {
                    interface_hardware.send(display_balance(msg.amount));
                    state=&atm::wait_for_action;
                }
                )
            .handle<cancel_pressed>(
                [&](cancel_pressed const& msg)
                {
                    state=&atm::done_processing;
                }
                );
    }

    void wait_for_action()
    {
```

```
        interface_hardware.send(display_withdrawal_options());
        incoming.wait()
            .handle<withdraw_pressed>(
                [&](withdraw_pressed const& msg)
                {
                    withdrawal_amount=msg.amount;
                    bank.send(withdraw(account,msg.amount,incoming));
                    state=&atm::process_withdrawal;
                }
                )
            .handle<balance_pressed>(
                [&](balance_pressed const& msg)
                {
                    bank.send(get_balance(account,incoming));
                    state=&atm::process_balance;
                }
                )
            .handle<cancel_pressed>(
                [&](cancel_pressed const& msg)
                {
                    state=&atm::done_processing;
                }
                );
    }
    void verifying_pin()
    {
        incoming.wait()
            .handle<pin_verified>(
                [&](pin_verified const& msg)
                {
                    state=&atm::wait_for_action;
                }
                )
            .handle<pin_incorrect>(
                [&](pin_incorrect const& msg)
                {
                    interface_hardware.send(
                        display_pin_incorrect_message());
                    state=&atm::done_processing;
                }
                )
            .handle<cancel_pressed>(
                [&](cancel_pressed const& msg)
                {
                    state=&atm::done_processing;
                }
                );
    }
    void getting_pin()
    {
        incoming.wait()
            .handle<digit_pressed>(
                [&](digit_pressed const& msg)
```

```
                {
                    unsigned const pin_length=4;
                    pin+=msg.digit;
                    if(pin.length()==pin_length)
                    {
                        bank.send(verify_pin(account,pin,incoming));
                        state=&atm::verifying_pin;
                    }
                }
                )
            .handle<clear_last_pressed>(
                [&](clear_last_pressed const& msg)
                {
                    if(!pin.empty())
                    {
                        pin.pop_back();
                    }
                }
                )
            .handle<cancel_pressed>(
                [&](cancel_pressed const& msg)
                {
                    state=&atm::done_processing;
                }
                );
    }

    void waiting_for_card()
    {
        interface_hardware.send(display_enter_card());
        incoming.wait()
            .handle<card_inserted>(
                [&](card_inserted const& msg)
                {
                    account=msg.account;
                    pin="";
                    interface_hardware.send(display_enter_pin());
                    state=&atm::getting_pin;
                }
                );
    }

    void done_processing()
    {
        interface_hardware.send(eject_card());
        state=&atm::waiting_for_card;
    }

    atm(atm const&)=delete;
    atm& operator=(atm const&)=delete;

public:
    atm(messaging::sender bank_,
        messaging::sender interface_hardware_):
        bank(bank_),interface_hardware(interface_hardware_)
    {}
```

```
    void done()
    {
        get_sender().send(messaging::close_queue());
    }

    void run()
    {
        state=&atm::waiting_for_card;
        try
        {
            for(;;)
            {
                (this->*state)();
            }
        }
        catch(messaging::close_queue const&)
        {
        }
    }

    messaging::sender get_sender()
    {
        return incoming;
    }
};
```

Listing C.8 The bank state machine

```
class bank_machine
{
    messaging::receiver incoming;
    unsigned balance;
public:
    bank_machine():
        balance(199)
    {}

    void done()
    {
        get_sender().send(messaging::close_queue());
    }

    void run()
    {
        try
        {
            for(;;)
            {
                incoming.wait()
                    .handle<verify_pin>(
                        [&](verify_pin const& msg)
                        {
                            if(msg.pin=="1937")
                            {
                                msg.atm_queue.send(pin_verified());
                            }
```

```
                    else
                    {
                        msg.atm_queue.send(pin_incorrect());
                    }
                }
                )
            .handle<withdraw>(
                [&](withdraw const& msg)
                {
                    if(balance>=msg.amount)
                    {
                        msg.atm_queue.send(withdraw_ok());
                        balance-=msg.amount;
                    }
                    else
                    {
                        msg.atm_queue.send(withdraw_denied());
                    }
                }
                )
            .handle<get_balance>(
                [&](get_balance const& msg)
                {
                    msg.atm_queue.send(::balance(balance));
                }
                )
            .handle<withdrawal_processed>(
                [&](withdrawal_processed const& msg)
                {
                }
                )
            .handle<cancel_withdrawal>(
                [&](cancel_withdrawal const& msg)
                {
                }
                );
            }
        }
        catch(messaging::close_queue const&)
        {
        }
    }

    messaging::sender get_sender()
    {
        return incoming;
    }
};
```

Listing C.9 The user-interface state machine

```
class interface_machine
{
    messaging::receiver incoming;
public:
```

```
void done()
{
    get_sender().send(messaging::close_queue());
}
void run()
{
    try
    {
        for(;;)
        {
            incoming.wait()
                .handle<issue_money>(
                    [&](issue_money const& msg)
                    {
                        {
                            std::lock_guard<std::mutex> lk(iom);
                            std::cout<<"Issuing "
                                     <<msg.amount<<std::endl;
                        }
                    }
                    )
                .handle<display_insufficient_funds>(
                    [&](display_insufficient_funds const& msg)
                    {
                        {
                            std::lock_guard<std::mutex> lk(iom);
                            std::cout<<"Insufficient funds"<<std::endl;
                        }
                    }
                    )
                .handle<display_enter_pin>(
                    [&](display_enter_pin const& msg)
                    {
                        {
                            std::lock_guard<std::mutex> lk(iom);
                            std::cout
                                <<"Please enter your PIN (0-9)"
                                <<std::endl;
                        }
                    }
                    )
                .handle<display_enter_card>(
                    [&](display_enter_card const& msg)
                    {
                        {
                            std::lock_guard<std::mutex> lk(iom);
                            std::cout<<"Please enter your card (I)"
                                     <<std::endl;
                        }
                    }
                    )
                .handle<display_balance>(
                    [&](display_balance const& msg)
                    {
```

```
                {
                    std::lock_guard<std::mutex> lk(iom);
                    std::cout
                        <<"The balance of your account is "
                        <<msg.amount<<std::endl;
                }
            }
            )
        .handle<display_withdrawal_options>(
            [&](display_withdrawal_options const& msg)
            {
                {
                    std::lock_guard<std::mutex> lk(iom);
                    std::cout<<"Withdraw 50? (w)"<<std::endl;
                    std::cout<<"Display Balance? (b)"
                             <<std::endl;
                    std::cout<<"Cancel? (c)"<<std::endl;
                }
            }
            )
        .handle<display_withdrawal_cancelled>(
            [&](display_withdrawal_cancelled const& msg)
            {
                {
                    std::lock_guard<std::mutex> lk(iom);
                    std::cout<<"Withdrawal cancelled"
                             <<std::endl;
                }
            }
            )
        .handle<display_pin_incorrect_message>(
            [&](display_pin_incorrect_message const& msg)
            {
                {
                    std::lock_guard<std::mutex> lk(iom);
                    std::cout<<"PIN incorrect"<<std::endl;
                }
            }
            )
        .handle<eject_card>(
            [&](eject_card const& msg)
            {
                {
                    std::lock_guard<std::mutex> lk(iom);
                    std::cout<<"Ejecting card"<<std::endl;
                }
            }
            );
        }
    }
    catch(messaging::close_queue&)
    {
    }
}
```

```
    messaging::sender get_sender()
    {
        return incoming;
    }
};
```

Listing C.10 The driving code

```
int main()
{
    bank_machine bank;
    interface_machine interface_hardware;

    atm machine(bank.get_sender(),interface_hardware.get_sender());

    std::thread bank_thread(&bank_machine::run,&bank);
    std::thread if_thread(&interface_machine::run,&interface_hardware);
    std::thread atm_thread(&atm::run,&machine);

    messaging::sender atmqueue(machine.get_sender());

    bool quit_pressed=false;

    while(!quit_pressed)
    {
        char c=getchar();
        switch(c)
        {
        case '0':
        case '1':
        case '2':
        case '3':
        case '4':
        case '5':
        case '6':
        case '7':
        case '8':
        case '9':
            atmqueue.send(digit_pressed(c));
            break;
        case 'b':
            atmqueue.send(balance_pressed());
            break;
        case 'w':
            atmqueue.send(withdraw_pressed(50));
            break;
        case 'c':
            atmqueue.send(cancel_pressed());
            break;
        case 'q':
            quit_pressed=true;
            break;
        case 'i':
            atmqueue.send(card_inserted("acc1234"));
            break;
        }
    }
```

```
    bank.done();
    machine.done();
    interface_hardware.done();
    atm_thread.join();
    bank_thread.join();
    if_thread.join();
}
```

appendix D C++ Thread Library reference

D.1 The <chrono> header

The `<chrono>` header provides classes for representing points in time and durations and clock classes, which act as a source of time_points. Each clock has an is_steady static data member, which indicates whether it's a *steady* clock that advances at a uniform rate (and can't be adjusted). The std::chrono::steady_clock class is the only clock guaranteed to be *steady*.

Header contents

```
namespace std
{
    namespace chrono
    {
        template<typename Rep,typename Period = ratio<1>>
        class duration;
        template<
            typename Clock,
            typename Duration = typename Clock::duration>
        class time_point;
        class system_clock;
        class steady_clock;
        typedef unspecified-clock-type high_resolution_clock;
    }
}
```

D.1.1 std::chrono::duration class template

The std::chrono::duration class template provides a facility for representing durations. The template parameters Rep and Period are the data type to store the duration value and an instantiation of the std::ratio class template indicating the length of time (as a fraction of a second) between successive "ticks," respectively. Thus `std::chrono::duration<int, std::milli>` is a count of milliseconds stored in a value of type `int`, whereas `std::chrono::duration<short, std::ratio<1,50>>` is a count of fiftieths of a second stored in a value of type `short`, and `std::chrono::duration <long long, std::ratio<60,1>>` is a count of minutes stored in a value of type `long long`.

Class definition

```
template <class Rep, class Period=ratio<1> >
class duration
{
public:
    typedef Rep rep;
    typedef Period period;

    constexpr duration() = default;
    ~duration() = default;

    duration(const duration&) = default;
    duration& operator=(const duration&) = default;

    template <class Rep2>
    constexpr explicit duration(const Rep2& r);

    template <class Rep2, class Period2>
    constexpr duration(const duration<Rep2, Period2>& d);

    constexpr rep count() const;
    constexpr duration operator+() const;
    constexpr duration operator-() const;
    duration& operator++();
    duration operator++(int);
    duration& operator--();
    duration operator--(int);
    duration& operator+=(const duration& d);
    duration& operator-=(const duration& d);
    duration& operator*=(const rep& rhs);
    duration& operator/=(const rep& rhs);
    duration& operator%=(const rep& rhs);
    duration& operator%=(const duration& rhs);
    static constexpr duration zero();
    static constexpr duration min();
    static constexpr duration max();
};

template <class Rep1, class Period1, class Rep2, class Period2>
constexpr bool operator==(
    const duration<Rep1, Period1>& lhs,
    const duration<Rep2, Period2>& rhs);

template <class Rep1, class Period1, class Rep2, class Period2>
constexpr bool operator!=(
    const duration<Rep1, Period1>& lhs,
    const duration<Rep2, Period2>& rhs);

template <class Rep1, class Period1, class Rep2, class Period2>
constexpr bool operator<(
```

```
    const duration<Rep1, Period1>& lhs,
    const duration<Rep2, Period2>& rhs);

template <class Rep1, class Period1, class Rep2, class Period2>
constexpr bool operator<=(
    const duration<Rep1, Period1>& lhs,
    const duration<Rep2, Period2>& rhs);

template <class Rep1, class Period1, class Rep2, class Period2>
constexpr bool operator>(
    const duration<Rep1, Period1>& lhs,
    const duration<Rep2, Period2>& rhs);

template <class Rep1, class Period1, class Rep2, class Period2>
constexpr bool operator>=(
    const duration<Rep1, Period1>& lhs,
    const duration<Rep2, Period2>& rhs);

template <class ToDuration, class Rep, class Period>
constexpr ToDuration duration_cast(const duration<Rep, Period>& d);
```

Requirements

`Rep` must be a built-in numeric type, or a number-like user-defined type. `Period` must be an instantiation of `std::ratio<>`.

STD::CHRONO::DURATION::REP TYPEDEF

This is a typedef for the type used to hold the number of ticks in a `duration` value.

Declaration

```
typedef Rep rep;
```

`rep` is the type of value used to hold the internal representation of the `duration` object.

STD::CHRONO::DURATION::PERIOD TYPEDEF

This typedef is for an instantiation of the `std::ratio` class template that specifies the fraction of a second represented by the duration count. For example, if `period` is `std::ratio<1,50>`, a `duration` value with a `count()` of *N* represents *N* fiftieths of a second.

Declaration

```
typedef Period period;
```

STD::CHRONO::DURATION DEFAULT CONSTRUCTOR

Constructs a `std::chrono::duration` instance with a default value.

Declaration

```
constexpr duration() = default;
```

Effects

The internal value of the `duration` (of type `rep`) is default initialized.

STD::CHRONO::DURATION CONVERTING CONSTRUCTOR FROM A COUNT VALUE

Constructs a `std::chrono::duration` instance with a specified count.

Declaration

```
template <class Rep2>
constexpr explicit duration(const Rep2& r);
```

Effects
The internal value of the duration object is initialized with static_cast<rep>(r).

Requirements
This constructor only participates in overload resolution if Rep2 is implicitly convertible to Rep and either Rep is a floating point type or Rep2 is *not* a floating point type.

Postcondition
this->count()==static_cast<rep>(r)

STD::CHRONO::DURATION CONVERTING CONSTRUCTOR FROM ANOTHER STD::CHRONO::DURATION VALUE

Constructs a std::chrono::duration instance by scaling the count value of another std::chrono::duration object.

Declaration

```
template <class Rep2, class Period2>
constexpr duration(const duration<Rep2,Period2>& d);
```

Effects
The internal value of the duration object is initialized with duration_cast<duration<Rep,Period>>(d).count().

Requirements
This constructor only participates in overload resolution if Rep is a floating point type or Rep2 is *not* a floating point type and Period2 is a whole number multiple of Period (that is, ratio_divide<Period2,Period>::den==1). This avoids accidental truncation (and corresponding loss of precision) from storing a duration with small periods in a variable representing a duration with a longer period.

Postcondition
this->count()==duration_cast<duration<Rep,Period>>(d).count()

Examples

```
duration<int,ratio<1,1000>> ms(5);           // 5 milliseconds
duration<int,ratio<1,1>> s(ms);              // Error: can't store ms as integral seconds
duration<double,ratio<1,1>> s2(ms);          // OK: s2.count()==0.005
duration<int,ratio<1,1000000>> us(ms);       // OK: us.count()==5000
```

STD::CHRONO::DURATION::COUNT MEMBER FUNCTION

Retrieves the value of the duration.

Declaration

```
constexpr rep count() const;
```

Returns
The internal value of the duration object, as a value of type rep.

STD::CHRONO::DURATION::OPERATOR+ UNARY PLUS OPERATOR

This is a no-op: it just returns a copy of *this.

Declaration

```
constexpr duration operator+() const;
```

Returns
*this

STD::CHRONO::DURATION::OPERATOR- UNARY MINUS OPERATOR

Returns a duration such that the `count()` value is the negative value of `this->count()`.

Declaration

```
constexpr duration operator-() const;
```

Returns

```
duration(-this->count());
```

STD::CHRONO::DURATION::OPERATOR++ PRE-INCREMENT OPERATOR

Increments the internal count.

Declaration

```
duration& operator++();
```

Effects

```
++this->internal_count;
```

Returns

```
*this
```

STD::CHRONO::DURATION::OPERATOR++ POST-INCREMENT OPERATOR

Increments the internal count and return the value of `*this` prior to the increment.

Declaration

```
duration operator++(int);
```

Effects

```
duration temp(*this);
++(*this);
return temp;
```

STD::CHRONO::DURATION::OPERATOR-- PRE-DECREMENT OPERATOR

Decrements the internal count.

Declaration

```
duration& operator--();
```

Effects

```
--this->internal_count;
```

Returns

```
*this
```

STD::CHRONO::DURATION::OPERATOR-- POST-DECREMENT OPERATOR

Decrements the internal count and return the value of `*this` prior to the decrement.

Declaration

```
duration operator--(int);
```

Effects

```
duration temp(*this);
--(*this);
return temp;
```

STD::CHRONO::DURATION::OPERATOR+= COMPOUND ASSIGNMENT OPERATOR

Adds the count for another duration object to the internal count for *this.

Declaration

```
duration& operator+=(duration const& other);
```

Effects

```
internal_count+=other.count();
```

Returns

```
*this
```

STD::CHRONO::DURATION::OPERATOR-= COMPOUND ASSIGNMENT OPERATOR

Subtracts the count for another duration object from the internal count for *this.

Declaration

```
duration& operator-=(duration const& other);
```

Effects

```
internal_count-=other.count();
```

Returns

```
*this
```

STD::CHRONO::DURATION::OPERATOR*= COMPOUND ASSIGNMENT OPERATOR

Multiplies the internal count for *this by the specified value.

Declaration

```
duration& operator*=(rep const& rhs);
```

Effects

```
internal_count*=rhs;
```

Returns

```
*this
```

STD::CHRONO::DURATION::OPERATOR/= COMPOUND ASSIGNMENT OPERATOR

Divides the internal count for *this by the specified value.

Declaration

```
duration& operator/=(rep const& rhs);
```

Effects

```
internal_count/=rhs;
```

Returns

```
*this
```

STD::CHRONO::DURATION::OPERATOR%= COMPOUND ASSIGNMENT OPERATOR

Adjusts the internal count for *this to be the remainder when divided by the specified value.

Declaration

```
duration& operator%=(rep const& rhs);
```

Effects

```
internal_count%=rhs;
```

Returns

```
*this
```

STD::CHRONO::DURATION::OPERATOR%= COMPOUND ASSIGNMENT OPERATOR

Adjusts the internal count for `*this` to be the remainder when divided by the count of the other `duration` object.

Declaration

```
duration& operator%=(duration const& rhs);
```

Effects

```
internal_count%=rhs.count();
```

Returns

```
*this
```

STD::CHRONO::DURATION::ZERO STATIC MEMBER FUNCTION

Returns a `duration` object representing a value of zero.

Declaration

```
constexpr duration zero();
```

Returns

```
duration(duration_values<rep>::zero());
```

STD::CHRONO::DURATION::MIN STATIC MEMBER FUNCTION

Returns a `duration` object holding the minimum possible value for the specified instantiation.

Declaration

```
constexpr duration min();
```

Returns

```
duration(duration_values<rep>::min());
```

STD::CHRONO::DURATION::MAX STATIC MEMBER FUNCTION

Returns a `duration` object holding the maximum possible value for the specified instantiation.

Declaration

```
constexpr duration max();
```

Returns

```
duration(duration_values<rep>::max());
```

STD::CHRONO::DURATION EQUALITY COMPARISON OPERATOR

Compares two `duration` objects for equality, even if they have distinct representations and/or periods.

Declaration

```
template <class Rep1, class Period1, class Rep2, class Period2>
constexpr bool operator==(
    const duration<Rep1, Period1>& lhs,
    const duration<Rep2, Period2>& rhs);
```

Requirements

Either `lhs` must be implicitly convertible to `rhs`, or vice versa. If neither can be implicitly converted to the other, or they are distinct instantiations of `duration` but each can implicitly convert to the other, the expression is ill formed.

Effects

If CommonDuration is a synonym for std::common_type< duration< Rep1, Period1>, duration< Rep2, Period2>>::type, then lhs==rhs returns CommonDuration(lhs).count()==CommonDuration(rhs).count().

STD::CHRONO::DURATION INEQUALITY COMPARISON OPERATOR

Compares two duration objects for inequality, even if they have distinct representations and/or periods.

Declaration

```
template <class Rep1, class Period1, class Rep2, class Period2>
constexpr bool operator!=(
    const duration<Rep1, Period1>& lhs,
    const duration<Rep2, Period2>& rhs);
```

Requirements

Either lhs must be implicitly convertible to rhs, or vice versa. If neither can be implicitly converted to the other, or they are distinct instantiations of duration but each can implicitly convert to the other, the expression is ill formed.

Returns

!(lhs==rhs)

STD::CHRONO::DURATION LESS-THAN COMPARISON OPERATOR

Compares two duration objects to see if one is less than the other, even if they have distinct representations and/or periods.

Declaration

```
template <class Rep1, class Period1, class Rep2, class Period2>
constexpr bool operator<(
    const duration<Rep1, Period1>& lhs,
    const duration<Rep2, Period2>& rhs);
```

Requirements

Either lhs must be implicitly convertible to rhs, or vice versa. If neither can be implicitly converted to the other, or they are distinct instantiations of duration but each can implicitly convert to the other, the expression is ill formed.

Effects

If CommonDuration is a synonym for std::common_type< duration< Rep1, Period1>, duration< Rep2, Period2>>::type, then lhs<rhs returns CommonDuration(lhs).count()<CommonDuration(rhs).count().

STD::CHRONO::DURATION GREATER-THAN COMPARISON OPERATOR

Compares two duration objects to see if one is greater than the other, even if they have distinct representations and/or periods.

Declaration

```
template <class Rep1, class Period1, class Rep2, class Period2>
constexpr bool operator>(
    const duration<Rep1, Period1>& lhs,
    const duration<Rep2, Period2>& rhs);
```

Requirements

Either `lhs` must be implicitly convertible to `rhs`, or vice versa. If neither can be implicitly converted to the other, or they are distinct instantiations of `duration` but each can implicitly convert to the other, the expression is ill formed.

Returns

```
rhs<lhs
```

STD::CHRONO::DURATION LESS-THAN-OR-EQUALS COMPARISON OPERATOR

Compares two `duration` objects to see if one is less than or equal to the other, even if they have distinct representations and/or periods.

Declaration

```
template <class Rep1, class Period1, class Rep2, class Period2>
constexpr bool operator<=(
    const duration<Rep1, Period1>& lhs,
    const duration<Rep2, Period2>& rhs);
```

Requirements

Either `lhs` must be implicitly convertible to `rhs`, or vice versa. If neither can be implicitly converted to the other, or they are distinct instantiations of `duration` but each can implicitly convert to the other, the expression is ill formed.

Returns

```
!(rhs<lhs)
```

STD::CHRONO::DURATION GREATER-THAN-OR-EQUALS COMPARISON OPERATOR

Compares two `duration` objects to see if one is greater than or equal to the other, even if they have distinct representations and/or periods.

Declaration

```
template <class Rep1, class Period1, class Rep2, class Period2>
constexpr bool operator>=(
    const duration<Rep1, Period1>& lhs,
    const duration<Rep2, Period2>& rhs);
```

Requirements

Either `lhs` must be implicitly convertible to `rhs`, or vice versa. If neither can be implicitly converted to the other, or they are distinct instantiations of `duration` but each can implicitly convert to the other, the expression is ill formed.

Returns

```
!(lhs<rhs)
```

STD::CHRONO::DURATION_CAST NONMEMBER FUNCTION

Explicitly converts a `std::chrono::duration` object to a specific `std::chrono::duration` instantiation.

Declaration

```
template <class ToDuration, class Rep, class Period>
constexpr ToDuration duration_cast(const duration<Rep, Period>& d);
```

Requirements

`ToDuration` must be an instantiation of `std::chrono::duration`.

Returns

The duration d converted to the duration type specified by ToDuration. This is done in such a way as to minimize any loss of precision resulting from conversions between different scales and representation types.

D.1.2 std::chrono::time_point class template

The std::chrono::time_point class template represents a point in time, as measured by a particular clock. It's specified as a duration since the *epoch* of that particular clock. The template parameter Clock identifies the clock (each distinct clock must have a unique type), whereas the Duration template parameter is the type to use for measuring the duration since the epoch and must be an instantiation of the std::chrono::duration class template. The Duration defaults to the default duration type of the Clock.

Class definition

```
template <class Clock,class Duration = typename Clock::duration>
class time_point
{
public:
    typedef Clock clock;
    typedef Duration duration;
    typedef typename duration::rep rep;
    typedef typename duration::period period;

    time_point();
    explicit time_point(const duration& d);

    template <class Duration2>
    time_point(const time_point<clock, Duration2>& t);

    duration time_since_epoch() const;

    time_point& operator+=(const duration& d);
    time_point& operator-=(const duration& d);

    static constexpr time_point min();
    static constexpr time_point max();
};
```

STD::CHRONO::TIME_POINT DEFAULT CONSTRUCTOR

Constructs a time_point representing the epoch of the associated Clock; the internal duration is initialized with Duration::zero().

Declaration

```
time_point();
```

Postcondition

For a newly default-constructed time_point object tp, tp.time_since_epoch() == tp::duration::zero().

STD::CHRONO::TIME_POINT DURATION CONSTRUCTOR

Constructs a time_point representing the specified duration since the epoch of the associated Clock.

Declaration

```
explicit time_point(const duration& d);
```

Postcondition

For a `time_point` object `tp`, constucted with `tp(d)` for some duration `d`, `tp.time_since_epoch()==d`.

STD::CHRONO::TIME_POINT CONVERSION CONSTRUCTOR

Constructs a `time_point` object from another `time_point` object with the same `Clock` but a distinct `Duration`.

Declaration

```
template <class Duration2>
time_point(const time_point<clock, Duration2>& t);
```

Requirements

`Duration2` shall be implicitly convertible to `Duration`.

Effects

As-if `time_point(t.time_since_epoch())`

The value returned from `t.time_since_epoch()` is implicitly converted to an object of type `Duration`, and that value is stored in the newly constructed `time_point` object.

STD::CHRONO::TIME_POINT::TIME_SINCE_EPOCH MEMBER FUNCTION

Retrieves the duration since the clock epoch for a particular `time_point` object.

Declaration

```
duration time_since_epoch() const;
```

Returns

The `duration` value stored in `*this`.

STD::CHRONO::TIME_POINT::OPERATOR+= COMPOUND ASSIGNMENT OPERATOR

Adds the specified `duration` to the value stored in the specified `time_point` object.

Declaration

```
time_point& operator+=(const duration& d);
```

Effects

Adds `d` to the internal `duration` object of `*this`, as-if

```
this->internal_duration += d;
```

Returns

`*this`

STD::CHRONO::TIME_POINT::OPERATOR-= COMPOUND ASSIGNMENT OPERATOR

Subtracts the specified `duration` from the value stored in the specified `time_point` object.

Declaration

```
time_point& operator-=(const duration& d);
```

Effects

Subtracts d from the internal duration object of *this, as-if

```
this->internal_duration -= d;
```

Returns

```
*this
```

STD::CHRONO::TIME_POINT::MIN STATIC MEMBER FUNCTION

Obtains a time_point object representing the minimum possible value for its type.

Declaration

```
static constexpr time_point min();
```

Returns

```
time_point(time_point::duration::min()) (see 11.1.1.15)
```

STD::CHRONO::TIME_POINT::MAX STATIC MEMBER FUNCTION

Obtains a time_point object representing the maximum possible value for its type.

Declaration

```
static constexpr time_point max();
```

Returns

```
time_point(time_point::duration::max()) (see 11.1.1.16)
```

D.1.3 std::chrono::system_clock class

The std::chrono::system_clock class provides a means of obtaining the current wall-clock time from the systemwide real-time clock. The current time can be obtained by calling std::chrono::system_clock::now(). Instances of std::chrono::system_clock::time_point can be converted to and from time_t with the std::chrono::system_clock::to_time_t() and std::chrono::system_clock::to_time_point() functions. The system clock isn't *steady*, so a subsequent call to std::chrono::system_clock::now() may return an earlier time than a previous call (for example, if the operating system clock is manually adjusted or synchronized with an external clock).

Class definition

```
class system_clock
{
public:
    typedef unspecified-integral-type rep;
    typedef std::ratio<unspecified,unspecified> period;
    typedef std::chrono::duration<rep,period> duration;
    typedef std::chrono::time_point<system_clock> time_point;
    static const bool is_steady=unspecified;

    static time_point now() noexcept;

    static time_t to_time_t(const time_point& t) noexcept;
    static time_point from_time_t(time_t t) noexcept;
};
```

STD::CHRONO::SYSTEM_CLOCK::REP TYPEDEF

A typedef for an integral type used to hold the number of ticks in a `duration` value.

Declaration

```
typedef unspecified-integral-type rep;
```

STD::CHRONO::SYSTEM_CLOCK::PERIOD TYPEDEF

A typedef for an instantiation of the `std::ratio` class template that specifies the smallest number of seconds (or fractions of a second) between distinct values of `duration` or `time_point`. The `period` specifies the *precision* of the clock, not the tick frequency.

Declaration

```
typedef std::ratio<unspecified,unspecified> period;
```

STD::CHRONO::SYSTEM_CLOCK::DURATION TYPEDEF

An instantiation of the `std::chrono::duration` class template that can hold the difference between any two time points returned by the systemwide real-time clock.

Declaration

```
typedef std::chrono::duration<
    std::chrono::system_clock::rep,
    std::chrono::system_clock::period> duration;
```

STD::CHRONO::SYSTEM_CLOCK::TIME_POINT TYPEDEF

An instantiation of the `std::chrono::time_point` class template that can hold time points returned by the systemwide real-time clock.

Declaration

```
typedef std::chrono::time_point<std::chrono::system_clock> time_point;
```

STD::CHRONO::SYSTEM_CLOCK::NOW STATIC MEMBER FUNCTION

Obtains the current wall-clock time from the systemwide real-time clock.

Declaration

```
time_point now() noexcept;
```

Returns

A `time_point` representing the current time of the systemwide real-time clock.

Throws

An exception of type `std::system_error` if an error occurs.

STD::CHRONO::SYSTEM_CLOCK::TO_TIME_T STATIC MEMBER FUNCTION

Converts an instance of `time_point` to `time_t`.

Declaration

```
time_t to_time_t(time_point const& t) noexcept;
```

Returns

A `time_t` value that represents the same point in time as `t` rounded or truncated to seconds precision.

Throws

An exception of type `std::system_error` if an error occurs.

STD::CHRONO::SYSTEM_CLOCK::FROM_TIME_T STATIC MEMBER FUNCTION

Converts an instance of `time_t` to `time_point`.

Declaration

```
time_point from_time_t(time_t const& t) noexcept;
```

Returns

A `time_point` value that represents the same point in time as `t`.

Throws

An exception of type `std::system_error` if an error occurs.

D.1.4 std::chrono::steady_clock class

The `std::chrono::steady_clock` class provides access to the systemwide steady clock. The current time can be obtained by calling `std::chrono::steady_clock::now()`. There is no fixed relationship between values returned by `std::chrono::steady_clock::now()` and wall-clock time. A steady clock can't go backwards, so if one call to `std::chrono::steady_clock::now()` happens-before another call to `std::chrono::steady_clock::now()`, the second call must return a time point equal to or later than the first. The clock advances at a uniform rate as far as possible.

Class definition

```
class steady_clock
{
public:
    typedef unspecified-integral-type rep;
    typedef std::ratio<
        unspecified,unspecified> period;
    typedef std::chrono::duration<rep,period> duration;
    typedef std::chrono::time_point<steady_clock>
        time_point;
    static const bool is_steady=true;

    static time_point now() noexcept;
};
```

STD::CHRONO::STEADY_CLOCK::REP TYPEDEF

This typedef is for an integral type used to hold the number of ticks in a `duration` value.

Declaration

```
typedef unspecified-integral-type rep;
```

STD::CHRONO::STEADY_CLOCK::PERIOD TYPEDEF

This is a typedef for an instantiation of the `std::ratio` class template that specifies the smallest number of seconds (or fractions of a second) between distinct values of `duration` or `time_point`. The `period` specifies the *precision* of the clock, not the tick frequency.

Declaration

```
typedef std::ratio<unspecified,unspecified> period;
```

STD::CHRONO::STEADY_CLOCK::DURATION TYPEDEF

This is an instantiation of the `std::chrono::duration` class template that can hold the difference between any two time points returned by the systemwide steady clock.

Declaration

```
typedef std::chrono::duration<
    std::chrono::steady_clock::rep,
    std::chrono::steady_clock::period> duration;
```

STD::CHRONO::STEADY_CLOCK::TIME_POINT TYPEDEF

This instantiation of the `std::chrono::time_point` class template can hold time points returned by the systemwide steady clock.

Declaration

```
typedef std::chrono::time_point<std::chrono::steady_clock> time_point;
```

STD::CHRONO::STEADY_CLOCK::NOW STATIC MEMBER FUNCTION

Obtains the current time from the systemwide steady clock.

Declaration

```
time_point now() noexcept;
```

Returns

A `time_point` representing the current time of the systemwide steady clock.

Throws

An exception of type `std::system_error` if an error occurs.

Synchronization

If one call to `std::chrono::steady_clock::now()` happens-before another, the `time_point` returned by the first call shall compare less-than or equal-to the `time_point` returned by the second call.

D.1.5 std::chrono::high_resolution_clock typedef

The `std::chrono::high_resolution_clock` class provides access to the systemwide clock with the highest resolution. As for all clocks, the current time can be obtained by calling `std::chrono::high_resolution_clock::now()`. `std::chrono::high_resolution_clock` may be a typedef for the `std::chrono::system_clock` class or `std::chrono::steady_clock` class, or it may be a separate type.

Although `std::chrono::high_resolution_clock` has the highest resolution of all the library-supplied clocks, `std::chrono::high_resolution_clock::now()` still takes a finite amount of time. You must take care to account for the overhead of calling `std::chrono::high_resolution_clock::now()` when timing short operations.

Class definition

```
class high_resolution_clock
{
public:
    typedef unspecified-integral-type rep;
    typedef std::ratio<
        unspecified,unspecified> period;
    typedef std::chrono::duration<rep,period> duration;
```

```
    typedef std::chrono::time_point<
        unspecified> time_point;
    static const bool is_steady=unspecified;

    static time_point now() noexcept;
};
```

D.2 <condition_variable> header

The `<condition_variable>` header provides condition variables. These are basic-level synchronization mechanisms that allow a thread to block until notified that some condition is true or a timeout period has elapsed.

Header contents

```
namespace std
{
    enum class cv_status { timeout, no_timeout };

    class condition_variable;
    class condition_variable_any;
}
```

D.2.1 std::condition_variable class

The `std::condition_variable` class allows a thread to wait for a condition to become `true`.

Instances of `std::condition_variable` aren't `CopyAssignable`, `CopyConstructible`, `MoveAssignable`, or `MoveConstructible`.

Class definition

```
class condition_variable
{
public:
    condition_variable();
    ~condition_variable();

    condition_variable(condition_variable const& ) = delete;
    condition_variable& operator=(condition_variable const& ) = delete;

    void notify_one() noexcept;
    void notify_all() noexcept;

    void wait(std::unique_lock<std::mutex>& lock);

    template <typename Predicate>
    void wait(std::unique_lock<std::mutex>& lock,Predicate pred);

    template <typename Clock, typename Duration>
    cv_status wait_until(
        std::unique_lock<std::mutex>& lock,
        const std::chrono::time_point<Clock, Duration>& absolute_time);

    template <typename Clock, typename Duration, typename Predicate>
    bool wait_until(
        std::unique_lock<std::mutex>& lock,
        const std::chrono::time_point<Clock, Duration>& absolute_time,
        Predicate pred);
```

```
    template <typename Rep, typename Period>
    cv_status wait_for(
        std::unique_lock<std::mutex>& lock,
        const std::chrono::duration<Rep, Period>& relative_time);

    template <typename Rep, typename Period, typename Predicate>
    bool wait_for(
        std::unique_lock<std::mutex>& lock,
        const std::chrono::duration<Rep, Period>& relative_time,
        Predicate pred);
};

void notify_all_at_thread_exit(condition_variable&,unique_lock<mutex>);
```

STD::CONDITION_VARIABLE DEFAULT CONSTRUCTOR

Constructs a `std::condition_variable` object.

Declaration

```
condition_variable();
```

Effects

Constructs a new `std::condition_variable` instance.

Throws

An exception of type `std::system_error` if the condition variable could not be constructed.

STD::CONDITION_VARIABLE DESTRUCTOR

Destroys a `std::condition_variable` object.

Declaration

```
~condition_variable();
```

Preconditions

There are no threads blocked on `*this` in a call to `wait()`, `wait_for()`, or `wait_until()`.

Effects

Destroys `*this`.

Throws

Nothing.

STD::CONDITION_VARIABLE::NOTIFY_ONE MEMBER FUNCTION

Wakes one of the threads currently waiting on a `std::condition_variable`.

Declaration

```
void notify_one() noexcept;
```

Effects

Wakes one of the threads waiting on `*this` at the point of the call. If there are no threads waiting, the call has no effect.

Throws

`std::system_error` if the effects can't be achieved.

Synchronization

Calls to `notify_one()`, `notify_all()`, `wait()`, `wait_for()`, and `wait_until()` on a single `std::condition_variable` instance are serialized. A call to `notify_one()` or `notify_all()` will only wake threads that started waiting *prior* to that call.

STD::CONDITION_VARIABLE::NOTIFY_ALL MEMBER FUNCTION

Wake all of the threads currently waiting on a `std::condition_variable`.

Declaration

```
void notify_all() noexcept;
```

Effects

Wakes all of the threads waiting on `*this` at the point of the call. If there are no threads waiting, the call has no effect.

Throws

`std::system_error` if the effects can't be achieved.

Synchronization

Calls to `notify_one()`, `notify_all()`, `wait()`, `wait_for()`, and `wait_until()` on a single `std::condition_variable` instance are serialized. A call to `notify_one()` or `notify_all()` will only wake threads that started waiting *prior* to that call.

STD::CONDITION_VARIABLE::WAIT MEMBER FUNCTION

Waits until the `std::condition_variable` is woken by a call to `notify_one()` or `notify_all()` or a spurious wakeup.

Declaration

```
void wait(std::unique_lock<std::mutex>& lock);
```

Preconditions

`lock.owns_lock()` is `true`, and the lock is owned by the calling thread.

Effects

Atomically unlocks the supplied `lock` object and block until the thread is woken by a call to `notify_one()` or `notify_all()` by another thread, or the thread is woken spuriously. The `lock` object is locked again before the call to `wait()` returns.

Throws

`std::system_error` if the effects can't be achieved. If the `lock` object is unlocked during the call to `wait()`, it's locked again on exit, even if the function exits via an exception.

> **NOTE** The spurious wakeups mean that a thread calling `wait()` may wake even though no thread has called `notify_one()` or `notify_all()`. It's therefore recommended that the overload of `wait()` that takes a predicate is used in preference where possible. Otherwise, it's recommended that `wait()` be called in a loop that tests the predicate associated with the condition variable.

Synchronization

Calls to notify_one(), notify_all(), wait(), wait_for(), and wait_until() on a single std::condition_variable instance are serialized. A call to notify_one() or notify_all() will only wake threads that started waiting *prior* to that call.

STD::CONDITION_VARIABLE::WAIT MEMBER FUNCTION OVERLOAD THAT TAKES A PREDICATE

Waits until the std::condition_variable is woken by a call to notify_one() or notify_all(), and the predicate is true.

Declaration

```
template<typename Predicate>
void wait(std::unique_lock<std::mutex>& lock,Predicate pred);
```

Preconditions

The expression pred() shall be valid and shall return a value that is convertible to bool. lock.owns_lock() shall be true, and the lock shall be owned by the thread calling wait().

Effects

As-if

```
while(!pred())
{
    wait(lock);
}
```

Throws

Any exception thrown by a call to pred, or std::system_error if the effects couldn't be achieved.

NOTE The potential for spurious wakeups means that it's unspecified how many times pred will be called. pred will always be invoked with the mutex referenced by lock locked, and the function shall return if (and only if) an evaluation of (bool)pred() returns true.

Synchronization

Calls to notify_one(), notify_all(), wait(), wait_for() and wait_until() on a single std::condition_variable instance are serialized. A call to notify_one() or notify_all() will only wake threads that started waiting *prior* to that call.

STD::CONDITION_VARIABLE::WAIT_FOR MEMBER FUNCTION

Waits until the std::condition_variable is notified by a call to notify_one() or notify_all(), or until a specified time period has elapsed or the thread is woken spuriously.

Declaration

```
template<typename Rep,typename Period>
cv_status wait_for(
    std::unique_lock<std::mutex>& lock,
    std::chrono::duration<Rep,Period> const& relative_time);
```

Preconditions

lock.owns_lock() is true, and the lock is owned by the calling thread.

Effects

Atomically unlocks the supplied lock object and block until the thread is woken by a call to notify_one() or notify_all() by another thread, or the time period specified by relative_time has elapsed or the thread is woken spuriously. The lock object is locked again before the call to wait_for() returns.

Returns

std::cv_status::no_timeout if the thread was woken by a call to notify_one() or notify_all() or a spurious wakeup, std::cv_status::timeout otherwise.

Throws

std::system_error if the effects can't be achieved. If the lock object is unlocked during the call to wait_for(), it's locked again on exit, even if the function exits via an exception.

NOTE The spurious wakeups mean that a thread calling wait_for() may wake even though no thread has called notify_one() or notify_all(). It's therefore recommended that the overload of wait_for() that takes a predicate is used in preference where possible. Otherwise, it's recommended that wait_for() be called in a loop that tests the predicate associated with the condition variable. Care must be taken when doing this to ensure that the timeout is still valid; wait_until() may be more appropriate in many circumstances. The thread may be blocked for longer than the specified duration. Where possible, the elapsed time is determined by a steady clock.

Synchronization

Calls to notify_one(), notify_all(), wait(), wait_for(), and wait_until() on a single std::condition_variable instance are serialized. A call to notify_one() or notify_all() will only wake threads that started waiting *prior* to that call.

STD::CONDITION_VARIABLE::WAIT_FOR MEMBER FUNCTION OVERLOAD THAT TAKES A PREDICATE

Wait until the std::condition_variable is woken by a call to notify_one() or notify_all() and the predicate is true, or until the specified time period has elapsed.

Declaration

```
template<typename Rep,typename Period,typename Predicate>
bool wait_for(
    std::unique_lock<std::mutex>& lock,
    std::chrono::duration<Rep,Period> const& relative_time,
    Predicate pred);
```

Preconditions

The expression pred() shall be valid and shall return a value that's convertible to bool. lock.owns_lock() shall be true, and the lock shall be owned by the thread calling wait().

Effects
As-if

```
internal_clock::time_point end=internal_clock::now()+relative_time;
while(!pred())
{
    std::chrono::duration<Rep,Period> remaining_time=
        end-internal_clock::now();
    if(wait_for(lock,remaining_time)==std::cv_status::timeout)
        return pred();
}
return true;
```

Returns
`true` if the most recent call to `pred()` returned `true`, `false` if the time period specified by `relative_time` has elapsed and `pred()` returned `false`.

NOTE The potential for spurious wakeups means that it's unspecified how many times `pred` will be called. `pred` will always be invoked with the mutex referenced by `lock` locked, and the function shall return if (and only if) an evaluation of `(bool)pred()` returns `true` or the time period specified by `relative_time` has elapsed. The thread may be blocked for longer than the specified duration. Where possible, the elapsed time is determined by a steady clock.

Throws
Any exception thrown by a call to `pred`, or `std::system_error` if the effects couldn't be achieved.

Synchronization
Calls to `notify_one()`, `notify_all()`, `wait()`, `wait_for()`, and `wait_until()` on a single `std::condition_variable` instance are serialized. A call to `notify_one()` or `notify_all()` will only wake threads that started waiting *prior* to that call.

STD::CONDITION_VARIABLE::WAIT_UNTIL MEMBER FUNCTION

Waits until the `std::condition_variable` is notified by a call to `notify_one()` or `notify_all()` or until a specified time has been reached or the thread is woken spuriously.

Declaration

```
template<typename Clock,typename Duration>
cv_status wait_until(
    std::unique_lock<std::mutex>& lock,
    std::chrono::time_point<Clock,Duration> const& absolute_time);
```

Preconditions
`lock.owns_lock()` is `true`, and the lock is owned by the calling thread.

Effects
Atomically unlocks the supplied `lock` object and block until the thread is woken by a call to `notify_one()` or `notify_all()` by another thread, or `Clock::now()`

returns a time equal to or later than `absolute_time` or the thread is woken spuriously. The `lock` object is locked again before the call to `wait_until()` returns.

Returns

`std::cv_status::no_timeout` if the thread was woken by a call to `notify_one()` or `notify_all()` or a spurious wakeup, `std::cv_status::timeout` otherwise.

Throws

`std::system_error` if the effects can't be achieved. If the `lock` object is unlocked during the call to `wait_until()`, it's locked again on exit, even if the function exits via an exception.

NOTE The spurious wakeups mean that a thread calling `wait_until()` may wake even though no thread has called `notify_one()` or `notify_all()`. It's therefore recommended that the overload of `wait_until()` that takes a predicate is used in preference where possible. Otherwise, it's recommended that `wait_until()` be called in a loop that tests the predicate associated with the condition variable. There's no guarantee as to how long the calling thread will be blocked, only that if the function returns `false`, then `Clock::now()` returns a time equal to or later than `absolute_time` at the point at which the thread became unblocked.

Synchronization

Calls to `notify_one()`, `notify_all()`, `wait()`, `wait_for()`, and `wait_until()` on a single `std::condition_variable` instance are serialized. A call to `notify_one()` or `notify_all()` will only wake threads that started waiting *prior* to that call.

STD::CONDITION_VARIABLE::WAIT_UNTIL MEMBER FUNCTION OVERLOAD THAT TAKES A PREDICATE

Wait until the `std::condition_variable` is woken by a call to `notify_one()` or `notify_all()` and the predicate is `true`, or until the specified time has been reached.

Declaration

```
template<typename Clock,typename Duration,typename Predicate>
bool wait_until(
    std::unique_lock<std::mutex>& lock,
    std::chrono::time_point<Clock,Duration> const& absolute_time,
    Predicate pred);
```

Preconditions

The expression `pred()` shall be valid and shall return a value that is convertible to `bool`. `lock.owns_lock()` shall be `true`, and the lock shall be owned by the thread calling `wait()`.

Effects

As-if

```
while(!pred())
{
    if(wait_until(lock,absolute_time)==std::cv_status::timeout)
        return pred();
}
return true;
```

Returns

true if the most recent call to pred() returned true, false if a call to Clock::now() returned a time equal to or later than the time specified by absolute_time and pred() returned false.

NOTE The potential for spurious wakeups means that it's unspecified how many times pred will be called. pred will always be invoked with the mutex referenced by lock locked, and the function shall return if (and only if) an evaluation of (bool)pred() returns true or Clock::now() returns a time equal to or later than absolute_time. There's no guarantee as to how long the calling thread will be blocked, only that if the function returns false, then Clock::now() returns a time equal to or later than absolute_time at the point at which the thread became unblocked.

Throws

Any exception thrown by a call to pred, or std::system_error if the effects couldn't be achieved.

Synchronization

Calls to notify_one(), notify_all(), wait(), wait_until(), and wait_until() on a single std::condition_variable instance are serialized. A call to notify_one() or notify_all() will wake only threads that started waiting *prior* to that call.

STD::NOTIFY_ALL_AT_THREAD_EXIT NONMEMBER FUNCTION

Wake all of the threads waiting on a std::condition_variable when the current thread exits.

Declaration

```
void notify_all_at_thread_exit(
    condition_variable& cv,unique_lock<mutex> lk);
```

Preconditions

lk.owns_lock() is true, and the lock is owned by the calling thread. lk.mutex() shall return the same value as for any of the lock objects supplied to wait(), wait_for(), or wait_until() on cv from concurrently waiting threads.

Effects

Transfers ownership of the lock held by lk into internal storage and schedules cv to be notified when the calling thread exits. This notification shall be as-if

```
lk.unlock();
cv.notify_all();
```

Throws

std::system_error if the effects can't be achieved.

NOTE The lock is held until the thread exits, so care must be taken to avoid deadlock. It's recommended that the calling thread should exit as soon as possible and that no blocking operations be performed on this thread.

The user should ensure that waiting threads don't erroneously assume that the thread has exited when they are woken, particularly with the potential for spurious wakeups. This can be achieved by testing a predicate on the waiting thread that's only made `true` by the notifying thread under the protection of the mutex and without releasing the lock on the mutex prior to the call of `notify_all_at_thread_exit`.std::condition_variable_any class.

D.2.2 std::condition_variable_any class

The `std::condition_variable_any` class allows a thread to wait for a condition to become `true`. Whereas `std::condition_variable` can be used only with `std::unique_lock<std::mutex>`, `std::condition_variable_any` can be used with *any* type that meets the `Lockable` requirements.

Instances of `std::condition_variable_any` aren't `CopyAssignable`, `CopyConstructible`, `MoveAssignable`, or `MoveConstructible`.

Class definition

```
class condition_variable_any
{
public:
    condition_variable_any();
    ~condition_variable_any();

    condition_variable_any(
        condition_variable_any const& ) = delete;
    condition_variable_any& operator=(
        condition_variable_any const& ) = delete;

    void notify_one() noexcept;
    void notify_all() noexcept;

    template<typename Lockable>
    void wait(Lockable& lock);

    template <typename Lockable, typename Predicate>
    void wait(Lockable& lock, Predicate pred);

    template <typename Lockable, typename Clock,typename Duration>
    std::cv_status wait_until(
        Lockable& lock,
        const std::chrono::time_point<Clock, Duration>& absolute_time);

    template <
        typename Lockable, typename Clock,
        typename Duration, typename Predicate>
    bool wait_until(
        Lockable& lock,
        const std::chrono::time_point<Clock, Duration>& absolute_time,
        Predicate pred);

    template <typename Lockable, typename Rep, typename Period>
    std::cv_status wait_for(
        Lockable& lock,
        const std::chrono::duration<Rep, Period>& relative_time);
```

```
    template <
        typename Lockable, typename Rep,
        typename Period, typename Predicate>
    bool wait_for(
        Lockable& lock,
        const std::chrono::duration<Rep, Period>& relative_time,
        Predicate pred);
};
```

STD::CONDITION_VARIABLE_ANY DEFAULT CONSTRUCTOR

Constructs a `std::condition_variable_any` object.

Declaration

```
condition_variable_any();
```

Effects

Constructs a new `std::condition_variable_any` instance.

Throws

An exception of type `std::system_error` if the condition variable couldn't be constructed.

STD::CONDITION_VARIABLE_ANY DESTRUCTOR

Destroys a `std::condition_variable_any` object.

Declaration

```
~condition_variable_any();
```

Preconditions

There are no threads blocked on `*this` in a call to `wait()`, `wait_for()`, or `wait_until()`.

Effects

Destroys `*this`.

Throws

Nothing.

STD::CONDITION_VARIABLE_ANY::NOTIFY_ONE MEMBER FUNCTION

Wakes one of the threads currently waiting on a `std::condition_variable_any`.

Declaration

```
void notify_one() noexcept;
```

Effects

Wakes one of the threads waiting on `*this` at the point of the call. If there are no threads waiting, the call has no effect.

Throws

`std::system_error` if the effects can't be achieved.

Synchronization

Calls to `notify_one()`, `notify_all()`, `wait()`, `wait_for()`, and `wait_until()` on a single `std::condition_variable_any` instance are serialized. A call to `notify_one()` or `notify_all()` will only wake threads that started waiting *prior* to that call.

STD::CONDITION_VARIABLE_ANY::NOTIFY_ALL MEMBER FUNCTION

Wakes all of the threads currently waiting on a `std::condition_variable_any`.

Declaration

```
void notify_all() noexcept;
```

Effects

Wakes all of the threads waiting on `*this` at the point of the call. If there are no threads waiting, the call has no effect.

Throws

`std::system_error` if the effects can't be achieved.

Synchronization

Calls to `notify_one()`, `notify_all()`, `wait()`, `wait_for()`, and `wait_until()` on a single `std::condition_variable_any` instance are serialized. A call to `notify_one()` or `notify_all()` will only wake threads that started waiting *prior* to that call.

STD::CONDITION_VARIABLE_ANY::WAIT MEMBER FUNCTION

Waits until the `std::condition_variable_any` is woken by a call to `notify_one()` or `notify_all()` or a spurious wakeup.

Declaration

```
template<typename Lockable>
void wait(Lockable& lock);
```

Preconditions

`Lockable` meets the `Lockable` requirements, and `lock` owns a lock.

Effects

Atomically unlocks the supplied `lock` object and block until the thread is woken by a call to `notify_one()` or `notify_all()` by another thread, or the thread is woken spuriously. The `lock` object is locked again before the call to `wait()` returns.

Throws

`std::system_error` if the effects can't be achieved. If the `lock` object is unlocked during the call to `wait()`, it's locked again on exit, even if the function exits via an exception.

NOTE The spurious wakeups mean that a thread calling `wait()` may wake even though no thread has called `notify_one()` or `notify_all()`. It's therefore recommended that the overload of `wait()` that takes a predicate is used in preference where possible. Otherwise, it's recommended that `wait()` be called in a loop that tests the predicate associated with the condition variable.

Synchronization

Calls to `notify_one()`, `notify_all()`, `wait()`, `wait_for()`, and `wait_until()` on a single `std::condition_variable_any` instance are serialized. A call to `notify_one()` or `notify_all()` will only wake threads that started waiting *prior* to that call.

STD::CONDITION_VARIABLE_ANY::WAIT MEMBER FUNCTION OVERLOAD THAT TAKES A PREDICATE

Waits until the `std::condition_variable_any` is woken by a call to `notify_one()` or `notify_all()` and the predicate is `true`.

Declaration

```
template<typename Lockable,typename Predicate>
void wait(Lockable& lock,Predicate pred);
```

Preconditions

The expression `pred()` shall be valid and shall return a value that's convertible to `bool`. `Lockable` meets the `Lockable` requirements, and `lock` owns a lock.

Effects

As-if

```
while(!pred())
{
    wait(lock);
}
```

Throws

Any exception thrown by a call to `pred`, or `std::system_error` if the effects could not be achieved.

NOTE The potential for spurious wakeups means that it's unspecified how many times `pred` will be called. `pred` will always be invoked with the mutex referenced by `lock` locked, and the function shall return if (and only if) an evaluation of `(bool)pred()` returns `true`.

Synchronization

Calls to `notify_one()`, `notify_all()`, `wait()`, `wait_for()`, and `wait_until()` on a single `std::condition_variable_any` instance are serialized. A call to `notify_one()` or `notify_all()` will only wake threads that started waiting *prior* to that call.

STD::CONDITION_VARIABLE_ANY::WAIT_FOR MEMBER FUNCTION

Waits until the `std::condition_variable_any` is notified by a call to `notify_one()` or `notify_all()` or until a specified time period has elapsed or the thread is woken spuriously.

Declaration

```
template<typename Lockable,typename Rep,typename Period>
std::cv_status wait_for(
    Lockable& lock,
    std::chrono::duration<Rep,Period> const& relative_time);
```

Preconditions

`Lockable` meets the `Lockable` requirements, and `lock` owns a lock.

Effects

Atomically unlocks the supplied `lock` object and block until the thread is woken by a call to `notify_one()` or `notify_all()` by another thread or the time period specified by `relative_time` has elapsed or the thread is woken spuriously. The `lock` object is locked again before the call to `wait_for()` returns.

Returns

std::cv_status::no_timeout if the thread was woken by a call to notify_one() or notify_all() or a spurious wakeup, std::cv_status::timeout otherwise.

Throws

std::system_error if the effects can't be achieved. If the lock object is unlocked during the call to wait_for(), it's locked again on exit, even if the function exits via an exception.

> **NOTE** The spurious wakeups mean that a thread calling wait_for() may wake even though no thread has called notify_one() or notify_all(). It's therefore recommended that the overload of wait_for() that takes a predicate is used in preference where possible. Otherwise, it's recommended that wait_for() be called in a loop that tests the predicate associated with the condition variable. Care must be taken when doing this to ensure that the timeout is still valid; wait_until() may be more appropriate in many circumstances. The thread may be blocked for longer than the specified duration. Where possible, the elapsed time is determined by a steady clock.

Synchronization

Calls to notify_one(), notify_all(), wait(), wait_for(), and wait_until() on a single std::condition_variable_any instance are serialized. A call to notify_one() or notify_all() will only wake threads that started waiting *prior* to that call.

STD::CONDITION_VARIABLE_ANY::WAIT_FOR MEMBER FUNCTION OVERLOAD THAT TAKES A PREDICATE

Waits until the std::condition_variable_any is woken by a call to notify_one() or notify_all() and the predicate is true, or until the specified time period has elapsed.

Declaration

```
template<typename Lockable,typename Rep,
    typename Period, typename Predicate>
bool wait_for(
    Lockable& lock,
    std::chrono::duration<Rep,Period> const& relative_time,
    Predicate pred);
```

Preconditions

The expression pred() shall be valid and shall return a value that's convertible to bool. Lockable meets the Lockable requirements, and lock owns a lock.

Effects

As-if

```
internal_clock::time_point end=internal_clock::now()+relative_time;
while(!pred())
{
    std::chrono::duration<Rep,Period> remaining_time=
        end-internal_clock::now();
    if(wait_for(lock,remaining_time)==std::cv_status::timeout)
        return pred();
}
return true;
```

Returns

true if the most recent call to pred() returned true, false if the time period specified by relative_time has elapsed and pred() returned false.

NOTE The potential for spurious wakeups means that it's unspecified how many times pred will be called. pred will always be invoked with the mutex referenced by lock locked, and the function shall return if (and only if) an evaluation of (bool)pred() returns true or the time period specified by relative_time has elapsed. The thread may be blocked for longer than the specified duration. Where possible, the elapsed time is determined by a steady clock.

Throws

Any exception thrown by a call to pred, or std::system_error if the effects couldn't be achieved.

Synchronization

Calls to notify_one(), notify_all(), wait(), wait_for(), and wait_until() on a single std::condition_variable_any instance are serialized. A call to notify_one() or notify_all() will only wake threads that started waiting *prior* to that call.

STD::CONDITION_VARIABLE_ANY::WAIT_UNTIL MEMBER FUNCTION

Waits until the std::condition_variable_any is notified by a call to notify_one() or notify_all() or until a specified time has been reached or the thread is woken spuriously.

Declaration

```
template<typename Lockable,typename Clock,typename Duration>
std::cv_status wait_until(
    Lockable& lock,
    std::chrono::time_point<Clock,Duration> const& absolute_time);
```

Preconditions

Lockable meets the Lockable requirements, and lock owns a lock.

Effects

Atomically unlocks the supplied lock object and block until the thread is woken by a call to notify_one() or notify_all() by another thread or Clock::now() returns a time equal to or later than absolute_time or the thread is woken spuriously. The lock object is locked again before the call to wait_until() returns.

Returns

std::cv_status::no_timeout if the thread was woken by a call to notify_one() or notify_all() or a spurious wakeup, std::cv_status::timeout otherwise.

Throws

std::system_error if the effects can't be achieved. If the lock object is unlocked during the call to wait_until(), it's locked again on exit, even if the function exits via an exception.

NOTE The spurious wakeups mean that a thread calling wait_until() may wake even though no thread has called notify_one() or notify_all(). It's therefore recommended that the overload of `wait_until()` that takes a predicate is used in preference where possible. Otherwise, it's recommended that `wait_until()` be called in a loop that tests the predicate associated with the condition variable. There's no guarantee as to how long the calling thread will be blocked, only that if the function returns `false`, then `Clock::now()` returns a time equal to or later than `absolute_time` at the point at which the thread became unblocked.

Synchronization

Calls to `notify_one()`, `notify_all()`, `wait()`, `wait_for()`, and `wait_until()` on a single `std::condition_variable_any` instance are serialized. A call to `notify_one()` or `notify_all()` will only wake threads that started waiting *prior* to that call.

STD::CONDITION_VARIABLE_ANY::WAIT_UNTIL MEMBER FUNCTION OVERLOAD THAT TAKES A PREDICATE

Waits until the `std::condition_variable_any` is woken by a call to `notify_one()` or `notify_all()` and the predicate is `true`, or until the specified time has been reached.

Declaration

```
template<typename Lockable,typename Clock,
    typename Duration, typename Predicate>
bool wait_until(
    Lockable& lock,
    std::chrono::time_point<Clock,Duration> const& absolute_time,
    Predicate pred);
```

Preconditions

The expression `pred()` shall be valid, and shall return a value that's convertible to `bool`. `Lockable` meets the `Lockable` requirements, and `lock` owns a lock.

Effects

As-if

```
while(!pred())
{
    if(wait_until(lock,absolute_time)==std::cv_status::timeout)
        return pred();
}
return true;
```

Returns

`true` if the most recent call to `pred()` returned `true`, `false` if a call to `Clock::now()` returned a time equal to or later than the time specified by `absolute_time`, and `pred()` returned `false`.

NOTE The potential for spurious wakeups means that it's unspecified how many times `pred` will be called. `pred` will always be invoked with the mutex referenced by `lock` locked, and the function shall return if (and only if) an evaluation of `(bool)pred()` returns `true` or `Clock::now()` returns a time equal to or later than `absolute_time`. There's no guarantee as to how long the calling thread will be blocked, only that if the function returns `false`, then `Clock::now()` returns a time equal to or later than `absolute_time` at the point at which the thread became unblocked.

Throws

Any exception thrown by a call to pred, or std::system_error if the effects couldn't be achieved.

Synchronization

Calls to notify_one(), notify_all(), wait(), wait_until(), and wait_until() on a single std::condition_variable_any instance are serialized. A call to notify_one() or notify_all() will only wake threads that started waiting *prior* to that call.

D.3 <atomic> header

The <atomic> header provides the set of basic atomic types and operations on those types and a class template for constructing an atomic version of a user-defined type that meets certain criteria.

Header contents

```
#define ATOMIC_BOOL_LOCK_FREE see description
#define ATOMIC_CHAR_LOCK_FREE see description
#define ATOMIC_SHORT_LOCK_FREE see description
#define ATOMIC_INT_LOCK_FREE see description
#define ATOMIC_LONG_LOCK_FREE see description
#define ATOMIC_LLONG_LOCK_FREE see description
#define ATOMIC_CHAR16_T_LOCK_FREE see description
#define ATOMIC_CHAR32_T_LOCK_FREE see description
#define ATOMIC_WCHAR_T_LOCK_FREE see description
#define ATOMIC_POINTER_LOCK_FREE see description

#define ATOMIC_VAR_INIT(value) see description

namespace std
{
    enum memory_order;

    struct atomic_flag;
    typedef see description atomic_bool;
    typedef see description atomic_char;
    typedef see description atomic_char16_t;
    typedef see description atomic_char32_t;
    typedef see description atomic_schar;
    typedef see description atomic_uchar;
    typedef see description atomic_short;
    typedef see description atomic_ushort;
    typedef see description atomic_int;
    typedef see description atomic_uint;
    typedef see description atomic_long;
    typedef see description atomic_ulong;
    typedef see description atomic_llong;
    typedef see description atomic_ullong;
    typedef see description atomic_wchar_t;

    typedef see description atomic_int_least8_t;
    typedef see description atomic_uint_least8_t;
    typedef see description atomic_int_least16_t;
    typedef see description atomic_uint_least16_t;
```

```
    typedef see description atomic_int_least32_t;
    typedef see description atomic_uint_least32_t;
    typedef see description atomic_int_least64_t;
    typedef see description atomic_uint_least64_t;
    typedef see description atomic_int_fast8_t;
    typedef see description atomic_uint_fast8_t;
    typedef see description atomic_int_fast16_t;
    typedef see description atomic_uint_fast16_t;
    typedef see description atomic_int_fast32_t;
    typedef see description atomic_uint_fast32_t;
    typedef see description atomic_int_fast64_t;
    typedef see description atomic_uint_fast64_t;
    typedef see description atomic_int8_t;
    typedef see description atomic_uint8_t;
    typedef see description atomic_int16_t;
    typedef see description atomic_uint16_t;
    typedef see description atomic_int32_t;
    typedef see description atomic_uint32_t;
    typedef see description atomic_int64_t;
    typedef see description atomic_uint64_t;
    typedef see description atomic_intptr_t;
    typedef see description atomic_uintptr_t;
    typedef see description atomic_size_t;
    typedef see description atomic_ssize_t;
    typedef see description atomic_ptrdiff_t;
    typedef see description atomic_intmax_t;
    typedef see description atomic_uintmax_t;

    template<typename T>
    struct atomic;

    extern "C" void atomic_thread_fence(memory_order order);
    extern "C" void atomic_signal_fence(memory_order order);

    template<typename T>
    T kill_dependency(T);
}
```

D.3.1 std::atomic_xxx typedefs

For compatibility with the forthcoming C Standard, typedefs for the atomic integral types are provided. These are either typedefs to the corresponding `std::atomic<T>` specialization or a base class of that specialization with the same interface.

Table D.1 Atomic typedefs and their corresponding `std::atomic<>` specializations

`std::atomic_itype`	`std::atomic<>` specialization
`std::atomic_char`	`std::atomic<char>`
`std::atomic_schar`	`std::atomic<signed char>`
`std::atomic_uchar`	`std::atomic<unsigned char>`
`std::atomic_short`	`std::atomic<short>`

Table D.1 Atomic typedefs and their corresponding `std::atomic<>` specializations *(continued)*

`std::atomic_itype`	`std::atomic<>` specialization
`std::atomic_ushort`	`std::atomic<unsigned short>`
`std::atomic_int`	`std::atomic<int>`
`std::atomic_uint`	`std::atomic<unsigned int>`
`std::atomic_long`	`std::atomic<long>`
`std::atomic_ulong`	`std::atomic<unsigned long>`
`std::atomic_llong`	`std::atomic<long long>`
`std::atomic_ullong`	`std::atomic<unsigned long long>`
`std::atomic_wchar_t`	`std::atomic<wchar_t>`
`std::atomic_char16_t`	`std::atomic<char16_t>`
`std::atomic_char32_t`	`std::atomic<char32_t>`

D.3.2 ATOMIC_xxx_LOCK_FREE macros

These macros specify whether the atomic types corresponding to particular built-in types are lock-free or not.

Macro declarations

```
#define ATOMIC_BOOL_LOCK_FREE see description
#define ATOMIC_CHAR_LOCK_FREE see description
#define ATOMIC_SHORT_LOCK_FREE see description
#define ATOMIC_INT_LOCK_FREE see description
#define ATOMIC_LONG_LOCK_FREE see description
#define ATOMIC_LLONG_LOCK_FREE see description
#define ATOMIC_CHAR16_T_LOCK_FREE see description
#define ATOMIC_CHAR32_T_LOCK_FREE see description
#define ATOMIC_WCHAR_T_LOCK_FREE see description
#define ATOMIC_POINTER_LOCK_FREE see description
```

The value of `ATOMIC_xxx_LOCK_FREE` is either 0, 1, or 2. A value of 0 means that operations on both the signed and unsigned atomic types corresponding to the named type are never lock-free, a value of 1 means that the operations may be lock-free for particular instances of those types and not for others, and a value of 2 means that the operations are always lock-free. For example, if `ATOMIC_INT_LOCK_FREE` is 2, operations on instances of `std::atomic<int>` and `std::atomic<unsigned>` are always lock-free.

The macro `ATOMIC_POINTER_LOCK_FREE` describes the lock-free property of operations on the atomic pointer specializations `std::atomic<T*>`.

D.3.3 ATOMIC_VAR_INIT macro

The `ATOMIC_VAR_INIT` macro provides a means of initializing an atomic variable to a particular value.

Declaration

```
#define ATOMIC_VAR_INIT(value) see description
```

The macro expands to a token sequence that can be used to initialize one of the standard atomic types with the specified value in an expression of the following form:

```
std::atomic<type> x = ATOMIC_VAR_INIT(val);
```

The specified value must be compatible with the nonatomic type corresponding to the atomic variable, for example:

```
std::atomic<int> i = ATOMIC_VAR_INIT(42);
std::string s;
std::atomic<std::string*> p = ATOMIC_VAR_INIT(&s);
```

Such initialization is not atomic, and any access by another thread to the variable being initialized where the initialization doesn't happen-before that access is a data race and thus undefined behavior.

D.3.4 std::memory_order enumeration

The `std::memory_order` enumeration is used to specify the ordering constraints of atomic operations.

Declaration

```
typedef enum memory_order
{
    memory_order_relaxed,memory_order_consume,
    memory_order_acquire,memory_order_release,
    memory_order_acq_rel,memory_order_seq_cst
} memory_order;
```

Operations tagged with the various memory order values behave as follows (see chapter 5 for detailed descriptions of the ordering constraints).

STD::MEMORY_ORDER_RELAXED

The operation doesn't provide any additional ordering constraints.

STD::MEMORY_ORDER_RELEASE

The operation is a release operation on the specified memory location. This therefore synchronizes-with an acquire operation on the same memory location that reads the stored value.

STD::MEMORY_ORDER_ACQUIRE

The operation is an acquire operation on the specified memory location. If the stored value was written by a release operation, that store synchronizes-with this operation.

STD::MEMORY_ORDER_ACQ_REL

The operation must be a read-modify-write operation, and it behaves as both `std::memory_order_acquire` and `std::memory_order_release` on the specified location.

STD::MEMORY_ORDER_SEQ_CST

The operation forms part of the single global total order of sequentially consistent operations. In addition, if it's a store, it behaves like a `std::memory_order_release` operation; if it's a load, it behaves like a `std::memory_order_acquire` operation; and if it's a read-modify-write operation, it behaves as both `std::memory_order_acquire` and `std::memory_order_release`. *This is the default for all operations.*

STD::MEMORY_ORDER_CONSUME

The operation is a consume operation on the specified memory location.

D.3.5 std::atomic_thread_fence function

The `std::atomic_thread_fence()` function inserts a "memory barrier" or "fence" in the code to force memory-ordering constraints between operations.

Declaration

```
extern "C" void atomic_thread_fence(std::memory_order order);
```

Effects

Inserts a fence with the required memory-ordering constraints.

A fence with an `order` of `std::memory_order_release`, `std::memory_order_acq_rel`, or `std::memory_order_seq_cst` synchronizes-with an acquire operation on the some memory location if that acquire operation reads a value stored by an atomic operation following the fence on the same thread as the fence.

A release operation synchronizes-with a fence with an `order` of `std::memory_order_acquire`, `std::memory_order_acq_rel`, or `std::memory_order_seq_cst` if that release operation stores a value that's read by an atomic operation prior to the fence on the same thread as the fence.

Throws

Nothing.

D.3.6 std::atomic_signal_fence function

The `std::atomic_signal_fence()` function inserts a memory barrier or fence in the code to force memory ordering constraints between operations on a thread and operations in a signal handler on that thread.

Declaration

```
extern "C" void atomic_signal_fence(std::memory_order order);
```

Effects

Inserts a fence with the required memory-ordering constraints. This is equivalent to `std::atomic_thread_fence(order)` except that the constraints apply only between a thread and a signal handler on the same thread.

Throws

Nothing.

D.3.7 std::atomic_flag class

The std::atomic_flag class provides a simple bare-bones atomic flag. It's the only data type that's *guaranteed* to be lock-free by the C++11 Standard (although many atomic types will be lock-free in most implementations).

An instance of std::atomic_flag is either *set* or *clear.*

Class definition

```
struct atomic_flag
{
    atomic_flag() noexcept = default;
    atomic_flag(const atomic_flag&) = delete;
    atomic_flag& operator=(const atomic_flag&) = delete;
    atomic_flag& operator=(const atomic_flag&) volatile = delete;

    bool test_and_set(memory_order = memory_order_seq_cst) volatile
     noexcept;
    bool test_and_set(memory_order = memory_order_seq_cst) noexcept;
    void clear(memory_order = memory_order_seq_cst) volatile noexcept;
    void clear(memory_order = memory_order_seq_cst) noexcept;
};

bool atomic_flag_test_and_set(volatile atomic_flag*) noexcept;
bool atomic_flag_test_and_set(atomic_flag*) noexcept;
bool atomic_flag_test_and_set_explicit(
    volatile atomic_flag*, memory_order) noexcept;
bool atomic_flag_test_and_set_explicit(
    atomic_flag*, memory_order) noexcept;
void atomic_flag_clear(volatile atomic_flag*) noexcept;
void atomic_flag_clear(atomic_flag*) noexcept;
void atomic_flag_clear_explicit(
    volatile atomic_flag*, memory_order) noexcept;
void atomic_flag_clear_explicit(
    atomic_flag*, memory_order) noexcept;

#define ATOMIC_FLAG_INIT unspecified
```

STD::ATOMIC_FLAG DEFAULT CONSTRUCTOR

It's unspecified whether a default-constructed instance of std::atomic_flag is *clear* or *set.* For objects of static storage duration, initialization shall be static initialization.

Declaration

```
std::atomic_flag() noexcept = default;
```

Effects

Constructs a new std::atomic_flag object in an unspecified state.

Throws

Nothing.

STD::ATOMIC_FLAG INITIALIZATION WITH ATOMIC_FLAG_INIT

An instance of std::atomic_flag may be initialized using the ATOMIC_FLAG_INIT macro, in which case it's initialized into the *clear* state. For objects of static storage duration, initialization shall be static initialization.

Declaration

```
#define ATOMIC_FLAG_INIT unspecified
```

Usage

```
std::atomic_flag flag=ATOMIC_FLAG_INIT;
```

Effects

Constructs a new `std::atomic_flag` object in the *clear* state.

Throws

Nothing.

STD::ATOMIC_FLAG::TEST_AND_SET MEMBER FUNCTION

Atomically sets the flag and checks whether or not it was set.

Declaration

```
bool test_and_set(memory_order order = memory_order_seq_cst) volatile
    noexcept;
bool test_and_set(memory_order order = memory_order_seq_cst) noexcept;
```

Effects

Atomically sets the flag.

Returns

`true` if the flag was set at the point of the call, `false` if the flag was clear.

Throws

Nothing.

NOTE This is an atomic read-modify-write operation for the memory location comprising `*this`.

STD::ATOMIC_FLAG_TEST_AND_SET NONMEMBER FUNCTION

Atomically sets the flag and checks whether or not it was set.

Declaration

```
bool atomic_flag_test_and_set(volatile atomic_flag* flag) noexcept;
bool atomic_flag_test_and_set(atomic_flag* flag) noexcept;
```

Effects

```
return flag->test_and_set();
```

STD::ATOMIC_FLAG_TEST_AND_SET_EXPLICIT NONMEMBER FUNCTION

Atomically sets the flag and checks whether or not it was set.

Declaration

```
bool atomic_flag_test_and_set_explicit(
    volatile atomic_flag* flag, memory_order order) noexcept;
bool atomic_flag_test_and_set_explicit(
    atomic_flag* flag, memory_order order) noexcept;
```

Effects

```
return flag->test_and_set(order);
```

STD::ATOMIC_FLAG::CLEAR MEMBER FUNCTION

Atomically clears the flag.

Declaration

```
void clear(memory_order order = memory_order_seq_cst) volatile noexcept;
void clear(memory_order order = memory_order_seq_cst) noexcept;
```

Preconditions
The supplied `order` must be one of `std::memory_order_relaxed`, `std::memory_order_release`, or `std::memory_order_seq_cst`.

Effects
Atomically clears the flag.

Throws
Nothing.

NOTE This is an atomic store operation for the memory location comprising `*this`.

STD::ATOMIC_FLAG_CLEAR NONMEMBER FUNCTION

Atomically clears the flag.

Declaration

```
void atomic_flag_clear(volatile atomic_flag* flag) noexcept;
void atomic_flag_clear(atomic_flag* flag) noexcept;
```

Effects

```
flag->clear();
```

STD::ATOMIC_FLAG_CLEAR_EXPLICIT NONMEMBER FUNCTION

Atomically clears the flag.

Declaration

```
void atomic_flag_clear_explicit(
    volatile atomic_flag* flag, memory_order order) noexcept;
void atomic_flag_clear_explicit(
    atomic_flag* flag, memory_order order) noexcept;
```

Effects

```
return flag->clear(order);
```

D.3.8 std::atomic class template

The `std::atomic` class provides a wrapper with atomic operations for any type that satisfies the following requirements.

The template parameter `BaseType` must

- Have a trivial default constructor
- Have a trivial copy-assignment operator
- Have a trivial destructor
- Be bitwise-equality comparable

This basically means that `std::atomic<some-built-in-type>` is fine, as is `std::atomic<some-simple-struct>`, but things like `std::atomic<std::string>` are not.

In addition to the primary template, there are specializations for the built-in integral types and pointers to provide additional operations such as `x++`.

Instances of `std::atomic` are not `CopyConstructible` or `CopyAssignable`, because these operations can't be performed as a single atomic operation.

Class definition

```
template<typename BaseType>
struct atomic
{
    atomic() noexcept = default;
    constexpr atomic(BaseType) noexcept;
    BaseType operator=(BaseType) volatile noexcept;
    BaseType operator=(BaseType) noexcept;

    atomic(const atomic&) = delete;
    atomic& operator=(const atomic&) = delete;
    atomic& operator=(const atomic&) volatile = delete;

    bool is_lock_free() const volatile noexcept;
    bool is_lock_free() const noexcept;
    void store(BaseType,memory_order = memory_order_seq_cst)
        volatile noexcept;
    void store(BaseType,memory_order = memory_order_seq_cst) noexcept;
    BaseType load(memory_order = memory_order_seq_cst)
        const volatile noexcept;
    BaseType load(memory_order = memory_order_seq_cst) const noexcept;
    BaseType exchange(BaseType,memory_order = memory_order_seq_cst)
        volatile noexcept;
    BaseType exchange(BaseType,memory_order = memory_order_seq_cst)
        noexcept;

    bool compare_exchange_strong(
        BaseType & old_value, BaseType new_value,
        memory_order order = memory_order_seq_cst) volatile noexcept;
    bool compare_exchange_strong(
        BaseType & old_value, BaseType new_value,
        memory_order order = memory_order_seq_cst) noexcept;
    bool compare_exchange_strong(
        BaseType & old_value, BaseType new_value,
        memory_order success_order,
        memory_order failure_order) volatile noexcept;
    bool compare_exchange_strong(
        BaseType & old_value, BaseType new_value,
        memory_order success_order,
        memory_order failure_order) noexcept;
    bool compare_exchange_weak(
        BaseType & old_value, BaseType new_value,
        memory_order order = memory_order_seq_cst)
        volatile noexcept;
    bool compare_exchange_weak(
        BaseType & old_value, BaseType new_value,
        memory_order order = memory_order_seq_cst) noexcept;
    bool compare_exchange_weak(
        BaseType & old_value, BaseType new_value,
        memory_order success_order,
        memory_order failure_order) volatile noexcept;
    bool compare_exchange_weak(
        BaseType & old_value, BaseType new_value,
        memory_order success_order,
        memory_order failure_order) noexcept;
```

```
    operator BaseType () const volatile noexcept;
    operator BaseType () const noexcept;
};
template<typename BaseType>
bool atomic_is_lock_free(volatile const atomic<BaseType>*) noexcept;
template<typename BaseType>
bool atomic_is_lock_free(const atomic<BaseType>*) noexcept;
template<typename BaseType>
void atomic_init(volatile atomic<BaseType>*, void*) noexcept;
template<typename BaseType>
void atomic_init(atomic<BaseType>*, void*) noexcept;
template<typename BaseType>
BaseType atomic_exchange(volatile atomic<BaseType>*, memory_order)
    noexcept;
template<typename BaseType>
BaseType atomic_exchange(atomic<BaseType>*, memory_order) noexcept;
template<typename BaseType>
BaseType atomic_exchange_explicit(
    volatile atomic<BaseType>*, memory_order) noexcept;
template<typename BaseType>
BaseType atomic_exchange_explicit(
    atomic<BaseType>*, memory_order) noexcept;
template<typename BaseType>
void atomic_store(volatile atomic<BaseType>*, BaseType) noexcept;
template<typename BaseType>
void atomic_store(atomic<BaseType>*, BaseType) noexcept;
template<typename BaseType>
void atomic_store_explicit(
    volatile atomic<BaseType>*, BaseType, memory_order) noexcept;
template<typename BaseType>
void atomic_store_explicit(
    atomic<BaseType>*, BaseType, memory_order) noexcept;
template<typename BaseType>
BaseType atomic_load(volatile const atomic<BaseType>*) noexcept;
template<typename BaseType>
BaseType atomic_load(const atomic<BaseType>*) noexcept;
template<typename BaseType>
BaseType atomic_load_explicit(
    volatile const atomic<BaseType>*, memory_order) noexcept;
template<typename BaseType>
BaseType atomic_load_explicit(
    const atomic<BaseType>*, memory_order) noexcept;
template<typename BaseType>
bool atomic_compare_exchange_strong(
    volatile atomic<BaseType>*,BaseType * old_value,
    BaseType new_value) noexcept;
template<typename BaseType>
bool atomic_compare_exchange_strong(
    atomic<BaseType>*,BaseType * old_value,
    BaseType new_value) noexcept;
template<typename BaseType>
bool atomic_compare_exchange_strong_explicit(
    volatile atomic<BaseType>*,BaseType * old_value,
    BaseType new_value, memory_order success_order,
    memory_order failure_order) noexcept;
```

```
template<typename BaseType>
bool atomic_compare_exchange_strong_explicit(
    atomic<BaseType>*,BaseType * old_value,
    BaseType new_value, memory_order success_order,
    memory_order failure_order) noexcept;
template<typename BaseType>
bool atomic_compare_exchange_weak(
    volatile atomic<BaseType>*,BaseType * old_value,BaseType new_value)
    noexcept;
template<typename BaseType>
bool atomic_compare_exchange_weak(
    atomic<BaseType>*,BaseType * old_value,BaseType new_value) noexcept;
template<typename BaseType>
bool atomic_compare_exchange_weak_explicit(
    volatile atomic<BaseType>*,BaseType * old_value,
    BaseType new_value, memory_order success_order,
    memory_order failure_order) noexcept;
template<typename BaseType>
bool atomic_compare_exchange_weak_explicit(
    atomic<BaseType>*,BaseType * old_value,
    BaseType new_value, memory_order success_order,
    memory_order failure_order) noexcept;
```

NOTE Although the nonmember functions are specified as templates, they may be provided as an overloaded set of functions, and explicit specification of the template arguments shouldn't be used.

STD::ATOMIC DEFAULT CONSTRUCTOR

Constructs an instance of `std::atomic` with a default-initialized value.

Declaration

```
atomic() noexcept;
```

Effects

Constructs a new `std::atomic` object with a default-initialized value. For objects with static storage duration this is static initialization.

NOTE Instances of `std::atomic` with nonstatic storage duration initialized with the default constructor can't be relied on to have a predictable value.

Throws

Nothing.

STD::ATOMIC_INIT NONMEMBER FUNCTION

Nonatomically stores the supplied value in an instance of `std::atomic<BaseType>`.

Declaration

```
template<typename BaseType>
void atomic_init(atomic<BaseType> volatile* p, BaseType v) noexcept;
template<typename BaseType>
void atomic_init(atomic<BaseType>* p, BaseType v) noexcept;
```

Effects
Nonatomically stores the value of v in *p. Invoking atomic_init() on an instance of atomic<BaseType> that hasn't been default constructed, or that has had any operations performed on it since construction, is undefined behavior.

NOTE Because this store is nonatomic, any concurrent access to the object pointed to by p from another thread (even with atomic operations) constitutes a data race.

Throws
Nothing.

STD::ATOMIC CONVERSION CONSTRUCTOR

Construct an instance of std::atomic with the supplied BaseType value.

Declaration
```
constexpr atomic(BaseType b) noexcept;
```

Effects
Constructs a new std::atomic object with a value of b. For objects with static storage duration this is static initialization.

Throws
Nothing.

STD::ATOMIC CONVERSION ASSIGNMENT OPERATOR

Stores a new value in *this.

Declaration
```
BaseType operator=(BaseType b) volatile noexcept;
BaseType operator=(BaseType b) noexcept;
```

Effects
```
return this->store(b);
```

STD::ATOMIC::IS_LOCK_FREE MEMBER FUNCTION

Determines if operations on *this are lock-free.

Declaration
```
bool is_lock_free() const volatile noexcept;
bool is_lock_free() const noexcept;
```

Returns
true if operations on *this are lock-free, false otherwise.

Throws
Nothing.

STD::ATOMIC_IS_LOCK_FREE NONMEMBER FUNCTION

Determine if operations on *this are lock-free.

Declaration
```
template<typename BaseType>
bool atomic_is_lock_free(volatile const atomic<BaseType>* p) noexcept;
```

```
template<typename BaseType>
bool atomic_is_lock_free(const atomic<BaseType>* p) noexcept;
```

Effects

```
return p->is_lock_free();
```

STD::ATOMIC::LOAD MEMBER FUNCTION

Atomically loads the current value of the `std::atomic` instance.

Declaration

```
BaseType load(memory_order order = memory_order_seq_cst)
    const volatile noexcept;
BaseType load(memory_order order = memory_order_seq_cst) const noexcept;
```

Preconditions

The supplied `order` must be one of `std::memory_order_relaxed`, `std::memory_order_acquire`, `std::memory_order_consume`, or `std::memory_order_seq_cst`.

Effects

Atomically loads the value stored in `*this`.

Returns

The value stored in `*this` at the point of the call.

Throws

Nothing.

NOTE This is an atomic load operation for the memory location comprising `*this`.

STD::ATOMIC_LOAD NONMEMBER FUNCTION

Atomically loads the current value of the `std::atomic` instance.

Declaration

```
template<typename BaseType>
BaseType atomic_load(volatile const atomic<BaseType>* p) noexcept;
template<typename BaseType>
BaseType atomic_load(const atomic<BaseType>* p) noexcept;
```

Effects

```
return p->load();
```

STD::ATOMIC_LOAD_EXPLICIT NONMEMBER FUNCTION

Atomically loads the current value of the `std::atomic` instance.

Declaration

```
template<typename BaseType>
BaseType atomic_load_explicit(
    volatile const atomic<BaseType>* p, memory_order order) noexcept;
template<typename BaseType>
BaseType atomic_load_explicit(
    const atomic<BaseType>* p, memory_order order) noexcept;
```

Effects

```
return p->load(order);
```

STD::ATOMIC::OPERATOR BASETYPE CONVERSION OPERATOR

Loads the value stored in `*this`.

Declaration

```
operator BaseType() const volatile noexcept;
operator BaseType() const noexcept;
```

Effects

```
return this->load();
```

STD::ATOMIC::STORE MEMBER FUNCTION

Atomically store a new value in an `atomic<BaseType>` instance.

Declaration

```
void store(BaseType new_value,memory_order order = memory_order_seq_cst)
    volatile noexcept;
void store(BaseType new_value,memory_order order = memory_order_seq_cst)
    noexcept;
```

Preconditions

The supplied `order` must be one of `std::memory_order_relaxed`, `std::memory_order_release`, or `std::memory_order_seq_cst`.

Effects

Atomically stores `new_value` in `*this`.

Throws

Nothing.

NOTE This is an atomic store operation for the memory location comprising `*this`.

STD::ATOMIC_STORE NONMEMBER FUNCTION

Atomically stores a new value in an `atomic<BaseType>` instance.

Declaration

```
template<typename BaseType>
void atomic_store(volatile atomic<BaseType>* p, BaseType new_value)
    noexcept;
template<typename BaseType>
void atomic_store(atomic<BaseType>* p, BaseType new_value) noexcept;
```

Effects

```
p->store(new_value);
```

STD::ATOMIC_STORE_EXPLICIT NONMEMBER FUNCTION

Atomically stores a new value in an `atomic<BaseType>` instance.

Declaration

```
template<typename BaseType>
void atomic_store_explicit(
    volatile atomic<BaseType>* p, BaseType new_value, memory_order order)
    noexcept;
template<typename BaseType>
void atomic_store_explicit(
    atomic<BaseType>* p, BaseType new_value, memory_order order) noexcept;
```

Effects

```
p->store(new_value,order);
```

STD::ATOMIC::EXCHANGE MEMBER FUNCTION

Atomically stores a new value and reads the old one.

Declaration

```
BaseType exchange(
    BaseType new_value,
    memory_order order = memory_order_seq_cst)
    volatile noexcept;
```

Effects

Atomically stores `new_value` in `*this` and retrieves the existing value of `*this`.

Returns

The value of `*this` immediately prior to the store.

Throws

Nothing.

NOTE This is an atomic read-modify-write operation for the memory location comprising `*this`.

STD::ATOMIC_EXCHANGE NONMEMBER FUNCTION

Atomically stores a new value in an `atomic<BaseType>` instance and reads the prior value.

Declaration

```
template<typename BaseType>
BaseType atomic_exchange(volatile atomic<BaseType>* p, BaseType new_value)
    noexcept;
template<typename BaseType>
BaseType atomic_exchange(atomic<BaseType>* p, BaseType new_value) noexcept;
```

Effects

```
return p->exchange(new_value);
```

STD::ATOMIC_EXCHANGE_EXPLICIT NONMEMBER FUNCTION

Atomically stores a new value in an `atomic<BaseType>` instance and reads the prior value.

Declaration

```
template<typename BaseType>
BaseType atomic_exchange_explicit(
    volatile atomic<BaseType>* p, BaseType new_value, memory_order order)
    noexcept;
template<typename BaseType>
BaseType atomic_exchange_explicit(
    atomic<BaseType>* p, BaseType new_value, memory_order order) noexcept;
```

Effects

```
return p->exchange(new_value,order);
```

STD::ATOMIC::COMPARE_EXCHANGE_STRONG MEMBER FUNCTION

Atomically compares the value to an expected value and stores a new value if the values are equal. If the values aren't equal, updates the expected value with the value read.

Declaration

```
bool compare_exchange_strong(
    BaseType& expected,BaseType new_value,
    memory_order order = std::memory_order_seq_cst) volatile noexcept;
bool compare_exchange_strong(
    BaseType& expected,BaseType new_value,
    memory_order order = std::memory_order_seq_cst) noexcept;
bool compare_exchange_strong(
    BaseType& expected,BaseType new_value,
    memory_order success_order,memory_order failure_order)
    volatile noexcept;
bool compare_exchange_strong(
    BaseType& expected,BaseType new_value,
    memory_order success_order,memory_order failure_order) noexcept;
```

Preconditions

`failure_order` shall not be `std::memory_order_release` or `std::memory_order_acq_rel`.

Effects

Atomically compares `expected` to the value stored in `*this` using bitwise comparison and stores `new_value` in `*this` if equal; otherwise updates `expected` to the value read.

Returns

`true` if the existing value of `*this` was equal to `expected`, `false` otherwise.

Throws

Nothing.

NOTE The three-parameter overload is equivalent to the four-parameter overload with `success_order==order` and `failure_order==order`, except that if `order` is `std::memory_order_acq_rel`, then `failure_order` is `std::memory_order_acquire`, and if `order` is `std::memory_order_release`, then `failure_order` is `std::memory_order_relaxed`.

NOTE This is an atomic read-modify-write operation for the memory location comprising `*this` if the result is `true`, with memory ordering `success_order`; otherwise, it's an atomic load operation for the memory location comprising `*this` with memory ordering `failure_order`.

STD::ATOMIC_COMPARE_EXCHANGE_STRONG NONMEMBER FUNCTION

Atomically compares the value to an expected value and stores a new value if the values are equal. If the values aren't equal, updates the expected value with the value read.

Declaration

```
template<typename BaseType>
bool atomic_compare_exchange_strong(
    volatile atomic<BaseType>* p,BaseType * old_value,BaseType new_value)
    noexcept;
template<typename BaseType>
bool atomic_compare_exchange_strong(
    atomic<BaseType>* p,BaseType * old_value,BaseType new_value) noexcept;
```

Effects

```
return p->compare_exchange_strong(*old_value,new_value);
```

STD::ATOMIC_COMPARE_EXCHANGE_STRONG_EXPLICIT NONMEMBER FUNCTION

Atomically compares the value to an expected value and stores a new value if the values are equal. If the values aren't equal, updates the expected value with the value read.

Declaration

```
template<typename BaseType>
bool atomic_compare_exchange_strong_explicit(
    volatile atomic<BaseType>* p,BaseType * old_value,
    BaseType new_value, memory_order success_order,
    memory_order failure_order) noexcept;
template<typename BaseType>
bool atomic_compare_exchange_strong_explicit(
    atomic<BaseType>* p,BaseType * old_value,
    BaseType new_value, memory_order success_order,
    memory_order failure_order) noexcept;
```

Effects

```
return p->compare_exchange_strong(
    *old_value,new_value,success_order,failure_order) noexcept;
```

STD::ATOMIC::COMPARE_EXCHANGE_WEAK MEMBER FUNCTION

Atomically compares the value to an expected value and stores a new value if the values are equal and the update can be done atomically. If the values aren't equal or the update can't be done atomically, updates the expected value with the value read.

Declaration

```
bool compare_exchange_weak(
    BaseType& expected,BaseType new_value,
    memory_order order = std::memory_order_seq_cst) volatile noexcept;
bool compare_exchange_weak(
    BaseType& expected,BaseType new_value,
    memory_order order = std::memory_order_seq_cst) noexcept;
bool compare_exchange_weak(
    BaseType& expected,BaseType new_value,
    memory_order success_order,memory_order failure_order)
    volatile noexcept;
bool compare_exchange_weak(
    BaseType& expected,BaseType new_value,
    memory_order success_order,memory_order failure_order) noexcept;
```

Preconditions

`failure_order` shall not be `std::memory_order_release` or `std::memory_order_acq_rel`.

Effects

Atomically compares `expected` to the value stored in `*this` using bitwise comparison and stores `new_value` in `*this` if equal. If the values aren't equal or the update can't be done atomically, updates `expected` to the value read.

Returns
true if the existing value of *this was equal to expected and new_value was successfully stored in *this, false otherwise.

Throws
Nothing.

NOTE The three-parameter overload is equivalent to the four-parameter overload with success_order==order and failure_order==order, except that if order is std::memory_order_acq_rel, then failure_order is std::memory_order_acquire, and if order is std::memory_order_release, then failure_order is std::memory_order_relaxed.

NOTE This is an atomic read-modify-write operation for the memory location comprising *this if the result is true, with memory ordering success_order; otherwise, it's an atomic load operation for the memory location comprising *this with memory ordering failure_order.

STD::ATOMIC_COMPARE_EXCHANGE_WEAK NONMEMBER FUNCTION

Atomically compares the value to an expected value and stores a new value if the values are equal and the update can be done atomically. If the values aren't equal or the update can't be done atomically, updates the expected value with the value read.

Declaration

```
template<typename BaseType>
bool atomic_compare_exchange_weak(
    volatile atomic<BaseType>* p,BaseType * old_value,BaseType new_value)
    noexcept;
template<typename BaseType>
bool atomic_compare_exchange_weak(
    atomic<BaseType>* p,BaseType * old_value,BaseType new_value) noexcept;
```

Effects

```
return p->compare_exchange_weak(*old_value,new_value);
```

STD::ATOMIC_COMPARE_EXCHANGE_WEAK_EXPLICIT NONMEMBER FUNCTION

Atomically compares the value to an expected value and stores a new value if the values are equal and the update can be done atomically. If the values aren't equal or the update can't be done atomically, updates the expected value with the value read.

Declaration

```
template<typename BaseType>
bool atomic_compare_exchange_weak_explicit(
    volatile atomic<BaseType>* p,BaseType * old_value,
    BaseType new_value, memory_order success_order,
    memory_order failure_order) noexcept;
template<typename BaseType>
bool atomic_compare_exchange_weak_explicit(
    atomic<BaseType>* p,BaseType * old_value,
    BaseType new_value, memory_order success_order,
    memory_order failure_order) noexcept;
```

Effects

```
return p->compare_exchange_weak(
    *old_value,new_value,success_order,failure_order);
```

D.3.9 Specializations of the std::atomic template

Specializations of the `std::atomic` class template are provided for the integral types and pointer types. For the integral types, these specializations provide atomic addition, subtraction, and bitwise operations in addition to the operations provided by the primary template. For pointer types, the specializations provide atomic pointer arithmetic in addition to the operations provided by the primary template.

Specializations are provided for the following integral types:

```
std::atomic<bool>
std::atomic<char>
std::atomic<signed char>
std::atomic<unsigned char>
std::atomic<short>
std::atomic<unsigned short>
std::atomic<int>
std::atomic<unsigned>
std::atomic<long>
std::atomic<unsigned long>
std::atomic<long long>
std::atomic<unsigned long long>
std::atomic<wchar_t>
std::atomic<char16_t>
std::atomic<char32_t>
```

and for `std::atomic<T*>` for all types `T`.

D.3.10 std::atomic<integral-type> specializations

The `std::atomic<`*`integral-type`*`>` specializations of the `std::atomic` class template provide an atomic integral data type for each fundamental integer type, with a comprehensive set of operations.

The following description applies to these specializations of the `std::atomic<>` class template:

```
std::atomic<char>
std::atomic<signed char>
std::atomic<unsigned char>
std::atomic<short>
std::atomic<unsigned short>
std::atomic<int>
std::atomic<unsigned>
std::atomic<long>
std::atomic<unsigned long>
std::atomic<long long>
std::atomic<unsigned long long>
std::atomic<wchar_t>
std::atomic<char16_t>
std::atomic<char32_t>
```

Instances of these specializations are not `CopyConstructible` or `CopyAssignable`, because these operations can't be performed as a single atomic operation.

Class definition

```
template<>
struct atomic<integral-type>
{
    atomic() noexcept = default;
    constexpr atomic(integral-type) noexcept;
    bool operator=(integral-type) volatile noexcept;

    atomic(const atomic&) = delete;
    atomic& operator=(const atomic&) = delete;
    atomic& operator=(const atomic&) volatile = delete;

    bool is_lock_free() const volatile noexcept;
    bool is_lock_free() const noexcept;

    void store(integral-type,memory_order = memory_order_seq_cst)
        volatile noexcept;
    void store(integral-type,memory_order = memory_order_seq_cst) noexcept;
    integral-type load(memory_order = memory_order_seq_cst)
        const volatile noexcept;
    integral-type load(memory_order = memory_order_seq_cst) const noexcept;
    integral-type exchange(
        integral-type,memory_order = memory_order_seq_cst)
        volatile noexcept;
    integral-type exchange(
        integral-type,memory_order = memory_order_seq_cst) noexcept;

    bool compare_exchange_strong(
        integral-type & old_value,integral-type new_value,
         memory_order order = memory_order_seq_cst) volatile noexcept;
    bool compare_exchange_strong(
        integral-type & old_value,integral-type new_value,
         memory_order order = memory_order_seq_cst) noexcept;
    bool compare_exchange_strong(
        integral-type & old_value,integral-type new_value,
        memory_order success_order,memory_order failure_order)
        volatile noexcept;
    bool compare_exchange_strong(
        integral-type & old_value,integral-type new_value,
        memory_order success_order,memory_order failure_order) noexcept;
    bool compare_exchange_weak(
        integral-type & old_value,integral-type new_value,
         memory_order order = memory_order_seq_cst) volatile noexcept;
    bool compare_exchange_weak(
        integral-type & old_value,integral-type new_value,
         memory_order order = memory_order_seq_cst) noexcept;
    bool compare_exchange_weak(
        integral-type & old_value,integral-type new_value,
        memory_order success_order,memory_order failure_order)
        volatile noexcept;
    bool compare_exchange_weak(
        integral-type & old_value,integral-type new_value,
        memory_order success_order,memory_order failure_order) noexcept;
```

```
    operator integral-type() const volatile noexcept;
    operator integral-type() const noexcept;

    integral-type fetch_add(
        integral-type,memory_order = memory_order_seq_cst)
        volatile noexcept;
    integral-type fetch_add(
        integral-type,memory_order = memory_order_seq_cst) noexcept;
    integral-type fetch_sub(
        integral-type,memory_order = memory_order_seq_cst)
        volatile noexcept;
    integral-type fetch_sub(
        integral-type,memory_order = memory_order_seq_cst) noexcept;
    integral-type fetch_and(
        integral-type,memory_order = memory_order_seq_cst)
        volatile noexcept;
    integral-type fetch_and(
        integral-type,memory_order = memory_order_seq_cst) noexcept;
    integral-type fetch_or(
        integral-type,memory_order = memory_order_seq_cst)
        volatile noexcept;
    integral-type fetch_or(
        integral-type,memory_order = memory_order_seq_cst) noexcept;
    integral-type fetch_xor(
        integral-type,memory_order = memory_order_seq_cst)
        volatile noexcept;
    integral-type fetch_xor(
        integral-type,memory_order = memory_order_seq_cst) noexcept;

    integral-type operator++() volatile noexcept;
    integral-type operator++() noexcept;
    integral-type operator++(int) volatile noexcept;
    integral-type operator++(int) noexcept;
    integral-type operator--() volatile noexcept;
    integral-type operator--() noexcept;
    integral-type operator--(int) volatile noexcept;
    integral-type operator--(int) noexcept;

    integral-type operator+=(integral-type) volatile noexcept;
    integral-type operator+=(integral-type) noexcept;
    integral-type operator-=(integral-type) volatile noexcept;
    integral-type operator-=(integral-type) noexcept;
    integral-type operator&=(integral-type) volatile noexcept;
    integral-type operator&=(integral-type) noexcept;
    integral-type operator|=(integral-type) volatile noexcept;
    integral-type operator|=(integral-type) noexcept;
    integral-type operator^=(integral-type) volatile noexcept;
    integral-type operator^=(integral-type) noexcept;
};

bool atomic_is_lock_free(volatile const atomic<integral-type>*) noexcept;
bool atomic_is_lock_free(const atomic<integral-type>*) noexcept;
void atomic_init(volatile atomic<integral-type>*,integral-type) noexcept;
void atomic_init(atomic<integral-type>*,integral-type) noexcept;
integral-type atomic_exchange(
    volatile atomic<integral-type>*,integral-type) noexcept;
integral-type atomic_exchange(
    atomic<integral-type>*,integral-type) noexcept;
```

```
integral-type atomic_exchange_explicit(
    volatile atomic<integral-type>*,integral-type, memory_order) noexcept;
integral-type atomic_exchange_explicit(
    atomic<integral-type>*,integral-type, memory_order) noexcept;
void atomic_store(volatile atomic<integral-type>*,integral-type) noexcept;
void atomic_store(atomic<integral-type>*,integral-type) noexcept;
void atomic_store_explicit(
    volatile atomic<integral-type>*,integral-type, memory_order) noexcept;
void atomic_store_explicit(
    atomic<integral-type>*,integral-type, memory_order) noexcept;
integral-type atomic_load(volatile const atomic<integral-type>*) noexcept;
integral-type atomic_load(const atomic<integral-type>*) noexcept;
integral-type atomic_load_explicit(
    volatile const atomic<integral-type>*,memory_order) noexcept;
integral-type atomic_load_explicit(
    const atomic<integral-type>*,memory_order) noexcept;
bool atomic_compare_exchange_strong(
    volatile atomic<integral-type>*,
    integral-type * old_value,integral-type new_value) noexcept;
bool atomic_compare_exchange_strong(
    atomic<integral-type>*,
    integral-type * old_value,integral-type new_value) noexcept;
bool atomic_compare_exchange_strong_explicit(
    volatile atomic<integral-type>*,
    integral-type * old_value,integral-type new_value,
    memory_order success_order,memory_order failure_order) noexcept;
bool atomic_compare_exchange_strong_explicit(
    atomic<integral-type>*,
    integral-type * old_value,integral-type new_value,
    memory_order success_order,memory_order failure_order) noexcept;
bool atomic_compare_exchange_weak(
    volatile atomic<integral-type>*,
    integral-type * old_value,integral-type new_value) noexcept;
bool atomic_compare_exchange_weak(
    atomic<integral-type>*,
    integral-type * old_value,integral-type new_value) noexcept;
bool atomic_compare_exchange_weak_explicit(
    volatile atomic<integral-type>*,
    integral-type * old_value,integral-type new_value,
    memory_order success_order,memory_order failure_order) noexcept;
bool atomic_compare_exchange_weak_explicit(
    atomic<integral-type>*,
    integral-type * old_value,integral-type new_value,
    memory_order success_order,memory_order failure_order) noexcept;

integral-type atomic_fetch_add(
    volatile atomic<integral-type>*,integral-type) noexcept;
integral-type atomic_fetch_add(
    atomic<integral-type>*,integral-type) noexcept;
integral-type atomic_fetch_add_explicit(
    volatile atomic<integral-type>*,integral-type, memory_order) noexcept;
integral-type atomic_fetch_add_explicit(
    atomic<integral-type>*,integral-type, memory_order) noexcept;
integral-type atomic_fetch_sub(
    volatile atomic<integral-type>*,integral-type) noexcept;
```

```
integral-type atomic_fetch_sub(
    atomic<integral-type>*,integral-type) noexcept;
integral-type atomic_fetch_sub_explicit(
    volatile atomic<integral-type>*,integral-type, memory_order) noexcept;
integral-type atomic_fetch_sub_explicit(
    atomic<integral-type>*,integral-type, memory_order) noexcept;
integral-type atomic_fetch_and(
    volatile atomic<integral-type>*,integral-type) noexcept;
integral-type atomic_fetch_and(
    atomic<integral-type>*,integral-type) noexcept;
integral-type atomic_fetch_and_explicit(
    volatile atomic<integral-type>*,integral-type, memory_order) noexcept;
integral-type atomic_fetch_and_explicit(
    atomic<integral-type>*,integral-type, memory_order) noexcept;
integral-type atomic_fetch_or(
    volatile atomic<integral-type>*,integral-type) noexcept;
integral-type atomic_fetch_or(
    atomic<integral-type>*,integral-type) noexcept;
integral-type atomic_fetch_or_explicit(
    volatile atomic<integral-type>*,integral-type, memory_order) noexcept;
integral-type atomic_fetch_or_explicit(
    atomic<integral-type>*,integral-type, memory_order) noexcept;
integral-type atomic_fetch_xor(
    volatile atomic<integral-type>*,integral-type) noexcept;
integral-type atomic_fetch_xor(
    atomic<integral-type>*,integral-type) noexcept;
integral-type atomic_fetch_xor_explicit(
    volatile atomic<integral-type>*,integral-type, memory_order) noexcept;
integral-type atomic_fetch_xor_explicit(
    atomic<integral-type>*,integral-type, memory_order) noexcept;
```

Those operations that are also provided by the primary template (see D.3.8) have the same semantics.

STD::ATOMIC<INTEGRAL-TYPE>::FETCH_ADD MEMBER FUNCTION

Atomically loads a value and replaces it with the sum of that value and the supplied value `i`.

Declaration

```
integral-type fetch_add(
    integral-type i,memory_order order = memory_order_seq_cst)
    volatile noexcept;
integral-type fetch_add(
    integral-type i,memory_order order = memory_order_seq_cst) noexcept;
```

Effects

Atomically retrieves the existing value of `*this` and stores *old-value* + `i` in `*this`.

Returns

The value of `*this` immediately prior to the store.

Throws

Nothing.

NOTE This is an atomic read-modify-write operation for the memory location comprising `*this`.

STD::ATOMIC_FETCH_ADD NONMEMBER FUNCTION

Atomically reads the value from an `atomic<integral-type>` instance and replaces it with that value plus the supplied value `i`.

Declaration

```
integral-type atomic_fetch_add(
    volatile atomic<integral-type>* p, integral-type i) noexcept;
integral-type atomic_fetch_add(
    atomic<integral-type>* p, integral-type i) noexcept;
```

Effects

```
return p->fetch_add(i);
```

STD::ATOMIC_FETCH_ADD_EXPLICIT NONMEMBER FUNCTION

Atomically reads the value from an `atomic<integral-type>` instance and replaces it with that value plus the supplied value `i`.

Declaration

```
integral-type atomic_fetch_add_explicit(
    volatile atomic<integral-type>* p, integral-type i,
    memory_order order) noexcept;
integral-type atomic_fetch_add_explicit(
    atomic<integral-type>* p, integral-type i, memory_order order)
    noexcept;
```

Effects

```
return p->fetch_add(i,order);
```

STD::ATOMIC<INTEGRAL-TYPE>::FETCH_SUB MEMBER FUNCTION

Atomically loads a value and replaces it with the sum of that value and the supplied value `i`.

Declaration

```
integral-type fetch_sub(
    integral-type i,memory_order order = memory_order_seq_cst)
    volatile noexcept;
integral-type fetch_sub(
    integral-type i,memory_order order = memory_order_seq_cst) noexcept;
```

Effects

Atomically retrieves the existing value of `*this` and stores *old-value* - `i` in `*this`.

Returns

The value of `*this` immediately prior to the store.

Throws

Nothing.

NOTE This is an atomic read-modify-write operation for the memory location comprising `*this`.

STD::ATOMIC_FETCH_SUB NONMEMBER FUNCTION

Atomically reads the value from an `atomic<integral-type>` instance and replaces it with that value minus the supplied value `i`.

Declaration

```
integral-type atomic_fetch_sub(
    volatile atomic<integral-type>* p, integral-type i) noexcept;
integral-type atomic_fetch_sub(
    atomic<integral-type>* p, integral-type i) noexcept;
```

Effects

```
return p->fetch_sub(i);
```

STD::ATOMIC_FETCH_SUB_EXPLICIT NONMEMBER FUNCTION

Atomically reads the value from an `atomic<integral-type>` instance and replaces it with that value minus the supplied value `i`.

Declaration

```
integral-type atomic_fetch_sub_explicit(
    volatile atomic<integral-type>* p, integral-type i,
    memory_order order) noexcept;
integral-type atomic_fetch_sub_explicit(
    atomic<integral-type>* p, integral-type i, memory_order order)
    noexcept;
```

Effects

```
return p->fetch_sub(i,order);
```

STD::ATOMIC<INTEGRAL-TYPE>::FETCH_AND MEMBER FUNCTION

Atomically loads a value and replaces it with the bitwise-and of that value and the supplied value `i`.

Declaration

```
integral-type fetch_and(
    integral-type i,memory_order order = memory_order_seq_cst)
    volatile noexcept;
integral-type fetch_and(
    integral-type i,memory_order order = memory_order_seq_cst) noexcept;
```

Effects

Atomically retrieves the existing value of `*this` and stores *old-value* `&` `i` in `*this`.

Returns

The value of `*this` immediately prior to the store.

Throws

Nothing.

NOTE This is an atomic read-modify-write operation for the memory location comprising `*this`.

STD::ATOMIC_FETCH_AND NONMEMBER FUNCTION

Atomically reads the value from an `atomic<integral-type>` instance and replaces it with the bitwise-and of that value and the supplied value `i`.

Declaration

```
integral-type atomic_fetch_and(
    volatile atomic<integral-type>* p, integral-type i) noexcept;
integral-type atomic_fetch_and(
    atomic<integral-type>* p, integral-type i) noexcept;
```

Effects

```
return p->fetch_and(i);
```

STD::ATOMIC_FETCH_AND_EXPLICIT NONMEMBER FUNCTION

Atomically reads the value from an `atomic<integral-type>` instance and replaces it with the bitwise-and of that value and the supplied value `i`.

Declaration

```
integral-type atomic_fetch_and_explicit(
    volatile atomic<integral-type>* p, integral-type i,
    memory_order order) noexcept;
integral-type atomic_fetch_and_explicit(
    atomic<integral-type>* p, integral-type i, memory_order order)
    noexcept;
```

Effects

```
return p->fetch_and(i,order);
```

STD::ATOMIC<INTEGRAL-TYPE>::FETCH_OR MEMBER FUNCTION

Atomically loads a value and replaces it with the bitwise-or of that value and the supplied value `i`.

Declaration

```
integral-type fetch_or(
    integral-type i,memory_order order = memory_order_seq_cst)
    volatile noexcept;
integral-type fetch_or(
    integral-type i,memory_order order = memory_order_seq_cst) noexcept;
```

Effects

Atomically retrieves the existing value of `*this` and stores *old-value* | `i` in `*this`.

Returns

The value of `*this` immediately prior to the store.

Throws

Nothing.

NOTE This is an atomic read-modify-write operation for the memory location comprising `*this`.

STD::ATOMIC_FETCH_OR NONMEMBER FUNCTION

Atomically reads the value from an `atomic<integral-type>` instance and replaces it with the bitwise-or of that value and the supplied value `i`.

Declaration

```
integral-type atomic_fetch_or(
    volatile atomic<integral-type>* p, integral-type i) noexcept;
integral-type atomic_fetch_or(
    atomic<integral-type>* p, integral-type i) noexcept;
```

Effects

```
return p->fetch_or(i);
```

STD::ATOMIC_FETCH_OR_EXPLICIT NONMEMBER FUNCTION

Atomically reads the value from an `atomic<integral-type>` instance and replaces it with the bitwise-or of that value and the supplied value `i`.

Declaration

```
integral-type atomic_fetch_or_explicit(
    volatile atomic<integral-type>* p, integral-type i,
    memory_order order) noexcept;
integral-type atomic_fetch_or_explicit(
    atomic<integral-type>* p, integral-type i, memory_order order)
    noexcept;
```

Effects

```
return p->fetch_or(i,order);
```

STD::ATOMIC<INTEGRAL-TYPE>::FETCH_XOR MEMBER FUNCTION

Atomically loads a value and replaces it with the bitwise-xor of that value and the supplied value `i`.

Declaration

```
integral-type fetch_xor(
    integral-type i,memory_order order = memory_order_seq_cst)
    volatile noexcept;
integral-type fetch_xor(
    integral-type i,memory_order order = memory_order_seq_cst) noexcept;
```

Effects

Atomically retrieves the existing value of `*this` and stores *old-value* `^ i` in `*this`.

Returns

The value of `*this` immediately prior to the store.

Throws

Nothing.

> **NOTE** This is an atomic read-modify-write operation for the memory location comprising `*this`.

STD::ATOMIC_FETCH_XOR NONMEMBER FUNCTION

Atomically reads the value from an `atomic<integral-type>` instance and replaces it with the bitwise-xor of that value and the supplied value `i`.

Declaration

```
integral-type atomic_fetch_xor(
    volatile atomic<integral-type>* p, integral-type i) noexcept;
integral-type atomic_fetch_xor(
    atomic<integral-type>* p, integral-type i) noexcept;
```

Effects

```
return p->fetch_xor(i);
```

STD::ATOMIC_FETCH_XOR_EXPLICIT NONMEMBER FUNCTION

Atomically reads the value from an `atomic<integral-type>` instance and replaces it with the bitwise-xor of that value and the supplied value `i`.

Declaration

```
integral-type atomic_fetch_xor_explicit(
    volatile atomic<integral-type>* p, integral-type i,
    memory_order order) noexcept;
integral-type atomic_fetch_xor_explicit(
    atomic<integral-type>* p, integral-type i, memory_order order)
    noexcept;
```

Effects

```
return p->fetch_xor(i,order);
```

STD::ATOMIC<INTEGRAL-TYPE>::OPERATOR++ PREINCREMENT OPERATOR

Atomically increments the value stored in `*this` and returns the new value.

Declaration

```
integral-type operator++() volatile noexcept;
integral-type operator++() noexcept;
```

Effects

```
return this->fetch_add(1) + 1;
```

STD::ATOMIC<INTEGRAL-TYPE>::OPERATOR++ POSTINCREMENT OPERATOR

Atomically increments the value stored in `*this` and returns the old value.

Declaration

```
integral-type operator++(int) volatile noexcept;
integral-type operator++(int) noexcept;
```

Effects

```
return this->fetch_add(1);
```

STD::ATOMIC<INTEGRAL-TYPE>::OPERATOR-- PREDECREMENT OPERATOR

Atomically decrements the value stored in `*this` and returns the new value.

Declaration

```
integral-type operator--() volatile noexcept;
integral-type operator--() noexcept;
```

Effects

```
return this->fetch_sub(1) - 1;
```

STD::ATOMIC<INTEGRAL-TYPE>::OPERATOR-- POSTDECREMENT OPERATOR

Atomically decrements the value stored in `*this` and returns the old value.

Declaration

```
integral-type operator--(int) volatile noexcept;
integral-type operator--(int) noexcept;
```

Effects

```
return this->fetch_sub(1);
```

STD::ATOMIC<INTEGRAL-TYPE>::OPERATOR+= COMPOUND ASSIGNMENT OPERATOR

Atomically adds the supplied value to the value stored in `*this` and returns the new value.

Declaration

```
integral-type operator+=(integral-type i) volatile noexcept;
integral-type operator+=(integral-type i) noexcept;
```

Effects

```
return this->fetch_add(i) + i;
```

STD::ATOMIC<INTEGRAL-TYPE>::OPERATOR-= COMPOUND ASSIGNMENT OPERATOR

Atomically subtracts the supplied value from the value stored in `*this` and returns the new value.

Declaration

```
integral-type operator-=(integral-type i) volatile noexcept;
integral-type operator-=(integral-type i) noexcept;
```

Effects

```
return this->fetch_sub(i,std::memory_order_seq_cst) - i;
```

STD::ATOMIC<INTEGRAL-TYPE>::OPERATOR&= COMPOUND ASSIGNMENT OPERATOR

Atomically replaces the value stored in `*this` with the bitwise-and of the supplied value and the value stored in `*this` and returns the new value.

Declaration

```
integral-type operator&=(integral-type i) volatile noexcept;
integral-type operator&=(integral-type i) noexcept;
```

Effects

```
return this->fetch_and(i) & i;
```

STD::ATOMIC<INTEGRAL-TYPE>::OPERATOR|= COMPOUND ASSIGNMENT OPERATOR

Atomically replaces the value stored in `*this` with the bitwise-or of the supplied value and the value stored in `*this` and returns the new value.

Declaration

```
integral-type operator|=(integral-type i) volatile noexcept;
integral-type operator|=(integral-type i) noexcept;
```

Effects

```
return this->fetch_or(i,std::memory_order_seq_cst) | i;
```

STD::ATOMIC<INTEGRAL-TYPE>::OPERATOR^= COMPOUND ASSIGNMENT OPERATOR

Atomically replaces the value stored in `*this` with the bitwise-xor of the supplied value and the value stored in `*this` and returns the new value.

Declaration

```
integral-type operator^=(integral-type i) volatile noexcept;
integral-type operator^=(integral-type i) noexcept;
```

Effects

```
return this->fetch_xor(i,std::memory_order_seq_cst) ^ i;
```

STD::ATOMIC<T*> PARTIAL SPECIALIZATION

The `std::atomic<T*>` partial specialization of the `std::atomic` class template provides an atomic data type for each pointer type, with a comprehensive set of operations.

Instances of these `std::atomic<T*>` are not `CopyConstructible` or `CopyAssignable`, because these operations can't be performed as a single atomic operation.

Class definition

```
template<typename T>
struct atomic<T*>
{
    atomic() noexcept = default;
    constexpr atomic(T*) noexcept;
    bool operator=(T*) volatile;
    bool operator=(T*);

    atomic(const atomic&) = delete;
    atomic& operator=(const atomic&) = delete;
    atomic& operator=(const atomic&) volatile = delete;

    bool is_lock_free() const volatile noexcept;
    bool is_lock_free() const noexcept;
    void store(T*,memory_order = memory_order_seq_cst) volatile noexcept;
    void store(T*,memory_order = memory_order_seq_cst) noexcept;
    T* load(memory_order = memory_order_seq_cst) const volatile noexcept;
    T* load(memory_order = memory_order_seq_cst) const noexcept;
    T* exchange(T*,memory_order = memory_order_seq_cst) volatile noexcept;
    T* exchange(T*,memory_order = memory_order_seq_cst) noexcept;

    bool compare_exchange_strong(
        T* & old_value, T* new_value,
        memory_order order = memory_order_seq_cst) volatile noexcept;
    bool compare_exchange_strong(
        T* & old_value, T* new_value,
        memory_order order = memory_order_seq_cst) noexcept;
    bool compare_exchange_strong(
        T* & old_value, T* new_value,
        memory_order success_order,memory_order failure_order)
        volatile noexcept;
    bool compare_exchange_strong(
        T* & old_value, T* new_value,
        memory_order success_order,memory_order failure_order) noexcept;
    bool compare_exchange_weak(
        T* & old_value, T* new_value,
        memory_order order = memory_order_seq_cst) volatile noexcept;
    bool compare_exchange_weak(
        T* & old_value, T* new_value,
        memory_order order = memory_order_seq_cst) noexcept;
    bool compare_exchange_weak(
        T* & old_value, T* new_value,
        memory_order success_order,memory_order failure_order)
        volatile noexcept;
    bool compare_exchange_weak(
        T* & old_value, T* new_value,
        memory_order success_order,memory_order failure_order) noexcept;

    operator T*() const volatile noexcept;
    operator T*() const noexcept;

    T* fetch_add(
        ptrdiff_t,memory_order = memory_order_seq_cst) volatile noexcept;
    T* fetch_add(
        ptrdiff_t,memory_order = memory_order_seq_cst) noexcept;
```

```
    T* fetch_sub(
        ptrdiff_t,memory_order = memory_order_seq_cst) volatile noexcept;
    T* fetch_sub(
        ptrdiff_t,memory_order = memory_order_seq_cst) noexcept;

    T* operator++() volatile noexcept;
    T* operator++() noexcept;
    T* operator++(int) volatile noexcept;
    T* operator++(int) noexcept;
    T* operator--() volatile noexcept;
    T* operator--() noexcept;
    T* operator--(int) volatile noexcept;
    T* operator--(int) noexcept;

    T* operator+=(ptrdiff_t) volatile noexcept;
    T* operator+=(ptrdiff_t) noexcept;
    T* operator-=(ptrdiff_t) volatile noexcept;
    T* operator-=(ptrdiff_t) noexcept;
};

bool atomic_is_lock_free(volatile const atomic<T*>*) noexcept;
bool atomic_is_lock_free(const atomic<T*>*) noexcept;
void atomic_init(volatile atomic<T*>*, T*) noexcept;
void atomic_init(atomic<T*>*, T*) noexcept;
T* atomic_exchange(volatile atomic<T*>*, T*) noexcept;
T* atomic_exchange(atomic<T*>*, T*) noexcept;
T* atomic_exchange_explicit(volatile atomic<T*>*, T*, memory_order)
    noexcept;
T* atomic_exchange_explicit(atomic<T*>*, T*, memory_order) noexcept;
void atomic_store(volatile atomic<T*>*, T*) noexcept;
void atomic_store(atomic<T*>*, T*) noexcept;
void atomic_store_explicit(volatile atomic<T*>*, T*, memory_order)
    noexcept;
void atomic_store_explicit(atomic<T*>*, T*, memory_order) noexcept;
T* atomic_load(volatile const atomic<T*>*) noexcept;
T* atomic_load(const atomic<T*>*) noexcept;
T* atomic_load_explicit(volatile const atomic<T*>*, memory_order) noexcept;
T* atomic_load_explicit(const atomic<T*>*, memory_order) noexcept;
bool atomic_compare_exchange_strong(
    volatile atomic<T*>*,T* * old_value,T* new_value) noexcept;
bool atomic_compare_exchange_strong(
    volatile atomic<T*>*,T* * old_value,T* new_value) noexcept;
bool atomic_compare_exchange_strong_explicit(
    atomic<T*>*,T* * old_value,T* new_value,
    memory_order success_order,memory_order failure_order) noexcept;
bool atomic_compare_exchange_strong_explicit(
    atomic<T*>*,T* * old_value,T* new_value,
    memory_order success_order,memory_order failure_order) noexcept;
bool atomic_compare_exchange_weak(
    volatile atomic<T*>*,T* * old_value,T* new_value) noexcept;
bool atomic_compare_exchange_weak(
    atomic<T*>*,T* * old_value,T* new_value) noexcept;
bool atomic_compare_exchange_weak_explicit(
    volatile atomic<T*>*,T* * old_value, T* new_value,
    memory_order success_order,memory_order failure_order) noexcept;
```

```
bool atomic_compare_exchange_weak_explicit(
    atomic<T*>*,T* * old_value, T* new_value,
    memory_order success_order,memory_order failure_order) noexcept;

T* atomic_fetch_add(volatile atomic<T*>*, ptrdiff_t) noexcept;
T* atomic_fetch_add(atomic<T*>*, ptrdiff_t) noexcept;
T* atomic_fetch_add_explicit(
    volatile atomic<T*>*, ptrdiff_t, memory_order) noexcept;
T* atomic_fetch_add_explicit(
    atomic<T*>*, ptrdiff_t, memory_order) noexcept;
T* atomic_fetch_sub(volatile atomic<T*>*, ptrdiff_t) noexcept;
T* atomic_fetch_sub(atomic<T*>*, ptrdiff_t) noexcept;
T* atomic_fetch_sub_explicit(
    volatile atomic<T*>*, ptrdiff_t, memory_order) noexcept;
T* atomic_fetch_sub_explicit(
    atomic<T*>*, ptrdiff_t, memory_order) noexcept;
```

Those operations that are also provided by the primary template (see 11.3.8) have the same semantics.

STD::ATOMIC<T*>::FETCH_ADD MEMBER FUNCTION

Atomically loads a value and replaces it with the sum of that value and the supplied value `i` using standard pointer arithmetic rules, and returns the old value.

Declaration

```
T* fetch_add(
    ptrdiff_t i,memory_order order = memory_order_seq_cst)
    volatile noexcept;
T* fetch_add(
    ptrdiff_t i,memory_order order = memory_order_seq_cst) noexcept;
```

Effects

Atomically retrieves the existing value of `*this` and stores *old-value* + `i` in `*this`.

Returns

The value of `*this` immediately prior to the store.

Throws

Nothing.

NOTE This is an atomic read-modify-write operation for the memory location comprising `*this`.

STD::ATOMIC_FETCH_ADD NONMEMBER FUNCTION

Atomically reads the value from an `atomic<T*>` instance and replaces it with that value plus the supplied value `i` using standard pointer arithmetic rules.

Declaration

```
T* atomic_fetch_add(volatile atomic<T*>* p, ptrdiff_t i) noexcept;
T* atomic_fetch_add(atomic<T*>* p, ptrdiff_t i) noexcept;
```

Effects

```
return p->fetch_add(i);
```

STD::ATOMIC_FETCH_ADD_EXPLICIT NONMEMBER FUNCTION

Atomically reads the value from an `atomic<T*>` instance and replaces it with that value plus the supplied value `i` using standard pointer arithmetic rules.

Declaration

```
T* atomic_fetch_add_explicit(
    volatile atomic<T*>* p, ptrdiff_t i,memory_order order) noexcept;
T* atomic_fetch_add_explicit(
    atomic<T*>* p, ptrdiff_t i, memory_order order) noexcept;
```

Effects

```
return p->fetch_add(i,order);
```

STD::ATOMIC<T*>::FETCH_SUB MEMBER FUNCTION

Atomically loads a value and replaces it with that value minus the supplied value `i` using standard pointer arithmetic rules, and returns the old value.

Declaration

```
T* fetch_sub(
    ptrdiff_t i,memory_order order = memory_order_seq_cst)
    volatile noexcept;
T* fetch_sub(
    ptrdiff_t i,memory_order order = memory_order_seq_cst) noexcept;
```

Effects

Atomically retrieves the existing value of `*this` and stores *old-value* - `i` in `*this`.

Returns

The value of `*this` immediately prior to the store.

Throws

Nothing.

NOTE This is an atomic read-modify-write operation for the memory location comprising `*this`.

STD::ATOMIC_FETCH_SUB NONMEMBER FUNCTION

Atomically reads the value from an `atomic<T*>` instance and replaces it with that value minus the supplied value `i` using standard pointer arithmetic rules.

Declaration

```
T* atomic_fetch_sub(volatile atomic<T*>* p, ptrdiff_t i) noexcept;
T* atomic_fetch_sub(atomic<T*>* p, ptrdiff_t i) noexcept;
```

Effects

```
return p->fetch_sub(i);
```

STD::ATOMIC_FETCH_SUB_EXPLICIT NONMEMBER FUNCTION

Atomically reads the value from an `atomic<T*>` instance and replaces it with that value minus the supplied value `i` using standard pointer arithmetic rules.

Declaration

```
T* atomic_fetch_sub_explicit(
    volatile atomic<T*>* p, ptrdiff_t i,memory_order order) noexcept;
```

```
T* atomic_fetch_sub_explicit(
    atomic<T*>* p, ptrdiff_t i, memory_order order) noexcept;
```

Effects

```
return p->fetch_sub(i,order);
```

STD::ATOMIC<T*>::OPERATOR++ PREINCREMENT OPERATOR

Atomically increments the value stored in `*this` using standard pointer arithmetic rules and returns the new value.

Declaration

```
T* operator++() volatile noexcept;
T* operator++() noexcept;
```

Effects

```
return this->fetch_add(1) + 1;
```

STD::ATOMIC<T*>::OPERATOR++ POSTINCREMENT OPERATOR

Atomically increments the value stored in `*this` and returns the old value.

Declaration

```
T* operator++(int) volatile noexcept;
T* operator++(int) noexcept;
```

Effects

```
return this->fetch_add(1);
```

STD::ATOMIC<T*>::OPERATOR-- PREDECREMENT OPERATOR

Atomically decrements the value stored in `*this` using standard pointer arithmetic rules and returns the new value.

Declaration

```
T* operator--() volatile noexcept;
T* operator--() noexcept;
```

Effects

```
return this->fetch_sub(1) - 1;
```

STD::ATOMIC<T*>::OPERATOR-- POSTDECREMENT OPERATOR

Atomically decrements the value stored in `*this` using standard pointer arithmetic rules and returns the old value.

Declaration

```
T* operator--(int) volatile noexcept;
T* operator--(int) noexcept;
```

Effects

```
return this->fetch_sub(1);
```

STD::ATOMIC<T*>::OPERATOR+= COMPOUND ASSIGNMENT OPERATOR

Atomically adds the supplied value to the value stored in `*this` using standard pointer arithmetic rules and returns the new value.

Declaration

```
T* operator+=(ptrdiff_t i) volatile noexcept;
T* operator+=(ptrdiff_t i) noexcept;
```

Effects

```
return this->fetch_add(i) + i;
```

STD::ATOMIC<T*>::OPERATOR-= COMPOUND ASSIGNMENT OPERATOR

Atomically subtracts the supplied value from the value stored in `*this` using standard pointer arithmetic rules and returns the new value.

Declaration

```
T* operator-=(ptrdiff_t i) volatile noexcept;
T* operator-=(ptrdiff_t i) noexcept;
```

Effects

```
return this->fetch_sub(i) - i;
```

D.4 <future> header

The `<future>` header provides facilities for handling asynchronous results from operations that may be performed on another thread.

Header contents

```
namespace std
{
    enum class future_status {
        ready, timeout, deferred };

    enum class future_errc
    {
        broken_promise,
        future_already_retrieved,
        promise_already_satisfied,
        no_state
    };

    class future_error;

    const error_category& future_category();

    error_code make_error_code(future_errc e);
    error_condition make_error_condition(future_errc e);

    template<typename ResultType>
    class future;

    template<typename ResultType>
    class shared_future;

    template<typename ResultType>
    class promise;

    template<typename FunctionSignature>
    class packaged_task; // no definition provided

    template<typename ResultType,typename ... Args>
    class packaged_task<ResultType (Args...)>;

    enum class launch {
        async, deferred
    };
```

```
    template<typename FunctionType,typename ... Args>
    future<result_of<FunctionType(Args...)>::type>
    async(FunctionType&& func,Args&& ... args);

    template<typename FunctionType,typename ... Args>
    future<result_of<FunctionType(Args...)>::type>
    async(std::launch policy,FunctionType&& func,Args&& ... args);
}
```

D.4.1 std::future class template

The `std::future` class template provides a means of waiting for an asynchronous result from another thread, in conjunction with the `std::promise` and `std::packaged_task` class templates and the `std::async` function template, which can be used to provide that asynchronous result. Only one `std::future` instance references any given asynchronous result at any time.

Instances of `std::future` are `MoveConstructible` and `MoveAssignable` but not `CopyConstructible` or `CopyAssignable`.

Class definition

```
template<typename ResultType>
class future
{
public:
    future() noexcept;
    future(future&&) noexcept;
    future& operator=(future&&) noexcept;
    ~future();

    future(future const&) = delete;
    future& operator=(future const&) = delete;

    shared_future<ResultType> share();

    bool valid() const noexcept;

    see description get();

    void wait();

    template<typename Rep,typename Period>
    future_status wait_for(
        std::chrono::duration<Rep,Period> const& relative_time);

    template<typename Clock,typename Duration>
    future_status wait_until(
        std::chrono::time_point<Clock,Duration> const& absolute_time);
};
```

STD::FUTURE DEFAULT CONSTRUCTOR

Constructs a `std::future` object without an associated asynchronous result.

Declaration

```
future() noexcept;
```

Effects

Constructs a new `std::future` instance.

Postconditions
valid() returns false.

Throws
Nothing.

STD::FUTURE MOVE CONSTRUCTOR

Constructs one std::future object from another, transferring ownership of the asynchronous result associated with the other std::future object to the newly constructed instance.

Declaration

```
future(future&& other) noexcept;
```

Effects
Move-constructs a new std::future instance from other.

Postconditions
The asynchronous result associated with other prior to the invocation of the constructor is associated with the newly constructed std::future object. other has no associated asynchronous result. this->valid() returns the same value that other.valid() returned before the invocation of this constructor. other.valid() returns false.

Throws
Nothing.

STD::FUTURE MOVE ASSIGNMENT OPERATOR

Transfers ownership of the asynchronous result associated with the one std::future object to another.

Declaration

```
future(future&& other) noexcept;
```

Effects
Transfers ownership of an asynchronous state between std::future instances.

Postconditions
The asynchronous result associated with other prior to the invocation of the constructor is associated with *this. other has no associated asynchronous result. The ownership of the asynchronous state (if any) associated with *this prior to the call is released, and the state destroyed if this is the last reference. this->valid() returns the same value that other.valid() returned before the invocation of this constructor. other.valid() returns false.

Throws
Nothing.

STD::FUTURE DESTRUCTOR

Destroys a std::future object.

Declaration

```
~future();
```

Effects
Destroys `*this`. If this is the last reference to the asynchronous result associated with `*this` (if any), then destroy that asynchronous result.

Throws
Nothing

STD::FUTURE::SHARE MEMBER FUNCTION

Constructs a new `std::shared_future` instance and transfers ownership of the asynchronous result associated with `*this` to this newly constructed `std::shared_future` instance.

Declaration

```
shared_future<ResultType> share();
```

Effects
As-if `shared_future<ResultType>(std::move(*this))`.

Postconditions
The asynchronous result associated with `*this` prior to the invocation of `share()` (if any) is associated with the newly constructed `std::shared_future` instance. `this->valid()` returns `false`.

Throws
Nothing.

STD::FUTURE::VALID MEMBER FUNCTION

Checks if a `std::future` instance is associated with an asynchronous result.

Declaration

```
bool valid() const noexcept;
```

Returns
`true` if the `*this` has an associated asynchronous result, `false` otherwise.

Throws
Nothing.

STD::FUTURE::WAIT MEMBER FUNCTION

If the state associated with `*this` contains a deferred function, invokes the deferred function. Otherwise, waits until the asynchronous result associated with an instance of `std::future` is ready.

Declaration

```
void wait();
```

Preconditions
`this->valid()` would return `true`.

Effects
If the associated state contains a deferred function, invokes the deferred function and stores the returned value or thrown exception as the asynchronous result. Otherwise, blocks until the asynchronous result associated with `*this` is *ready*.

Throws
Nothing.

STD::FUTURE::WAIT_FOR MEMBER FUNCTION

Waits until the asynchronous result associated with an instance of `std::future` is ready or until a specified time period has elapsed.

Declaration

```
template<typename Rep,typename Period>
future_status wait_for(
    std::chrono::duration<Rep,Period> const& relative_time);
```

Preconditions

`this->valid()` would return `true`.

Effects

If the asynchronous result associated with `*this` contains a deferred function arising from a call to `std::async` that hasn't yet started execution, returns immediately without blocking. Otherwise blocks until the asynchronous result associated with `*this` is *ready* or the time period specified by `relative_time` has elapsed.

Returns

`std::future_status::deferred` if the asynchronous result associated with `*this` contains a deferred function arising from a call to `std::async` that hasn't yet started execution, `std::future_status::ready` if the asynchronous result associated with `*this` is *ready*, `std::future_status::timeout` if the time period specified by `relative_time` has elapsed.

NOTE The thread may be blocked for longer than the specified duration. Where possible, the elapsed time is determined by a steady clock.

Throws

Nothing.

STD::FUTURE::WAIT_UNTIL MEMBER FUNCTION

Waits until the asynchronous result associated with an instance of `std::future` is ready or until a specified time period has elapsed.

Declaration

```
template<typename Clock,typename Duration>
future_status wait_until(
    std::chrono::time_point<Clock,Duration> const& absolute_time);
```

Preconditions

`this->valid()` would return `true`.

Effects

If the asynchronous result associated with `*this` contains a deferred function arising from a call to `std::async` that hasn't yet started execution, returns immediately without blocking. Otherwise blocks until the asynchronous result associated with `*this` is *ready* or `Clock::now()` returns a time equal to or later than `absolute_time`.

Returns

`std::future_status::deferred` if the asynchronous result associated with `*this` contains a deferred function arising from a call to `std::async` that hasn't yet started execution, `std::future_status::ready` if the asynchronous result associated with `*this` is *ready*, `std::future_status::timeout` if `Clock::now()` returns a time equal to or later than `absolute_time`.

NOTE There's no guarantee as to how long the calling thread will be blocked, only that if the function returns `std::future_status::timeout`, then `Clock::now()` returns a time equal to or later than `absolute_time` at the point at which the thread became unblocked.

Throws
Nothing.

STD::FUTURE::GET MEMBER FUNCTION

If the associated state contains a deferred function from a call to `std::async`, invokes that function and returns the result; otherwise, waits until the asynchronous result associated with an instance of `std::future` is ready, and then returns the stored value or throw the stored exception.

Declaration

```
void future<void>::get();
R& future<R&>::get();
R future<R>::get();
```

Preconditions
`this->valid()` would return `true`.

Effects
If the state associated with `*this` contains a deferred function, invokes the deferred function and returns the result or propagates any thrown exception.

Otherwise, blocks until the asynchronous result associated with `*this` is *ready*. If the result is a stored exception, throws that exception. Otherwise, returns the stored value.

Returns
If the associated state contains a deferred function, the result of the function invocation is returned. Otherwise, if `ResultType` is `void`, the call returns normally. If `ResultType` is `R&` for some type `R`, the stored reference is returned. Otherwise, the stored value is returned.

Throws
The exception thrown by the deferred exception or stored in the asynchronous result, if any.

Postcondition
`this->valid()==false`

D.4.2 std::shared_future class template

The `std::shared_future` class template provides a means of waiting for an asynchronous result from another thread, in conjunction with the `std::promise` and `std::packaged_task` class templates and `std::async` function template, which can be used to provide that asynchronous result. Multiple `std::shared_future` instances can reference the same asynchronous result.

Instances of `std::shared_future` are `CopyConstructible` and `CopyAssignable`. You can also move-construct a `std::shared_future` from a `std::future` with the same `ResultType`.

Accesses to a given instance of `std::shared_future` aren't synchronized. It's therefore *not safe* for multiple threads to access the same `std::shared_future` instance without external synchronization. But accesses to the associated state are synchronized, so it *is* safe for multiple threads to each access separate instances of `std::shared_future` that share the same associated state without external synchronization.

Class definition

```
template<typename ResultType>
class shared_future
{
public:
    shared_future() noexcept;
    shared_future(future<ResultType>&&) noexcept;

    shared_future(shared_future&&) noexcept;
    shared_future(shared_future const&);
    shared_future& operator=(shared_future const&);
    shared_future& operator=(shared_future&&) noexcept;
    ~shared_future();

    bool valid() const noexcept;

    see description get() const;

    void wait() const;

    template<typename Rep,typename Period>
    future_status wait_for(
        std::chrono::duration<Rep,Period> const& relative_time) const;

    template<typename Clock,typename Duration>
    future_status wait_until(
        std::chrono::time_point<Clock,Duration> const& absolute_time)
      const;
};
```

STD::SHARED_FUTURE DEFAULT CONSTRUCTOR

Constructs a `std::shared_future` object without an associated asynchronous result.

Declaration

```
shared_future() noexcept;
```

Effects

Constructs a new `std::shared_future` instance.

Postconditions

`valid()` returns `false` for the newly constructed instance.

Throws

Nothing.

STD::SHARED_FUTURE MOVE CONSTRUCTOR

Constructs one `std::shared_future` object from another, transferring ownership of the asynchronous result associated with the other `std::shared_future` object to the newly constructed instance.

Declaration

```
shared_future(shared_future&& other) noexcept;
```

Effects

Constructs a new `std::shared_future` instance.

Postconditions

The asynchronous result associated with `other` prior to the invocation of the constructor is associated with the newly constructed `std::shared_future` object. `other` has no associated asynchronous result.

Throws

Nothing.

STD::SHARED_FUTURE MOVE-FROM-STD::FUTURE CONSTRUCTOR

Constructs a `std::shared_future` object from a `std::future`, transferring ownership of the asynchronous result associated with the `std::future` object to the newly constructed `std::shared_future`.

Declaration

```
shared_future(std::future<ResultType>&& other) noexcept;
```

Effects

Constructs a new `std::shared_future` instance.

Postconditions

The asynchronous result associated with `other` prior to the invocation of the constructor is associated with the newly constructed `std::shared_future` object. `other` has no associated asynchronous result.

Throws

Nothing.

STD::SHARED_FUTURE COPY CONSTRUCTOR

Constructs one `std::shared_future` object from another, so that both the source and the copy refer to the asynchronous result associated with the source `std::shared_future` object, if any.

Declaration

```
shared_future(shared_future const& other);
```

Effects

Constructs a new `std::shared_future` instance.

Postconditions

The asynchronous result associated with `other` prior to the invocation of the constructor is associated with the newly constructed `std::shared_future` object *and* `other`.

Throws

Nothing.

STD::SHARED_FUTURE DESTRUCTOR

Destroys a `std::shared_future` object.

Declaration

```
~shared_future();
```

Effects

Destroys `*this`. If there's no longer a `std::promise` or `std::packaged_task` instance associated with the asynchronous result associated with `*this`, and this is the last `std::shared_future` instance associated with that asynchronous result, destroys that asynchronous result.

Throws

Nothing.

STD::SHARED_FUTURE::VALID MEMBER FUNCTION

Checks if a `std::shared_future` instance is associated with an asynchronous result.

Declaration

```
bool valid() const noexcept;
```

Returns

`true` if the `*this` has an associated asynchronous result, `false` otherwise.

Throws

Nothing.

STD::SHARED_FUTURE::WAIT MEMBER FUNCTION

If the state associated with `*this` contains a deferred function, invokes the deferred function. Otherwise, waits until the asynchronous result associated with an instance of `std::shared_future` is ready.

Declaration

```
void wait() const;
```

Preconditions

`this->valid()` would return `true`.

Effects

Calls to `get()` and `wait()` from multiple threads on `std::shared_future` instances that share the same associated state are serialized. If the associated state contains a deferred function, the first call to `get()` or `wait()` invokes the deferred function and stores the returned value or thrown exception as the asynchronous result.

Blocks until the asynchronous result associated with `*this` is *ready*.

Throws

Nothing.

STD::SHARED_FUTURE::WAIT_FOR MEMBER FUNCTION

Waits until the asynchronous result associated with an instance of `std::shared_future` is ready or until a specified time period has elapsed.

Declaration

```
template<typename Rep,typename Period>
future_status wait_for(
    std::chrono::duration<Rep,Period> const& relative_time) const;
```

Preconditions

`this->valid()` would return `true`.

Effects

If the asynchronous result associated with `*this` contains a deferred function arising from a call to `std::async` that has not yet started execution, returns immediately without blocking. Otherwise, blocks until the asynchronous result associated with `*this` is *ready* or the time period specified by `relative_time` has elapsed.

Returns

`std::future_status::deferred` if the asynchronous result associated with `*this` contains a deferred function arising from a call to `std::async` that hasn't yet started execution, `std::future_status::ready` if the asynchronous result associated with `*this` is *ready*, `std::future_status::timeout` if the time period specified by `relative_time` has elapsed.

NOTE The thread may be blocked for longer than the specified duration. Where possible, the elapsed time is determined by a steady clock.

Throws

Nothing.

STD::SHARED_FUTURE::WAIT_UNTIL MEMBER FUNCTION

Waits until the asynchronous result associated with an instance of `std::shared_future` is ready or until a specified time period has elapsed.

Declaration

```
template<typename Clock,typename Duration>
bool wait_until(
    std::chrono::time_point<Clock,Duration> const& absolute_time) const;
```

Preconditions

`this->valid()` would return `true`.

Effects

If the asynchronous result associated with `*this` contains a deferred function arising from a call to `std::async` that hasn't yet started execution, returns immediately without blocking. Otherwise, blocks until the asynchronous result associated with `*this` is *ready* or `Clock::now()` returns a time equal to or later than `absolute_time`.

Returns

`std::future_status::deferred` if the asynchronous result associated with `*this` contains a deferred function arising from a call to `std::async` that hasn't yet started execution, `std::future_status::ready` if the asynchronous result associated with `*this` is *ready*, `std::future_status::timeout` if `Clock::now()` returns a time equal to or later than `absolute_time`.

NOTE There's no guarantee as to how long the calling thread will be blocked, only that if the function returns `std::future_status::timeout`, then `Clock::now()` returns a time equal to or later than `absolute_time` at the point at which the thread became unblocked.

Throws
Nothing.

STD::SHARED_FUTURE::GET MEMBER FUNCTION

If the associated state contains a deferred function from a call to `std::async`, invokes that function and return the result. Otherwise, waits until the asynchronous result associated with an instance of `std::shared_future` is ready, and then returns the stored value or throws the stored exception.

Declaration

```
void shared_future<void>::get() const;
R& shared_future<R&>::get() const;
R const& shared_future<R>::get() const;
```

Preconditions
`this->valid()` would return `true`.

Effects
Calls to `get()` and `wait()` from multiple threads on `std::shared_future` instances that share the same associated state are serialized. If the associated state contains a deferred function, the first call to `get()` or `wait()` invokes the deferred function and stores the returned value or thrown exception as the asynchronous result.

Blocks until the asynchronous result associated with `*this` is *ready*. If the asynchronous result is a stored exception, throws that exception. Otherwise, returns the stored value.

Returns
If `ResultType` is `void`, returns normally. If `ResultType` is `R&` for some type `R`, returns the stored reference. Otherwise, returns a `const` reference to the stored value.

Throws
The stored exception, if any.

D.4.3 std::packaged_task class template

The `std::packaged_task` class template packages a function or other callable object so that when the function is invoked through the `std::packaged_task` instance, the result is stored as an asynchronous result for retrieval through an instance of `std::future`.

Instances of `std::packaged_task` are `MoveConstructible` and `MoveAssignable` but not `CopyConstructible` or `CopyAssignable`.

Class definition

```
template<typename FunctionType>
class packaged_task; // undefined

template<typename ResultType,typename... ArgTypes>
class packaged_task<ResultType(ArgTypes...)>
```

```
{
public:
    packaged_task() noexcept;
    packaged_task(packaged_task&&) noexcept;
    ~packaged_task();

    packaged_task& operator=(packaged_task&&) noexcept;

    packaged_task(packaged_task const&) = delete;
    packaged_task& operator=(packaged_task const&) = delete;

    void swap(packaged_task&) noexcept;

    template<typename Callable>
    explicit packaged_task(Callable&& func);

    template<typename Callable,typename Allocator>
    packaged_task(std::allocator_arg_t, const Allocator&,Callable&&);

    bool valid() const noexcept;
    std::future<ResultType> get_future();
    void operator()(ArgTypes...);
    void make_ready_at_thread_exit(ArgTypes...);
    void reset();
};
```

STD::PACKAGED_TASK DEFAULT CONSTRUCTOR

Constructs a `std::packaged_task` object.

Declaration

```
packaged_task() noexcept;
```

Effects

Constructs a `std::packaged_task` instance with no associated task or asynchronous result.

Throws

Nothing.

STD::PACKAGED_TASK CONSTRUCTION FROM A CALLABLE OBJECT

Constructsa `std::packaged_task` object with an associated task and asynchronous result.

Declaration

```
template<typename Callable>
packaged_task(Callable&& func);
```

Preconditions

The expression `func(args...)` shall be valid, where each element `args-i` in `args...` shall be a value of the corresponding type `ArgTypes-i` in `ArgTypes...`. The return value shall be convertible to `ResultType`.

Effects

Constructs a `std::packaged_task` instance with an associated asynchronous result of type `ResultType` that isn't *ready* and an associated task of type `Callable` that's a copy of `func`.

Throws

An exception of type `std::bad_alloc` if the constructor is unable to allocate memory for the asynchronous result. Any exception thrown by the copy or move constructor of `Callable`.

STD::PACKAGED_TASK CONSTRUCTION FROM A CALLABLE OBJECT WITH AN ALLOCATOR

Constructs a `std::packaged_task` object with an associated task and asynchronous result, using the supplied allocator to allocate memory for the associated asynchronous result and task.

Declaration

```
template<typename Allocator,typename Callable>
packaged_task(
    std::allocator_arg_t, Allocator const& alloc,Callable&& func);
```

Preconditions

The expression `func(args...)` shall be valid, where each element `args-i` in `args...` shall be a value of the corresponding type `ArgTypes-i` in `ArgTypes...`. The return value shall be convertible to `ResultType`.

Effects

Constructs a `std::packaged_task` instance with an associated asynchronous result of type `ResultType` that isn't *ready* and an associated task of type `Callable` that's a copy of `func`. The memory for the asynchronous result and task is allocated through the allocator `alloc` or a copy thereof.

Throws

Any exception thrown by the allocator when trying to allocate memory for the asynchronous result or task. Any exception thrown by the copy or move constructor of `Callable`.

STD::PACKAGED_TASK MOVE CONSTRUCTOR

Constructs one `std::packaged_task` object from another, transferring ownership of the asynchronous result and task associated with the other `std::packaged_task` object to the newly constructed instance.

Declaration

```
packaged_task(packaged_task&& other) noexcept;
```

Effects

Constructs a new `std::packaged_task` instance.

Postconditions

The asynchronous result and task associated with `other` prior to the invocation of the constructor is associated with the newly constructed `std::packaged_task` object. `other` has no associated asynchronous result.

Throws

Nothing.

STD::PACKAGED_TASK MOVE-ASSIGNMENT OPERATOR

Transfers ownership of the asynchronous result associated with one `std::packaged_task` object to another.

Declaration

```
packaged_task& operator=(packaged_task&& other) noexcept;
```

Effects

Transfers ownership of the asynchronous result and task associated with `other` to `*this`, and discards any prior asynchronous result, as-if `std::packaged_task(other).swap(*this)`.

Postconditions

The asynchronous result and task associated with `other` prior to the invocation of the move-assignment operator is associated with the `*this`. `other` has no associated asynchronous result.

Returns

`*this`

Throws

Nothing.

STD::PACKAGED_TASK::SWAP MEMBER FUNCTION

Exchanges ownership of the asynchronous results associated with two `std::packaged_task` objects.

Declaration

```
void swap(packaged_task& other) noexcept;
```

Effects

Exchanges ownership of the asynchronous results and tasks associated with `other` and `*this`.

Postconditions

The asynchronous result and task associated with `other` prior to the invocation of `swap` (if any) is associated with `*this`. The asynchronous result and task associated with `*this` prior to the invocation of `swap` (if any) is associated with `other`.

Throws

Nothing.

STD::PACKAGED_TASK DESTRUCTOR

Destroys a `std::packaged_task` object.

Declaration

```
~packaged_task();
```

Effects

Destroys `*this`. If `*this` has an associated asynchronous result, and that result doesn't have a stored task or exception, then that result becomes *ready* with a `std::future_error` exception with an error code of `std::future_errc::broken_promise`.

Throws

Nothing.

STD::PACKAGED_TASK::GET_FUTURE MEMBER FUNCTION

Retrieves a `std::future` instance for the asynchronous result associated with `*this`.

Declaration

```
std::future<ResultType> get_future();
```

Preconditions

`*this` has an associated asynchronous result.

Returns

A `std::future` instance for the asynchronous result associated with `*this`.

Throws

An exception of type `std::future_error` with an error code of `std::future_errc::future_already_retrieved` if a `std::future` has already been obtained for this asynchronous result through a prior call to `get_future()`.

STD::PACKAGED_TASK::RESET MEMBER FUNCTION

Associates a `std::packaged_task` instance with a new asynchronous result for the same task.

Declaration

```
void reset();
```

Preconditions

`*this` has an associated asynchronous task.

Effects

As-if `*this=packaged_task(std::move(f))`, where `f` is the stored task associated with `*this`.

Throws

An exception of type `std::bad_alloc` if memory couldn't be allocated for the new asynchronous result.

STD::PACKAGED_TASK::VALID MEMBER FUNCTION

Checks whether `*this` has an associated task and asynchronous result.

Declaration

```
bool valid() const noexcept;
```

Returns

`true` if `*this` has an associated task and asynchronous result, `false` otherwise.

Throws

Nothing.

STD::PACKAGED_TASK::OPERATOR() FUNCTION CALL OPERATOR

Invokes the task associated with a `std::packaged_task` instance, and stores the return value or exception in the associated asynchronous result.

Declaration

```
void operator()(ArgTypes... args);
```

Preconditions

`*this` has an associated task.

Effects
Invokes the associated task `func` as-if `INVOKE(func,args...)`. If the invocation returns normally, stores the return value in the asynchronous result associated with `*this`. If the invocation returns with an exception, stores the exception in the asynchronous result associated with `*this`.

Postconditions
The asynchronous result associated with `*this` is *ready* with a stored value or exception. Any threads blocked waiting for the asynchronous result are unblocked.

Throws
An exception of type `std::future_error` with an error code of `std::future_errc::promise_already_satisfied` if the asynchronous result already has a stored value or exception.

Synchronization
A successful call to the function call operator synchronizes-with a call to `std::future<ResultType>::get()` or `std::shared_future<ResultType>::get()`, which retrieves the value or exception stored.

STD::PACKAGED_TASK::MAKE_READY_AT_THREAD_EXIT MEMBER FUNCTION

Invokes the task associated with a `std::packaged_task` instance, and stores the return value or exception in the associated asynchronous result without making the associated asynchronous result *ready* until thread exit.

Declaration

```
void make_ready_at_thread_exit(ArgTypes... args);
```

Preconditions
`*this` has an associated task.

Effects
Invokes the associated task `func` as-if `INVOKE(func,args...)`. If the invocation returns normally, stores the return value in the asynchronous result associated with `*this`. If the invocation returns with an exception, stores the exception in the asynchronous result associated with `*this`. Schedules the associated asynchronous state to be made *ready* when the current thread exits.

Postconditions
The asynchronous result associated with `*this` has a stored value or exception but isn't *ready* until the current thread exits. Threads blocked waiting for the asynchronous result will be unblocked when the current thread exits.

Throws
An exception of type `std::future_error` with an error code of `std::future_errc::promise_already_satisfied` if the asynchronous result already has a stored value or exception. An exception of type `std::future_error` with an error code of `std::future_errc::no_state` if `*this` has no associated asynchronous state.

Synchronization

The completion of the thread that made a successful call to `make_ready_at_thread_exit()` synchronizes-with a call to `std::future<ResultType>::get()` or `std::shared_future<ResultType>::get()`, which retrieves the value or exception stored.

D.4.4 std::promise class template

The `std::promise` class template provides a means of setting an asynchronous result, which may be retrieved from another thread through an instance of `std::future`.

The `ResultType` template parameter is the type of the value that can be stored in the asynchronous result.

A `std::future` associated with the asynchronous result of a particular `std::promise` instance can be obtained by calling the `get_future()` member function. The asynchronous result is set either to a value of type `ResultType` with the `set_value()` member function or to an exception with the `set_exception()` member function.

Instances of `std::promise` are `MoveConstructible` and `MoveAssignable` but not `CopyConstructible` or `CopyAssignable`.

Class definition

```
template<typename ResultType>
class promise
{
public:
    promise();
    promise(promise&&) noexcept;
    ~promise();
    promise& operator=(promise&&) noexcept;

    template<typename Allocator>
    promise(std::allocator_arg_t, Allocator const&);

    promise(promise const&) = delete;
    promise& operator=(promise const&) = delete;

    void swap(promise& ) noexcept;

    std::future<ResultType> get_future();

    void set_value(see description);
    void set_exception(std::exception_ptr p);
};
```

STD::PROMISE DEFAULT CONSTRUCTOR

Constructs a `std::promise` object.

Declaration

```
promise();
```

Effects

Constructs a `std::promise` instance with an associated asynchronous result of type `ResultType` that's not *ready*.

Throws
An exception of type `std::bad_alloc` if the constructor is unable to allocate memory for the asynchronous result.

STD::PROMISE ALLOCATOR CONSTRUCTOR

Constructs a `std::promise` object, using the supplied allocator to allocate memory for the associated asynchronous result.

Declaration

```
template<typename Allocator>
promise(std::allocator_arg_t, Allocator const& alloc);
```

Effects
Constructs a `std::promise` instance with an associated asynchronous result of type `ResultType` that isn't *ready*. The memory for the asynchronous result is allocated through the allocator `alloc`.

Throws
Any exception thrown by the allocator when attempting to allocate memory for the asynchronous result.

STD::PROMISE MOVE CONSTRUCTOR

Constructs one `std::promise` object from another, transferring ownership of the asynchronous result associated with the other `std::promise` object to the newly constructed instance.

Declaration

```
promise(promise&& other) noexcept;
```

Effects
Constructs a new `std::promise` instance.

Postconditions
The asynchronous result associated with `other` prior to the invocation of the constructor is associated with the newly constructed `std::promise` object. `other` has no associated asynchronous result.

Throws
Nothing.

STD::PROMISE MOVE-ASSIGNMENT OPERATOR

Transfers ownership of the asynchronous result associated with one `std::promise` object to another.

Declaration

```
promise& operator=(promise&& other) noexcept;
```

Effects
Transfers ownership of the asynchronous result associated with `other` to `*this`. If `*this` already had an associated asynchronous result, that asynchronous result is made *ready* with an exception of type `std::future_error` and an error code of `std::future_errc::broken_promise`.

Postconditions
The asynchronous result associated with `other` prior to the invocation of the move-assignment operator is associated with the `*this`. `other` has no associated asynchronous result.

Returns
`*this`

Throws
Nothing.

STD::PROMISE::SWAP MEMBER FUNCTION

Exchanges ownership of the asynchronous results associated with two `std::promise` objects.

Declaration
```
void swap(promise& other);
```

Effects
Exchanges ownership of the asynchronous results associated with `other` and `*this`.

Postconditions
The asynchronous result associated with `other` prior to the invocation of `swap` (if any) is associated with `*this`. The asynchronous result associated with `*this` prior to the invocation of `swap` (if any) is associated with `other`.

Throws
Nothing.

STD::PROMISE DESTRUCTOR

Destroys a `std::promise` object.

Declaration
```
~promise();
```

Effects
Destroys `*this`. If `*this` has an associated asynchronous result, and that result doesn't have a stored value or exception, that result becomes *ready* with a `std::future_error` exception with an error code of `std::future_errc::broken_promise`.

Throws
Nothing.

STD::PROMISE::GET_FUTURE MEMBER FUNCTION

Retrieves a `std::future` instance for the asynchronous result associated with `*this`.

Declaration
```
std::future<ResultType> get_future();
```

Preconditions
`*this` has an associated asynchronous result.

Returns
A `std::future` instance for the asynchronous result associated with `*this`.

Throws

An exception of type `std::future_error` with an error code of `std::future_errc::future_already_retrieved` if a `std::future` has already been obtained for this asynchronous result through a prior call to `get_future()`.

STD::PROMISE::SET_VALUE MEMBER FUNCTION

Stores a value in the asynchronous result associated with `*this`.

Declaration

```
void promise<void>::set_value();
void promise<R&>::set_value(R& r);
void promise<R>::set_value(R const& r);
void promise<R>::set_value(R&& r);
```

Preconditions

`*this` has an associated asynchronous result.

Effects

Stores `r` in the asynchronous result associated with `*this` if `ResultType` isn't `void`.

Postconditions

The asynchronous result associated with `*this` is *ready* with a stored value. Any threads blocked waiting for the asynchronous result are unblocked.

Throws

An exception of type `std::future_error` with an error code of `std::future_errc::promise_already_satisfied` if the asynchronous result already has a stored value or exception. Any exceptions thrown by the copy-constructor or move-constructor of `r`.

Synchronization

Multiple concurrent calls to `set_value()`, `set_value_at_thread_exit()`, `set_exception()`, and `set_exception_at_thread_exit()` are serialized. A successful call to `set_value()` happens-before a call to `std::future<ResultType>::get()` or `std::shared_future<ResultType>::get()`, which retrieves the value stored.

STD::PROMISE::SET_VALUE_AT_THREAD_EXIT MEMBER FUNCTION

Stores a value in the asynchronous result associated with `*this` without making that result *ready* until the current thread exits.

Declaration

```
void promise<void>::set_value_at_thread_exit();
void promise<R&>::set_value_at_thread_exit(R& r);
void promise<R>::set_value_at_thread_exit(R const& r);
void promise<R>::set_value_at_thread_exit(R&& r);
```

Preconditions

`*this` has an associated asynchronous result.

Effects

Stores `r` in the asynchronous result associated with `*this` if `ResultType` isn't `void`. Marks the asynchronous result as having a stored value. Schedules the associated asynchronous result to be made *ready* when the current thread exits.

Postconditions

The asynchronous result associated with `*this` has a stored value but isn't *ready* until the current thread exits. Threads blocked waiting for the asynchronous result will be unblocked when the current thread exits.

Throws

An exception of type `std::future_error` with an error code of `std::future_errc::promise_already_satisfied` if the asynchronous result already has a stored value or exception. Any exceptions thrown by the copy-constructor or move-constructor of `r`.

Synchronization

Multiple concurrent calls to `set_value()`, `set_value_at_thread_exit()`, `set_exception()`, and `set_exception_at_thread_exit()` are serialized. The completion of the thread that made a successful call to `set_value_at_thread_exit()` happens-before a call to `std::future<ResultType>::get()` or `std::shared_future<ResultType>::get()`, which retrieves the exception stored.

STD::PROMISE::SET_EXCEPTION MEMBER FUNCTION

Stores an exception in the asynchronous result associated with `*this`.

Declaration

```
void set_exception(std::exception_ptr e);
```

Preconditions

`*this` has an associated asynchronous result. `(bool)e` is `true`.

Effects

Stores `e` in the asynchronous result associated with `*this`.

Postconditions

The asynchronous result associated with `*this` is *ready* with a stored exception. Any threads blocked waiting for the asynchronous result are unblocked.

Throws

An exception of type `std::future_error` with an error code of `std::future_errc::promise_already_satisfied` if the asynchronous result already has a stored value or exception.

Synchronization

Multiple concurrent calls to `set_value()` and `set_exception()` are serialized. A successful call to `set_exception()` happens-before a call to `std::future<ResultType>::get()` or `std::shared_future<ResultType>::get()`, which retrieves the exception stored.

STD::PROMISE::SET_EXCEPTION_AT_THREAD_EXIT MEMBER FUNCTION

Stores an exception in the asynchronous result associated with `*this` without making that result *ready* until the current thread exits.

Declaration

```
void set_exception_at_thread_exit(std::exception_ptr e);
```

Preconditions

`*this` has an associated asynchronous result. `(bool)e` is `true`.

Effects

Stores `e` in the asynchronous result associated with `*this`. Schedules the associated asynchronous result to be made *ready* when the current thread exits.

Postconditions

The asynchronous result associated with `*this` has a stored exception but isn't *ready* until the current thread exits. Threads blocked waiting for the asynchronous result will be unblocked when the current thread exits.

Throws

An exception of type `std::future_error` with an error code of `std::future_errc::promise_already_satisfied` if the asynchronous result already has a stored value or exception.

Synchronization

Multiple concurrent calls to `set_value()`, `set_value_at_thread_exit()`, `set_exception()`, and `set_exception_at_thread_exit()` are serialized. The completion of the thread that made a successful call to `set_exception_at_thread_exit()` happens-before a call to `std::future<ResultType>::get()` or `std::shared_future<ResultType>::get()`, which retrieves the exception stored.

D.4.5 std::async function template

`std::async` is a simple way of running self-contained asynchronous tasks to make use of the available hardware concurrency. A call to `std::async` returns a `std::future` that will contain the result of the task. Depending on the launch policy, the task is either run asynchronously on its own thread or synchronously on whichever thread calls the `wait()` or `get()` member functions on that future.

Declaration

```
enum class launch
{
    async,deferred
};

template<typename Callable,typename ... Args>
future<result_of<Callable(Args...)>::type>
async(Callable&& func,Args&& ... args);

template<typename Callable,typename ... Args>
future<result_of<Callable(Args...)>::type>
async(launch policy,Callable&& func,Args&& ... args);
```

Preconditions

The expression `INVOKE(func,args)` is valid for the supplied values of `func` and `args`. `Callable` and every member of `Args` are `MoveConstructible`.

Effects

Constructs copies of `func` and `args...` in internal storage (denoted by `fff` and `xyz...` respectively).

If `policy` is `std::launch::async`, runs `INVOKE(fff,xyz...)` on its own thread. The returned `std::future` will become *ready* when this thread is complete and will hold either the return value or exception thrown by the function invocation. The destructor of the last future object associated with the asynchronous state of the returned `std::future` blocks until the future is *ready*.

If `policy` is `std::launch::deferred`, `fff` and `xyz...` are stored in the returned `std::future` as a deferred function call. The first call to the `wait()` or `get()` member functions on a future that shares the same associated state will execute `INVOKE(fff,xyz...)` synchronously on the thread that called `wait()` or `get()`.

The value returned or exception thrown by the execution of `INVOKE(fff, xyz...)` will be returned from a call to `get()` on that `std::future`.

If `policy` is `std::launch::async | std::launch::deferred` or the `policy` argument is omitted, the behavior is as-if either `std::launch::async` or `std::launch::deferred` had been specified. The implementation will choose the behavior on a call-by-call basis in order to take advantage of the available hardware concurrency without excessive oversubscription.

In all cases, the `std::async` call returns immediately.

Synchronization

The completion of the function invocation happens-before a successful return from a call to `wait()`, `get()`, `wait_for()`, or `wait_until()` on any `std::future` or `std::shared_future` instance that references the same associated state as the `std::future` object returned from the `std::async` call. In the case of a `policy` of `std::launch::async`, the completion of the thread on which the function invocation occurs also happens-before the successful return from these calls.

Throws

`std::bad_alloc` if the required internal storage can't be allocated, otherwise `std::future_error` when the effects can't be achieved, or any exception thrown during the construction of `fff` or `xyz...`.

D.5 <mutex> header

The `<mutex>` header provides facilities for ensuring mutual exclusion: mutex types, lock types and functions, and a mechanism for ensuring an operation is performed exactly once.

Header contents

```
namespace std
{
    class mutex;
    class recursive_mutex;
    class timed_mutex;
    class recursive_timed_mutex;
```

```
    struct adopt_lock_t;
    struct defer_lock_t;
    struct try_to_lock_t;

    constexpr adopt_lock_t adopt_lock{};
    constexpr defer_lock_t defer_lock{};
    constexpr try_to_lock_t try_to_lock{};

    template<typename LockableType>
    class lock_guard;

    template<typename LockableType>
    class unique_lock;

    template<typename LockableType1,typename... LockableType2>
    void lock(LockableType1& m1,LockableType2& m2...);

    template<typename LockableType1,typename... LockableType2>
    int try_lock(LockableType1& m1,LockableType2& m2...);

    struct once_flag;

    template<typename Callable,typename... Args>
    void call_once(once_flag& flag,Callable func,Args args...);
}
```

D.5.1 std::mutex class

The `std::mutex` class provides a basic mutual exclusion and synchronization facility for threads that can be used to protect shared data. Prior to accessing the data protected by the mutex, the mutex must be *locked* by calling `lock()` or `try_lock()`. Only one thread may hold the lock at a time, so if another thread also tries to lock the mutex, it will fail (`try_lock()`) or block (`lock()`) as appropriate. Once a thread is done accessing the shared data, it then must call `unlock()` to release the lock and allow other threads to acquire it.

`std::mutex` meets the `Lockable` requirements.

Class definition

```
class mutex
{
public:
    mutex(mutex const&)=delete;
    mutex& operator=(mutex const&)=delete;

    constexpr mutex() noexcept;
    ~mutex();

    void lock();
    void unlock();
    bool try_lock();
};
```

STD::MUTEX DEFAULT CONSTRUCTOR

Constructs a `std::mutex` object.

Declaration

```
constexpr mutex() noexcept;
```

Effects
Constructs a `std::mutex` instance.

Postconditions
The newly constructed `std::mutex` object is initially unlocked.

Throws
Nothing.

STD::MUTEX DESTRUCTOR

Destroys a `std::mutex` object.

Declaration

```
~mutex();
```

Preconditions
`*this` must not be locked.

Effects
Destroys `*this`.

Throws
Nothing.

STD::MUTEX::LOCK MEMBER FUNCTION

Acquires a lock on a `std::mutex` object for the current thread.

Declaration

```
void lock();
```

Preconditions
The calling thread must not hold a lock on `*this`.

Effects
Blocks the current thread until a lock on `*this` can be obtained.

Postconditions
`*this` is locked by the calling thread.

Throws
An exception of type `std::system_error` if an error occurs.

STD::MUTEX::TRY_LOCK MEMBER FUNCTION

Attempts to acquire a lock on a `std::mutex` object for the current thread.

Declaration

```
bool try_lock();
```

Preconditions
The calling thread must not hold a lock on `*this`.

Effects
Attempts to acquire a lock on `*this` for the calling thread without blocking.

Returns
`true` if a lock was obtained for the calling thread, `false` otherwise.

Postconditions
`*this` is locked by the calling thread if the function returns `true`.

Throws
Nothing.

NOTE The function may fail to acquire the lock (and return `false`) even if no other thread holds a lock on `*this`.

STD::MUTEX::UNLOCK MEMBER FUNCTION

Releases a lock on a `std::mutex` object held by the current thread.

Declaration

```
void unlock();
```

Preconditions
The calling thread must hold a lock on `*this`.

Effects
Releases the lock on `*this` held by the current thread. If any threads are blocked waiting to acquire a lock on `*this`, unblocks one of them.

Postconditions
`*this` is not locked by the calling thread.

Throws
Nothing.

D.5.2 std::recursive_mutex class

The `std::recursive_mutex` class provides a basic mutual exclusion and synchronization facility for threads that can be used to protect shared data. Prior to accessing the data protected by the mutex, the mutex must be *locked* by calling `lock()` or `try_lock()`. Only one thread may hold the lock at a time, so if another thread also tries to lock the `recursive_mutex`, it will fail (`try_lock`) or block (`lock`) as appropriate. Once a thread is done accessing the shared data, it then must call `unlock()` to release the lock and allow other threads to acquire it.

This mutex is *recursive* so a thread that holds a lock on a particular `std::recursive_mutex` instance may make further calls `lock()` or `try_lock()` to increase the lock count. The mutex can't be locked by another thread until the thread that acquired the locks has called `unlock` once for each successful call to `lock()` or `try_lock()`.

`std::recursive_mutex` meets the `Lockable` requirements.

Class definition

```
class recursive_mutex
{
public:
    recursive_mutex(recursive_mutex const&)=delete;
    recursive_mutex& operator=(recursive_mutex const&)=delete;

    recursive_mutex() noexcept;
    ~recursive_mutex();
```

```
    void lock();
    void unlock();
    bool try_lock() noexcept;
};
```

STD::RECURSIVE_MUTEX DEFAULT CONSTRUCTOR

Constructs a `std::recursive_mutex` object.

Declaration

```
recursive_mutex() noexcept;
```

Effects

Constructs a `std::recursive_mutex` instance.

Postconditions

The newly constructed `std::recursive_mutex` object is initially unlocked.

Throws

An exception of type `std::system_error` if unable to create a new `std::recursive_mutex` instance.

STD::RECURSIVE_MUTEX DESTRUCTOR

Destroys a `std::recursive_mutex` object.

Declaration

```
~recursive_mutex();
```

Preconditions

`*this` must not be locked.

Effects

Destroys `*this`.

Throws

Nothing.

STD::RECURSIVE_MUTEX::LOCK MEMBER FUNCTION

Acquires a lock on a `std::recursive_mutex` object for the current thread.

Declaration

```
void lock();
```

Effects

Blocks the current thread until a lock on `*this` can be obtained.

Postconditions

`*this` is locked by the calling thread. If the calling thread already held a lock on `*this`, the lock count is increased by one.

Throws

An exception of type `std::system_error` if an error occurs.

STD::RECURSIVE_MUTEX::TRY_LOCK MEMBER FUNCTION

Attempts to acquire a lock on a `std::recursive_mutex` object for the current thread.

Declaration

```
bool try_lock() noexcept;
```

Effects
Attempts to acquire a lock on `*this` for the calling thread without blocking.

Returns
`true` if a lock was obtained for the calling thread, `false` otherwise.

Postconditions
A new lock on `*this` has been obtained for the calling thread if the function returns `true`.

Throws
Nothing.

NOTE If the calling thread already holds the lock on `*this`, the function returns `true` and the count of locks on `*this` held by the calling thread is increased by one. If the current thread doesn't already hold a lock on `*this`, the function may fail to acquire the lock (and return `false`) even if no other thread holds a lock on `*this`.

STD::RECURSIVE_MUTEX::UNLOCK MEMBER FUNCTION

Releases a lock on a `std::recursive_mutex` object held by the current thread.

Declaration
```
void unlock();
```

Preconditions
The calling thread must hold a lock on `*this`.

Effects
Releases a lock on `*this` held by the current thread. If this is the last lock on `*this` held by the calling thread, any threads are blocked waiting to acquire a lock on `*this`. Unblocks one of them.

Postconditions
The number of locks on `*this` held by the calling thread is reduced by one.

Throws
Nothing.

D.5.3 std::timed_mutex class

The `std::timed_mutex` class provides support for locks with timeouts on top of the basic mutual exclusion and synchronization facility provided by `std::mutex`. Prior to accessing the data protected by the mutex, the mutex must be *locked* by calling `lock()`, `try_lock()`, `try_lock_for()`, or `try_lock_until()`. If a lock is already held by another thread, an attempt to acquire the lock will fail (`try_lock()`), block until the lock can be acquired (`lock()`), or block until the lock can be acquired or the lock attempt times out (`try_lock_for()` or `try_lock_until()`). Once a lock has been acquired (whichever function was used to acquire it), it must be released by calling `unlock()` before another thread can acquire the lock on the mutex.

`std::timed_mutex` meets the `TimedLockable` requirements.

Class definition

```
class timed_mutex
{
public:
    timed_mutex(timed_mutex const&)=delete;
    timed_mutex& operator=(timed_mutex const&)=delete;

    timed_mutex();
    ~timed_mutex();

    void lock();
    void unlock();
    bool try_lock();

    template<typename Rep,typename Period>
    bool try_lock_for(
        std::chrono::duration<Rep,Period> const& relative_time);

    template<typename Clock,typename Duration>
    bool try_lock_until(
        std::chrono::time_point<Clock,Duration> const& absolute_time);
};
```

STD::TIMED_MUTEX DEFAULT CONSTRUCTOR

Constructs a `std::timed_mutex` object.

Declaration

```
timed_mutex();
```

Effects

Constructs a `std::timed_mutex` instance.

Postconditions

The newly constructed `std::timed_mutex` object is initially unlocked.

Throws

An exception of type `std::system_error` if unable to create a new `std::timed_mutex` instance.

STD::TIMED_MUTEX DESTRUCTOR

Destroys a `std::timed_mutex` object.

Declaration

```
~timed_mutex();
```

Preconditions

`*this` must not be locked.

Effects

Destroys `*this`.

Throws

Nothing.

STD::TIMED_MUTEX::LOCK MEMBER FUNCTION

Acquires a lock on a `std::timed_mutex` object for the current thread.

Declaration

```
void lock();
```

Preconditions
The calling thread must not hold a lock on `*this`.

Effects
Blocks the current thread until a lock on `*this` can be obtained.

Postconditions
`*this` is locked by the calling thread.

Throws
An exception of type `std::system_error` if an error occurs.

STD::TIMED_MUTEX::TRY_LOCK MEMBER FUNCTION

Attempts to acquire a lock on a `std::timed_mutex` object for the current thread.

Declaration

```
bool try_lock();
```

Preconditions
The calling thread must not hold a lock on `*this`.

Effects
Attempts to acquire a lock on `*this` for the calling thread without blocking.

Returns
`true` if a lock was obtained for the calling thread, `false` otherwise.

Postconditions
`*this` is locked by the calling thread if the function returns `true`.

Throws
Nothing.

NOTE The function may fail to acquire the lock (and return `false`) even if no other thread holds a lock on `*this`.

STD::TIMED_MUTEX::TRY_LOCK_FOR MEMBER FUNCTION

Attempts to acquire a lock on a `std::timed_mutex` object for the current thread.

Declaration

```
template<typename Rep,typename Period>
bool try_lock_for(
    std::chrono::duration<Rep,Period> const& relative_time);
```

Preconditions
The calling thread must not hold a lock on `*this`.

Effects
Attempts to acquire a lock on `*this` for the calling thread within the time specified by `relative_time`. If `relative_time.count()` is zero or negative, the call will return immediately, as if it was a call to `try_lock()`. Otherwise, the call blocks until either the lock has been acquired or the time period specified by `relative_time` has elapsed.

Returns
`true` if a lock was obtained for the calling thread, `false` otherwise.

Postconditions
`*this` is locked by the calling thread if the function returns `true`.

Throws
Nothing.

NOTE The function may fail to acquire the lock (and return `false`) even if no other thread holds a lock on `*this`. The thread may be blocked for longer than the specified duration. Where possible, the elapsed time is determined by a steady clock.

STD::TIMED_MUTEX::TRY_LOCK_UNTIL MEMBER FUNCTION

Attempts to acquire a lock on a `std::timed_mutex` object for the current thread.

Declaration

```
template<typename Clock,typename Duration>
bool try_lock_until(
    std::chrono::time_point<Clock,Duration> const& absolute_time);
```

Preconditions
The calling thread must not hold a lock on `*this`.

Effects
Attempts to acquire a lock on `*this` for the calling thread before the time specified by `absolute_time`. If `absolute_time<=Clock::now()` on entry, the call will return immediately, as if it was a call to `try_lock()`. Otherwise, the call blocks until either the lock has been acquired or `Clock::now()` returns a time equal to or later than `absolute_time`.

Returns
`true` if a lock was obtained for the calling thread, `false` otherwise.

Postconditions
`*this` is locked by the calling thread if the function returns `true`.

Throws
Nothing.

NOTE The function may fail to acquire the lock (and return `false`) even if no other thread holds a lock on `*this`. There's no guarantee as to how long the calling thread will be blocked, only that if the function returns `false`, then `Clock::now()` returns a time equal to or later than `absolute_time` at the point at which the thread became unblocked.

STD::TIMED_MUTEX::UNLOCK MEMBER FUNCTION

Releases a lock on a `std::timed_mutex` object held by the current thread.

Declaration

```
void unlock();
```

Preconditions
The calling thread must hold a lock on `*this`.

Effects
Releases the lock on `*this` held by the current thread. If any threads are blocked waiting to acquire a lock on `*this`, unblocks one of them.

Postconditions
`*this` is not locked by the calling thread.

Throws
Nothing.

D.5.4 std::recursive_timed_mutex class

The `std::recursive_timed_mutex` class provides support for locks with timeouts on top of the mutual exclusion and synchronization facility provided by `std::recursive_mutex`. Prior to accessing the data protected by the mutex, the mutex must be *locked* by calling `lock()`, `try_lock()`, `try_lock_for()`, or `try_lock_until()`. If a lock is already held by another thread, an attempt to acquire the lock will fail (`try_lock()`), block until the lock can be acquired (`lock()`), or block until the lock can be acquired or the lock attempt times out (`try_lock_for()` or `try_lock_until()`). Once a lock has been acquired (whichever function was used to acquire it) it must be released by calling `unlock()` before another thread can acquire the lock on the mutex.

This mutex is *recursive*, so a thread that holds a lock on a particular instance of `std::recursive_timed_mutex` may acquire additional locks on that instance through any of the lock functions. All of these locks must be released by a corresponding call to `unlock()` before another thread can acquire a lock on that instance.

`std::recursive_timed_mutex` meets the `TimedLockable` requirements.

Class definition

```
class recursive_timed_mutex
{
public:
    recursive_timed_mutex(recursive_timed_mutex const&)=delete;
    recursive_timed_mutex& operator=(recursive_timed_mutex const&)=delete;

    recursive_timed_mutex();
    ~recursive_timed_mutex();

    void lock();
    void unlock();
    bool try_lock() noexcept;

    template<typename Rep,typename Period>
    bool try_lock_for(
        std::chrono::duration<Rep,Period> const& relative_time);

    template<typename Clock,typename Duration>
    bool try_lock_until(
        std::chrono::time_point<Clock,Duration> const& absolute_time);
};
```

STD::RECURSIVE_TIMED_MUTEX DEFAULT CONSTRUCTOR

Constructs a `std::recursive_timed_mutex` object.

Declaration

```
recursive_timed_mutex();
```

Effects

Constructs a `std::recursive_timed_mutex` instance.

Postconditions

The newly constructed `std::recursive_timed_mutex` object is initially unlocked.

Throws

An exception of type `std::system_error` if unable to create a new `std::recursive_timed_mutex` instance.

STD::RECURSIVE_TIMED_MUTEX DESTRUCTOR

Destroys a `std::recursive_timed_mutex` object.

Declaration

```
~recursive_timed_mutex();
```

Preconditions

`*this` must not be locked.

Effects

Destroys `*this`.

Throws

Nothing.

STD::RECURSIVE_TIMED_MUTEX::LOCK MEMBER FUNCTION

Acquires a lock on a `std::recursive_timed_mutex` object for the current thread.

Declaration

```
void lock();
```

Preconditions

The calling thread must not hold a lock on `*this`.

Effects

Blocks the current thread until a lock on `*this` can be obtained.

Postconditions

`*this` is locked by the calling thread. If the calling thread already held a lock on `*this`, the lock count is increased by one.

Throws

An exception of type `std::system_error` if an error occurs.

STD::RECURSIVE_TIMED_MUTEX::TRY_LOCK MEMBER FUNCTION

Attempts to acquire a lock on a `std::recursive_timed_mutex` object for the current thread.

Declaration

```
bool try_lock() noexcept;
```

Effects
Attempts to acquire a lock on *this for the calling thread without blocking.

Returns
true if a lock was obtained for the calling thread, false otherwise.

Postconditions
*this is locked by the calling thread if the function returns true.

Throws
Nothing.

NOTE If the calling thread already holds the lock on *this, the function returns true and the count of locks on *this held by the calling thread is increased by one. If the current thread doesn't already hold a lock on *this, the function may fail to acquire the lock (and return false) even if no other thread holds a lock on *this.

STD::RECURSIVE_TIMED_MUTEX::TRY_LOCK_FOR MEMBER FUNCTION

Attempts to acquire a lock on a std::recursive_timed_mutex object for the current thread.

Declaration

```
template<typename Rep,typename Period>
bool try_lock_for(
    std::chrono::duration<Rep,Period> const& relative_time);
```

Effects
Attempts to acquire a lock on *this for the calling thread within the time specified by relative_time. If relative_time.count() is zero or negative, the call will return immediately, as if it was a call to try_lock(). Otherwise, the call blocks until either the lock has been acquired or the time period specified by relative_time has elapsed.

Returns
true if a lock was obtained for the calling thread, false otherwise.

Postconditions
*this is locked by the calling thread if the function returns true.

Throws
Nothing.

NOTE If the calling thread already holds the lock on *this, the function returns true and the count of locks on *this held by the calling thread is increased by one. If the current thread doesn't already hold a lock on *this, the function may fail to acquire the lock (and return false) even if no other thread holds a lock on *this. The thread may be blocked for longer than the specified duration. Where possible, the elapsed time is determined by a steady clock.

STD::RECURSIVE_TIMED_MUTEX::TRY_LOCK_UNTIL MEMBER FUNCTION

Attempts to acquire a lock on a `std::recursive_timed_mutex` object for the current thread.

Declaration

```
template<typename Clock,typename Duration>
bool try_lock_until(
    std::chrono::time_point<Clock,Duration> const& absolute_time);
```

Effects

Attempts to acquire a lock on `*this` for the calling thread before the time specified by `absolute_time`. If `absolute_time<=Clock::now()` on entry, the call will return immediately, as if it was a call to `try_lock()`. Otherwise, the call blocks until either the lock has been acquired or `Clock::now()` returns a time equal to or later than `absolute_time`.

Returns

`true` if a lock was obtained for the calling thread, `false` otherwise.

Postconditions

`*this` is locked by the calling thread if the function returns `true`.

Throws

Nothing.

NOTE If the calling thread already holds the lock on `*this`, the function returns `true` and the count of locks on `*this` held by the calling thread is increased by one. If the current thread doesn't already hold a lock on `*this`, the function may fail to acquire the lock (and return `false`) even if no other thread holds a lock on `*this`. There's no guarantee as to how long the calling thread will be blocked, only that if the function returns `false`, then `Clock::now()` returns a time equal to or later than `absolute_time` at the point at which the thread became unblocked.

STD::RECURSIVE_TIMED_MUTEX::UNLOCK MEMBER FUNCTION

Releases a lock on a `std::recursive_timed_mutex` object held by the current thread.

Declaration

```
void unlock();
```

Preconditions

The calling thread must hold a lock on `*this`.

Effects

Releases a lock on `*this` held by the current thread. If this is the last lock on `*this` held by the calling thread, any threads are blocked waiting to acquire a lock on `*this`. Unblocks one of them.

Postconditions

The number of locks on `*this` held by the calling thread is reduced by one.

Throws

Nothing.

D.5.5 std::lock_guard class template

The std::lock_guard class template provides a basic lock ownership wrapper. The type of mutex being locked is specified by template parameter Mutex and must meet the Lockable requirements. The specified mutex is locked in the constructor and unlocked in the destructor. This provides a simple means of locking a mutex for a block of code and ensuring that the mutex is unlocked when the block is left, whether that's by running off the end, by the use of a control flow statement such as break or return, or by throwing an exception.

Instances of std::lock_guard are not MoveConstructible, CopyConstructible, or CopyAssignable.

Class definition

```
template <class Mutex>
class lock_guard
{
public:
    typedef Mutex mutex_type;

    explicit lock_guard(mutex_type& m);
    lock_guard(mutex_type& m, adopt_lock_t);
    ~lock_guard();

    lock_guard(lock_guard const& ) = delete;
    lock_guard& operator=(lock_guard const& ) = delete;
};
```

STD::LOCK_GUARD LOCKING CONSTRUCTOR

Constructs a std::lock_guard instance that locks the supplied mutex.

Declaration

```
explicit lock_guard(mutex_type& m);
```

Effects

Constructs a std::lock_guard instance that references the supplied mutex. Calls m.lock().

Throws

Any exceptions thrown by m.lock().

Postconditions

*this owns a lock on m.

STD::LOCK_GUARD LOCK-ADOPTING CONSTRUCTOR

Constructs a std::lock_guard instance that owns the lock on the supplied mutex.

Declaration

```
lock_guard(mutex_type& m,std::adopt_lock_t);
```

Preconditions

The calling thread must own a lock on m.

Effects

Constructs a std::lock_guard instance that references the supplied mutex and takes ownership of the lock on m held by the calling thread.

Throws

Nothing.

Postconditions

`*this` owns the lock on `m` held by the calling thread.

STD::LOCK_GUARD DESTRUCTOR

Destroys a `std::lock_guard` instance and unlocks the corresponding mutex.

Declaration

```
~lock_guard();
```

Effects

Calls `m.unlock()` for the mutex instance `m` supplied when `*this` was constructed.

Throws

Nothing.

D.5.6 std::unique_lock class template

The `std::unique_lock` class template provides a more general lock ownership wrapper than `std::lock_guard`. The type of mutex being locked is specified by the template parameter `Mutex`, which must meet the `BasicLockable` requirements. In general, the specified mutex is locked in the constructor and unlocked in the destructor, although additional constructors and member functions are provided to allow other possibilities. This provides a means of locking a mutex for a block of code and ensuring that the mutex is unlocked when the block is left, whether that's by running off the end, by the use of a control flow statement such as `break` or `return`, or by throwing an exception. The wait functions of `std::condition_variable` require an instance of `std::unique_lock<std::mutex>`, and all instantiations of `std::unique_lock` are suitable for use with the `Lockable` parameter for the `std::condition_variable_any` wait functions.

If the supplied `Mutex` type meets the `Lockable` requirements, then `std::unique_lock<Mutex>` also meets the `Lockable` requirements. If, in addition, the supplied `Mutex` type meets the `TimedLockable` requirements, then `std::unique_lock<Mutex>` also meets the `TimedLockable` requirements.

Instances of `std::unique_lock` are `MoveConstructible` and `MoveAssignable` but not `CopyConstructible` or `CopyAssignable`.

Class definition

```
template <class Mutex>
class unique_lock
{
public:
    typedef Mutex mutex_type;

    unique_lock() noexcept;
    explicit unique_lock(mutex_type& m);
    unique_lock(mutex_type& m, adopt_lock_t);
    unique_lock(mutex_type& m, defer_lock_t) noexcept;
    unique_lock(mutex_type& m, try_to_lock_t);
```

```
    template<typename Clock,typename Duration>
    unique_lock(
        mutex_type& m,
        std::chrono::time_point<Clock,Duration> const& absolute_time);

    template<typename Rep,typename Period>
    unique_lock(
        mutex_type& m,
        std::chrono::duration<Rep,Period> const& relative_time);

    ~unique_lock();

    unique_lock(unique_lock const& ) = delete;
    unique_lock& operator=(unique_lock const& ) = delete;

    unique_lock(unique_lock&& );
    unique_lock& operator=(unique_lock&& );

    void swap(unique_lock& other) noexcept;

    void lock();
    bool try_lock();
    template<typename Rep, typename Period>
    bool try_lock_for(
        std::chrono::duration<Rep,Period> const& relative_time);
    template<typename Clock, typename Duration>
    bool try_lock_until(
        std::chrono::time_point<Clock,Duration> const& absolute_time);
    void unlock();

    explicit operator bool() const noexcept;
    bool owns_lock() const noexcept;
    Mutex* mutex() const noexcept;
    Mutex* release() noexcept;
};
```

STD::UNIQUE_LOCK DEFAULT CONSTRUCTOR

Constructs a `std::unique_lock` instance with no associated mutex.

Declaration

```
unique_lock() noexcept;
```

Effects

Constructs a `std::unique_lock` instance that has no associated mutex.

Postconditions

`this->mutex()==NULL, this->owns_lock()==false.`

STD::UNIQUE_LOCK LOCKING CONSTRUCTOR

Constructs a `std::unique_lock` instance that locks the supplied mutex.

Declaration

```
explicit unique_lock(mutex_type& m);
```

Effects

Constructs a `std::unique_lock` instance that references the supplied mutex. Calls `m.lock()`.

Throws
Any exceptions thrown by `m.lock()`.

Postconditions
`this->owns_lock()==true, this->mutex()==&m.`

STD::UNIQUE_LOCK LOCK-ADOPTING CONSTRUCTOR

Constructs a `std::unique_lock` instance that owns the lock on the supplied mutex.

Declaration

```
unique_lock(mutex_type& m,std::adopt_lock_t);
```

Preconditions
The calling thread must own a lock on `m`.

Effects
Constructs a `std::unique_lock` instance that references the supplied mutex and takes ownership of the lock on `m` held by the calling thread.

Throws
Nothing.

Postconditions
`this->owns_lock()==true, this->mutex()==&m.`

STD::UNIQUE_LOCK DEFERRED-LOCK CONSTRUCTOR

Constructs a `std::unique_lock` instance that doesn't own the lock on the supplied mutex.

Declaration

```
unique_lock(mutex_type& m,std::defer_lock_t) noexcept;
```

Effects
Constructs a `std::unique_lock` instance that references the supplied mutex.

Throws
Nothing.

Postconditions
`this->owns_lock()==false, this->mutex()==&m.`

STD::UNIQUE_LOCK TRY-TO-LOCK CONSTRUCTOR

Constructs a `std::unique_lock` instance associated with the supplied mutex and tries to acquire a lock on that mutex.

Declaration

```
unique_lock(mutex_type& m,std::try_to_lock_t);
```

Preconditions
The `Mutex` type used to instantiate `std::unique_lock` must meet the `Lockable` requirements.

Effects
Constructs a `std::unique_lock` instance that references the supplied mutex. Calls `m.try_lock()`.

Throws

Nothing.

Postconditions

`this->owns_lock()` returns the result of the `m.try_lock()` call, `this->mutex()==&m`.

STD::UNIQUE_LOCK TRY-TO-LOCK CONSTRUCTOR WITH A DURATION TIMEOUT

Constructs a `std::unique_lock` instance associated with the supplied mutex and tries to acquire a lock on that mutex.

Declaration

```
template<typename Rep,typename Period>
unique_lock(
    mutex_type& m,
    std::chrono::duration<Rep,Period> const& relative_time);
```

Preconditions

The `Mutex` type used to instantiate `std::unique_lock` must meet the `TimedLockable` requirements.

Effects

Constructs a `std::unique_lock` instance that references the supplied mutex. Calls `m.try_lock_for(relative_time)`.

Throws

Nothing.

Postconditions

`this->owns_lock()` returns the result of the `m.try_lock_for()` call, `this->mutex()==&m`.

STD::UNIQUE_LOCK TRY-TO-LOCK CONSTRUCTOR WITH A TIME_POINT TIMEOUT

Constructs a `std::unique_lock` instance associated with the supplied mutex and tries to acquire a lock on that mutex.

Declaration

```
template<typename Clock,typename Duration>
unique_lock(
    mutex_type& m,
    std::chrono::time_point<Clock,Duration> const& absolute_time);
```

Preconditions

The `Mutex` type used to instantiate `std::unique_lock` must meet the `TimedLockable` requirements.

Effects

Constructs a `std::unique_lock` instance that references the supplied mutex. Calls `m.try_lock_until(absolute_time)`.

Throws

Nothing.

Postconditions
`this->owns_lock()` returns the result of the `m.try_lock_until()` call, `this->mutex()==&m`.

STD::UNIQUE_LOCK MOVE-CONSTRUCTOR

Transfers ownership of a lock from one `std::unique_lock` object to a newly created `std::unique_lock` object.

Declaration

```
unique_lock(unique_lock&& other) noexcept;
```

Effects
Constructs a `std::unique_lock` instance. If `other` owned a lock on a mutex prior to the constructor invocation, that lock is now owned by the newly created `std::unique_lock` object.

Postconditions
For a newly constructed `std::unique_lock` object `x`, `x.mutex()` is equal to the value of `other.mutex()` prior to the constructor invocation, and `x.owns_lock()` is equal to the value of `other.owns_lock()` prior to the constructor invocation. `other.mutex()==NULL`, `other.owns_lock()==false`.

Throws
Nothing.

NOTE `std::unique_lock` objects are *not* `CopyConstructible`, so there's no copy constructor, only this move constructor.

STD::UNIQUE_LOCK MOVE-ASSIGNMENT OPERATOR

Transfers ownership of a lock from one `std::unique_lock` object to another `std::unique_lock` object.

Declaration

```
unique_lock& operator=(unique_lock&& other) noexcept;
```

Effects
If `this->owns_lock()` returns `true` prior to the call, calls `this->unlock()`. If `other` owned a lock on a mutex prior to the assignment, that lock is now owned by `*this`.

Postconditions
`this->mutex()` is equal to the value of `other.mutex()` prior to the assignment, and `this->owns_lock()` is equal to the value of `other.owns_lock()` prior to the assignment. `other.mutex()==NULL`, `other.owns_lock()==false`.

Throws
Nothing.

NOTE `std::unique_lock` objects are *not* `CopyAssignable`, so there's no copy-assignment operator, only this move-assignment operator.

STD::UNIQUE_LOCK DESTRUCTOR

Destroys a `std::unique_lock` instance and unlocks the corresponding mutex if it's owned by the destroyed instance.

Declaration

```
~unique_lock();
```

Effects

If `this->owns_lock()` returns `true`, calls `this->mutex()->unlock()`.

Throws

Nothing.

STD::UNIQUE_LOCK::SWAP MEMBER FUNCTION

Exchanges ownership of their associated `unique_locks` of execution between two `std::unique_lock` objects.

Declaration

```
void swap(unique_lock& other) noexcept;
```

Effects

If `other` owns a lock on a mutex prior to the call, that lock is now owned by `*this`. If `*this` owns a lock on a mutex prior to the call, that lock is now owned by `other`.

Postconditions

`this->mutex()` is equal to the value of `other.mutex()` prior to the call. `other.mutex()` is equal to the value of `this->mutex()` prior to the call. `this->owns_lock()` is equal to the value of `other.owns_lock()` prior to the call. `other.owns_lock()` is equal to the value of `this->owns_lock()` prior to the call.

Throws

Nothing.

SWAP NONMEMBER FUNCTION FOR STD::UNIQUE_LOCK

Exchanges ownership of their associated mutex locks between two `std::unique_lock` objects.

Declaration

```
void swap(unique_lock& lhs,unique_lock& rhs) noexcept;
```

Effects

`lhs.swap(rhs)`

Throws

Nothing.

STD::UNIQUE_LOCK::LOCK MEMBER FUNCTION

Acquires a lock on the mutex associated with `*this`.

Declaration

```
void lock();
```

Preconditions

`this->mutex()!=NULL, this->owns_lock()==false.`

Effects
Calls `this->mutex()->lock()`.

Throws
Any exceptions thrown by `this->mutex()->lock()`. `std::system_error` with an error code of `std::errc::operation_not_permitted` if `this->mutex()==NULL`. `std::system_error` with an error code of `std::errc::resource_deadlock_would_occur` if `this->owns_lock()==true` on entry.

Postconditions
`this->owns_lock()==true`.

STD::UNIQUE_LOCK::TRY_LOCK MEMBER FUNCTION

Attempts to acquire a lock on the mutex associated with `*this`.

Declaration
```
bool try_lock();
```

Preconditions
The `Mutex` type used to instantiate `std::unique_lock` must meet the `Lockable` requirements. `this->mutex()!=NULL`, `this->owns_lock()==false`.

Effects
Calls `this->mutex()->try_lock()`.

Returns
`true` if the call to `this->mutex()->try_lock()` returned `true`, `false` otherwise.

Throws
Any exceptions thrown by `this->mutex()->try_lock()`. `std::system_error` with an error code of `std::errc::operation_not_permitted` if `this->mutex()==NULL`. `std::system_error` with an error code of `std::errc::resource_deadlock_would_occur` if `this->owns_lock()==true` on entry.

Postconditions
If the function returns `true`, `this->owns_lock()==true`, otherwise `this->owns_lock()==false`.

STD::UNIQUE_LOCK::UNLOCK MEMBER FUNCTION

Releases a lock on the mutex associated with `*this`.

Declaration
```
void unlock();
```

Preconditions
`this->mutex()!=NULL, this->owns_lock()==true`.

Effects
Calls `this->mutex()->unlock()`.

Throws
Any exceptions thrown by `this->mutex()->unlock()`. `std::system_error` with an error code of `std::errc::operation_not_permitted` if `this->owns_lock()== false` on entry.

Postconditions
this->owns_lock()==false.

STD::UNIQUE_LOCK::TRY_LOCK_FOR MEMBER FUNCTION

Attempts to acquire a lock on the mutex associated with *this within the time specified.

Declaration

```
template<typename Rep, typename Period>
bool try_lock_for(
    std::chrono::duration<Rep,Period> const& relative_time);
```

Preconditions
The Mutex type used to instantiate std::unique_lock must meet the TimedLockable requirements. this->mutex()!=NULL, this->owns_lock()==false.

Effects
Calls this->mutex()->try_lock_for(relative_time).

Returns
true if the call to this->mutex()->try_lock_for() returned true, false otherwise.

Throws
Any exceptions thrown by this->mutex()->try_lock_for(). std::system_error with an error code of std::errc::operation_not_permitted if this->mutex()== NULL. std::system_error with an error code of std::errc::resource_deadlock_would_occur if this->owns_lock()==true on entry.

Postconditions
If the function returns true, this->owns_lock()==true, otherwise this->owns_lock()==false.

STD::UNIQUE_LOCK::TRY_LOCK_UNTIL MEMBER FUNCTION

Attempts to acquire a lock on the mutex associated with *this within the time specified.

Declaration

```
template<typename Clock, typename Duration>
bool try_lock_until(
    std::chrono::time_point<Clock,Duration> const& absolute_time);
```

Preconditions
The Mutex type used to instantiate std::unique_lock must meet the TimedLockable requirements. this->mutex()!=NULL, this->owns_lock()==false.

Effects
Calls this->mutex()->try_lock_until(absolute_time).

Returns
true if the call to this->mutex()->try_lock_until() returned true, false otherwise.

Throws
Any exceptions thrown by `this->mutex()->try_lock_until()`. `std::system_error` with an error code of `std::errc::operation_not_permitted` if `this->mutex()==NULL`. `std::system_error` with an error code of `std::errc::resource_deadlock_would_occur` if `this->owns_lock()==true` on entry.

Postcondition
If the function returns `true`, `this->owns_lock()==true`, otherwise `this->owns_lock()==false`.

STD::UNIQUE_LOCK::OPERATOR BOOL MEMBER FUNCTION

Checks whether or not `*this` owns a lock on a mutex.

Declaration
```
explicit operator bool() const noexcept;
```

Returns
`this->owns_lock()`.

Throws
Nothing.

NOTE This is an `explicit` conversion operator, so it's only implicitly called in contexts where the result is used as a Boolean and not where the result would be treated as an integer value 0 or 1.

STD::UNIQUE_LOCK::OWNS_LOCK MEMBER FUNCTION

Checks whether or not `*this` owns a lock on a mutex.

Declaration
```
bool owns_lock() const noexcept;
```

Returns
`true` if `*this` owns a lock on a mutex, `false` otherwise.

Throws
Nothing.

STD::UNIQUE_LOCK::MUTEX MEMBER FUNCTION

Returns the mutex associated with `*this` if any.

Declaration
```
mutex_type* mutex() const noexcept;
```

Returns
A pointer to the mutex associated with `*this` if any, `NULL` otherwise.

Throws
Nothing.

STD::UNIQUE_LOCK::RELEASE MEMBER FUNCTION

Returns the mutex associated with `*this` if any, and releases that association.

Declaration
```
mutex_type* release() noexcept;
```

Effects

Breaks the association of the mutex with `*this` without unlocking any locks held.

Returns

A pointer to the mutex associated with `*this` prior to the call if any, `NULL` otherwise.

Postconditions

`this->mutex()==NULL, this->owns_lock()==false.`

Throws

Nothing.

NOTE If `this->owns_lock()` would have returned `true` prior to the call, the caller would now be responsible for unlocking the mutex.

D.5.7 std::lock function template

The `std::lock` function template provides a means of locking more than one mutex at the same time, without risk of deadlock resulting from inconsistent lock orders.

Declaration

```
template<typename LockableType1,typename... LockableType2>
void lock(LockableType1& m1,LockableType2& m2...);
```

Preconditions

The types of the supplied lockable objects `LockableType1`, `LockableType2`, ... shall conform to the `Lockable` requirements.

Effects

Acquires a lock on each of the supplied lockable objects `m1`, `m2`, ... by an unspecified sequence of calls to the `lock()`, `try_lock()`, and `unlock()` members of those types that avoid deadlock.

Postconditions

The current thread owns a lock on each of the supplied lockable objects.

Throws

Any exceptions thrown by the calls to `lock()`, `try_lock()`, and `unlock()`.

NOTE If an exception propagates out of the call to `std::lock`, then `unlock()` shall have been called for any of the objects `m1`, `m2`, ... for which a lock has been acquired in the function by a call to `lock()` or `try_lock()`.

D.5.8 std::try_lock function template

The `std::try_lock` function template allows you to try to lock a set of lockable objects in one go, so either they are all locked or none are locked.

Declaration

```
template<typename LockableType1,typename... LockableType2>
int try_lock(LockableType1& m1,LockableType2& m2...);
```

Preconditions
The types of the supplied lockable objects `LockableType1`, `LockableType2`, ... shall conform to the `Lockable` requirements.

Effects
Tries to acquires a lock on each of the supplied lockable objects `m1`, `m2`, ... by calling `try_lock()` on each in turn. If a call to `try_lock()` returns `false` or throws an exception, locks already acquired are released by calling `unlock()` on the corresponding lockable object.

Returns
`-1` if all locks were acquired (each call to `try_lock()` returned `true`), otherwise the zero-based index of the object for which the call to `try_lock()` returned `false`.

Postconditions
If the function returns `-1`, the current thread owns a lock on each of the supplied lockable objects. Otherwise, any locks acquired by this call have been released.

Throws
Any exceptions thrown by the calls to `try_lock()`.

NOTE If an exception propagates out of the call to `std::try_lock`, then `unlock()` shall have been called for any of the objects `m1`, `m2`, ... for which a lock has been acquired in the function by a call to `try_lock()`.

D.5.9 std::once_flag class

Instances of `std::once_flag` are used with `std::call_once` to ensure that a particular function is called exactly once, even if multiple threads invoke the call concurrently.

Instances of `std::once_flag` are not `CopyConstructible`, `CopyAssignable`, `MoveConstructible`, or `MoveAssignable`.

Class definition
```
struct once_flag
{
    constexpr once_flag() noexcept;

    once_flag(once_flag const& ) = delete;
    once_flag& operator=(once_flag const& ) = delete;
};
```

STD::ONCE_FLAG DEFAULT CONSTRUCTOR

The `std::once_flag` default constructor creates a new `std::once_flag` instance in a state, which indicates that the associated function hasn't been called.

Declaration
```
constexpr once_flag() noexcept;
```

Effects
Constructs a new `std::once_flag` instance in a state, which indicates that the associated function hasn't been called. Because this is a `constexpr` constructor, an instance with static storage duration is constructed as part of the static initialization phase, which avoids race conditions and order-of-initialization problems.

D.5.10 std::call_once function template

`std::call_once` is used with an instance of `std::once_flag` to ensure that a particular function is called exactly once, even if multiple threads invoke the call concurrently.

Declaration

```
template<typename Callable,typename... Args>
void call_once(std::once_flag& flag,Callable func,Args args...);
```

Preconditions

The expression `INVOKE(func,args)` is valid for the supplied values of `func` and `args`. `Callable` and every member of `Args` are `MoveConstructible`.

Effects

Invocations of `std::call_once` on the same `std::once_flag` object are serialized. If there has been no prior effective `std::call_once` invocation on the same `std::once_flag` object, the argument `func` (or a copy thereof) is called as-if by *`INVOKE`*`(func,args)`, and the invocation of `std::call_once` is effective if and only if the invocation of `func` returns without throwing an exception. If an exception is thrown, the exception is propagated to the caller. If there has been a prior effective `std::call_once` on the same `std::once_flag` object, the invocation of `std::call_once` returns without invoking `func`.

Synchronization

The completion of an effective `std::call_once` invocation on a `std::once_flag` object happens-before all subsequent `std::call_once` invocations on the same `std::once_flag` object.

Throws

`std::system_error` when the effects can't be achieved or for any exception propagated from the invocation of `func`.

D.6 <ratio> header

The `<ratio>` header provides support for compile-time rational arithmetic.

Header contents

```
namespace std
{
    template<intmax_t N,intmax_t D=1>
    class ratio;

    // ratio arithmetic
    template <class R1, class R2>
    using ratio_add = see description;

    template <class R1, class R2>
    using ratio_subtract = see description;

    template <class R1, class R2>
    using ratio_multiply = see description;

    template <class R1, class R2>
    using ratio_divide = see description;
```

```
    // ratio comparison
    template <class R1, class R2>
    struct ratio_equal;

    template <class R1, class R2>
    struct ratio_not_equal;

    template <class R1, class R2>
    struct ratio_less;

    template <class R1, class R2>
    struct ratio_less_equal;

    template <class R1, class R2>
    struct ratio_greater;

    template <class R1, class R2>
    struct ratio_greater_equal;

    typedef ratio<1, 1000000000000000000> atto;
    typedef ratio<1, 1000000000000000> femto;
    typedef ratio<1, 1000000000000> pico;
    typedef ratio<1, 1000000000> nano;
    typedef ratio<1, 1000000> micro;
    typedef ratio<1, 1000> milli;
    typedef ratio<1, 100> centi;
    typedef ratio<1, 10> deci;
    typedef ratio<10, 1> deca;
    typedef ratio<100, 1> hecto;
    typedef ratio<1000, 1> kilo;
    typedef ratio<1000000, 1> mega;
    typedef ratio<1000000000, 1> giga;
    typedef ratio<1000000000000, 1> tera;
    typedef ratio<1000000000000000, 1> peta;
    typedef ratio<1000000000000000000, 1> exa;
}
```

D.6.1 std::ratio class template

The `std::ratio` class template provides a mechanism for compile-time arithmetic involving rational values such as one half (`std::ratio<1,2>`), two thirds (`std::ratio<2,3>`) or fifteen forty-thirds (`std::ratio<15,43>`). It's used within the C++ Standard Library for specifying the period for instantiating the `std::chrono::duration` class template.

Class definition

```
template <intmax_t N, intmax_t D = 1>
class ratio
{
public:
    typedef ratio<num, den> type;
    static constexpr intmax_t num= see below;
    static constexpr intmax_t den= see below;
};
```

Requirements

`D` may not be zero.

Description

num and den are the numerator and denominator of the fraction N/D reduced to lowest terms. den is always positive. If N and D are the same sign, num is positive; otherwise num is negative.

Examples

```
ratio<4,6>::num == 2
ratio<4,6>::den == 3
ratio<4,-6>::num == -2
ratio<4,-6>::den == 3
```

D.6.2 std::ratio_add template alias

The std::ratio_add template alias provides a mechanism for adding two std::ratio values at compile time, using rational arithmetic.

Definition

```
template <class R1, class R2>
using ratio_add = std::ratio<see below>;
```

Preconditions

R1 and R2 must be instantiations of the std::ratio class template.

Effects

ratio_add<R1,R2> is defined as an alias for an instantiation of std::ratio that represents the sum of the fractions represented by R1 and R2 if that sum can be calculated without overflow. If the calculation of the result overflows, the program is ill formed. In the absence of arithmetic overflow, std::ratio_add<R1,R2> shall have the same num and den values as std::ratio<R1::num * R2::den + R2::num * R1::den, R1::den * R2::den>.

Examples

```
std::ratio_add<std::ratio<1,3>, std::ratio<2,5> >::num == 11
std::ratio_add<std::ratio<1,3>, std::ratio<2,5> >::den == 15

std::ratio_add<std::ratio<1,3>, std::ratio<7,6> >::num == 3
std::ratio_add<std::ratio<1,3>, std::ratio<7,6> >::den == 2
```

D.6.3 std::ratio_subtract template alias

The std::ratio_subtract template alias provides a mechanism for subtracting two std::ratio values at compile time, using rational arithmetic.

Definition

```
template <class R1, class R2>
using ratio_subtract = std::ratio<see below>;
```

Preconditions

R1 and R2 must be instantiations of the std::ratio class template.

Effects

ratio_subtract<R1,R2> is defined as an alias for an instantiation of std::ratio that represents the difference of the fractions represented by R1 and R2 if that difference can be calculated without overflow. If the calculation of the result overflows, the program is ill formed. In the absence of arithmetic overflow, `std::ratio_subtract<R1,R2>` shall have the same `num` and `den` values as `std::ratio<R1::num * R2::den - R2::num * R1::den, R1::den * R2::den>`.

Examples

```
std::ratio_subtract<std::ratio<1,3>, std::ratio<1,5> >::num == 2
std::ratio_subtract<std::ratio<1,3>, std::ratio<1,5> >::den == 15

std::ratio_subtract<std::ratio<1,3>, std::ratio<7,6> >::num == -5
std::ratio_subtract<std::ratio<1,3>, std::ratio<7,6> >::den == 6
```

D.6.4 std::ratio_multiply template alias

The `std::ratio_multiply` template alias provides a mechanism for multiplying two `std::ratio` values at compile time, using rational arithmetic.

Definition

```
template <class R1, class R2>
using ratio_multiply = std::ratio<see below>;
```

Preconditions

`R1` and `R2` must be instantiations of the `std::ratio` class template.

Effects

`ratio_multiply<R1,R2>` is defined as an alias for an instantiation of `std::ratio` that represents the product of the fractions represented by `R1` and `R2` if that product can be calculated without overflow. If the calculation of the result overflows, the program is ill formed. In the absence of arithmetic overflow, `std::ratio_multiply<R1,R2>` shall have the same `num` and `den` values as `std::ratio<R1::num * R2::num, R1::den * R2::den>`.

Examples

```
std::ratio_multiply<std::ratio<1,3>, std::ratio<2,5> >::num == 2
std::ratio_multiply<std::ratio<1,3>, std::ratio<2,5> >::den == 15

std::ratio_multiply<std::ratio<1,3>, std::ratio<15,7> >::num == 5
std::ratio_multiply<std::ratio<1,3>, std::ratio<15,7> >::den == 7
```

D.6.5 std::ratio_divide template alias

The `std::ratio_divide` template alias provides a mechanism for dividing two `std::ratio` values at compile time, using rational arithmetic.

Definition

```
template <class R1, class R2>
using ratio_divide = std::ratio<see below>;
```

Preconditions

`R1` and `R2` must be instantiations of the `std::ratio` class template.

Effects

`ratio_divide<R1,R2>` is defined as an alias for an instantiation of `std::ratio` that represents the result of dividing the fractions represented by `R1` and `R2` if that result can be calculated without overflow. If the calculation overflows, the program is ill formed. In the absence of arithmetic overflow, `std::ratio_divide<R1,R2>` shall have the same `num` and `den` values as `std::ratio<R1::num * R2::den, R1::den * R2::num>`.

Examples

```
std::ratio_divide<std::ratio<1,3>, std::ratio<2,5> >::num == 5
std::ratio_divide<std::ratio<1,3>, std::ratio<2,5> >::den == 6

std::ratio_divide<std::ratio<1,3>, std::ratio<15,7> >::num == 7
std::ratio_divide<std::ratio<1,3>, std::ratio<15,7> >::den == 45
```

D.6.6 std::ratio_equal class template

The `std::ratio_equal` class template provides a mechanism for comparing two `std::ratio` values for equality at compile time, using rational arithmetic.

Class definition

```
template <class R1, class R2>
class ratio_equal:
    public std::integral_constant<
        bool,(R1::num == R2::num) && (R1::den == R2::den)>
{};
```

Preconditions

`R1` and `R2` must be instantiations of the `std::ratio` class template.

Examples

```
std::ratio_equal<std::ratio<1,3>, std::ratio<2,6> >::value == true
std::ratio_equal<std::ratio<1,3>, std::ratio<1,6> >::value == false
std::ratio_equal<std::ratio<1,3>, std::ratio<2,3> >::value == false
std::ratio_equal<std::ratio<1,3>, std::ratio<1,3> >::value == true
```

D.6.7 std::ratio_not_equal class template

The `std::ratio_not_equal` class template provides a mechanism for comparing two `std::ratio` values for inequality at compile time, using rational arithmetic.

Class definition

```
template <class R1, class R2>
class ratio_not_equal:
    public std::integral_constant<bool,!ratio_equal<R1,R2>::value>
{};
```

Preconditions

`R1` and `R2` must be instantiations of the `std::ratio` class template.

Examples

```
std::ratio_not_equal<std::ratio<1,3>, std::ratio<2,6> >::value == false
std::ratio_not_equal<std::ratio<1,3>, std::ratio<1,6> >::value == true
std::ratio_not_equal<std::ratio<1,3>, std::ratio<2,3> >::value == true
std::ratio_not_equal<std::ratio<1,3>, std::ratio<1,3> >::value == false
```

D.6.8 std::ratio_less class template

The `std::ratio_less` class template provides a mechanism for comparing two `std::ratio` values at compile time, using rational arithmetic.

Class definition

```
template <class R1, class R2>
class ratio_less:
    public std::integral_constant<bool,see below>
{};
```

Preconditions

R1 and R2 must be instantiations of the `std::ratio` class template.

Effects

`std::ratio_less<R1,R2>` derives from `std::integral_constant<bool, value >`, where *value* is `(R1::num*R2::den) < (R2::num*R1::den)`. Where possible, implementations shall use a method of calculating the result that avoids overflow. If overflow occurs, the program is ill formed.

Examples

```
std::ratio_less<std::ratio<1,3>, std::ratio<2,6> >::value == false
std::ratio_less<std::ratio<1,6>, std::ratio<1,3> >::value == true
std::ratio_less<
    std::ratio<999999999,1000000000>,
    std::ratio<1000000001,1000000000> >::value == true
std::ratio_less<
    std::ratio<1000000001,1000000000>,
    std::ratio<999999999,1000000000> >::value == false
```

D.6.9 std::ratio_greater class template

The `std::ratio_greater` class template provides a mechanism for comparing two `std::ratio` values at compile time, using rational arithmetic.

Class definition

```
template <class R1, class R2>
class ratio_greater:
    public std::integral_constant<bool,ratio_less<R2,R1>::value>
{};
```

Preconditions

R1 and R2 must be instantiations of the `std::ratio` class template.

D.6.10 std::ratio_less_equal class template

The `std::ratio_less_equal` class template provides a mechanism for comparing two `std::ratio` values at compile time, using rational arithmetic.

Class definition

```
template <class R1, class R2>
class ratio_less_equal:
    public std::integral_constant<bool,!ratio_less<R2,R1>::value>
{};
```

Preconditions

R1 and R2 must be instantiations of the `std::ratio` class template.

D.6.11 std::ratio_greater_equal class template

The `std::ratio_greater_equal` class template provides a mechanism for comparing two `std::ratio` values at compile time, using rational arithmetic.

Class definition

```
template <class R1, class R2>
class ratio_greater_equal:
    public std::integral_constant<bool,!ratio_less<R1,R2>::value>
{};
```

Preconditions

`R1` and `R2` must be instantiations of the `std::ratio` class template.

D.7 <thread> header

The `<thread>` header provides facilities for managing and identifying threads and provides functions for making the current thread sleep.

Header contents

```
namespace std
{
    class thread;

    namespace this_thread
    {
        thread::id get_id() noexcept;

        void yield() noexcept;

        template<typename Rep,typename Period>
        void sleep_for(
            std::chrono::duration<Rep,Period> sleep_duration);

        template<typename Clock,typename Duration>
        void sleep_until(
            std::chrono::time_point<Clock,Duration> wake_time);
    }
}
```

D.7.1 std::thread class

The `std::thread` class is used to manage a thread of execution. It provides a means of starting a new thread of execution and waiting for the completion of a thread of execution. It also provides a means for identifying and provides other functions for managing threads of execution.

Class definition

```
class thread
{
public:
    // Types
    class id;
    typedef implementation-defined native_handle_type; // optional

    // Construction and Destruction
    thread() noexcept;
```

```
    ~thread();

    template<typename Callable,typename Args...>
    explicit thread(Callable&& func,Args&&... args);

    // Copying and Moving
    thread(thread const& other) = delete;
    thread(thread&& other) noexcept;

    thread& operator=(thread const& other) = delete;
    thread& operator=(thread&& other) noexcept;

    void swap(thread& other) noexcept;

    void join();
    void detach();
    bool joinable() const noexcept;

    id get_id() const noexcept;

    native_handle_type native_handle();

    static unsigned hardware_concurrency() noexcept;
};

void swap(thread& lhs,thread& rhs);
```

STD::THREAD::ID CLASS

An instance of `std::thread::id` identifies a particular thread of execution.

Class definition

```
class thread::id
{
public:
    id() noexcept;
};

bool operator==(thread::id x, thread::id y) noexcept;
bool operator!=(thread::id x, thread::id y) noexcept;
bool operator<(thread::id x, thread::id y) noexcept;
bool operator<=(thread::id x, thread::id y) noexcept;
bool operator>(thread::id x, thread::id y) noexcept;
bool operator>=(thread::id x, thread::id y) noexcept;

template<typename charT, typename traits>
basic_ostream<charT, traits>&
operator<< (basic_ostream<charT, traits>&& out, thread::id id);
```

Notes

The `std::thread::id` value that identifies a particular thread of execution shall be distinct from the value of a default-constructed `std::thread::id` instance and from any value that represents another thread of execution.

The `std::thread::id` values for particular threads aren't predictable and may vary between executions of the same program.

`std::thread::id` is `CopyConstructible` and `CopyAssignable`, so instances of `std::thread::id` may be freely copied and assigned.

STD::THREAD::ID DEFAULT CONSTRUCTOR

Constructs a `std::thread::id` object that doesn't represent any thread of execution.

Declaration

```
id() noexcept;
```

Effects

Constructs a `std::thread::id` instance that has the singular *not any thread* value.

Throws

Nothing.

NOTE All default-constructed `std::thread::id` instances store the same value.

STD::THREAD::ID EQUALITY COMPARISON OPERATOR

Compares two instances of `std::thread::id` to see if they represent the same thread of execution.

Declaration

```
bool operator==(std::thread::id lhs,std::thread::id rhs) noexcept;
```

Returns

`true` if both `lhs` and `rhs` represent the same thread of execution or both have the singular *not any thread* value. `false` if `lhs` and `rhs` represent different threads of execution or one represents a thread of execution and the other has the singular *not any thread* value.

Throws

Nothing.

STD::THREAD::ID INEQUALITY COMPARISON OPERATOR

Compares two instances of `std::thread::id` to see if they represent different threads of execution.

Declaration

```
bool operator!=(std::thread::id lhs,std::thread::id rhs) noexcept;
```

Returns

```
!(lhs==rhs)
```

Throws

Nothing.

STD::THREAD::ID LESS-THAN COMPARISON OPERATOR

Compares two instances of `std::thread::id` to see if one lies before the other in the total ordering of thread ID values.

Declaration

```
bool operator<(std::thread::id lhs,std::thread::id rhs) noexcept;
```

Returns
true if the value of lhs occurs before the value of rhs in the total ordering of thread ID values. If lhs!=rhs, exactly one of lhs<rhs or rhs<lhs returns true and the other returns false. If lhs==rhs, lhs<rhs and rhs<lhs both return false.

Throws
Nothing.

NOTE The singular *not any thread* value held by a default-constructed std::thread::id instance compares less than any std::thread::id instance that represents a thread of execution. If two instances of std::thread::id are equal, neither is less than the other. Any set of distinct std::thread::id values forms a total order, which is consistent throughout an execution of a program. This order may vary between executions of the same program.

STD::THREAD::ID LESS-THAN OR EQUAL COMPARISON OPERATOR

Compares two instances of std::thread::id to see if one lies before the other in the total ordering of thread ID values or is equal to it.

Declaration
```
bool operator<=(std::thread::id lhs,std::thread::id rhs) noexcept;
```

Returns
```
!(rhs<lhs)
```

Throws
Nothing.

STD::THREAD::ID GREATER-THAN COMPARISON OPERATOR

Compares two instances of std::thread::id to see if one lies after the other in the total ordering of thread ID values.

Declaration
```
bool operator>(std::thread::id lhs,std::thread::id rhs) noexcept;
```

Returns
```
rhs<lhs
```

Throws
Nothing.

STD::THREAD::ID GREATER-THAN OR EQUAL COMPARISON OPERATOR

Compares two instances of std::thread::id to see if one lies after the other in the total ordering of thread ID values or is equal to it.

Declaration
```
bool operator>=(std::thread::id lhs,std::thread::id rhs) noexcept;
```

Returns
```
!(lhs<rhs)
```

Throws
Nothing.

STD::THREAD::ID STREAM INSERTION OPERATOR

Writes a string representation of the `std::thread::id` value into the specified stream.

Declaration

```
template<typename charT, typename traits>
basic_ostream<charT, traits>&
operator<< (basic_ostream<charT, traits>&& out, thread::id id);
```

Effects

Inserts a string representation of the `std::thread::id` value into the specified stream.

Returns

`out`

Throws

Nothing.

NOTE The format of the string representation isn't specified. Instances of `std::thread::id` that compare equal have the same representation, and instances that aren't equal have distinct representations.

STD::THREAD::NATIVE_HANDLE_TYPE TYPEDEF

`native_handle_type` is a typedef to a type that can be used with platform-specific APIs.

Declaration

```
typedef implementation-defined native_handle_type;
```

NOTE This typedef is *optional.* If present, the implementation should provide a type that's suitable for use with native platform-specific APIs.

STD::THREAD::NATIVE_HANDLE MEMBER FUNCTION

Returns a value of type `native_handle_type` that represents the thread of execution associated with `*this`.

Declaration

```
native_handle_type native_handle();
```

NOTE This function is *optional.* If present, the value returned should be suitable for use with the native platform-specific APIs.

STD::THREAD DEFAULT CONSTRUCTOR

Constructs a `std::thread` object without an associated thread of execution.

Declaration

```
thread() noexcept;
```

Effects

Constructs a `std::thread` instance that has no associated thread of execution.

Postconditions

For a newly constructed `std::thread` object `x`, `x.get_id()==id()`.

Throws

Nothing.

STD::THREAD CONSTRUCTOR

Constructs a `std::thread` object associated with a new thread of execution.

Declaration

```
template<typename Callable,typename Args...>
explicit thread(Callable&& func,Args&&... args);
```

Preconditions

`func` and each element of `args` must be `MoveConstructible`.

Effects

Constructs a `std::thread` instance and associates it with a newly created thread of execution. Copies or moves `func` and each element of `args` into internal storage that persists for the lifetime of the new thread of execution. Performs *INVOKE* *(copy-of-*`func`*,copy-of-*`args`*)* on the new thread of execution.

Postconditions

For a newly constructed `std::thread` object `x`, `x.get_id()!=id()`.

Throws

An exception of type `std::system_error` if unable to start the new thread. Any exception thrown by copying `func` or `args` into internal storage.

Synchronization

The invocation of the constructor happens-before the execution of the supplied function on the newly created thread of execution.

STD::THREAD MOVE-CONSTRUCTOR

Transfers ownership of a thread of execution from one `std::thread` object to a newly created `std::thread` object.

Declaration

```
thread(thread&& other) noexcept;
```

Effects

Constructs a `std::thread` instance. If `other` has an associated thread of execution prior to the constructor invocation, that thread of execution is now associated with the newly created `std::thread` object. Otherwise, the newly created `std::thread` object has no associated thread of execution.

Postconditions

For a newly constructed `std::thread` object `x`, `x.get_id()` is equal to the value of `other.get_id()` prior to the constructor invocation. `other.get_id()==id()`.

Throws

Nothing.

NOTE `std::thread` objects are *not* `CopyConstructible`, so there's no copy constructor, only this move constructor.

STD::THREAD DESTRUCTOR

Destroys a `std::thread` object.

Declaration

```
~thread();
```

Effects
Destroys `*this`. If `*this` has an associated thread of execution (`this->joinable()` would return `true`), calls `std::terminate()` to abort the program.

Throws
Nothing.

STD::THREAD MOVE-ASSIGNMENT OPERATOR

Transfers ownership of a thread of execution from one `std::thread` object to another `std::thread` object.

Declaration

```
thread& operator=(thread&& other) noexcept;
```

Effects
If `this->joinable()` returns `true` prior to the call, calls `std::terminate()` to abort the program. If `other` has an associated thread of execution prior to the assignment, that thread of execution is now associated with `*this`. Otherwise `*this` has no associated thread of execution.

Postconditions
`this->get_id()` is equal to the value of `other.get_id()` prior to the call. `other.get_id()==id()`.

Throws
Nothing.

NOTE `std::thread` objects are *not* `CopyAssignable`, so there's no copy-assignment operator, only this move-assignment operator.

STD::THREAD::SWAP MEMBER FUNCTION

Exchanges ownership of their associated threads of execution between two `std::thread` objects.

Declaration

```
void swap(thread& other) noexcept;
```

Effects
If `other` has an associated thread of execution prior to the call, that thread of execution is now associated with `*this`. Otherwise `*this` has no associated thread of execution. If `*this` has an associated thread of execution prior to the call, that thread of execution is now associated with `other`. Otherwise `other` has no associated thread of execution.

Postconditions
`this->get_id()` is equal to the value of `other.get_id()` prior to the call. `other.get_id()` is equal to the value of `this->get_id()` prior to the call.

Throws
Nothing.

SWAP NONMEMBER FUNCTION FOR STD::THREADS

Exchanges ownership of their associated threads of execution between two `std::thread` objects.

Declaration

```
void swap(thread& lhs,thread& rhs) noexcept;
```

Effects

`lhs.swap(rhs)`

Throws

Nothing.

STD::THREAD::JOINABLE MEMBER FUNCTION

Queries whether or not `*this` has an associated thread of execution.

Declaration

```
bool joinable() const noexcept;
```

Returns

`true` if `*this` has an associated thread of execution, `false` otherwise.

Throws

Nothing.

STD::THREAD::JOIN MEMBER FUNCTION

Waits for the thread of execution associated with `*this` to finish.

Declaration

```
void join();
```

Preconditions

`this->joinable()` would return `true`.

Effects

Blocks the current thread until the thread of execution associated with `*this` has finished.

Postconditions

`this->get_id()==id()`. The thread of execution associated with `*this` prior to the call has finished.

Synchronization

The completion of the thread of execution associated with `*this` prior to the call happens-before the call to `join()` returns.

Throws

`std::system_error` if the effects can't be achieved or `this->joinable()` returns `false`.

STD::THREAD::DETACH MEMBER FUNCTION

Detaches the thread of execution associated with `*this` to finish.

Declaration

```
void detach();
```

Preconditions
`this->joinable()` returns `true`.

Effects
Detaches the thread of execution associated with `*this`.

Postconditions
`this->get_id()==id(), this->joinable()==false`

The thread of execution associated with `*this` prior to the call is detached and no longer has an associated `std::thread` object.

Throws
`std::system_error` if the effects can't be achieved or `this->joinable()` returns `false` on invocation.

STD::THREAD::GET_ID MEMBER FUNCTION

Returns a value of type `std::thread::id` that identifies the thread of execution associated with `*this`.

Declaration

```
thread::id get_id() const noexcept;
```

Returns
If `*this` has an associated thread of execution, returns an instance of `std::thread::id` that identifies that thread. Otherwise returns a default-constructed `std::thread::id`.

Throws
Nothing.

STD::THREAD::HARDWARE_CONCURRENCY STATIC MEMBER FUNCTION

Returns a hint as to the number of threads that can run concurrently on the current hardware.

Declaration

```
unsigned hardware_concurrency() noexcept;
```

Returns
The number of threads that can run concurrently on the current hardware. This may be the number of processors in the system, for example. Where this information is not available or well defined, this function returns `0`.

Throws
Nothing.

D.7.2 Namespace this_thread

The functions in the `std::this_thread` namespace operate on the calling thread.

STD::THIS_THREAD::GET_ID NONMEMBER FUNCTION

Returns a value of type `std::thread::id` that identifies the current thread of execution.

Declaration

```
thread::id get_id() noexcept;
```

Returns
An instance of `std::thread::id` that identifies the current thread.

Throws
Nothing.

STD::THIS_THREAD::YIELD NONMEMBER FUNCTION

Used to inform the library that the thread that invoked the function doesn't need to run at the point of the call. Commonly used in tight loops to avoid consuming excessive CPU time.

Declaration

```
void yield() noexcept;
```

Effects
Provides the library an opportunity to schedule something else in place of the current thread.

Throws
Nothing.

STD::THIS_THREAD::SLEEP_FOR NONMEMBER FUNCTION

Suspends execution of the current thread for the specified duration.

Declaration

```
template<typename Rep,typename Period>
void sleep_for(std::chrono::duration<Rep,Period> const& relative_time);
```

Effects
Blocks the current thread until the specified `relative_time` has elapsed.

NOTE The thread may be blocked for longer than the specified duration. Where possible, the elapsed time is determined by a steady clock.

Throws
Nothing.

STD::THIS_THREAD::SLEEP_UNTIL NONMEMBER FUNCTION

Suspends execution of the current thread until the specified time point has been reached.

Declaration

```
template<typename Clock,typename Duration>
void sleep_until(
    std::chrono::time_point<Clock,Duration> const& absolute_time);
```

Effects
Blocks the current thread until the specified `absolute_time` has been reached for the specified `Clock`.

NOTE There's no guarantee as to how long the calling thread will be blocked for, only that `Clock::now()` returned a time equal to or later than `absolute_time` at the point at which the thread became unblocked.

Throws
Nothing.

resources

Print resources

Cargill, Tom, "Exception Handling: A False Sense of Security," in *C++ Report* 6, no. 9, (November-December 1994). Also available at http://www.informit.com/content/images/020163371x/supplements/Exception_Handling_Article.html.

Hoare, C.A.R., *Communicating Sequential Processes* (Prentice Hall International, 1985), ISBN 0131532898. Also available at http://www.usingcsp.com/cspbook.pdf.

Michael, Maged M., "Safe Memory Reclamation for Dynamic Lock-Free Objects Using Atomic Reads and Writes" in *PODC '02: Proceedings of the Twenty-first Annual Symposium on Principles of Distributed Computing* (2002), ISBN 1-58113-485-1.

———. U.S. Patent and Trademark Office application 20040107227, "Method for efficient implementation of dynamic lock-free data structures with safe memory reclamation."

Sutter, Herb, *Exceptional C++: 47 Engineering Puzzles, Programming Problems, and Solutions* (Addison Wesley Professional, 1999), ISBN 0-201-61562-2.

———. "The Free Lunch Is Over: A Fundamental Turn Toward Concurrency in Software," in *Dr. Dobb's Journal* 30, no. 3 (March 2005). Also available at http://www.gotw.ca/publications/concurrency-ddj.htm.

Online resources

Atomic Ptr Plus Project Home, http://atomic-ptr-plus.sourceforge.net/.

Boost C++ library collection, http://www.boost.org.

C++0x/C++11 Support in GCC, http://gcc.gnu.org/projects/cxx0x.html.

C++11—The Recently Approved New ISO C++ Standard, http://www.research.att.com/~bs/C++0xFAQ.html.

Erlang Programming Language, http://www.erlang.org/.

GNU General Public License, http://www.gnu.org/licenses/gpl.html.

Haskell Programming Language, http://www.haskell.org/.

IBM Statement of Non-Assertion of Named Patents Against OSS, http://www.ibm.com/ibm/licensing/patents/pledgedpatents.pdf.

Intel Building Blocks for Open Source, http://threadingbuildingblocks.org/.

The just::thread Implementation of the C++ Standard Thread Library, http://www.stdthread.co.uk.

Message Passing Interface Forum, http://www.mpi-forum.org/.

Multithreading API for C++0X—A Layered Approach, C++ Standards Committee Paper N2094, http://www.open-std.org/jtc1/sc22/wg21/docs/papers/2006/n2094.html.

OpenMP, http://www.openmp.org/.

SETI@Home, http://setiathome.ssl.berkeley.edu/.

index

Symbols

A

B

C

D

E

F

G

H

I

J

L

M

N

O

P

T

U

V

W